シーボルト蒐集和書目録

A Listing of Siebold's Collection of Japanese Books
―Papers on Siebold and Japanese Translation of Latin Used―

【監修】中野三敏　【編集】高杉志緒／宮崎克則
【ラテン語和訳】家入敏光
【執筆】山口隆男／マティ・フォラー
【英訳】マティ・フォラー／デビット・キャリシャー

八木書店

Yagi Bookstore Ltd.
Tokyo, Japan

序　文

中野　三敏

　此の度、ライデン大学とライデン国立民族学博物館に遺るフィリップ・フランツ・バルタザール・フォン・シーボルトの蒐集和本目録の監修及び緒言を乞われた。

　この所十数年にわたり、海外に遺された和本の数々を尋ね歩くこと幾度か、その都度、和本の質と量にはひたすら驚くこと多く、特に大英博物館とボストン美術館の絵本コレクションは、恐らく日本国内の図書館・美術館を三十年かけて経廻っても、殆ど及びもつかぬ豊富さである。所がどういう訳か、未だに、四百年に及ぶ江戸との繋がりに裏打ちされた御本家オランダだけには、どうしても手が届かなかった。一つには、シーボルト蒐集和書は海外に渡った最も早い和書群として、殆ど調べ尽くされているだろうという安心感があった所以である。流石に近年は長時間の外国訪書には堪えきれなくなってきた今、その目録が、しかも豊富な図版（カラー80頁・モノクロ64頁）と共に出刊されるという。以て喜ばざる可けん哉。雀躍に勝えずして引き受けざる可けん哉。

　さらにその目録には、元熊本大学理学部教授の山口隆男氏の遺稿も附載される。恐らく山口氏ほどシーボルト・コレクションの全容に通じた方は得られまい。仄聞するに古都ライデンでも最高の評価を得た邦人であるという。その方の総説と解説は、到底余人の及ぶ所ではなかろう。以て依らざる可けん哉。

　また、シーボルトによる序文と助手ヨハン・ヨセフ・ホフマンによる目録本文はラテン語で書かれているため、その翻訳は、編者の一人である美術史の専家高杉志緒氏（下関短期大学准教授）の伯父上に当る元天理大学教授（中世ラテン語）の家入敏光氏に御引き受け戴いた。もう一人の編者は、シーボルト著『NIPPON』の研究を端緒として異文化交流史で知られた九州大学大学院文学研究科史学専攻出身の中堅宮崎克則氏（西南学院大学教授）である。国史と美術史の両専家が数度にわたるライデン詣でを重ねた本書の内容と出来栄えは以て信頼するに足る。革めて言おう。喜ばざる可けん哉。依らざる可けん哉。信ぜざる可けん哉。

（なかの　みつとし・九州大学名誉教授）

Preface

Dr. Mitsutoshi Nakano, Professor Emeritus, Kyushu University

This publication concerns Pfilipp Franz Barlthasar von Siebold's collection of Japanese books preserved at Leiden University and the National Museum of Ethnology, Leiden. On this occasion, I was requested to supervise the compilation of this publication and write its preface.

For the past ten or twenty years I have conducted research on a number of occasions on Japanese hand written publications of the Edo Era, which exist outside of Japan. On each occasion, I have been astonished at the quality and size of such publications. In particular, the illustrated publications of the Edo Era housed at the British Museum and the Museum of Fine Arts, Boston are so rich and plentiful that I doubt if I could come close to researching such a sizeable collection even if I visited all the libraries and museums in Japan over a period of thirty years.

Strangely enough, I have never conducted any research on the Netherlands, the only country in all of Europe and the United States to maintained international relations with Japan for 400 years since the Edo Era. One reason for this is my conviction that Siebold's collection of Japanese publications, being the earliest of its kind to leave Japan, has already been thoroughly researched.

Now after putting my 77th birthday behind me and being at an age where I no longer can endure lengthy overseas travel to research books, I am informed that this publication will come with a rich selection of illustrations (80 pages in color and 64 pages in black and white). Now how could I not be overjoyed with this news and how could I ever refuse the opportunity of supervising the compilation of such a publication?

Furthermore, included in this publication will be the posthumous manuscript of the late Takao Yamaguchi, formerly a professor of the Faculty of Science of Kumamoto University. Perhaps no one is as comprehensively knowledgeable with Siebold's entire collection as Dr. Yamaguchi was. I hear his reputation was highly esteemed even by those in Leiden back in the Netherlands. I doubt if anyone could match or equal the professionalism of his remarks and commentary on the subject. He is definitely an authoritative source on the subject matter.

Because the preface written by Siebold and the text by Johann Joseph Hoffman, his assistant, are written in Latin, Mr. Toshimitsu Ieiri, a professor formerly with Tenri University (with a specialization in Medieval Latin) agreed to do the translation. Mr. Ieiri is the uncle to Shio Takasugi, an associate professor at Shimonoseki Junior College with a specialization in Fine Arts History and a member of the editorial staff of this publication. Another editor of this publication is Katsunori Miyazaki, a professor at Seinan Gakuin University who holds a doctorate in History from the Graduate School of Letters of Kyushu University and who began his studies in the history of intercultural relations by researching "*NIPPON*" written by Siebold, himself.

The content and workmanship, which went into this publication where specialists in Japanese History as well as Fine Art History both made trips to Leiden on a number of occasions, is indeed credible and trustworthy. Let me emphasize that the publication should definitely bring joy to scholars as a trustworthy and reliable piece of research material.

(English Trans. by David Kalischer)

目　次

序文 …………………………………………………………中野三敏	i
〔英訳〕Preface ……………………………………Mitsutoshi Nakano	ii
凡例 ………………………………………………………………………	vii
山口博士の遺稿英訳にあたって ………………………マティ・フォラー	1
〔英文〕Preliminary remarks to the translation of two posthumous articles by Dr. Yamaguchi Takao ………………Matthi Forrer	3
シーボルトの初回来日と収集書籍類について ……………山口隆男	5
〔英訳〕Siebold's first journey to Japan–with special emphasis on his collection of books. ……………………………Takao Yamaguchi	21
「シーボルトの初回来日と収集書籍類について」に対する脚註・追記 ……………………………………………マティ・フォラー	32
原文影印　CATALOGUS LIBRORUM ET MANUSCRIPTORUM JAPONICORUM …	35
日本語訳 ……………………………………………………家入敏光	99
シーボルトの日本収集書籍コレクションの概略について ………山口隆男	161
〔英訳〕Overview of the books collected by Siebold …Takao Yamaguchi	197
「シーボルトの日本収集書籍コレクションの概略について」に対する脚註・追記 ……………………………………マティ・フォラー	213
Bibliography—Two posthumous articles by Dr. Yamaguchi Takao— …Matthi Forrer	215
シーボルトがフィッセルから借用した書籍一覧 ………マティ・フォラー	220
（A Provisional List of the Books Collected by Overmeer Fisscher, now to be found in the Siebold Collection by Matthi Forrer）	
掲載図版一覧（List of the Illustrative Plates）………………………………	225
索引（Index）………………………………………………………………	231
書名索引（Title Index）…………………………………………………	232
人名索引（Personal name Index）………………………………………	251
図版（Illustrative Plates）…………………………………………………	*1*
カラー図版（Color Illustrative Plates）…………………………………	*3*
モノクロ図版（Black-and-white Illustrative Plates）…………………………	*83*

凡　例

1. 本書の主題は、フィリップ・フランツ・バルタザール・フォン・シーボルト（Philipp Franz Balthasar von Siebold、1796年生～1866年没）が、初回来日（1823年～1829年）時に蒐集した和書資料（特にオランダ国ライデン現存分）およびシーボルトがそれら蒐集資料に対して作成した"*Catalogus librorum et manuscriptorum Japonicorum a Ph. Fr. de Siebold collectorum, annexa enumeratione illorum, qui in Museo Regio Hagano servantur*"（邦訳『シーボルト蒐集日本書籍目録、並びにハーグ王立博物館所蔵日本書籍および手稿類目録』、1845年刊）である。

2. 本書の内容は、（1）シーボルト蒐集和書資料をめぐる論文・考察（山口隆男執筆、マティ・フォラー英訳・註記・追記）、（2）"*Catalogus librorum et manuscriptorum Japonicorum a Ph. Fr. de Siebold collectorum, annexa enumeratione illorum, qui in Museo Regio Hagano servantur*"（公益財団法人東洋文庫所蔵）の影印、（3）上記（2）のラテン語本文日本語訳（家入敏光）、（4）和書資料図版（ライデン大学図書館・ライデン国立民族学博物館所蔵）、以上4部分を主軸としている。

3. 論文および論文英訳・註記等については、マティ・フォラー「山口博士の遺稿英訳にあたって」を参照されたい。

4. 原文影印、日本語訳、図版については別途、凡例を作成して各項の冒頭に記した。

5. 本文（論文、原文影印、日本語訳）中に掲載された書名・人名については、巻末にアルファベット順の索引を掲載した。なお、和書の書名・日本人名はヘボン式ローマ字で記し、アクセント・音節の長短記号は省略した。

6. 本書に掲載した図版（論文・註に掲載した図版を含む）については別途「掲載図版一覧」を作成した。巻末の図版掲載資料は、ライデン大学図書館・ライデン国立民族学博物館の所蔵資料である。シーボルト初回来日時の蒐集和書資料はオランダ国外（オーストリア国立図書館、フランス国立図書館等）にも現存していることが知られるが、現存資料の書誌情報等については「第一次滞在シーボルト日本書籍コレクション所蔵機関別現存書目録」（人間文化研究機構　国文学研究資料館編『シーボルト日本書籍コレクション現存書目録と研究』勉誠出版、2014

凡　　例

　年）を参照されたい。

7. 本書作成における担当は以下の通りである（順不同・敬称略）。
　・監修・序文作成・資料調査指導・掲載図版資料選定：中野三敏（九州大学名誉教授）
　・ラテン語翻訳：家入敏光（元天理大学教授）
　・論文執筆・図版資料写真撮影：山口隆男（元熊本大学教授）
　・論文英訳・註記・追記・「シーボルトがフィッセルから借用した書籍一覧」・論文参考文献一覧作成：マティ・フォラー（Matthias Franciscus Maria Forrer、ライデン国立民族学博物館・元ライデン大学特任教授）
　・序文英訳：デビット・キャリシャー（David Calischer、福岡市総合図書館）
　・原文影印底本調査・選定：高杉志緒（下関短期大学准教授）
　・編集・図版資料写真撮影：高杉志緒・宮崎克則（西南学院大学教授）

8. 本書は、公益財団法人　三菱財団「第39回　三菱財団人文科学研究助成事業」における共同研究「ライデンに現存するシーボルト収集和古書の書誌学的研究」の研究成果報告書として作成した。

山口博士の遺稿英訳にあたって

マティ・フォラー
（Matthi Forrer）

　故山口隆男博士（2013年5月27日没）は、大場秀章東京大学名誉教授と私が2006年から座長を務める国際シーボルトコレクション会議に欠かせない存在であった。山口博士の他界を心から遺憾に思う。縁があって、編集担当の高杉志緒氏から、博士が亡くなる数週間前に同氏の依頼で仕上げた原稿英訳の依頼を受けた。山口博士が、シーボルトの書籍コレクションの研究をされていたことをその時、初めて知った。山口博士らしいと感じたとともに、ご生前に博士と書籍コレクションについて意見交換が出来なかったことを、今さらながら残念に思う。

　私は、ライデン国立民族学博物館に所属する研究者で、これまでシーボルトの書籍コレクションについては、調査を進める一方、日本の研究者からは無数の問い合わせを受けてきた。山口博士が、すでに遺稿に見られるような知見を持っておられたことには、正直なところ驚いた。参考文献に頼られているのは、残念であるが、これは書籍研究が山口博士の専門分野でないことを鑑みれば、致し方ないことであろう。それ以上に、私は、山口博士がシーボルトコレクションの「包括的な研究」を提言し、遺稿に明らかなように、それを自ら地道に実行されていたことに心から敬意を表するものである。

　本文に関しては、可能な限り原本に忠実な翻訳を試みた。私の立場から追記する必要があると判断した場合、脚註、または便宜上文中に記したが、それは山口博士が望んだであろうと信じている。イニシャル「MF」で始まるのが、私の追記である（原文の論文のための追記を下に列挙した。＊は、原文に注がなく、私が追記のために新たに加えた註を示す）。

　出典に関しては、日本語文献を原文のまま表記し、後に英訳を記した。ページ表記は、まばらであるが、翻訳者としては参照しかねる部分が多いので、原文にページ記載があるものだけ、記載した（Bibliography：本書215〜219頁、参照のこと）。山口博士は、注でかなり多くの書物を紹介されているが、これは最期のご論文で、幅広く後輩の研究者に道筋をつけようとされたからであろう。

　山口博士は、シーボルトの『日本書籍目録』に収められた書物にブロムホフ、または、フィッセルのコレクションが混在していることに言及し、さらに、その数についてはシーボルト自

身の見解とホフマンの見解が違っていることを正当に指摘している。これは、私の立場からすれば、実にありがたい。ライデンに調査に来る日本人研究者は、この点、つまり、コレクションの成り立ちについて、ほとんど頓着がなかったからだ。

　しかし、それ以上に興味深いのは、たとえば目録中の借用書籍について言及すれば、博士がシーボルトの収集品として疑わなかった『和漢三才図会』をはじめ、学術文献の執筆に欠かせない主要参考書籍が実際はシーボルトのものではなく、フィッセルのコレクションからの借用書籍であったことだろう。フィッセルの収集書籍とは、それほどに充実したものであった。山口博士のご遺稿の刊行にあたり、ここに、まだ現在進行中の作業で恐縮だが、私が作成している「シーボルトがフィッセルから借用した書籍一覧」を添える（本書221〜225頁、参照のこと）。

　シーボルトが『NIPPON』執筆にあたり、ブロムホフやフィッセルから借用したものは書籍に限らない。そのため、この全貌の解明が急がれるが、書籍借用については、近年、国立国会図書館の奥田倫子氏が、ライデン大学に納めた修士論文で言及されていることをここに記しておく。

　ライデン国立民族学博物館をはじめ、オランダ、ドイツに散在するシーボルトコレクションの成り立ちは複雑である。山口博士は、それを早くから気にかけ、シーボルトの収集品について「包括的な調査」を目指された。このバトンを受け取るかのように、近年（2010年）、国立歴史民俗学博物館の久留島浩教授が「日本関連在外資料調査研究事業」プロジェクト（大学共同利用機関法人　人間文化研究機構）を立ち上げ、シーボルトコレクションを含む在外研究資源の共有化、また、在外の日本コレクションの形成についての認識の共有化に取り組んでいる。これは、いわばシーボルト研究のためのインフラを充実させるものであり、このプロジェクトの成果を土台に、今後ますます活発な研究報告が、山口博士が担当医師に阻まれるまで毎年参加されたシーボルトコレクション会議で、実現されることを願うものである。

Preliminary remarks to the translation of two posthumous articles by Dr. Yamaguchi Takao

Dr. Matthi Forrer

It was almost impossible to image any of the International Siebold Collection Conferences that were organized and chaired each year since 2006 by Dr. Ohba Hideaki, honorary professor of the University of Tokyo and myself, without the late doctor Yamaguchi Takao attending – he never missed a single one. His passing away came as a great shock and I deeply regret we have to do without this fine scholar.

It was only when Dr. Takasugi Shio, the editor of this volume, asked me to help translate these two articles which Dr. Yamaguchi finished shortly before his death, that I first came to know that Dr. Yamaguchi also engaged in the research of Siebold's collection of books. Although I feel that this is something that could be expected of Dr. Yamaguchi, at the same time I also regret that I didn't have an occasion to exchange my thoughts with him when he was still with us.

As a researcher with the National Museum of Ethnology I have until now received many inquiries about the books collected by Siebold, while also conducting my own research. I was honestly surprised with the insight and knowledge that Dr. Yamaguchi as a Japanese researcher demonstrates in his articles. It is only a pity that he mainly relied upon secondary reference works. However, we can hardly blame him for this as this is not his primary field of expertise. I may add that I very much respect and support his call for a comprehensive research of the Siebold collections.

In my translations, I tried to provide you with a text that would be as faithful to the original as possible. Whenever there is something to add or comment from my position, I do so either in the footnotes or at the end of some sentence, whichever is most convenient, as I belief that this is something that also Dr. Yamaguchi would have welcomed. These annotations always start with my initials, MF.

As for the footnotes, I quote the Japanese references as they are, followed by my English translation. As for the indication of the relevant pages, these were mostly given by Dr. Yamaguchi, but not always. For a translator, it is rather impossible to check everything, so I left these indications as they were given in the Japanese original. The circumstance that Dr. Yamaguchi introduced rather an abundance of references in his footnotes must probably be seen as his intention in his last articles to show the way to the younger generation of researchers.

Dr. Yamaguchi was correct in pointing out clearly that the *Catalogus* also contains books collected by Blomhoff and by Fisscher. He was also correct in pointing out that there is at least some difference of opinion between Siebold and Hoffmann as regards the number of the books collected by Blomhoff and Fisscher that are listed in the *Catalogus*. From my position this is very meaningful since not many Japanese researchers seem to be aware of this. However, I must add that even Dr. Yamaguchi didn't suspect that some of the major publications that were indispensable for Siebold when writing his scientific articles, among others *Wakan sanzai zue*, were originally part of the collection of books made by Fisscher. On the occasion of this publication of the two last articles by the late Dr. Yamaguchi, I will add a provisional list of the books collected by Fisscher that were borrowed by Siebold.

It was not only books that Siebold borrowed from Blomhoff and Fisscher in order to write his *Nippon*. We should really work hard on a complete inventory of all the items that Siebold borrowed from these two earlier collections in the Royal Cabinet of Curiosities. As for the books, such an inventory was already made by Ms. Okuda Tomoko of the National Diet Library, as part of the research for her MA-thesis, submitted to Leiden University.

It really is a puzzle how the Siebold Collection came to be scattered, first in the Leiden National Museum of Ethnology, then both in the Netherlands, in Germany, and elsewhere. Dr. Yamaguchi was quick to notice this and so he focused on his comprehensive investigation of the collections made by Siebold. One may well say that it is Professor Kurushima Hiroshi of the National Museum of Japanese History who has in recent years taken over the baton with his research project of an Investigation of Japanese Collections Outside of Japan, funded by the National Institute for the Humanities. This project not only aims to make the various Japanese collections outside of Japan accessible, including the Siebold collections, it also aims to share an understanding of the collection forming. This is meant to provide an infrastructure for further Siebold research. I sincerely hope that the results of this project may serve as a basis for lively discussions during the Siebold Collection Conferences that the late Dr. Yamaguchi attended annually, until his doctor advised him not to do so any longer.

シーボルトの初回来日と収集書籍類について

山 口 隆 男

※本稿の（MF脚註番号）は、マティ・フォラーによる脚註・追記（英訳21～31頁、和文32～34頁）に対応している。

1. はじめに

　フィリップ・フランツ・バルタザール・フォン・シーボルト（Philipp Franz Barlthasar von Siebold　1796年生～1866年没）は、生涯2度にわたって来日している。それは、1823年（文政6）～1829年（文政12）すなわちシーボルト27歳～33歳と、1859年（安政6）～1862年（文久2）・シーボルト63歳～66歳の2回である。

　1845年、シーボルトは、自分の研究助手であるヨハン・ヨセフ・ホフマン（Johann Joseph Hoffmann　1805年生～1878年没）と共に、日本の書籍類目録『Catalogus librorum et manuscriptorum Japonicorum a Ph. Fr. de Siebold collectorum, annexa enumeratione illorum, qui in Museo Regio Hagano servantur』（邦訳『シーボルト収集日本書籍目録、並びにハーグ王立博物館所蔵日本書籍および写本類目録』、以下『日本書籍目録』と略記）を作成して、刊行した。

　この目録は、彼が初回来日時に収集した図書資料が中心を占めており、オランダのライデンで125部発行された。本文はラテン語で記述・リストされ、書籍の名前・著者名・刊行年・内容の簡単な紹介などが示されている。ホフマンは語学の天才で日本語のかな文字、漢文など各種の文献を読み、内容を知ることができた。この目録には、郭成章（Ko Tsching Dschang）が書いた漢字と日本語による書目一覧表（石版刷・16葉）が附属している。
[p.34 写真*Figs. 1a MF, 1b MF, 2b MF]

　そこで本稿では以下、本目録成立の背景として「2. シーボルトの初回来日と日本書籍類の収集」「3. シーボルトとホフマン」「4. シーボルトと郭成章」という三つの観点について述べた後、結語として「5. シーボルトの三大著作と収集書籍について」2013年4月現在、確認できたシーボルト研究の現状をふまえた概観を行い、今後の研究提言として「6. おわりに」を記す。

2. シーボルトの初回来日と日本書籍類の収集

　1796年2月17日（太陰暦1月9日）、フィリップ・フランツ・シーボルトは、ヴュルツブルグ大学医学部教授であった父ヨハン・ゲオルグ・クリストフ・シーボルト（Johann Georg Christoph Siebold）、母アポロニア（Apollonia 旧姓Lotz）の次男として生まれた。1798年に父が他界し、兄と姉も夭折したので、1805年、彼は母と共に、伯父（フランツ・ヨーゼフ・ロッツ Franz Joseph Lotz）の住むハイディングスフェルトに身を寄せた。

　1820年、彼は父が勤めたヴュルツブルグ大学で内科学・外科学・産科学博士の学位を受けた後、同年にハイディングスフェルトで開業。しかし、彼は開業医として暮らすことを望まず、1822年、バイエルン国籍（現ドイツ連邦共和国バイエルン州の前身）保持のままオランダ勤務の許可を得て、オランダ領東インド陸軍外科軍医少佐に任命された。シーボルトは、同年内にヨーロッパ内の自然科学アカデミーや学会会員資格（ゲンセンベルク自然研究学会の通信会員、帝立レオポルト・カロリン自然研究者アカデミー会員、ヴェタラウ全博物学会正会員）を入手。翌1823年2月13日（太陰暦1月3日）、バタヴィア（オランダ領ジャワ島）に到着後、東インド自然科学調査官兼任となった。その後、自らが日本研究を希望した結果、同年4月18日（太陰暦3月8日）長崎出島の商館医員に任じられ、8月12日（太陰暦七夕）長崎の出島に上陸した。[1]

　このように、シーボルトの来日時の肩書きは単に「長崎出島の商館付き医員」だけではなく、「自然科学調査官」でもあった。[2] 1820年、ライデンに設立された国立自然史博物館では日本産の標本を欲しがっていた。シーボルトには様々な任務があったが、日本の動植物の標本を収集し、オランダのライデンへの標本発送・東インドへの日本の生きた植物の送付等もその一つであったのである。

　来日後、シーボルトには様々な制約があった。1826年（文政9）の江戸参府旅行を除くと、出島から自由に出歩くことなど許されず、採集のために長崎郊外にでることができたのは僅かに日帰りの3回だけだったという。[3] 彼は何かにつけて不便な生活していたにもかかわらず、動植物の標本だけでなく、多数の書籍も入手していた。

　シーボルトは、出島のオランダ商館付医師として滞在していた時から、日本に関した本を刊行することを考えていた。それは、1824年（文政7）11月、オランダ国立自然史博物館初代館長のコンラート・ヤコブ・テンミンク（Coenraad Jacob Tenminck　1778年生～1858年没　鳥類学者）に宛てた手紙からも窺える。「私の計画は日本に関する広範な叙述をすることで、その仕事は既にはじめられ、いくつかの試作はすでに印刷に付されています。その中に短いけれど日本の有益な植物、動物、鉱物に関する事柄が付加されています。」[4]

シーボルトは、政府の指示に従ってライデンに標本を送るという任務を遂行するだけではなく、動物・植物に関したもの、日本の様々な面を総合的に紹介し、教養に関した包括的な著作をいずれ刊行するという構想を抱いていたことが分かる。野心的な彼は、日本に滞在できる機会を活用して、自分の研究を発展させ、記録として残そうと考えたのである。

ヨーロッパでは、19世紀は自然史の黄金時代であった。美麗な図版を沢山含む豪華な出版物によって、世界各地の様々な動植物が紹介されていた。日本に関するそのような書物を刊行することは大きな意義があるとシーボルトは考えたのである。シーボルトは、動植物の標本のほかに、写生画の収集も重視した。美麗な図版を含む書籍刊行には写生画が不可欠であった。動植物は標本にすると、色彩が失われたり、形が崩れたりするためである。そこで彼は、出島に出入りした絵師・川原慶賀に植物写生画をはじめとした様々な画を描かせたことが知られる。[5]

また、シーボルトは、動植物の写生画以外にも日本の風景・風俗が分かる肉筆画を収集した。収集肉筆画で最も有名なのは、日本人の生活習慣を描いた葛飾北斎による風俗画であろう。現在、27図がライデン国立民族学博物館に所蔵されている。[6]（MF脚註6追記）

このようにシーボルトは、写生画・肉筆画だけでなく、研究書物刊行に必要と考えられる日本の書籍類（板本・写本）は可能な限り集めるという方針にそって、購入・収集を行っていた。それが『日本書籍目録』の母体となったのである。

シーボルトの日本滞在任期終了について、1827年（文政10）9月10日（太陰暦9月4日）、ジャワのオランダ領東インド政庁は、彼をバタヴィアに帰国させることを決定。シーボルトは、翌年、長崎から出帆するオランダへの交易船に乗ることにしていた。

残念なことに、帰国予定の1828年（文政11）、「シーボルト事件」が発覚するというシーボルト本人が予想していなかったことが起きてしまった。[7]

同年5月11日（太陽暦3月28日）、シーボルトからの手紙を受け取った江戸の高橋景安（当時、書物奉行兼天文方筆頭）の身辺を中心に幕府の探索が始まった。また、同年秋9月18日（太陰暦8月10日）には「シーボルト台風」と呼ばれる猛烈な台風が長崎に襲来した。そのため、同年8月6日（太陰暦6月26日）に長崎へ入港し、10月1日（太陰暦8月23日）に出帆予定であった交易船のコルネリス・ハウトマン号は稲佐山下の海岸に乗り上げて座礁。離礁させるのに手間取り、出航が大幅に遅れるという事態になった。

翌1929年（文政12）2月24日（太陰暦1月21日）、ハウトマン号は出帆したが、シーボルトはそれに乗ることはできなかった。シーボルト事件の取り調べがあり、彼の処置が決まるまで、出国が許されなかったからである。同年10月22日（太陰暦9月25日）に判決が下ったが、それは「日本御構」（判決後最も早い出帆船での日本出国、および再入国禁止）であった。

シーボルトは1829年2月13日（太陰暦1月10日）付でジャワのオランダ領東インド政庁に

宛てて、自分が出島で行ってきた調査研究活動、業績の一覧表を作成して提出している。それには彼がコレクションしたリストも含まれている。「学術調査のための日本珍奇品収集リスト」(8)には、五つの項目があるが（Ⅰ書籍類、Ⅱ絵画とスケッチ、Ⅲ鋳貨、Ⅳ道具、Ⅴ工芸品、Ⅵ周辺諸国の書物品）、書籍類収集に関する部分は次の通りである。

　Ⅰ　書籍、地図、木版絵図などのコレクション
　　A　言語学（Ⅰ）
　　　約30の日本語、中国語、朝鮮語、アイヌ語、満州語、サンスクリット語のさまざまな辞書および語学書を含む
　　B　宗教（Ⅱ）　神道、仏道に関する著作、10
　　C　技芸および学術（Ⅲ）　約80の著作。それらの大部分には木版画の挿絵あり
　　D　自然学（Ⅳ）　約70の著作。それらの大部分には木版画の挿絵あり
　　E　地図、絵図、展望図など（Ⅴ）。約110の著作
　　F　地誌および歴史（Ⅵ）　日本および周辺諸国に関する50の著作。このなかには種々の手稿も含まれる
　　G　（欠）
　　H　画帖、美しい風景（名所）、服装、道具類の有名な日本画の書写を含む約90の作品および種々の物品の写生図のコレクション（Ⅶ）
　　Ｉ　雑（Ⅷ）　ここには上の諸項目に分類できない種々の著作が含まれる。
　　　少なくとも、冊子1,200からなるこの書籍コレクションは教養ある日本人により分類され、簡単な目録が付されており、全体的に非常によい保存状態である。これらの書籍のうち約400の著作は2部ずつあり、まず（バタフィア）当局の承認をえてから、このようなコレクションと調査に多大な学術上の援助を乞わねばならないパリ・アジア協会に向けられる

　シーボルト自身による本報告によって、彼が日本滞在中、地図・絵図類110、画帖・写生90、技芸・学芸が80、自然史関連70という数の書籍資料を「学術調査のため」収集していたことがわかる。（MF脚註*9）

　1830年（天保元）1月3日（太陰暦1829年12月7日）、シーボルトは離日し、1月28日（太陰暦1月4日）バタヴィア到着後、同地に約2箇月滞在。3月15日（太陰暦2月15日）、オランダに向けて出発。同年7月7日（太陰暦5月17日）オランダのフリッシング港に帰港。オランダ到着から10日目の7月17日（太陰暦5月27日）、シーボルトは、アントワープの旅先で本目録の共著者となったホフマンに出会うこととなった。

3. シーボルトとホフマン

　ヨハン・ヨセフ・ホフマンは、1805年（文化2）、ドイツのヴェルツブルクで裁判所奉仕員アダム・ホフマン（Adam Hoffmann）の息子として生まれた。[写真1参照：ヨセフ・ホフマン（ライデン大学蔵）]
　シーボルトとホフマンの思いがけない出会いについて杉本つとむは、次のように記述している。少し長くなるが、以下に引用する。(MF脚註11追記)

　　（シーボルトこと）彼はオランダのライデンに落着く途中、ベルギー北部の美しい港町、アントワープ（アンベルス）に旅宿の疲れを癒した。一八三〇年七月である。シーボルトはバタヴィアでしりあった中国人、郭成章 Ko Tsching Dschang をともなっていた。郭はシーボルトにとって、中国語や漢字を教授する強力な協力者であった。（とともに、やがてホフマンにとっても大切な指導者となる）。そしてこの旅宿に、売り出し中のオペラ歌手、ホフマンもまた、休息の一夜をすごすことになった。ホフマンは天性、美しい声を神から授けられたという。自ら進んでオペラ歌手の道で大成せんとして、この道を進んでいたのである。ホフマンはこの旅宿の娯楽室で、一人の男が、ドイツ語にオランダ語やフランス語、マライ語までまじえて何やら得意になって話しているのをみた。職業柄、耳にしたことばのなまりから、この男が自分と同郷のものであろうことを推測することができた。しかもその話しの内容から、この男が日本で数年をすごしたこともしった。──やがてホフマンの日本とは？　という問いによって、二人の出あいは永久の師弟関係をもって結ばれることとなるのであった。このときホフマンは二十六歳、すでに五年間、オペラ歌手として修業をかさねていた。しかし、シーボルトからきいた日本や日本語は若いホフマンに一大衝撃を与えた。魅せられたこの青年は、ついに自分の歩まんとしたオペラ歌手の道を断念、シーボルトに従ってライデンにおもむき、日本語研究に志すことを決意した。（中略）ホフマンはシーボルトから日本語の手ほどきを受け、その持ち前のすぐれた感覚、言語能力がもりあがり、次第に未知の日本語の世界をわがものとするようになっていった。元来、声楽家として耳と声には自信があり、格別に他にぬきんでていた彼の資質は、基本的に人間の声を研究対象にする言語の学にはよくむいていたわけである。

　こうしてホフマンは、1830年7月17日にシーボルトと出会ったことによって5年間の歌手生活に区切りをつけ、シーボルトの助手として日本研究に携わることになった。
　古田啓は、ホフマンの生涯を　①学生時代まで（1805～1825年）、②歌手時代（1825～1830

年)、③専業助手時代（1830〜1845年)、④植民省翻訳局時代（1846〜1854年)、⑤ライデン大学正教授時代Ⅰ（1855〜1861年)、⑥ライデン大学正教授時代Ⅱ（1862〜1878年）という6期に分けて述べているが、30代以降の後半生を日本語研究に捧げる契機をつくったのはシーボルトとの出会いであった。

　この出会いは、ホフマンが日本語研究を始める契機になった。驚くべきことに、彼は速やかに日本語文献を自由に読むことができるようになった。シーボルトの日本研究の右腕ともいうべき、無くてはならない存在になったことは、彼が15年も「専業助手」を務めたことからも明らかである。

　1855年、ライデン大学に日本語の講座が設置された折、ホフマンは初代正教授として就任し、晩年まで務めた。古田啓が「ライデン大学正教授時代」を二分しているのは、1862年（文久2）幕府から派遣された遣欧使節一行と出会ったことによる。ホフマンが日本人と直接面談したのはこれが最初であり、会談は主に筆談に頼ったという。ホフマンはこの折、福沢諭吉ら遣欧使節に対する接待係兼世話役を務めた。また、1863年（文久3）からオランダに滞在した幕府留学生15名に対しても親身な世話を行った。

　ホフマンの日本語研究成果の代表として挙げられるのが、ホフマンの補筆によってライデンで出版されたD.クルチュス（J. H. Donker Curtius）『Proeve Eener Japansche Spraakkunst』（『日本文法試論』、扉題「日本文典」、1857年刊）と、ホフマンの単著『Japansche Spraakleer』（『日本文典』、蘭文・英文、1867〜1868年刊）である。

　杉本つとむは、後者『日本文典』の「序論」はホフマンの日本語観を示しており「文語と口語、古代日本語と現代日本語という史的観点からの考察など他の研究者の追随を許さぬ」「系統論に筆を入れている。明治以降の日本語研究に先鞭をつけるもの」と評し、同著が「日本の文字・発音の考察」等も行ったことに注目している。

　ホフマンは人柄が良いことでも知られており、「最も控え目な、最も気取らぬ学者」であったと追悼文で評された。

　ホフマンのような特殊な能力の持ち主はどこにでもいるわけではない。全くの奇遇でそうした特別な人と出会い、自分の研究助手に雇うことができたシーボルトは幸運であった。

4. シーボルトと郭成章

　広東地方出身の知識人である郭成章（生没年未詳）について、残念ながら筆者はほとんど何も知らない。日本の学術的書物の多くが漢文で記されているので、シーボルトがそれらを理解するためには、中国の知識人の協力が必要であった。［写真2参照：　郭成章『Nippon』Ⅰ（福岡県立図書館蔵)］

郭成章は、広東省大埔県出身。号は乾草堂主人。先に述べたように、1830年、シーボルトは約2箇月バタヴィアに滞在したが、その時に郭と知り合い、彼を連れてきたのであった。彼の月俸は100グルデンであった。シーボルトは自分で負担していたが、やがてオランダ政府が肩代わりしてくれた。(MF脚註*18) 郭成章は約6年間、シーボルトのもとで中国服・弁髪のままライデンで暮らしたという。(16) 郭は、シーボルトの助手であっただけでなく、ホフマンにとって漢字・中国語の先生でもあった。郭は、中国語とマレー語しか出来なかったので、ホフマンは双方学習した。(17)

　1854年、『日本書籍目録』を刊行した時、郭成章はオランダにいなかった。(MF脚註*21) 郭成章が漢字と和名の書目一覧表を書くためには、彼がオランダを去る前に、シーボルトとホフマンは書物類の整理を終えていなければならなかった。

　郭成章はシーボルトと共に、日本語学習において重要な書物を著した。それらは『千字文』("Mille literae ideograpicae" 1833年刊)、『和漢音釋書言字考 Wakan won seki sio gen zi ko』("Thesaurus linguae japonicae" 1833年刊)、『新増字林玉篇 Zilin gjok ben』("Novus et auctus literarum ideographicarum thesaus" 1834年刊) (MF脚註*22) である。

　『千字文』は、各漢字に片仮名とハングル文字の読みが添えられている。『和漢音釋書言字考』は、『日本書籍目録』の第301番目にリストされている槇島昭武編『和漢音釈書言字考節用集』(初版1698年刊、1802年刊)の解説である。『新増字林玉篇』は、日本で収集した『和漢音釈書言字考節用集』などを用いて、漢字と片仮名による読みが示されたものである。これらの書物は、漢文あるいは漢字混じりの日本の書物を読み、理解する上で役に立つものであった。3冊に掲載される漢字と片仮名は、郭成章が書いている。つまり郭は、ホフマンに中国語を教え、各種文献類の解読面でシーボルトを助けただけでなく、日本語学習のための基礎書物の編集を行ったことになる。

　前章で触れたように、ホフマンは漢字を中国音ではなく、日本式の発音で読むことができた。たとえ語学の天才であっても、何故オランダで学習・研究ができたのか、筆者にとって謎の一つになっていた。それは、シーボルトが漢字・熟語の日本語読みを記述した書籍を入手していたことも一因であろう。

　例えば、杉本つとむは、ホフマンの日本語研究における参考文献として、寺島良庵『和漢三才図会』、『頭書訓蒙図彙（大成）』を挙げているが、(18) これは『日本書籍目録』の第1番目、2・3番目にリストされている（1『和漢三才図会』、2『頭書増補訓蒙図彙』、3『頭書増補訓蒙図彙大成』）。(MF脚註23追記)

　その他、ホフマンが日本語習得に活用した文献として杉本つとむは「シーボルトが持参した『和漢音釈書言字考節用集』も有効だったようである。これは江戸時代、もっとも典型的な漢和辞書であった。何よりも語彙が豊かであり、片仮名ですべての語彙に振り仮字が与えられて

いる点、外国人には有益であったと思う」と指摘している。先述したように、シーボルトは日本で収集した『和漢音釈書言字考節用集』を郭成章に調べさせて、新たに『和漢音釋書言字考』を編集刊行した。シーボルトの書籍収集が網羅的で優れていたことを示す一例と言えよう。

5. シーボルトの三大著作と収集書籍について ―現状の研究成果を踏まえて―

　シーボルトはオランダに戻ってから、三大著作と言われている大著の刊行を開始した。『Nippon』(『日本』、20分冊　1832～1859年頃)、『Fauna Japonica』(『日本動物誌』、5巻　1833～1850年)、『Flora Japonica』(『日本植物誌』、1巻　1835～1841年、2巻 1842～1844年・1879年) であるが、全て「未完の大著」となった。彼の後半生は、三大著作の刊行と、彼が興味を抱いた日本産の各種の園芸・庭園植物のオランダへの導入に費やされたといっても過言ではなかろう。三大著作はいずれも多数の図版を含む豪華なものであったから、多大な出版経費が必要であった。自費出版物として刊行したので、出版費用の捻出には色々な苦労があった。

　『Fauna Japonica』(日本動物誌)、『Flora Japonica』(日本植物誌) の主体は標本掲載であった。彼が入手した自然史関係の書籍や写生画（写本類を含む）は、参考資料としてそれなりに役に立っている。しかし、最も重要であったのは標本そのものであった。

　『Nippon』(日本) の場合は、シーボルトが出島で調べて記録・作成していた各種のデータや文書類、門人に執筆してもらった草稿類、川原慶賀に指示して描かせた写生図類、そして、持ち帰った書籍と地図類が執筆に用いられた。(22)(MF脚註27追記)

　例えば、『Nippon』の第5部「Pantheon von Nippon」の執筆にあたり『日本書籍目録』の第1番目にリストされている『和漢三才図会』も参照された。各種の仏像を図示した「Buddha-Pantheon von Nippon, Buts zo dsu i」という章の挿絵については『日本書籍目録』の第343番目にリストされた土佐秀信『増補諸宗　仏像図彙』にある各種の仏像の絵が使用された。(23)(MF脚註28追記) [写真3参照：『仏像図彙』挿絵と『NIPPON』の図版]

　また、先にふれたように、シーボルトは葛飾北斎の肉筆画も収集していたことが知られる。文政9年 (1826) の江戸滞在中、北斎と面会したとされ、肉筆画・浮世絵版画をはじめ『日本書籍目録』の第547番目にリストされている『北斎漫画』の挿絵が『Nippon』に借用されたことが指摘されている。(24)(MF脚註29追記)

　更に、『Nippon』には妙義山、愛宕山、御嶽山などの風景画が含まれている。それらの挿絵は、『日本書籍目録』の第149番目にリストされた谷文晁『名山図譜』(1804年刊) を活用して描かれたことが研究されている。(25) [写真4参照：『名山図譜』挿絵と『Nippon』の図版]

6. おわりに ―今後の研究課題について―

　シーボルトが来日時に入手した書籍類・写生画類・草稿類をどのように研究・執筆に活用したかについて、専門家各氏によって調査研究が行われている。しかし、現状では十分とはいえないだろう。専門家諸氏は、それぞれ自分が関心を抱く事柄、分野の範囲における調査研究を行ったに過ぎない。そのため、かなり深く調査研究が行われた分野がある一方で、全く何も行われていない分野がある。シーボルトは、日本にとって重要な功績を遺した人物の一人であることに対して、異論はなかろう。1996年には、生誕200年を記念して日本とドイツ連邦共和国において同一デザインの記念切手が発行された程、一般にも周知されている[26]。ところが、シーボルトに関した総合的な学術研究は未だに実施されていない。それを企画して文部科学省に補助金の交付を申請した人や研究グループはあったが、どれも採択されなかったのである。

　個人研究歴の回顧になり恐縮だが、筆者は元来、動物形態学・動物生態学を専門としてきた。1979年にオランダのライデンにある国立自然史博物館でカニの標本を調査したことがきっかけとなり、1985年以来シーボルト収集の動物と植物の標本の調査を行って今日（2013年4月）に至っている。オランダに滞在してシーボルト収集の動物と植物の標本調査研究を行った人は筆者以前にもいた。しかし、それは部分的な調査であり、総合的なものではなかった。自然史に関した総合的な調査研究は筆者が初めて行ったことになる。しかし、調査経費の確保に多大な苦労があった。当初は文部科学省の科学研究費を貰うことができた。しかし、中途で交付が打ち切られてしまい、その後は再三申請しても、採択されることが無かった。筆者はオランダのライデンに計42回渡航して調査したが、科研費による調査は10回分だけであった。6回分については航空運賃の補助があったが、現地滞在費の大部分は個人負担だった。残り26回は山口の私的調査で、渡航費・滞在費の全部を個人的に負担したのである。筆者は研究に必要な文献だけでなく、調査に必要なカメラ・フィルム・コンピューターの購入にもかなりの金額を費やした。

　筆者は、シーボルトについては各方面の専門家を集めた総合的学術調査が必要と信じている。シーボルトは決して過去の人ではない。江戸期に彼が収集した資料群は、今後益々重要性を増すばかりである。例えば、彼が収集した日本の民族学的標本・資料は、急速に日本の社会が変化しつつある今日では、ますます収集困難なものになっている。自然史的収集品は自然破壊が進み、多くの日本産動植物が絶滅に瀕している現在では、より貴重なものになった。彼の偉業がまだ十分に研究されていないのは全く残念である。書籍類・写生画類・草稿類についても、包括的な調査・研究が行われることを強く望むものである。

【 注 】

(1) シーボルトの伝記に関する記述は多数あり、呉秀三『シーボルト先生其生涯及功業』1～3 平凡社 1967～1968 年、板沢武雄『シーボルト』人物叢書 吉川弘文館 1960 年、ハンス・ケルナー著 竹内精一訳『シーボルト父子伝』創造社 1974 年、等が挙げられる。本稿では、石山禎一「シーボルト生涯・業績および関係年表」『新・シーボルト研究』八坂書房 2003 年、石山禎一・宮崎克則「シーボルトの生涯とその業績関係年表１（1796～1832 年）」『西南学院大学国際文化論集』26 巻 1 号 西南学院大学学術研究所 2011 年 9 月を主に参照した。

(2) シーボルト第 1 回目の来日目的が単に「長崎出島の商館付き医員」ではなかったことは早くから指摘されている。例えば、板澤武雄は、シーボルトがバタヴィアの東インド会社総督府に宛てた報告書類で度々用いた肩書 "De chirurgijn Majoor, belast met het natuurkundig onderzoek in dit Rijk, Dr. von Siebold" に注目して「万有学 Naturhistorische Wissenschaft の上から研究する使命を帯びてきた」としている（板澤武雄「シーボルトの第一回渡来の使命と彼の日本研究特に日蘭貿易の検討について」『シーボルト研究』岩波書店、1936 年）。また、大場秀章はシーボルトが用いた同じ肩書を視野に「自然科学的調査の使命を帯びた外科少佐」という面を視野に日本植物研究について述べている（大場秀章「シーボルトと彼の日本植物研究」『新・シーボルト研究Ⅰ』八坂書房 2003 年）。なお、秦新二氏は、シーボルト来日の目的を「博物学的調査、貿易的調査、政治的調査」の 3 点と指摘している（秦新二「一五〇年前の"現代人"」『ヨーロッパに眠る日本の宝』長崎県立美術博物館 1990 年）。

(3) 宮坂正英「研究ノート：シーボルトの日誌「漁村小瀬戸への調査の旅（草稿）」について」『鳴滝紀要』創刊号 長崎市シーボルト記念館 1991 年。

(4) 1824 年 11 月 15 日（太陰暦 9 月 25 日）付シーボルト作成テンミンク宛て手紙文の和訳は、以下の書を引用。Ｌ・Ｂ・ホルサイス 酒井恒『シーボルトと日本動物誌―日本動物史の黎明』学術書出版会 1970 年 248～250 頁。なお、「いくつかの試作」の具体例については、1823 年（文政 6）に脱稿した論文「日本国博物誌」（ラテン語、1824 年 10 月、バタヴィアで出版）が挙げられよう。

(5) 川原慶賀についての図書（図録）は、古賀十二郎『長崎絵画全史』北光書房 1933 年、『川原慶賀展 鎖国の窓を開く・出島の絵師』西武美術館 1980 年、金子厚男『シーボルトの絵師―埋れていた三人の画業』青潮社 1982 年、『川原慶賀展：幕末の"日本"を伝えるシーボルトの絵師』西武美術館 1987 年、影里鐵郎『日本の美術 329 号 川原慶賀と長崎派』至文堂 1993 年、兼重護『シーボルトと町絵師慶賀』長崎新聞社 2003 年、等がある。自然史画と川原慶賀の論文は、木村陽二郎「シーボルトと川原慶賀―植物図の関連」『蘭学資料研究会研究報告』309 号 1976 年、拙稿「ライデンにある川原慶賀の自然史画（1996 年度〔洋学史学会〕大会記録（長崎））」『洋学』5 号 洋学史学会 1996 年、拙稿「川原慶賀と日本の自然史研究：Ⅰ シーボ

ルト・ビュルゲルと「ファウナ・ヤポニカ魚類編」」『Calanus：合津臨海実験所報』12号　熊本大学理学部附属合津臨海実験所　1997年1月、等がある。

(6) マティ・フォラー「葛飾北斎とシーボルトの出会い」『北斎』東京新聞、2007年。

(7) シーボルト事件に関する研究は多数ある。例えば、中西啓「シーボルト事件判決時の法的根拠」『鳴滝紀要』9号　1999年、梶輝行「シーボルト事件―商館長メイランの日記を中心に」『新・シーボルト研究Ⅱ』八坂書房　2003年、等がある。

(8) 1829年2月13日（太陰暦1月10日）シーボルト作成「一八二三年より一八二八年十月一日まで、日本における博物学調査のために宛てられ、（交付された）調査費の使途明細報告総括」における「付録五　下名の計算（支払い）で収集し、差し当たり王立博物館に宛てた、学術調査のための日本珍奇品収集リスト」。翻訳の引用は以下の書による。栗原福也翻訳『シーボルトの日本報告』東洋文庫784　平凡社　2009年　293～299頁。

(9) ホフマン伝の邦文主要論文は以下の通りである。幸田成友「ヨハン・ヨゼフ・ホフマン」『科学ペン』15巻12号　1940年12月、「ヨハン・ヨゼフ・ホフマン―ライデンの日本語学者―」『法政大学部教養部紀要　人文科学編』50号　1984年1月、フランツ・バビンガー　古田啓訳「日本語学者列伝　ホフマン伝(1)～(3)」『日本語学』44～46号　明治書院　1986年6月～9月、古田啓「ヨハン・ヨーゼフ・ホフマン―生涯と業績」『お茶の水女子大学人文科学紀要』57号　2004年3月。

(10) 杉本つとむ『杉本つとむ著作選集　10巻　西洋人の日本語研究』八坂書房　1999年　352～354頁。

(11) 古田啓「ヨハン・ヨーゼフ・ホフマン―生涯と業績―」『お茶の水女子大学人文科学紀要』57号　2004年3月。

(12) 前掲「ヨハン・ヨゼフ・ホフマン―ライデンの日本語学者―」138～145頁。

(13) 杉本つとむは、『Proeve Eener Japansche Spraakkunst』（1957年刊）に対し、『Japansche Spraakleer』（1867～68年刊）と区別のため『日本文法試論』と邦訳しているが（前掲『西洋人の日本語研究』）、吉田啓は『日本語文典稿本』と邦訳している（前掲「ヨハン・ヨーゼフ・ホフマン―生涯と業績―」）。

(14) 前掲『杉本つとむ著作選集　10巻　西洋人の日本語研究』353～383頁。

(15) イギリスの雑誌『Ashiniamu』（アスィニーアム）1878年2月9日掲載（前掲論文「ヨハン・ヨゼフ・ホフマン―ライデンの日本語学者―」148頁）。

(16) 前掲「ヨハン・ヨゼフ・ホフマン―ライデンの日本語学者―」124頁。

(17) フランツ・バビンガー　古田啓訳「ホフマン伝(2)―ヴェルツブルクの一東洋学者―」『日本語学』45号　明治書院　1986年7月。

(18) 前掲『杉本つとむ著作選集　10巻　西洋人の日本語研究』387～389頁。

(19) 前掲『杉本つとむ著作選集　10巻　西洋人の日本語研究』390頁。

(20) 『Nippon』刊行・配布時期については、斉藤信「シーボルト『日本』の最終刊行年とその全体構想について」『シーボルトと日本』6巻　雄松堂　1979年、マティ・フォラー他『シーボルトと日本』Hotei出版　2000年、宮崎克則「復元　シーボルト『NIPPON』の配本」『九州大学総合研究博物館研究報告』3号　2005年3月、等の考察がある。なお、『Fauna Japonica』の刊行については、ホルトハウス・酒井恒『シーボルトと日本動物誌―日本動物史の黎明』学術書出版会　1970年、『Flora Japonica』については、木村陽二郎『シーボルトと日本の植物　東西文化交流の源泉』恒和出版　1981年、木村陽二郎・大場秀章『シーボルト「フローラ・ヤポニカ」日本植物誌』八坂書房　2000年、等に詳しい。

(21) シーボルト収集標本類の重要性とその活用については、山口隆男編『シーボルトと日本の博物学　甲殻類』日本甲殻類学会　1993年、山口隆男「シーボルトと日本の動物学」『鳴滝紀要』6号　シーボルト記念館　1996年3月、山口隆男「シーボルト、ビュルガー、川原慶賀と日本の魚類学」『鳴滝紀要』17号　2007年3月等で言及している。

(22) ドイツのブランデンシュタイン城に保存されている江戸参府に随行した川原慶賀の写生画や『Nippon』下絵について、宮崎克則「シーボルト『NIPPON』の原画・下絵・図版」『九州大学総合研究博物館研究報告』9号　2011年3月、に報告がある。

(23) 岩生成一監修『シーボルト「日本」の研究と解説』講談社　1977年、末木文美士「『仏像図彙』解説」『シーボルト　日本』6巻　雄松堂書店　1979年、末木文美士「シーボルト／ホフマンと日本宗教」『季刊日本思想史』55号　ぺりかん社　1999年11月。なお、宮崎克則氏は、「シーボルト『NIPPON』の色つき図版」『九州大学総合研究博物館研究報告』5号　2007年1月　46頁、において、シーボルトが収集した『増補諸宗　仏像図彙』1796年刊　5冊は、現在ライデン大学図書館の所蔵であることを報告している。

(24) シーボルトと北斎肉筆画の関係については、前掲「葛飾北斎とシーボルトの出会い」に詳しい。また、北斎肉筆画・浮世絵や『北斎漫画』に基づいた『NIPPON』挿絵作成に関する指摘については、前掲『北斎展』図版解説や、橋本健一郎「『北斎漫画』考　その成立と影響―シーボルト著『NIPPON』図版篇を中心として―」『北斎研究所　研究紀要』5集　2013年1月、等がある。

(25) 宮崎克則「シーボルト『NIPPON』の山々と谷文晁『名山図譜』」『九州大学総合研究博物館研究報告』4号　2006年。

(26) 日本におけるシーボルト顕彰については、『鳴滝紀要』6号（シーボルト記念館　1996年3月）に掲載された、沓沢宣賢「シーボルト渡来百年記念祭に関する一考察―外務省外交資料館所蔵史料を中心に―」や五貫淳「シーボルト生誕二百周年の歩み―シーボルトと長崎―」に詳しい。

写真1：ヨセフ・ホフマン Johann Joseph Hoffmann　1805〜1878（ライデン大学蔵）
Fig. 1—A portrait of Johann Joseph Hoffmann. Courtesy Leiden University.

写真2：郭成章　Ko Tsching Dschang　『Nippon』Ⅰ（福岡県立図書館蔵）
Fig. 2—A portrait of Ko-tsching Dschang. From *Nippon*. Courtesy Fukuoka Prefectural Library.

写真３：『仏像図彙』（ライデン大学図書館蔵）挿絵と『Nippon』Ⅴ（福岡県立図書館蔵）の図版
（上『仏像図彙』の原図、下『Nippon』Ⅴにある複製画）
Fig. 3—A comparison of the illustrations in *Butsuzō zui* and in *Nippon*.

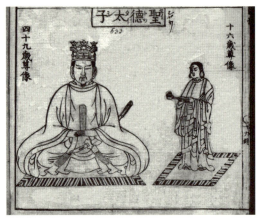

「343. Zôbô sjosiu, Butszô dsui」(UL, Ser. 592)

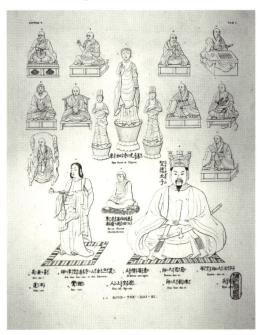

「Buddha-Pantheon von Nippon Buts zo dsu i」
(*Nippon* V, Fukuoka Prefectual Library)

【343.『増補諸宗　仏像図彙』（L .Serrurier 目録№. 592、ライデン大学図書館蔵）】

　シーボルト『Nippon』（ニッポン）には、ホフマン著として「Buddha-Pantheon von Nippon Buts zo dsu i」のタイトルで様々な仏像を紹介、解説している論文がある。図の出典は『増補諸宗仏像図彙』であった。絵は土佐秀信が描いている。全5巻で、各種の仏像だけではなく、神社に神として祀られている人々、仏になったとされる名僧など実にさまざまなものが図示されている。ライデン大学図書館本は Serrurier によると 1796 年刊の第 3 版である。

　ホフマンは 40 頁の図版によって、全部ではないが、かなりの数の仏や神を図示している。

　聖徳太子の画像は『仏像図彙』第 4 巻の最後にあるが、ホフマンは第 1 図版に含めている。第 1 図版は日本の仏教の発展、振興に功績があった人たちの画像集で、聖徳太子の他に弘法大師、伝教大師、日蓮、親鸞などの画像がある。ホフマンはいろいろな仏や神像を調べて、グループごとにまとめて図示している。

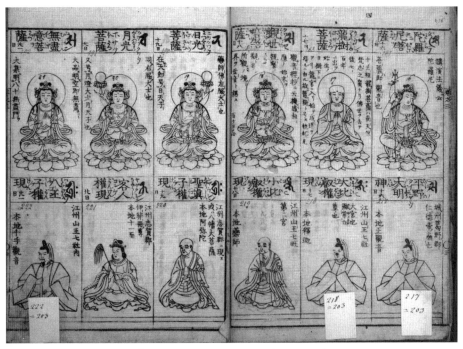

「343. Zôbô sjosiu, Butszô dsui」（UL, Ser. 592）

「Buddha-Pantheon von Nippon Buts zo dsu i」
（*Nippon* Ⅴ, Fukuoka Prefectual Library）

写真4：『名山図譜』（ライデン大学図書館館）挿絵と『Nippon』Ⅵ（福岡県立図書館蔵）の図版
（左「筥根嶺」と「HAKONE-TOGE」、右「御嶽」と「MI-TAKE」）
Fig. 4—A comparison of the illustrations in Tani Bunchō's *Meizan zufu* and those in *Nippon*.

 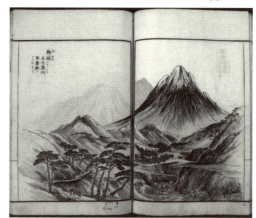

（2巻、4図）　「149. Mei san dsu bu」(UL, Ser. 365)　（1巻、15図）

（*Nippon* Ⅵ）

【149. 『名山図譜』（L. Serrurier 目録№365、ライデン大学図書館蔵）】
　シーボルト『Nippon』Ⅵの図版には次のような日本各地の山の絵がある（所在地・標高は山口による加筆）。
1）妙義山（群馬県、1104 m）、2）箱根（神奈川県、1438 m）、3）愛宕山（京都市、924 m）、4）吾田多良山（安達太良山、あだたらやまのこと、福島県、1728 m）、5）小野岳（福島県、1383 m）、6）御嶽（長野県、3067 m）7）白山（石川 - 岐阜県、2702 m）、8）霧島山（鹿児島 - 宮崎県、1700 m）、9）浅間山（長野県、2568 m）、10）阿蘇山（熊本県、1592 m）、11）鳥海山（秋田 - 山形県、2236 m）、12）富士山（静岡 - 山梨県、3776 m）、13）巌鷲山（岩手県の岩手山のことである。2038 m）、14）巌木山（岩木山のこと、青森県、1625 m）、15）御駒岳（宮城。秋田、岩手県境、1627 m）、16）大山（鳥取県、1729 m）、17）御嶽（この場合は鹿児島県の桜島のこと、1117 m）、18）雲仙岳（長崎県、1483 m）、19）金華山（宮城県、445 m）、20）五剣山（香川県、375 m）の20山である。
　全て谷文晁（1763-1841）が描いた『名山図譜』3冊に含まれる絵の模写である。この『名山図譜』は、江戸の将軍の侍医の桂川甫賢がシーボルトに贈った。1804年刊行の初版本である。これらのうちの御嶽（桜島）は原画とかなり異なり、海上にあることがよりよく判るように修正がなされている。他の19図は原画に準拠して作成された。しかし、全く同じではなく、細部に変更が加えられている。なお、シーボルト旧蔵『名山図譜』は手彩色がほどこされているが、『Nippon』の図版はいずれも白黒である。『名山図譜』と『Nippon』に掲載された各図版と実景の比較については、宮崎克則「シーボルト『NIPPON』の山々と谷文晁『名山図譜』」（『九州大学総合研究博物館研究報告』4号　2006年）に詳しい。

Siebold's first journey to Japan – with special emphasis on his collection of books.

Dr. Takao Yamaguchi

I. Preliminary

Philipp Franz von Siebold (1796-1866) visited Japan twice, first from 1823 to 1829 (that is from Bunsei 6 to Bunsei 12), from the age of 27 to 33 years, and again from 1859 to 1862 (Ansei 6 to Bunkyū 2), when he was 63 to 66 years old. In between these two journeys, in 1845, he published the *Catalogus librorum et manuscriptorum japonicorum a Ph. Fr. de Siebold collectorum, annexa enumeratione illorum, qui in Museo Regio Hagano servantur*, a catalogue compiled together with his research assistant Johann Joseph Hoffmann (1805-1878). According to the title-page, it lists the books and manuscripts that Siebold had collected during his first journey to Japan as well as the books collected earlier by Jan Cock Blomhoff (1779-1853) and Johannes van Overmeer Fisscher (1800-1848) that the King of the Netherlands had purchased for his Cabinet at The Hague. [p. 34*Figs. 1aMF, 1bMF, 2b MF] The list gives titles, names of authors, year of publication, and summary contents of each book in Latin. This catalogue was published in Leyden in an impression of 125 copies. The just mentioned Hoffmann was a genius in languages who could read both *kana* syllables and Chinese characters, as well as understand their meaning. The catalogue was complemented by a list of the titles of the books in Chinese characters, written by Ko-tsching Dschang (dates unknown) and printed on 16-lithographed sheets.

In this contribution, I would like to discuss the background of this catalogue and how it came into being, notably from three viewpoints: Siebold's first visit to Japan and his collection of books will be discussed in paragraph II; Siebold and Hoffmann in paragraph III; and Siebold and Ko-tsching Dschang in paragraph IV. I will then proceed with a discussion of Siebold's three *opera magna* and their relation to his collection of books, in paragraph V. By way of conclusion I would then like to come up with some suggestions for possible further research – to be viewed in the light of those researches known to me at the time of writing this, April 2013.

II. Siebold's first stay in Japan and his collection of books

Philipp Franz Balthasar von Siebold was born on February 17th, 1796 (the 1st month, 9th day in the lunar calendar), as the second son of Johann Georg Christoph Siebold, professor of medicine at Würzburg University, and Apollonia Lotz. When his father died in 1798, and also his brother and sister had died young, his mother moved in with her brother Franz Joseph Lotz in Heidingsfeld, where the young Siebold would grow up from 1805. In 1820 he obtained a doctorate in internal surgery and obstetrics at Würzburg University, where also his father had been teaching, and later that year he started practicing as a medical doctor in Heidingsfeld.

However, not wishing to simply spend the rest of his life as a medical doctor, he managed to find a position as Surgeon-Major with the Netherlands East Indian Army in 1822, retaining his Bavarian nationality. In the same year he was appointed corresponding member of both the Senckenbergisches Naturforschendes Gesellschaft and of the Kaiserliche Leopoldinisch- Carolinische Akademie der Naturforscher, as well as of the Wetterauische Gesellschaft. And so, the following year, on February 13th, 1823 (1/3 in the lunar calendar), he arrived at Batavia (present-day Jakarta) on the island of Java in the Dutch East Indies. Shortly after his arrival, he was also made responsible for the natural history research there. When he himself expressed his desire to conduct research in Japan, he was appointed medical doctor with the Deshima Factory on April 18th, 1823 (3/8). Consequently, he would arrive at Deshima, Nagasaki, on August 12th (7/7)[1]. Besides 'factory doctor', he was also responsible for investigating the natural history of Japan[2]. The National Museum of Natural History, established in Leyden in 1820, was anxious to obtain specimens from that country. And so, collecting and sending Japanese plants to the Netherlands Indies was only one of Siebold's various diverse tasks, he was also responsible for collecting specimens of Japanese flora and fauna and shipping these to Leyden. However, upon his arrival at Deshima, Siebold was subjected to strict regulations. Except for the Court Journey to Edo in 1826 (Bunsei 9), he was not allowed to freely leave the island of Deshima. Indeed, it is said that he was only three times allowed a day's trip to the outskirts of Nagasaki to collect plants[3]. Yet, although he had to spend the time in limited freedom, he not only collected many specimens of Japanese flora and fauna as we will see in the following, but he even made a quite sizeable collection of books.

From a letter written to Conrad Jacob Temminck (1778-1858), ornithologist and the first director of the National Museum of Natural History in the Netherlands, it appears that Siebold already conceived his plan to publish a book on Japan as early as 1824 (Bunsei 7), when still at Deshima:

> My plan is to make a comprehensive description of Japan. I have already started this work and some pieces have even appeared in print. To these, I appended

---

(1) There are many descriptions of Siebold's life, such as, Kure 1967-68; Itazawa 1960; Körner/Takeuchi 1974. When writing this contribution, I primarily used: *New Siebold Research* 2003; Ishiyama/Miyazaki 2011.

(2) It has been remarked earlier that the purpose of Siebold's first sojourn was not only to be a factory doctor, as was discussed by, for example, Itazawa Takeo on the basis of the signature that Siebold used in his documents sent to the government, signing: 'De chirurgijn-majoor belast met het natuurkundige onderzoek in dit Rijk, Dr. Von Siebold' (Itazawa 1938). Also Ohba Hideaki discussed Siebold's natural history research from this perspective (Ohba 2003); Hata Shinji gave the following three reasons for Siebold's coming to Japan: museological research, trade related research, and politics (Hata 1990).

(3) Miyasaka 1991.

some remarks in regard to the useful plants, animals and minerals of Japan[4].

It thus appears that Siebold was not only fulfilling his task of sending specimens to the Netherlands, but that he also cherished a greater plan to introduce Japan in Europe, including its flora and fauna, through his publications. Ambitious as he was, he always tried to further his own research and to submit the results of it, benefiting from the opportunities that were given to him.

In Europe, the nineteenth century was really the golden age of natural history. The flora and fauna of diverse parts of the world were introduced in richly illustrated publications. Siebold found it very important to be able to also publish such a book on Japan. Consequently, he realized the importance to have illustrations made of the specimens that he collected. Illustrations after life of these specimens were not only indispensable when publishing such a book, we must also realize that plants and animals would loose both their colours and their form when they were made into specimens. As is now well known, it was exactly for that reason that Siebold commissioned the painter Kawahara Keiga (1786-1860s) to make paintings of all plants and animals[5].

In addition to the paintings of flora and fauna, Siebold also made a collection of paintings of landscapes and customs of Japan. Among these, the group of genre paintings by Katsushika Hokusai – some 27 such paintings have been preserved in the National Museum of Ethnology, Leyden – is best known[6]. In addition to these paintings and drawings, he also tried to bring together as many books as he could – both printed and manuscripts – that might be meaningful and important for his future research. These were the basis for the earlier mentioned *Catalogus librorum et manuscriptorum japonicorum*, henceforth referred to as *Catalogus librorum*.

On September 10th, 1827 (Bunsei 10, lunar 7/20), the Government in Java decided to call an end to Siebold's stay in Japan and make him return to Batavia. Consequently, he prepared for his return journey to Batavia in the following year, 1828. It is a pity though that there was an incident that year that came to be known as the 'Siebold Incident.'[7] On May 11th (3/28), 1828, Takahashi Kageyasu (1785-1829), the head of the astronomical office, was being investigated. Later that year, on September 18th (8/10), a severe typhoon – that came to be known as the 'Siebold Typhoon' – hit upon Nagasaki. Consequently, the *Cornelis Houtman*, the ship that arrived at Nagasaki on August 6th (6/26) and was to sail back to Batavia on October 1st (8/23), was thrown onto the coast. Its return journey was then delayed

---

(4) The letter dates from November 15th, 1824 (lunar 9/25) and is here quoted after Holthuis/Sakai 1970, pp. 248-250. As concerns these several pieces of writing, one example would be *De historiae naturalis in Japonia statu* (Batavia, 1824).

(5) As for Keiga, see for example J. Koga 1933; Exhibition Catalogue 1980; Kaneko 1982; Exhibition Catalogue 1987; Kagesato 1993; Kaneshige 2003. As for Keiga and his natural history paintings, see for example Kimura 1976; Yamaguchi 1996b; Yamaguchi 1997.

(6) See Forrer 2007. [MF: Actually, as is also suggested in that publication, the group in the Leyden collection would only number 17 at most, including some four paintings attributable to Hokusai's pupil Totoya Hokkei.]

(7) Understandably, there are quite a few studies of the incident, such as: Nakanishi 1999; Kaji 2003.

considerably as it was difficult to get the ship out of the shallow waters. It was only the following year 1829 (Bunsei 12), on February 24th (1/21), that the *Cornelis Houtman* could sail out, however, without Siebold on board. He didn't get permission to leave the country until the Siebold Incident had been fully investigated. It was only later that year, on October 22nd (9/25), that Siebold was sentenced to leave Japan with the first possible ship, to be banned forever.

By then, Siebold had made up an extensive overview of his activities for the Dutch government concerned with his research of the natural history of Japan conducted at Deshima, dated February 13th (1/10), 1829. This report is also comprised of an overview of the collections that he managed to make in Japan[8]. Under the heading of *Overview of the collection of Japanese rarities to serve in the scientific research*, this document is subdivided into five categories, as follows: I Books, maps, and prints; II Paintings and drawings; III Coins; IV Utensils; V Works of craftsmanship; VI Objects from neighbouring countries.

In the following I will elaborate on category I, the collection of Books, Maps, and Prints, that is again subdivided and annotated as follows:

A Linguistics (I) – Circa 30 dictionaries and linguistic treatises on Japanese, Chinese, Korean, Ainu, Manchu, and Sanskrit.

B Religion (II) – 10 books on Shintō and Buddhism.

C Technique and Science (III) – Circa 80 works, most of these illustrated with woodblock printed images.

D Natural History (IV) – Some 70 works, most of these with woodblock printed illustrations.

E Maps, Plans and Views (V) – Circa 110 works.

F Geography and History (VI) – Circa 50 works on Japan and the neighbouring countries.

Among these also various MSS.

G (blank)

H Albums of paintings, famous views, costumes, and tools, including copies after famous Japanese paintings (VII) – More than 90 works, also including depictions of collections of various objects.

I Miscellaneous (VIII) – In this group figure those books that cannot be included in the above categories.

This collection of books of at least 1200 volumes was arranged by a learned Japanese and complemented by simple annotations. They are in excellent condition.

More than 40 works in this collection are in duplicate copies. When permission of the authorities is obtained, these will be destined for the Société asiatique of Paris, which is in need of large scientific support for this kind of collection and research.

From this report[9], made up by Siebold himself, it is clear that he assembled some

---

(8) This list, made up by Siebold himself and dated February 13th, 1829 (1/10), is titled in full *Overview of the collection of Japanese rarities, to serve in the scientific research, brought together at the expense of the undersigned, and provisionally destined for the museum of His Majesty the King*. More precisely, it is Appendix No. 5, to complement his *General overview and account of the budget of DFl. 42.974 from 1823 until October 1st, 1828, in support of the natural history research on Japan*, in which Siebold specifies which sums were used as payments to whom and for what, covering the period from 1823 until October 1st, 1828. Here cited after Kurihara (tr.) 2009, pp. 293-299.

110 maps and plans, some 90 illustrated albums, some 80 works on technique and science, and some 70 on natural history, all collected during his stay in Japan for his scientific research.

On January 3rd, 1830 (Tenpō 1, 1829, lunar 12/9), Siebold would leave Japan to arrive in Batavia on January 28th, (1/4), where he would stay some two months (MF: actually rather a month and a half). On March 15th (2/21) he then departs for the Netherlands where he would arrive on July 7th (5/17) of the same year 1830, in the harbour of Flushing. Only ten days later, on July 17th (5/27), in Antwerp, Siebold first meets with J.J. Hoffmann with whom he would later make the catalogue of his collection of books.

III. Siebold and Hoffmann

Johann Joseph Hoffmann was born in 1805 (Bunka 2), the son of Adam Hoffmann who had some position with the court at Würzburg[10]. [Fig. 1] Sugimoto Tsutomu provides an account of the unexpected meeting of Siebold with Hoffmann[11]. Even though it may be a bit long, I would like to cite it here in full:

He [Siebold] was on his way to Leyden in the Netherlands when he took a break at Antwerp, a beautiful harbour city in the north of Belgium. It was July of 1830. Siebold was accompanied by Ko-tsching Dschang, a Chinese whom he had met and got to know in Batavia. Ko was an important collaborator for Siebold, who taught him Chinese and Chinese characters, much like he would later also be an important teacher for Hoffmann.

Then Hoffmann, who just started getting some fame as an opera singer, came to the same inn for a night of rest. Of Hoffmann it has always been said that he had received his beautiful voice from God. He had the ambition to make a real reputation as an opera singer. That evening, Hoffmann saw a man in the resting room of the inn who proudly spoke German, Dutch, French, and even Malay. He not only started to guess from his accent that the man came from the same region as he himself, he also came to understand from his stories that the man had spent several years in Japan – Japan? Soon it would also be Hoffmann's Japan. When his questions

---

(9) MF: These annotations are written in Japanese, mostly in *katakana* script, on small pieces of Dutch paper, taking the format of an indication where the work would fit in some systematical ordering, followed by details such as 1: Title of the work, 2: Author, 3: Place of publication, 4: Year of publication, and 5: Number of volumes. [*Fig. 1c MF] They are normally pasted on the inside front-cover. Obviously, these labels are the only means to positively identify those books that Siebold originally collected during his stay on Deshima in the years 1823 through 1829. That there is a considerable difference between this original collection of some 440 titles in 1200 volumes (Brug Brandenstein Archives, SAM 3-23; Cf. Kurihara (tr.) 2009) – as per 1829 – becomes directly clear from the number of volumes represented in the 1845 *Catalogus librorum*, totaling some 1800 volumes.

(10) The main articles dealing with the life of Hoffmann are among others: Kōda 1940; Miyanaga 1984; Barbinger/Furuta 1986; Furuta 2004.

(11) Sugimoto 1999, pp. 352-354. [MF: However nice this surprise meeting may sound, it must be said though, that Hoffmann had already sought contact with Siebold as early as January 1829 and even as shortly before this meeting as in April 1830 (Cf. Ishiyama/Miyazaki 2011, pp. 206 and 212). Moreover, it is highly unlikely that also Ko would be present at this meeting on July 17th, as he only left Batavia almost two months later than Siebold, early May 1830, and on a different ship, the *Jonge Adriana*, as Medhurst writes to Siebold in a letter preserved in the Burg Brandenstein Archives (15B-168)]

had been answered, the meeting of the two men changed into the teacher-student relation that would bind them forever. At the time, Hoffmann was 26 years old and had been training as an opera singer for some five years. However, the stories that he heard from Siebold about Japan and the Japanese language so much impressed the young Hoffmann that he gave up his career of an opera singer and decided to follow Siebold to Leyden in order to study the Japanese language. /…/

Hoffmann was then taught the Japanese language by Siebold and came to familiarize himself with this unknown world, thanks to his natural feeling for linguistics. By nature and as a singer, Hoffmann was convinced of his hearing and voice, and these excellent talents made him suited for the study of languages.

So far the story of their meeting as recounted by Sugimoto. In this way, there came an end to Hoffmann's five years as an opera singer, on July 17th, 1830, and he started a new life as a Japan-researcher, the assistant of Siebold.

Furuta Kei distinguishes six periods in the life of Hoffmann, setting the start of his Japanese studies in the second part of his life, in his thirties, as the result of his meeting with Siebold[12].

1. From his youth until the end of his studies, 1805-25
2. As a singer, 1825-30
3. Assistant of Siebold, 1830-45
4. Translator for the Dutch Ministry of Colonies, 1846-54
5. Full professor at the University of Leyden I, 1855-61
6. Full professor at the University of Leyden II, 1862-78

To everybody's amazement, Hoffmann quickly learned to read Japanese reference works. That he served as the right hand of Siebold in the Japan research of the latter, being indispensable as such, can be inferred from the circumstance that he worked as his exclusive assistant for some fifteen years.

In 1858, when the University of Leyden installed a chair in Japanology, Hoffmann was nominated its first professor, a position he kept until his death. Furuta Kei's subdividing his professorship at Leyden into two periods is based on Hoffmann's meeting in 1862 (Bunkyū 2) with a delegation sent by the Japanese *bakufu*. This would be his first occasion to meet with living Japanese while their discussions would be mainly conducted in the form of a written conversation. On this occasion Hoffmann acted as the host, being in charge of the delegation, among whom Fukuzawa Yukichi[13]. In 1863 (Bunkyū 3), he would again take care of a group of Japanese students, no less than fifteen this time, also sent to the Netherlands by the *bakufu*[14].

Hoffmann's most important contributions to the research of the Japanese language would be his editing of a publication by J.H.

---

[12] Furuta 2004.
[13] MF: Fukuzawa Yukichi (1834-1901) was one of Japan's foremost reformers, travelling to the United States in 1860 and in 1867, and to Europe in 1861. In 1868 he founded Keiō University.
[14] Miyanaga 1984, pp. 138-145.

Donker Curtius, *Proeve eener Japansche spraakkunst* (Leyden, 1857), as well as his own *Japansche spraakleer* that was published both in Dutch and in English (Leyden, 1867 and 1868)[15]. In regard to the *Japansche spraakleer*, Sugimoto remarks that Hoffmann laid down his views of the Japanese language in the preface. He appreciates this, as it demonstrates that Hoffmann is unique in not only treating equally both written and spoken Japanese, but also both classical and modern Japanese. Moreover, he would also pay attention to the characters used in writing Japanese, as well as to their pronunciation[16].

Hoffmann was also known for his personality and in his obituaries he was praised as both the most modest as well as the least arrogant scientist[17]. One cannot easily find another such talented person as Hoffmann. As for that, Siebold was especially lucky to meet with such a person by sheer accidence and moreover managing to employ him as his research assistant.

IV. Siebold and Ko-tsching Dschang

It is quite annoying to have to admit that I hardly know anything about Ko-tsching Dschang (or Kuo Ch'êng-chang) – a learned man from Canton, but years of birth and death not known. Since many of the scientific books in Japan were written in classical Chinese, or *kanbun*, Siebold needed some learned Chinese. [Fig. 2] Ko-tsching Dschang was born in Canton, and his literary name was Kansōdō Shujin. As already remarked above, Siebold got to know Ko during the almost two months he spent in Batavia, in early 1830, whereupon he brought him with him to Leyden. He was paid a salary of Dutch Florins 100 per month. Initially, Siebold paid him out of his own pocket, but later the Dutch Government would take over this responsibility[18]. Ko appears to have been working with Siebold some six years, always keeping up his traditional life, that is clad in Chinese dress and his hair in the Chinese style[19]. Ko was not only Siebold's assistant, he was also the teacher of Hoffmann for his studies of Chinese characters and of the Chinese language. As Ko only knew Chinese and Malay, Hoffmann was obliged to learn both these languages too[20].

When the *Catalogus librorum* was published in 1845, Ko was no longer in the Nether-

---

(15) Sugimoto Tsutomu translates *Proeve eener Japansche spraakkunst* in his *Japanese Studies by Europeans* as *Nihon bunpō shiron*『日本文法試論』, so as to distinguish it from Hoffmann's *Japansche spraakleer*『日本語文法』(Sugimoto 1999). Furuta translates the '*Proeve*' as *Nihongo bunten kōhon*『日本語文典稿本』(Furuta 2004). [MF: J.H. Donker Curtius (1813-1879) was the last Opperhoofd at Deshima, acting in this function from 1852-1860.]
(16) Sugimoto 1999, pp. 353-83.
(17) See *Atheneum*, dd February 9th, 1878, after Miyanaga 1984, p. 148.
(18) MF: In his account of expenses related to his publications in the period from July 1830 to the end of June, 1837, Siebold specifies DFl 1.500 and DFl 1.600 as 'supporting costs' for Ko for 1834 and 1835 respectively. The total for the period 1830-35, including the costs involved in Ko's coming over from Batavia, is given as DFl 6.745,20. In the same account, he also specifies the financial support provided by the Dutch Government, at a total of DFl 6.745,20. It may well have been that Siebold advanced the payments for Ko, however, in the end all costs were borne by the Dutch Government (Burg Brandenstein Archives 15A-146).
(19) See Miyanaga 1984, p. 124.
(20) See: Babinger/Furuta 1986 (2) in *Japanology* 45.

lands[21]. We can thus conclude that Ko must have written the list of titles of the books and maps in Japanese and Chinese characters before he left the country. Consequently, Siebold and Hoffmann would have had to arrange the books systematically well before the publication of the *Catalogus librorum*, so that Ko would have ample time and opportunity to neatly write the 16-pages list of titles.

With Siebold, Ko-tsching Dschang also authored some important books for the study of Japanese, such as the *Senjimon*, published as the *Mille literae ideographicae* in 1833 and the *Wakan onshaku shogen jikō*, issued under the title of *Thesaurus linguae japonicae*, both in 1833, as well as the *Shinzō - Jirin gyokuhen*, published as *Novus et auctus literarum ideographicarum thesaurus*, in 1834[22]. In the *Mille litterae*, each of the *kanji* characters is complemented with the reading in both *katakana* and in the Korean *hangŭl*. The *Thesaurus linguae japonicae* is an explanation of the *Wakan onshaku shogen jikō* (1st ed. 1698, most recent ed. 1802), figuring as No. 301 in the *Catalogus librorum*. Thus the *Thesaurus linguae japonicae* is in fact a new edition, complemented with *kana* and *kanji*, based on the *Wakan onshaku shogen jikō*. These books were useful aids for reading Japanese books completely written in Chinese or in Chinese characters. Each has the Chinese characters or *kana* written by Ko-tsching Dschang. In summary, Ko not only taught Chinese to Hoffmann and helped Siebold to read various works in Japanese, but he also edited some important works for the study of the Japanese language.

As already remarked in the previous paragraph, Hoffmann could only read the Chinese characters in the Japanese pronunciation, not in the Chinese pronunciation. For me it remains kind of a puzzle how he could learn this in the Netherlands. However, this is probably thanks to the fact that Siebold collected books that provided a reading and an explanation of the Chinese characters and the Chinese compounds in Japanese. Sugimoto Tsutomu, for example, mentions both the *Wakan sansai zue* (Cat. 1) and the *Kinmō zui* (Cat. 3) as reference works for Hoffmann's study of the Japanese language[23]. It is not for nothing that these works figure as Nos. 1 and 3 in the *Catalogus librorum*. Moreover, as Sugimoto maintains, also the already mentioned *Wakan onshaku shogen jikō* that Siebold brought with him from Japan, was of great use for Hoffmann's studies. It was the most common Sino-Japanese dictionary in the Edo period, containing an exceptionally large vocabulary with every word provided with the reading in *furigana*. Sugimoto estimates that it was especially useful for foreigners[24]. As

---

(21) MF: Ko, it seems, returned to Batavia late in 1835. This is apparent from the overview of costs mentioned in note 18 above. See also R. Effert, *Volkenkundig verzamelen*, Ph.D. Thesis Leiden University, 2003, p. 128, note 72.

(22) MF: The *Mille literae ideographicae* is actually a translation of the *Kunten senjimon* of 1715 in *Catalogus* 320. It must be said though that both the *Wakan onshaku shogen jikō* and the *Shinzō - Jirin gyokuhen* originally belonged to the Fisscher Collection of books (Nos. 33 and 5 in his MS catalogue), only to become part of the Siebold collection when Siebold failed to return these as well as many other books that were lent to him by the Royal Cabinet of Curiosities. (*Fig. 2a MF)

(23) See Sugimoto 1999, pp. 387-389. [MF: Siebold only acquired a complete set of the *Wakan sansai zue* later – initially he must have worked with the (incomplete) copy in the Fisscher collection.]

I remarked before, Siebold had Ko-tsching Dschang investigate the *Wakan onshaku shogen jikō* that he acquired in Japan and he himself then published a new edition of this work in 1833 under the title of *Thesaurus linguae japonicae*. This is just one example to illustrate how comprehensive and excellent Siebold's collection of books was.

V. Siebold's magna opera in relation to his collection of books (taking into account the results of investigations until now)

After Siebold returned to the Netherlands, he started the publication of the books that are now known as his three *magna opera*, that is *Nippon* (20 cahiers, from 1832 until *c*. 1859), the *Fauna japonica* (5 vols., 1833-50), and the *Flora japonica* (vol. 1, 1835-41; vol. 2, 1842-44, 1879). All of these are actually 'unfinished *magna opera*.'[25] It is then not too farfetched to say that he spent the second half of his life publishing his three *magna opera* on the one hand, and introducing Japanese horticulture into the Netherlands on the other. Each of these three *magna opera* has a large number of illustrations and, as a consequence, he needed quite some money. Moreover, it must be said that these works were published at his own expense, and so he really had to work hard to get the necessary funds for their publication.

Most important for both the *Fauna japonica* and *Flora japonica* was the incorporation of specimens. The books on natural history that he had collected and the drawings he had assembled were very useful and, indeed, fundamental sources. However, most important were the specimens themselves[26]. As for *Nippon*, Siebold could avail himself of the data and documents that he had gathered on Deshima, of the many theses written by his pupils, of the drawings that he commissioned from Kawahara Keiga, as well as of his collection of books and maps[27]. For example, when writing Part V of *Nippon*, on the 'Pantheon,' he made reference to *Wakan sansai zue* that figured as No. 1 in his *Catalogus librorum*. Moreover, he then of course also used Tosa Hidenobu's *Zōho shoshū - Butsuzō zui*, listed as No. 343 in the same *Catalogus librorum*[28]. **[Fig. 3]**

As already remarked above, Siebold is also known to have collected paintings of Katsushika Hokusai. In 1826 (Bunsei 9), during his sojourn in Edo, it is assumed that he did

---

(24) Sugimoto 1999, p. 390.
(25) As for the date of publication and the distribution of *Nippon*, there are studies such as Saitō 1979; Forrer/Kouwenhoven 2000; Miyazaki 2005. As for the publication of the *Fauna Japonica*, see Holthuis/ Sakai 1970. As for the *Flora Japonica*, see the discussion in Kimura 1981; Kimura/Ohba 2000.
(26) Some studies have been dedicated to the importance of the specimens collected by Siebold and their use, such as Yamaguchi (ed.) 1993; Yamaguchi 1996a; Yamaguchi 1997.
(27) There is a report by Miyazaki Katsunori (Miyazaki 2011) about the drawings for *Nippon* made by Kawahara Keiga during the court journey to Edo. These drawings are preserved in Burg Brandenstein. [MF: In addition, at least 33 paintings made by Keiga to document views of the 1826 Court Journey are preserved in the National Museum of Ethnology, Leyden.]
(28) Iwao (ed.) 1977; Sueki 1979; Sueki. As concerns *Butsuzō zui* (5 vols., 1796), Miyazaki Katsunori (Miyazaki 2011) reports that it is preserved in the Siebold collection in Leyden University Library (UB Ser 592). [MF: Another copy with the Siebold inventory no. 1-4339, but actually the copy that figures as No. 36 in the Fisscher MS catalogue of his books, is in the National Museum of Ethnology, Leyden.]

meet with Hokusai and, in addition to Hokusai's paintings and prints, also the *Hokusai manga*, listed as No. 547 in the *Catalogus*, was used for *Nippon*[29]. Moreover, *Nippon* also contains landscape views of mountains, such as Myōgizan, Atagoyama, Mitakesan, &tc. Thanks to the research of Miyazaki Katsunori, it is now known that these illustrations can be traced back to Tani Bunchō's *Meizan zufu*, listed as No. 149 in the *Catalogus*[30]. [Fig. 4]

VI. Concluding remarks – Suggestions for further research

Various experts are engaged in research trying to find out how Siebold made use of the books, manuscripts and drawings that he collected during his stay in Japan for his later research and writings. However, I am afraid that this may not be sufficient. These experts, it should be said, don't conduct any research beyond their own area of interest. Consequently, intensive research has been done in some areas, whereas, on the other hand, there are also areas with no investigations whatsoever.

Nobody would object to consider Siebold as one of the persons to have made a large contribution to Japanese studies. This was publicly confirmed when his 200th anniversary was celebrated with the joint issue of a special postage stamp by both Japan and the Bundesrepublik[31]. However, anything like a general scientific research of Siebold has not been conducted so far. Although some projects have been formulated in the past by researchers or groups of researchers who applied for so-called *kakkenhi* support of the Ministry of Education, Culture, Sports, Science, and Technology, none of these have been awarded.

I here must also excuse myself. In retrospect, I must say that my own history of research started in the field of my original specialty, the morphology of flora and fauna. Following my research of the crustaceans in the Naturalis Biodiversity Centre in Leyden in 1979, I have from 1985 until now, that is April 2013, conducted research on the specimens of flora and fauna that Siebold collected. Certainly, there were researchers before me, who also came to visit the Netherlands to research the fauna and flora in the Siebold collection. However, what they would usually accomplish was only some kind of partial research, no comprehensive research.

As for that, I am the first to conduct a general research of the natural history collections made by Siebold. I have gone at great length to obtain financial support for my researches. Initially my costs were covered by *kakkenhi* support, but later this government support was terminated. Ever since, I continued applying for *kakkenhi* support, but my applications were never again honoured. In the end, I travelled a total 42 times to the Netherlands for research of the Siebold col-

---

(29) The relation between Siebold and Hokusai's paintings is discussed into detail in the aforementioned *Hokusai. Siebold and Hokusai & Co*. On the illustrations in *Nippon* based on both paintings and prints by Hokusai, as well as on the illustrations in the *Hokusai manga*, see Hashimoto 2013. [MF: As for the *Hokusai manga*, this, again, is an acquisition of Fisscher, there is no copy in the Siebold collection.]

(30) See Miyazaki 2006.

(31) On the one-hundredth commemoration of Siebold's arrival in Japan, see Kutsuzawa 1996 and Inuki 1996.

lection material, with only ten such research trips with funding. On six occasions, my air ticket got funded, but the remaining costs for my stay and research would have to be paid by myself. Consequently, some 26 times, my research trips were completely at my own costs. In addition to paying the necessary costs for his research journeys, this writer was also obliged to invest and buy the necessary equipment, such as cameras, films, and a computer.

This writer also believes that Siebold deserves, even needs, a general scientific research conducted by experts in various disciplines. Siebold is not just a man of the past. The material that he collected during the Edo period increases in importance every day. For example, the ethnographical collection that he assembled is increasingly impossible to obtain in the quickly changing Japanese society. His natural history collection is presently even more important, especially since we live in a world where nature is threatened and large parts of the flora and fauna of Japan are being endangered. It is too sad that Siebold's contribution has not yet been fully researched. I strongly wish that real comprehensive research into the books, drawings, paintings, and manuscripts that Siebold collected will be conducted one day.

Captions for the Figures (pp. 17-20)

Fig. 1 The University Library at Leyden.

Fig. 2 A portrait of Ko-tsching Dschang. From *Nippon*. Courtesy Fukuoka Prefectural Library.

Fig. 3 A comparison of the illustrations in *Butsuzō zui* and in *Nippon*.

Fig. 4 A comparison of the illustrations in Tani Bunchō's *Meizan zufu* and those in *Nippon*.

(English Trans. by Matthi Forrer)

Captions for the Figures (p. 34)

*Fig. 1a MF: The stamp identifying books from the Blomhoff Collection, reading De verzameling van Cock Blomhoff.

*Fig. 1b MF: The stamp identifying books from the Fisscher Collection, reading De verzameling Overmeer Fisscher.

*Fig. 1c MF: A sample note of the kind prepared by some learned Japanese to help identify and classify the books in the original Siebold Collection.

*Fig. 2a MF: The Fisscher Catalogue of his books collected in Japan. Courtesy National Museum of Ethnology, Leiden.

*Fig. 2b MF: A sample Ex libris, designed by Fisscher, and normally pasted on the back cover of all books in the Fisscher Collection. Courtesy National Museum of Ethnology, Leiden.

「シーボルトの初回来日と収集書籍類について」
に対する脚註・追記

マティ・フォラー
(Matthi Forrer)

※　本稿の註番号はマティ・フォラーによる英訳脚註番号（6～30頁）に対応しており、
「*」は、原文に注（写真）がないため、追記として新たに付したことを示す。

写真：*Figs. 1a MF、1b MF、2b MF

　山口氏のもう1つの論文「シーボルトの日本収集書籍コレクションの概要について」の冒頭でも紹介しているように、『日本書籍目録』は、シーボルトが収集した書籍の他、出島商館長を務めたブロンホフの収集書籍（*Fig. 1a MF）、フィッセルの収集書籍（*Fig. 1b MF、*Fig. 2b MF）も含まれている。

脚註6追記

MF：実際は、私が当該出版物にも示したように、この絵画のグループは、ライデン国立民族学博物館には17点しかない。さらにこの数は、北斎の弟子、魚屋北渓作とされる絵画4点を含むものである。

脚註*9

MF：この書籍蒐集リストは、シーボルトが1823年から1829年に滞在した際に蒐集した書籍で、数えてみると、440タイトル、少なくとも1200巻からなる（ブランデンシュタイン家文書 SAM 3-23、和訳は栗原2003参照のこと）。この分類は、日本人が行ったもので、これらの書籍にはそれぞれ、表紙の裏側に「付箋」が貼られている。この付箋とは、オランダ紙の断片で、そこにカタカナ書きで、まず、書物の分類（ローマ数字でI-VIII）、続いて、1）書名、2）著者、3）出版地、4）出版年、5）巻数が記されている［写真（*Fig. 1c MF）参照］。換言すれば、この付箋のない書物は、シーボルトが第一回の日本滞在時に蒐集した書物ではないことになる（後年、付箋が取れてしまった場合は除く）。すなわち、シーボルトが、1829年付けでバタヴィア政庁に「日本で蒐集した」と報告した書物が440タイトル（1200巻）であるのに対し、『日本書籍目録』（1845年）には、一つの番号下の複数の書物や、重複分をすべて計算すると、総数615タイトル（1800巻強）が集録されている。

脚註11追記

MF：この偶然の出会いについては、ホフマンはそれより以前に、少なくとも2度、シーボルトに書簡を送っていることを書き添えておく（Ishiyama/Miyazaki 2011, pp. 206 and 212参照）。さらに、郭成章が1830年7月17日の出会いに居合わせたというのも不思議な話だ。郭は、英国人宣教師メドハーストがシーボルトに宛てた手紙によれば、1830年5月初旬、〈若きアドリアナ〉でバタヴィアを出立している（ブランデンシュタイン家文書15B-168）。

脚註*13

MF：福沢諭吉（1834-1901）は、日本の誇る啓蒙思想家、教育者であり、1860年と1867年にアメリカを1861年にはヨーロッパを訪れている。1868年諭吉は、慶應大学を創設した。

脚註15追記

MF：J. H. ドンケル・クルティウス（1813-1879）は、和蘭出島商館の最後の商館長（1852-1860）を務めた。

脚註＊18

MF：シーボルトの1830年7月から1837年6月の間の勘定帳によれば、シーボルトは、1834年と1835年、郭成章の生活援助費として、それぞれ1500ギルダー、1600ギルダーを支払っている。また、1830年から1835年にかけて郭に支払った合計金額は、バタヴィアからの渡航費も含め、6745,20ギルダーであった。シーボルトはこの金額を前払いしたが、後にオランダ政府が全額をシーボルトに払い戻している（ブランデンシュタイン家文書15A-146）。

脚註＊21

MF：郭成章は1835年の終わりにバタヴィア（現ジャカルタ）に戻ったとものと見られる。これは、前出の勘定帳からも明らかに見てとれる。また、エフェルト氏の学位論文（R. Effert, *Volkenkundige verzamelen*, Leyden, 2003, p. 128, 注 72）も参照されたし。

脚註＊22

MF：『千字文』（ライデン、1833年）は、『訓点千字文』（1715年刊、ホフマン320）を基にしたものである。また『和漢音釋書言字節用集』（ホフマン301）と『新増字林玉篇』（ホフマン297）の2冊は、フィッセルが持ち帰ったもので、シーボルトがハーグの王立骨董陳列室から借用した図書であったことを明記しておく（フィッセル自身の手稿［写真（*Fig. 2a MF）参照］には、それぞれ33番、5番とある）。

脚註23 追記

MF：シーボルトの『和漢三才図会』には、シーボルトが日本出立前に貼らせた付箋がない。このためシーボルトが、『和漢三才図会』を入手したのは、日本滞在時ではなく、オランダに戻ってからだということになる。シーボルトは『NIPPON』執筆に、まずはフィッセルが持ち帰った『和漢三才図会』を利用していたと考えるべきである。

脚註27 追記

MF：加えて、慶賀が1826年の江戸参府道中で描いた絵画が、少なくとも33点、ライデン国立民族学博物館に残されている。

脚註28 追記

『仏像図彙』はライデン国立民族学博物館にもあり、フィッセルが持ち帰ったものである（RMvV 1-4339）。ライデン大学図書館が所蔵する『仏像図彙』は、シーボルトコレクションであるが、付箋の貼ってあった形跡がなく、『和漢三才図会』の場合と同様に、シーボルトがオランダに戻ってから入手したものと考えられる。

脚註29 追記

MF：『北斎漫画』は、フィッセルが持ち帰ったものである。シーボルトのコレクションに『北斎漫画』は存在しない。

「シーボルトの初回来日と収集書籍類について」に対する脚註・追記

*Fig. 1a MF：ライデン国立民族学博物館蔵
ブロムホフコレクションの蔵書印
The stamp identifying books from the Blomhoff Collection—RMvV

*Fig. 1b MF：ライデン国立民族学博物館蔵
フィッセルコレクションの蔵書印
The stamp identifying books from the Fisscher Collection—RMvV

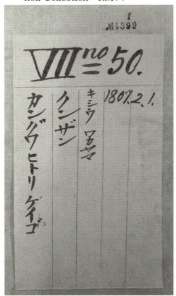

*Fig. 1c MF：シーボルトが、1829年のバタヴィア政庁に「蒐集図書」として報告した書籍に貼られている「付箋」の一例、オリジナルのシーボルト蒐集図書とオランダに戻ってからシーボルトコレクションに加わった図書（ブロムホフ、フィッセルからの借用図書を含む）の区別に役立つ。
A sample note of the books in the original Siebold Collection—RMvV

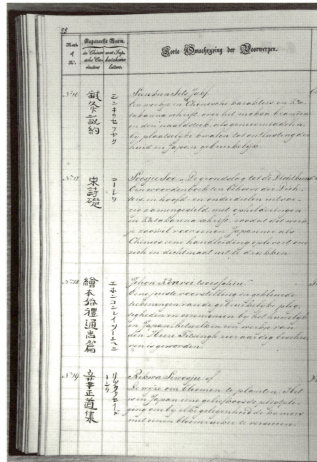

*Fig. 2a MF：フィッセルの手稿目録から書籍部分
（ライデン国立民族学博物館蔵）
The Fisscher Catalogue of his books collected in Japan—RMvV

*Fig. 2b MF：フィッセルが自分で作成した石版の蔵書ラベル、たいていは裏表紙に貼り付けられている（ライデン国立民族学博物館蔵）。
A sample Ex libris, designed by Fisscher—RMvV

原文影印

CATALOGUS
LIBRORUM ET MANUSCRIPTORUM JAPONICORUM

《凡例》

1. 掲載資料概略
   (1) 影印掲載は、公益財団法人東洋文庫が所蔵する下記2冊の原本 "*Catalogus librorum et manuscriptorum Japonicorum a Ph. Fr. de Siebold collectorum, annexa enumeratione illorum, qui in Museo Regio Hagano servantur*" を校合して使用した。
   (2) 本書に掲載した原本2冊における所蔵館請求番号（掲載箇所）は、以下の通りである。
      ・La-62（扉p3、刊記p4、緒言pp.5〜8、目次pp.9〜10、石版刷目録pp.47〜63）
      ・XVII-1-A-12（ラテン語解説本文pp.11〜46）
   (3) 本書における掲載順については、石版刷目録（原資料も左綴じ）を含め、原本の掲載順に従った。
   (4) 原文影印に加え、本書の頁番号（奇数頁は右下隅・偶数頁は左下隅）と、影印内容（奇数頁は右上隅・偶数頁は左上隅）を付した。

2. 底本書誌
   (1) 所蔵館（資料請求記号）：公益財団法人東洋文庫（請求記号 La-62、XVII-1-A-12）
   (2) 原題（版元、刊行年次、所蔵館受入）："*Catalogus librorum et manuscriptorum Japonicorum a Ph. Fr. de Siebold collectorum, annexa enumeratione illorum, qui in Museo Regio Hagano servantur*"（J.G. LA LAU. 1845年刊 125部印刷、東洋文庫の受入時期は未詳）

   ○請求番号　La-62
      ・表紙　縦38.5cm　横28.3cm（白地無模様の洋紙に扉頁と同様の印刷有、背のみ別紙補強有）
      ・構成　表紙（表見返し白紙）、遊紙（白紙2頁）、扉（内題1頁、1845年）、刊記「EX TYPOGRAPHEO J.G.LA LAU.」(1頁)、「PREMISSA」（緒言4頁、1845年2月）、「LIBRORUM ORDO.」（目次2頁）、ラテン語解説本文（35頁）、白紙（1頁）、漢字・仮名による石版刷書籍目録（17頁）、白紙（1

原文影印（凡例）

頁）、遊紙（白紙2頁）、裏表紙（裏見返し白紙）
- 印記　扉頁：王冠・紋章を中心にライオン2頭が向かい合い「RIJKS ETHNOG-RAPHISCH MUSEUM」と記される青色の円印（ライデン民族学博物館受入印）1顆有
- 挟込資料　「Veirreda」（底本のラテン語緒言のオランダ語訳、両面刷罫紙・ペン書・3枚1組）有

○請求番号　XVII-1-A-12
- 表紙　縦36.6cm　横27.6cm（青・白・黒の大理石模様紙を使用、背と四隅は革張）
- 構成　表紙（表見返し白紙）、遊紙（現存白紙6頁）、扉（内題1頁、1845年）、刊記「EX TYPOGRAPHEO J.G.LA LAU.」（1頁）、「PREMISSA」（緒言4頁、1845年2月）、「LIBRORUM ORDO.」（目次2頁）、ラテン語解説本文（35頁）、白紙（1頁）、漢字・仮名による石版刷書籍目録（16頁）、遊紙（白紙38頁）、裏表紙（裏見返し白紙）
- 印記　扉頁：紫色円印（印文不鮮明）1顆有
- 挟込資料　無

3. 底本選択の方針

　第一の底本とした資料（請求番号La-62）の特徴として、①ライデン民族学博物館（現在のライデン国立民族学博物館）の受入印があること、②扉頁に「AGCEDUNT TABULAE LITHOGRAPHICAE ⅩⅥ」（石版刷16枚付）と印刷されるのに対し17頁（17枚分）あること、③ラテン語解説本文にインクが飛び散った跡が散見され番号部分に鉛筆の書き込みがあること、④オランダ語の緒言の挟込があること、以上4点が挙げられる。

　以上を勘案して、オランダのライデン民族学博物館で使用された可能性が高く、石版刷目録17頁目が含まれる原本（請求番号　La-62）を主軸に影印掲載した。

　但し、第一の底本とした資料（請求番号La-62）のラテン語解説本文は、ペンや鉛筆の書き込みがあり文字が読みにくい部分があるため、ラテン語解説本文は全く書き込みがなく同内容の原本（請求番号　XVII-1-A-12）の影印掲載を行った。

CATALOGUS

LIBRORUM ET MANUSCRIPTORUM JAPONICORUM

A PH. FR. DE SIEBOLD COLLECTORUM,

ANNEXA ENUMERATIONE ILLORUM, QUI IN MUSEO REGIO HAGANO SERVANTUR.

AUCTORE

PH. FR. DE SIEBOLD

LIBROS DESCRIPSIT

J. HOFFMANN.

ACCEDUNT TABULAE LITHOGRAPHICAE XVI.

LUGDUNI-BATAVORUM,
APUD AUCTOREM.
1845.
IMPRESSA CXXV EXEMPLA.

原文影印（扉裏・刊記）

EX TYPOGRAPHEO J. G. LA LAU.

PRAEMISSA.

Quum libri Japonici ad finem usque proximi seculi inter rarissima literarum Orientalium monumenta haberentur, vix minuta quaedam eorum fragmenta in celeberrimis Europae bibliothecis reperiebantur. Et primus quidem fuit medicus illustris ANDREAS CLEYER, annis 1683—1686, Batavorum in Japonia commercio praefectus, qui admonente Electore FREDERICO WILHELMO M., Bibliothecae Berolinensi libros aliquot Sinicos, ac delineationes botanicas Japonicas inferret.

Ampliorem deinceps ex Japonia librorum supellectilem advexit ANGELBERTUS KAEMPFER, istius regionis tunc temporis (1691, 1692) perscrutator felicissimus; quae quum constaret 49 operibus xylographicis compluribusque delineationibus, post mortem viri celeberrimi (1716) 33 ex his opera in possessionem venerunt Equitis JOHANNIS SLOANE, cetera in diversas Bibliothecas migrarunt. Spectabatur autem tunc potissimum externa librorum Japonicorum forma, quos huiusmodi rerum curiosi tanquam rarissima artis typographicae in Japonia specimina custodiebant, neque erant qui inspicerent atque interpreterentur, indeque cognitionem morum ac disciplinarum cultissimae gentis peterent. Itaque hos libros male sedula bibliomaniacorum curiositas oblivioni tradidit.

Ab illo inde tempore per centum fere annos nulla scriptorum ex Japonia allatorum mentio fit, quod dubium est tribuendumne sit severitati legum eius populi, quae hospites Europaeos ab explorandis rebus suis excluderent, an incuriae potius ac negligentiae paucorum eruditorum, qui tunc Mare Indicum trajicerent, ultimique Orientis literas despicerent. Harum certe studium diutissime jacuit, ac ne initia quidem operae collocatae in addiscenda lingua a Missionariis propagandae religionis Christianae vim habuerunt ad eruenda incognitarum rerum desideria:

itaque CAROLUS PETRUS THUNBERG, vir praeclarus, cui aliquam certe linguae Japonicae scientiam debemus, magis explorandae naturae illarum regionum incubuit, quam investigandis colligendisque literarum speciminibus: paucos tantum libros de re botanica in Itinerario suo recensuit, eosque titulis mutilatis, pauciora etiam volumina secum advexit.

Tandem exstitit vir diligentissimus, deque historia gentis Japonicae praeclare meritus ISACUS TITSINGH, annis 1780—1782 Batavorum in Japonia commercio praefectus. Hic insignem librorum, tabularum geographicarum ac delineationum copiam sibi comparavit, scripsitque commentationes, ac Belgicas versiones operum praestantissimorum, adiuvantibus interpretibus indigenis: quarum omnium, in patriam redux, splendidum exemplar Amstelodami deposuit in bibliotheca Instituti Regii. Ipse, quo labentem valetudinem sub mitiori coelo confirmaret, Parisios se contulit, metitabatur autem Imperii Japonici descriptionem uberrimam, eratque ad hanc rem, siquis alius, praestantissimus ab accurata doctrina ingeniique acumine, et laboris constantia plane singulari; inopinata mors triginta annorum laborem intercepit, priusquam fructum eius eruditis impartiretur; quodque haud minus dolendum est, scripta eius, tabulae, pretiosa numorum supellex, caetera usa sunt infelicissimo fato: quippe totus hic thesaurus, pro quo Regimen Indiae Orientalis Britanicum ducenta quinquaginta millia florenorum auctori obtulerat, sex totos annos Parisiis absconditus latuit. Haec persequi nolim, quamquam possim: habeant sibi facti conscientiam, quorum nefanda cupiditas alienis bonis inhiavit, vel turpis invidia immortalis viri memoriam sceleste obscurare conata est.

Factum est tandem editionis initium a bibliopola NEPVEU, qui indicio usus LANGLESII, viri clarissimi (ita enim ipse rem narrat) scripta quaedam aliaque documenta TITSINGHII indagavit sibique comparavit anno 1818: itaque huius operum posthumorum edidit volumen primum anno 1819. Depromitur autem in illo primo volumine, tum in Vol. XXIV Annalium Itinerum *Malte-Brunii* Index Collectionis Titsinghianae. Ibi codices quidem aliquot manuscripti recensentur, tum tabulae geographicae, aliaeque delineationes, paucissimi vero libri typis impressi, quamquam ego in Bibliothecis tum publicis tum privatis deprehendi complures libros de historia, de geographia, de re numismatica, quibus inscriptae notae autographae TITSINGHII testabantur, eum ex hoc quoque genere apparatu instructum ex Oriente domum rediisse.

Ostendimus, opinor, doctam TITSINGHII supellectilem minutim discerptam esse isigni literarum detrimento coniuncto cum existimationis Titsinghianae deminutione: quo magis dolendum est, alterum operum eius exemplar, cuius supra mentionem iniecimus, quodque ille in Instituti Regii Museo deposuit, ibi religiose quidem, sed veluti vellus quoddam aureum custodiri.

Interea studium rerum Japonicarum sensim incrementum cepit, mihique copiose Interpretes laudaverunt virum nobilissimum JOHANNEN FRIDERICUM VAN RHEEDE, annis 1786—1789 in Japonia commercio praefectum, utpote librorum aliarumque rerum curiosissimum investigatorem, quibus ego ut facile credidi, ita in nulla adhuc eius specimina incidi. Verum singuli libri, ab aliis alii, tabulae geographicae, aliarumque rerum adumbratae effigies identidem ab rerum exoticarum amantibus advectae sunt, repositaeque in Museis Bibliothecisque publicis ac privatis. Itaque Bibliotheca Regia Parisiensis habet Encyclopaediam amplissimam, vocabularia Japonica ac mappas geographicas; Museum Asiaticum Petropolitanum libros rarissimos de Numismatica, ac tabulas Geographicas: Viennae, Dresdae, Vinariae, Gothae inque aliis publicis Museis servantur pretiosae delineationes operaque geographica, historica, philologica, in Bibliotheca Regia Berolinensi CLEYERI, in Museo Britanico Londinensi KAEMPFERI, in Bibliotheca denique Upsalensi THUNBERGII apparatus fragmenta, cum aliis quibusdam literarum Japonicarum speciminibus. Privatorum Bibliotheca KLAPROTHII longe fuit ditissima.

In Bibliothecis autem Batavis publicis, quae ceteroquin ditissimae sunt, libris Orientalibus tum manu tum arte typographica exaratis, vix ullum librorum Japonicorum exemplum reperiebatur ante Equitem JOHANNEM COCK BLOMHOFF, cuius incredebile studium fuit rerum Japonicarum, quae quidem ad vitam publicam privatamque, victum, cultum, artes denique istius populi pertinerent; quibus ille explorandis quum multos annos, Commercio Praefectus, insumsisset, solutum apparatum, diuturni laboris fructum anno 1824 in patriam detulit; quo quidem insigni incremento auctum est Museum Regium Haganum. In his igitur libris tabulisque geographicis opera exstant viginti novem, quorum mihi exempla in Japonia comparare non potui; haec autem in nostro Catalogo asterisco (*) designavimus.

Eo denique tempore, quo nos iussu Magistratus Indiae terram Japonicam explorabamus, vir sagacissimus VAN OVERMEER FISSCHER, Commercio Subpraefectus, idem consilium agitabat, neque successu caruit eius industria: etenim insignem copiam librorum, tabularum geographicarum aliarumque rerum pictas imagines patriae obtulit (1831), quae quidem munificentia Serenissimi Regis Museo Hagano accessit. In hoc autem apparatu Fisscheriano librorum volumina circiter 117 sunt, quorum sexaginta novis operibus Catalogum nostrum locupletavimus, addita hac nota (†).

Et nos quoque, quantum potuimus, operam dedimus, collegimusque 525 opera in septem annorum decursu (1823—1830) quos in illis regionibus transegimus, omniaque Reipublicae Batavae cessimus, ut erigatur literarum Japonicarum monumentum. Hoc ut composuimus eo ordine, quem librorum argumenta acquirebant, ita effecisse speramus, ut literarum Orientalium amantes, quique in disciplina Geographica et Ethnographica studium coleant, uniuscuiusque scripti pretium ac virtutes aestimare possint. Exemplaria autem quae superfuere, quosque hactenus e Japonia ac alicunde nobis comparavimus libros ac codices manuscriptos, partim in Bibliotheca Imperiali Viennae partim in Bibliotheca Regia Parisiis deposuimus: hoc quidem consilio, ut ducibus illustrissimis Sinologis, viris Celeberrimis STEPHANO ENDLICHER ac STANISLASIO JULIEN, literae Japonicae coleantur scientiarumque Orientalium augeatur studium.

Quod autem in hunc Catalogum non nostra sola inclusimus, recipimusque ex aliorum supellectile, quae in nostra dessent, hoc ideo factum est, ut uno quasi conspectu pateret quantum divitiarum eruditarum Batavi paucis abhinc annis ex remotissima illa terra deportaverint, essetque simul enumeratio ac censura quaedam subsidiorum ad iuvanda studia rerum Japonicarum.

Plerique librorum tituli ab ipsis scriptoribus literis ideographicis exarati sunt: hos igitur in Tabulis lithographicis manu amici nostri Sinensis KO TSCHING DSCHANG descriptos reddidimus, addito auctoris nomine voluminumque numero. Libros autem descripsit et illustravit vir nobis amicissimus Dr. J. HOFFMANN.

Propositum fuit, ut haec res plane quidem sed quam brevissime absolveretur.

Si liber est origine Sinicus in Japonia autem sine mutatione repetitus, titulus nonnisi Sinice legitur et literis Itallicis exaratus est (Conf. n°. 11).

Si vero liber origine quidem Sinicus, sed in usum Japonensium additamentis et commentariis auctus est, uti n°. 197, Japonicam tituli lectionem expressam habes, addita non nunquam pronuntiatione Sinica, quae dicitur Mandarinorum, uncis inclusa.

Saepe quoque titulus Sinicis quidem literis expressus sermone mere Japonica reddendus fuit, in quo Japonensium morem secuti sumus. Titulo proxime addita est versio quam potuit accuratissima, nec nisi quum obscuri quid inesse aut aliquid cognitu necessarium non omittendum videbatur, pauca illustrandi causa addebantur.

Scripsi in secessu prope ab urbe Lugduni-Batavorum **DE SIEBOLD.**
mense Februario MDCCCXLV.

LIBRORUM ORDO.

SECTIO I. Libri encyclopaedici. . . . . 1—12.
SECTIO II. Libri historici et geographici.
    A. Historici.
        a. Mythologici. . . . . 13—15.
        b. Historici. . . . . 16—27.
        c. Tabulae chronologicae. . . . . 28—33.
    B. Historico-geographici. . . . . 34—53.
    C. Mappae geographicae.
        a. Generales. . . . . 54—59.
        b. Speciales. . . . . 60—91.
    D. Libri topographici.
        a. Topographiam spectantes urbis *Mijako*. . . . . 92—104.
        b. » » » *Jedo*. . . . . 105—124.
        c. » » » *Ohosaka*. . . . . 125—134.
        d. » » » *Nagasaki* cet. . . . . 135—139.
    E. Urbium regionumque prospectus. . . . . 140—160.
    F. Itineraria. 161—173.
    G. Coloniarum tributariorumque populorum libri geographici et historici. 174—190.
    H. Mappae geographicae auctorum Europaeorum Japonice redditae. . . 191—193.
SECTIO III. Libri physici.
    A. De historia naturali generales.
        a. Sinici denuo in Japonia impressi. . . . . 194—206.
        b. Japonici. 207—223.
    B. De historia naturali speciales.
        a. Monographiae botanicae ac zoologicae. . . . . 224—247.
        b. Adumbrationes botanicae, MS^{tae}. . . . . 248—265.
        c. » zoologicae, MS^{tae}. . . . . 266—283.
        d. Dissertationes miscellaneae. . . . . , 284—293.
SECTIO IV. Libri grammatici et lexicographici.
    A. Dictionaria.
        a. Sinica et Sinico-Japonica. . . . . 294—300.
        b. Japonico-Sinica. . . . . 301—304.
        c. Synonymarum. . . . . 305—306.
        d. Japonica antiquita. . . . . 307—308.
        e. Japonico-Batava. ⎫
        f. Batavo-Japonica. ⎭ . . . . 324—327.

B. Vocabularia.
    a. Linguae Aino. . . . . 328—329.
    b. » Côraianae. . . . . 330—332.
    c. » Sanscritae. . . . . 333—334.
    d. » Mandschu. . . . . 335—336.
C. Libri grammatici. . . . . 309—323.

SECTIO V. **Libri theologici et morales.**
  A. De cultu Buddhaico. . . . . 337—343, 335^b—336^b.
  B. De cultu Sjuto. . . . . 337^b—340^b.
  C. Praecepta moralia, historiae fictae et miscellanea. . . . 341^b—343^b, 344—372.

SECTIO VI. **Poetae.**
  A. Poesis dramatica. 373—382.
  B. » lyrica, cui nomen Uta. . . . . 383—400.
  C. » cui nomen Haïkaï. . . . . 401—406.
  D. » Sinica. 407—410.

SECTIO VII. **Libri de populo ac civitate.**
  A. De moribus et consuetudinibus. . . . . 411—421.
  B. De civitatis et imperii forma et administratione. . . . . . 422—427.
  C. De politia. . . . . 428—431.
  D. De re militari. . . . . 434—437.
  E. De architectura. . . . . 432—433.

SECTIO VIII. **Libri oeconomici.**
  A. De agricultura. . . . . 438—448.
  B. De artibus et mercatura. . . . . 449—472.

SECTIO IX. **Libri numismatici.** . . . . 473—485.

SECTIO X. **Libri medici et pharmaceutici.** . . . . 486—499.

SECTIO XI. **Tabulae xylographicae.**
  A. Praecepta ac rudimenta artis pingendi. . . . . 500—505.
  B. Imitationes xylographicae celebrium tabularum pictarum.
    a. Sinensium. . . . . 506—512.
    b. Japonicarum. 513—562.
  C. Libri picturarum.
    a. Historicarum. 563—573.
    b. Regionum aedificiorumque delineationes. . . . . 574—577.
    c. Vestimentorum delineationes. . . . . 578—594.

CORRIGENDA.

Pag. 20. *c. n.* 334. *l.* 333.
» » *n.* 335. *l.* 334.
» 26. E. *n.* 431. *l.* 432.

Sectio I. **LIBRI ENCYCLOPAEDICI.**

1. **Wa Kan san sai dsu e** (Sinice *Hô Hán sân ts'aî t'û hoeï*) i. e. Japonensium et Sinarum tria principia (coelum, terra, homo), adumbrata auctore *Simajosi Ankô*. 105 *kiuén* (tomi) in 80 voll. in 8° Ed. 1714. Hoc opus, quod Encyclopaedia magna sinico-japonica nuncupari solet, Cl. *Abel Remusat* recensuit. V. Notices et extraits des Manuscrits, tom. XI.

2. **Kasira gaki, zô-bo, Kin mô dsu i**, adumbrationes in usum tironum cum explicatione figurarum superiori paginarum parte posita. 1661, 21 *kiuén* in 8°. Opera Nis 2, 3 et 4 adlegata libros esse elementarios imaginibus ornatos scias; rerum enim omnium, quae ad naturam, artem victumque pertinent, imagines adsunt, et quidquid de rerum usu et origine nosse opus est, paucis absolvitur. Sinae pariter ac Japonenses hujusmodi libris uti solent, quibus tirones communi rerum cognitione imbuant.

3. **Kasira gaki, zô bo, Kin mô dsu i dai sei**, i. e. perfecta adumbrationum collectio in usum tironum. 1666, 21 tomi in 9 voll. in 8°. Repetita libri praecedentis editio denuo elaborata atque aucta.

4. **Morokosi kin-mô dsu i**, rerum sinensium imagines in usum tironum collectae et descriptae auctore *Firazumi Senan*. Mijako 1719. 14 *kiuén* in 10 voll. in 8°.

5. **Kjok-kai sets-jô zi-rin zô**, i. e. mare rerum praetiosarum, sive receptacula apte collocata literarum, quae maxime necessariae sunt. 1789, 3 voll. in 4° cum imaginibus. In hoc libro encyclopaedico, qui japonice quoque audit »*Tamano umi fodojoku motsijuru asanano fajasino kura*", varias invenies materias, quae ad historiam, geographiam, victum cultumque pertinent; accedit vocabularium linguae japonicae, quo tertium operis volumen absolvitur.

† 6. **Man-kai sets-jô zi fuk-zô**, i. e. decies mille maria sive receptacula literarum, quae maxime sunt necessariae. Hic liber, 13° annorum, qui *Bunkwa* nominantur (1817), editus in uno volumine, accedit ad similitudinem operis praecedentis.

† 7. **To-kwai sets-jô fjak-ka tsû**, liber encyclopaedicus cum vocabulario in usum hominum omnium ordinum conscriptus, anno 1801 primum editus curantibus collegiis, quae in urbibus primariis (Mijako, Jedo, Okosaka) florent; denuo typis expressus A°. 1819. Non multum differt a libris illis, quos 5° et 6° loco laudavimus.

* 8. **Man-bô sets-jô fu-ki zô**, i. e. dives et illustre receptaculum rerum omnium praetiosarum, quas nosse opus est. Liber encyclopaedicus cum imaginibus annexo vocabulario linguae japonicae, cui titulus: *Kwô-jeki zits jô zi rin*, i. e. nemus auctum literarum, quae in usu quotidiano sunt. Ed. prima A°. 1788, altera A°. 1811. 1 vol. 4°.

† 9. Wa-Kan sets-jô mu-sô bukuro, i. e. saccus incomparabilis, quo continentur notitiae maxime necessariae rerum japonicarum et sinensium. A°. 1799, 1 vol.

10. Fak buts zen, i. e. ampla rerum nassa. Compendiosa encyclopaedia japonica, auct. *Lanzai Jama saki Ujemon*. 1768, 1 vol. 351 foliorum transvers. in 8° min. Operis materia in 13 capita digesta ad alphabetum japonicum disposita est, explicatio autem linguâ japonicâ conscripta admixtis characteribus sinensibus.

† 11. *Wei kĕ schŭ mŭ*, librorum sub imperio Mandschu-co in Sinis impressorum catalogus, editus quarto annorum *Kiâ king* (1799) a *Kú sieû lo*, in Japonia vero denuo typis exscriptus A° 1818, 10. voll. in 8° min.

12. Wa-Kan sjo kwa itsi ran, i. e. conspectus scriptorum et pictorum tam japonensium quam sinicorum. *Ohosaka* 1786, 1 vol. transvers. in 12°. Editio V^{ta} A° 1821. In hoc libello non solum laudati sunt, qui arte scribendi et pingendi excelluere, sed medici quoque illustres et clerici Buddhaici comparent, de quorum origine et vita mentionem brevem fecit auctor.

Sectio II. **LIBRI HISTORICI ET GEOGRAPHICI.**

A. *Historici.*

a. *Mythologici.*

13. Kami-jo-bumi asikabi, i. e. cannarum gemmae sive initia annalium, in quibus Deorum (*Kami*) res gestae relatae sunt. 3 voll. in 8°. *Kurida Toman*, japonensis sacrorum antistes, quae in variis scriptis mythologicis notione digna reperit, in hunc librum contulit animadversionibusque illustravit. Praefationem libri 8° annorum *Bunkwa* (1811) scripsit.

14. Kami jono masa koto, i. e. vera de Deorum generationibus. Monuit *Motoworino Norinaga*, sacrorum in templo regionis *Ise* antistes. 1789, 3 voll. in 8°.

15. Ko si-kei dsu, tabula genealogiae antiquae sive stemma imperatorum a Diis deductum. Scripsit *Tairano Atsutane*, 1815, 1 vol. 8°.

b. *Libri Historici.*

16. Nippon wô-dai itsi-ran, i. e. conspectus successionum regni japonici. Scripsit *Sjunzai Rinsjo*, religiosus Buddhaicus, 1652. Ed. *Ohosaka*. 1795, 10 voll. in 8°.

† 17. Jamato fumi sive Nippon sjo ki. Annales japonici inde ab anno 661 ante Chr. n. usque ad annum 696 post C. n. Lingua sinensi conscripsit *Oho Ason Amaro*, imperatoris *Tenmu* filius minor, et imperatori *Gensio* obtulit A° 720; typis autem primum mandati sunt A° 1228. Exemplum huius operis A° 1709 denuo typis exscriptum a Cl. *V. O. Fisscher* allatum est. 30 *kiuén* in 15 voll. in 8°. Praecedunt tomi duo, in quibus de mythologia japonica agitur.

18. Wa-Kan nen-kei (*Hô-Hán nién-k'ï*). Chronologiae japonicae et sinicae concordia, auctore *Asija Jamabito*. Mijako, A° 1797. 1 vol. 8°. Eam libri partem, quae historiam japonicam spectat, denuo typis exscriptam *Bibliothecae Japonicae* inseruimus addita versione in linguam germanam. Liber inscriptus est *Wa nen kei*, sive Annales japonici.

† 19. **Sjô-tsiu Wa-Kan nen kei.** Libri praecedentis exemplum pugillare, in quo enumerati sunt imperatores japonici et sinici, aeque ac nomina annorum, quae in utroque regno in usu fuere. Accedit succinctus rerum gestarum index. 1801, 1 vol. in 12°.

20. **Jamato nen-dai kwô-ki kwai-sjô,** annales japonici in usum principum imaginibus illustrati, 3 tomi in 1 vol. Succinctam regum historiam usque ad annum 887 literis, quae *Firakana* dicuntur, scriptam continent.

† 21. **Dai-fei ki,** historia pacis (recuperatae) sive de rebus bello gestis inde ab anno 1320 usque ad annum 1393. Accedunt capita duo de bello ab imperatrice *Zingu* in terram Coreanam illato, et de infausto isto imperatoris Mongolici *Kublaikhan* anno 1281 adversus Japoniam impetu. Scribendi genus idem atque in annalibus Nippon wôdai itsi ran. Ed. 1631, 40 *kiuén* in 39 voll. in 8°.

† 22. **Kô-jô gun kan,** speculum militare *Kôjô*nicum (*), sive de bellis a *Takeda Singen*, principe regionis *Kai*, gestis adversus principes regionum *Sinano, Suwô, Jetsigo, Suruga* cet. inde ab anno 1535 usque ad annum 1586, quo *Tojodomi Fidejosi* ad principatum pervenit. Ed. Mijako 1659, 20 *kiuén* in 18 voll. in 8°. Literae, quibus liber scriptus est, abbreviatae eiusque generis sunt, quod *Ts'aò* et *Firakana* dicitur.

(*) Urbs primaria provinciae *Kai* vel *Kôsju* a poëtis nominatur *Kôjô*, vulgo autem *Futsiu*.

† 23. **Fei-ke monogatari,** historia familiae imperialis *Feike* sive *Daira*. Ed. A°. 1710, 12 *kiuén* cum imaginibus. Liber literis *Firakana* scriptus. — *Feike mono gatari* est epos Japonensium longe celebratissimum a *Jukinaga*, principe provinciae *Sinano*, compositum, qui exstincta *Feike* familia (1186) vitae monastricae se addixerat. Hoc epos caecus iis temporibus rhapsodus, cui nomen *Seô buts*, memoriae mandatum primus in foro cecinit.

† 24. **Simabaraki,** historia *Simabara*-na sive de Christianorum in Simabara seditione et excidio annis 1637—1639. Scripsit dux quidam militum imperii japonici, qui ipse rei interfuit. 3 voll. in 8°. Liber literis *Firakana* scriptus.

25. **Hon-tsjô kok-gun ken-tsi jen-kak dsu-sets,** orbis Japonici descriptio seu divisio per provincias varia variis temporibus, illustrata a *Itsi sai Satô*. Jedo, 1823, 1 vol. in 4°.

26. **Dai Nippon Dai-fei-ki mei-sjô bu-jû kurabe,** tabula, qua belli duces inclyti et viri bello egregii, quorum mentio facta est in libro *Dai fei ki* (N. 21) alius alii contenduntur.

27. **Dai Nippon tsi-zin mei sjô jû si kagami,** speculum (conspectus) belli ducum atque heroum imperii japonici, qui sapientiâ et pietate magnam sui famam reliquere.

c. *Tabulae chronologicae.*

28. **Katsu-si zjun kwan dsu,** circulatio cycli sexagenarii descripta, sive cycli sexagenarii viginti, qui per orbem mobilem circulos suos conficiunt, totidemque circulis exteris respondent, per quos annorum successio juxta aerarum japonicarum nomina (*Nengo*) disposita est. Re ita instituta auctor *Kwan gjok siu nin* supellectilem lectori paravit, cuius ope varia temporis intervalla brevi ad calculos vocare possit. Mijako, 1820.

29. **Nen-dai ki,** aerarum descriptio. Tabula eadem ratione, quam supra indicavimus, descripta, chalcographiae japonicae periculum. Ed. A°. 1824.

† 30. **Ki nen si sjô,** anni ad numerorum signa redacti et quasi in palma manus indicati. Est autem tabula aerarum japonicarum, quae inde a quarto annorum *Bunsei* enumerantur.

31. **Wa-Kan nen reki zen.** *Suvara Movei,* chronologiae japonicae ac sinicae libellus. Brevi in conspectu posita sunt imperatorum et annorum in Japonia atque in Sinis nomina, notitiis quibusdam historicis adiectis. Accedit brevis terrae japonicae descriptio, et conspectus imperatorum Sjôgun, neque omissa sunt, quae ad astronomiam, astrologiam, fastos, stemmaque spectant. Jedo, 1823, 1 vol. in 12°.

32. **Man-bô ni-men kagami**, speculum duplex rerum pretiosarum. Folium habes notitiis omnis generis in usum plebis dotatum.

33. **Man-reki rjô-men kagami**, i. e. speculum duplex centies mille cognitionum. Folium unum parum differens a supra dicto »duplici rerum pretiosarum speculo." Ed. a *Sivoja Kisuke*, Okosaka, 1825.

B. *Libri historico-geographici.*

34. **Jamato mei-sjô dsu-e**, i. e. descriptiones rerum provinciae Jamato memorabilium in librum redactae, sive topographia provinciae *Jamato*. Auctor *Fulanzai*, cui nomen quoque *Akizato Ritô* est, cunctas circuli *Gokinai*-ci provincias descripsit librosque suos historico-chorographicos tabulis ornavit, quae locorum memorabilium, templorum, monumentorumque imagines a pictoribus peritissimis delineatas exhibent. Imaginum huius libri auctor est *Takebara Sjun tsjô zai*. Ed. in urbe Mijako, 1800, 7 voll. in 8°.

35. **Kawatsi mei-sjo dsu-e**, topographia provinciae *Kawatsi*, auctore *Akizato Ritô*. Accedunt imagines a *Tôkei*, pictore *Tanba*-no. 1801, 6 voll. in 8°.

36. **Idsumi mei-sjô dsu-e**, topographia provinciae *Idsumi*, auct. *Akizato Ritô*, imaginibus illustrata a *Takebara Sjun tsjô zai*. Ed. 1769, 4 voll. in 8°.

37. **Setsu-jô gun-tan**, i. e. discursus Ohosakani. Auctor *Okada Roksuke* latius et uberius descripsit provinciam *Setsu* imaginibusque illustravit. Ed. 1717, 17 voll. in 8°.

38. **Setsu mei-sjo dsu-e**, topographia provinciae *Setsu*, auct. *Akizato Ritô*. 1794, 16 voll. in 8°. Primum volumen.

39. **Tô-kai-dô mei-sjô dsu-e**, topographia regionis *Tôkaidô*, per cuius provincias iter est ab urbe Mijako ad urbem Jedo. Auct. *Akizato Ritô*. 1797, 6 voll. in 8°.

40. **Musasino banasi**, loquelae *Musasianae*, sive quae topographiam provinciae *Musasi* spectant. Scripsit *Kwakki Sensei*, civis *Tokorosawa*nus eiusdem provinciae. 1816, 4 voll. in 8°.

41. **Omi mei-sjo dsu-e**, topographia provinciae *Omi*, auct. *Akizato Ritô*, cum imag. 1815, 4 vol. in 8°.

42. **Kisodsi mei-sjo dsu-e**, topographia regionis *Kisodsi* (*), auct. *Akizato Ritô*, cum imag. a *Fô kiô Tsiuwa*, religioso quodam, delineatis. 1805, 6 voll., quorum primum deest.

(*) *Kisodsi* nomen Japonenses imposuerunt viae, quae ex provincia *Kôdske* ad vallem *Kisogawa*nam, praeterque fluminis ripam in provinciam *Mino* fert.

43. **Kiino kuni mei-sjo dsu-e**, topographia provinciae Kii, auct. *Akizato Ritô*. 1812, 5 voll. in 8°.

44. **Halima mei-sjo sjun-ran-dsu e**, loca memorabilia et quaecunque ab iis, qui per provinciam *Halima* iter faciunt, spectari solent, descripta et adumbrata ab *Akizato Ritô*. 1812, 5 voll. in 8°.

45. **Nagasaki gjô-jak nitsi-ki**, diarium officialis ex provincia *Fidatsi* in urbem *Nagasaki* delegati A°. 1769. Ed. 1805, 1 vol. in 8°. Auctor *Seki sui Sensei* sive *Gensju*, qui centurio fuit civitatis *Mito*, complures libros geographicos et intineraria scripsit, mappasque geographicas a Batavis communicatas japonice edidit, quorum operum index huic libro adiectus est.

46. **Tsikusi ki-kô**, itineris in regionem *Tsikusi* (†) descriptio, sive diarium Cl. *Fisija Fei sitsi*, qui quum ex provinciae *Owari*anae capite *Nagoja* urbem *Nagasaki* peteret, quaecunque memoratu digna occurrerunt, fusa oratione descripsit, domumque reversus A°. 1802 publice edidit in 10 voll. in 8°.

(†) Occidentalis insulae *Kiusiu* pars olim *Tsikusi* nomen tulit.

47. **Sai-ju ki**, ambulationum occidentalium libri 5. Ed. *Tatsi bana Nan kei si*, medicus *Kamakura*nus, 1794.

48. Tô-ju ki, ambulationum orientalium libri quinque, auct. eodem.
49. Nan-ju ki, ambulationum australium libri quinque, (eorum primus tantum est). Auctor est idem *Tatsi bana Nan keisi*, qui quum Ambulationum septentrionalium quoque libros quinque scripsisset, provinciis imperii sane omnibus percognitis, operis sui titulis praescripsit verba Sjo kok kei tan (*Tschu kuĕ ki tan*) i. e. rara provinciarum omnium memoria.
50. Wô Tsjô ni siu no ki, de provinciis *Wô siu* (*Suwo*) atque *Tsjô siu* sive *Nagáto*, vol. MS.
51. San rjô si, memoriale tumulorum, quibus Mikadones inlati sunt. Auct. *Kamo-u Fide sane*. Jedo 1822, 2 *kiuén* in 1 vol. in 8°.
52. Ko san-rjôno dsu-e, antiquorum, quibus Mikadones inlati sunt, tumulorum imagines, manu pictae.
53. Sjo kok tate-jokoki koto; gohori sirono kazu tsuku, provinciae cuiusque japonicae longitudo et latitudo ab astronomis imperatoris observatae; accedit regionum (*gohori*) et praemunitarum vallo urbium enumeratio, 1 vol. in 8° MS.

C. *Mappae geographicae.*

a. *Generales.*

54. Dai Nippon sai-ken si-sjô zen-dsu, i. e. imperium japonicum magnum ad minutam scalam geometricam redactum et accurate descriptum. Supplevit *Tori kavi Tô zai*; examinavit vir peritissimus *Tatsi bana Nan keisi* (conf. n°. 47). Tabula denuo typis exscripta quinto annorum *Bunkwa* (A°. 1808).
55. Kai-sei Nippon dsu, descriptio regni jap. emendata. Ed. 1812.
56. Kai-sei Nippon jo-dsi-ro-tei zen-dsu, descriptio regni japonici emendata. In viis indicatae sunt locorum inter se distantiae. Ed. civitatis *Mito*-nicae centurio, cui nomen *Gensiu siwô* (conf. n°. 45) A°. 1812.
57. Sin ban, Nippon-kok oho je-dsu, regni japonici tabula nova; ed. A°. 1744.
58. Nippon fen-kai rjak-dsu, regni japonici terrarumque confinium tabula minor, aeri incisa.
59. Kiusiu no dsu, Kiusiu insulae descriptio geographica. Nagasaki 1822.

b. *Speciales.*

60. Jamasirono kuni je dsu, mappa geogr. provinciae *Jamásiro* MS. In mappis geogr. specialibus magni sane aestimandae sunt tabulae manuscriptae, quarum dimensio ea ratione facta est, ut milliare japonicum partibus quindecim mensurae gallicae centrimetrae respondeat.
61. Jamátono kuni je dsu, map. geogr. provinciae *Jamáto*, MS.
62. Jamátono kuni sai-ken je-dsu, map. geogr. provinciae *Jamáto*. Ed. *Nakamura Kan zi sai*. 1775.
63. Kawátsino kuni sai ken sjo dsu, map. geogr. prov. *Kawátsi* minor, auct. *Niva Tokei*. Ed. 1776, iterum 1801.
64. Kawátsino kuni je-dsu, map. geogr. prov. *Kawátsi*, MS.
65. Idsumino kuni oho je-dsu, map. geogr. prov. *Idsumi* major. Ed. *Takebara Sjun tsjô sai* ante annum 1769.
66. Idsumino kuni je dsu, map. geogr. provinciae *Idsumi*, MS.

67. Setsno kuni mei-sjo oho je dsu, mappa geogr. provinciae *Sets* major.
68. Simano kuni je dsu, map. geogr. provinciae *Sima*, MS.
69. Owarino kuni je dsu, mappa geogr. prov. *Owari*, tab. 2, MSS.
70. Mikawano kuni je dsu, mappa geogr. prov. *Mikáwa*, MS.
71. Awano kuni je dsu, map. geogr. prov. *Awa*, MS.
72. Musasino rjak-dsu, map. geogr. prov. *Musasi* minor. Ed. *Iwasaki Tsunemasa*. Jedo 1824.
73. Ômino kuni oho-jedsu, map. geogr. prov. *Ômi* major, auct. *Jamasita Sigemasa*. Ohosaka 1742. Denuo typis excusa 1824.
74. Omino kuni jedsu, mappa geogr. prov. *Omi*, tabulae binae, MSS.
75. Mimasakano (*) kuni jedsu, mappa geogr. prov. *Mimasaka*, MS.
    (*) Exemplo ipsi, per errorem, provinciae *Mino* titulus inscriptus est.
76. Notono kuni jedsu, map. geogr. prov. *Noto*, MS.
77. Jetsigono kuni jedsu, map. geogr. prov. *Jetsi go*.
78. Sadono kuni jedsu, map. geogr. prov. *Sado*.
79. Tanbano kuni jedsu, map. geogr. prov. *Tanba*. Auct. *Jano Sadatosi*, *Mijako* 1799.
80. Tangono kuni jedsu, map. geogr. prov. *Tango*. Auct. *Saito Sin sajemon*, Ed. *Asano javei*. Ohosaka 1817.
81. Tangono kuni jedsu, map. geogr. prov. *Tango*, MS.
82. Tatsimano kuni jedsu, map. geogr. prov. *Tatsima* 1782.
83. Fokino kuni jedsu, map. geogr. prov. *Foki*.
84. Iwamino kuni jedsu, map. geogr. prov. *Iwami*, tab. tres MSS.
85. Okino kuni jedsu, map. geogr. prov. (insulae) *Oki*, MS.
86. Inabano kuni jedsu, map. geogr. prov. *Inaba*, MS.
87. Halimano kuni jedsu, map. geogr. prov. *Halima*, MS.
88. Halimano kuni oho jedsu, map. geogr. prov. Halima major. Ed. *Kawatsi ja Gisuke*, Ohosaka 1749.
89. Bizenno kuni jedsu, map. geogr. prov *Bizen*, MS.
90. Bitsiuno kuni jedsu, map. geogr. prov. *Bitsiu*, MS.
91. Awadsino kuni jedsu, map. geogr. prov. *Awadsi*, MS.

91. *b.* Additamenti loco allatas quoque ab equite *J. C. Blomhoff* provinciarum jap. tabulas attingo manuscriptas, quae in Museo regio Hagano servantur, atque exempla esse videntur manu japonica cursim ad minorem scalam redacta.

D. *Libri Topographici.*

a. *Topographiam spectantes urbis Mijako.*

92. Mijako mei sjo dsu e, descriptio rerum memorabilium urbis, in qua est sedes imperatorum Mikadonum. Auct. *Akizato Ritô* cum adumbr. a *Takebara Sjun tsjô sai*, delin. 1780, 11 voll. in 8°.
93. Mijako rin sen mei sjo dsu e, descriptio fanorum, fontium rerumque memorabilium, quae urbi Mijako ornatui sunt. Auct. *Akizato Ritô*. Accedunt delineationes diversorum auctorum. 1798, 5 voll. in 8°.

94. **Kjô midsu**, i. e. aqua sive fontes *Mijak*onenses. Urbis Mijako descriptio auct. *Akizato Sjunfuk*, Ed. A°. 1791, 2. voll.

    Vol. I. Descriptio aulae regiae, cui Dairi nomen est.

    Vol. II. Descript. urbis Mijako in partem orientalem (*Rak-jô*) atque occidentalem (*Tsjô-an*) divisae.

95. **Kjôto meguri**, i. e. ambulationes *Mijak*onenses auct. *Kaibara Toksin*. Liber typis exscriptus A°. 1784, iterum 1815, 2 voll. in 8°. Libri conscribendi ratio fuit, ut qui urbem regiam adiret, per omnia, quae sive in ipsa urbe sive locis circumiacentibus visu digna essent, septendecim duceretur ambulationibus diurnis.

96. **Mijako si-sja zen-dsu**, imagines templorum buddhaicorum aediumque sacrarum, quae urbem Mijako ornant, tabulis ligneis exscriptae a *Jasida Kitsifei*. 1730, 4 voll.

97. **Zô-bô je-ire, Mijako mei-sjo kuruma**, *Kaibara Toksin*; currus rerum memorabilium Mijakonensium, sive topographia urbis regiae, aucta, imaginibusque locupl. 1714, 1 vol. Est autem accuratior aulae regiae nec non templorum aediumque sacrarum descriptio, ad quam enumeratio fastorum accedit, qui sancte et religiose celebrari solent. Praemittitur index viarum, quae intra et extra urbem sunt.

98. **Mijako oho je-dsu**, urbis Mijako locorumque adiacentium adumbratio. Ed. prima A°. 1666, 1 fol. maj. Ed. emend. A°. 1741, 2 foll., quorum unum in libris Cl. equitis *J. C. Blomhoff* servatur, alterum in Museo Regio Hagano suspensum est.

99. **Kjôto si-sjô no dsu**, accurata ubis regiae (Mijako) adumbratio. Ed. correct. A°. 1812, 1 fol.

100. *a*. **Sin-zô sai-ken Kjôno je-dsu**, nova et aucta urbis regiae adumbratio subtilis. Ed. 1811, denuo typis exarat. 1813, 1 fol.

100. *b*. **Kwai bô Kjôno jedsu**, in sinu recondenda urbis Mijako adumbratio, ad mensuram minorem redacta; ed. 1774. Indicata reperies templa, aedes sacras, locos conspicuos monumentorum reliquias, quae intra et extra urbem adsunt.

101. **Kwa-rak itsi-ran dsu**, urbis Mijako imago universa (Panorama); delin. *Wô kwa san* pictor; ed. *Kazawori Masaka*. Mijako 1809, 1 fol.

102. **Sin kai, Dairi no dsu**, nov. et emend. aulae regiae adumbratio. Ed. 1817, 1 fol.

* 103. **Sin bô, Kjôno dsu**, nov. et emend. urbis Mijako adumbratio, ed. 1684, 1 fol. Tabulam si evolvis, titulus tibi prolatus est alius quo »denuo exscripta urbis *Fei an* (Mijako) locorumque adiacentium adumbratio designatur.

104. **Sin fan, Fijei-san Jenraksi**, prospectus templi *Jenraksi* in monte *Fijeisan*, regionisque adiacentis. 1 fol. magn.

b. *Topographiam spectantes urbis Jedo.*

105. **Bun-ken Jedo oho jedsu**, magna urbis Jedo adumbratio (Plan) ad mensuram $\frac{1}{7560}$ facta, singulum enim *Bun* (centesima pars pedis japonici) respondet duodenis *Ken* ($75\frac{6}{10}$ ped. jap. Ed. prima A°. 1732. Adsunt exempla quoque ed. A°. 1775 et 1826, 1 fol.

106. **Bun-ken, won Jedo no je**, urbis imperialis Jedo adumbratio ad mensuram ita descripta ut singulum *Bun* respondeat tricenis *Ken* ($\frac{1}{18,900}$). Ed. 1804, 1 fol.

107. **Bun-ken kwai-bô, won Jedo no jedsu**, in sinu recondenda urbis imperialis *Jedo* adumbratio ad mensuram deducta. Ed. 1825, 1 fol.

* 108. **Sai-fan sin-kai, won Jedo no jedsu**, imperialis urbis Jedo adumbratio nova et emend. denuo typis exscripta A°. 1797, 1 fol.

* 109. **Bun-kwa kai sei, won Jedo no jedsu**, imperialis urbis Jedo adumbratio annis *Bunkwa* (1804 et seqq.) facta. Tabulae sub num. 108 indicatae editio est nova.

* 110. **Sai fan, Sin kai won Jedo no jedsu**, imperialis urbis Jedo adumbratio nova et emend. denuo typis exscripta A°. 1804 et 1818, 1 fol. Tabula litteris *Firakana* scripta est.

† 111. **Bun-sei kai sei, won Jedo oho jedsu**, imperialis urbis Jedo adumbratio ampla, annis *Bunsei*. 1818 et seqq. emendata, 1 fol. Tab. literis *Katakana* scripta.

112. **Fô-sjô no Udsijasu zidai Bu-siu Jedo no jedsu**, urbs Jedo, qualis *Fô-sjô no Udsijasu* principis tempore (1540—1561) fuit, adumbrata. Ed. 1804.

113—120. Adumbrationes diversarum urbis Jedo partium. **Sita-ja Asagusa kata no dsu**, adumbratio partis cui nomen est Sitaja Asagusa. 1767.

114. **Janaka Motomimaru jama Woisigawa kata no dsu**, adumbratio partis cui nomen est Janaka M. Woisigawa. 1770.

115. **Suruga tai Wogawa matsi no dsu**, adumbratio partis cui nomen, Suruga tai Wogawa matsi.

116. **(Tôdo) Nagada matsi no jedsu**, Nagada matsi nominatae partis adumbratio. 1759.

117. **Ban tsjô no jedsu**, adumbratio partis cui nomen Bantsjô. 1752.

118. **Fama-tsjo, Kanda, Nippon-basi kita no dsu**, adumbratio partium Famatsjô Kanda, Nippon basi kita. 1770.

119. **Siba, Atago sita kata no dsu**, adumbr. partium Siba, Atagosita. 1766.

120. **Tsuku dsi, Batsjô fori, Nipponbasi minami no dsu**, adumbratio partium Tsukudsi, Batsjô fori, Nipponbasi minami. 1775.

121. **Sin fan, won Jedo mei-sjo fitori annai ki**, rerum urbis imperialis Jedo memorabilium monstrator solitarius. Ed. nov. 1 vol.

122. *a*. **Irofa wake fitori annai, Jedo matsi tsukusi**, index viarum urbis Jedo in usum solivagorum secundum *Irofa* dispositus. 1821. Accedunt *b*. libellus inscriptus **Sai ken** (*si hién*) i. e. conspectus minutus, sive Indicium quanti quae ad viam *Josiwara* florent sacerdotes Veneriae aestimentur, quanti venire soleant. 1826. *c*. quaedam de conditione civitatis Jedo interna notitiae MSS.

123. **Jedo won metsuke rjak dsu**, imperiales urbis Jedo vigiliae breviter descriptae.

124. **Jedo go sjô nai go sumai no dsu**, imperialium arcis Jedonicae aedium adumbr.

c. Topographiam spectantes urbis Ohosaka.

125. **Inisive jori imajomade Naniva Ohosaka zjŭ ni dsu**, tabulae duodecim topographicae MSS. urbis Ohosaka antiquam et hodiernam conditionem exhibentes.

† * 126. **Zô-sin, Ohosaka si sjô dsu**, urbis Ohosaka descriptio distincta, addita fluminis *Sumida gawa* adumbratione, 1 tab. auct. et ornata. 1794. Urbs ad mensuram ita descripta est, ut 1 *Bun* (centesima pars pedis) respondeat 24 *Ken* (ped. $151\frac{2}{10}$). Accedit index rerum, quas urbs Ohosaka profert, itemque pontium primariorum eorumque mensurarum.

127. **Sin-ban zô-bô, Ohosaka no dsu**, tab. topogr. urbis Ohosaka denuo typis exscripta atque aucta. A°. 1787.

* 128. **Zo-siu kai-sei, Setsiu Ohosaka dsi no dsu**, tab. topogr. urbis Ohosaka, quae est caput provinciae *Sets*, auct. et emend. Haec urbis Ohosaka delineatio imperatoris iussu A°. 1778 ad maiorem mensuram instituta, A°. 1807 ad finem perducta est.

129. **Bun-sei sin kai, Setsiu Ohosakano zen dsu**, tab. topogr. urbis Ohosaka omnibus numeris absoluta, VIII° annorum *Bunsei* (1825) denuo typis exscripta. Exemplum est tabulae praecedentis ad mensuram dimidio minorem redactum, ita ut centesima pars pedis (unum *Bun*) respondeat pedibus $75\frac{6}{10}$ sive 12 *Ken*.

130. **Ohosaka matsi kagami**, viarum *Ohosaka*narum speculum, sive index ad alphabetum dispositus. Ed. 1756, libellus pusillus.

131. **Ohosaka sirono dsu**, *a*. Arcis *Ohosaka*nae tabulae topogr. duae MSS., in quarum minore locorum dimensiones indicatae sunt. *b*. **Ohosaka Abeno katsuseno no dsu**, imagines duae ad arcis *Ohosaka*nae A°. 1615. oppugnationem spectantes.

132. **Kai-sei, Fito-me sen-gen**, mille delectationum sive rerum memorabilium *Ohosaka*narum conspectus. 1 vol. emend.

133. **Kwan-sei kai-sei, Miwodsukusi**, signum (*) rerum memorabilium *Ohosaka*narum annis *Kwansei* (1789—1801) emend. 1 vol.

(*) Vocabulo *Miwodsuki* signum indicatur, quod navigantibus tutum monstrat ingressum in portum.

134. *a*. **Ohosaka matsi-tsiu Ohoso tsumori-mune san-jô**, computatio incolarum, quibus urbs *Ohosaka* gaudet. Ed. ineunte aera *Bunsei* (1818). 1 fol.

b. **Ohosaka rjô-gave te-kata fen-ran**, negotiatores argentarii, qui in urbe *Ohosaka* florent, indicati.

c. **Ohosaka Mijako mei-buts awase sumô**, tabula, qua urbium *Ohosaka* atque *Mijako* res memorabiles comparantur.

d. **Tsume sirusi**, indicatio foeminarum sive sacerdotum Veneriarum, quae in urbe *Ohosaka* florent. 1819, 1 vol. in 12°.

d. Topographiam spectantes urbis Nagasaki atque locorum aliorum.

135. **Fisiu Nagasakino dsu**, tabula topogr. urbis *Nagasaki* in provincia *Fizen* sitae. Ed. 1778, iterum 1802, denuo 1821.

136. **Halima Fimedsino dsu**, tab. topogr. urbis *Fimedsi* in prov. *Halima* sitae, MS.

137. **Simôsa kunino Nikwôsan no dsu**, tab. topogr. montis *Nikwôsan* in prov. *Simôsa*.

138. **Nikwô won-san sôno jedsu**, totius montis imperialis, cui nomen *Nikwó*, templorumque in illo erectorum adumbratio.

139. **Kamakura seô kaino dsu**, loci *Kamakura*ni adumbratio. Tabula haec topographica a pictore *Fata kasimaru* A°. 1798 delineata descriptionem exhibet templi *Tsuru oka Fatsiman mija* regionisque in qua situm est.

E. *Urbium regionumque prospectus.*

140. **Nippon mei-sjo no je**, imago locorum Japoniae memorabilium, sive tabula terrae japonicae prospectum procul exhibens, auct. *Kunsai seôsin*, pictore *Jedo*nensi.

141. **Tô-kai dô mei-sjo itsi ran**, conspectus locorum regionis *Tôkaidô* memorabilium, auct. *Hoksai*, inter pictores *Jedo*nenses principe. 1818.

142. **Tô-tsiu ki**, itinerarium *Tôkaidô*-nicum, 2 voll, quorum prius inde ab urbe *Mijako* usque ad *Arai*, alterum autem inde a *Tenriu gawa Jedo* tenus quae sunt visu digna indicat.

143. **Wa siu Josino jama mei-sjo dsu**, locorum regionis montanae, cui nomen est *Josino jama*, memorabilium conspectus. Ed. 1713. Accedit locorum, qui reliquis praestant, descriptio.

144. **Akino kuni Itsukusima kei**, insulae *Itsukusima*, quae ad provinciam *Aki* pertinet, prospectus, a *Kaibara Toksin* explicatus. Ed. 1789.

145. **Tangono kuni Amanobasi tateno dsu**, prospectus, qui a ponte *Amanobasi* (prov. *Tango*) patet.

146. Mitsinôku kuni Sivokama Matsusimano dsu, pulcherrimus, qui a vicis *Sivokama* et *Matsusima* est, prospectus maris insularumque. Ed. 1729. Vici dicti prope ab urbe *Sendai* provinciae *Mutsu* sunt.

147. Jedo Sumidagawa rjô-gan itsi ran dsu, fluminis, quo aqua *Sumida*na per urbem *Jedo* in mare labitur, ripae utriusque conspectus. Delin. *Tsuruoka Rosui*, A°. 1781. 2 voll.

148. Jodogawa rjô-gan sjô-kei dsu-e, fluminis *Jodogawa* ripae utruisque prospectus. Delin. *Keô sjô sei*. 1824, 2 voll.

149. Mei san dsu bu, montium memorabilium tum japonensium tum jezonensium adumbrationes. Auct. *Buntsjô* 1804, 3 voll. in 8°.

150. San-sui ki-kwan, rari regionum prospectus auct *Gjokkô*, *Jedo* 1800, 4 voll.

151. Fusijamano dsu, *Fusi*, montis ignivomi, singulis anni mensibus specie variantis, prospectus duodecim. Auct. *Kobajasi Tsjôsiu*, 1822, 1 vol.

152. Fusino kei, *Fusi* montis prospectus novem a diversis provinciarum *Suruga* atque *Sagami* locis. Accedunt quatuor huius montis, uti quatuor anni tempestatibus facie variat, imagines coloribus in tela serica adumbratae, vol. 1, in 4°.

153. Sai zô kan bits, *Ninomija Komaki* Japonis Σκιαγραφήματα MSS. versicoloria subitaria, quae prospectum exhibent insulae *Sakurasima*, montis *Asojama* atque *Takatsifo* insulaeque *Fanagasima*.

154. Kiino san-sui kei kwan, nonnullarum provinciae *Kii* regionum prospectus rari MSS.; spectant inprimis ad *Fasimoto*, *Kii gawa*, portum *Wakafama*num, sinumque *Wakaura*num.

155. Omino fatsi kei dsu, octo lacus *Omi*anae prospectus; pinxit *Wôsiu* Mijakonensis, tab. 1.

156. Fansiu Akasi Maikono famano dsu, prospectus litoris *Maikono fama* prope urbem *Akasi* provinciae *Halima*, tab. 1. xylographica.

157. Kôjasan sai ken jedsu, prospectus montis *Kôja*, qui in provincia *Kii* jacet. Delin. *Tatsibana Tô siun*, 1813. Tab. major xylogr. coloribus adumbrata.

158. Kisiu Kôjasan Kongô busi saiken dsu, prospectus templi *Kôjasan*ensis, cui nomen *Kongôbusi*. Delin. *Tatsibana Kuniwô*, pictor Ohosakanus, 1784, tab. 1. xylogr.

159. Si ten wô si Karanno dsu, prospectus templi regibus quatuor coelestibus sacri monasteriique adiacentis (locus prope ab urbe *Ohosaka* est). Delin. *Takebara sinfan* Ohosakanus.

160. Daisaifu Ten man gu won kei naino jedsu, prospectus templi *Tenmangu* una cum locis adiunctis. Templum ad urbem *Daisaifu* in provincia *Tsikugo* pertinet, 1819, 1 tab. xylogr.

F. *Itineraria*.

161. Tôkaidô bun-ken jedsu, viae *Tôkaidô*, quae ab urbe *Mijako* ducit *Jedo*ne tenus, adumbratio (ut dicitur) ad mensuram facta. Exempla adsunt annis 1752, 1772, 1774 typis exscripta.

162. Tôkai, Kiso rjô-dô-tsiu kwai bô dsu kan, prospectus in sinu recondendus rerum, quae iis, qui vias *Tôkaido* atque *Kisodsi* meant, spectandae sunt. Ed. 1807, 1 vol.

163. Dai Nippon dô-tsiu kô-tei sai-ken ki, urbium locorumque japonicorum intervalla accurate descripta. Ed. 1804, 1 vol.

164. Dai Nippon dô-tsiu kô-tei si-nan-kuruma, pyxis nautica imperii jap., sive index quantum loci inter se distent. Ed. 1820, 1 vol.

* 165. Dai Nippon kai riku tsû ran, itinera Japoniae maritima et terranea (inde a *Matsumaë* usque ad *Fusankai*, portum Koreanum) descripta. Ed. 1804, 1 vol.

166. Dô-tsiu fitori an-nai, itineris dux solitarius, sive tab. geogr. inde a *Nagasaki* usque ad *Matsumaë* mansiones cursus publici earumque intervalla indicans, 1 vol.

167. Sai-kok zjun-rei sai-ken dai sen, provinciarum occidentalium sive insulae *Sikok* loci, quos religionis causa pervagari solent, accurate indicati. 1825, 1 vol. cum tab. geogr.

168. Si-kok ben-reino dsu, insulae *Sikok* circuitus in usum eorum, qui locos sacros adeunt, descriptus. 1763.

169. Si-kok ben-reino dsu, tabula parum differens ab ea, quae praecedit.

170. Ni-kwô jeki-ro ri-sû no beô, viae, qua itur *Jedo*ne ad montem *Nikwôsan*, mansionum milliariorumque index (Europaeorum more conscriptus). *Jedo* 1226, 1 tab.

171. Tô-kai-dô jeki ro-ri-sû no beô, viae *Tôkaidô* mansionum milliariorumque index, MS.

172. Zô-bô Nippon sivodsino ki, itinera Japoniae marina descripta, auct. *Takada Masanori* 1796, 1 vol. in 12°.

173. Ohosakano gawa-kutsi jori Nagasaki madeno sen-ro, navium litora legentium via inde a fluminis *Ohosaka*ni ore usque ad urbem *Nagasaki* indicata, tab. MS.

G. *De Coloniis tributariisque populis libri geographici et historici.*

174. San-kok tsu-ran dsu ki, descriptio trium regnorum (scil. *Jezo, Liukiu* atque *Tschaosiën*) cum adumbrationibus et mappis 4 geogr. auct. *Fajasi Sivei*, civi *Sendai*ano 1785, 1 vol. MS.

175. Jezo tan fitsu ki, *Sugano Jôfo*, Japonensis adnotata de insula *Jezo*, MS. A°. 1710, 1 vol.

† 176. Jezo sju wi, notitiarum Insulae Jezo supplementum, 1 vol. MS.

177. Jezono dsu, *Mogami Toknai*, geographi Jap. illustrissimi mappae geographicae MSS. quinque, quarum tres terram *Jezo* duae autem terram *Karafuto* exhibent.

178. Matsumaë Jezono dsu, tab. geogr. MS. exhibens meridionalem insulae *Jezo* partem, cuius caput est *Matsumaë*.

179. Jezo kai binno kei, litorum *Jezo*nensium pars ea, quae inde a *Wodalnai* ad promontorium *Sója*num tendit, coloribus adumbrata, 1 vol. MS.

180. Karafuto sima, *Mogami Toknai*, geographus celeberrimus de insula *Karafuto*, vol. 1. MS.

181. Săgalen simano dsu, tab. geogr. insulae *Krafuto* MS. auct. *Mogami Toknai*.

182. Kok-riu-kô tsiu-siu, (*Hé lûng-kiâng tschung-tscheû*), tab. geogr. in gradus descripta exhibens terram in ostio fluminis *Amur* sitam (scil. *Karafuto*) auct. *Mamija Rinzô* MS. *Amur* flumen a Sinensibus flumen draconis nigri (*Hélûng kiâng*) dicitur.

† 183. Karafuto simano dsu, mappa geogr. insulae *Karafuto*.

184. Liukiu dan, *Morisima Tsiurô*, de insulis *Liukiu* dissertatio. A°. 1790, vol. 1.

185. Tsjôsen monogatari, *Kimura Rijemon*, historiae Koreanae libri quinque. Ed. Jedo 1750. Quae in his libris dicuntur, iam reddita sunt in ea operis *Nippon Archiv* sectione, cui titulus: »*Nachrichten über Kôrai, Japan's Bezüge mit der Kôraischen Halbinsel und mit Schina.*"

186. Sân-tsʻaí ï-kuân tʻû, rerum coelestium, terrestrium atque humanarum quidquid cognitione dignissimum est in tabulam unam coniectum auct. *Lù-fu Ngân schi*, qui vicum *Sin tschang hien* prope urbem *Tschao hing fu* in prov. *Tschĕkiang* incoluit.

187. *Wán-kuĕ tá tsʻiuén tʻú*, tabula omnium regnorum magna et perfecta. Est autem mappa geogr. imperii Sinensis regionumque confinium, 1663.

188. *Lĭ tai ssé-tsi̇̆ tʻú*, i. e. generationum sibi invicem succedentium vestigia historica adumbrata. Titulus, quam explicavi, mappam geogr. regni Sinensis spectat, quae A°. 1659 in urbe *Peking* edita et in Japonia anno 1749 denuo typis exscripta est.

189. *Tá-Tsʻing wan-niên ĭ-tʻóng tí-li tsʻiuén tʻú*, tab. geographica universum imperium *Mandschu*cum exhibens.

† 190. *Kù-kin jên-kĕ tí-tú*, *Akamidsu*, centurionis *Mito*nensis tabulae 13, orbem sinensem exhibentes antiquum et novum. Jedo 1788, 1 vol. in 4°.

Tabularum conspectus: Tab. 1. Orbis sinensis indicata urbium distantia terra marique. 2. Orb. sin. sub imperio *Hia*, 2207 ante Chr. n. 3. Orb. sin. sub imperio *Tscheu*, ante Chr. n. 1122. 4. Orb. sin. ad illustrandam Confucii historiam *Tschʻün tsieu*. 5. Regna bellantia. 6. Imperium *Tsʻin*, 256—207 ante Chr. n. 7. Imperium *Si Han*. 8. Imp. *Tung Han*. 9. *San kuĕ*. 10. Imp. *Tsin* duplex. 11. Imp. *Tʻang*. 12. *Tá Ming*. 13. Generalis Asiae orientalis et Archipelagi Indici descriptio.

II. *Mappae geographicae auctorum Europaeorum Japonice redditae.*

191. O-lan sin-jeki tsi-kiu zen dsu, hemisphaerium utrumque origine batavum; japonice reddidit notasque adiecit *Akamidsu* centurio civitatis *Mito* 1769, 1 vol. in 4°.

192. Kan-tsa-ka no dsu, tab. geogr. terrae *Kamtschatka* origine russica; japonice reddidit *Mogami Toknai*.

193. Fŏ kai (*Pé hai*), mare glaciale, tabula origine russica; japonice reddidit *Mogami Toknai*. Accedunt eiusdem auctoris 3 voll. MSS., in quibus notitiae quaedam insularum *Jezo*, *Karafuto* cet. nec non imperii russici collectae sunt.

Sectio III. LIBRI PHYSICI.

A. *De historia naturali generales.*

a. *Sinici, denuo in Japonia impressi.*

194. *Tá-kuon Tsching-lui pèn-tsʻaò*, historia naturalis in justiorem ordinem redacta denuoque elaborata annis *Tá kuon* dictis (1107—1110) auctore sinensi *Tʻang Schin wi*. Prospectum huius libri jam J. Klaproth in opere illo, cui titulus *Verzeichniss der Chinesischen und Mandshuischen Bücher und Handschriften der K. Bibliothek zu Berlin*, pag. 164 inseruit. Opus nostrum cura collegii medici, quod in urbe *Jedo* floret, denuo typis exscriptum A°. 1769, 31 *kiuén* sive tomi in 26 voll.

195. Historia naturalis, cui titulus *Pen tsʻaò kang mŭ*, auctore *Li Schi tsching* exeunte saeculo XVI conscripta et cum praefatione doctissimi *Wang Schi tschin* edita A°. 1596. Hoc in opere, quod alterius A°. 1603 in Sina factae editionis exemplum est, in usum Japonum flexio vocum Japonensium addita est, complectitur 52 *kiuén* in 25 tomis. Recentior huius operis editio Japonica, cui titulus est *Sin* (i. e. novum) *Pèn-tsʻaò kang-mŭ*, a Clar. v. O. Fisscher adlata, continet 61 *kiuén*.

196. *Pèn ts'aò hoeï*, i. e. vasa naturae sive doctrina de medicamentis adhibendis auct. sinensi *Niên ngó Li siën seng*, Edidit *Kuŏ Fu lan*, 1666. Opus in Japonia denuo typis exscriptum, adiectis versionis japonicae notis, 18 tom. in 8°. Fasciculi octo priores de morbis eorumque remediis agunt; fasc. 9. 10, 11 et 12, de herbis officinalibus, fasc. 13. de variis frumentis et oleribus; fasc. 14. de fructibus, fasc. 15 et 16. de arboribus; fasc. 17. de insectis, conchyliis, avibus et quadrupedibus; fasc. 18. de materiis a corpore humano depromtis, de fossilibus, aqua, igni et terra quatenus usui medicinali inserviunt.

197. **Môsi sô mok teo ziu gjô so**, (*Maôschi ts'aò mŭ niaò scheŭ tsch'ŭng jü sù*), i. e. illustratio herbarum, arborum, avium, quadrupedum, insectorum, piscium, de quibus in antiquorum carminum collectione, quam *Maôschi* (i. e. carmina, quibus animalium et herbarum laudes celebrantur) sive *Schi-king* dicunt, agitur. Scripsit *Lŭ ki*, Sinensis. Denuo typis expressit, notasque lectionis japonicae adiecit *Matsusita Kenrin*, 1698, 1 vol. 8°.

198. **Môsi, Liksi sô mok so dsu kai**, (*Maôschi, Lŭ-schi ts'aò-mŭ sŭ t'ŭ kiaì*), descriptio herbarum et arborum, quarum mentio fit in *Maôschi* dicta sinensium carminum collectione, adumbrationibus illustrata auctore *Lŭ schi* vel *Lŭ ki*. Exemplum quod praesto est, denuo in Japonia typis exscriptum, prodiit in urbe Jedo, 1778, 5 voll. in 8° curante *Futsi Zai kwan*, qui annotationibus librum illustravit japonicaque rerum nomina adiecit. In volume 5to agitur de suppellectile, instrumentis musicis, vasis, vexillis, curriculis cet., et quum praeclarae quoque res bello gestae in dicto carminum libro celebratae sint, commentario suo quaedam de re bellica et agminum dispositione adiunxit auctor.

199. **Môsi bin-buts dsu kô**, (*Maôschi p'ĭn-wŭ t'ŭ k'aò*), i. e. res, quae antiquis carminibus celebrantur, in classes reductae, figuris adumbratae et descriptae auctore *Oka Genfô*, civi *Ohosaka*no 1786, 3 voll. in 8°.

200. *Maôschi mĭng-wŭ t'ŭ jŭe*, sive res notabiles, quae carminibus antiquis celebrantur, depictae et illustratae auctore *U Tschŭng siŭ tĭng*, Sinensi 1771, 2 voll., typis denuo exscripta et edita curante Collegio medico, quod in urbe *Jedo* floret. A°. 1808.

201. *Kieŭ-hoáng pen-ts'aò*, i. e. vegetabilia annonae levandae. Descripsit *Tscheŭ-fán Hiĕn wang*, qui vixit sub imperio *Ming*. Auxit animadversionesque adiecit *Jaô K'ò tsching* 1715, 9 voll. in 8°.

202. *Schi wù pèn ts'aò*, descriptio plantarum edulium auctore *Tung jen Li kaò*, qui vixit sub imperio Mongolico. Recens. *Ts'iën jŭn tschi* imperante dynastia *Ming*. Ed. Japonica 1651, 2 voll. in 8°.

203. *T'ŭng tschi kuên tsch'ŏng ts'aò mŭ liŏ*, compendium Faunae et Florae terrae sinensis. Ed. *Tsching kiă tsi*, regnante dynastia *Song*; typis denuo exprimi curavit *Wono Lanzan*, Japonensis, 1785, 2 voll. in 8°.

204. *Hoâ kîng*, speculum florum, auctore *Tsch'ing fù jaó*, 1688, exempl. MS. 6 voll. in 8°.

205. *Pèn ts'aò weijén*, collectanea botanica. Quae principes sinensium medici ac physici de rerum natura et usu medico docuerunt, collata a *Ni tschŭ mu*, qui vixit sub imperio *Ming*. Exemplum MS. a Japonensi *Matsuoka Tsiu an*, 6 voll.

206. *Nân fang ts'aò mŭ tschoáng*, herbae et arbores regionum australium (prov. *Kuang tung* atque Cochinchinae). Descripsit *Hi hán*, qui fuit belli dux sub imperatore *Wuti* 274. Lectionis japonicae notas addidit, denuoque typis exprimi curavit *Firasumi Senan* 1725, 2 voll. in 8°.

b. *Japonici*.

207. **Honzô kômok kei mô**, rudimenta physices. Docuit *Wono Lanzan*, scripsit *Tsunenori*, nepos eius. Mijako, Jedo 1804, 5 voll. in 8°.

208. **Honzô keimô meisu**, operis praecedentis nomenclatio, statuit Dr. *Wono Lansan*, redegit *Tsunenori*, nepos eius, 1809, 8 voll. in 8°.

209. **Honzô gensi** (*Pèntsʻaò juênschî*), elementa physices auct. *Lui kungpao*. Ed. Jap. 1698, 5 voll. in 12°.

210. **Honzô Wakai**, explicatio japonica historiae naturalis, scripsit *Dosan*, medicus Academiae *Mijak*onensis celeberrimus, auxit *Ohoje Fensen*. Ohosaka 1712, 2 voll. in 12°.

211. **Jamato honzô sinkiôsei**, Japonica historia naturae denuo correcta auct. *Kaibara Toksin*, literarum studioso *Tsikuzen*iano 1708, 10 voll. in 8°. Doctrina de natura rerum, quam operis auctor praecipit, de libris sinicis atque japonicis deprompta, botanicen spectat praecipuam.

212. **Kwô Jamato honzô**, Japonica historia naturae ampliata auct. *Tsiok Kairiu*. Mijako 1759, 12 voll. in 8°.

213. **Sjaben jorok**, *Tojoda Jokei*, Medici *Suwón*ensis, supplementum enumerationis et descriptionis rariorum, quae in collectione eius servantur. 1761, 1 vol. in 8°.

214. **Butsrui bin sits**, collectiones rerum naturalium in classes divisae. Descripsit *Fatotani Firaki sensei*. Ohosaka 1763, 6 voll. in 8°.

215. **Kwa wi**, species florum (topiariorum) diversae. Descripsit et adumbravit *Jônan Densiu*. Mijako 1759, iterum 1765, 8 voll. in 8° maj.

216. **Sômok seifu**, *Kijovara Tsiukjo*, de natura herbarum et arborum. Owari 1823—1827, 3 voll. in 8° majori. Opus curante naturae indagatorum societate, quae in urbe *Owari* floret, editum est.

217. **Judok honzô dsusets**, *Kijovara Tsiukjo*, descriptio arborum et herbarum venenatarum cum adumbr. Owari 1827, 2 voll. in 8° majori.

218. **Honzô Wameô**, nomina rerum naturalium japonica, explicavit *Fukaje Fozin*. 1797, 2 voll. in 8°.

219. **Butsbin sikimei**, rerum nomina nota, sive *Wono Lansan*, physici celeberrimi nomenclatura rerum naturalium. Scripsit *Midsutani Fófun Sukerok* 1809, 4 voll. in 12°.

220. **Honzô Jakmei bikô Wagun seô**, medicaminum sive rerum omnium naturalium nomina japonica secundum *Irofa* disposita. Examinavit atque nomina sinica adiecit *Tanba Jorisudsi*. Mijako 1807, 7 voll. in 8°. Medici tam sinenses quam japonici, quum quidquid natura productum sit, officinale esse censeant, de omnibus rebus naturalibus in hoc libro mentio facta est.

221. **Sôkwa siki**, specimina herbarum florumque. Delineavit et descripsit *Fokiô Farugava* 1820, 3 voll. in 8°.

222. **Unkonsi**, de crystallis atque rebus in lapidem versis, quae in diversis collectionibus servantur. Scripsit *Kinoudsi Seôban* in vico *Jamadawura* prov. *Omi* 1772—1801, 15 voll. in 8°.

223. **Daisai honzô meisu**, synopsis florae origine Europaeae. Est autem synopsis plantarum japonicarum a celeberrimo *C. P. Thunberg* recognitarum. Ed. *Itô Keiske*, Botanicus *Owari*ensis 1828, 3 voll. in 8°.

B. *De historia naturali speciales.*

a. *Monographiae botanicae ac zoologicae.*

224. **Fjak kikno fu**, monographia Chrysanthemi indici generis cum adumbr. auct. *Zisôzen* 1735, 2 voll. in 8°.

225. **Kwadan jôkik siu**, de Chrysanthemi indici varietatibus, quae in floralibus cultivari solent; auct. *Simidsu Kanzi*, 2 voll. in 12°.

226. Kengo bin, monographia generis Ipomoeae trilobae, cum adumbr., auct. *Minokisi Rjôfo*. Ohosaka 1819, 2 voll.

227. Tsjôsei kwarin seô, nemus Azaliarum; est autem monographia Azaliarum generis, auct. *Somewi Itô Ifei*. Jedo 1733, 5 voll.

228. Asagavo no fu, monographia generis Ipomoeae trilobae. Scripsit *Akimidsu Tsjareo Sensei*, adumbr. *Tsjô Tansai*. Jedo 1818, 1 vol. in 12°.

229. Kwadan Asagavo no dsu, monographia generis Ipomoeae trilobae, quo floralia ornari solent. Scripsit *Kotendono sjunin*, adumbr. *Mori Sjunkei*. Jedo 1815, 2 voll. in 12°.

230. Bai bin, monographia generis Pruni, auct. *Matsuoka Gendats*. Mijako 1760, 2 voll. in 12°.

231. Ikansai ranbin, monographia Orchidearum atque Iridearum, quae specie sunt venustiori, auct. *Matsuoka Gendats (Dsiôan)*. Mijako 1772, 2 voll. in 8° majori.

232. Ikansai ôbin, monographia Cerassi varietatum, quarum flores specie sunt eximia, auct. *Matsuoka Gendats*. Mijako 1758, 1 vol. in 12°.

233. Sômok kibin kagami, herbarum arborumque specierum rararum speculum sive monographia plantarum foliis argenteo vel aurato variegatis, cum adumbr. Edidit *Kinda*. Jedo 1827, 2 voll. in 8°.

234. Tatsibana binrui kô, monographia generis Bladhiae, auct. *Kei an Kimura Sjuntok*. Mijako 1797, 2 voll. in 8°.

235. *Kitsbin*, monographia generis Bladhiae. Scripsit *Rôkwateino Sjuzin*, i. e. Horto botanico in Mijako praefectus; erat autem nomine *Wutagawa Joan*. Mijako 1797, 1 vol. in 12°.

236. Kwôjeki zôbô, Tsikin seô, de ornatu terrae, sive florula coronaria auct. *Itô Ifei*. Jedonico 1710, 1719, 20 voll. in 12°.

237. Kwadan daizen, de cultura florum (praecipue Poeoniarum, Cerassorum, Camelliarum) liber integer. Scripsit *Kwakiuken Sjuzin*. 1756, iterum 1798, 5 kiuén in 1 vol. in 12°. Adest aliud huius opusculi exemplum, cui titulus est *Kwadan sômok je bu*, i. e. descriptio arborum, quibus horti topiarii ornari solent, cum adumbr., 5 voll. in 12°.

238. Sasiki sasibana no atsumé, index florum, qui in conclavia ornatus causa transponi solent, juxta tempus florescentiae dispositus. Scripsit *Fôtei Jazin*, adumbr. *Ivasaki Tokiva*. Jedo 1824, 1 vol. in 12°.

239. Kokon takano koto, de Falconibus atque re accipitraria notitiae ex libris antiquis et novis collectae cum adumbr., 1 vol. in 8° literis *Firakana* scriptum.

240. Rikbuts sinsi, novi quiddam de rebus sex, quae sunt Monoceros, Crocus, Nux moschata, cadavera Aegyptiorum more condita, Boletus laricis, ex Batava in linguam jap. versum ab interprete *Ohodsuki Gendak*, revisum a *Sugida*, medico in provincia *Wakasa*. Ed. 1759, 1 vol. in 8°.

241. Ranjen tekifô, anthologia floralium sive plantarum rariorum descriptio. Continet liber excerpta ex batavis de naturae historia libris a *Ohodsuki Gendak* in linguam japonicam versa; tractat autem praecipue herbas, arbores, animalia terrarum peregrinarum atque medicamenta, quae in Japoniam induci solent. Jedo 1804, 3 voll. in 8°.

242. *Ĭkiŏ tsuàn k'aò*, eiusdem auctoris de Monocerote compendium, ex Batava in ling. sinicam versum. 1786, 1 voll. in 8°.

243. Keisi (*K'ingtschi*), monographia Balnearum, auct. *Nanki Njosui*. Ohosaka 1758, 1 vol. in 8°.

244. Ikansai kai bin, descriptio crustatorum, quae specie sunt venusta, cum adumbr. auct. *Matsuoka Dsiôan*. Mijako 1758, 1 vol. in 8°.

245. Musi no kagami, speculum vermium, sive observationes circa vermes intestinales atque insecta quaedam. Scripsit *Kô Genriu*, physicus in provincia *Kawatsi*, 1807, ed. altera 1809, 1 vol. in 8°.

246. Kasô tôtsiu no dsu, de herba quaedam aestiva, ex qua insectum nascitur hyeme, cum adumbr. 1801, 1 vol. in 8°. Est autem disquisitio circa Fungos clavatos, qui ex cadaveribus insectorum enascuntur.

247. Sendai Kinko no ki, de Holothuria ea, quae ad litus provinciae *Sendai* a piscatoribus capta, *Sendai-kinko* vocatur. Scripsit *Okodsuki Gendak*. Jedo, 1 vol. in 8°.

b. *Adumbrationes botanicae* MS^ptae.

248. Honzô sjasin, adumbrationes botanicae ad naturam del. *Midsutani Sukerok*. 2 voll.

249. Honzô sjasin, adumbr. botanicae ad naturam del. *Udagawa Jôan*. 1 vol.

250. Honzô sjasin, adumbrationes botanicae ad naturam del. *Kadsuragawa Hoken*. 1 vol. in folio.

251. Ninzin sjasin, panax quinque folium, ad nat. delineavit *Kadsuragawa Hoken*. 1 vol.

252. Nippon no kusaki, Flora japonica, ad naturam pinxit *Kadsuragawa Hoken*. 2 voll.

253. Mume sakura no rui kwa sjasin, flores variarum pruni et cerasi specierum ad naturam delineati. 1 vol. in fol.

254. Jezo honzô no dsu, Flora *Jezonensis*; ad nat. pinxit *Kadsuragawa Hoken*. 2 voll. in fol.

255. Liukiu honzô no dsu, Flora *Liukiu*ensis; ad nat. pinxit *Kadsuragawa Hoken*. 2 voll. in fol.

256. Liukiu sômok sjasin so kô, herbae atque arbores insularum *Liukiu* ad naturam paucis descriptae. 1 vol. in fol.

257. Nikwôsan sômok sjasin, Flora montis *Nikwôsan*; ad nat. del. *Itô Keiske*. 2 vol.

258. *Honzô sjasin*, adumbrationes botanicae, ad nat. del. *Midsutani Sukerok*. 1 vol.

259. Honzô batsusui (*Pèn ts'aò pă ts'uì*), selecta botanica, sive plantae rariores japonicae; adumbravit *Midsutani Sukerok*. 5 voll.

260. Honzô bătsusui, selecta botan., adumbravit *Ohokubo Dafeije*. 5 voll.

261. Honzô batssui, selecta botanica, adumbr. *Udagawa Jôan*. 1 vol.

262. Seisjok (*) zensjo, rerum vegetabilium descriptio. Est autem adumbratio plantarum rariorum auct. *Udagawa Jôan*. 1 vol. 8°.

(*) In titulorum enumeratione legendum est 生植.

263. Jamasakura no sets, dissertatio de Ceraso silvestri cum adumbr. 1 vol. in fol.

264. Sô kwa no dsu, adumbrationes plantarum diversarum, communicavit *Mogami Toknai* 1 voll.

265. Osiba suri, herbarum arborumque folia sicca; colore expressit *Kadsura Reian*. 2 voll.

c. *Adumbrationes zoologicae* MS^ptae.

266. Zju kin tsiu sjasin, quadrupedum, avium, insectorum imagines, ad nat. delineatae. 3 voll. in folio.

267. Kaika rui sjasin, diversae Crustaceorum species, ad nat. del. *Kadsuragawa Kurimoto Suiken*. 2 voll. in fol.

268. Tsui kai no dsu, *Tessan*, pictoris *Ohosaka*ni imagines insectorum atque cancrorum. 1 vol. fol.

269. Teô nizju sjasin, papiliones viginti ad nat. del. 1 vol. fol.

270. Tsiurui sjasju, insecta diversa ad nat. del. *Ohokôtsi Sonsin*. 1 vol. in 8°.

271. Tsiurui setsdsu, aranei japonici; descripsit et adumbr. *Ohokubo Sjôsanrô.* 1 vol. in 12°.

272. Gjorui sjasin, pisces diversi; ad naturam delineavit *Kadsuragawa Kurimoto Suiken.* 3 voll. in folio.

273. Kaigjo kô dsu-e, pisces marini accurate depicti a *Mutsi Konsai.* 2 voll., MSS.

274. Kaigjo sjasin, pisces marini; ad nat. delineavit *Udagawa Jôan.* 1 vol. in 8°, MS.

275. Sjasin suisju, rerum variarum adumbrationes ad nat. factae auct. *Udagawa Jôan.* 1 vol. MS.

276. Siugjo sjuksja, quadrupedum atque piscium imagines cursim factae. 1 vol., MS.

277. Kin siu gjo sjasin, aves, quadrupedes, pisces ad nat. delineati. 1 vol., MS.

278. Sjasin nagakuzirano dsu, balaenae ad nat. delineatae. 1 vol., MS.

279. Karafutono ivajuru Likinkamŭi, Tsŭnakai ni-siuno dsu, adumbratio quadrupedum amborum, quae ab incolis terrae Karafuto vocantur *Tsunakai* et *Likinkamŭi*; est autem Moschus moschiferus et Cervus tarandus.

280. Sjakotsno sjasin, i. e. serpens sceleta, anno 1814 eruta prope vicum *Tsuje* (circa 130° 45. long. or., 33° 12. lat.) provinciae *Bungo*, ad nat. del., MS.

281. *Tájuĕ keŭtschung tschŭ'i scheŭ kiŏ kŏ t'ŭ*, cornua et ossa quadrupedis miri (Cervi fossilis) eruta loco, quo fossa ducebatur, ad nat. del. 1 vol., MS.

282. Isininaru uwono dsu, piscis in lapidem conversi adumbratio.

283. Tenguno tsumeisi satsukô, disceptationes miscellae de lapidibus, qui »ungues canis coelestis" vocantur. Agitur de squali dentibus in lapidem versis, quos *Kiutsi Tsiukjô* japonicus naturae indagator hoc titulo descripsit atque adumbravit, MS.

d. *Dissertationes miscellaneae.*

284. Honzô itsika gen, i. e. verba physici cuiusdam, sive historia naturae, a *Matsuoka Dsjoan* explic. 4 voll. in 8°, MSS.

285. Honzô Wameô sju, rerum naturalium nomina japonica. 2 voll. in 8°, MSS.

286. Kin fu, *Sakawi Liusei*, commentatio de fungis, cum adumbr. 1814, 1 vol. in 8°, MS.

287. Siujôdô Honzôkwai mokrok, acta societatis naturae curiosorum, qui A°. 1827 in aula *Siujôdô* convenerant. Scripsit *Itô Keiske.* 1 vol., MS.

288. Seiseidô Honzô kwai mokrok, acta societatis naturae curiosorum, qui in aula *Seiseidô* convenerant. Scripsit *Ohokôtsi Sonsin.* 1 vol., MS.

289. Honzôkwai mokrok, acta societatis naturae curiosorum, quae in urbe *Owari* floret. 1 vol., MS.

290. Kaisiu (*Haì ts'ieŭ*), i. e. anguillae marinae. Agitur de balaenis, quarum notitias ex libris variis transcripsit auctor anonymus. 1 vol., MS.

291. Teobinrui seoki, avium ordines brevi descripti, MS.

292. Nippon sjokin sinsja, aves japonici ad naturam depicti; accedunt avium nomina japonica. 2 voll. in fol., MSS.

293. Sigi zjufatsibin sinsja, avium grallatarum, quibus nomen *Sigi*, species 18, ad nat. delineavit *Midsutani Sukerok.* 1828, 1 vol., MS.

18

SECTIO IV. LIBRI GRAMMATICI ET LEXICOGRAPHI.

A. *Dictionaria*.

a. *Sinico-Japonica*.

294. **Tsé lui** vel **Tsé wei**, i. e. collectio characterum, auct. *Mei ing tsù*. 1615, (Vide *Fourmont*, *Catal. librorum Bibl. regiae sinicorum*, I. porro *J. Klaproth*, *Verzeichniss der chinesischen und Mandshuischen Bücher und Handschriften der Königl. Bibl. zu Berlin*, pag. 122). Opus in Japonia denuo typis exscriptum est addita characterum pronuntiatione japonica. 9 voll. in 8° maj.

295. **K'áng hi tsé tièn**, doctrina literarum annis *K'áng hi* scripta. (Vid. *J. Klaproth*, *Verzeichniss*, p. 125). 30 voll. in 12°.

296. **Zô sjok dai kwôjeki Gjok ben** (*Tséng sù tá kuang ï Jŭ piên*), i. e. folia pretiosa, accedit continuum et admodum auctum supplementum. Dictionarium est characterum sinensium addita versione japonica. Ed. *Mori Teisai*, doctor privatus *Mijako*nensis. 1691, 12 voll. in 8°.

297. **Sinzô Zilin gjok ben**, (*Sin tséng Tsé lin jŭ p'iên*), novus et auctus literarum ideographicarum thesaurus, auct. *Kamada Teisan* 1797. Ed. nova 1820, 1 vol. in 8°.

298. **Si sei zilin sju in** (*Sse sching Tsé lin tsī jùn*), sylva characterum, quorum toni et vocum exitus indicati sunt. Auct. *Kwan sai Kamada*. 1803, iterum 1815, 1 vol. in 12°.

299. **San tei zô bô seo zii** (*Sân ting tséng pù siaò tsé wei*), parva characterum collectio, emendata et aucta. 1 vol. in 16°.

† 300. **Sinzi gjok ben dai sei** (*Tschin tsé jŭ p'iên tá tsch'ing*), pretiosa literarum verarum (scripturae *Lì*) folia in librum collecta; accedunt toni atque versio japonica. 1819, 1 vol. in 12°.

b. *Japonico-Sinica*.

301. **Wa Kan won seki sio gen zi kô**, thesaurus linguae japonicae, sive illustratio omnium, quae libris recepta, verborum ac dictionum loquelae tam japonicae, quam sinensis, addita synonymarum literarum ideographicarum copia. Auct. *Makino sima Teru take*, Jedo 1698. Recens. *Koma tani San zin*. 1802, 10 voll. in 8°.

302. **Kana fiki setsjô sju**, dictionarium japonico-sinicum secundum *Irofa* (hoc nomen literarum est ordini) diopositum. Scriptum est literis cursoriis, quibus nomen est *Ts'aò* atque *Firakana*, accedunt autem literae quoque rectae, quae *Hing schu* atque *Katakana* vocantur. Scripsit *Danaka Nobu*. 1803, 1 vol. in 8°.

303. **Dai sen fajabiki setsjô sju**, collectio verborum necessariorum magna, completa, expedita. 1817, 1 vol. in 8°.

† 304. **Fajabiki setsjô sju**, expedita verborum necessariorum collectio. Literis cursoriis, quibus liber scriptus est, adiunctae sunt literae rectae. Ed. *Jorigiri Sanzin*. 1823, 1 vol. in 8°.

c. *Synonymarum*.

305. **Zô bô Simon tsiu bô ki**, vocabularium dictionum poeticarum secundum *Irofa* dispositum. Auct. *Sin Kôsei*. 1733, 1 vol. in 12°.

† 306. **Jeki mon zen**, nassa characterum traductorum. Est collectio vocabulorum sinensium similem sensum habentium. Explicavit *Sorai Sensei*. Ed. 1715, 3 voll. in 8°.

d. Japonica antiqua.

307. **Furukotono basi**, scala ad linguam antiquam. Ed. *Fudsivarano Umaki*. 1765, 1 vol. in 8°.

308. **Gagen kazi kak**, exemplar elegantium linguae japonicae vocabulorum. Ed. *Itsi oka Takefiko*. 1814, 1 vol. in 12°. Mutato titulo est nova libri praecedentis editio, vocabulorum numero quidem aucta, explicatione vero mutilata.

C. Libri grammatici.

309. **Jamato kotoba**, i. e. lingua japonica (pura). 1759, 1 vol. in 12°. Est autem vocabulorum et dictionum, quae in epigrammatibus carminibusque antiquis praevalent, sermone vulgari explicatorum collectio, librique sequentis exemplum novum.

310. **Jamato kotoba**, lingua jap. sive voces poeticae sermone vulgari explicatae. 1727, 1 vol. in 12°.

311. **Sinsen Jamato kotoba**, vocabulorum jap. nova collectio. Est autem periculum grammaticae jap. auct. *Tôkwa Sekkei* atque *Watanave no Kuruvu*. Mijako 1711, iterum 1729, 2 voll. in 8°.

312. **Sôzi rui ben**, vocabula composita, secundum *Irofa* disposita. Ed. *Fan ai dô no Sju zin*. 1764. 2 voll. in 8°.

313. **Gakgoron** (*Hiôjù lun*), est collectio vocabulorum compositorum sinensium cum versione japonica. Ed. *Tsikuzjô*. 1772, 2 voll. in 12°.

314. **Irofa ten ri seo**, de natura alphabeti *Irofa*. Scripsit Samanaeus *Rjôban*. 1677, 2 voll. in 8°.

315. **Irofa zi kôrok**, disputationes de alphabeto *Irofa*. Scripsit *Zen tsjô*, religiosus Buddhaicus. 1736, 2 voll. in 8°.

316. **Irofa no gorui**, alphabetum *Irofa* quincuplex. 1 vol.

* 317. **Kôkai no Irofa**, specimen alphabeti *Irofa*, quod presbyter *Kôkai* vel *Kobô daisi* A°. 809 principi Sin mjô kô sin wô obtulisse dicitur.

318. **Mâ kuâng jún king**, vocum similiter cadentium speculum politum et splendens. 1744, 2 voll. in 8°. Est autem systema vocum linguae sinensis in usum Japonensium scriptum a *Bun iu Sokei*, monasterii *Ren sjo si* in urbe *Mijako* Samanaeo, qui, ut veram linguae sinensis elocutionem cognosceret, per decem annos in ipsa Sina peregrinatus est.

319. **Sen zi mon** (*Tsiän dsü wên*), libellus mille verborum, MS. Conf. Isagoge in Biblioth. Jap. pag. 6.

320. **Gunden senzimon**, libellus mille verborum. Versionis japonicae notas adiecit doct. *Mogami Sansi*. Jedo 1515, 1 vol. in 8°.

† 321. **Kwa in zju tai senzimon kômôk**, libellus mille verborum praemisso characterum indice. Accedunt 1. variae cuiusvis literae formae, 2. synopsis clavium scripturae sinensis, quae tam antiquis quam recentioribus signis expressae sunt, 3. synopsis praenominum (*nanori*) japonicorum. Conscripsit et illustravit *Nisi kame son*, qui versionem quoque japonicam addidit, quae, uti in vocabulariis usus est, verbum verbo reddit. Mijako 1756, 1 vol. in 8°.

322. *Wâng jeû tün tschì schú Tsiän dsü wên*, libellus mille verborum, quem clar. *Wâng jeû tün* scripsit. 1 vol. 8°. Literae colore albo tabulis nigris pictae sunt, opus autem calligraphiae sinensis specimen habetur.

323. *Mì Nân kûng tù liŭ mĕ t'iĕ*, specimen autographon philosophi *Mì Nan kung*, Confucio coaevi, literis albis in charta nigra expressum. 1 vol. in 4°.

[A.] e, f. *Dictionaria Japonico-Batava et Batavo-Japonica.*

324. *a.* Nieuw verzameld Japans en Hollandsch Woordenboek door den Vorst van het Landschap Nakats, *Minamoto Masataka*, gedrukt bij zijn dienaar *Kaija Filojosi*. 1810, 5 voll. in 4°. Est autem vocabularium ling. jap. cum versione batava, conscriptum ab interprete *B. Sadajosi*, editum jussu et sumptibus principis dicti.

324. *b.* Jakken (*ī ki'èn*), interpretis clavis. Dict. bat.-jap. ed. a *Fudsibajasi Daisuke*. Mijako, 2 voll. in 4°.

325. *a.* Jedo-Halma, dict. batavo-jap. MS., 14 voll. in 8° maj. Est autem manuscriptum operis sequentis exemplum.

325. *b.* Jedo-Halma, dict. Bat. auct. Halma in jap. versum. Jedo, 20 voll. in 4°. De huius dictionarii origine et ratione uberius disputatum est in libro illo, cui titulus *Isagoge in Biblioth. Jap.*, pag. 20, 21.

326. Wa Lan kotoba sjo, liber vocabulorum jap. et bat., de cuius origine et ratione disputatum est loco citato (*Isag. in Bibl. Jap.*), pag. 23.

327. Bango sen, i. e. index linguae peregrinae (batavae) literis *Katakana* scriptus. Ed. *Kadsuragawa Fosan*. 1798, 1 vol. in 12°.

B. *Vocabularia.*

a. *Linguae Aino.*

328. Jezo fôgen, vocabularium linguae *Aino*. Ed. *Siranizi sai*. 1804, 1 vol. in 12°. Libro titulus quoque inscriptus est *Mosivo kusa*, i. e. plantae salsae muscosae.

329. Jezogasima kotoba, vocab. linguae *Aino* MS. cum explic. jap. auct. *Mogami Toknai*. Accedit versio germana.

b. *Linguae Côraianae.*

330. Tsiändsüwèn, tápèn, scriptura mille verborum in folio. Opus sinicum origine cum interpretatione côraiana (imperfecta) in peninsula côraiana impressum. (Conf. *Isagoge in Bibl. Jap.*, p. 6).

331. Luihŏ, vocabularium sinense in côraianum versum. (Conf. *Isagoge in Bibl. Jap.*, p. 7).

332. Tsjozen zisjo, miscellanea nonnulla linguam spectantia côraianam. 1 vol. MS. in fol.

c. *Linguae Sanscritae.*

334. Sitvan mata tiwen, i. e. vocales et consonantes sanscritae, sive sacra Buddhaicorum scriptura, illustrata auctore *Genseô Rôzin*, Samanaeo indico. 1695. Ed. 1789, 1 vol.

335. Fangonatsume, vocabula sanscrita ex libris buddhaicis collecta, cum explic. sinica. Auct. *Mogami Toknai*. 1 vol. MS.

d. *Linguae Mandschu.*

335. *Sin k'ĕ Ts'ing schŭ ts'iuên tsĭ*, institutio scripturae mandshucae, denuo typis expressa, auct *Wâng Hŏ sün*. 1699, 3 voll. in 8° maj. Est autem operis origine sinici exemplum MS. In volumine 1° elementa literarum tradita sunt, volumen 2 et 3 vocabularium continet mandshuco sinicum.

336. *Ts'ing jutsĭ*, vocabulorum mandshucorum collectio, MS. 1 vol. 12°.

21

Sectio V. LIBRI THEOLOGICI ET MORALES.

A. *De cultu Buddhaico.*

337. Rjôbu Sindô kukets sjô (*Liàngpú schîntao K'eù kiuĕ tschaó*), dissertatio in bifarium spirituum cultum (origine indicum sive buddhaicum et japonicum) cum commentario, auct. *Kôgen Keian*. 1716. Ed. altera 1795, 6 voll. in 8°.

338. Jemŭma finagata, i. e. specimina equorum pictorum, sive tabularum votivarum, quibus templa Japonensium ornari solent. 1750, 1 vol. in 8°.

339. Benkak kivan, specimina tabularum votivarum, quae in templo *Giwon* suspensae sunt; collegerunt *Avigawa Minkwa* et *Kitagawa Sjunsei*. 1819, 1 vol. in 8°.

* 340. Tsûsin kwabu, imagines miraculosae; pinxit *Avigawa Minkwa*. 1819, 1 vol. in 8°.

341. Saiken Wotokojama Fôzjôje dsurok, animalium manumissionis solemnia, quae quotannis in templo *Javata mija* provinciae *Jamato* celebrantur, accuratissime adumbrata a pictore *Faja midsu Sjun geô sai*. 1 vol.

342. Nizjusĭbai sjunbaidsue, viginti quatuor loci, qui religionis causa frequentari solent; descripsit *Sjak Reôtei*, religiosus templi *Tengeôsi* provinciae *Kawatsi*, adumbravit *Takebara Sjun sensai*. 1803, 5 voll. in 4°.

343. Zôbô sjosiu, Butszô dsui, adumbrationes imaginum buddhaicarum, conditorumque sectarum theologicarum. Delineavit *Tosano seôsô Kino Fidenobu*. 1690, 5 voll. in 8°. Ed. altera 1696.

[335. *b.*] (*Tĭschĭ*) *Tá pan shŏ li ts'ŭ fén*, Hymni indici, cui titulus *Mahâ pradschnâ ritsch*, in sinicum versi pars decima, complectens tomum 578^{vum} libri inscripti *Tá pan shŏ po lo mi to king* (Mahâ pradschnâ pâramita sûtra? i. e. liber sacer de liberatione per magnam intelligentiam). In sinicum vertit *Hiuén tsàng fùng*, Sinensis, doctrinaeque universae (buddhaicae) praeceptor. 1 vol.

[336. *b.*] Sjuso teô fô ki, regulae artis magicae, auct. *Kik kiu Kwa san zin*. Mijako 1780, 1 vol. in 12°.

B. *Libri de cultu Sjutô (Shû tao) sive qui literariam Sinensium sectam spectant.*

[† 337. *b.*] Sisjo (*Sséschû*), Libri Quatuor. Textus sinicus cum versione japonica interlineari. Owari 1812, 3 voll. in 8°.

[338. *b.*] Kôkjô (*Hiao king*), Liber de pietate. Textus sinensis cum commentario. Jedo 1730; ed. altera 1789, 1 vol. 4°.

[339. *b.*] Rongo (*Lûnjù*), Dialogorum textus sinensis, cui notas jap. adscripsit *To sjun*; 1 vol. imperf.

[340. *b.*] Rongo ikun makino fazime (*Lûnjù ĭ hiŭn kiuén tschi scheù*), Dialogorum textus cum commentariis, 24 voll. in 8°. Edidit *Mogami Toknai*, Jedo 1822. Adest primum huius operis volumen, in quo de Editionibus libri laudati eiusque commentariis agitur.

C. *Praecepta moralia; historiae fictae et miscellanea.*

[341. *b.*] Sai kon dan (*Ts'aĭ kên t'ân*), i. e. disputationes, in quibus olera et radices (scil. animi ingeniique pabulum) sunt. Scripsit *Húng tsé tsch'ĭng*, Sinensis, qui sub imperio *Ming* vixit. Opus in Japonia denuo typis exscriptum est A°. 1825. 2 voll. 8°.

[† 342. *b.*] **Jehon Kôfuno ten**, narratiunculae foeminarum piarum. Liber imaginibus distinctus. Mijako 1806, 1 vol. in 8°.

[343. *b.*] **Reikjok Fjaknin itsusju adsumanisigi**, summa eorum, quibus educatio institutioque puellarum continetur. Liber nitidissimus, ornatus centum poetarum imaginibus, quibus singulis unus ex ipsorum carminibus versus adscriptus est. 1811, 1 vol. in 4°.

† 344. **Ruijevu Fjaknin itsusju keomonko**, i. e. thesaurus institutionis cum anthologia centum poetarum, in usum liberorum et nepotum. 1817, 1 vol.

345. **Dsjojô sibo Mijako meisjo tsukusi**, descriptio rerum urbis Mijako memorabilium. In usum puellarum edidit *Ikeda Tourisai*. Mijako 1824, 1 vol. in 16°.

346. **Teika sen kinjevu seô**, *Teika* poetae celeberrimi (*) carmina selecta, quae foliis variegatis inscripta sunt. Ohosaka 1814, 1 vol. in 4°.

(*) Obiit 1241.

† 347. **Zatwa, Keokun Kagami**, speculum disciplinae, sive narrationes variae, quae pro disciplina et praeceptis haberi possunt. 1776, 5 voll.

† 348. **Konze tei fu zen**, vitae foeminarum, quae proximo tempore virtutis gloria excelluerunt. 1800, 5 voll. Titulo mutato operis sub N°. 347 citati exemplum habes anno 1800 denuo impressum.

† 349. **Sedan zavusets**, dissertationes rerum (et mythologiam et historiam spectantium), quae ab omnibus percelebrari solent. 1754, 5 voll.

† 350. **Tsuredsure gusa**, narratiunculae horridae. 1737, 2 voll. cum adumbr.

† 351. **Jehon Kinkwa dan**, liber floris aurei imaginibus distinctus, sive vita principis *Iwagi Fiogono kami Fidekatsu*, qui eodem tempore vixit cum imperatore *Minamoto Joritomo*. 1806, 12 voll.

† 352. **Jehon Kagamijama retzjokô**, illustria virginis *Kagamijama*nae facinora, sive vita puellae *Wonoë Ofats*. Liber imaginibus illustratus. In usum juventutis edidit *Kavaseki Wizju*. 1803, 5 voll.

† 353. **Koseno Kanaoka Meiki tsutave**, *Koseno Kanaoka* pictoris opera maxime celebrata. 1808, 2 voll. in 8° cum adumbr.

† 354. **Isemonogatari**, historia *Isena*, denuo typis exscripta. 1804, 2 voll. in 8°.

† 355. **Honteôfiki monogatari**, selectae historiae japonicae. 1774, 1 vol. in 8°.

† 356. **Wotsino siranami**, longinqua unda alba, sive historia cuiusdam piratae, cui nomen *Itsufon Dajemon*. 3 voll. in 8°.

* 357. **Sitsi-fuk sitsi-nan dsu-e**, septem res secundae et septem res adversae adumbratae. Scripsit *Seisei Suima*, *Ohosaka*nus, adumbravit *Ohada Tôseki*, civis urbis *Akasi*. 1808, 5 voll. in 8°.

† 358. **Wakan kokon kakwi dan**, de rebus magnitudine eximiis, quae inde a temporibus antiquissimis ad hunc usque diem in terra sinica atque japonica observatae et descriptae sunt. Auct. *Kikuoka Kwasanziu*. 1748, 5 voll. in 8°.

† 359. **Jenkwak dsuran**, de lautitiae studio in foeminis aucto. Narratiunculis illustravit *Tôra Sanzin*. 1800, 5 voll. in 8°.

† 360. **Matsukage kwaidan** (*Sûngîn K'uai t'ân*), sub umbra abietis requiescentium confabulationes hilares. Sunt autem commentationes variae lingua sinensi scriptae a *Tojojama Nagano Sensei*. Mijako 1821, 2 voll. in 8°.

† 361. **Tôjûsi**, viri docti commentationes diversae. 1 vol., lacsum atque imperf.

† 362. *Hiên ts'ing ngeù ki*, sententiae otiosae casu obiectae. Edidit *Hû Schángli*. 2 voll. in 8°.

† 363. *Siáofu*, thesaurus ridiculus, sive rerum ridicularum narratiunculae; sinice edidit et lectionis japonicae notas adscripsit *Bok kan sai Sju zin*. 1 vol. in 12°.

364. U k i j o s i n k a t a r o k m a i b j ô f u, tabulatum, quod adversus auram permeantem poni solet, scutis sex compositum, quae novis figuris aetatem nunc florentem spectantibus ornatae sunt (*). Hoc titulo urbis Jedo incolis liber annualis offertur a *Riutei Tanefiko* compositus cum adumbrationibus manu pictoris *Tojokuni* factis. Adsunt 2 voll. anno 1820 edita.

(*) Simplicius Germanice vertas: »Sechsblätteriger Windschirm mit neuen Figuren aus der flotten Welt."

365. O t o b a T a n s i t s i. W o m i n a b e s i T a t o v e n o a v a s i m a, amores inter *Otoba* puellam et mercatorem *Tansitsi*. Liber annualis auct. *Riutei Tanefiko*. Jedo 1822, 2 voll.

366. S e ô h o n s i t a t e s i t s i b e n, archetyporum fasciculus septimus. Auct. *Riutei Tanefiko*. Jedo 1825, 2 voll.

367. S e ô h o n s i t a t e f a t s i b e n, operis praemissi fasc. octavus. Jedo 1826, 2 voll.

368. S a s a i r o n o t s j o k u k o j o m i d e, operis eiusdem fasciculus anno 1826 editus. 2 voll.

* 369. O s o m e F i s a m a t s u F a n a k u r a b e u k i n a n o j o m i u r i, amores quos *Osome Fisamatsu* sectatus est. Jedo 1822, 3 voll.

370. S e n g a i k j ô (*Schān hai king*), liber de montibus maribusque, geographia antiqua regionum exterarum auctore *Kuŏ p'ŏ* admodum fabulosa, in Japonia denuo typis exscripta. 18 tomi in 7 voll.

371. K i b u n e n o h o n d s i, *Kibune* antiquum, sive historia rerum in regione, cui nomen *Kibune*, gestarum. 3 voll. pretiosa, MSS., imaginibus ornata.

372. T s j ô k o n u t a (*Tsch'áng hén kó*), *Tsch'áng hén* (sive *Jang Kueifei*, filia nobilis, quam imperator sinensis *Hiuên tsûng* A°. 745 in matrimonium duxit). Carmen lyricum ling. jap. scriptum. 3 voll. pretiosa, MSS., cum imaginibus.

SECTIO VI. POETAE.

A. *Poesis dramatica.*

373. I m o s e j a m a, drama historicum nomine montis *Imose* appellatum. 5 voll. in 8°.

374. D a n n o u r a k a b u t o - k u n, exercitus galeatus in campo *Dannoura*no. Habemus unum huius dramatis historici actum, qui *Koto semeno tan* vocatur. Mikadonis *Antok* interitus, adverso prope *Dannoura*m proelio facto (A°. 1185), huius dramatis argumentum est.

† 375. I t s i n o t a n i f u t a b a k u n k i, clades in valle *Itsinotani* (Prov. *Setsu*) accepta A°. 1184. Scripsit *Tojotake Jetsizen Seorok*, atque edidit A°. 1751. Ed. altera 1764. 1 vol.

† 376. H o n m a t s i I t o j a m u s u m e, *Wakagusa* et *Fatsne*, filiae domus *Honmatsi Itoja*. Drama historicum auctoris eiusdem; ed. 1814. 1 vol.

† 377. O m i G e n s i s e n d s i n J a k á t a, i. e. praecursorum exercitus, qui causam secutus est familiae *Gen*, in provincia *Omi* hospitium. Ed. 1769, 2 voll.

† 378. K a n a t e h o n T s i u s i n g u r a, i. e. thesaurus praefectis fidelis. 1748, 1 vol.

† 379. F u t a t s t e ô t e ô k u r u w a k i, moenia papilionum coniunctarum. 1749, 1 vol.

† 380. S u g a v a r a t e n z j u t e n a r a v i k a g a m i, speculum institutionis a *Sugavara* communicatum. 1746, 1 vol.

† 381. **Kjôto kabuki sin kjôgen ge-tai nen kan**, index poematum dithyrambicorum (*Kjôgen*), ad quorum modos moveri solent saltatores urbis *Mijako*. Enumerantur poemata huius generis inde ab anno 1719 usque ad annum 1826 scripta. 1 folium.

382. **Kuniguni sibawi vanjei sumô**, theatrorum in Japonia enumeratio. 1 fol.

B. *Poesis lyrica, cui nomen* Uta.

383. **Kokin sju tovokagami**, speculum longinquum eius carminum collectionis, quae anno 905 primum edita, et inscripta est *Kokin sju* i. e. rerum antiquarum et novarum collectio; continet autem decem millia distichorum. Horum carminum speculi auctor, *Motowi Nori take*, eruditus artis poeticae iudex erat. 1816, 6 voll. in 8°.

384. **Fjaknin itsu sju mineno kakebasi**, scala ad fastigium carminum japonicorum. Est autem ad Parnassum japonicum gradus, sive introductio in artem poeticam, annexo commentario carminum a centum poetis scriptorum. Scripsit *Motowi Nori take*. Edidit *Koromogava Dai nin*. 1806, 2 voll. in 8°.

† 385. **Kadômei mok seô**, de arte poetica libri 3 auct. *Utsiufen Suke motsi*. 1713, 3 voll. in 8°.

† 386. **Sjôtets no monogatari**, poetae *Sjôtets* (*) vita et carmina. 1790, 2 voll. in 8°.
   (*) Obiit 1459.

387. **Manjo sju**, h. e. collectio decies mille foliorum, sive carminum antiquorum; inchoavit *Tatsibana Moroje* (qui obiit A°. 757), complevit *Udaiven Jakamotsi*. Ed. Mijako 1684—1686, 30 voll. in 8°.

388. **Jamato uta Rinja sju**, carmina japonica ruralia; redegit *Kijobarano Ogaze*. 1806, 12 voll. in 8°, quorum 6 inscripta sunt »quatuor anni tempestates," in ceteris autem sunt carmina erotica et miscellanea.

* 389. **Karin zatsmok seô**, variae carminum nemoris arbores, sive carminum collectio. Mijako 1696, 8 voll. in 8°. In vol. 1 et 2 sunt carmina ad Verem, in vol. 3 ad Aestatem, in vol. 4 et 5 ad Autumnum, in vol. 6 ad hyemem, in vol. 7 ad amorem et amicitiam, in vol. 8 miscellanea.

390. **Sjoksengin Waka sju rui tai**, carminum jap. collectio; digesta sunt secundum anni tempestates titulisque praedita. 1800, 1 vol. in 8°.

391. **Senkô bansi**, carmina japonica. Collegit *Sjoksan Sensei*. 1817, 1 vol. in 8° min.

392. **Fjaknin itsu sju kokura monko**, anthologia centum poetarum. Liber pusillus.

393. **Fjaknin itsu sju**, anthologia centum poetarum. 1 vol. in 16°.

394. **Fô gjok Fjaknin itsu sju**, i. e. pretiosa centum poetarum anthologia. 1 vol. in 12°.

395. **Jehon Fjaknin itsu sju**, anthologia centum poetarum, imaginibus distincta. 2 voll. in 8°.

396. **Jehon Waka awase**, collectio versuum japonicorum cum imaginibus. Edidit *Fudsi tani Mitsuje*. 1819, 1 vol. in 8°.

397. **Jehon Waka awase**, collectio versuum japonicorum cum imaginibus. 1 vol.

398. **Kaitsukusi urano nisigi**, praetextus litori ornatus, sive concharum margaritiferarum (versuum) collectio, auct. *Fan kwa an*, *Noto*nico. 1 vol. 8°.

399. **Sanzjurok utano atsume**, collectio 36 carminum japonicorum. Eadem sunt carmina, quae libello praecedenti continentur.

400. **Jamaka sju, rui tai**, carminum collectio *Jamaka*na (hoc nomen est urbis Provinciae *Tanba*). In classes redegit titulosque adiecit *Saigjô sjônin*, Religiosus. 1813, 1 vol. in 8° min.

C. *Poesis cui nomen Haï kaï* (p'aï hiaï).

401. Haikai sitsibu atsume, poemata epica in septem capita redacta. 1774, 2 voll. in 12°.
402. Javeno jamabiko, i. e. echo bis quadruplex. 1804, 2 voll. in 8°.
403. Kjô kate gotono bana, flosculi ex poetis epigrammaticis delibati. Ed. *Bunjano Sigetada.* 1810, 2 voll. in 8° min.
404. Kjôka je ziman, epigrammata imaginibus illustrata a *Hokkei Sensei.* 3 voll.
† 405. Kjôka Kwantô fjaktai sju, centum epigrammatum collectio *Jedo*nica dicta. Ed. *Tonton tei.* Jedo 1805, 2 voll. in 8°.
† 406. Kjôka Fusan sju, epigrammatum collectio dicta japonica. 2 voll. in 8°.

D. *Poesis Sinica.*

† 407. *Sŭng schĭ ts'ĭng tsiuĕ*, carmina lectissima sub imperio *Sŭng* facta. Accedunt extrema lectionis japonicae lineamenta. Ed. *Kaja aki Njo tei.* Jedo 1814, 1 vol.
† 408. Sô zino fasira (*Sŭng schĭ ts'ŭ*), fundamenta carminum sub imperio *Sŭng* conditorum. Ed. *Ohokubo gjô.* Jedo 1803, 2 voll. Verbis similiter cadentibus, uti *tŭng* (oriens), *fŭng* (ventus), in capita dispositis variae dicendi formulae adiectae sunt.
† 409. Ziso genkai (*Schĭ ts'ŭ jén kiaĭ*), dicendi formulae, in quibus versuum fundamenta sunt, cum explicatione japonica. Accedunt versus copulati (*liên kiŭ*). Ed. *Murase Kaibo.* 1 vol.
† 410. Siutsinrjak in daisei, (*Sieŭ tschîn liŏ jŭn tá tsch'ĭng*), lexicon verborum similiter cadentium. Accedunt phrases ternis verbis compositae cum interpretatione japonica. 4 voll.

SECTIO VII. **LIBRI DE POPULO AC CIVITATE.**

A. *De moribus et institutis.*

† 411. Sei do dsû (*Tschĭ tú t'ŭng*), regulae et institutiones sinicae atque japonicae; pertractavit *Itô Tsjô in.* 1724, 16 *kiuén* MS. in 6 voll. in 8°.
412. Kot tô sju (*Kŏ tòng tsĭ*), *Seisai*, de rebus notatu dignis, sive de priscorum Japonensium victu cultuque, cum adumbr. 1815, 5 voll. in 8°.
413. Jomeiri dankô basira (*K'iá schĭ t'án hŏ tschŭ*), i. e. columnae nuptiarum conciliatoris, sive quid in nuptiis conciliandis observandum sit; praecepit *Kwafô Sonzin, Mijak*onensis. Ohosaka, 2 voll. in 8° cum adumbr.
414. Sanrei kukets (*Sán lĭ k'eŭ kiuĕ*), *Kaibara Toksin*, dissertatio de tribus ritibus, sive quid observandum sit in epulis, theae compotatione atque scribendo. 1688, 2 voll. in 12°.
415. Tôfû Wakok fjaknjo (*Táng fŭng Hŏ kuĕ pĕ niŭ*), foeminae japonicae omnium ordinum novae consuetudinis cultu ornatae. Descripsit et adumbravit *Fizi gawa Moro nobu.* 1 vol. in 8° maj.
† 416. Wokasavara sjo rei daizen, *Fokjô Wŏ san*, de moribus et consuetudinibus jap. praecepit *Sada mune Kiutaka*, princeps ex domo *Wokasawara*, sanxit Mikado *Godaiko*. Ed. 1810, 3 voll. in 8° cum adumbr.

† 417. Mijako Ohosaka tsjaja sjobunteôfô ki, descriptio tabernarum urbium *Mijako* atque *Ohosaka*, in quibus theae potus venditur. 1 vol. in 16°.

418. Seôzok dsu siki (*Tschoáng schŏ t'û schŭ*), adumbratio vestium magnificarum quibus Mikado eiusque aulici indui solent. 1692, 2 voll. in 8°.

419. Kasaneno irome, conspectus colorum binorum, quos in vestibus conferre moris est. Ed. *Suwara ja movei*. Jedo 1826, 1 vol.

420. Gajû man rok (*Jà jeu moénlŭ*), supellectilis concinnae et elegantis conspectus cum adumbr. Auctor est *Ohojeda Riûfô*. Ohosaka 1755, 5 voll. in 8°.

421. Gunsjo ruiseô (*Kiun tschu lui ts'óng*), collectana ex variis libris in classes digesta a *Ken kjô Fomi itsi*. 1683. Exstat huius operis tomus 171us tribus constans voluminibus, in quibus agitur de apparatu conviviali, domo instruendo atque varia supellectile.

B. *De civitatis et imperii forma et administratione.*

422. Bunsei Bu kan, i. e. speculum rei militaris in annos *Bunsei* dictos (1818 et seqq.) 5 voll. in 12°. Hoc autem in libro accuratissime descripta sunt quaecunque spectant ad imperii formam et administrationem, familiae *Sjôgun*, principum, universique ordinis equestris genealogiam, disciplinam, officia.

423. On gen buk Gjo kiû ni mairu Gjo jôke gjo jak nin tsuku, descriptio comitatus aulici, qui filio imperatoris *Sjôgun* natu majori post assumtam togam virilem adiunctus est A°. 1826. 1 vol. in 16°.

424. Mantai fôkan (*Wán tai paò kién*), i. e. speculum pretiosum in decies mille successiones. Est autem succincta totius reipublicae japonicae corporis descriptio. Jedo 1826, 1 vol.

425. Gwatsrei fak buts zen (*Juĕ ling pŏ wŭ ts'iuên*), h. e. ampla rerum singulis mensibus convenientium nassa, sive fastorum japonensium libri 14 in 12°. Auct. *Kaibara Toksin*, Ohosaka 1804. Quidquid ad Japonensium cultum victumque pertinet in his libris indicatum est.

426. Bunsei zjuitsi nen rjakrekiko, calendarium in annum undecimum aerae *Bunsei* (1828).

427. Bunsei zjuitsi (tsutsi nojeneno) tosi rjakreki zjusitsini kô, calendarium in annum supradictum.

C. *De politia.*

† 428. Jorodsujo Jedomatsino kagami, h. e. speculum vicorum (*matsi*) urbis *Jedo* in decies mille successiones. Agitur de provinciarum excubitoriis (*Sjo kok Go seki sjo*), quae imperator militibus suis tuenda tradidit, de vicorum magistris (*Matsi Gobugjô*), de universa publicae disciplinae ac securitatis in urbe *Jedo* cura.

429. Matsi fikesi bangumi, conspectus excubiarum adversus incendia per urbem Jedo institutarum.

430. Kuwazi on sjutsjak, conspectus excubitorum adversus incendium arcis imperialis in urbe *Jedo*.

431. Irofa kumi matove tsukusi, conspectus signorum, quibus excubiae adversus incendium in urbe Jedo notatae sunt.

E. *De architectura.*

431. Daiku finagata, exempla architectonica sive de architectura libri quinque. Jedo 1717.
    Tom. I. Mija finagata, sive palatiorum aediumque sacrarum lineamenta.
    Tom. II. Buke finagata, lineamenta aedium, quae ad usum belli pertinent.

Tom. III. Tana finagata, exempla tabulamentorum.
Tom. IV. Sukija finagata, norma architecturae civilis.
Tom. V. Seôfei nori, regulae supellectilis.

433. Do reô kô sets tô (*Tŏ liáng héng schuĕ t'òng*), *Mogami Toknai*, dissertatio brevis de mensuris et ponderibus. Jedo 1824, 3 voll. in 8°.

D. *De re militari.*

434. Dsu kai, Bu jô ben rjak (*Tú kiai, Wù jùng pién liŏ*), disputatio de re militari, adumbrationibus illustrata. Auct. *Konosita Jositomo*. Jedo 1747, 8 voll. in 8°.

435. Kattsiu tsjakjô ben (*Kiă tscheù tschŏ júng pién*), quomodo thoracem et galeam induere oporteat. Scripsit *Winouve Okina*. 1803, 3 voll.

436. Ko Gun ki no dsu kai (*Kù kiûn k'ï tschi t'ú kiai*), antiqua supellex militaris adumbrata. Tab. manupicta.

437. Sumô seô sets, Kwats kongô den, de arte luctandi, sive virorum, qui corporis duritia sunt adamantina, laudes. Scripsit *Seô zju rô Sjuzin*. Jedo 1822, 2 voll. in 8° cum adumbr.

Sectio VIII. LIBRI OECONOMICI.

A. *De agricultura.*

438. Fai bun kô sjokno dsu (*Pei wén Kéng tschĭ t'û*), culturae agrorum e bombycum adumbratio cum literis ipsius imperatoris manu scriptis. Opus est jussu imperatoris *K'ang hi* A°. 1696 scriptum et a successore eius *Schi tsung* epigrammatis ornatum, quibus munera figuris expressa illustrantur. Est autem exemplum A°. 1807 in urbe *Jedo* typis denuo redditum. 2 voll. in folio.

439. Nari katatsi no dsu sets (*Tsch'ing hing t'û schuĕ*), i. e. res, quae natura gignuntur vel arte formantur, adumbratae et descriptae. Liber universam agriculturam japonicam complectens, imperatoris jussu confectus et editus. Praefatio a Cl. *Fudsivara Kunifasira* scripta est A°. 1804. 30 voll.

440. Nô geo zensjo (*Núng niĕ ts'iuén schü*), rei agrariae tractatio auct. *Mijasaki Antei*. Mijako 1696, 8 voll. in 8°.

441. Nô ka jeki (*Núng kiá ĭ*), h. e. in usum agricolarum. Huius operis 22 voluminibus constantis tria volumina adsunt, in quibus agitur de cultura Rhus succedaneae et praeparanda cera vegetabili. Auctor est *Ohokura Nagatsune*. Ohosaka 1820.

442. Nô ka geo zi (*Núng kiá niĕ ssé*), agricolarum occupationes; descripsit *Kosima Zjo sui*. Ohosaka 1793, 5 voll. in 8°.

443. Sankai mei san dsu e (*Schân hai míng ts'án t'û hoeï*), rerum praecipuarum, quae terra marique gignuntur, descriptio cum adumbr. Scripsit *Kimura Kô kjô*. Ohosaka 1799, 5 voll. in 8°.

444. Nippon sankai mei buts dsu e, rerum praecipuarum japonicarum, quae terra marique efferuntur, descriptio cum adumbr. Scripsit *Firase Tetsusai*. Ohosaka 1753, 5 voll. in 8°.

445. Bukô sanbuts si (*Wù kiâng ts'àn wŭ tschi*), *Ivasaki Tokiva*, historia rerum, quas provincia *Musasi* producit. 1824, 1 vol. in 12°.

446. Inzen takujô (*Inschén ts'ĕjao*), alimenta japonica. Enumeravit et descripsit *Wono Lansan*. Ed. 1814, 1 vol. in 16°.

447. Jchon beiwon rok (*Hoei pèn mìngēn lŭ*), de oryzae beneficio liber imaginibus distinctus. In usum tironum scripsit *Nakagawa Aritsune*. Mijako 1802, 5 voll.

448. Nitsu siu jôfôno dsu, adumbratio rei apiariae *Fiuga*nae aeri incisa. Explicavit *Mogami Toknai*.

B. *De artibus et mercatura*.

449. Sjoknin tsukusi, fotsuku avase, conspectus sive adumbratio opificum; accedunt initiales epigrammatum, quae eo pertinent, versus. Ed. *Kanten Si kô kei*. Jedo 1797, 2 voll. in 8°.

450. Jedo sjoknin, uta avase, opifices *Jed*onici carminibus celebrati. Owari 1808, 2 voll. in 8°.

† 451. Meôzjuts fakbuts zen, ampla artium reconditarum nassa. Sunt libri technologici 7 a *Kaibara Toksin* editi.

452. Sôken kisjô (*Tschoâng kién kî schàng*) h. e. fabrorum gladiariorum laus. Scripsit *Inaba Mitsidatsu Sinjemon*, *Ohosaka*nus 1781, 7 voll. in 8°. Fabrorum gladiariorum nomine jam etiam continentur caelatores aeris et ligni.

453. Kotô dsurok, ars metallorum efodiendorum et purgandorum. Scripsit Masida kô. 1 vol. in 8°.

454. Samekava seikan rok, ars perficiendi raiae corii, quo capuli gladiorum ornantur. Ohosaka 1759, 1 vol. in 8°.

455. Kotsukei mankwa, h. e. effusio imaginum ironicarum, quae nondum digestae omnes turbatae et confusae iacent. Exempla sunt ad artem acu pingendi exercendam. Ed. *Kjô Seô sei*. Jedo 1823, 1 vol.

456. Osije fajageiko, i. e. exprimendarum imaginum doctrina matutina in usum puellarum. Ed. *Fori Seiken*. Mijako 1825, 1 vol. in 8°.

457. Kagjok Fana musubi, Tamano asobi, ludus pretiosus, sive ars nodorum artificiose nectendorum. Ed. *Okava Kiufo*. Ohosaka 1817, 1 vol. in 8°.

458. Ikebana fidenno jamano nisigi, i. e. montium camporumque tela floribus aureis contexta. Agitur de serviarum in vasis conservatione. Ed. *Kimura Siu tok*. Ohosaka 1730, 2 voll. in folio.

459. Ikebana dsui, florum in situlis positorum adumbrationes. Ed. *Jamanaka Tsiu Sajemon*. 1698, 2 voll. in folio.

460. Ikebana dsuzen, florum situlis insertorum adumbrationes. 1 vol. in 8°.

461. Ikebana tsisuzino fumoto, i. e. radices montium mille floribus vivis consitae. Est ars florum situlis inserendorum, auct. *Irije Kjoksen*. Jedo 1768, 3 voll. in 8°.

462. Ikebana koromonoka, floribus ornatarum vestium fragantia. Est ars florum situlis inserendorum auctore *Satomatsu sai Itsiba*. Jedo 1801, 8 voll. in 8°.

† 463. Ritsukwa seidô sju, regulae rectae sertorum e floribus faciendorum. 1684, 4 voll.

464. Nippon someirono fô, quomodo telae coloribus inficiantur in Japonia. 1 vol. MS.

465. *a.* Somemono no fô, de arte tinctoria.
    b. Wase tsukuri nori, de oryza praecoce curanda.
    c. Tsja tsukûri nori, de thea aptanda. 1 vol. MS. in 12°.
466. Sake tsukûru koto, de cerevisia, cui nomen *sake*, temperanda. 1 vol. MS., in 8°.
467. Kami tsukûru fô, ars opificis chartarii. 1 vol. MS., in 8°.
468. Nuru fô, vasorum vernice obducendorum ratio. 1 vol. MS.
469. Sju gjok tsije kai, (*Schĭjŭ tschî hoeĭ haĭ*), i. e. pretiosum sapientiae et beneficii mare, ampliatum. Libri cuiusdam technologici, cui titulus hic inscriptus est, volumen alterum, in quo multa de arte magica et incantamentis disseruntur.
470. Nippon motsimaru teôzja sju, mercatorum Japoniae praecipuorum index.
471. Tsjôko sunadori, balaenarum capturae adumbratio. 1 vol. in fol. MS.
472. Sifo tsukûru fô dsu, artis salinariae adumbratio. 1 vol. MS.

Sectio IX. LIBRI NUMISMATICI.

473. Tsinkwa kôfô kan, liber monetalis, seu speculum numorum aeneorum, qui foramine quadrangulo percussi sunt. Auct. *Nakatani Kôsan.* Ohosaka 1730, 1 vol. in 8°.

† 474. Kwan sei kôfô kan, speculum numorum aeneorum, quos *Riuseki Anu* annis *Kwan sei* dictis (1789—1800) collegit. 1 vol. in 8°.

475. Kai sei kôfô dsu kan, speculum, quo imagines numorum aeneorum correctae exhibentur. Edidit *Wozawa Tô itsi* 1785, 1 vol. in 8°. Est autem alterum libri, cui numerum 477 inscripsimus, exemplum.

† 476. Tsinsen kibin dsurok (*Tschîn ts'iên kí p'in t'ú lŭ*), adumbrationes omnium rariorum numorum tam japonicorum quam sinensium (inde a numo *Puan liang* dicto usque ad monetam *Wadôkai tsin*). Ed. *Ohomura Naritomi.* 1 vol. in 8°.

477. Kôfô dsu kan (*K'ùng fàng t'ú kién*), conspectus adumbrationum numorum aeneorum. Edidit *Wozawa Tô itsi.* 1789, 1 vol. in 8°.

478. Kokon senkwa kan (*Kù kin t'siuên hò kién*), conspectus numorum antiquorum atque recentiorum. Auct. *Wozawa Tô itsi.* 1804, 12 voll. in 8°.

479. Wa Kan sen wi, collectio numorum japonicorum atque sinensium. Ed. *Fô gawa Zin ujemon.* 1793, 1 vol. in 8°.

480. Kingin dsurok, adumbratio et descriptio numorum aureorum atque argenteorum. Ed. *Kon tô Ziudsiû.* Jedo 1810, 7 voll. in 8°.

481. Tai sen fu (*Tuì tsiuên p'ù*), series numorum, quorum utraque pars literis est inscripta. Scrips. *Burôden Motonari.* Jedo 1814, 1 vol. in 8°.

* † 482. Ko sen, atavi tsuku, numi antiqui, accedit valoris indicatio.

* 483. Sen van (*Ts'iên fàn*), lex monetalis, sive conspectus numorum in Japonia usitatorum. 1794, 1 vol. in 8°.

484. Kwaibo tsinsen kagami, numorum, qui habentur amuleta, conspectus.

485. Seijô sen bu, (*Si jang ts'ien p'ù*), de numis exteris (europaeis) dissertatio. Scripsit *Wozawa Tô itsi.* 1 vol. in 8°.

Sectio X. LIBRI MEDICI ET PHARMACEUTICI.

486. **Sin kiu fatsu sui dai sei** (*Tschîn kieù păts'uĭ tă tsching*), de praestantia acupuncturae et moxae. Scripsit *Okamoto Itsufôsi*. Mijako 1699, 7 voll. in 8°.

487. **Sin kiu kwô keô sin gu sju** (*Tschîn kieù Kuang hiŭ schîn kiŭ tsĭ*), de apparatu divino acupuncturae et moxae. Ed. *Unrô si*. Jedo 1819, 1 vol. in 8°.

488. **Sin kiu setsjak** (*Tschîn kieù schuĕjŏ*), acupuncturae et moxae explicatio in compendium redacta. Ed. *Isisaka Sôtets*, princeps imperatoris medicus. Jedo 1812, 1 vol. in 12°.

489. **Kwô sin sets**, de Panacis quinquefolii radice dissertatio auct. *Sjokkô*. 1 vol. in 8°.

490. **Jak mei sjô ko** (*Jŏ ming tsch'ing hu*), mille medicamentorum nomina sinica atque japonica. Ed. *Kivara Sôtei*. Mijako 1823, 1 vol. in 12°.

491. **Nin men zô dsu sets**, de tumore crurum, cui nomen *Ninmen* h. e. facies humana, dissertatio cum adumbr. Scripsit *Kadsura gawa Hoken*.

492. **Kai zô dsu fu** (*Kiaì tsáng t'û fù*), adumbrationes anatomicae origine europaea. Ed. *Ikeda Josijuki Tózó*. Mijako 1821, 1 vol. in 8°.

493. **Wa lan zen ku nai gwai bun no dsu**, adumbrationes anatomicae omnium corporis humani partium. Opus origine Batavum, japonice vertit *Motoki sii*, interpres *Nagasaki*nensis, edidit *Suzuki Sôun*, medicus provinciae *Suwô*. 1774, 2 voll. in 8°.

494. **Jei jei tsiu kei no dsu** (*Ing wei tschúng king t'û*), tabulae ad angeologiam spectantes duae. Ed. *Kan sei Sen sei*. 1825.

495. **Ja bin wô siu rok**, h. e. medicamentorum index promtus. Continet autem nomina herbarum rerumque naturalium, quae penes nos in usu officinali sunt. Scripsit *Kô Rjô sai*, med. stud. ex provincia *Awa*, praeceptore de Siebold, cuius sumptibus hicce libellus typis expressus est. Ohosaka 1826, 1 vol. in 16°.

496. **Sin kiu dsu kai** (*Tschîn kieù t'û kiaì*), tabulae duae spectantes artem acu pungendi et inurendi. Accedunt tabulae anatomicae 4 aeri incisae.

497. **Tsi jô itsi gen**, *Isisaka Sôtets*, medici *Jedo*nici dissertatio medica, MS. 1 vol.

498. **Kutsin no sets** (*Kieù tschîn tschi schuĕ*), *Isisaka Sôtets*, dissertatio de acupunctura. 1 vol. MS.

499. **Fu nin kwan bjô sio** (*Fù schîn huán p'ing schu*), historia morbi cuiusdam foeminae. 1 vol. MS.

Sectio XI. TABULAE XYLOGRAPHICAE.

A. *Libri de arte pingendi.*

500. **Kan gwa si nan** (*Hán hoà tschì nan*), ars picturae linearis more sinico. Ed. *Kenrjô tai*, cui titulus *Môkô Kanjô sai*, Japonensis. 1776, iterum 1802, 2 voll. in 8°.

* 501. **Kan gwa si nan ni ben**, operis eiusdem series altera. 3 voll. in 8°.

502. **Kan gwa fitori keiko**, ars picturae sinensis in usum tironis, qui sua ipsius opera illam addiscere vult. Ed. *Kunzan Kiu kei*. 1807, 2 voll. in 8°.

503. **Kwa zen**, pictoris nassa, seu praecipuae cuiusvis generis picturae in librum collectae. Ed *Fajasi Moriatsu*, pictor jap. 1721, 6 voll. in 8°.

504. **Kwa teo gwa siki**, specimina florum aviumque. Ed. *Asaina Júkavo*. 1813, 1 vol. in 8°.
505. **Jehon dsiksi bô**, *Tatsibana Morikuni*, pictoris celeberrimi, ars picturae rationi consentanea. 1744, 9 voll. in 8°.

B. *Imitationes xylographicae celebrium tabularum pictarum.*

a. *Picturarum sinensium.*

506. **Sô Siseki kwabu**, series picturarum Cl. *Sô Siseki*, pictoris *Jedonici*, cui *Setskei* nomen quoque fuit. Sunt autem et adumbrationes rerum sinensium et imitamina picturarum sinensium, quas auctor adeptus est in urbe *Nagasaki*, quum multum esset cum *Tschîn Nânpin*, pictore quodam sinensi. 1762, 13 voll. in 8°.
507. **Sô Siseki kwabu**, libri eiusdem suppl. 3 voll. in 8°.
508. **Gwa si kwai jô**, pinacothekae compendium. Edidit *Farubok Itsuwo*. 1751, 6 voll. in 8°.
509. **Siu tsin gwa teo**, picturarum eximiarum libri tres in 4°. Ed. *Kunseô sai*. 1802. Tabularum pictarum, quarum imitationes xylographicae hic congestae sunt, auctor est *Taniu*, inter pictores jap. celeberrimus.
510. **Osijeno tekagami**, speculum picturarum impressarum, sive collectio imaginum ligno incisarum. Ed. *Ohooka Mitsinobu*. 1736, 3 voll. in 8°.
511. **Sinkok Kinsi kwabu**, ars picturae more pictoris *Kinsi*. Ed. *Kiufou Keiden*. 1813, 1 vol. 8° maj.
* 512. **Gen Mei kwateo** (*Juên Ming hoá tiaò*), imagines florum aviumque a pictoribus, qui sub Dynastiis *Juên* atque *Ming* floruerunt, factae. Ed. jap. 1764, 2 voll. in 8°.

b. *Picturarum japonicarum.*

513. **Meika kwabu**, series picturarum artificum celebrium. Ed. *Tokei Sensei*. 1812. 2 voll. in 8°.
514. **Jehon fitsjô**, imagines sane utiles ex picturarum libris collatae a *Nakadsi Undsiku*. Mijako 1751, 2 voll. in 8°.
515. **Takeda Keibo kwabu**, series picturarum celeberrimi *Takeda Keibo*, qui floruit circa aeram *Kwanjen* (1750). Ed. 1800, 4 voll. in 8°.
516. **Sjo sjok kwakan**, speculum, quo imagines opificum exhibentur. Ed. *Keisai Kitawo Masajosi*. Jedo 1796, 1 vol. in 8°.
517. **Keisai sokwa**, imagines rudes pictoris *Keisai*. 1 vol. in 8°.
518. **Sô kwa rjak gwa siki**, specimina herbarum florumque paucis descripta. Auct. *Keisai*. 1818, 1 vol. in 8°.
519. **Fito mono rjak gwa siki**, specimina figurae humanae paucis descripta. Auct. *Keisai*. 1799, 1 vol. in 8°.
520. **Tsikubu sjôrok**, arundinum index distinctus, auct. *Soksai Tôzin*. Mijako 1757, 2 voll. in 8°. Est autem ars arundinum delineandarum.
521. **Kensi kwajen**, pictoris *Kensi* hortus tabularum, sive collectio tabularum, quas celeberrimus *Kenrjô tai*, cui titulus *Kanjo sai* (conf. n°. 500), pinxit. 1765, 3 voll. in 8°.
522. **Kensi kwajen kai sak dsu**, pictoris eiusdem hortus tabularum continens adumbrationes piscium marinorum. 1 vol. in 8°.

523. Jehon jei buts sen, rerum carminibus celebratarum adumbrationes. Delineavit *Foken Tatsibana Jasukuni*. 1779, 5 voll. in 8°.

524. Jehon no jamagusa, pictoris eiusdem adumbratio plantarum silvestrium. 1755, 5 voll. in 8°.

525. Tei to gakei itsiran, pulcherrimi urbis Mijako prospectus, del. *Kavamura Bunbô*. 1807—1814, 4 voll. in 8°.

526. Bunbô sansui kwabu, pictoris *Bunbô* prospectus regionum. Mijako 1824, 1 vol. in 8°.

527. Sotsjun kwabu, pictoris *Jamagutsi Sotsiun* tabulae, quae plantas floresque exhibent. 1806, 3 voll. in 8°.

528. Jehon keiko tsjô, cortinae sive tabulae ad discendam artem delineandi; exhibent autem specimina telis imprimenda. Ed. *Wimura Katsukits*. 1718, 3 voll. in 8°.

529. Sjasei kedamonono dsue, (*Sièseng scheu t'û hoá*), quadrupedum imagines ad naturam delineatae. Mijako 1718, 2 voll. in 8°.

530. Kwado fjak kwateô, flores avesque delineatae a *Jama sita Sekitsiu*. 1728, 4 voll. in 8°.

531. Jehon musino crabi (*Hoápèn tsch'ùng tschuén*), insectorum collectio; est autem liber insectorum imaginibus distinctus epigrammatisque ornatus. Ed. *Kitagawa Utamaro*. Jedo 1799, 2 voll. in 8°.

532. Jehon tebiki nogusa, praecepta artis rerum penicillo adumbrandarum. Mijako 1735, 1 vol. in 8°.

533. Jehon fudeno nisiki, pictoris *Kitawo Sigemasa* bicolores avium et quadrupedum imagines. 2 voll. in 8°.

534. Sjasei kwateô Sjosin fasira date, imagines ad naturam delineatae in librum collectae, sive initia artis pingendi. Mijako 1818, 1 vol. in 8°.

535. Sakurabana kwateô, cerassi florum adumbrationes. 1 vol. in 8°.

536. Jehon mumei, collectio picturarum, quarum auctores ignoti sunt. 1 vol. in 8°.

537. Keisjô kwajen, hortus picturarum Mijakonensium, sive pictorum Mijakonensium celebriorum tabulae in librum collectae. Mijako 1814, 1 vol. in 8°.

* 538. Wôton kwabu, tabularum a celeberrimo *Wôton* pictarum series. Ed. 1817, 1 vol. in 8°.

* 539. Kwôrin fjak dsu, celeberrimi pictoris *Kwôrin* tabulae centum. 2 vol. in 8°.

* 540. Nanfei, Bunbô kaido sôkwa, i. e. pictorum *Nanfei* et *Bunbô* tabulae binae procedentes. 1811, 1 vol. in 8°.

541. Jehon te kagami, manuale imaginum speculum. Ed. *Fokio Sjunbok*. 1728, 1 vol. in 8° maj.

542. Jehon sinnôno tane, i. e. semina in animo colenda, libri 2 varias continentes adumbrationes.

543. Kwateô sjasin dsue, flores avesque ad naturam delineatae. 2 voll. in 8°.

* 544. Kwateô kwabu, florum aviumque adumbrationes. 1 vol. in 8°.

* 545. Kwateô kwateô, adumbrationes florum aviumque. 1819, 1 vol. in 8°.

* 546. Teôsiu rjak gwasiki, avium atque quadrupedum paucis describendorum specimina. Ed. *Keisai*. 1797, 1 vol. in 8°.

547. *Hoksai mangwa*, *Hoksai* pictoris celeberrimi imagines rerum mire turbatae. Jedo 1812, 10 voll. in 8°.

548. Boksen sôgwa, pictoris *Boksen (Hoksai)* adumbrationes rerum promiscuae. Jedo 1815, 1 vol. in 8°.

549. Santai kwabu, pictoris *Hoksai* adumbrationes rerum triplici modo factae. Jedo 1815, 1 vol. in 8°.

550. Hoksai sjasin gwabu, *Hoksai* pictoris adumbrationes rerum ad naturam delineatae. Jedo 1813, 1 vol. in 8°.

551. Itsubits gwabu, adumbrationes uno penicilli ductu factae. Ed. *Hoksai*. Jedo 1823, 1 vol. in 8°.

552. Jehon rjô bits, penicilli bini, sive liber imaginum a pictoribus *Hoksai* atque *Riu Kosai* adumbratarum. 1 vol. in 8°.

553. Jeijû dsue, priscorum Japoniae heroum imagines. Ed. *Genrjusai Taito*. 1 vol. in 8°.

† 554. Hoksai gwasiki, *Hoksai* pictoris regulae pingendi. 1820, 1 vol. in 8°.

* 555. Siugwa itsiran, conspectus picturarum elegantium. Ed. *Hoksai*. 1 vol. in 8°.

* 556. Jehon Zjôruri zetsuku, carmen eroticum, cui nomen *Zjôruri*, imaginibus illustratum. Accedit strophae cuiusque, quam adumbratio quaeque spectat, versus primus et ultimus. Ed. *Hoksai*. 1 vol. in 8°. *Zjôruri fime* nomen est puellae, quam princeps *Minamato Jositsune* (1184), mirifice dilexit caramque habuit.

557. Hokun mangwa, *Hokun* pictoris imagines rerum mire turbatae. 1 vol. in 8°.

* 558. Torijama Sekijengwa, pictoris *Torijama Sekijen* tabulae, quae spectant res historicas. 1772, 1 vol. in 8°.

† 559. Jehon sjabô fukuro, saccus rerum pretiosarum ad naturam delineatarum, auct. *Tatsibana Jusei*. 1805, 10 voll. in 8°.

560. Jedsu fjakki Tsuredsure fukuro, saccus fabulis horrificis spectrisque adumbratis repletus. Ed. *Torijama Sekijen Tojofusa*. Jedo 1805, 3 voll. in 8°.

561. Kokon jedsu, Tsukudsugu fjaktsuki, narratiunculae de spectris cum adumbr. antiq. et nov. Ed. *Torijama Tojofusa*. 3 voll. in 8°.

562. Fûriu jeavase, Tebikinosono, hortus institutionis, sive imagines cultum victumque spectantes. Ed. *Kinuja Uvei*, Ohosaka 1824, 3 voll. in 8°.

C. *Libri picturarum*.

a. *Historicarum*.

563. Jehon, Gen Fei musja sorove, pugnatores, qui causam familiae *Gen* secuti sunt, comparati cum illis qui *Fei*anae partis fuerunt. Liber imaginibus distinctus. Ed. *Fotsutari Seki*. Mijako 1816, 2 voll. in 8°.

564. Jehon, Joritomo itsu seô ki, vita imperatoris *Joritomo* figuris illustrata. Ed. *Kino Josinobu*. 1799, 2 voll.

565. Jehon siu tsiu, Fina Gensirok zju dsjô, liber pusillus imaginibus sexaginta distinctus, quae historiam familiae *Gen* (*Minamoto*) spectant. 1 vol. in 16°.

* 566. Jehon, Gensjô meijo zô, gloria imperatorum ex familia *Gen* (*Minamoto*) paucis descripta cum adumbr. Ed. *Kjoktei Makin*. 1804, 2 voll. in 8°.

* 567. Jehon, Mukô sakura, decus virorum rerum gestarum gloria praestantium; liber imaginibus distinctus. Ed. *Fasegawa Mitsinobu*. 1756, 2 voll. in 8°.

† 568. Jehon, Tabuno mine, de rebus in monte *Tabuno mine* (provinciae *Jamato*) gestis, cum adumbr. Ed. *Kôsuigen Sigemasa*. 1793, 3 voll. in 8°.

* 569. Jehon, **Musja waratsi**, militum calcei straminei. Liber imaginibus distinctus res bello gestas spectantibus. 2 voll. in 8°.

† 570. Jehon, **Usuguijadorumume**, prunus, in qua luscinia nidulatur. Liber imaginibus distinctus. Ed. *Tatsibana Morikuni*. 1740, 7 voll. in 8°.

† 571. Jehon, **Futsibakama**, eupatorium chinense. Narrationes promiscuae adumbrationibus illustratae. Ed. *Fôsan*. 2 voll. in 8°.

572. **Musja kagami**, speculum militare. 3 voll. in 8°.

573. Jehon, **Konrei mitsisirube**, de ritu nuptiarum cum imag. a pictore *Forida Rensan* factis. Mijako 1813, 2 voll. in 8°.

b. *Regionum aedificiorumque.*

* 574. Jehon, **Sumidagawa rjôgan itsiran**, conspectus ripae utriusque fluminis, cui nomen *Sumidagawa*. Del. *Kozju Rôseian*. 3 voll. (conf. N°. 147).

* 575. Jehon, **Jedosakura**, cerassi Jedonicae, sive adumbrationes partium urbis Jedo. 1803, 2 voll. in 8°.

* 576. Jehon, **Adsumaasobi**, ambulationes Jedonicae, sive prospectus diversarum urbis *Jedo* partium. Ed. *Hoksai*. 1802, 3 voll. in 8°.

* 577. **Jedo katsikei itsiran**, praeclariores ad aspectum urbis Jedo situs; adumbravit *Hoksai*. 1815, 2 voll. in 8°.

c. *Vestimentorum.*

578. **Sjôgun nizjugo mijei**, imagines 25 imperatorum *Sjôgun* nonnullorumque imperii principum.

579. **Wakok fjaknjo**, vide N°. 415.

† 580. **Kwajônjo sjoknin kagami**, speculum seu adumbratio foeminarum florentium atque opificum. Descriptio est rerum domesticarum, edita a *Nisikowori Matsubuts*. 2 voll.

581. **Tsjanojuno dsu**, ritus theae potus parandi adumbratus. 1 vol. in 4°.

582. **Sarugakno dsu**, chorea simiae adumbrata. 1 vol. in 4°. Quae quidem chorea, a *Sjôtok Daisi* ineunte saeculo VII. inducta ad mythologiam buddhaicam (indicam) referenda esse videtur.

583. **Jedo fû bizin sugata**, imagines foeminarum elegantium, quae *Jedonico* cultu ornatae sunt. 1 vol. in 8°.

584. **Adsumanisigi je**, adumbratio *Jedonici* vestium habitus. 1 vol.

585. **Adsumanisigi je, bizin sugata**, descriptio *Jedonici* vestium habitus, hominumque ornatorum imagines. 1 vol. in fol. maj.

586. **Imajo bizinno kagami**, speculum foeminarum elegantium, quae hodierno vestium cultu ornatae sunt. 1 vol. in fol. maj.

587. **Tôsei bizin gwateo**, adumbrationes foeminarum elegantium temporis novissimi. 1 vol. in fol. maj.

588. **Josivara bizin midate gozjusan tsugi**, quinquaginta tres stationes in quibus elegantes viae *Josivara* foeminae prostant. 1 vol. in fol. maj.

589. **Josivara keisei Jedo bizin je**, imagines venerearum viae Josivara sacerdotum elegantiumque foeminarum *Jedonicarum*. 1 vol. in fol.

590. **Jedo fatsu kei**, prospectus amoeni urbis Jedo. 3 voll.
591. **Bizin je gozju san tsugi**, quinquaginta tres stationes, quae hominum elegantium imaginibus ornatae sunt.
592. **Adsuma nisigi je atsume**, descriptio varii vestium habitus *Jed*onici.
593. **Jedo fu kei**, praeclariores ad aspectum urbis *Jedo* situs. 2 voll.
594. **Tôkaidô gozju san jeki**, quinquaginta tres mansiones viae *Tôkaidô*.

Additamentum ad ea quae de libro *Schân hai king* sub N°. 370 laudato dicta sunt.

Vasa illa novem, quae *Ju*, auctor primae imperialis familiae *Hia* A° 2207 ante C. n. velut novem provinciarum monumenta fudit, figuris ornata erant rerum externarum, montium, marium, herbarum, arborum, avium, quadrupedum cet., quae iis temporibus Sinarum genti memoratu digna videbantur. Has figuras vasis illis caelatas Sinensis quidam, cui nomen *Tʼaìssè Tschung kù*, delineavit et descripsit in libro, cui titulum *Schân hai king* inscripsit, qui quidem liber, subductus igni, ad quem imperator *Schi Hoang ti* libros omnes praeter medicos et judicarios (A° 222 ante C. n.) damnaverat, seriori tempore, quum imperialis familia *Tsin* floreret, a *Kuŏpŏ* denuo typis expressus et in vulgus editus est, scripturae formâ antiqua in novam versa.

原文影印（白）

1	和漢三才圖會	攝陽城醫法橋寺島良安尚順編	全百五卷
2	頭書增補訓蒙圖彙		廿一卷
3	頭書增補訓蒙圖彙大成		廿一卷
4	唐土訓蒙圖彙	平住專菴先生著	十四卷
5	新增廣益萬會節用玉海節用字林藏		全三册
6	文化補刻萬海節用字福藏		全一册
7	新刻文林節用筆海大全		全三册
8	新增廣益萬會節用百家選		全一册
9	增廣百倍萬寶節用富貴藏		全一册
10	新撰增補都會節用百家通		全一册
11	字彙增倭漢節用無雙囊	華文軒主人述	全一册
12	博物筌	蘭齋山崎右衞門	全一册
13	彙刻書目		全十册
14	增補和漢書畫一覽		全一册
15	神代正語	伊勢人本居宣長	全三册
16	神代紀葦牙	栗田土滿大人著	全三册
17	古史系圖	平篤胤	一册
18	日本王代一覽	法眼春齋林恕	全十册
19	日本書紀		全卅卷
20	和漢年契	攝陽蘆屋山人著	全一册
21	掌中和漢年契		全一册
22	和年代皇紀繪章		三册
23	太平記		全四十卷
24	甲陽軍鑑		全二十卷
25	平家物語		全十二卷
26	島原記		全三册
27	本朝國郡建置沿革圖說	二齋佐藤	全二册
28	大日本太平記名將武勇競		
29	大日本知仁名將勇鑑		
30	甲子循環圖	觀嶽主人著	
31	年代記		
32	紀年指掌		全一册
33	和漢年歷笺		
34	萬寶二面鑑		
35	萬歷兩面鑑		
36	大和名所圖會	秋里籬嶋佩蘭清	全七册
37	河内名所圖會	竹原春朝齋畫丹羽桃溪畫	全六册
38	和泉名所圖會	竹原春朝齋畫 同	全四册
39	攝陽群談	攝西陳人岡田氏陸助	全十七册

50. 防長二州之記	49. 同 南遊記	48. 同 東遊記	47. 諸國奇談 西遊記 橘南谿子	46. 筑紫紀行 菱屋平七	45. 長崎行役日記 常州水戸長玄珠記	44. 播磨名所巡覧圖會 同	43. 紀伊國名所圖會 秋里離嶌	42. 木曽路名所圖會	41. 近江名所圖會 秋里離嶌	40. 武藏野話 鶴磯	39. 東海道名所圖會 同	38. 攝津名所圖會 秋里離島
	全五冊	全五冊	全五冊	全十冊	全一冊	全五冊	全五冊	全六冊	全四冊	全四冊	全六冊	全十六冊
63. 河内國細見小圖 丹羽桃溪	62. 大和國細見繪圖 中村敢旱斎	61. 大和國繪圖	60. 山城國繪圖	59. 九州之圖	58. 日本邊界略圖	57. 新板 日本國大繪圖	56. 改正日本輿地路程全圖 常州水戸長玄珠子玉又	55. 改正日本圖	54. 大日本細見指掌全圖	53. 諸國經緯郡城數附	52. 古山陵之圖	51. 山陵志 蒲生秀實
												全一冊
76. 能登國繪圖	75. 美濃繪圖	74. 近江國繪圖	73. 近江國大繪圖 河内敢人山下重政	72. 武江畧圖 岩埼常正	71. 阿波國繪圖	70. 叁河國繪圖	69. 尾張國繪圖	68. 志摩國繪圖	67. 攝津國名所大繪圖	66. 和泉國繪圖	65. 和泉國大繪圖	64. 河内國繪圖
		二冊				二冊						

原文影印（石版刷目錄）

77.	越後國繪圖		
78.	佐渡國繪圖		
79.	丹波國繪圖		
80.	丹後國繪圖		
81.	同		
82.	但馬國繪圖		
83.	伯耆國繪圖		
84.	石見國繪圖		
85.	隱岐國繪圖		
86.	因幡國繪圖		
87.	播磨國繪圖		
88.	播磨國大繪圖		
89.	備前國繪圖		
90.	備中國繪圖		
91.	淡路國繪圖		
92.	都名所圖會	秋里籬嶌 竹原春朝齋画	全十一冊
93.	都林泉名勝圖會	秋里籬嶌同 諸名家画	全五冊
94.	京之水	秋里舜福	全二冊
95.	再板 京都めぐり	貝原篤信	全二冊
96.	都寺社全圖		全四冊
97.	增補繪入都名所車		全一冊
98.	新撰增補京大繪圖		全一冊
99.	文化改正京都指掌圖		全一冊
100.	文化改正新增細見京繪圖		全一冊
101.	花洛一覽圖	發行風折政香 画工黃華山	全一冊
102.	新改內裏圖		全一冊
103.	補新京之圖		全一冊
104.	板新比叡山延曆寺		
105.	分間江戶大繪圖		全一冊
106.	分間御江戶繪		全一冊
107.	再版新改御江戶繪圖		
108.	文化改正御江戶繪圖		
109.	再版新改御江戶繪圖		
110.	文政改正御江戶大繪圖		
111.	改正御江戶大繪圖		
112.	北條氏康時代武州江戶繪圖		
113.	下谷淺草邊之圖		
114.	谷中本鄉丸山小石川邊之圖		
115.	駿河臺小川町之圖		

116. 東都永町之繪圖	117. 東都番町之繪圖	118. 濱町神田日本橋北之圖	119. 芝愛岩下邊之圖	120. 築地八町堀日本橋南之圖	121. 新板御繪江戸名所獨案内記	122. いろは分 獨案内 江戸町ほくし	123. 江戸御見附略圖	124. 江戸御城内御住屋之圖	125. 自上古到今世難波大坂十二圖	126. 修增 大坂指掌圖 附川画圖 全一册	127. 增補新板 大坂之圖 全	128. 新板增修改正 攝州大坂地圖 全

129. 文政新改 攝州大坂全圖 全	130. 大坂町鑑 全	131. 大坂城之圖 軍政之圖 安部之合戰之圖	132. 改ヒトメセンゲン 正 一目千軒 全一册	133. 寛政改正 繁花 みをつくし 市中 大凡積胸筭用 全一册	135. 肥州長嵜圖	136. 播磨姫路之圖	137. 下野國日光山之圖	138. 日光御山總繪圖	139. 鎌倉勝槩圖 秦檍丸圖	140. 日本名所之繪 江戸重齋紹真筆	141. 東海道名所一覽 北齋

142. 道中記 東海道 全二卷	143. 和洲吉野山名勝圖	144. 安藝國嚴嶋景	145. 丹後國天橋立之圖	146. 陸奧國鹽竈松島圖	147. 江戸隅田川兩岸一覽圖會 曉鐘成画圖 全二册 鶴岡蘆水	148. 澗州兩岸 勝景圖會 全二册	149. 名山圖譜 淡海谷文晁繪圖 全三册	150. 山水奇觀 旭江著	151. 富士山圖 小林長周 全一册	152. 富士之景	153. 采草閒筆 二宮熊木	154. 紀伊山水奇觀

155. 淡海八景圖 平安應受寫	168. 四國徧禮之圖	181. 薩哈連島之圖 最上德內
156. 明石舞子濱之圖 播州	169. 四國徧禮里數之表	182. 黑龍江中之洲並天度 間宮氏
157. 高野山細見繪圖 橘保春	170. 日光驛路里數之表	183. 唐太島之圖
158. 高野山金剛峯寺細見圖 浪華橋園雄圖 紀州	171. 東海道驛路里數之表	184. 琉球談 森島中良
159. 四天王寺伽藍圖 浪華春朝齋竹原信繁圖	172. 增補日本汐路之記 高田政度	185. 朝鮮物語 全五冊
160. 太宰府天滿宮御境內之繪圖	173. 大坂川口ヨリ長崎迄舟路 全一冊	186. 三才一貫圖 淅紹新昌呂撫安世輯
161. 東海道分間繪圖	174. 三國通覽圖記 仙臺林子平圖並記 全一冊	187. 萬國大全圖
162. 東海木曾兩道中懷寶圖鑑	175. 蝦夷談筆記 藤仍繩 全一冊	188. 歷代事跡圖
163. 大日本道中行程細見記	176. 蝦夷拾遺	189. 大清萬年一統地理全圖
164. 大日本道中行程指南車	177. 蝦夷圖 最上德內	190. 古今沿革地圖 水戶長赤水
165. 大日本海陸通覽 カイリクツウラン	178. 松前蝦夷之圖 全五枚	191. 喝蘭新譯地球全圖 水戶赤水長閣
166. 道中獨案內 だうちうひとりあんない	179. 蝦夷海濱之景	192. 東察加之圖 最上德內
167. 西國順禮細見大全 さいこくじゅんれいさいけんだいぜん 一冊	180. 唐太島 最上德內 全二冊	193. 北海 同

194. 大觀證類本草 唐愼微 江戶醫官 全卅卷	195. 校正本草綱目 明李時珍 全廿五冊	196. 本草滙 吳門郊西郭佩蘭章宜篤纂輯 全十八冊	197. 毛詩草木鳥獸蟲魚疏 唐吳郡陸璣著 全一冊	198. 毛詩陸氏艸木疏圖解 淵在寬述 全五冊	199. 毛詩品物圖攷 浪華岡元鳳 全三冊	200. 毛詩名物圖說 吳中徐鼎實夫纂 全二冊	201. 救荒本草 明王西樓輯 姚可成補 全九冊	202. 食物本草 元東垣李杲編輯 明吳郡錢允治校訂 全二冊	203. 通志昆蟲艸木略 宋鄭夾漈著 日本蘭山先生校 全三冊	204. 花鏡 西湖陳扶搖彙輯 全六冊	205. 本草彙言 明錢塘倪朱謨選集 松岡恕菴先生抄錄 全六冊	206. 南方草木狀 全二冊
207. 本草綱目啓蒙 蘭山小野先生口授 孫小野職寺士德錄 全五冊	208. 本草啓蒙名疏 小野蘭山鑑定 孫職編輯 全八冊	209. 本草原始 合雷公炮 全五冊	210. 本草和解 大江顧軒 全二冊	211. 大和本草新校正 貝原篤信 全十冊	212. 廣稭本草 直海龍 全十二冊	213. 赭鞭餘錄 豐田養慶 全一冊	214. 物類品隲 鳩溪平賀先生著 全六冊	215. 花彙 雍南田充房 全八冊	216. 草木性譜 張府舍人清原丕撰 全三冊	217. 有毒本草圖說 同 全三冊	218. 本草和名 深江輔仁 全二冊	219. 物品識名 尾張水谷豐文 全四冊
220. 本草藥名備考和訓鈔 丹波賴理 全七冊	221. 草花式 法橋春川筆 全三冊	222. 雲根志 同前後編 江州山田浦木内小繁先生著 共七五冊	223. 泰西本草名疏 尾張伊藤舜民藏堯編 全三冊	224. 百菊譜 兒素仙 全二冊	225. 花壇養菊集 志水閑事 全二冊	226. 牽牛品 峰岸龍父著 全二冊	227. 長生花林抄 東都深井伊藤兵衛著 全五冊	228. 朝顏譜 濃淡齋森春溪画 全一冊	229. 花壇朝顏通 怡顏齋松岡玄達先生撰 全二冊	230. 梅品 怡顏齋松岡玄達成章撰 全二冊	231. 怡顏齋蘭品 松岡玄達成章撰 全二冊	232. 怡顏齋櫻品 同 全一冊

245. 蟲蛆鏡 高玄龍 全一冊	244. 怡顔齋介 松岡玄達先生成章撰 全五冊	243. 鯨志 南紀如水軒 全一冊	242. 一角纂考 同 全一冊	241. 蘭畹摘芳 同 全三冊	240. 六物新志 大槻茂質 全二冊	239. 古今鷹之事 全一冊	238. 茶席挿花集 芳亭野人 岩崎常正寫 全一冊	237. 花壇大全	236. 廣益增補 地錦抄 伊藤伊兵衛 全七八冊	235. 橘品 弄花亭 全一冊	234. 橘品類考 桂菴木村 全二冊	233. 草木奇品家雅見 金太著 全三冊
258. 本草寫真 水谷助六 一冊	257. 日光山草木寫真 伊藤舜民ケイスケ 二冊	256. 琉球草木寫真素稿 一冊	255. 琉球本草寫真之圖 同 二冊	254. 蝦夷本草之圖 桂川甫賢 二冊	253. 梅櫻類花寫真 一冊	252. 日本草木 同 二冊	251. 人參寫真 同 一冊	250. 同 桂川甫賢 一冊	249. 同 宇田川榕菴 一冊	248. 本草寫真 水谷助六 二冊	247. 臺きんきの記 大槻茂質 一冊	246. 夏草冬蟲圖 抽木常翌 一冊
271. 蛛類説圖 尾藩大窪舒三郎昌章寫 一冊	270. 蟲蛆類寫集 一冊	269. 蝶二十寫真 一冊	268. 蟲蟹之圖 浪華鐵山画 一冊	267. 蟹鰕類寫真 桂川栗本瑞兀 二冊	266. 獸禽蟲寫真 全三冊	265. 腊葉摺 薜茘菴 二冊	264. 草花之圖 春溪寫 一冊	263. 山櫻説 筑前候所著 一冊	262. 生檀全書 同 一冊	261. 同 宇田川榕菴 五冊	260. 同 大窪太兵衛 五冊	259. 本草拔萃 同 五冊

272. 魚類寫真 桂川栗本瑞元 三册	273. 海魚考圖繪 鞭近齋 二册	274. 海魚寫真 宇田川搉菴 一册	275. 寫真隨集 同 一册	276. 獸魚縮寫 一册	277. 禽獸魚寫真 一册	278. 寫真長鯨圖 一册	279. 唐夫人所謂 リキンカムビ 二獸之圖 ツナカイ	280. 蛇骨寫真	281. 打越溝中出異獸角骨圖	282. 石ニ化ヲノ魚之圖 ナルウヲノ	283. 天狗爪石雜考 木内重曉	284. 本州一家言 松岡恕菴 全四册 Ms

285. 本草和名集 全二册 Ms	286. 菌譜 酒井立生 一册 Ms	287. 修養堂 本草會目錄 伊藤舜民ケイスケ 一册 Ms	288. 生堂 本草會目錄 大河內存眞 Ms	289. 草會目錄 同 Ms	290. 海鮹 Ms	291. 鳥品類小記	292. 日本諸禽眞寫 附名 全二本	293. 鷸十八品眞寫 水谷助六 全一册	294. 字彙 梅膺祚 全九册	295. 康熙字典 全卅册

296. 增續大廣益玉篇 洛濱隱士毛利 全十一册	297. 增字林玉篇 鎌田禎 全一册	298. 四聲字林集韻 鎌田禎刪補 全一册	299. 删定增補小字彙 全一册	300. 急用間合 眞字玉篇大成 平仄校正 訓譯改訂 全一册	301. 和漢音釋書言字考節用集 駒谷散人檜郁輯 全十册	302. 假名引節用集 田仲宣 全一册	303. 大全早引節用集 全一册	304. 早引節用集 據梧散人 眞字附 全一册	305. 增補詩文重寶記 信雯生 全一册	306. 譯文筌 全三册	307. 古言梯 取魚彥 全一册

308. 雅言假字格 市岡孟彦補訂 全一册	321. 画引十體千字文 綱目 西嶼孫玉顯編輯 全一册	334. 梵言集 一册
309. 大和詞 全一册	322. 汪由敦揩書千字文 全一册	335. 新刻清書全集 重鐫錢塘同學弟汪鶴孫撰 全三册
310. 屋まひとの詞 全一册	323. 米南宮杜律墨帖 全一册	336. 清語集 全一册
311. 新撰大和詞 東華切磋 全二册	324. 譯鍵 全二册	337. 改正兩部神道口決鈔 江源慶安 全六册
312. 雜字類編 氾愛堂 全二册	325. 江戸ハルマ 全十六册	338. 繪馬雛形 全一册
313. 學語論 全二册	326. 和蘭辞書 一册	339. 扁額軌範 此川春成先生 合川珉和先生 合摸 全一册
314. イロハ天理鈔 全二册	327. 蠻語箋 全一册	340. 通神画譜 合川亭眠和画 全一册
315. 以呂波字考錄 全二册	328. 蝦夷方言 白虹齊 全一册	341. 細見男山放生會圖會 速水春曉齊 全一册
316. 以呂波之五類 全一册	329. 蝦夷ヶ嶋言語 全一册	342. 二十四輩順拜圖會 河州專教寺隱擇了貞 竹原春泉齋画 全五册
317. 空海之いろは 全一册	330. 千字文 大本 全一册	343. 增補諸宗佛像圖彙 浪華土佐將曹紀秀信画 全五册
318. 麻光韻鏡 京師子蓮淨寺沙門文雄僧谿述 全二册	331. 類合 全一册	
319. 千字文 全一册	332. 朝鮮辞書 全一册	
320. 訓点千字文 山子点 全一册	333. 摩多體文 西海蓮華沙門源昭 一册	

原文影印（石版刷目録）

346	345	344	343	342	341	340	339	338	337	336	335
定家撰錦葉鈔 テイカセンキンエフセフ	女用至寶 都名所盡	類葉百人一首敎文庫	文化新版 麗玉百人一首吾妻錦 合川珉和画圖	繪本孝婦傳	菜根譚 明ノ洪自誠	論語彙訓卷之省 最上德内著	論語 道春點	孝經 漢魯人孔安國傳 日本信陽太宰純音	四書	增補 咒咀調法記 菊丘卧山人	大般若理趣分 大唐三藏法師玄奘奉詔譯 大般若波羅蜜多經卷第五百七十八
全一冊	全一冊	全一冊	全一冊	全一冊	全二冊	一冊	一冊	一冊	一冊	一冊	一冊

359	358	357	356	355	354	353	352	351	350	349	348	347
艶廓通覽 浪華洞籬山人著	和漢古今角偉談 菊丘卧山人江匡弼文坡	七福七難圖會 浪華生々瑞馬著赤石岡田東帛画	遠乃白浪 ヲチノシラナミ	文化新板 本朝蘿物語 ホンテウモノガタリ	伊勢物語	巨勢金岡名技傳	繪本鏡山列女功 川関惟充	繪本金花談	泄せく莨	世談雜說	近世貞婦傳	雜話敎訓鑑
全五冊	全五冊	全五冊	全三冊	一冊	全二冊	全二冊	全五冊	全十三冊	全二冊	全五冊	全五冊	全五冊

372	371	370	369	368	367	366	365	364	363	362	361	360
長恨歌	キフ子本地	山海經晉記室參軍郭璞傳	久松花競浮名之讀販	笹邑廼猪口屑手	正本製八編	正本製七編	音羽七女郎花喩粟島 歌川国貞画	浮世新形六枚屏風 柳亭種彦作 豊國画	笑府 墨憨齋主人編	閨情偶寄 湖上李漁著	東庸子	松陰快談 豐山長野先生著
全三冊	三卷	全十八冊	全三冊	全二冊	同全二冊	同全二冊	同全二冊	全二冊	一冊	二冊	一冊	全二冊

385.	384.	383.	382.	381.	380.	379.	378.	377.	376.	375.	374.	373.
歌道名目鈔 右中辨資任	百人一首峯のうけしほ 衣川久人著	古今集遠鏡 本居宣長	都國芝居繁榮數望	京都歌舞妓新狂言外題年鑑	菅原傳授手習鑑 同	双蝶蝶曲輪日記 竹本義太夫直傳	假名手本忠臣藏 竹田因幡椽後様 竹本松後様直傳 全冊	近江源氏先陣舘 竹田新松 竹本義太夫直傳	妹背音 本町糸屋娘	一谷嫩軍記 豊竹越前少椽	壇浦兜軍 琴責段	妹背山 玉水源次郎
全三冊	全三冊	全六冊	全一冊	全一冊	全一冊	全一冊		全一冊	全一冊	一	一	五冊

398	397	396	395	394	393	392	391	390	389	388	387	386
浦のみつぎ 伴花菴	同	繪本和歌合	繪本百人一首	寶玉百人一首	百人一首	百人一首小倉文庫	千紅萬紫 蜀山先生集	續撰吟和歌集韻	歌林雜木抄	歌怜野集 清原雄風大夫編輯 四季 六冊 戀雜 六冊	萬葉集 橘諸兄公集	正徹物語
全一冊	一冊	全一冊	全二冊	全二冊	全一	一小冊	一冊				全三冊	全二冊

	410	409	408	407	406	405	404	403	402	401	400	399
	袖珍畧韻大成	詩礎諺解 附 聯句 村瀬海輔輯解	宋詩礎 江戸大窪行	宋詩清絶 江戸柏昶如亭撰	狂歌扶桑集 六樹園 菊榮亭兩撰	狂歌関東百題集 鈍々亭撰	狂歌画自滿	狂歌手毎之花 文屋茂鶯	八重山婦	俳諧七部集	山家集類題 西行上人歌集	三十六歌集 同
	全四冊	全一冊	全二冊	全一冊	全二冊	全二冊	全三冊	全二冊	全二冊	全二冊	全一冊	全一冊

423	422	421	420	419	418	417	416	415	414	413	412	411
御元服 御宮参 御用掛 御役人附	文政武鑑	群書類従 撿拔保己一集 卷第四百七十下迄	雅遊漫録 大枝流芳著	かさ祢のいろ尓	装束圖式	京大坂茶屋諸分調方記	小笠原諸礼大全 法橋王山著	風和國百女 菱川師宣	三禮口訣 貝原篤信	新板後篇 嫁入談合桂 平安華鳳山著	骨董集 醒齋輯	制度通 伊藤長胤輯
全一冊	全四冊	三冊	全五冊	全一冊	全二冊	全一冊	三冊	全一冊	全二冊	全二冊	全五冊	全六冊

433	432	431	430	429	428	427	426	425	424
度量衡説統 最上德内	宮雛形 武家雛形 棚雛 敷寄屋雛形 小坪矩尺	江戸本所深川 いろは組纏はくし兩面摺	火事御出役 定火消御役 御大名火消 御塲所附 イロハ番組	町火消番組	萬世江戸町鑑	文政十二子年略暦十七二候	文政十一年略暦候	月令博物筌	萬代寶鑑
全三冊	全五冊			全二冊		全十四冊		全一冊	

446	445	444	443	442	441	440	439	438	437	436	435	434
飲膳摘要 小野蕙畋	武江産物志 岩崎常正	日本山海名物圖會	山海名産圖會	農家嫁業事 兒島如水翁著	農家益 大藏永常著	農業全書 筑州後學宮崎安貞	成形圖説 臣藤原國柱	佩文耕織圖 江戸櫻井雪鮮	詳説角觚 活金剛傳 松壽樓主人撰	古軍器之圖解	甲冑著用辨 井上老先生著	圖解武用辨略 大樹戸木下義俊編輯
全二冊	全一冊	全五冊	全五冊	全五冊	全三冊	全八冊	全卅冊	全二冊	全二冊	全一冊	全二冊	全八冊

459	458	457	456	455	454	453	452	451	450	449	448	447
瓶花圖彙	生花秘傳野山錦	雅曲花娘玉みがきおし	押繪早稽古	滑稽漫画	鮫皮精鑒錄 浅尾遠視	鼓銅圖錄 浪華住友氏奴隷増田綱謹撰	装劍奇賞 浪華稻葉通龍新右衛門著	妙術博物筌 貝原先生	江戶職人歌合 藤原泰圖	職人盡發句合 關田子蕭蹊	日州養蜂圖	教訓繪本米恩錄 中川有恒 速水春曉齋縮画
全二冊	全二冊	全一冊	全一冊	全一冊	全一冊	全一冊	全七冊	全七冊	全二冊	全二冊	一	全五冊

471	470	469	468	467	466	465	464	463	462	461	460
張公捕魚	日本持丸長者集	拾玉智惠海	塗之法	紙作之法	酒作之事	染物之法 早稻作法 茶製法	日本漆邑法	立華正道集	挿花衣之香 真松斎米一馬	挿花千筋之麓 入江玉蟾	瓶花圖全
			一	一	一	全一冊	一	全四冊	全四冊	全三冊	一

483	482	481	480	479	478	477	476	475	474	473	472
錢範	古錢價附	對泉譜 文樓田元成	金銀圖錄 近藤守重	和漢泉彙 芳川甚右門	古今泉貨鑑	孔方圖鑑 小澤東市	珍錢奇品圖錄 大村成富	改正孔方圖鑑 小澤東市	寬政孔方圖鑑 流石菴羽積	珍貨孔方圖鑑 中谷顧山	造壜法圖
全一冊	全	全一冊	全七冊	全十二冊	全一冊	全一冊	全一冊	全一冊	全一冊	全一冊	

495	494	493	492	491	490	489	488	487	486	485	484
藥品應手錄 高良齋	榮衞中經圖 竿齋先生著 周防鈴木宗云撰次	和蘭全軀內外分圖 長崎本木子意翻譯	解臟圖賦 池田義之冬藏	人面瘡圖説 桂川甫賢	藥名稱呼 木原宗眞	廣參説臟考	鍼灸説約 石坂宗哲先生著	鍼灸廣狹神俱集 雲樓子著 石坂宗哲校	鍼灸援翠大成 岡本一抱子	西洋錢譜 小澤東市	懷寶珍錢鑑 タイホウチンセンカヾミ
一	全二板	全一冊	全一冊	全一冊	全一冊	全一冊	全一冊	全一冊	全七冊		全一冊

505	504	503	502	*501	500	499	498	497	496
繪本直指寶 橘守國	花鳥畫式 朝比奈夕顔	畫筌 筑前魯軒林守篤	漢畫獨稽古 君山宮瓊	漢畫指南二編 寒葉齋	漢畫指南 東都建凌岱孟喬著述		婦人患病書	九鍼之説 石坂宗哲	知要一言	鍼灸圖解
全九冊	全一冊	全六冊	全二冊	三冊	二冊		一	一	二枚

518	517	516	515	514	513	*512	511	510	509	508	507	506
草花畧畫式	蕙齋鹿畫	諸職畫鑑 蕙齋北尾政美	高田敬甫畫譜	画本必用 中路雲岬	名家畫譜 桃溪	元明華鳥	新刻金氏畫譜 尾張九峰寄田延選撰	押畫手鑑 大岡道信	聚珍畫帖 薫杉軒葦寫	畫史會要 春卜翁集	宋紫石畫譜	宋紫石畫譜
全一冊	全一冊	全一冊	全四冊	全二冊	全二冊	全二冊	全一冊	全三冊	全三冊	全六冊	全三冊	全十三冊

519	人物畧画式		全一冊
520	竹譜詳録	息斎李	全二冊
521	建氏画苑	寒葉斎	全三冊
522	建氏画苑海錯圖	同	全一冊
523	繪本詠物選	法眼橘保国	全五冊
524	繪本野山草	同	全五冊
525	帝都雅景一覧	河邑文鳳	全四冊
526	文鳳山水画譜		全一冊
527	素絢画譜	山口素絢画 草花之部	三冊
528	繪本稽古帳	井村勝吉	全三冊
529	寫生獸圖画		全二冊
530	画圖百花鳥	山下石仲	全四冊
531	画本虫撰	喜多川歌麿呂	全二冊
532	繪本手引草		全一冊
533	繪本筆二邑	北尾重政	全二冊
534	寫生画帖 初心柱立		全一冊
535	櫻花画帖		全一冊
536	画本無名		全一冊
537	京城画苑	文徴堂輯	全一冊
538	鶯邪画譜		全一冊
539	光琳百圖		全一冊
540	南兵衛街道雙画	文鳳	全二冊
541	繪本手鑑	法橋春ト	一冊
542	繪本心農種		全二冊
543	花鳥寫眞圖會		三冊
544	花鳥画譜		全一冊
545	花鳥画帖		全一冊
546	鳥獸畧画式	蕙斎	全二冊
547	北斎漫画		全十冊
548	寫真學筆 墨僊叢画	北斎	全一冊
549	北斎寫真画譜		全一冊
550	三體画譜	同	全一冊
551	一筆画譜		全一冊
552	繪本兩筆	立好斎	全一冊
553	英雄圖會	玄龍斎戴斗	一
554	北斎画式	北斎	全二冊
555	秀画一覧	同	全一冊
556	繪本淨瑠璃絕句	同	全一冊
557	北雲漫画編		全一冊

570. 繪本鶯宿梅 橘守国	569. 繪本武者鞋	568. 繪本多武峯 北尾紅翠軒重政	567. 繪本武勇櫻 長谷川光信	566. 繪本源將名譽草 曲亭馬琴	565. 繪袖中雛源氏	564. 繪本賴朝一生記	563. 繪本源平武者揃	562. 風流繪合手引北園	561. 今昔画圖續百鬼	560. 画圖百器徒然袋 鳥山石燕豐房	559. 画本寫寶袋 橘有税	558. 鳥山石燕画
全七册	全二册	全三册	全二册	二册	全一册	全二册	全二册	全三册	全三册	全三册	全十册	全一册

582. 猿樂之圖	581. 茶湯之圖	580. 花容女職人鑑 西來居未佛	579. 倭國百女 菱川師宣	578. 將軍二十五容貌	577. 東都勝景一覽 同	576. 画本東都遊 北斎	575. 繪本江都櫻	574. 繪本隅田川兩岸一覽 壺十樓成安	573. 繪本婚禮道シルベ 堀田連山 南里亭其樂	572. 武者鑑	571. 繪本フチハカマ 縫山撰 柳川重山画
全一册	全一册		全二册	全一册		全二册	全三册	全二册	全三册	全二册	全三册	全二册

594. 東海道五十三驛	593. 江戶風景	592. 東錦繪集	591. 美人繪五十三驛	590. 江戶八景	589. 吉原傾城江戶美人画	588. 吉原美人見立五十三驛	587. 當世美人画帖	586. 今樣美人鏡	585. 東錦繪美人容貌	584. 東錦繪	583. 江戶風美人姿
二册				三册							

17.

604.	603.	602.	601.	600.		599.	598.	597.	596.	595.
萬廓笑面鑑	晝夜いろなちみ光ぐに 化粧 青樓兩面鏡	新エドダウチウメイショヅヱ 板江戸道中名所圖會	佛法雙文	官職昇進雙六 スゴロク 二册		花畫	當世画工帖集	草花之圖	草華之圖	笠亭晴岩兩先生妙品

原文影印（白）

日本語訳

家入敏光

《凡例》

1. 底本・日本語訳方針

　本書に掲載した日本語訳の底本および翻訳部分は、"*Catalogus librorum et manuscriptorum Japonicorum a Ph. Fr. de Siebold collectorum, annexa enumeratione illorum, qui in Museo Regio Hagano servantur*"（公益財団法人東洋文庫所蔵、請求番号　La-62：扉 p 3、刊記 p 4、緒言 pp. 5〜8、目次 pp. 9〜10・XVII-1-A-12：ラテン語解説本文 pp. 11〜46）である。日本語訳は、底本の掲載順に従って掲載した。ラテン語本文中、日本語の固有名詞の表記には誤記もみられる。その際、正しい名詞が明白な場合には漢字で該当する名詞をあてることを旨とした。以下 2〜4 では、ラテン語解説本文の日本語訳について記す。

2. 資料番号表記

　ラテン語本文に記している記号・番号（アラビア数字・アルファベット）のまま記した。但し、石版刷目録にない番号には〔　〕を付し、間違えて付されていると思われる場合には番号の上に（ママ）と付した。なお、冒頭の記号「＊」印はブロンホフ旧蔵、「＋」印はフィッセル旧蔵を意味する。

　　　　　（例）1.　　＊8　　＋11.　　〔324.a〕　　334.（ママ）

3. 書名（表題・資料名）

（1）書名は、原文（ローマ字表記）記載に基づき、番号に続けて漢字・仮名交じりになおした表記（ゴチック体・新字の漢字）で表記した。石版刷目録にあってラテン語本文にない部分は〔　〕、石版刷目録にはなくラテン語本文にある部分は【　】で記した。

　　　　　（例）＋6.〔**文化補刻**〕**万海節用字福蔵**　　　244. **怡顔斎介【品】**

（2）書名に用いる漢字の表記は、旧字体漢字を新字体に改めることを原則とした。

（3）漢字書名表記の次に（　）内に平仮名　原文アルファベット　の順で表記した。

　　　　書名（読み　ローマ字表記［中国語読み］〔通行の日本語読み〕）

　　　　　（例）424. **万代宝鑑**（まんたいほうかん　Mantai fôkan［*Wàntai paò kièn*］〔ばんだいほうかん〕）

日本語訳（凡例）

  (4) 書名ローマ字表記による平仮名読みにおける原文の濁音・促音等の有無は無視して、日本語通行の読みを表記した。なお「Nippon」の読みは「にっぽん」に統一した。
      （例）10. **博物筌**（はくぶつせん　Fak buts zen）
  (5) 書名表記の原文がイタリック体による中国語読み表記を行っている場合、（　）内に原文表記〔平仮名日本語読み〕の順で記し、原文アルファベットに日本語・中国語、双方の読みが記される場合は、中国語表記に〔　〕を付した。
      （例）+11. **彙刻書目**（*Wei ke schû mû*〔いこくしょもく〕）
           209. **本草原始**（ほんぞうげんし　Honzo genshi［*Pènts'aô juénsci*］）
  (6) 書名に対して原文の読み方が明らかに誤記の場合、現在『国書総目録』に記してある読みを平仮名で（　）内の末尾に〔　〕で付した。
      （例）53. **諸国経緯郡城数附**（しょこくたてよこきこと；ごほりしろのかずつく Sjo kok tate-jokoki koto；gohori sirono kazu tsuku〔しょこくけいいぐんじょうすうづけ〕）
  (7) 324a. は石版刷目録にはなく、原文が蘭語題名のため、冒頭「　」内に書名の和訳を表記し、『　』内に今日通行の和文書名を記した。
      （例）〔324a.〕「**新輯和蘭辞書**」（Nieuw verzameld Japans en Hollandsch woorden-boek door den Vorst van het Landschap Nakats『蘭語訳撰』）

4. 説明文
  (1) ラテン語本文における書誌事項（冊数・巻数、木版・活版の区別、成立年代等）、内容解説（書名の説明、著作者名、資料内容等）等、記述内容が誤記と判断される場合や文意が汲み取りにくい表現もあるが、本文の内容を正確に伝えることを重視して原文に忠実な日本語訳を試みた。
  (2) 書名表記に続くラテン語による説明本文中、（　）内に説明がある場合は和訳文中においても（　）を使って該当部分の日本語訳を記した。
  (3) 説明文中に記される人名は、通常日本語で記される表記（日本・中国の人物は漢字使用、欧米人は片仮名）で記した後、原文の表記を（　）内にイタリック体で記した。
      （例）最上徳内（*Mogami Toknai*）　　李時珍（*Li Schi tsching*）
           C.P. トゥーンベリ（*C.P. Thunberug*）
  (4) 説明文中に記される書名は、通常日本語で記される表記（日本・中国の資料は漢字使用、欧米の資料は日本語に和訳表記）で「　」あるいは『　』内に記した後、原文の表記を（　）内に記した。
      （例）「毛詩」（*Maôschî*）　　「日本蔵書」（Bibliothecae Japonicae）
  (5) 人名・書名の原文表記が明らかに誤記と分かる場合、人名表記の略記、地名等が分かりにくい場合は、〔　〕内に正しい読みや人名を補った。
      （例）太朝臣安万侶（*Ohu Ason Amaro*）〔おおのあそんやすまろ〕
           平〔田〕篤胤（*Tairano Atutane*）
  (6) 書誌説明に関する基本的な語彙（略語）は以下のような日本語訳を行った。
      Auct.（auctore）：著　　　　Ed.（edidit）：編、撰
      MS.（manuscript）：手稿　　 Tab.（Tabula）：表、図表、絵図
      typis：活字刷り、活版　　　 xylogr.：木版刷り、木版

日本書籍及び写本目録

フィリップ・フランツ フォン・シーボルト収集による
付・ハーグ王立博物館所蔵日本関係図書

フィリップ・フランツ・フォン・シーボルト（PH. FR. DE SIEBOLD）著
ヨハン・ホフマン（J. HOFFMANN.）解説

石版刷 16 枚付
ライデン
著者
1845
125 部印刷

印刷　J. G. LA LAU.

緒　言

　日本の書籍は前世紀〔17世紀〕の終り頃までは、東洋に関する文献中極めて稀有の記念品と見なされ、ヨーロッパの大変有名な図書館ですら、これらの断片さえ見出されるのは皆無に近いものでした。1683年から1686年の間日本に於けるオランダの商館長であった有名な医師アンドレアス・クライエル（ANDREAS CLEYER）は、フリードリヒ・ウィルヘルム（FREDERICO WILHELMO）大選定侯のすすめによって、ベルリン図書館に23冊の中国図書と日本植物図書とを贈りましたが、これが最初のものでした。

　次いで日本から多数の書籍を持ち帰ったのはエンゲルベルト・ケンペル（ANGELBERTUS KAEMPFER）でした。同氏は当時（1691、1692）における日本の大変恵まれた精通者で、これらの書籍は全部で49冊の木版本と多くの図絵でした。有名人ケンペルの死後（1716）、右の書籍中33冊は、ハンス・スローン（JOHANNIS SLOANE）卿の手に帰し、他は諸々の図書館に散佚しました。そのときこれらの日本書籍の外装が特に人目を引き、収集家はこのようなもの

日本語訳（緒言）

を日本印刷術の見本として珍重したものでした。彼らは点検もしなければ説明もせず、そのために彼らは大変な文化人〔日本人〕の諸風俗、規律の考えを追求もしませんでした。それゆえ蔵書狂たちの熱心な好奇心は、これらの書籍を悪くも忘れ去りました。

　それ以来、ほとんど百年間、日本から書籍が来たという話を聞いていません。それはあるいは外国人が日本の事物を研究する事を締め出した、この国〔日本〕の厳重な法律に帰因するのか、あるいは当時インド洋を横断していながら、この極東の文書の研究に注目しなかった無関心、むしろ怠慢に帰すべきか、とにかくこれらの研究は大変長年の間、等閑に付されていました。また宣教師たちがキリスト教布教のために学んだ初歩の語学は、この見知らぬ事物に対する興味を起こさせる力を持っていませんでした。有名なカール・ペーテル・トゥーンベリ（CAROLUS PETRUS THUNBERG）は、日本語研究には確かに功労があったとせねばならない人ではありますが、同氏はどちらかと云えば、日本の代表的著作を探し求めて収集すると云う人ではなく、むしろこの国の自然界の研究に没頭した人です。氏はその旅行記に、植物に関する少数の書籍を挙げていますが、これらも省略された表題のみで、彼自身が持ち帰った書籍も極く少数です。

　次いで遂にイサーク・ティツイング（ISACUS TITSINGH）氏は非常な熱心家で、日本歴史の研究には多大の貢献をもたらしました。彼は1780-1782年の間、日本でのオランダ商館長でした。彼は非常に沢山の書籍、地図、及び図絵を収集し、かつこれらの解説を試み、しかも大変重要な書籍は日本人の通訳の助けを借りて、これらをベルギー語に翻訳しました。帰国に際しては、彼はこれら総ての書物を持ち帰り、その見事な見本をアムステルダムの王立学校図書館に寄贈しました。

　ティツイング自身は後に健康を損ねて、温暖なパリに静養に行くことに決め、そこで日本帝国に関する浩瀚な著述をしようと考えていました。もし誰か別の者がいればとにかく、彼はこの仕事に適した人で、学識も博く理知も鋭く、確かに仕事に対する特有の根気を持っていましたが、突然の死によって、30年間の仕事はその博識の成果を見ることなく、中止の止むなきに至りました。それに劣らず残念なのは、彼の著書、図絵並びに収集した貴重な貨幣その他が、大変不幸な運命に陥ったことです。すなわちこの全宝物に対して、東インドの英政府は25万グルデンを提供したのですが、それらは満6年の間に、パリで陰をひそめてしまいました。私はそれ以上の事情を知っていますが、追求しますまい。卑しい欲に駆られて他人の財宝をうかがい、あるいは恥ずべき嫉妬の念をもって、この不朽の人物の記念物を、犯罪的に行方不明とすることを企てた者こそ、己の行為を知るがよいのです。

　その後やっと、書籍商ネープブー（NEPVEU）がティツイングの出版を始めました。（彼自身の語るところによると）彼は大変有名なラングレス（LANGLESII）の指導に従って、1818年にティツイングの少数の著書とその他の書類を探して準備し、こうして翌1819年に作者の遺

稿としてティツイング集（*Titsinghianae*）第1巻を出版しました。この第1巻にも、またマルテ・ブルン（*Malte-Brunii*）〔編〕「旅行年代記」（Annalium Itinerum）第24巻〔1824年〕にも、ティツイングのコレクションの索引が載っています。そこには多少の写本、地図、その他の図絵が収録され、又極めて少数の刊本も収録されています。なお私は公立及び私立図書館において、ティツイングの歴史、地誌及び貨幣史についての多くの著作を見出しました。これらを見ても、彼がこの種の書物を東洋から持ち帰ったことを知り得ます。

　私たちはティツイングの天与の才能と評価が極端にまで破壊され、これが学問に対する著しい損失であり、またティツイングの名誉をも毀損したと前にも述べたと信じていますが、なお一層悲しむべきことは、上記の王立学校図書館に寄贈された別の見本が、確かに良心的に保存されてはいますが、それはちょうど金の羊皮〔奥深くしまい込まれた宝の意〕同様に取扱われていることです。

　日本研究熱は、この間に徐々に増して来ました。多くの通訳たちは、しばしば私に1786-1789年の間、日本で大変高貴な商館長であったヨハン・フレデリック・ファン・レーデ（*JO-HANNEN FREDERICUM VAN RHEEDE*）が書籍その他の事物の大変熱心な研究者だ、と云って褒めてくれました。私はこれらを容易に信じましたが、まだその事例を自身で確かめてはいません。しかし単行書その他種々・雑多の書物、地図、種々のスケッチが度々好事家たちの手によって持ち帰られ、博物館や公私の図書館に納められました。こうしてパリの王立図書館は浩瀚なるエンサイクロペディア〔百科事典〕、日本語辞書（Vocabularia Japonica）、地図を所有し、ペテルブルクのアジア博物館には大変珍しい貨幣に関する書物及び地図があり、ウイーン、ドレスデン、ワイマール、ゴータその他にある公立図書館は、それぞれ高価な図、地理書、歴史及び言語学的著述を保有しています。ベルリンの王立図書館には、クライエル（*CLEYERI*）の持ち帰ったもの、ロンドンの大英博物館にはケンペルのもの、ウプサラの図書館にはトゥーンベリの持ち帰った断篇および日本書籍の代表作より成る収集物があります。私立図書館の中ではクラプロート（*KLAPROTHII*）のが一番豊富でした。

　更に蔵書の大変豊富なことで知られるオランダ公立図書館には、勲爵士ヤン・コック・ブロムホフ（*JOHANNEN COCK BLOMHOFF*）の帰国前は、その備付の東洋の写本及び刊本中に、未だ日本の書籍の例を見出せませんでした。ブロムホフは非常な努力で日本文化、日本人の公私生活、その生計、国民の宗教並びに芸術に関して研究しました。彼は長年の間、商館長として日本に滞在してこの研究をなし、その責任を果して1824年に長年の研究成果を携えて帰国しました。ハーグの王立博物館はこれによって、著しい成長による書籍の増加を見ました。これらの書籍並びに地図の中の29冊を、すでに私は日本において購入することはできませんでした。私たちが目録の中で（＊）印を付したものがそれです。

　それにまた、私たちがインド政庁の委託を受けて、日本へ研究の目的をもって旅立った当

日本語訳（緒言）

時、同地にはファン・オーフェルメール・フィッセル（VAN OVERMEER FISSCHER）と云う大変賢明な人が副商館長を勤めていて、同じ目的を抱いて熱心に努力していました。彼の努力は報いられ、彼はすでに1831年に書籍、地図その他多数の図絵を祖国へ持ち帰りました。これらの惜しみなさは、ハーグ王立博物館に納められました。フィッセルの集めたこの品目は、およそ117冊から成っています。私たちはその中の60冊を、私たちのカタログの中に新しく取り入れ、（+）印を付して豊かにしました。

私たちもできるだけの努力を払って、日本に滞在していた7年間（1823-1830）に、525冊の書籍を集めて、これらをすべてオランダ国に寄贈しました。それと云うのも、同国に特に日本に関する文献だけの収蔵記念文庫が出来ればと思ったからです。また私たちはこれらをその著作内容に応じて整理したのですが、これで東洋に関する文献愛好家、あるいは地理学、民族学研究者たちに、その書籍の価値と意義をよりよく知らせることが出来たと信じています。私たちがこれまで日本、あるいはその他の国で集めた諸々の書籍並びに写本で残存したものは、一部はウイーンの帝室図書館に、一部はパリの王立図書館に贈りました。これは有名な中国学者ステファン・エントリッヘル（STEPHANO ENDLICHER）及びスタニスラス・ジュリアン（STANISLASIO JULIEN）両氏の指導の下に、日本に関する文献が尊重され、ひいては東洋学の研究が促進されることを目的としたのです。

この目録の中に、私たちが自分達の収集書籍だけでなく、私たちの収集書籍に存在していない他人の収書をも加えたのは、いかに多数の学問上の至宝が数年の間に、しかも大変な遠隔地からオランダに集められ得たかを、まさしく目前に示すと同時に、日本文化研究に役立つ資料の列挙と評価価値でもあることを、明らかにしようとしたためです。

これらの書籍における大部分の表題は、作者自身が日本文字をもって書き下した通りのものを採用しました。つまりそれらは私たちの中国の友人郭成章（KO TSCHING DSCHANG）が書いたのを石版に刷ったものです。著者名および巻数も記載しておきました。書籍の記載、解説は、最も親愛なる友人ヨハン・J・ホフマン博士（Dr. J. HOFFMANN）が記述しました。

明瞭にしかも極めて簡潔にこれらを解明することを意図しました。

書籍が中国のものが原本であり、それがそのまま日本で翻刻された場合、その表題は中国語読みのままにし、それはイタリック体で印刷しておきました（第11番参照）。

また本来、中国文字で表わされた表題が、しばしば日本の習慣に従って、日本語にしなければならないことがありましたが、この場合には表題にできるだけ正確な翻訳を加えました。ただ内容が余り判然としないと思われる場合、あるいはなにか必要な理解を省略すべきでないと思われた場合には、これに少々解説を加えておきました。

　　　　ライデン市付近の別荘にて誌す
　　　　　1845年2月　フォン・シーボルト（DE SIEBOLD）

目　次

第Ⅰ部　百科辞典 …………………………………………………………1—12
第Ⅱ部　歴史書と地理書
　　A．歴史
　　　　a．神話 ………………………………………………………13—15
　　　　b．歴史 ………………………………………………………16—27
　　　　c．年表 ………………………………………………………28—33
　　B．歴史地理 ………………………………………………………34—53
　　C．地図
　　　　a．一般地図 …………………………………………………54—59
　　　　b．地方地図 …………………………………………………60—91
　　D．地誌
　　　　a．京都地誌 …………………………………………………92—104
　　　　b．江戸地誌 …………………………………………………105—124
　　　　c．大坂地誌 …………………………………………………125—134
　　　　d．長崎地誌其他 ……………………………………………135—139
　　E．都市及び地方案内記 …………………………………………140—160
　　F．旅行記 …………………………………………………………161—173
　　G．植民地と租税を納める義務の国民についての地理書と歴史書 ……174—190
　　H．欧州の著者による地図で日本語に翻刻されたもの …………191—193
第Ⅲ部　自然科学書
　　A．一般博物学
　　　　a．中国書で日本にて再版されたもの ……………………194—206
　　　　b．和書 ………………………………………………………207—223
　　B．特殊自然科学
　　　　a．植物書、動物書 …………………………………………224—247
　　　　b．植物写生図、手稿 ………………………………………248—265
　　　　c．動物写生図、手稿 ………………………………………266—283
　　　　d．雑論 ………………………………………………………284—293
第Ⅳ部　文法書と辞書

日本語訳（目次）

      A．辞書
          a．漢和辞書 …………………………………………294—300
          b．和漢辞書 …………………………………………301—304
          c．同義語辞書 ………………………………………305—306
          d．日本古語辞書 ……………………………………307—308
          e．和蘭辞書
                       ………………………………………324—327
          f．蘭和辞書
      B．語彙
          a．アイヌ語 …………………………………………328—329
          b．高麗語 ……………………………………………330—332
          c．サンスクリット …………………………………333—334
          d．満州語 ……………………………………………335—336
      C．文法書 ………………………………………………309—323

第Ⅴ部　神学書と道徳書
      A．仏教……………………………………337—343、335b—336b
      B．神道………………………………………………337b—340b
      C．道徳教訓書；小説と雑書 ………………341b—343b、344—372

第Ⅵ部　詩
      A．劇詩…………………………………………………373—382
      B．歌〔和歌〕という叙情詩…………………………383—400
      C．俳諧という歌 ………………………………………401—406
      D．漢詩…………………………………………………407—410

第Ⅶ部　国民と諸制度
      A．風習と習慣 …………………………………………411—421
      B．都市・国家組織と行政 ……………………………422—427
      C．政治…………………………………………………428—431
      D．軍事…………………………………………………434—437
      E．建築…………………………………………………432—443

第Ⅷ部　経済書
      A．農業…………………………………………………438—448
      B．商工…………………………………………………449—472

第Ⅸ部　貨幣書……………………………………………………473—485

第Ⅹ部　医学書と薬学書…………………………………………486—499

第XI部　木版図
　　A. 絵画指南書 ……………………………………………………………500—505
　　B. 有名な絵画の木版複製
　　　　a. 中国 ……………………………………………………………506—512
　　　　b. 日本 ……………………………………………………………513—562
　　C. 絵画書
　　　　a. 歴史画書 ………………………………………………………563—573
　　　　b. 風景と建築図 …………………………………………………574—577
　　　　c. 服飾図 …………………………………………………………578—594

第Ⅰ部　百科辞典

1. **和漢三才図会**（わかんさんさいずえ　Wa Kan san sai dsu e、［中国語 *Hô Han san ts'ai tû hoei*］）。つまり日本人と中国人の三原理（天、地、人）を、著者〔寺〕島良安（*Simajosi Ankô*）〔てらしまりょうあん〕によって図解したもの。105巻80冊8折判1714年刊。本書は中国・日本大百科辞典として称されるを常とする。分類はアベル・レミューザ（*Abel Remusat*）が検した。第11巻手稿の注・抜粋を見よ。

2. **頭書増補 訓蒙図彙**（かしらがき、ぞうほ、きんもうずい　Kasira gaki, zo-bo, Kin mô dsu i）。頁上部（欄）に挿絵の説明をした啓蒙的概略図辞典。21巻8折判1661年刊。巻2、3、4で教唆された作品は図像で飾られた入門書であると分かる。自然、生活術に関するすべての図画がそこにあり、また事物の利用、起源について知る必要があるすべてについて簡単に解説されている。中国人同様、日本人もこの種の書籍を利用する習慣があり、それによって入門書は事物の共通知識を得ている。

3. **頭書増補 訓蒙図彙大成**（かしらがき、ぞうほ、きんもうずいたいせい　Kasira gaki, zo bo, Kin mô dsu i dai sei）。つまり入門用簡略図大成辞典。21巻9冊8折判。前述書の再増補版。

4. **唐土訓蒙図彙**（もろこしきんもうずい　Morokosi kin-mô dsu i）。入門用に著書平住専庵（*Firazumi Senan*）によって集められた、中国の事物の図説。京都、1719年、14巻10冊8折判。

5. **玉海節用字林蔵**（きょくかいせつようじりんぞう　Kjok-kai sets-jô zi-rin zô）。つまり貴重な事物の海、あるいは極めて必要な文書を適切に収集した文庫。1789年、3冊4折判、図入り。この百科辞典では、日本語でも「タマノウミホドヨクモチユルマサナノハヤシノクラ」（Tamano umi fodo joku motsijuru asanano fajasino kura）と添えてあり歴史、地理、文化生活に関する多様な文献を見るだろう。付・日本語彙は第3巻に見られる。

＋6．〔文化補刻〕**万海節用字福蔵**（まんかいせつようじふくぞう　Man-kai sets-jô zi fuk-zô）。つまり極めて必要な文献の何万倍もの海または蔵。本書は文化13年（1817）1冊刊、前述書に図を付す。

＋7．〔新撰増益〕**都会節用百家通**（とかいせつようひゃっかつう　To-kwai sets-jô fjak-ka tsû）。人々の全階層用に書かれた語彙をもつ百科辞典。第一の都市（都、江戸、大坂）の書物仲間と手配して、1801年に初版刊。1819年再版。No.5、6で言及した書籍と大差はない。

＊8．〔増字百倍〕**万宝節用富貴蔵**（まんぽうせつようふうきぞう　Man-bô sets-jo fu-ki zô）。知る必要ある全貴重事の豊富で明確な文庫。「広益実用字林」つまり、日用文献の増大した森という表題の日本語彙に、図入りの百科辞典。1788年初版、1811年再版。1冊、4折判。

＋9．〔増字〕**倭漢節用無雙囊**（わかんせつようむそうぶくろ　Wa-Kan sets-jô mu-sô bukuro）。つまり比類のない袋であり、そこには日本人と中国人の最も必要としている事物の知識が入れてある。1799年、1冊。

10．**博物筌**（はくぶつせん　Fak buts zen）。つまり事物の広いかたまり。蘭斎山崎右衛門（*Lanzai Jamasaki Ujemon*）著の簡潔な日本語百科辞典。1768年、1冊。351葉におよぶ、小8折判。著作資料は、日本の五十音順によって13章に類別されているが、説明は漢字をまじえた日本語でなされている。

＋11．**彙刻書目**（*Wei kʻe schû mû*〔いこくしょもく〕）。中国の満州下で活字に刷られた書目。嘉慶4年（1799）、顧修郎（*Kû sieû lo*）〔顧修〕によって発行されたが、日本では新たに1818年に10冊、8折小型判で模刻刊行された。

12．〔増補〕**和漢書画一覧**（わかんしょがいちらん　Wa-Kan sjo kwa itsi ran）。つまり中国人同様、日本人作者と画家に注目している。大坂1786年、1冊、12折判の変型。1821年5版。本小冊子では、ただ単に書法、画法で、すぐれた人が褒められているだけでなく、有名な医家、仏僧も同等で、著者は彼らの祖先と生涯について短評している。

第Ⅱ部　歴史書と地理書

A．歴史

a．神話

13．**神代紀葦牙**（かみよぶみあしかび　Kami-jo-bumi asikabi〔じんだいきあしかび〕）。つまり葦の芽、あるいは年代の始まりであり、そこで神の業績が語られている。3冊8折判。日本人神職栗田土満（*Kurida Toman*）は多様な神話的著作の中に知るにふさわしいものを見出し、本

書に採り入れ、注意して明らかにした。彼は文化8年（1811）自序を記した。

14. **神代正語**（かみよのまさこと　Kami jono masa koto）。つまり神々の誕生についての真実。伊勢国の神宮の神職本居宣長（*Motoworino Noringa*）は真理を告げ知らせた。1789年、3冊、8折判。

15. **古史系図**（こしけいず　ko si-kei dsu）。古系図（史伝）。平〔田〕篤胤（*Tairano Atsutane*）、1815年、1冊、8折判。

b. 歴史

16. **日本王代一覧**（にっぽんおうだいいちらん　Nippon wô-dai itsi-ran）。つまり日本の王家の系図一覧。仏僧春齋林恕（*Sjunzai Rinsjo*）〔林春斎〕書、1652年。大坂、1795年版、10冊、8折判。

+17. **日本書紀**（やまとふみ、または　にほんしょき　Jamato fumi, Nippon sjoki）。紀元前661年から紀元後696年までの日本の年代。天武天皇（*imperatoris Tenmu*）の臣下太朝臣安万侶（*Ohu Ason Amaro*）〔おおのあそんやすまろ〕が漢文で書き上げて、720年元正天皇（*imperatori Gensio*）に献上した。ところで1228年に初めて活字に記録された。本著作の見本は1709年に著名なV・O・フィッセルによって、新たな活字に書き留められたものがもたらされた。30巻15冊、8折判。先行2巻では、日本神話について記されている。

18. **和漢年契**（わかんねんけい　Wa-Kan nen-kei [*Hó-Hán nién-k'i*]）。日中用語索引、芦屋山人（*Asija Jamabito*）〔高安芦屋〕著。京都、1797年、1冊、8折判。本書の日本史の関係箇所を、私たちは更に活版で書き留められた「日本蔵書」（Bibliothecae Japonicae）にドイツ語訳を付して挿入した。本書は「和年契」（*Wa nen kei*）、または「日本年代記」（Annelcs japonici）と題されている。

+19. **掌中和漢年契**（しょうちゅうわかんねんけい　Sjô-tsiu Wa-Kan nen kei）。前掲書の掌中型で、その中に日本と中国の天皇、帝王、両国で使われた年号が列挙されている。付・史実索引。1801年、1冊、12折判。

20. **和年代皇紀絵章**（やまとねんだいこうきえしょう　Jamato nen-dai kwô-ki kwai-sjô）。天皇家用の図絵で表わされた日本年代記、3巻1冊。887年までの簡潔な天皇史を平仮名といわれる文字で書かれたものを含む。

+21. **太平記**（たいへいき　Dai-fei ki）。（取り戻された）平和の歴史、または1320年から1393年に至る戦記について。神功皇后（*imperatrice Zingu*）による高麗侵攻戦と、蒙古王忽必烈汗（*imperatoris Mongolici Kublaikhan*）の1281年の日本への不幸な攻撃の二つの戦役についての章が加わっている。年代記「日本王代一覧」（にっぽんおうだいいちらん　Nippon wôdai itsi ran）でも同じ書き方。1631年、40巻39冊8折判。

+22. 甲陽軍鑑（こうようぐんかん　Kô-jô gun kan）。甲斐国（＊）の軍の鏡、かんがみる手本。あるいは甲斐国の首領武田信玄（Takeda Singen）によって信濃・諏訪・越後・駿河などの国の首領に対してなされた戦、つまり1535年から豊臣秀吉（Tojotomi Fidejosi）が天下をとるに至る1586年までの戦について。京都、1659年刊、20巻18冊8折判。本書が書かれている文字は草字と平仮名といわれている簡略字体である。

（＊）甲斐あるいは甲州地方の歌人には甲陽、一般には府中と云われている都市。

+23. 平家物語（へいけものがたり　Fei-ke monogatari）。平家または平（たいら）の王族史。1710年刊、12巻、付・画。平仮名文字で書かれた書。平家物語は平氏一族の滅亡（1186）後、信濃の前の国司〔信濃前司（しなののぜんじ）〕行長（ゆきなが）（Jukinaga）によって記された、大変有名な日本の長文の叙事詩である。その当時生仏（しょうぶつ）（Seô buts）という名の盲目の吟誦叙事詩人は、この叙事詩を憶えて公開広場で吟誦した。

+24. 島原記（しまばらき　Simabaraki）。島原の乱、あるいは1637〜1639年の島原でのキリシタンの反乱と破滅についての歴史。自ら関係した日本の幕府軍のある武将が書いた。3冊8折判。本書は平仮名文字で書かれている。

25. 本朝国郡建置沿革図説（ほんちょうこくぐんけんちえんかくずせつ　Hon-tsjô kok-gun ken-tsi jen-kak dsu-sets）。一斎佐藤（Itsi sai Satô）〔佐藤一斎〕が明らかにした日本国叙述、あるいは諸時代の多様な領地区分。江戸、1823年、1冊、4折判。

26. 大日本太平記名将武勇競（だいにっぽんたいへいきめいしょうぶゆうくらべ　Dai Nippon Dai-fei-ki mei-sjô bu-jû kurabe）。「太平記」（Dai fei ki, №21）で言及されている名将・武勇者たちは別々に説かれている。

27. 大日本知仁名将勇士鑑（だいにほんちじんめいしょうゆうしかがみ　Dai Nippon tsi-zin mei sjô jû si kagami）。知と仁で大きな名誉を残した日本国の名将・勇士たちの鏡（手本）。

c. 年表

28. 甲子循環図（かつしじゅんかんず　Katsu-si zjun kwan dsu）。記述された60周期の循環、あるいは移動するその周期によってその軌道を構成し、同数の周期で外界に相応する60の周期20の循環。それらによって年々の継承は、日本の時代に従って名（年号）が当てられている。事柄をそのように設定して、著者観嶽主人（Kwan gjok siu nin）は材料を読者に用意し、その多様な作業によって、時の短い間隔で計算できるようにしている。京都、1820年。

29. 年代記（ねんだいき　Nen-dai Ki）。年代記述。私たちが上述した同じ説明で記した年表は、日本の青銅図表の試みとなっている。1824年刊。

+30. 紀年指掌（きねんししょう　Ki nen si sjô）。紀元年数のしるしのため、掌中に示されたような年数。しかし日本の年表は、それゆえ文政4年で記されている。

31. **和漢年歴箋**（わかんねんれきせん　Wa-Kan nen reki zen）。須原茂兵衛（*Suvara Movei*）による日本・中国年表の小冊子。日本と中国の帝王名、年号が簡潔に見られ、いくつかの歴史知識を付してある。日本領土の簡単な記述と、将軍たちの考察が続き、天文学・占星術・暦・系図についても省略されていない。江戸、1823年、1冊、12折判。

32. **万宝二面鑑**（まんぽうにめんかがみ　Man-bô ni-men kagami）。貴重事項の両面刷鑑手本。一般用全種類の注記を備えた2折判1枚。

33. **万歴両面鑑**（まんれきりょうめんかがみ　Man-reki rjô-men kagami）。つまり多数の知識事項の両面刷鑑手本。前掲の「万宝二面鑑」とは少し違った2折判1枚。大坂、1825年、塩屋義助（*Sivoja Kisuke*）刊。

B. 歴史地理

34. **大和名所図会**（やまとめいしょずえ　Jamato mei-sjô dsu-e）。つまり著者は佩蘭斎（*Fulan-zai*）、またの名は秋里籬島（*Akizato Ritô*）であり、彼は五畿内地方全域を記し、またその歴史―地誌書を図で飾った。それらは名所・社寺・遺跡を大変熟練した絵で描いたものを示している。本書の絵師は竹原春朝斎（*Takebara Sjun tsjô zai*）である。京都、1800年刊、7冊、8折判。

35. **河内名所図会**（かわちめいしょずえ　Kwatsi mei-sjo dsu-e）。河内国の地誌。秋里籬島（*Akizato Ritô*）著、丹羽桃渓（*Tanba-no Tôkei*）〔にわとうけい〕画。1801年、6冊、8折判。

36. **和泉名所図会**（いずみめいしょずえ　Idsumi mei-sjo dsu-e）。和泉国地誌。秋里籬島（*Akizato Ritô*）著、竹原春朝斎（*Takebara Sjun tsjô zai*）画、1769年刊、4冊、8折判。

37. **摂陽群談**（せつようぐんだん　Setsu-jô gun-tan）。つまり大坂の談話。著者岡田陸助（*Okada Roksuke*）が摂津国をもっと広く豊かに記述し、画で明らかにした。1717年刊、17冊。

38. **摂津名所図会**（せっつめいしょずえ　Setsu mei-sjo dsu-e）。摂津国地誌。秋里籬島（*Akizato Ritô*）著、1794年、16冊、8折判。第1巻。

39. **東海道名所図会**（とうかいどうめいしょずえ　Tô-kai-dô mei-sjo dsu-e）。東海道地方地誌。その諸国を通る道は、都から江戸市までである。秋里籬島（*Akizato Ritô*）著。1797年、6冊、8折判。

40. **武蔵野話**（むさしのばなし　Musasino banasi）。つまり武蔵国を見ている。同国所沢市民〔斉藤〕鶴磯先生（*Kwakki Sensei*）著。1816年、4冊、8折判。

41. **近江名所図会**（おうみめいしょずえ　Omi mei-sjo dsu-e）。近江国地誌。秋里籬島（*Akizato Ritô*）著。付・画。1815年、4冊、8折判。

42. **木曽路名所図会**（きそじめいしょずえ　Kisodsi mei-sjo dsu-e）。木曾路（*）地方の地誌。秋里籬島（*Akizato Ritô*）著。付・一人の僧〔西村〕法橋中和（*Fôkiô Tsiuwa*）によって描かれ

た画。1805年、6冊、内第1巻欠。

　　　（＊）木曾路の名を、日本人は上野国から木曾川谷へ川岸を通って美濃国へ至る街道に与えた。

43. 紀伊国名所図会（きいのくにめいしょずえ　Kiino kuni mei-sjo dsu-e）。紀伊国地誌。秋里籬島（*Akizato Ritô*）著。1812年、5冊、8折判。

44. 播磨名所巡覧図会（はりまめいしょじゅんらんずえ　Halima mei-sjo sjun-ran-dsu e）。よく播磨国を旅なれている者たちが見物している名所と各地が、秋里籬島（*Akizato Ritô*）によって記され、概要が述べられている。1812年、5冊、8折判。

45. 長崎行役日記（ながさきぎょうやくにっき　Nagasaki gjô-jak nitsi-ki〔ながさきこうえきにっき〕）。1769年に常陸国から長崎市へ派遣された公務日記。1805年刊、1冊、8折判。著者〔長久保〕赤水先生（*Seki sui Sensei*）または玄珠（*Gensju*）は水戸藩の藩主の侍講であった。彼は多くの地理書や旅行記を書き、またバタヴィアから伝えられた地図を日本語で発行し、その著作の索引が本書に付け加えられている。

46. 筑紫紀行（ちくしきこう　Tsikusi ki-kô）。筑紫（＋）地方への旅行記、あるいは著名な菱屋平七（*Fisija Feisitsi*）の日記。彼は尾張国の首都名古屋から長崎へ来たとき、記憶にふさわしい起ったことのすべてを冗長な言葉で記し、帰宅して1802年、10冊、8折判で公刊した。

　　　（＋）九州西部は昔は筑紫という名をもっていた。

47. 〔諸国奇談〕西遊記（さいゆうき　Sai-ju ki）。西国（近畿から西の諸国）旅行記、5冊。鎌倉の医者　橘　南谿子（*Tatsi bana Nan kei si*）、1794刊。

48. 〔同〕東遊記（とうゆうき　Tô-ju ki）。東国（都から東の諸国）旅行記、5冊。著者同前。

49. 〔同〕南遊記（なんゆうき　Nan-ju ki）。南海道旅行記、5冊（その第1冊だけあり）。著者は同じく橘南谿子（*Tatsi bana Nan kei si*）。彼は北国（信濃・北陸・奥羽）旅行記5冊を書いたとき、日本国全国をも周知して、その著作の表題に諸国畸談（Sjo kok kei tan）（中国畸談 Tschu kuē ki tan）、つまり全国のまれな記憶と名づけた。

50. 防長二州之記（ぼうちょうにしゅうのき　Wô Tsjô ni siu no ki）。防州（周防）国と長州国または長門国について。写本。

51. 山陵志（さんりょうし　San rjô si）。天皇（*Mikadones*）が埋葬されている墓の記念物。著者は蒲生秀実（*Kamo-u Fidesane*）。江戸1822年、2巻1冊、8折判。

52. 古山陵之図（こさんりょうのず　Ko san-rjôno dsu-e）。天皇（*Mikadones*）が埋葬されている古代墳墓図。写本。

53. 諸国経緯郡城数附（しょこくたてよこきこと；ごほりしろのかずつく　Sjo kok tate-jokoki koto; gohori sirono kazu tsuku〔しょこくけいいぐんじょうすうづけ〕）。君侯の諸国の天文学者によって観測された日本各国の経度と緯度。付・諸都市の濠と防・堡塁の数。1冊、8折判、写

本。

C. 地図

a. 一般地図

54. 大日本細見指掌全図（だいにっぽんさいけんししょうぜんず　Dai Nippon sai-ken si-sjô zen-dsu）。大日本国を幾何学的小階段状にし、入念に記述したもの。鳥飼洞斎（*Torikavi Tô zai*）が補完した。非常な経験者橘南谿子（*Tatsibana Nan keisi*）（№47 参照）が校閲した。表は文化〔5 年〕（1808 年）、新たに書き留められた。

55. 改正日本図（かいせいにっぽんず　Kai-sei Nippon dsu）。改正された日本国の記述。1812 年刊。

56. 改正日本輿地路程全図（かいせいにっぽんよちろていぜんず　Kai-sei Nippon jo-dsi-ro-tei zen-dsu）。改正された日本国記述。街道では、場所（地点）の相互距離が示されている。水戸藩主の侍講、その名は〔長久保〕玄珠子王（*Gensiu siwô*）（№45 参照）撰。1812 年。

57. 新板日本国大絵図（しんばん、にっぽんこくおおえず　Sin ban, Nippon-kok oho je-dsu）。日本国の新しい絵図。1744 年刊。

58. 日本辺界略図（にっぽんへんかいりゃくず　Nippon fen-kai rjak-dsu）。日本国とその周辺界の銅板小絵図。

59. 九州之図（きゅうしゅうのず　Kiusiuno dsu）。地理上の九州島記述。長崎、1822 年。

b. 地方地図

60. 山城国絵図（やましろのくにえず　Jamasirono kuni je dsu）。山城国地図、手稿。この地方地図では、手稿絵図が確かに大いに評価されるべきである。その寸法は、日本の里程表がフランスの 15 cm（quindecim mensurae）に相応するようにされているためである。

61. 大和国絵図（やまとのくにえず　Jamátono kuni je dsu）。大和国地図、手稿。

62. 大和国細見絵図（やまとのくにさいけんえず　Jamátono kuni sai-ken je-dsu）。大和国地図。中村敢耳斎（*Nakamura Kan zi sai*）編。1775 年。

63. 河内国細見小図（かわちのくにさいけんしょうず　Kawátsino kuni sai ken sjo dsu）。小河内国の地図。著者丹羽桃渓（*Niva Tokei*）。1776 年刊、1801 年再版。

64. 河内国絵図（かわちのくにえず　Kawátsino kuni je-dsu）。河内国地図、手稿。

65. 和泉国大絵図（いずみのくにおおえず　Idsumino kuni oho je-dsu）。和泉国地図。竹原春朝斎（*Takebara Sjun tsjô sai*）編、1769 年以前。

日本語訳（Ⅱ歴史書と地理書）

66. 和泉国絵図（いずみのくにえず Idsumino kuni je dsu）。和泉国地図、手稿。

67. 摂津国名所大絵図（せっつのくにめいしょおおえず Setsno kuni mei-sjo oho je dsu）。大摂津国の地図。

68. 志摩国絵図（しまのくにえず Simano kuni je dsu）。志摩国地図、手稿。

69. 尾張国絵図（おわりのくにえず Owarino kuni je dsu）。尾張国地図、2表。手稿。

70. 参河国絵図（みかわのくにえず Mikawano kuni je dsu）。三河国地図、手稿。

71. 阿波国絵図（あわのくにえず Awano kuni je dsu）。阿波国地図、手稿。

72. 武江略図（むさしのりゃくず Musasino rjak-dsu）。小武蔵国地図。岩崎常正（*Iwasaki Tsunemasa*）編。江戸、1824年。

73. 近江国大絵図（おうみのくにおおえず Ômino kuni oho-jedsu）。大近江国地図。著者山下重政（*Jamasita Sigemasa*）。大坂、1742年。1824年再版。

74. 近江国絵図（おうみのくにえず Omino kuni jedsu）。近江国地図、一覧表1対、手稿。

75. 美作〔濃〕（＊）国絵図（みまさかのくにえず Mimasakano kuni jedsu）。美作国地図、手稿。

（＊）例自体では、誤って美濃国の表題が記されている。

76. 能登国絵図（のとのくにえず Notono kuni jedsu）。能登国地図、手稿。

77. 越後国絵図（えちごのくにえず Jetsigono kuni jedsu）。越後国地図。

78. 佐渡国絵図（さどのくにえず Sadono kuni jedsu）。佐渡国地図。

79. 丹波国絵図（たんばのくにえず Tanbano kuni jedsu）。丹波国地図。矢野貞利（*Jano Sadatosi*）著。京都1799年。

80. 丹後国絵図（たんごのくにえず Tangono kuni jedsu）。丹後国地図。斎藤甚左衛門（*Saito Sin sajemon*）著、浅野弥兵衛（*Asano Javei*）刊。大坂、1817年。

81. 丹後国絵図（たんごのくにえず Tangono kuni jedsu）。丹後国地図、手稿。

82. 但馬国絵図（たじまのくにえず Tatsimano kuni jedsu）。但馬国地図、1782年。

83. 伯耆国絵図（ほうきのくにえず Fokino kuni jedsu）。伯耆国地図。

84. 石見国絵図（いわみのくにえず Iwamino kuni jedsu）。石見国地図、3表、手稿。

85. 隠岐国絵図（おきのくにえず Okino kuni jedsu）。隠岐（島）国地図、手稿。

86. 因幡国絵図（いなばのくにえず Inabano kuni jedsu）。因幡国地図、手稿。

87. 播磨国絵図（はりまのくにえず Halimano kuni jedsu）。播磨国地図、手稿。

88. 播磨国大絵図（はりまのくにおおえず Halimano kuni oho jedsu）。大播磨国地図。河内屋儀助（*Kawatsi ja Gisuke*）刊。大坂、1749年。

89. 備前国絵図（びぜんのくにえず Bizenno kuni jedsu）。備前国地図、手稿。

90. 備中国絵図（びっちゅうのくにえず Bitsiuno kuni jedsu）。備中国地図、手稿。

91. **淡路国絵図**（あわじのくにえず　Awadsino kuni jedsu）。淡路国地図、手稿。

91b. J.C. ブロムホフ勲爵士商館長（J.C. Blomhoff）によって追加箇所に加えられた日本国一覧を、私は写本と関連させています。それらはハーグ王立博物館に保存されていて、手本は日本人の手で急いで、より小さい縮尺にされていると思われます。

D. 地誌

a. 京都地誌

92. **都名所図会**（みやこめいしょずえ　Mijako mei sjo dsu e）。皇居がある都の記念物の記述。著者秋里籬島（Akizato Ritô）、竹原春朝斎（Takebara Sjun tsjô sai）画、1780年刊、11冊、8折判。

93. **都林泉名勝図会**（みやこりんせんめいしょうずえ　Mijako rin sen mei sjo dsu e）。京都を飾っている神社仏閣・泉水池・記念行事の記述。著者秋里籬島（Akizato Ritô）。付・諸名家の記述。1798年、5冊、8折判。

94. **京之水**（きょうみず　Kjô midsu〔きょうのみず〕）。つまり都の庭園または泉水・池。都の描写。著書秋里舜福（Akizato Sjunfuk）。1791年刊、2冊。

第1巻：内裏という名の宮廷の描写。

第2巻：東の部分（洛陽 Rak-jô）と西の部分（長安 Tsjō-an）に分けられた都の記述。

95. 〔天明再板〕**京都めぐり**（きょうとめぐり　Kjôto meguri）。つまり京都の散歩。著者貝原篤信（Kaibara Toksin）。本書は1784年に文字で刷られ、1815年再版、8折判。この書物が作られている理由は、帝の都を訪れる者が、都自体あるいは近郊地を見物するにふさわしいすべてに関して、都の街を17箇所、散歩に案内されるためであった。

96. **都寺社全図**（みやこじしゃぜんず　Mijako si-sja zen-dsu）。都の街を飾っている仏寺・神社の絵図。安田吉兵衛（Jasida Kitsifei）。1730年、4冊。

97. **増補絵入 都名所車**（ぞうほえいり、みやこめいしょくるま　Zô-bô je-ire, Mijako mei-sjo kuruma）。貝原篤信（Kaibara Toksin）〔かいばらあつのぶ〕〔著〕。都の記念物の乗り物巡り、あるいは都の街の地誌の絵入増補版。1714年、1冊。御所や聖なる諸寺院の記述はより一層詳細で、それに聖なる宗教行事が通例挙行される祭事暦が書きそえてある。街の内外にある街路の索引が先付になっている。

98. 〔新撰増補〕**京大絵図**（みやこおおえず　Mijako oho je-dsu）。京都の街と付近の名所案内。1666年初版、1枚大2折判。1741年、2枚2折判。その1枚は著名なJ.C. ブロムホフ（J. C. Blomhoff）勲爵士の書籍中に保存され、もう一枚はハーグの王立博物館に掛けられている。

99. 〔文化改正〕京都指掌図（きょうとししょうのず　Kjôto si-sjô no dsu）。天皇の都市（都 Mijako）の詳細図。1812 年改正版、1 枚 2 折判。

100a. 〔文化改正〕新増細見京絵図（しんぞうさいけんきょうのえず　Sin-zô sai-ken Kjôno jedsu）。天皇の都市の新しく増補された詳細図。1811 年刊、活字再版 1813 年、1 枚 2 折判。

100b. 懐宝京絵図（かいほうきょうのえず　Kwai bô Kjôno jedsu）。より小さい大きさにまとめられた、懐にしまっておかれる京の都の絵図。1774 年刊。都の内外にある神社、仏閣、諸記念物の顕著な場所、遺跡を見られるであろう。

101. 花洛一覧図（からくいちらんず　Kwa-rak itsi-ran dsu）。都の街の全景図。黄華山（*Wô kwa san*）画。風折政香（*Kazawori Masaka*）発行。京都、1809 年、1 枚 2 折判。

102. 新改 内裏図（しんかいだいりのず　Sin kai, Dairino dsu）。内裏の新改図。1817 年発行。1 枚 2 折判。

＊103. 新補京之図（しんぽ、きょうのず　Sin bô, Kjôno dsu）。都の街の新補図。1684 年発行。1 枚 2 折判。もしあなたが図表を広げて読むなら、別の表題「平安の都市（都 Mijako）の名所と近郊の新しく書き記された図が示されている」ということが提示されている。

104. 新板 比叡山延暦寺（しんぱん、ひえいさんえんりゃくじ　Sin fan, Fijei-san Jenraksi）。比叡山延暦寺とその周辺地の様子。大型 1 枚 2 折判。

b. 江戸地誌

105. 分間江戸大絵図（ぶんけんえどおおえず　Bun-ken Jedo oho jedsu）。大江戸の測定（量）は $\frac{1}{7,560}$ にされた絵図。なぜなら 1 分（日本の歩の 100 分の 1）が 12 間（日本の歩 $75\frac{6}{10}$）だからである。1732 年初版。1775 年と 1826 年版の見本もある、1 枚 2 つ折判。

106. 分間御江戸絵（ぶんけん、おんえどのえ　Bun-ken, won Jedo no je）。将軍の江戸の街の絵図は測量において、1 分が 30 間（$\frac{1}{18,900}$）に相当している。1804 年刊、1 枚の 2 折判。

107. 分間 懐宝御江戸絵図（ぶんけんかいほう、おんえどのえず　Bun-ken kwai-bô, won Jedono jedsu）。将軍の都市江戸の懐で、測量のために作成された、保管されるべき概略絵図。1825 年刊、2 折判 1 枚。

＊108. 再版 新改御江戸絵図（さいはんしんかい、おんえどのえず　Sai-fan sin-kai, won Jedo no jedsu）。将軍の都市江戸の新しく改められ、もう一度活字で書かれ、1797 年刊、2 折判 1 枚。

109. 文化改正 御江戸絵図（ぶんかかいせい、おんえどえず　Bun-kwa kai sei, won Jedo no jedsu）。文化年間（1804 年と続年）に作成された将軍の都市江戸の絵図。No. 108 の下方に記された表の版は新しい。

110. 再版 新改御江戸絵図（さいはん、しんかいおんえどのえず　Sai fan, Sin kai won Jedono jedsu）。将軍の都市の新しく改定された絵図。もう一度活字で書かれ 1804 年、1818 年刊、1 枚 2

折判。表は平仮名文字で書かれている。

+111. 文政改正 御江戸大絵図（ぶんせいかいせい、おんえどおおえず Bun-sei kai sei, won Jedo oho jedsu）。江戸の将軍の都市の大絵図。文政1818年と続く年に改正された。1枚2折判。表は片仮名文字で書かれる。

112. 北條氏康時代武州江戸絵図（ほうじょうのうじやすじだいぶしゅうえどのえず Fô-sjôno Udsijasu zidai Bu-siu Jedo no jedsu）。北條氏康（Fô-sjô no Udsi jasu）が領主時代（1540年–1561年）だった江戸の街の絵図。1804年刊。

113–120. 江戸の街の諸地域絵図。下谷浅草辺之図（したやあさくさかたのず Sita-ja Asagusa katano dsu〔したやあさくさへんのず〕）、下谷・浅草という名の地域の絵図。1767年。

114. 谷中本郷丸山小石川辺之図（やなかもとみまるやまおいしがわかたのず Janaka Motomi-marujama Woisigawa katanodsu〔やなかほんごうまるやまこいしかわへんのず〕）。小石川という名の絵図。1770年。

115. 駿河台小川町之図（するがだいおがわまちのず Suruga tai Wogawa matsino dsu）。駿河台小川町という名の地の絵図。

116. （東都）永【田】町之絵図（とうとながたまちのえず (Tôdo) Nagada matsino jedsu）。永田町という名の絵図。1759年。

117. 〔東都〕番町之絵図（ばんちょうのえず Ban tsjôno jedsu）。番町という名の地の絵図。1752年。

118. 浜町神田日本橋北之図（はまちょう、かんだ、にっぽんばしきたのず Fama-tsjo Kanda, Nippon-basi kita no dsu）。浜町、神田、日本橋北の地の図。1770年。

119. 芝愛宕下辺之図（しば、あたごしたかたのず Siba, Atago sita katano dsu〔しば、あたごしたへんのず〕）。芝、愛宕下の図。1766年。

120. 築地八丁堀日本橋南之図（つきじ、はっちょうほり、にっぽんばしみなみのず Tsuku dsi, Batsjô fori, Nipponbasi minami no dsu）。築地、八町堀、日本橋南の図。1775年。

121. 新板 御江戸名所独案内記（しんぱん、おんえどめいしょひとりあんないき Sin fan, won Jedo mei-sjo fitori annai ki）。将軍の都市江戸の名所の独案内者。新版1冊。

122 a. いろは分独案内 江戸町づくし（いろはわけひとりあんない、えどまちづくし Irofa wake fitori annai, Jedo matsi tsukusi）。いろは順江戸市案内索引。

b. 小冊子表記「細見（Sai ken）」。つまり細かい観察、あるいは吉原街で繁昌して性的女郎たちが通いなじんでいる限りのものを評価している報告。1826年。

c. 江戸市の状態についてのある評判、手稿。

123. 江戸御見附略図（えどおんみつけりゃくず Jedo won metsuke rjak dsu）。江戸市の将軍の見附が簡単に記されている。

124. **江戸御城内御住屋之図**（えどごじょうないごすまいのず Jedo go sjô nai go sumaino dsu)。江戸の将軍の城内の住居の図。

c. 大坂地誌

125. **自上古到今世難波大坂十二図**（いにしえよりいまよまでなにわおおさかじゅうにず Ini-sive jori imajomade Naniva Ohsaka zjū ni dsu)。上古と近代の大坂市の状態を示している12表の地誌、手稿。

＋*126. **増修 大坂指掌図**（ぞうしん、おおさかししょうず Zô-sin, Ohosaka si sjô dsu〔ぞうしゅう、おおさかししょうず〕)。大坂市中を明白に示した図。付「隅田川 *Sumida gawa*」の絵図。図表は著者によって飾られている、1図表、1794年。市と測量は1分（歩の100分の1）は24間（$151\frac{2}{10}$歩）に相当する。付・事項索引。それらを大坂市中が示しており、また同じく主要な橋とその寸法も記している。

127. **新板増補 大坂之図**（しんばんぞうほ、おおさかのず Sin-ban zô-bô, Ohosakano dsu)。新たに刷られ増補された大坂市中の地誌図表。1787年。

*128. **増修改正 摂州大坂地図**（ぞうしゅうかいせい、せっしゅうおおさかちず Zo-siu kai-sei, Setsiu Ohosaka dsino dsu)。摂津国の首府大坂市の地誌の増修改正版。大坂市のこの図は1778年、将軍の命によって大地図にされ、1807年完成された。

129. **文政新改 摂州大坂全図**（ぶんせいしんかい、せっしゅうおおさかぜんず Bun-sei sin kai, Setsiu Ohosakano zen dsu)。文政8年（1825）新版にされ、全数を完成させた大坂市地誌。例は前述の表を半分小さくされている。それゆえ歩の100分の1（1分）は$75\frac{6}{10}$または12間に相当する。

130. **大坂町鑑**（おおさかまちかがみ Ohosaka matsi kagami)。大坂の道路の手本、または、あいうえお順索引。1756年刊、極小冊子。

131. **大坂城之図**（おおさかしろのず Ohosaka siro no dsu〔おおさかじょうのず〕)。a.〔軍攻之図、安部之合戦之図〕：大坂城の2軍攻図、手稿。小図には場所の絵図が示されている。b. **大坂安部之合戦之図**（Ohosaka Abeno katsusen no dsu）大坂城合戦図2図、1615年。

132. **改正 一目千軒**（かいせい、ひとめせんげん Kai-sei, Fito-me sen-gen)。大坂の千軒の娯楽・名所一覧。1冊、改正版。

133. **寛政改正 みをつくし**（かんせいかいせい、みおつくし Kwan-sei kai-sei, Miwodsukusi)。大坂名所になっている寛政年間（1789年–1801年）の水路標（＊）。改正版、1冊。

（＊）「みおつくし」という語は、通行する船に、港へ安全な水路を示している立て杭のこと。

134　a. **繁花市中 大凡積胸算用**（〔おおさかまちじゅうおおよそつもりむねさんよう Ohosaka

matsi-tsiu Ohoso tsumori-mune san-jô)。大坂市が喜ぶ住民勘定。文政年代（1818年）より、1枚。

b. **大坂両替手形便覧**（おおさかりょうがえてがたべんらん　Ohosaka rjô-gave te-kata fen-ran)。大坂市で栄えている両替屋が示されている。

c. **大坂京都名物合角力**（おおさかみやこめいぶつあわせすもう　Ohosaka Mijako mei-buts awase sumô)。大坂市と京都の名所が表で比較されている。

d. **爪印**（つめしるし　Tsumesirusi〔つまじるし〕)。大坂市で繁昌している女性や女郎のしるし。1819年、1冊、12折判。

d. 長崎市地誌その他

135. **肥州長崎図**（ひしゅうながさきのず　Fisiu Nagasakino dsu)。肥前国長崎市地誌図。1778年版、1802年再版、1821年再々刊。

136. **播磨姫路之図**（はりまひめじのず　Halima Fimedsino dsu)。播磨国姫路市地図表、手稿。

137. **下総〔野〕国日光山之図**（しもうさのくにのにっこうさんのず　Simôsa kunino Nikwôsan-no dsu〔しもつけのくににっこうさんのず〕)。下総（*Shimôsa*）国日光山の地誌。

138. **日光御山総絵図**（にっこうおんさんそうのえず　Nikwô won-san sôno jedsu)。日光という名の将軍の総本山とそこに建立された〔東照〕宮の絵図。

139. **鎌倉勝概図**（かまくらしょうがいのず　Kamakura seô kaino dsu)。鎌倉の地の絵図。この地誌図表は、絵師秦檍丸（*Fata Kasimaru*）によって、鶴岡八幡宮とその地域の記述が1798年に画かれた。

E. 都市及び地方案内記

140. **日本名所之絵**（にっぽんめいしょのえ　Nippon mei-sjo no je)。日本名所絵図、または日本領土の景色を遠く離れて見せている絵図。江戸の絵師、蕙斎紹真（*Kunsai Seôsin*）〔けいさいつぐざね〕筆。

141. **東海道名所一覧**（とうかいどうめいしょいちらん　Tô-kai dô mei-sjo itsi ran)。東海道地方名所一覧。江戸の絵師達の中における重鎮の北斎（*Hoksai*）画。1818年。

142. **道中記〔東海道〕**（どうちゅうき　Tô-tsiu ki)。東海道旅行記、2冊。第1巻は京都から新井まで、第2巻は天竜川から江戸まで。それは見物に価するものを示している。

143. **和州吉野山名勝図**（わしゅうよしのやまめいしょうず　Wa siu Josino jama mei-sjo dsu)。吉野山という名の山地の名勝図。1713年刊。付・他の名勝図。

144. **安芸国厳島景**（あきのくにいつくしまけい　Akino kuni Itsukusima kei)。安芸国にある厳

島の景色。貝原篤信（*Kaibara Toksin*）〔かいばらあつのぶ〕説明。1789年刊。

145. 丹後国天橋立之図（たんごのくにあまのばしたてのず　Tangono kuni Amanobasi tateno dsu〔たんごのくにあまのはしだてのず〕）。丹後国天橋の橋から見える眺望。

146. 陸奥国塩釜松島図（みちのうくくにしおがままつしまのず　Mitsinôku kuni Sivokama Matsusimano dsu）〔むつのくにしおがままつしまのず〕。塩釜と松島の地からの海と島々の大変美しい眺め。1729年刊。前述の地は陸奥国の仙台市の近くにある。

147. 江戸隅田川両岸一覧図（えどすみだがわりょうがんいちらんず　Jedo Sumidagawa rjô-gan itsi ran dsu）。隅田川の水が江戸市を流れて海に注ぐ、両岸の光景。鶴岡蘆水（*Tsuruoka Rosui*）画、1781年、2冊。

148. 澱川両岸勝景図会（よどがわりょうがんしょうけいずえ　Jodogawa ryô-gan sjô-kei dsu-e）。淀川の両岸の光景。暁鐘成（*Keô sjô sei*）〔あかつきのかねなり〕画。1824年、2冊。

149. 名山図譜（めいざんずふ　Mei san dsu bu）。日本、蝦夷の名山の絵図。〔谷〕文晁（*Buntsjô*）筆。1804年、3冊、8折判。

150. 山水奇観（さんすいきかん　San-sui ki-kwan）。各地の珍しい風景。〔淵上〕旭江（*Gjokkô*）〔きょっこう〕著、江戸1800年、4冊。

151. 富士山図（ふじやまのず　Fusijama no dsu）。富士火山の様々な年の毎月の容姿、12景観。小林長周（*Kobajasi Tsjôsiu*）著、1822年、1冊。

152. 富士之景（ふじのけい　Fusino kei）。駿河国と相模国の各地からの富士山の九景。年の季節で四つの外観で変っているように、絹布の中に色彩で描かれた、富士山の四つの絵図が続いている。1冊、4折判。

153. 采草閑筆（さいそうかんひつ　Sai zô kan bits）。日本人、二宮熊木（*Ninomija Komaki*）の急ごしらえの多彩な、陰影をつけた遠近感によって描いた手稿。それらは桜島、阿蘇山、高千穂、種子島の展望を示している。

154. 紀伊山水景〔奇〕観（きいのさんすいけいかん　Kiino san-sui kei kwan）。紀伊国地方の少なからぬ山水の奇観、手稿。それらは主に橋本、和歌山港、和歌浦湾方面へ及んでいる。

155. 淡海八景図（おうみのはちけいず　Omino fatsikei dsu）。近江の湖の八つの風景。都の〔円山〕応受（*Wôsiu*）画、1面。

156. 播州明石舞子浜之図（ばんしゅうあかしまいこのはまのず　Fansiu Akasi Maikono famano dsu）。播磨国明石市近郊舞子浜海岸図。1面、木版。

157. 高野山細見絵図（こうやさんさいけんえず　Kôjasan sai ken jedsu）。紀伊国にある高野山図。橘保春（*Tatsibana Tô siun*）〔たちばなやすはる〕画、1813年。大きい木版色彩絵図表。

158. 紀州高野山金剛峯寺細見図（きしゅうこうやさんこんごうぶじさいけんず　Kisiu Kôjasan Kongô busi saiken dsu）。金剛峯寺という高野山寺の絵図。大坂の画人橘国雄（*Tatsibana Kuni-*

wô）図、1784年、木版、1面。

159. 四天王寺伽藍図（してんのうじがらんのず Si ten wô si Karanno dsu）。（大坂市近郊にある）四聖天の僧房に隣接している伽藍図。大坂の竹原信繁（Takebara sinfan）〔たけはらのぶしげ〕図。

160. 太宰府天満宮御境内之絵図（だざいふてんまんぐうおんけいだいのず Daisaifu Ten man gu won kei naino jedsu）。天満宮と付属地絵図。筑後国太宰府市神社に関している、1819年、木版、1面。

F. 旅行記

161. 東海道分間絵図（とうかいどうぶんけんえず Tôkaidô bun-ken jedsu）。京都から江戸へ行く東海道街道の、いわゆる次の宿場までなされた旅。1752年、1772年、1774年に版行された例がある。

162. 東海木曽両道中懐宝図鑑（とうかい、きそりょうどうちゅうかいほうずかん Tôkai, Kiso rjô-dô-tsiu kwai bô dsu kan）。東海道と木曾路で見物すべきものを懐中にしまっておくべき景色。1807年刊、1冊。

163. 大日本道中行程細見記（だいにっぽんどうちゅうこうていさいけんき Dai Nippon dô-tsiu kô-tei sai-ken ki）。日本の諸都市、土地間の行程が詳しく記されている。1804年刊、1冊。

164. 大日本道中行程指南車（だいにっぽんどうちゅうこうていしなんくるま Dai Nippon dô-tsiu kô-tei si-nan–kuruma〔だいにほんどうちゅうこうていしなんしゃ〕）。日本国の乗船の小箱、または場所間距離索引。1820年刊、1冊。

＊165. 大日本海陸通覧（だいにっぽんかいりくつうらん Dai Nippon kai riku tsû ran）。日本の陸地と海の行程（それゆえ松前から韓国の港釜山まで）が記されている。1804年刊、1冊。

166. 道中独案内（どうちゅうひとりあんない Dô-tsiu fitori an-nai）。一人旅の案内者、あるいは長崎から松前宿場までの公の旅程と、それらの間隔を示す地理表。1冊。

167. 西国順礼細見大全（さいこくじゅんれいさいけんたいぜん Sai-kok zjun-rei sai-ken dai sen）。信心のために巡礼するを常としている西国、あるいは四国の霊場が細かに示されている。1825年、1冊、付・地図。

168. 四国徧礼之図（しこくへんれいのず Si-kok ben-reino dsu）。霊場をめぐり歩く人々のために記された四国の徧路。1763年。

169. 四国徧礼之図（しこくへんれいのず Si-kok ben-reino dsu）。図表は前書と少し異なっている。

170. 日光駅路里数之表（にっこうえきろりすうのひょう Ni-kwô jeki-ro ri-sûno beô）。江戸か

ら日光山へ通じる街道と宿場の里程標の索引。江戸、1226 年、1 面。

171. **東海道駅路里数之表**（とうかいどうえきろりすうのひょう　Tô-kai-dô jeki ro-ri-sûno beô）。東海道の宿場と里程表の索引、手稿。

172. 増補 **日本汐路之記**（ぞうほにっぽんしおじのき　Zô-bô Nippon sivodsino ki）。日本の海路の記述。高田政度（*Takada Masanori*）著、1796 年、1 冊、12 折判。

173. **大坂川口ヨリ長崎迄舟路**（おおさかのかわぐちよりながさきまでのせんろ　Ohosakano gawa-kutsi jori Nagasaki madeno sen-ro）。大坂の川口から長崎市への船で行く旅の航路名が記されている。図表、手稿。

G. 植民地と租税を納める義務の国民についての地理書と歴史書

174. **三国通覧図記**（さんごくつうらんずき　San-kok tsu-ran dsu ki）。三国（つまり蝦夷、琉球、朝鮮）の描写。付・絵図と 4 地図。仙台市民林子平（*Fajasi Sivei*）著。1785 年、1 冊、手稿。

175. **蝦夷談筆記**（えぞだんひつき　Jezo tan fitsu ki）。蝦夷島について、日本人菅縄（*Sugano Jôfo*）〔松宮観山〕が書きつけた手稿、1710 年、1 冊。

+176. **蝦夷拾遺**（えぞしゅうい　Jezo sju wi）。蝦夷島紹介の補足。1 冊、手稿。

177. **蝦夷図**（えぞのず　Jezo no dsu）。日本の地理学者最上徳内（*Mogami Toknai*）の地図の手稿 5 枚、その 3 枚は蝦夷を、2 枚は樺太を示している。

178. **松前蝦夷之図**（まつまええぞのず　Matsumaë Jezo no dsu）。その首府は松前である、蝦夷島南部を示している地図、手稿。

179. **蝦夷海浜之景**（えぞかいひんのけい　Jezo kai bin no kei）。小樽から宗谷岬へ至る所を色彩で描いた、蝦夷の海岸風景、1 冊、手稿。

180. **唐太島**（からふとしま　Karafuto sima）。樺太島について、最も著名な地理学者最上徳内（*Mogami Toknai*）。1 冊、手稿。

181. **薩哈連島之図**（さはりんしまのず　Sāgalen sima no dsu）。最上徳内（*Mogami Toknai*）著。樺太島地図、手稿。

182. **黒竜江中之洲〔并天度〕**（こくりゅうこうちゅうしゅう　Kok-riu-kô tsiu-siu〔こくりゅうこうなかのすならびにてんど〕）。アムール川河口（つまり樺太の近く）に位置する土地を示す、緯度で記した地図。間宮林蔵（*Mamija Rinzô*）著、手稿。アムール川は、中国人からは黒竜江と言われている。

+183. **唐太島之図**（からふとしまのず　Karafuto simano dsu）。樺太島地図。

184. **琉球談**（りゅうきゅうだん　Liukiu dan）。琉球島についての森島中良（*Morisima Tsiurô*

談。1790年、1冊。

185. **朝鮮物語**（ちょうせんものがたり　Tsjôsen monogatari）。木村理右衛門（*Kimura Rijemon*）著、韓国史5冊、江戸、1750年刊。本書に述べられていることは、すでに "Nippon Archiv"〔日本古文書〕という書物の当該箇所中に報告されている。その書名は "Nachrichten über Kôrai, Japan's Bezüge mit Kôraischen Halbinsel und mit Schina"〔高麗についての報告：日本の朝鮮半島及び中国との関係〕。

186. **三才一貫図**（さんさいいっかんず　*Sân-ts'aí ĭ-kuân t'û*）。天・地・人の事柄のすべての知識に最もふさわしいことが一つの表にまとめてある。呂撫安世（*Lù-fù Ngân schî*）輯。彼は浙江省紹興府近くの新昌の別荘に住んでいた。

187. **万国大全図**（*Wàn-kuĕ tà ts'iuén t'û*〔ばんこくだいぜんず〕）。中国全土の完全な大地図。しかし地図は中国の隣接諸国である。1663年。

188. **歴代事跡図**（*Lĭ taí ssé –tsī t'û*〔れきだいじせきず〕）。つまり互いに継承している歴代の歴史上の事跡が図示されている。私が説明した表題は、中国の地図を目指している。それは1659年北京市で刊行され、1749年日本で新たに活字印刷されている。

189. **大清万年一統地理全図**（*Tà-Ts'ing wan-niên ĭt'ông tĭ-li ts'iuén t'û*〔だいしんまんねんいっとうちりぜんず〕）。地図は満州国全体を示している。

+190. **古今沿革地図**（*Kù-kin jên-kĕ tĭ-tû*〔ここんえんかくちず〕）。水戸の〔長久保〕赤水（*Akamidsu*）〔せきすい〕著。古代と現代の中国を示している地図13面。江戸1788年、1冊、4折判。

図表概略：表1：諸都市の陸海間距離を示す中国世界。表2：前2207年、夏王朝下の中国世界。表3：前1122年、周王朝下の中国世界。表4：孔子（*Contueii*）の史書 "*Tsch'ün tsieu*"〔春秋〕を示す中国世界。表5：戦国時代。表6：前256年-207年、秦王朝。表7：前漢王朝。表8：後漢王朝。表9：三国時代。表10：両〔東・西〕晋。表11：唐王朝。表12：宋・明王朝。表13：極東とインド群島の絵図。

H. 欧州の著者による地図で日本語に翻刻されたもの

191. **嗊蘭新訳地球全図**（おうらんしんえきちきゅうぜんず　O-lan sin-jeki tsi-kiu zen dsu〔おらんだしんやくちきゅうぜんず〕）。オランダの両半球領土図。水戸市の〔長久保〕赤水（*Akamidsu*）〔せきすい〕が日本語に訳し、註を付す。1769年、1冊、4折判。

192. **東察加之図**（カムチャッカのず　Kan-tsa-ka no dsu）。ロシア領カムチャッカの領土地図。最上徳内（*Mogami Toknai*）が日本語に訳した。

193. **北海**（ほっかい　Fō kai (Pē hai)）。ロシア領絵図、氷の海。最上徳内（*Mogami Toknai*）

が日本語に訳した。付：同著者の3冊の手稿。その中で蝦夷、樺太島等についての注記、ロシア国のそれも集められている。

第Ⅲ部　自然科学書

A．一般博物学

a．中国書で日本にて再版されたもの

194. **大観証類本草**（*Tà-kuon Tsching-lui pèn-ts'aô*〔たいかんしょうるいほんぞう〕）。本書はより正しい階層にまとめられ、中国の著者唐慎微（*T'ang Schin wi*）によって、いわゆる大観年代（1107年～1110年）に新たに作成された博物学書である。本書の概略を、すでにJ．クラプロート（*J. Klaproth*）はその著書 "*Verzeichniss der Chinesischen und Mandschuischen Bücher und Handschriften der K. Bibliothek zu Berlin*"（ベルリン王立図書館の中国語と満州語図書・手稿目録）の164頁に挿入した。私たちの図書は、江戸で活躍した医官の配慮により、新たに活字にして刊行された。1769年、31巻、または26巻。

195. 〔校正 **本草綱目**〕（*Historia naturalis*）〔ほんぞうこうもく〕。李時珍（*Li Schi tsching*）著による「本草綱目」（*Pen ts'aô kang mŭ*）という表題の博物学書は、前の16世紀に作られ、大変賢明な王世貞（*Wang Schi tschin*）が1596年に序言を付けて刊行した博物学書。1603年に中国で作られた版の別の見本があり、それは日本用に日本読みの適用が付され、52巻、25冊になっている。本書のより新しい日本語版は、「新（新しい）本草綱目」（*Sin Pèn-ts'aô kang-mŭ*）という表題であり、著明な van O．フィッセル（*v. O. Fisscher*）によって持参された。61巻より成る。

196. **本草滙**（*Pèn ts'aô hoèi*〔ほんぞうかい〕）。つまり薬物施す際の自然の道具または教え。中国人の佩蘭章宜（*Nièn ngô Li siën seng*）撰、郭佩蘭（*Kuō Fu lan*）刊、1666年。本書は日本で新たに活字に刷られ、日本語注記が付された。18冊、8折判。

前部8小冊子は、慣用とその療法についての処方について。第9、10、11、12小冊子は製造所の薬草について。第13小冊子は多様な穀物と青物について。第14小冊子は果実について。第15、16小冊子は樹木について。第17小冊子は昆虫について。第18小冊子は医療用に役立つ限りでの人体から取り出された材料や掘り出されたもの、水、火、土について。

197. **毛詩草木鳥獣虫魚疏**（もうしそうもくちょうじゅうちゅうぎょそ　*Môsi sô mok teo ziu gjô so,*〔*Maôschî ts'aô mŭ niaò scheù tsch'ûng jŭ sŭ*〕）。つまり「毛詩」（*Maôschî*）（すなわち動植物が称えられている詩）や「詩経」（*Schî-king*）が言っている、古代詩集成の中でなされている草木

鳥獣虫魚の説明。中国人の陸璣（Lǔ ki）筆。松下見林（Matsusita Kenrin）が更に活字刷りをし、日本語読みの注を付けた。1698年、1冊、8折判。

198. **毛詩陸氏草木疏図解**（もうし、りくしそうもくそずかい　Môsi, Liksi sô mok so dsu kai, [Maôschî, Lǔ-schî ts'aô-mū sū t'û kiai]）。中国詩の集成なる「毛詩」（Maôschî）の中で言及されている草木の記述。陸氏（Lǔ schî）または陸璣（Lǔ ki）によって例示された絵図。例示絵図は日本で更に活字に刷られ、淵在寛（Futsi Zai kwan）の配慮により江戸、1778年刊、5冊、8折判。彼は注記で本書を説明し、事物に日本名を付した。第5巻では品物、楽器、容器、軍旗、戦車などが述べられている。そして前述の毛詩（詩経）で祝われている戦争でのことが輝かしいとき、著者はその注釈で戦争や進軍の配置について付記している。

199. **毛詩品物図攷**（もうしひんぶつずこう　Môsi bin-buts dsu kô, [Maôschî p'in-wū t'û k'aô]）。つまり古代の毛詩で祝われていた品物が（草木鳥獣虫魚に）分けられ、図解して記述されている。大坂の岡元鳳（Oka Genfô）〔岡澹斎〕撰、1786年、3冊、8折判。
おかげんぽう

200. **毛詩名物図説**（Maôschî ming-wū t'ù jūe〔もうしめいぶつずせつ〕）。古代詩で祝されている名物が（鳥・獣・虫・魚・草・木に分けられ）、著者：中国人呉中〔蘇州市〕の徐鼎（Tschùng siû tìng）による図説、1771年、2冊。江戸で栄えていた医学所の配慮で再び活字刷りにして刊行された。1808年。
じょてい

201. **救荒本草**（Kieù-hoàng pen-ts'aò〔きゅうこうほんぞう〕）。つまり穀物などの年間収穫を救済すべき野菜。明王朝下の人王西楼（Tscheû-fàn Hièn wamg）編輯。姚可成（Jaô K'ò tsch-ing）補、吟味追加、1715年、9冊、8折判。

202. **食物本草**（Schīwū pen-ts'aò〔しょくもつほんぞう〕）。食用植物の記述。著者：東垣李杲（Tungjen Likaò）。彼は元朝下の人。明王朝期の銭允治（Ts'iën jùn tschi）校訂。日本発行1651年、2冊、8折判。

203. **通志昆虫草木略**（T'ûngtschi kuèntsch'ông ts'aòmū lió〔つうしこんちゅうそうもくりゃく〕）。中国の地の動物相・植物相の要約。宋朝期の鄭夾漈（Tsching kiā tsi）著。日本人小野蘭山（Wono Lanzan）が活字版再刊行、1785年、2冊、8折判。

204. **花鏡**（Hoù king〔かきょう〕）。花の鏡、手本。陳扶揺（Tsch'ing fû jaô）著、1688年、手稿、6冊、8折判。

205. **本草彙言**（Pèn ts'aô weijên〔ほんぞういげん〕）。植物の分類収集。中国の主だった医者、博物学者が事物の本性と薬用について教えたものを明朝下の人倪朱謨（Nitschū mu）が記述した。日本人松岡恕菴（Matsuoka Tsiuan）による手稿の範例。6冊。

206. **南方草木状**（Nânfang ts'aòmū tschoáng〔なんぽうそうもくじょう〕）。（コーチシナから広東省）南方〔嶺南〕地方の草木。武帝274年下の将軍であった嵇含（Hîhan）撰。平住専庵（Firasumi Senan）が日本語読みの注記をつけ、更に活字刷りにするように配慮した。1725年、2
けいがん

125

冊、8折判。

b. 和書

207. **本草綱目啓蒙**（ほんぞうこうもくけいもう　Honzô kômok keimô）。自然科学入門。小野蘭山（*Wono Lanzan*）口授、孫の蕙畝（*Tsunenori*）編、京都・江戸 1804 年、5 冊、8 折判。

208. **本草啓蒙名疏**（ほんぞうけいもうめいそ　Honzô keimô meisu）。前述書の一覧表。小野蘭山（*Wono Lanzan*）博士監定、孫の蕙畝（*Tsunenori*）編。1809 年、8 冊、8 折判。

209. **本草原始**（ほんぞうげんし　Honzô gensi〔*Pènts'aô juênschi*〕）。自然科学初歩。雷公炮（*Lui kung pao*）著。日本版、1698 年、5 冊、12 折判。

210. **本草和解**（ほんぞうわかい　Honzô Wakai〔ほんぞうわげ〕）。博物学の日本語説明。京都の学林の大変有名な医師〔曲直瀬〕道三（*Dosan*）著、大江頤軒（*Ohoje Fensen*）〔おおえいけん、中江藤樹〕増補。大坂、1712 年。2 冊、12 折判。

211. **大和本草新校正**（やまとほんぞうしんこうせい　Jamato honzô sinkiôsei）。日本語の博物学は筑前の文学研究者貝原篤信（*Kaibara Toksin*）〔かいばらあつのぶ〕によって更に校正された。1708 年、10 冊、8 折判。本書の著者が指示している事物の本性について中国書と和書で取り上げている教えは、主として植物に関している。

212. **広倭〔稜〕本草**（こうやまとほんぞう　Kwô Jamato honzô）。直海龍（*Tsiok Kairiu*）〔なおみりゅう、直海元周〕による日本語の博物学で増大した版。京都、1759 年、12 冊、8 折判。

213. **赭鞭余録**（しゃべんよろく　Sjaben jorok）。周防の医者豊田養慶（*Tojoda Jokei*）による本草書に収録されている稀少なものの列挙と記述の補足。

214. **物類品隲**（ぶつるいひんしつ　Butsruibinsits）。類に分けられた自然の事物の収録。鳩渓平賀先生（*Fatotani Firaki Sensei*）〔きゅうけいひらが、平賀源内〕著。大坂、1763 年、6 冊、8 折判。

215. **花彙**（かい　Kwa wi）。花（装飾庭園）の様々な種類。雍南田充（*Jônan Densiu*）〔島田光房〕による記述と図。京都、1759 年、再版 1765 年、8 冊大 8 折判。

216. **草木性譜**（そうもくせいふ　Sômok seifu）。草木の本性について。清原重巨（*Kijovara Tsiukjo*）〔きよはらしげなお〕撰。尾張、1823 年-1827 年、3 冊、大 8 折判。著作は尾張市で栄えていた探求者仲間の配慮によって刊行された。

217. **有毒本草図説**（ゆうどくほんぞうずせつ　Judok honzô dsusets）。清原重巨（*Kijovara Tsiukjo*）〔きよはらしげなお〕の有毒草木の性格についての図説。尾張、1827 年、2 冊、大 8 折判。

218. **本草和名**（ほんぞうわみょう　Honzô Wameô）。自然の事物の日本語名を深江輔仁（*Fukaje Fozin*）が説明。1797 年、2 冊、8 折判。

219. **物品識名**（ぶっぴんしきめい　Butsbin sikimei）。事物の注記名、または大変著名な自然

科学者小野蘭山（Wono Lansan）による自然の事物の分類命名。水谷豊文助六（Midsutani Fôfun Sukerok）筆、1809年、4冊、12折判。

220. **本草薬名備考和訓鈔**（ほんぞうやくめいびこうわくんしょう　Honzô Jakmei bikô Wagun seô）。薬物または全博物のいろは順日本語名。丹波頼理（Tanba Jorisudsi）が吟味し、中国語名を付加した。京都、1807年、7冊、8折判。中国人と日本人医者は、すべて薬物が製造されたとき、本書中に言及されている全品質については、公式であると見なしている。

221. **草花式**（そうかしき　Sôkwa siki）。草花の手本。法橋〔大岡〕春川（Fokiô Farugawa）〔しゅんせん〕図説。1820年、3冊、8折判。

222. **雲根志同〔前後編〕**（うんこんし　Unkonsi）。種々の集録中に保存されている水晶、石に書きしるしたものについて。近江国山田浦村にて木内小繁（Kinoudsi Seôban）著。1772年－1801年、15冊、8折判。

223. **泰西本草名疏**（たいせいほんぞうめいそ　Daisai honzô meisu）。ヨーロッパ産植物相概要。大変著名なC. P. トゥーンベリ（C.P. Thunberg）によって認められた日本の植物相概要もある。尾張の植物学者伊藤圭介（Itô Keiske）編、1828年、3冊、8折判。

B. 特殊自然科学書

a. 植物書、動物書

224. **百菊譜**（ひゃくきくふ　Fjak kikno fu）。インド種属の菊の本。付・児素仙（Zisôzen）図説。1735年、2冊、8折判。

225. **花壇養菊集**（かだんようきくしゅう　Kwadan jôkik siu）。花栽培を常とするインド菊の多様性について。志水閑事（Simidsu Kanzi）著。2冊、12折判。

226. **牽牛品**（けんぎゅうひん　Kengo bin）。三葉の牽牛花（朝顔）の書。峰岸龍父（Minokisi Rjôfo）〔みねぎしりゅうほ〕著。大坂、1819年、2冊。

227. **長生花林抄**（ちょうせいかりんしょう　Tsjôsei kwarin seô）。躑躅の群生林；つつじの種類の書である。伊藤伊兵衛（Itô Ifei）著。江戸、1733年、5冊。

228. **朝顔譜**（あさがおのふ　Asagavono fu）。三葉の朝顔の種についての書。秋水茶寮（Akimidsu Tsjareo）先生著、濃淡斎（Tsjô Tansai）画。江戸、1818年、1冊、18折判。

229. **花壇朝顔通**（かだんあさがおつう　Kwadan Asagavono dsu）。花壇を飾る慣わしの三葉の朝顔種の書。壺天堂主人（Kotendono sjunin）〔こてんどうしゅじん〕著、森春渓（Mori Sjunkei）画。江戸、1815年、2冊、12折判。

230. **梅品**（ばいひん　Baibin）。梅種属の書。松岡玄達（Matsuoka Gendats）撰。京都、1760年、2冊、12折判。

231. **怡顔斎蘭品**（いがんさいらんぴん　Ikansai ranbin）。種属でより一層優美な蘭とあやめの書。松岡玄達（成章）（Matsuoka Gendats〔Dsiôan〕）撰。京都1772年、2冊、大8折判。

232. **怡顔斎桜品**（いがんさいおうひん　Ikansai ôbin）。その花が見事な種の桜の多種多様さの書。松岡玄達（Matsuoka Gendats）撰。京都1758年、1冊、12折判。

233. **草木奇品家雅見**（そうもくきひんかがみ　Sômok kibin kagami）。草木の珍しい種類の見本、または金・銀色の様々な色の葉をもつ植物の本。付・画。〔種樹家〕金太（Kinda）著。江戸、1827年、2冊、8折判。

234. **橘品類考**（たちばなひんるいこう　Tatsibana binrui kô〔きつひんるいこう〕）。柑橘類の本。桂菴木村俊篤（Kei an Kimura Sjuntok）著。京都、1797年、2冊、8折判。

235. **橘品**（きつひん　Kitsbin）。柑橘類の一般書。弄花亭主人（Rôkwateino Sjuzin）著、つまり京都植物園主催、宇田川榕菴（Wutagawa Joan）という名でもあった。京都、1797年、1冊、12折判。

236. **広益増補 地錦抄**（こうえきぞうほ、じきんしょう　Kwôjeki zôbô, Tsikin seô）。地面の美しい飾り、または花冠について。伊藤伊兵衛（Itô Ifei）著。江戸、1710年、1719年、20冊、12折判。

237. **花壇大全**（かだんたいぜん　Kwadan daizen〔じきんしょう〕）。花壇（主に松、桜、椿の）全書。華文軒風子主人（Kwakiuken Sjuzin）〔中西敬房〕撰。1756年、再版1798年、5巻1冊、12折判。本小冊子の別見本あり、その表題：「花壇草木絵図」（Kwadan sômok jebu）、つまり造園師たちが飾ることを常としている草木図説。5冊、12折判。

238. **茶席挿花集**（させきさしばなのあつめ　Sasiki sasibanano atsumé〔ちゃせきそうかしゅう〕）。茶席の挿花のために移されるのを常とする、挿花の季節によって配置された諸花の指針。芳亭野人（Fôtei Jazin）著、岩崎常正（Ivasaki Tokiva）写図。江戸、1824年、1冊、12折判。

239. **古今鷹之事**（ここんたかのこと　Kokon takano koto）。鷹と鷹狩りのことについて、古代と新しい書物から集められた図説。平仮名文字で書かれた1冊、8折判。

240. **六物新志**（りくぶつしんし　Rikbuts sinsi）。6つの博物（それは一角獣、サフラン、肉豆蔲、エジプトの屍体保存法（木乃伊）、エブリコ、人魚）についての新しいもの。オランダ語からの和訳。大槻玄沢（Ohodsuki Gendak）〔茂質〕解釈、若狭国の医者杉田（Sugida）〔玄白〕改訂。1759年刊、1冊、8折刊。

241. **蘭畹摘方**（らんえんてきほう　Ranjen tekifô）。珍しい草花植物の記述選集。本書は博物学書について、大槻玄沢（Ohodsuki Gendak）によってオランダ語から和訳された抜粋を含んでいる。それは主として草木、日本へ移入されるのを常とする外国の動物・薬物を取り扱っている。江戸、1804年、3冊、8折判。

242. 一角纂考（Ĭkiō tsuàn k'aò〔いっかくさんこう〕）。同著者による一角獣概説書。オランダ語からの中国語訳。1786 年、1 冊、8 折判。

243. 鯨志（げいし　Keisi〔K'ingtschi〕）。鯨の種類の本。著者：南紀如水（Nanki Njosui）〔梶取屋次右衛門〕。大坂、1758 年、1 冊、8 折判。

244. 怡顔斎介【品】（いがんさいかいひん　Ikansai kai bin）。美しい種類の貝（甲殻）類の記述。付・図。著者：松岡恕庵（Matsuoka Dsiôun）〔玄達〕。京都、1758 年、1 冊、8 折判。

245. 虫〔鏡〕鑑（むしのかがみ　Musino kagami〔むしかがみ〕）。または腸の回虫とある虫についての観察。河内国の医者高玄竜（Kô Genriu）著。1807 年、再版 1809 年、1 冊、8 折判。

246. 夏草冬虫図（かそうとうちゅうのず　Kasô tôtsiu no dsu）。ある夏草から、冬に昆虫が生れることについて。付・図。1801 年、1 冊、8 折判。昆虫の死体から生ずる紫の縞をつけたキノコについての記述がある。

247. 仙台 きんこの記（せんだいきんこのき　Sendai Kinko no ki）。仙台地方の海岸で漁師によって捕られた、仙台キンコと云われるナマコ〔海鼠〕について。大槻玄沢（Okodsuki Gendak）〔茂質〕著。江戸、1 冊、8 折判。

b. 植物写生図（手稿）

248. 本草写真（ほんぞうしゃしん　Honzô sjasin）。水谷助六（Midsutani Sukerok）の自然な植物図、2 冊。

249. 本草写真（ほんぞうしゃしん　Honzô sjasin）。宇田川榕菴（Udagawa Jôan）による自然の植物図。1 冊。

250. 本草写真（ほんぞうしゃしん　Honzô sjasin）。桂川甫賢（Kadsuragawa Hoken）による自然の植物図。1 冊、2 折判。

251. 人参写真（にんじんしゃしん　Ninzin sjasin）。桂川甫賢（Kadsuragawa Hoken）が描いた自然の植物図、2 折判、5 つの人参。1 冊。

252. 日本草木（にっぽんのくさき　Nippon no kusaki）。自然の日本植物相を桂川甫賢（Kadsuragawa Hoken）が描いた。2 冊

253. 梅桜類花写真（うめさくらのるいかしゃしん　Mume sakurano rui kwa sjasin）。梅桜類の自然の種々の花が描かれている。1 冊、2 折判。

254. 蝦夷本草之図（えぞほんぞうのず　Jezo honzô no dsu）。桂川甫賢（Kadsuragawa Hoken）が自然の蝦夷の植物相を描いた。2 冊、2 折判。

255. 琉球本草之図（りゅうきゅうほんぞうのず　Liukiu honzô no dsu）。桂川甫賢（Kadsuragawa Hoken）が自然の琉球の植物相を描いた。2 冊、2 折判。

256. 琉球草木写真素稿（りゅうきゅうそうもくしゃしんそこう　Liukiu sômok sjasin so kô）。

琉球島の自然の草木が少し描かれている。1冊、2折判。

257. **日光山草木写真**（にっこうさんそうもくしゃしん　Nikwôsan sômok sjasin）。伊藤圭介（*Itô Keiske*）による自然の日光山の植物相。2冊。

258. **本草写真**（ほんぞうしゃしん　Honzô sjasin）。水谷助六（*Midsutani Sukerok*）による自然の植物図。1冊。

259. **本草抜萃**（ほんぞうばっすい　Honzô batsusui [*Pèn ts'aò pā ts'ui*]）。植物抜粋、あるいは日本の珍しい植物。水谷助六（*Midsutani Sukerok*）画。5冊。

260. **本草抜萃**（ほんぞうばっすい　Honzô bātsusui）。植物抜粋。大窪太兵衛（*Ohokubo Dafeije*）画。5冊。

261. **本草抜萃**（ほんぞうばっすい　Honzô batssui）。植物抜粋。宇田川榕菴（*Udagawa Jôan*）画。1冊。

262. **生植**（＊）〔檀〕**全書**（せいしょくぜんしょ　Seisjok zensjo）。植物性のものの記述。珍しい植物の図である。宇田川榕菴（*Udagawa Jôan*）著。1冊、8折判。

　　　（＊）表題目録は「生植」と読まれるべきである。

263. **山桜説**（やまざくらのせつ　Jamasakurano sets）。樹木の茂った山中に咲くサクラの木についての論。付・図。1冊、2折判。

264. **草花之図**（そうかのず　Sô kwano dsu）。様々な植物図。最上徳内（*Mogami Toknai*）が伝えた。1冊。

265. **腊葉揚**（おしばすり　Osiba suri）。（本などの間にはさんで押さえて）乾かした草木の葉。薜茘菴（かずられいあん）（*Kadsura Reian*）が色彩で示した。2冊。

c. 動物写生図（手稿）

266. **獣禽虫写真**（じゅうきんちゅうしゃしん　Zju kin tsiu sjasin）。四足獣、鳥、虫の自然の種類の図。3冊、2折判。

267. **蟹蝦類写真**（かいかるいしゃしん　Kaika rui sjasin）。桂川（*Kadsuragawa*）栗本瑞見（*Kurimoto Suiken*）によって描かれた自然の甲殻類。2冊、2折判。

268. **虫蟹之図**（ちゅうかいのず　Tsui kaino dsu）。大坂の絵師鉄山（*Tessan*）の昆虫と甲殻類の絵。1冊、2折判。

269. **蝶二十写真**（ちょうにじゅうしゃしん　Teô nizju sjasin）。自然の蝶20。1冊、2折判。

270. **虫類写集**（ちゅうるいしゃしゅう　Tsiurui sjasju）。自然の様々な昆虫。大河内存真（おおこうちぞんしん）（*Ohokôtsi Sonsin*）図説。1冊、8折判。

271. **蛛類説図**（ちゅうるいせつず　Tsiurui setsdsu）。日本のクモ。大窪舒三郎（*Ohokubo Sjôsanrô*）図説。1冊、12折判。

272. 魚類写真（ぎょるいしゃしん　Gjorui sjasin）。様々な魚類。桂川（Kadsuragawa）栗本瑞見（Kurimoto Suiken）が自然に即して描いた。3冊、2折判。

273. 海魚考図絵（かいぎょこうずえ　Kaigjo kô dsu-e）。鞭近斎（Mutsi Konsai）が海の魚類を入念に描いた。2冊、手稿。

274. 海魚写真（かいぎょしゃしん　Kaigjo sjasin）。海中の魚類。宇田川榕菴（Udagawa Jôan）が自然に描いた。1冊、8折判、手稿。

275. 写真随集（しゃしんずいしゅう　Sjasin suisju）。様々な事物の絵が自然に描かれている。宇田川榕菴（Udagawa Jôan）著。1冊、手稿。

276. 獣魚縮写（じゅうぎょしゅくしゃ　Siugjo sjuksja）。四足獣と魚の絵が走り書かれている。1冊、手稿。

277. 禽獣魚写真（きんじゅうぎょしゃしん　Kin siu gjo sjasin）。鳥、四足獣、魚が自然に描かれている。1冊、手稿。

278. 写真長鯨【之】図（しゃしんながくじらのず　Sjasin nagakuzirano dsu〔しゃしんちょうげいず〕）。鯨が自然に描かれている。1冊、手稿。

279. 唐夫人所謂 リキンカムヒ ツナカヒ二獣之図（からふとのいわゆるりきんかむい、つなかい、にじゅうのず　Karafutono ivajuru Likinkamūi, Tsūnakai ni-siuno dsu）。樺太の地の住民から馴鹿、リキンカムイ；アイヌ人の神と云われている両四足獣の画。それは燃えたモスク〔麝香鹿〕とトナカイ〔馴鹿〕である。

280. 蛇骨之写真（じゃこつしゃしん　Sjakotsno sjasin）。つまり豊後国津江村付近（凡そ東経130°45′、北緯33°12′）で1814年に発掘された蛇の骨。自然に即して。手稿。

281. 打越溝中出異獣角骨図（〔Tàjuĕ keŭtschung tschŭ i scheù kiō kō t'ŭ〕〔うちこしこうちゅうしゅついじゅうつのほねず〕）。溝が通されていた場所で掘り出された、不思議な四足獣（化石の鹿）の角と骨。自然に描かれた。1冊、手稿。

282. 石ニ化魚之図（いしになるうおのず　Isininaru uwono dsu）。石になった魚の図。

283. 天狗爪石雑考（てんぐのつめいしざっこう　Tenguno tsumeisi satsukô）。「天狗爪石」と云われている石についての雑録。石になった鮫の歯についての話。日本人の博物探求者の木内重暁（Kiutsi Tsiukjô）は、この話をこの表題で図説した。手稿。

d. 雑論

284. 本草一家言（ほんぞういっかげん　Honzô itsika gen）。ある自然科学者の言葉、あるいは博物史。松岡恕菴（Matsuoka Dsjoan）述。4冊、8折判、手稿。

285. 本草和名集（ほんぞうわみょうしゅう　Honzô Wameô sju）。自然の事物の日本語名。2冊、8折判、手稿。

286. 菌譜（きんふ　Kin fu）。酒井立生（Sakawi Liusei）による菌類・きのこについての解説。付・絵図。1814年、1冊、8折判、手稿。

287. 修養堂 本草会目録（しゅうようどうほんぞうかいもくろく　Siujôdô Honzôkwai mokrok）。1827年に修養堂館に参集した博物会の同好者たちの報告。伊藤圭介（Itô Keiske）著。1冊、手稿。

288. 生々堂 本草会目録（せいせいどうほんぞうかいもくろく　Seiseidô Honzô kwai mokrok）。尾張市で起っている博物会の同好者たちの報告。大河内存真（Ohokôtsi Sonsin）著。1冊、手稿。

289. 【本】草会目録（ほんぞうかいもくろく　Honzôkwai mokrok）。尾張市で起っている博物会の同好者たちの報告。1冊、手稿

290. 海鰌（かいしゅう　Kaisiu [Hai ts'ieŭ]）。つまり海のウナギ（せみくじら）。鯨について記されている。筆者不明。様々な書から鯨についての知識を書き写した。1冊、手稿。

291. 鳥品類小記（ちょうひんるいしょうき　Teo binrui seoki）。鳥類について簡単に記述されている。手稿。

292. 日本諸禽真写（にほんしょきんしんしゃ　Nippon sjokin sinsja）。日本の鳥類が自然に描かれている。付・鳥の日本名。2冊、2折判、手稿。

293. 鷸十八品真写（しぎじゅうはちひんしんしゃ　Sigi zjufatsibin sinsja）。しぎという名の足が細長い渉禽18種。水谷助六（Midsutani Sukerok）が自然に描いている。1828年、1冊、手稿。

第Ⅳ部　文法書と辞書

A. 辞書

a. 漢和辞書

294. 字彙（Tsèlui 又は Tsèwei〔じい〕）。つまり文字を集めた本。梅膺祚（Meiîngtsŭ）著。1615年（参照：Fourmont, "Catal. librorum Bibl. regiae sinicorum"、1〔E. フールモン「王立図書館の中国書目録」1〕．更に Heinrich Julius. Klaproth, "Verzeichniss der chinesischen und Mandshuischen Bücher und Handschriften der Königl. Bibl. zu Berlin", pag. 122。〔H.J. クラプロート「ベルリン王立図書館蔵中国語と満州語書籍と手稿本目録」〕122頁。）本書は文字の日本語の発音を付して、日本で新たに活字で書き留められた。9冊、大8折判。

295. 康熙字典（K'ânghî tsètièn〔こうきじてん〕）。康熙年間に書きあげられた字書。（参照：294：H.J. クラプロート：同前掲書。J. Klaproth 125頁）。30冊、12折判。

296. 増続大広益玉篇（ぞうぞくだいこうえきぎょくへん　Zôsjok daikwôjeki Gjokben [*Tsêng sŭ tá kuangī Jŭpiên*]）。つまり貴重な紙葉。続けて、増補されている書。辞書は漢字であり、和訳が付加されている。京都の儒学者毛利貞斎（*Mori Teisai*）編。1691年、12冊、8折判。

297. 新増 字林玉篇（しんぞうじりんぎょくへん　Sinzô Zilin gjokben [*Sin tsêng Tsèlîn jŭp'iên*]）。表意文字辞典新増版。鎌田禎斎（*Kamada Teisan*）〔かまたていさい、環斎〕著、1797年。新版、1820年、1冊、8折判。

298. 四声字林集韻（しせいじりんしゅういん　Sisei zilin sjuin [*Sseschîng Tsèlîn tsījùn*]）。四声が示されている漢字を集めて解釈をほどこした音韻書。環斎鎌田（*Kwansai Kamada*）著。1803年。1815年再版、1冊、12折判。

299. 刪定増補小字彙（さんていぞうほしょうじい　Santei zôbô seo zii [*Sânting tsêngpù siaò tsèwei*]）。文字を集めた小辞書（文章の不要な字句を削り取って整理してある）。増補版、1冊、16折判。

+300. 〔急用問合〕真字玉篇大成（しんじぎょくへんたいせい　Sinzi gjokben daisei [*Tschîn tsè jŭp'iên tátsch'îng*]）〔真字引玉篇大成〕。真字（真書楷書）（"理"[*Li*]の字）の貴重な紙葉が本書に集められている。付：韻（四声）と日本語訳。1819年、1冊、12折判。

b. 和漢辞書

301. 和漢音釈 書言字考〔節用集〕（わかんおんしゃくしょげんじこう　Wa Kan wonseki siogen zikô）。日本語語彙辞典あるいは中国語同様日本語の語彙と会話用語。付：類義語・同義語の表意文字の手段。著者：槙島昭武（*Makinosima Terutake*）〔まきしまてるたけ〕。江戸、1698年。駒谷散人（*Komatani Sanzin*）〔こまやさんじん、槙島昭武〕校訂。1802年、10冊、8折判。

302. 仮名引節用集（かなびきせつようしゅう　Kanafiki setsjô sju）。いろは順（この名は文字順である）に排列された和漢辞書。草と平仮名の名がある書体である。行書、片仮名と言われている楷書文字も付けられている。田仲宣（*Danaka Nobu*）〔でんちゅうせん、田宮仲宣〕著。1803年、1冊、8折判。

303. 大全早引節用集（たいぜんはやびきせつようしゅう　Daisen fajabiki setsjô sju）。必要語を早くさがす便利な大辞書。1817年、1冊、8折判。

+304. 早引節用集（はやびきせつようしゅう　Fajabiki setsjô sju）。必要語を早くさがす便利な辞書。本書が書かれている草書体に、楷書体が添えられている。據梧散人（*Jorigiri Sanzin*）編。1823年、1冊、8折判。

c. 同義語辞書

305. 増補詩文重宝記（ぞうほしぶんちょうほうき　Zôbô Simon tsiubô ki）。いろは順排列詩文

用語集。信更生（Sin Kôsei）著。1733年、1冊、12折判。

+306. **訳文筌**（やくもんぜん　Jeki mon zen）〔訳文筌蹄〕。訳された文字のわな。中国語の類義語手引書である。〔荻生〕徂徠先生（Sorai Sensei）解説。1715年編、3冊、8折判。

d. 日本古語辞書

307. **古言梯**（ふることのばし　Furukotono basi〔こげんてい〕）古語への階段・手引書。藤原宇万伎（Fudsivara no Umaki）編。1765年、1冊、8折判。

308. **雅言仮字格**（がげんかじかく　Gagen kazikak）。日本語の雅言の手本。市岡孟彦（Itsioka Takefiko）補訂。1814年、1冊、12折判。前掲書の表題を変えた補訂版。語彙数は増加されているが、説明は切断して縮少されている。

C. 文法書

309. **大和詞**（やまとことば　Jamatokotoba）。つまり日本の（固有の純粋な）ことば。1759年、1冊、12折判。古代の警句、歌謡ではやっている語彙や言い回しの一般的なことばを集めている書。次掲書の新しい本。

310. **やまと詞**（やまとことば　Jamatokotoba）。日本語、または一般のことばで説明されている詩的な声をもったことば。1727年、1冊、12折判。

311. **新撰大和詞**（しんせんやまとことば　Sinsen Jamatokotoba）。日本の古語の新しい語彙集。日本語文法の試みである。著者：東華切稽（Tôkwa Sekkei）〔東華坊、各務支考〕（ママ）、渡部狂（Watanave no Kuruvu）〔くるう〕。京都、1711年、再版1729年、2冊、8折判。

312. **雑字類編**（そうじるいへん　Sôzi ruiben〔ざつじるいへん〕）。いろは順に排列した複合語。汎愛堂主人（Fan ai dô no Sjuzin）編。1764年、2冊、8折判。

313. **学語論**（がくごろん　Gakgoron〔Hiöjùlun〕）〔学語編〕（がくごへん）。本書は日本語訳をつけた中国語の複合語語彙集。竺常（Tsikuzjô）〔大典顕常〕編。1772年、2冊、12折判。

314. **イロハ天理鈔**（いろはてんりしょう　Irofa tenri seo）。いろはアルファベットの本質について。僧の良鑁（Rjôban）著。1677年、2冊、8折判。

315. **以呂波字考録**（いろはじこうろく　Irofazi kôrok）。いろはアルファベット論。仏僧の全長（Zentsjô）編。1736年、2冊、8折判。

316. **以呂波之五類**（いろはのごるい　Irofano gorui）。5紙葉のいろはアルファベット。1冊。

*317. **空海之いろは**（くうかいのいろは　Kôkaino Irofa）。僧の空海（Kôkai）、または弘法大師（Kobô daisi）が809年に真如法親王（Sin mjô kô sin wô）に書を奉ったと云われる、アルファベットの「いろは」の見本。

318. **麻光韻鏡**（Mâkuâng júnking〔まこういんきょう〕）類似音で終わっている、清く澄んだ手本。1744年、2冊、8折判。本書は、中国語の真の朗読法を学ぶために、10年間中国自体へ渡航した京都の了蓮寺の僧の文雄僧谿（*Buniu Sokei*）によって中国語が和訳された。

319. **千字文**（せんじもん　Sen zi mon〔*Tsiän dsü wên*〕）。漢字千字からなる小冊子、手稿。（参照："Isagoge in Biblioth. Jap."〔「日本語蔵書への序説」〕pag. 6、№ 325b、326）。

320. **訓点千字文**（くんてんせんじもん　Gunden senzimon）。漢字千字からなる小冊子。最上山子（*Mogami Sansi*）〔片山兼山〕が日本語訳の注記を添えている。江戸、1515年、1冊、8折判。

+321. **画引十体千字文綱目**（がいんじったいせんじもんこうもく　Kwain zjutai senzimon kômōk〔かくびきじったいせんじもんこうもく〕）。前置きの部首索引による、漢字千字からなる小冊子。1. 各漢字の様々な形。2. 古代同様近代の記号（サイン）で表されている、部首一覧。3. 日本人の「名乗り」（称している）一覧。西甌孫（*Nisikame son*）〔孫丕顕〕が作成し説明した。彼は語彙で使用しているように、語句を語句で示している。京都、1756年、1冊、8折判。

322. **汪由敦楷書千字文**（*Wângjeŭ tûntschischû Tsiän dsü wên*〔おうゆとんかいしょせんじもん〕）。漢字千字からなる小冊子。本書を著名な汪由敦（*Wângjeŭtün*）が書いた。1冊、8折判。文字は黒板に白色で記されている。しかし本書は中国の見事な筆蹟の見本とされている。

323. **米南宮杜律墨帖**（*Mi Nân kŭng tŭliŭ mēt'iē*〔べいなんきゅうとりつぼくちょう〕）。黒色の紙に白色の文字で書かれた孔子（*Confucio*）と同時代の哲人米南宮（*Mi Nan kung*）〔宋時代の米芾〕の自伝見本。1冊、4折判。

〔A.〕e, f.　日本語—オランダ語辞書とオランダ語—日本語辞書

〔324a.〕**「新輯和蘭辞書」**（Nieuw verzameld Japans en Hollandsch Woordenboek door den Vorst van het Landschap Nakats『蘭語訳撰』）。中津地方の君侯、源〔奥平〕昌高（*Minamoto Masataka*）によって与えられ、家臣神谷弘孝（*Kaija Filojosi*）によって編纂された。1810年、5冊、4折判。和・蘭語彙は通詞馬〔場〕貞由（*B. Sadajosi*）により、先述の君侯の命と支援によって編集された。

324b. **訳鍵**（やくけん　Jakken〔*īki'èn*〕）。翻訳の手がかり。蘭和辞書。藤林泰助（*Fudsibajasi Daisuke*）編。京都、2冊、4折判。

〔325a.〕**江戸ハルマ**（えどはるま　Jedo-Halma）。蘭和辞書。手稿、14冊、大8折判。本稿は次の書物の例である。

325b. **江戸ハルマ**（えどはるま　Jedo-Halma）。ハルマが著者の蘭和訳辞書。江戸、20冊、4折判。本辞書の起源と理由については、表題"*Isagoge in Biblioth. Jap.*"（「日本語蔵書への序

説」20、21頁）という書物の中でより一層豊かに論じられている。

326. **和蘭辞書**（わらんことばしょ　Wa Lan kotoba sjo〔わらんじしょ〕）。日本とオランダの言葉の本。本辞書の起源と理由については、前述箇所（"*Isag. in Bibl. Jap.*"）（「日本語蔵書への序説」、23頁）に論じられている。

327. **蛮語箋**（ばんごせん　Bango sen）。つまり片仮名で書かれた異国（オランダ）語紙片・索引。桂川甫三（*Kadsuragawa Fosan*）編。1798年、1冊、12折判。

B. 語彙

a. アイヌ語

328. **蝦夷方言**（えぞほうげん　Jezo fôgen）。アイヌ語語彙。白虹斎（*Siranizi sai*）〔はっこうさい、最上徳内〕編。1804年、1冊、12折判。本書の表題は次のようにも書かれている。「モシボクサ」（*Mo sivo kusa*）、つまりこけにおおわれた塩気のある植物。

329. **蝦夷ヶ嶋言語**（えぞがしまことば　Jezo gasima kotoba）。アイヌ語語彙手稿。著者最上徳内（*Mogami Tokunai*）の日本語説明を付す。真実の訳語を添えている。

b. 高麗語

330. **千字文大本**（Tsiän dsü wên, tápèn〔せんじもんおおほん〕）。千字の語彙の2つ折判。中国語〔中国六朝の梁の周興嗣が武帝の命により撰した韻文〕が起源の本書は、朝鮮半島で印刷され、（不完全な）高麗語解釈を付したもの。（参照："*Isagoge in Bibl. Jap.*"（「日本語蔵書への序説」）6頁）

331. **類合**（Luihō〔るいごう〕）。中国語を高麗語に訳したもの。（参照："*Isagoge in Bibl. Jap.*"（「日本語蔵書への序説」）7頁）。

332. **朝鮮辞書**（ちょうせんじしょ　Tsjozen zisjo）。高麗語を考慮するいくつかの雑録。1冊、手稿、2折判。

c. サンスクリット

334.(ママ) **悉曇摩多体文**（しつたんまたいもん　Sitvan mata tiwen）。つまりサンスクリットの母音と子音、あるいは聖なる仏陀（*Buddha*）の文言。インドの三蔵法師玄奘老人（*Genseô Rôzin*）によって解説されている。1695年。1789年刊、1冊。

335.(ママ) **梵言集**（ぼんごあつめ　Fangonatsume〔ぼんごしゅう〕）。仏典から集められたサンスクリット語彙。付：中国語の説明。著者：最上徳内（*Mogami Toknai*）。1冊、手稿。

d. 満州語

335. **新刻清書全集**（Sînk'ē Ts'îng schû ts'iuên tsī〔しんこくしんしょぜんしゅう〕）。再び活字で表わされた、満州文書の慣例。著者：汪鶴孫（Wâng Hōsün）。1699年、3冊、大8折判。本書の起源について、中国語の見本の手稿がある。第1巻では文字の要素が伝えられている。第2、3巻では、満州語・中国語の語彙を入れている。

336. **清語集**（Ts'îngjutsī〔しんごしゅう〕）。満州語語彙集。手稿、1冊、12折判。

第Ⅴ部　神学書と道徳書

A．仏教

337. 〔改正〕**両部神道口決鈔**（りょうぶしんとうくけつしょう　Rjôbu Sindô kukets Sjô [Liàngpú schîntao K'eŭkiuē tschaó]）。二様（インドあるいは仏教と日本起源）の神霊礼拝への論述。付：注釈。著者：江源慶安（Kôgen Keian）〔源慶安〕。1716年。再版1795年、6冊、8折判。

338. **絵馬雛形**（えまひながた　Jemūma finagata）。つまり馬の絵の手本、あるいは奉納額。それによって日本人の神社・寺は飾られるのを常とした。1750年、1冊、8折判。

339. **扁額軌範**（へんがくきはん　Benkak Kivan）。祇園神社〔京都の八坂神社〕に掛けられている、横長の奉納額。合川珉和（Avigawa Minkwa）、北川春成（Kitagawa Sjunsei）共撰。1819年、1冊、8折判。

＊340. **通神画譜**（つうしんがふ　Tsûsin kwabu）不思議な画譜。合川珉和（Avigawa Minkwa）画。1819年、1冊、8折判。

341. **細見男山放生会図録**（さいけんおとこやまほうじょうえずろく　Saiken Wotokojama Fôzjôje dsurok）。毎年大和国八幡宮で法会される捕えた生き物を放してやる法会。絵師速水春暁斎（Fajamidsu Sjungeôsai）〔はやみしゅんぎょうさい〕によって大変入念に描かれている。1冊。

342. **二十四輩順拝図会**（にじゅうしはいじゅんぱいずえ　Nizjusibai sjunbaidsue）。信仰心から諸方の社寺を参拝して回っている二十四の霊場。河内国の専教寺住職の釈了貞（Sjak Reôtei）記述、絵師竹原春泉斎（Takebara Sjunsensai）画。1803年、5冊、4折判。

343. **増補諸宗 仏像図彙**（ぞうほしょしゅうぶつぞうづい　Zôbô sjosiu, Butszô dsui）。仏像と諸宗派の創建者の図彙。土佐将曹紀秀信（Kino Fidenobu）画。1690年、5冊、8折判。再版1696年。

[335b] **（大唐）大般若理趣分**（[Tischī〔だいとう〕] Tápanshō lits'úfên〔だいはんにゃりしゅぶ

ん〕)。「大般若理趣」(*Mahâpradschnâritsch*) という表題のインドの経文。中国語の経(仏陀の教えを説いた書物)の第十部分。「大般若波羅蜜多」(*Tápanshōpolomitoking*)(つまり大きな悟りによって、現実の迷いの境地を離れることについての聖典)と書かれた書物の第578巻を含んでいる。中国人で、(仏教の)普遍的教義に深く通じた人、玄奘三蔵(*Hiuên tsàng fùng*)が、中国語に訳した。1冊。

[336b]〔増補〕**呪詛調法記**(じゅそちょうほうき Sjuso teôfôki)。神仏に祈願して人をのろう術。菊丘臥山人(*Kikkiu Kwasanzin*)著。京都、1780年、1冊、12折判。

B. 神道または中国の諸派

[+337b] **四書**(ししょ Sisjo [*Ssè schû*])。四種の儒教の教典〔大学、中庸、論語、孟子〕。中国語本文に、行間に書いた日本語訳が付されている。尾張、1812年、3冊、8折判。

[338b] **孝経**(こうきょう Kôkjô [*Hiao king*])。孝行の道についての書。中国語本文に注釈を付けてある。江戸、1730年。再版1789年、1冊、4折判。

[339b] **論語**(ろんご Rongo [*Lûnjù*])。中国語の対話が本文。本書の日本語の注記を道春(*Tosjun*)〔林羅山〕が書き加えた。1冊。

[340b] **論語彝訓巻之首**(ろんごいくんまきのはじめ Rongo ikun makino fazime [*Lûnjù ihiún kiuén tschi scheù*])。〔論語の〕対話が本文。注釈つき。24冊、8折判。最上徳内(*Mogami Toknai*)編著。江戸、1822年。そこには本書の首巻があり、その中で言及されている書物の版とその注釈について記されている。

C. 道徳教訓書;小説と雑書

[341b] **菜根譚**(さいこんたん Sai kou dan [*Ts'aí kên t'ùn*])。つまり草木、野菜の根(すなわち精霊や才ある者の糧)がその中にあるという論議。明朝下にいた中国人洪自誠(*Hŭng tsé tsch'ing*)編。本書は日本で1825年、再び活字に書き留められた。2冊、8折判。

[+342b] **絵本孝婦伝**(えほんこうふのでん Jehon kôfuno ten)。敬けんな婦人たちの小伝。絵本で特色のある本。京都、1806年、1冊、8折判。

[343b]〔文化新版〕**麗玉百人一首吾妻錦**(れいぎょくひゃくにんいっしゅあずまにしき Reikjok Fjaknin itsusju adsumanisigi)。少女の教養教育のための要約。百人の歌人の絵が描かれ、それら歌人の和歌各一首が書かれている。大変美しい本。1811年、1冊、4折判。

+344. **類葉百人一首教文庫**(るいようひゃくにんいっしゅきょうぶんこ Ruijevu Fjaknin itsusju keomonko)。つまり子供、孫たちのための百人の歌人の撰集教本の語彙辞典。1817年、1冊。

日本語訳（V神学書と道徳書）

345. **女用至宝都名所尽**（みやこめいしょつくし Dsjojô sibo Mijako Meisjo tsukusi）。京都名所図。少女用に池田東籬斎（Ikeda Tourisai）〔池田東籬亭〕が編集した。京都、1824年、1冊、16折判。

346. **定家撰錦葉鈔**（ていかせんきんようしょう Teika sen kinjevu seô）。大変有名な歌人定家（Teika）（*）の和歌選。彩色2つ折判で書かれている。大坂、1814年、1冊、4折判。

　　　　（*）1241年没。

+347. **雑話教訓鑑**（ざつわきょうくんかん Zatwa, Keokun Kagami）。修養規律の手本、あるいは諸々の行動規律と見なされうる様々な訓話。1776年、5冊。

+348. **近世貞婦伝**（こんぜていふでん konze tei fu zen〔きんせいていふでん〕）。最近の有徳で傑出した婦人たちの伝記。1800年、5冊。No.347に述べられた書名を変えて、1800年に再版された見本あなたは入手できよう。

+349. **世談雑説**（せだんぞうせつ Sedan zavusets〔せだんざつせつ〕）。皆から非常によく話題にされていることの諸説（や観客の作り話や実話）。1754年、5冊。

+350. **つれづれ草**（つれづれぐさ Tsuredsure gusa）。何もせず所存ない、耳ざわりなちょっとした話。1737年、2冊。付・画。

+351. **絵本金花談**（えほんきんかだん Jehon Kinkwa dan）。美しい黄金の花の物語絵本、または源頼朝（Minamoto Joritomo）将軍と同時代に生きた岩城兵庫守秀勝（Iwagi Fiogono Kami Fidekatsu）王の生涯。1806年、12冊。

+352. **絵本鏡山烈〔列〕女功**（えほんかがみやまれつじょこう Jehon Kagamijama retzjokô〔えほんかがみやまれつじょのいさおし〕）。加々見山列女の最もすばらしい行為、あるいは列女尾上おはつ（Wonoë Ofats）の生涯。若者用に川関惟充（Kavaseki Wizju）撰。1803年、5冊。

+353. **巨勢金岡 名技伝**（こせのかなおかめいぎつたえ Koseno Kanaoka Meiki tsutave〔こせのかなおかめいぎでん〕）。巨勢金岡（Koseno Kanaoka）絵師の最も有名な作品。1808年、2冊、付絵。8折判。

+354. **〔文化新板〕伊勢物語**（いせものがたり Isemonogatari）。伊勢の物語。再び活字に付されたもの。1804年、2冊、8折判。

+355. **本朝蘗物語**（ほんちょうひきものがたり Honteôfiki monogatari）。日本史選。1774年、1冊、8折判。

+356. **遠乃白波**（おちのしらなみ Wotsino siranami）。遠方の白波、または（Itsufon Dajemon）〔日本左衛門〕という名のある海賊の物語。3冊、8折判。

*357. **七福七難図会**（しちふくしちなんずえ Sitsi-fuk sitsi-nan dsu-e）。順境と逆境の七福七難図。大坂の人　生々瑞馬（Seisei Suima）〔せいせいずいば〕著、明石の人　岡田東虎（Ohada Tôseki）〔おかだとうこ〕画。5冊、8折判。

+358. 和漢古今角偉談（わかんここんかくわいだん　Wakan kokon kakwi dan）。古代から現代まで中国と日本での、特別な大事件について考察し記述されている。著者菊丘臥山人（Kikuoka Kwasanziu）。1748年、5冊、8折判。

+359. 艶廓通覧（えんかくつうらん　Jenkwak dsuran）。女性たちの間での豪奢についての盛んな観察。洞羅山人（Tôra Sanzin）が小話で説明したもの。1800年、5冊、8折判。

+360. 松陰快談（まつかげかいだん　Matsukage kwaidan〔Sûngîn K'uaìt'ân〕〔しょういんかいだん〕）。陰に捨てられ、眠りについた者たちの愉快な話。中国語で書かれた豊山長野先生（Tojojama Nagano Sensei）〔長野豊山〕による様々な論評である。京都、1821年、2冊、8折判。

+361. 東牖子（とうゆうし　Tôjûsi）。賢い男の多様な注釈。1冊、欠損、未完本。

+362. 間情偶寄（Hiênts'ing ngeù ki〔かんじょうぐうき〕）。ふとして起こったことの暇な感想。湖上李（Hû Schángli）〔李漁〕編。2冊、8折判。

+363. 笑府（しょうふ　Siáofu）。笑話辞典。笑話、落語小話。墨憨斎主人（Bok kan sai Sjuzin）が中国語版と日本語読みの注を記した。1冊、12折判。

364. 浮世新形六枚屏風（うきよしんがたろくまいびょうぶ　Ukijo sinkata rok mai bjôfu）。金色の普通六枚から成る新形の屏風。それらはその時代の流行を見る者に、新しい容姿で飾られている（*）。柳亭種彦（Riutei Tanefiko）作、絵師〔歌川〕豊国（Tojokuni）の手によって描かれて翌年、刊本は江戸の市民にこの表題で提供されている。2冊、1820年刊。

*ドイツ語簡約表題："Sechsblätteriger Windschirm mit neuen Figuren aus der flotten Welt."（浮世〔現世〕の新しい容姿の六枚屏風）

365. 音羽丹七女郎花喩粟島（おとわたんしちおみなえしたとえのあわしま　Otoba Tansitsi. Womina besi Tatoveno avasima）。女郎音羽（Otoba）と商人丹七（Tansitsi）との間の色事。柳亭種彦（Riutei Tanefiko）作、年間書。江戸、1822年、2冊。

366. 正本製七編（しょうほんじたてしちへん　Seôhon sitate sitsiben）。〔歌舞伎の〕原本・台本七編。柳亭種彦（Riutei Tanefiko）作。江戸、1825年、2冊。

367. 正本製八編（しょうほんじたてはちへん　Seôhon sitate fatsiben）。前掲書の小冊子の八編。8折判。江戸、1826年、2冊。

368. 笹色〔酒〕猪口暦手（ささいろのちょくこよみで　Sasairono tsjoku kojomide〔ささいろのちょくはこよみで〕）。同書の小冊子。1826年刊、2冊。

*369. おそめ久松 花競浮名の読販（おそめひさまつはなくらべうきなのよみうり　Osome Fisamatsu Fanakurabe ukinano jomiuri）。おそめ（Osome）久松（Fisamatsu）が追い求めた恋人たち。江戸、1822年、3冊。

370. 山海経（せんがいきょう　Sengaikjô〔Schân hai kîng〕）。郭璞（Kuōp'ō）著とされる外国の陸地、海についての、まったく古い伝説的地理書が、再び日本で活字にされたもの。18

巻、7冊。

371. **キフ子本地**（きふねのほんじ　Kibuneno Hondsi）。昔の貴船、または貴船という地で行われた諸行事。3冊。貴重な手稿。付絵図。

372. **長恨歌**（ちょうごんか　Tsjôkon uta〔*Tsch'ânghén kô*〕）。「長恨」（あるいは中国の皇帝玄宗（*Jang Kueifei*）が、745年に貴妃にした高貴な娘楊貴妃（*Hiuên tsûng*）の日本語訳された長篇叙事詩。3冊。絵付き、貴重な手稿。

第Ⅵ部　詩

A. 劇詩

373. **妹背山**（いもせやま　Imose jama）。妹背山という名で言われている史劇。5冊、8折判。

374. **壇浦兜軍**（だんのうらかぶとぐん　Dannoura kabuto-kun）。壇浦の戦での兜軍。私たちは「〔阿古屋〕琴責めの段」（*Koto semeno tan*）と云われているこの史劇の一幕をもっている。壇浦付近の決戦（1185年）安徳天皇（*Mikadouis Antok interitus*）の死去がこの劇の論拠である。

+375. **一谷嫩軍記**（いちのたにふたばぐんき　Itsinotani futaba kun ki）。1184年（摂津国）一谷合戦での敗北。豊竹越前少禄〔掾〕（*Tojotake Jetsizen Seorok*）著。1751年刊、再刊1764年、1冊。

+376. 〔姉若草妹初音〕**本町糸屋娘**（ほんまちいとやむすめ　Honmatsi Itoja musume）。若草（*Wakagusa*）と初音（*Fatsne*）、本町糸屋の史劇。1814年刊、1冊。

+377. **近江源氏先陣館**（おうみげんじせんじんやかた　Omi Gensi sendsin Jakáta）。つまり源家に備えて追い、近江国で詰めている、先陣たちの陣屋。1769年刊、2冊。

+378. **仮名手本忠臣蔵**（かなてほんちゅうしんぐら　kanatehon Tsiusingura）。つまり忠義を尽くす家来がしまってある所。1748年、1冊。

+379. **双蝶蝶曲輪記**（ふたつちょうちょうくるわき　Futats teôteô kuruwaki）〔双蝶蝶曲輪日記〕。結ばれた二匹の蝶の館。1749年、1冊。

+380. **菅原伝授手習鑑**（すがわらでんじゅてならいかがみ　Sugavara tenzju tenaravi kagami）。菅原（*Sugavara*）〔道真〕によって伝えられた寺子屋修業の手本。1746年、1冊。

+381. **京都歌舞伎〔妓〕新狂言外題年鑑**（きょうとかぶきしんきょうげんげだいねんかん　Kjôto kabuki sin kjôgen ge-tai nen kan）。京都の役者たちが動き回るのを常とする狂言の標題の索引。1719年～1826年に書かれた、この種の狂言が列挙されている。1枚。2つ折判。

382. **諸〔都〕国芝居繁栄数望**（くにぐにしばいはんえいずもう　Kuniguni sibawi vanjei

sumô)。日本での演劇の列挙。1冊。

B. 歌(うた)〔和歌〕という叙情詩

383. **古今集遠鏡**（こきんしゅうとおかがみ Kokin sju tovokagami）。古今集（Kokin sju）が905年に最初に撰されて成った和歌集の長期にわたる手本。つまり古い歌と新しいうたの集成。それは二行連句一万を入れている。これらの和歌の手本の撰者本居宣長（*Motowi Noritake*）〔もとおり のりなが〕は詩論の学識ある評価者であった。1816年、6冊、8折判。

384. **百人一首峯のかけはし**（ひゃくにんいっしゅみねのかけはし Fjakninitsu sju mineno kakebasi）。日本の和歌の高みへの階段。日本のパルナソスへの階段、あるいは百人の歌人によって和歌の注釈と結びついた詩論への入門。本居宣長（*Motowi Noritake*）〔もとおり のりなが〕著。衣川大人（*Koromogava Dainin*）編。1806年、2冊、8折判。

+385. **歌道名目抄〔鈔〕**（かどうめいもくしょう Kadômei mok seô〔かどうみょうもくしょう〕）。詩論3巻。右中辨資任（*Utsiufen Sukemotsi*）著。1713年、3冊、8折判。

+386. **正徹物語**（しょうてつのものがたり Sjôtetsno monogatari）。詩人正徹（*Sjôtets*）（＊）の生涯と歌。1790年、2冊、8折判。

（＊）正徹は1459年没。

387. **万葉集**（まんようしゅう Manjo sju）。本書は多数紙葉の古代の歌集。橘諸兄（*Tatsibana Moroje*）（757年没）が着手し、右大弁〔大伴〕家持（*Udaiven Jakamotsi*）が終えた。京都1684年-1686年、30冊、8折判。

388. **和歌怜野集**（やまとうたれいやしゅう Jamato uta Rinja sju）。日本の田園詩。清原雄風（*Kijobarano Ogaze*）撰。1806年、12冊、8折判、6表題あり、「四季（春・夏・秋・冬）」と他は恋歌と雑歌である。

＊389. **歌林雑木抄**（かりんざつもくしょう Karin zatsmok seô）。森の歌の様々な樹木、あるいは和歌集。京都、1696年、8冊、8折判。第1、2冊 春の歌。第3冊 夏。第4、5冊 秋。第6冊 冬。第7冊 恋、友情。第8冊 雑。

390. **続撰吟和歌集類題〔韻〕**（しょくせんぎんわかしゅうるいだい Sjoksengin Wakasju rui tai）。和歌集。四季と表題で分けられている。1800年、1冊、8折判。

391. **千紅万紫**（せんこうばんし Senkô bansi）。深紅色の和歌。蜀山先生（*Sjoksan Sensei*）編集。1817年、1冊、小8折判。

392. **百人一首小倉文庫**（ひゃくにんいっしゅこくらもんこ Fjaknin itsu sju Kokura monko〔ひゃくにんいっしゅおぐらぶんこ〕）。百人の歌人の歌各一首の選集。ごく小さい書。

393. **百人一首**（ひゃくにんいっしゅ Fjaknin itsu sju）。百人の歌人の歌各一首の選集。1

冊、16 折判。

394. 宝玉百人一首（ほうぎょくひゃくにんいっしゅ Fôgjok Fjaknin itsu sju）。つまり百人の歌人の歌各一首の貴重な選集。1 冊、12 折判。

395. 絵本百人一首（えほんひゃくにんいっしゅ Jehon Fjaknin itsu sju）。百人の歌人の歌各一首を、絵本にした選集。2 冊、8 折判。

396. 絵本和歌合（えほんわかあわせ Jehon Waka awase）。絵本にした和歌集。富士谷御杖（*Fudsitani Mitsuje*）編、1819 年、1 冊、8 折判。

397. 絵本和歌合（えほんわかあわせ Jehon Waka awase）。絵本にした和歌集。1 冊。

398. 貝ツクシ浦のにしき（かいつくしうらのにしき Kaitsukusi urano nisigi）。海辺で貝を集めて歌った口実、あるいは真珠貝（詩歌）集。能登の伴花菴（*Fan Kwa an*）著。1 冊、8 折判。

399. 三十六歌集（さんじゅうろくうたのあつめ Sanzjurok utano atsume〔さんじゅうろっかしゅう〕）。和歌三十六首集。前掲書に入れられている歌と同じである。

400. 山家集類題（さんかしゅうるいだい Jamakasju, rui tai）。山家「*Jamakana*」〔やまが〕（この名は丹波国の山中にある家の名）の歌集。法師の西行上人（*Saigjô sjônin*）が種類分けして表題を付加している。1813 年、1 冊、小 8 折判。

C. 俳諧という歌

401. 俳諧七部集（はいかいしちぶあつめ Haikai sitsibu atsume〔はいかいしちぶしゅう〕）。七部に分けられた俳諧撰集。1774 年、2 冊、12 折判。

402. 八重山彦〔婦〕（やえのやまびこ Javeno jamabiko）〔八重山吹〕。つまり数多く重なったこだま。1804 年、2 冊、8 折判。

403. 狂歌手毎之花（きょうかてごとのはな Kjô kate gotono bana）。狂歌作者たちから汲み出された小詞花。文屋茂喬（*Bunjano Sigetada*）編。1810 年、2 冊、小 8 折判。

404. 狂歌画自満（きょうかえじまん Kjôka je ziman）。〔魚屋〕北渓先生（*Hokkei Sensei*）によって図解され狂歌。3 冊。

+405. 狂歌関東百題集（きょうかかんとうひゃくだいしゅう Kjôka Kwantô fjaktai sju）。江戸で歌われた百狂歌集。鈍々亭（*Tontontei*）〔和樽〕編。江戸、1805 年、2 冊、8 折判。

+406. 狂歌扶桑集（きょうかふそうしゅう Kjôka Fusan sju）。日本で歌われた狂歌集。2 冊、8 折判。

D. 漢詩

+407. **宋詩清絶**（Súng schî ts'íng tsiuē〔そうしせいぜつ〕）。宋朝下に作られ、最も読まれた漢詩。付・日本語読みの最大特徴。柏木如亭（Kajaaki Njotei）編。江戸、1814年、1冊。

+408. **宋詩礎**（そうしのはしら Sôzino fasira〔そうしそ〕[Súng schî ts'ǔ]）。宋朝下に作られた詩歌の基礎。大窪行（Ohokubo gjô）〔詩仏〕編。江戸、1803年、2冊。束、風のように、押韻を章節に配置して、多様な表現形式が添えられている。

+409. **詩礎諺解**（しそげんかい Ziso genkai [Schîts'ǔ jén kiai]）。漢詩の基礎である表現形式が日本語の説明なされている。聯句が添えられている。村瀬海輔（Murase Kaibo）編。1冊。

+410. **袖珍略韻大成**（しゅうちんりゃくいんたいせい Siutsinrjak in daisei,[Sieú tschîn liōjún tá tsch'îng]）。押韻の韻語語彙辞書。三語句の漢詩音が日本語説明で添えられている。4冊。

第Ⅶ部 国民と諸制度

A. 風習と制度

+411. **制度通**（せいどつう Sei do dsû [Tschí tú t'ûng]）。中国と日本の諸法令と制度。伊藤長胤（Itô Tsjôin）輯。1724年、16巻、手稿、6冊、8折判。

412. **骨董集**（こっとうしゅう Kot tô sju [Kōtòng tsī]）。収集・美術鑑賞に値する品々、あるいは日本の古物の生活様式・道具。付・図。1815年、5冊、8折判。

413. 〔新板後篇〕**嫁入談合柱**（よめいりだんごうばしら Jomeiri dankô basira [Kiáschī t'ân hō tschǔ]）。結婚仲人の中心あるいは結婚を取り決めるのに何が守られるべきかということ。都の華鳳山人（Kwafô Sonzin）著。大坂、2冊、8折判。付・画。

414. **三礼口訣**（さんれいくけつ Sanrei Kukets [Sân li k'eǔkiuē]）。貝原篤信（Kaibara Toksin）〔かいばらあつのぶ〕著。三礼についての説明、あるいは飲食、茶事、書礼について守るべきこと。1688年、2冊、12折。

415. **当風和国百女**（とうふうわこくひゃくじょ Tôfû Wakok fjaknjo [Táng fûng Hôkuē pēniǔ]）。新流行様式で飾られた全日本女性層。菱川師宣（Fizi gawa Moro nobu）著。1冊、大8折判。

+416. **小笠原諸礼大全**（おがさわらしょれいたいぜん Wokasa vara sjorei daizen）。法橋王山（Fokjô Wôsan）〔岡田玉山（ぎょくざん）〕著。日本の風習と制度について、小笠原（Wokasawara）家の門主貞宗弓高（Sadamune Kiutaka）〔小笠原貞宗〕が命じ、後醍醐天皇（Mikado Godaiko）が認可し

た。1810 年刊、3 冊、8 折判。付・図。

　+417.　京大坂茶屋諸分調方記（みやこおおさかちゃやしょぶんちょうほうき　Mijako Ohosaka tsjaja sjo bunteôfô ki〔茶屋諸分調方記〕）。飲料茶が販売されている京・大坂の茶屋の記述。1 冊、16 折判。

　418.　装束図式（しょうぞくずしき　Seô zok dsu siki〔Tschoâng schō t'û schĭ〕）。天皇とその宮廷人がよく着る礼服の図。1692 年、2 冊、8 折判。

　419.　かさねのいろめ（Kasaneno irome）。衣装に重ねて着用する習慣の一対の地色の配合。須原屋茂兵衛（Suwara ja movei）編、江戸、1826 年、1 冊。

　420.　雅遊漫録（がゆうまんろく　Gajù man rok〔Jà jeu moénlū〕）。適切優雅な什器図。大枝流芳著。大坂、1755 年、5 冊、8 折判。

　421.　群書類従（ぐんしょるいじゅう　Gunsjo ruiseô〔Kiuntschu luits'ông〕）。様々な書を部門に分類して収められた叢書。検校〔塙〕保己一（Kenkjô Fomiitsi）編。1683 年。本叢書は 171 巻 3 冊から成り、その中に神祇、多様な律令、公事（遊戯・飲食）が記されている。

B. 都市・国家組織と行政

　422.　文政武鑑（ぶんせいぶかん　Bunsei Bu kan）。いわゆる文政年間（1818 年～）の武事手本。5 冊、12 折判。本書には幕府国家の形態、行政、将軍家、諸侯、全武士階級の系譜、心得、役目に関する各々の規則が大変詳細に記述されている。

　423.　御元服御宮参御用掛御役人附（おんげんぷくぎょきゅうにまいる〔ごげんぷくおみやまいり おやくにん〕ごようがかりおやくにんづけ　On gen buk Gjo kiûni mairu Gjo jôke gjo jaknin tsuku）。将軍家の男の長子が誕生して、成人服を着用した後の公家侍臣の記述。1826 年、1 冊、16 折判。

　424.　万代宝鑑（まんたいほうかん　Mantai fôkan〔Wàntaí paò kièn〕〔ばんだいほうかん〕）。それは万代継承に貴重な手本である。しかしそれは日本国全体の記述が施されている。江戸、1826 年、1 冊。

　425.　月令博物筌（げつれいはくぶつせん　Gwatsrei fakbutszen〔Juĕlíng pōwŭts'iuên〕）。本書は年間の歳時故事を四季別各月に、ふさわしく集めた豊富なやな（方法・手引き）、あるいは日本人の年中行事の暦表、14 冊、12 折判。貝原篤信（Kaibara Toksin）〔かいばらあつのぶ〕著。大坂、1804 年。これらの書には、日本人の故事、生活に関して何でも示されている。

　426.　文政十一年略暦候（ぶんせいじゅういちねんりゃくれきこう　Bunsei zjuitsi nen rjakrekiko）。文政 11 年暦（1828 年）。

　427.　文政十一（戊子）年略暦十七二候（ぶんせいじゅういち（つちのえの）としりゃくれき

じゅうしちにこう　Bunsei zjuitsi（tsutsinoje ne no）tosi rjakreki zjusitsini kô）。前掲書年暦。

C. 政治

+428. **万世江戸町鑑**（よろずよえどまちのかがみ　Jorodsujo Jedo matsino kagami〔ばんせいえどちょうかん〕）。つまり地域組合での江戸町の手本。町奉行について、江戸町内においての全体の風紀、安全な治安について、奉行の守るべきことを伝えた諸国御関所について書かれている。

429. **町火消番組**（まちひけしばんぐみ　Matsi fikesi ban gumi)。江戸の町の火災に対して定められた見張番摘要。

430. **火事御出役**〔定火消御役御大名火消 御場所附 イロハ番組〕（かじおんしゅつやく　Kuwazi on sjutsjak)。江戸の町で大名屋敷の火災に対して定められた見張番摘要。

431. 〔江戸本所深川〕**いろは組纏つくし**〔両面摺〕（いろはぐみまといつくし　Irofa kumi matove tsukusi)。江戸の町の火災に対して、見張番に注意されている合図の摘要。

E. 建築

431. **大工雛形**（だいくひながた　Daiku finagata)。建築の手本、あるいは建築について、5冊。江戸、1717年。

第1巻. **宮雛形**（Mija finagata)、または神殿・聖殿の特徴見本。

第2巻. **武家雛形**（Buke finagata)、武家向家の特徴見本。

第3巻. **棚雛形**（Tana finagata)、床張りの見本。

第4巻. **数寄屋雛形**（Sukija finagata)、市民の茶室風建築基準。

第5巻. **小坪規矩**（Seôfei nori)〔こつぼきく〕、什器の基準。

433. **度量衡説統**（どりょうこうせっとう　Doreôkô sets tô [Tŏliànghêng schuĕ t'ŏng]）。長さ・容積・目方についての簡単な説明。最上徳内（*Mogami Toknai*)。江戸、1824年、3冊、8折判。

D. 軍事

434. **図解武用弁略**（ずかいぶようべんりゃく　Dsukai, Bujô benrjak [*Tûkiaí, Wùjúng pién liŏ*]）。軍事についての図解。木下義俊（*Kinosita Jositomo*)〔きのしたよしとし〕著。江戸、1747年、8冊、8折判。

435. **甲冑着**〔著〕**用弁**（かっちゅうちゃくようべん　Kattsiu tsjakjô ben [*Kiătscheú tschôjúng*

pién〕)。どんなふうに甲冑を着用する必要があるか。井上翁（Winouve Okina）〔井上直〕著。1803年、3冊。

436. **古軍器之図解**（こぐんきのずかい　Ko Gunkino dsu kai〔Kù kiûn k'ítschi t'ù kiaí〕)。昔の軍の装備図。図表。手稿。

437. **角觝詳説活金剛伝**（すもうしょうせつ、かつこんごうでん　Sumô seôsets, Kwats kongô den)。相撲について、または体のたくましさが金剛力士であることを、称える。松寿楼主人（Seôzjurô Sjuzin）撰。江戸、1822年、2冊、8折判、付・図。

第Ⅷ部　経済書

A. 農業

438. **佩文耕織図**（はいぶんこうしょくず　Fai bun kô sjokno dsu〔Peíwên Kêngtschī t'û〕)。皇帝の自筆を付した農耕図と蚕織図。本書は康熙（K'ang hi）帝の命令によって1696年に書かれ、後継者世宗（Schi tsung）の警句で飾られ、その形でその任務が示されている。見本は1807年、江戸で再び活字にされたもの。2冊、2折判。

439. **成形図説**（なりかたちのずせつ　Nari katatsino dsu sets〔Tsch'îng hîng t'û schuĕ〕〔せいけいずせつ〕)。つまり自然に形をつくりまたは手を加えて実るものが図説されている。国主〔島津重豪〕の命令で作成して発行された、日本の全農業を包含している書。序文は有名な藤原〔白尾〕国柱（Fudsivara Kunifasira）によって書かれている。1804年、30冊。

440. **農業全書**（のうぎょうぜんしょ　Nôgeo zensjo〔Nûngniĕ ts'iuên schŭ〕)。農業冊子。宮崎安貞（Mijasaki Antei）著。京都、1696年、8冊、8折判。

441. **農家益**（のうかえき　Nôka jeki〔Nûng kiá i〕)。つまり農業の有益性に関して。22冊中3冊があるが、その中では黄櫨の木を犠牲にする農耕と植物性蠟を準備することについて。著者、大蔵永常（Ohokura Nagatsune）。大坂、1820年。

442. **農嫁〔稼〕業事**（のうかぎょうじ　Nôka geozi〔Nûng kiá niĕ ssé〕)。農家の仕事・商売。児島如水（Kosima Zjo sui）著。大坂、1793年、5冊、8折判。

443. **山海名産図会**（さんかいめいさんずえ　Sankai meisan dsu e〔Schân hai mîngts'àn t'û hoeí〕)。陸・海産物の主要物。木村孔恭（Kimura Kôkjô）著。付・図。大坂、1799年、5冊、8折判。

444. **日本山海名物図会**（にっぽんさんかいめいぶつずえ　Nippon sankai meibuts dsu e)。日本の陸・海産物の主要物。付・図。平瀬徹斎（Firase Tetsusai）著。大坂、1753年、5冊、8折判。

445. **武江産物志**（ぶこうさんぶつし　Bukô san buts si [Wŭkiâng ts'àn wŭ tschì]）。武蔵国の産物誌。岩崎常正（Ivasaki Tokiva）〔いわさきつねまさ〕著。1824年、1冊、12折判。

446. **飲膳摘要**（いんぜんてきよう　Inzen takujô [Inschén ts'ējao]）。日本の食膳。小野蘭山（Wono Lansan）が列挙し記述した。1814年刊、1冊、16折判。

447. 〔童蒙教訓〕**絵本米恩録**（えほんべいおんろく　Jehon beiwon rok [Hoeí pèn mingēn lŭ]）。豊年米の恩の書。絵本で示されている。中川有恒（Nakagawa Aritsūne）が児童向に書いた。京都、1802年、5冊。

448. **日州養蜂図**（にっしゅうようほうのず　Nitsu sin jôfono dsu）。日向国の養蜂所の銅刻図。最上徳内（Mogami Toknai）図説。

B. 商工

449. **職人尽発句合**（しょくにんつくしほっくあわせ　Sjoknin tsukusi, fotsuku avase）。職人への関心または図。職人にかかわる警句の発句が続いている。閑田子蒿蹊（Kanten Si kôkei）〔伴蒿蹊〕撰。江戸、1797年、2冊、8折判。

450. **江戸職人歌合**（えどしょくにんうたあわせ　Jedo sjoknin, utaavase）。江戸の職人が歌に作られ、組み合わされている。尾張、1808年、2冊、8折判。

+451. **妙術博物筌**（みょうじゅつはくぶつせん　Meôzjuts fakbuts zen）。隠された秘術についての豊富な宝鑑。貝原篤信（Kaibara Toksin）〔かいばらあつのぶ〕によって編纂された技法7冊書。

452. **装剣奇賞**（そうけんきしょう　Sôken kisjô [Tschoâng kién kî schàng]）。つまり架空芝居の剣士たちの珍しい賞賛。大坂の人　稲葉通龍新右衛門（Inaba Mitsidatsu Sinjemon）著。1781年、7冊、8折判。芝居の剣士名は、すでに銅版や木の浮彫り細工師が入れている。

453. **鼓銅図録**（こどうずろく　Kotô dsurok）。鉱石を採掘して洗浄する術。増田綱（Masida kô）著。1冊、8折判。

454. **鮫皮精鑑録**（さめがわせいかんろく　Samekava seikan rok）。サメの皮の研磨術。その皮で剣士の刀の柄は飾られている。大坂、1759年、1冊、8折判。

455. **滑稽漫画**（こっけいまんが　Kotsukei mankwa）。つまりまだその全あら筋が動揺と混乱におとしいれていない、道化風刺画の発散表現。見本は核心の表出術にある。暁鐘成（Kjô seô sei）〔あかつきのかねなり〕編。江戸、1823年、1冊。

456. **押絵早稽古**（おしえはやげいこ　Osije fajageiko）。つまり押絵〔中に綿を入れて他の物に張りつけた押し出し絵〕の少女用早期の教え。堀井軒（Fori Seiken）編。京都、1825年、1冊、8折判。

457. 雅曲花結〔娘〕玉のあそび（がきょくはなむすび、たまのあそび　Kagjok Fana musubi, Tamano asobi）。高価な演出、あるいは結び目を功妙に編んで作る術。雄川丘甫（*Okava Kiufo*）編。大坂、1817年、1冊、8折判。

458. 生花秘伝 野山錦（いけばなひでんのやまにしき　Ikebana fiden no jama no nisigi）。つまり野山の花の錦で織り合わされた生花。花器の中の主軸・従属軸を守ることについて記されている。木村周篤（*Kimura Siutok*）編。大坂、1730年、2冊、2折判。

459. 瓶花図彙（いけばなずい　Ikebana dsui〔へいかずい〕）。瓶に入れた花の図。山中忠左衛門（*Jamanaka Tsiu Sajemon*）編。1698年、2冊、2折判。

460. 瓶花図全（いけばなずぜん　Ikebana dsuzen〔へいかずぜん〕）。瓶に入れた花の図。1冊、8折判。

461. 挿花 千筋之麓（いけばなちすじのふもと　Ikebana tsisuzino fumoto〔そうかちすじのふもと〕）。つまり山の麓の根本は多くの生きた花から成っている。瓶に入れるための華道。入江玉蟾（*Irije Kjoksen*）著。江戸、1768年、3冊、8折判。

462. 挿花衣之香（いけばなころものか　Ikebana koromonoka〔そうかころものか〕）。花で飾られた衣装の芳香。びんに入れるための華道。貞松斎一馬（*Satomatsu sai Itsiba*）〔ていしょうさいいちば〕著。江戸、1801年、8冊、8折判。

+463. 立華正道集（りっかせいどうしゅう　Ritsukwa seidô sju）。形を整えて、立てた生け花からなされるべき正しい規則。1684年、4冊。

464. 日本染色法（にっぽんそめいろのほう　Nippon someirono fô〔にほんせんしょくほう〕）。布を染めることは、日本ではどのように着色されるか。1冊。手稿。

465. a. 染物の法（そめもののほう　Somemonono fô）。染色方法について。
　　b. 早稲作法（わせつくりのりほう　Wase tsukuri nori〔わせさくほう〕）。早く実る品種の稲作法について。
　　c. 茶製法（ちゃつくりのり　Tsja tsukûri nori〔ちゃせいほう〕）。茶の葉を飲料用とする加工法について。1冊、12折判。手稿。

466. 酒作之事（さけつくること　Sake tsukûru koto〔さけつくりのこと〕）。酒という名の飲料を醸造することについて。1冊、手稿、8折判。

467. 紙作之法（かみつくるほう　Kami tsukûru fô〔かみつくりのほう〕）。紙の製法。1冊、手稿、8折判。

468. 塗之法（ぬるほう　Nuru fô〔ぬりのほう〕）。容器に漆・ニスを塗る方法、理由。1冊。手稿。

469. 拾玉智恵海（しゅうぎょくちえかい　Sjugjok tsije kai [*Schijūtschi hoeí hai*]〔しゅうぎょくちえのうみ〕）。つまり英知と利益の貴重な海の称揚。ここで書かれている表題の　ある技術

者の書。別巻では、魔術・呪文について論じられている。

470. **日本持丸長者集**（にっぽんもちまるちょうじゃしゅう　Nippon motsimaru teôzja sju）。日本の主な商人番付。

471. **張公捕魚**（ちょうこうすなどり　Tsjôko sunadori〔ちょうこうほぎょ〕）。捕鯨図。1冊、2折判。手稿。

472. **造塩法図**（しおつくるほうず　Sifo tsukûru fô dsu〔ぞうえんほうず〕）。製塩図。1冊。手稿。

第IX部　貨幣書

473. **珍貨孔方鑑**（ちんかこうほうかん　Tsinkwa kôfô kan）。通貨書、または四角孔で刻印された青銅貨見本。中谷顧山（*Nakatani Kôsan*）著。大坂、1730年、1冊、8折判。

+474. **寛政孔方鑑**（かんせいこうほうかん　Kwansei kôfô kan）。流石庵（*Riuseki Anu*）〔りゅうせきあん、河村羽積〕が、いわゆる寛政年間（1789年-1800年）に集めた青銅貨幣見本。1冊、8折判。

475. **改正孔方図鑑**（かいせいこうほうずかん　Kaisei kôfô dsu kan）。その見本によって改正された青銅貨幣図像が提示されている。小沢〔辰元〕東市（*Wozawa Tôitsi*）編。1785年、1冊、8折判。別本見本あり、それは番号477に私たちは記した。

+476. **珍銭奇品図録**（ちんせんきひんずろく　Tsin sen kibin dsurok〔*Tschîn ts'iên kîp'in t'û lû*〕）。日本と同じく中国の珍奇な青銅貨幣（それゆえ古銭半両によって、今日まで和銅開珎銭と言われている）。大村成富（*Ohomura Naritomi*）編。1冊、8折判。

477. **孔方図鑑**（こうほうずかん　Kôfô dsu kan〔*K'ùngfâng t'û kién*〕）。青銅貨幣図鑑。小沢〔辰元〕東市（*Wozawa Tôitsi*）編。1789年、1冊、8折判。

478. **古今泉貨鑑**（ここんせんかかん　Kokon senkwa kan〔*Kùkin t'siuênhó kién*〕〔ここんせんかかがみ〕）。昔と今の貨幣概観。小沢〔辰元〕東市（*Wozawa Tôitsi*）編〔序〕。1804年、12冊、8折判。

479. **和漢泉彙**（わかんせんい　Wa Kan sen wi）。日本と中国の貨幣集。芳川〔維堅〕甚右衛門（*Fôgawa Zinujemon*）編〔序〕。1793年、1冊、8折判。

480. **金銀図録**（きんぎんずろく　Kingin dsurok）。金貨と銀貨の図録。近藤重蔵（*Kontô Ziudsiû*）編。江戸、1810年、7冊、8折判。

481. **対泉譜**（たいせんふ　Taisen fu〔*Tuí tsiuên p'ù*〕〔ついせんふ〕）。文字と刻文の両方の一連の貨幣。文楼田元成（*Burôden Motonari*）〔文桜、田元成、加保茶元成〕著。江戸、1814

年、1冊、8折判。

　＊＋482. **古銭価附**（こせんあたいつく　Ko sen, atavi tsuku〔こせんあたいづけ〕）。値段が記してある古銭。

　＊483. **銭範**（せんぱん　Sen van〔Ts'iên fán〕）。通貨のならうべき一定のしきたり、あるいは日本で使用された通貨概観。

　484. **懐宝珍銭鑑**（かいほうちんせんかがみ　Kwaibo tsinsen kagami）。ふところに入れるお守りとみなされている通貨概観。

　485. **西洋銭譜**（せいようせんぷ　Seijô sen bu〔Sijang ts'ien p'ŭ〕）。外国（ヨーロッパ）の通貨小論。小沢〔辰元〕東市（Wozawa Tôitsi）著〔凡例〕、〔朽木昌綱著〕。1冊、8折判。

第X部　医学書と薬学書

　486. **鍼灸抜粋大成**（しんきゅうばっすいたいせい　Sinkiu fatsusui daisei〔Tschînkieù pāts'uí tátsching〕）。鍼術と艾〔灸〕の卓越性について。岡本一抱子（Okamoto Itsufôsi）著。京都、1699年、7冊、8折判。

　487. **鍼灸広狭神倶集**（しんきゅうこうきょうしんぐしゅう　Sinkiu kwôkeô singu sju〔Tschîn kieù Kuang hiă schînkiû tsï〕）。鍼術と灸の神的そなえ。雲桜子（Unrôsi）〔雲棲子〕編。江戸、1819年、1冊、8折判。

　488. **鍼灸説約**（しんきゅうせつやく　Sinkiu setsjak〔Tschîn kieù schuějō〕）。鍼術と灸の説明の簡単なまとめ。国主の侍医石坂宗哲（Isisaka Sôtets）編。江戸、1812年、1冊、12折判。

　489. **広参説**（こうしんせつ　Kwôsin sets〔こうさんせつ〕）。五葉、オタネニンジンの根についての小論。〔小野〕職孝（Sjok kô）〔職孝は跋文記載。正しくは職博、蘭山〕著。1冊、8折判。

　490. **薬名称呼**（やくめいしょうこ　Jak mei sjô ko〔Jŏ mîng tsch'îng hu〕）。多数の薬名の中国語・日本語称呼。木原宗真（Kivara Sôtei）〔きはらむねざね〕編。京都、1823年、1冊、12折判。

　491. **人面瘡図説**（にんめんそうずせつ　Nin men zô dsu sets）。人面（Nin men）つまり人間の顔という名のすねのはれものについての図説。桂川甫賢（Kadsuragawa Hoken）著。

　492. **解臓図賦〔譜〕**（かいぞうずふ　Kaizô dsu fu〔Kiaì tsáng t'ŭ fú〕）。ヨーロッパ起源の解剖図。池田義之冬蔵（Ikeda Josijuki Tôzô）編。京都、1821年、1冊、8折判。

　493. **和蘭全体内外分図**（わらんぜんくないがいぶんのず　Walan zenku naigwaibun no dsu）〔和蘭全軀内外分合図〕。人体全部分の解剖図。オランダ語原書を長崎の通詞本木子意（Motoki

si i)〔本木 了意(りょうい)〕が和訳し、周防国医師鈴木宗云（*Suzuki Sôun*）が編した。1774 年、2 冊、8 折判。

494. 栄衛中経図（えいえいちゅうけいのず　Jeijei tsiukeino dsu [*Ingweï tschûng kîng t'ú*]）。脈管学に関する二表。竿斎先生（*Kan sei Sen seï*）〔石坂宗哲〕編。1825 年。

495. 薬品応手録（やくひんおうしゅろく　Jabinwô siu rok）。本書は薬品の容易な指標。私たちの手許の薬用の薬草・博物名を含んでいる。阿波国生れの医師で、シーボルト（*Siebold*）に師事した高 良斎(こうりょうさい)（*Kô Rjô sai*）著。シーボルトの支援で本書は刊行された。大坂、1826 年、1 冊、16 折判。

496. 鍼灸図解（しんきゅうずかい　Sinkiu dsu kai [*Tschín kieù t'û kiai*]）。医療用針を刺し、また焼くことに関する二つの図表。4 銅板に刻印された解剖表が添えてある。

497. 知要一言（ちょういちげん　Tsijô itsigen）。江戸の医師石坂宗哲（*Isisaka Sôtets*）の医学小論。手稿。1 冊。

498. 九鍼之説（きゅうしんのせつ　Kutsin no sets [*Kieú tschîn tschi schuĕ*]）。鍼術・針治療小論。石坂宗哲（*Isisaka Sôtets*）著。1 冊、手稿。

499. 婦人患病書（ふじんかんびょうしょ　Funin kwanbjô sio [*Fùschín huánpíng schu*]）。一婦人の病歴。1 冊、手稿。

第XI部　木版図

A. 絵画指南書

500. 漢画指南（かんがしなん　Kangwa sinan [*Hánhoá tschi nan*]）。中国風の線画術案内。建凌岱(りょうたい)（*Kenrjô tai*）編。彼の日本人の称号は孟喬寒葉斎(もうきょうかんようさい)（*Môkô Kanjô sai*）〔建部綾足(たけべあやたり)〕である。1776 年、再版 1802 年、2 冊、8 折判。

＊501. 漢画指南二編（かんがしなんにへん　Kangwa sinan niben）。同著者書の別の続き物。3 冊、8 折判。

502. 漢画独稽古（かんがひとりげいこ　Kangwa fitori keiko）。初心者が独習することを望む、初心用中国画技法。〔宮本〕君山宮瓊（*Kunzan Kiukei*）編。1807 年、2 冊、8 折判。

503. 画筌（がせん　Kwazen）。画家の手引き。または各任意の種類の主な画が書物に集められている。日本人絵師林守篤（*Fajasi Moriatsu*）編。1721 年、6 冊、8 折判。

504. 花鳥画式（かちょうがしき　Kwa teo gwa siki）。絵画の対象としての花と鳥の手本。朝比奈夕顔（*Asaina Jûkavo*）〔あさいなせきがん〕編。1813 年、1 冊、8 折判。

505. 絵本直指宝（えほんじきしほう　Jehon dsik si bô）。大変有名な絵師橘守国（Tatsibana Morikuni）の合理的な画術至宝。1744年、9冊、8折判。

B. 有名な絵画の木版複製

a. 中国画

506. 宋紫石画譜（そうしせきがふ　Sô Siseki kwabu）。雪渓（Setskei）という名でもあった、著名な江戸の絵師宋紫石（Sô Siseki）の一連の画譜。それらは中国の事物や絵画の模倣図であるが、宋紫石がある中国人画家〔宋紫岩〕と沈南蘋（Tschîn Nânpîn）の堂に一緒に長くいたとき、長﨑で入手した。1762年、13冊、8折判。

507. 宋紫石画譜（そうしせきがふ　Sô Siseki kwabu）。同前掲書の補遺。3冊、8折判。

508. 画史会要（がしかいよう　Gwasikwaijô）。絵画の館の要所。〔大岡〕春卜一翁（Farubok Itsuwo）〔しゅんぼくいおう〕著。1751年、6冊、8折判。

509. 聚珍画帖（しゅうちんがじょう　Siutsin gwateo）。えりぬきの画帖、3冊、4折判。薫松斎（Kunseô sai）〔石川大浪〕画。1802年。ここにある諸絵図の木版刷模写は、日本の絵師中大変有名な〔狩野〕探幽（Taniu）の作である。

510. 押画手鑑（おしえのてかがみ　Osijeno tekagami〔おしえてかがみ〕）。花鳥・人物などの形の押し絵の手本、あるいは木に刻まれた画集。大岡道信（Ohooka Mitsinobu）編。1736年、3冊、8折判。

511. 新刻 金氏画譜（しんこくきんしがふ　Sinkok Kinsi kwabu）。絵師金氏（Kinsi）風画法。九峰寄田（Kjufou Keiden）〔寄田九峯〕編。1813年、1冊、大8折判。

＊512. 元明華鳥（げんめいかちょう　Gen Mei kwateo〔Juên Ming hoá tiaŏ〕）。元・明朝下に活躍した画家たちによって描かれた花鳥画。日本版、1764年、2冊、8折判。

b. 日本画

513. 名家画譜（めいかがふ　Meika kwabu）。一連の名家の絵画。〔真野〕桃渓先生（Tokei Sensei）編。1812年、2冊、8折判。

514. 画本必用（えほんひつよう　Jehon fitsjô）。絵画書から集められた有益な絵。中路雲軸（Nakadsi Undsiku）著。京都、1751年、2冊、8折判。

515. 高田敬輔〔甫〕画譜（たけだけいほがふ　Takeda Keibo kwabu〔たかだけいほがふ〕）〔敬輔画譜〕。大変有名な高田敬輔（Takeda Keibo）〔たかだけいほ〕の画譜。彼は寛延年間（1750年）に活躍した。1800年刊、4冊、8折判。

日本語訳（XI 木版図）

516. 諸職画鑑（しょしょくがかん　Sjosjok kwakan）。諸職人の画が示されている手本。蕙斎北尾政美（*Keisai Kitawo Masajosi*）編。江戸、1796 年、1 冊、8 折判。

517. 蕙斎麁画（けいさいそが　Keisai sokwa）。絵師の蕙斎（*Keisai*）のおおまかな画。1 冊、8 折判。

518. 草花略画式（くさばなりゃくがしき　Sôkwa rjakgwa siki）。草花を簡略に描いた手本。蕙斎（*Keisai*）著。1799 年、1 冊、8 折判。

519. 人物略画式（ひとものりゃくがしき　Fitomono rjakgwa siki〔じんぶつりゃくがしき〕）。人物を簡略に描いた手本。蕙斎（*Keisai*）著。1799 年、1 冊、8 折判。

520. 竹譜詳録（ちくふしょうろく　Tsikubu sjôrok）。葦・竹の区分された索引。著者：息斎道人（*Soksai Tôzin*）。京都、1757 年、2 冊、8 折判。葦・竹で輪郭を描く技法である。

521. 建氏画苑（けんしがえん　Kensi kwajen）。絵師の建氏（*Kensi*）の画苑、あるいは寒葉斎（*Kan jo sai*）という称号（参照：№500）の大変有名な建凌岱（*Ken rjô tai*）が描いた版画集。1765 年、3 冊、8 折判。

522. 建氏画苑海錯図（けんしがえんかいさくず　Kensi kwajen kai sak dsu）。同前掲絵師の画苑で、海中魚図を入れている。1 冊、8 折判。

523. 絵本詠物選（えほんえいぶつせん　Jehon jeibuts sen）。詩歌で花・鳥・風・月など物に託して歌った作品画。法眼橘保国（*Foken Tatsibana Jasukuni*）撰画。1779 年、5 冊、8 折判。

524. 絵本野山草（えほんのやまぐさ　Jehon no jamagusa）。同前掲絵師の野山の植物画。1755 年、5 冊、8 折判。

525. 帝都雅景一覧（ていとがけいいちらん　Teito gakei itsiran）。都の大変美しい展望。河村文鳳（*Kavamura Bunbô*）著。1807 年-1814 年、4 冊、8 折判。

526. 文鳳山水画譜（ぶんぽうさんすいがふ　Bunbô bsansui kwa bu）。絵師の文鳳（*Bunbô*）の山水画譜。京都、1824 年、1 冊、8 折判。

527. 素絢画譜（そけんがふ　So tsjun kwa bu）。絵師の山口素絢（*Jamagutsi So tsiun*）〔やまぐちそけん〕の草花画譜。1806 年、3 冊、8 折判。

528. 絵本稽古帳（えほんけいこちょう　Jehon keiko tsjô）。輪郭画法を習うための三脚台または画板。それらは布地〔画布〕に示されるべき見本を示している。井村勝吉（*Wimura Katsukits*）編。1718 年、3 冊、8 折判。

529. 写生獣図画（しゃせいけだもののずえ　Sjasei kedamono no dsu e〔*Sièseng scheú t'û hoá*〕〔しゃせいけだものずが〕）。自然のままの輪郭で描かれた四足獣の画。京都、1718 年、2 冊、8 折判。

530. 画図百花鳥（がとひゃっかちょう　Kwado fjak kwa teô）。山下石仲（*Jamasita Sekitsiu*）〔石仲子守範〕による花鳥輪郭図。1728 年、4 冊、8 折判。

531. 画本虫撰（えほんむしのえらみ　Jehon musino erabi［Hoá pèn tsch'ùng tschuén］〔えほんむしえらみ〕）。昆虫画。昆虫画で明示され、警句で飾られている。喜多川歌麿（Kitagawa Utamaro）編。江戸、1799年、2冊、8折判。

532. 絵本手引草（えほんてびきぐさ　Jehon tebikinogusa）。絵筆で事物を描く手引書。京都、1735年、1冊、8折判。

533. 絵本筆二色（えほんふでのにしき　Jehon fudeno nisiki）。絵師北尾重政（Kitawo Sigemasa）の鳥・四足獣の二色の絵画。2冊、8折判。

534. 写生画帖 初心柱立（しゃせいがちょうしょしんはしらだて　Sjasei kwateô Sjo sin fasira date〔絵本初心柱立〕）。自然のままの輪郭で描かれた画集、あるいは画法入門。京都、1818年、1冊、8折判。

535. 桜花画帖（さくらばながちょう　Sakurabana kwateô）。桜花の図。1冊、8折判。

536. 画本無名（えほんむめい　Jehon mumei）。名が書いていない画集。1冊、8折判。

537. 京城画苑（けいじょうがえん　Keisjô kwajen）。都の人々の絵画の園、または都のより著明な絵師たちを書物にまとめた一覧表。京都、1814年、1冊、8折判。

＊538. 鶯邨画譜（おうとんがふ　Wôton kwabu〔おうそんがふ〕）。大変有名な鶯邨（Wôton）〔おうそん、酒井抱一〕の一連の絵の表。1817年刊、1冊、8折判。

＊539. 光琳百図（こうりんひゃくず　Kwôrin fjak dsu）。大変有名な絵師の〔尾形〕光琳（Kwôrin）による一連の絵画の表。1817年編（撰）。2冊、8折判。

＊540. 南兵文鳳 街道双画（なんへいぶんぽうかいどうそうが　Nanfei, Bunbô kaido sôkwa）〔南岳文鳳街道双画〕。つまり絵師の南兵（Nanfei）〔渡辺南岳〕と文鳳（Bunbô）の両名の街道画。1811年、1冊、8折判。

541. 絵本手鑑（えほんてかがみ　Jehon te kagami）。絵本鑑賞手本。法橋春卜（Fokio Sjunbok）〔大岡春卜〕編。1728年、1冊、大八折判。

542. 絵本心農種（えほんしんのうのたね　Jehon sinnôno tane〔えほんこころのたね〕）。つまり心に涵養すべき種。様々な絵を入れている。2冊。

543. 花鳥写真図会（かちょうしゃしんずえ　Kwateô sjasin dsu e）。自然のままの輪郭で描かれた花鳥図。2冊、8折判。

＊544. 花鳥画譜（かちょうがふ　Kwateô kwabu）。花鳥図。1冊、8折判。

＊545. 花鳥画帖（かちょうがちょう　Kwateô kwateô）。花鳥の画帖。1冊、8折判。

＊546. 鳥獣略画式（ちょうじゅうりゃくがしき　Teôsiu rjak gwasiki）。簡単に描く鳥獣の手本。蕙斎（Keisai）編。1797年、1冊、8折判。

547. 北斎漫画（ほくさいまんが　Hoksai mangwa）。大変有名な絵師の北斎（Hoksai）の驚くほどの波立図。江戸、1812年、10冊、8折判。

日本語訳（XI 木版図）

548. 〔写真学筆〕墨僊叢画（ぼくせんそうが Boksen sôgwa）。墨僊（Boksen）（北斎［Hoksai］）絵師の区別なしの一般事物画。江戸、1815 年、1 冊、8 折判。

549. 三体画譜（さんたいがふ San tai kwa bu）。絵師の北斎（Hoksai）の三つの方法で描かれた画。江戸、1815 年、1 冊、8 折判。

550. 北斎写真画譜（ほくさいしゃしんがふ Hoksai sjasin gwabu）。絵師の北斎（Hoksai）による自然の事物の輪郭で描かれた図。江戸、1813 年、1 冊、8 折判。

551. 一筆画譜（いっぴつがふ Itsubits gwabu）。一本の絵筆で書かれた画。北斎（Hoksai）編。江戸、1823 年、1 冊、8 折判。

552. 絵本両筆（えほんりょうひつ Jehon rjô bits）。一対の絵筆、あるいは北斎（Hoksai）と流好斎（Riu Kosai）両絵師によって描かれた想像画書。1 冊、8 折判。

553. 英雄図会（えいゆうずえ Jeijû dsu e）。日本の古代の英雄図。〔葛飾〕玄龍斎戴斗（Genrjusai Taito）編。1 冊、8 折判。

+554. 北斎画式（ほくさいがしき Hoksai gwasiki）。絵師の北斎（Hoksai）の画法。1820 年、1 冊、8 折判。

*555. 秀画一覧（しゅうがいちらん Siugwa itsiran）。優美な絵一覧。北斎（Hoksai）編。1 冊、8 折判。

*556. 絵本浄瑠璃絶句（えほんじょうるりぜっく Jehon Zjôruri zetsuku）。想像画による浄瑠璃という名の恋歌が絵で明らかにされている。各々の絵に見る各節の最初と最後の詩句が更に加わっている。北斎（Hoksai）編。1 冊、8 折判。浄瑠璃姫（Zjôruri fime）という名は主君の源義経（Minamato Jositsune）公（1184 年）が、この上なく愛して大切にした女性である。

557. 北雲漫画（ほくうんまんが Hokun mangwa）。絵師の〔葛飾〕北雲（Hokun）が諸々の事象に驚くばかり混乱している漫画。1 冊、8 折判。

*558. 鳥山石燕画（とりやませきえんが Torijama Sekijen gwa）〔鳥山石燕画譜〕。歴史画に目を向けている、絵師鳥山石燕（Torijama Sekijen）の画。1772 年、1 冊、8 折判。

+559. 画本写宝袋（えほんしゃほうふくろ Jehon sjabô fukuro）。自然を写生している貴重な事物の画の入れもの。橘有税（Tatsibana Jusei）〔宇国〕著。1805 年、10 冊、8 折判。

560. 画図百器 徒然袋（えずひゃっきつれづれふくろ Jedsu fjakki Tsuredsure fukuro〔がずひゃっきつれづれぶくろ〕）。恐ろしい寓話や幽霊図で満ちた袋。鳥山石燕豊房（Torijama Sekijen Tojofusa）編。江戸、1805 年、3 冊、8 折判。

561. 古今〔今昔〕画図続百鬼（ここんえずつくづくひゃっき Kokon jedsu, Tsukudsugu fjaktsuki〔こんじゃくがずぞくひゃっき〕）。いろいろな化け物についての小話。付・昔と今の画図。鳥山豊房（Torijama Tojofusa）編。3 冊、8 折判。

562. 風流絵合 手引の園（ふうりゅうえあわせてびきのその Fûriu jeavase, Tebikino sono）。手

引の園。世界、あるいは文化、生活様式にかかわる図説。杵屋右兵衛（*Kinuja Uvei*）編。

C. 絵画書

a. 歴史画書

563. **絵本源平武者揃**（えほんげんぺいむしゃそろえ　Jehon, Gen Fei musja sorove）。源（*Gen*）〔みなもと〕家の一族のために追討した武者たちが、平家の味方だった者たちと比較されている。諸々の絵で明示された書。堀田里席（*Fotsutari Seki*）〔ほったりせき、堀田連山〕編、京都、1816年、2冊、8折判。

564. **絵本頼朝一生記**（えほんよりともいっしょうき　Jehon, Joritomo itsu seô ki）。将軍〔源〕頼朝（*Joritomo*）の一生の絵本。紀信吉（*Kino Josinobu*）編。1799年、2冊。

565. 〔**絵本袖中 雛源氏**〕**六十帖**（えほんしゅうちゅうひなげんじ　Jehon, siu tsiu, Fina Gen si rok zju dsjô）。源（*Gen*）（源〔*Minamoto*〕）家の歴史に注目した、六十帖の袖中絵本。1冊、16折判。

＊566. **絵本源将名誉草**（えほんげんしょうめいよそう　Jehon, Gensjô meijo zô〔えほんげんしょうめいよぐさ〕）。源（*Gen*）（源〔*Minamoto*〕）氏族出身将軍たちの光栄が、簡潔に記されている。付・図。曲亭馬琴（*Kjoktei Makin*）〔きょくていばきん〕編。1804年、2冊、8折判。

＊567. **絵本武勇桜**（えほんむこうさくら　Jehon, Mukô sakura〔えほんぶゆうざくら〕）。武勇者たちの栄誉。絵図で明らかにした書。長谷川光信（*Fasegawa Mitsinobu*）編。1756年、2冊、8折判。

+568. **絵本多武峯**（えほんたぶのみね　Jehon, Tabuno mine〔えほんとうのみね〕）。（大和国の）多武峯山での行事。付・図。〔北尾〕紅翠軒重政（*Kôsuigen Sigemasa*）〔こうすいけんしげまさ〕編。1793年、3冊、8折判。

＊569. **絵本武者鞋**（えほんむしゃわらじ　Johon, Musja waratsi）。武士たちのわらじ。戦争を見る者に絵で明らかな書。2冊、8折判。

+570. **絵本鶯宿梅**（えほんうすぐいやどるうめ　Jehon, Usuguijadoru mume〔えほんおうしゅくばい〕）。うぐいすが小さな巣宿りをしている梅の木。想像の図書。橘守国（*Tatsibana Morikuni*）編。1740年、7冊、8折判。

+571. **絵本フチハカマ**（えほんふちばかま　Jehon, Futsibakama〔えほんふじばかま〕）。雑色のきんみずひき。絵本で示された入り交じった物語。縫山（*Fôsan*）〔縫山、小枝 繁（こうざん　さえだしげる）〕撰。2冊、8折判。

572. **武者鑑**（むしゃかがみ　Musja kagami）。武士の手本。3冊、8折判。

573. **絵本婚礼道シルベ**（えほんこんれいみちしるべ　Jehon, Konrei mitsisirube）。結婚の儀式について。付・図。堀田連山（*Forida Rensan*）〔ほったれんざん〕著、京都、1813年、2冊、8

日本語訳（XI 木版図）

折判。

b. 風景と建築図

＊574. 絵本隅田川 両岸一覧（えほんすみだがわりょうがんいちらん　Jehon, Sumidagawa rjôgan itsiran）。隅田川の両岸の絵。壺十楼成安（*Kozju Rôseian*）画〔序〕。3冊（参照：No. 147）。

＊575. 絵本江戸桜（えほんえどさくら　Jehon, Jedo sakura）。江戸の桜、または江戸の町の部分図。1803年、2冊、8折判。

＊576. 画本東都遊（えほんあずまあそび　Jehon, Adsuma asobi）。江戸の絵、または江戸の町の様々場所図。北斎（*Hoksai*）撰。1802年、3冊、8折判。

＊577. 東都勝景一覧（えどかちけいいちらん　Jedo katsikei itsiran〔とうとしょうけいいちらん〕）。江戸の町のすぐれた景色地一覧。北斎（*Hoksai*）画。1815年、2冊、8折判。

c. 服飾図

578. 将軍二十五容貌（しょうぐんにじゅうごみえい　Sjôgun nizjugo mijei）。25名の将軍と何人かの大名図像。

579. 和〔倭〕国百女（わこくひゃくにょ　Wakok fjaknjo〔わこくひゃくじょ〕）。No. 415参照。

+580. 花容女職人鑑（かようじょしょくにんかがみ　Kwajônjo sjoknin kagami〔はながたちおんなしょくにんかがみ〕）。女盛りと女手の鑑または絵図。西來居未仏（*Nisikowori Matsubuts*）撰。2冊。

581. 茶湯之図（ちゃのゆのず　Tsjanojuno dsu）。抹茶をたてて客に勧める茶道図。1冊、4折判。

582. 猿楽之図（さるがくのず　Sarugakno dsu）。猿のものまねの輪舞・言葉芸。1冊、4折判。確かにその輪舞・言葉芸は、聖徳太子（*Sjôtok Daisi*）によって、7世紀以後導入され、（インド）仏教神話に言及されているべきだと思われる。

583. 江戸風美人姿（えどふうびじんすがた　Jedo fû bizin sugata）。江戸の生活風で着飾った優雅な婦人図。1冊、8折判。

584. 東錦絵（あずまにしきえ　Adsuma nisigi je）。江戸の人の着物姿図。1冊。

585. 東錦絵美人容貌（あずまにしきえびじんすがた　Adsuma nisigi je, bizin sugata）。江戸の人の着物姿図と華美に着飾った人々の絵図。1冊、大2折判。

586. 今様美人鑑（いまようびじんのかがみ　Imajo bizinno kagami）。当世風衣装で飾られている、優雅な美女の鑑。1冊、大2折判。

587. 当世美人画帖（とうせいびじんがちょう　Tôsei bizin gwateo）。ごく最近の美人画帖。1冊、大2折判。

588. 吉原美人見立五十三駅（よしはらびじんみたてごじゅうさんつぎ　Josivara bizin midate gozjusan tsugi）。吉原の街で美女たちが商売している五十三宿駅。1冊、大2折判。

589. 吉原傾城江戸美人画（よしはらけいせいえどびじんえ　Josivara keisei Jedo bizin je）。吉原の遊女、江戸の美人画。1冊、2折判。

590. 江戸八景（えどはっけい　Jedo fatsukei）。江戸の街の美しい景色の所。3冊。

591. 美人絵五十三駅（びじんえごじゅうさんつぎ　Bizin je gozjusan tsugi）。美人絵で飾られている五十三の宿駅。

592. 東錦絵集（あずまにしきえあつめ　Adsuma nisigi je atsume）。多色刷りの華美な江戸の浮世絵版画。

593. 江戸風景（えどふうけい　Jedo fukei）。江戸の街の眺めのよりよい場所。2冊。

594. 東海道五十三駅（とうかいどうごしゅうさんえき　Tôkaidô gozjusan jeki）。東海道の五十三宿駅。

追記：№370「山海経」（Schân hai king）書籍について称賛して言われていること

紀元前2207年に、初代王朝夏の創始者禹（Ju）が九属国の記念として創設したその9つの器は、山・海・草・樹木・鳥・四足獣など、当時中国の民族にとって、記憶に値いされるべきことと思われていた。それらの器につけられた絵図と大宛（T'aiseè）、帝台（Tschung kù）というある中国人が書物の中で輪郭を描いて記述した。

その表題を「山海経」（Schân hai king）と記した書物は焚書にされた。紀元前222年に、始皇帝（Schi Hoang ti）は医学書、法学書を除く全書を断罪にしたが、後代に王族と共に晋王朝が栄えたとき、郭璞（Kuōpō）によって再び文字に付され、俗用に昔の書の形態で新しく発行された。

シーボルトの日本収集書籍コレクションの概略について

山口　隆男

※本稿の（MF脚註番号）は、マティ・フォラーによる脚註・追記（英訳197〜212頁、和文213〜214頁）に対応している。

1. はじめに

1845年に刊行された『Catalogus librorum et manuscriptorum Japonicorum a Ph. Fr. de Siebold collectorum, annexa enumeratione illorum, qui in Museo Regio Hagano servantur』（邦訳『シーボルト収集日本書籍目録、並びにハーグ王立博物館所蔵日本書籍および写本類目録』、以下『日本書籍目録』と略記）は、掲載書籍・資料にそれぞれ1から始まり、594で終わる通し番号が与えられている。

この『日本書籍目録』は題名通り、シーボルトが収集した以外の書籍、即ち出島の事務官であったフィッセル（J.F. van Overmeer Fisscher、1800年生〜1848年没）と出島商館長を勤めたブロムホフ（Jan Cock Blomhoff、1779年生〜1866年没）が集めたものも含まれている。オランダ国王ウィレムⅠ世は、両名が日本で集めていた民族学的コレクションを購入してくれた。その中に書籍類が含まれていたのである。

『日本書籍目録』の本文をみると、フィッセル収集書籍は通し番号の前に（＋）が付けられた70タイトル、ブロムホフ収集書籍は通し番号の前に（＊）が付けられた31タイトルあり、両名が共に入手していたのは3タイトルが存在する。『日本書籍目録』にシーボルトが記した「序言」では、フィッセル収集書籍60冊、ブロムホフ収集書籍29冊と記すため、ホフマンによる解説本文と食い違いがあり、双方の把握がずれていたことになるが、その理由については後考を俟ちたい。

それらを除いたシーボルトの収集品は503タイトルである。リストは594で終わっているが、重複番号が9点あるので、実際にリストされている書目は603である（MF脚註＊1）。シーボルトが入手したものの中には、1.『和漢三才図会』のように105巻81冊で構成されているものがある。それには及ばないとしても、3.『訓蒙図彙大成』（21巻9冊）、439.『成形図説』（30冊）などの冊数が多いものがあった（資料名の前に付記した番号は『日本書籍目録』の通し番号、以下同様）。そのため、冊子数ではシーボルト収集資料はおよそ1,500冊を数える量的にはかなりのもので

(MF脚註＊2)
ある。

『日本書籍目録』は、著作内容ごとに11の分類を行い、解説本文を掲載している（Ⅰ百科事典類、Ⅱ歴史書・地理書、Ⅲ自然科学書、Ⅳ文法書及び辞書、Ⅴ神学書及び道徳書、Ⅵ詩、Ⅶ市井風俗並びに制度、Ⅷ経済書、Ⅸ貨幣書、Ⅹ医書・薬書、Ⅺ木版図）。

筆者は、この分類では分かりにくい「シーボルト収集書籍の特徴について」（2章）述べた後、シーボルト没後の収集和古書のゆくえについて「シーボルト収集和古書とライデンにおける整理と現状」（3章）において一端を紹介し、本稿の締めくくりとして「おわりに ―総合的調査研究の必要性について―」（4章）、今後のシーボルト研究に対する展望を記す。

2. シーボルト収集書籍の特徴について

『日本書籍目録』は、著作内容ごとに11の分類を行っているが、本章では、この分類ではみえにくいシーボルト収集書籍の特徴について以下の観点から述べる。それは、ⅰ事典類、ⅱ日本語・アイヌ語書籍、ⅲ地図類、ⅳ自然史関連、ⅴ門人たちの草稿類の種本として用いられたもの、ⅵ最上徳内からの贈り物、以上6つの観点である。

ⅰ．事典類

『日本書籍目録』リストの最初に「Ⅰ百科事典類」がある。1.『和漢三才図会』、2.『頭書増訓蒙図彙』、3.『頭書増訓蒙図彙大成』、4.『唐土訓蒙図彙』の4点がある。後述するように、シーボルトは1.『和漢三才図会』を重視したことが窺える。杉本つとむは3.『頭書増訓蒙図彙大成』もホフマンにとって役に立ったと述べている。(1)

1.『和漢三才図会』は大坂の医師の寺島良安（1654年生〜没年未詳）が編集した画期的な大著である。三才というのは「天・地・人」のことで、多種の事項を記述した項目別事典である。漢文で記されているが、比較的平易であり、漢文の素養が無い人でも内容の理解は困難ではない。現代でも役に立つ多岐にわたった記述がある。「図会」とあるように図が数多く含まれていることも特徴である。

シーボルトにとって1.『和漢三才図会』は、便利で役に立つ重要な文献であったといえる。それは、彼の著書『Nippon』（日本）の執筆時、何かにつけて参照していたことが窺えるためである。(2) シーボルトは、漢文を読むことはできなかった。しかし、ホフマンや郭成章に手伝ってもらうことができた。［写真5参照：『和漢三才図会』表紙、その他（ライデン大学図書館蔵）］

ⅱ．日本語・アイヌ語書籍

シーボルトは日本語そのものに関心を抱いた。残念なことに、彼は語学に関した才能にはあ

まり恵まれていなかった。通常の人よりははるかに高い能力があったが、語学の歴史に名を残すような才能は持ち合わせていなかった。しかし、当時の長崎には吉雄権之助のような、極めて高い語学力の持ち主の通詞たちがいた。権之助らから日本語の基礎、日本語の特色について学ぶことができた。⁽³⁾

シーボルトが出島に着任する前にドゥフ（Hendrick Doeff、1777年生～1835年没）が商館長として出島にいた。彼は長い出島勤務期間の間に日本語が上達した。そして、吉雄権之助らに手伝ってもらい、蘭日辞書の編集を行ったのである。それは『ズーフ・ハルマ辞書』（Doeff-Halma）と呼ばれるもので、その後の日蘭文化交流に大きな役割を果たすことになった。

ドゥフは離日してオランダに戻る途上で船が遭難し、船荷の全てと妻を失った。彼自身の収集だけでなく、多くの日本人と交友があったから多様な品物を貰っていたはずである。その中には、各種の価値の高い品物があったに違いない。また、自分が努力して編集していた蘭日辞書の草稿類もあった筈である。それら全てが海の藻屑となってしまった。⁽⁴⁾

ドゥフは蘭日辞書編集の先駆者であるが、シーボルトはより広い範囲を研究対象にしていた。例えば、「日本語要略」（『バタヴィア学芸協会誌』11号、1826年）では日本語の文字・発音・各品詞や文法を解説し、「日本人系統論」（『バタヴィア学芸協会誌』13号、1832年）では日本人の起源を身体・宗教・言語などから論じ、巻末の表に中国語・朝鮮語・満洲語・アイヌ語・日本語・琉球語の語彙比較を行っている。⁽⁵⁾二人の間には、日本語への接し方に大きな違いがあったことは注目すべきであろう。シーボルトは辞書の編纂ではなく、日本語の特色・日本語の構造やより広範な日本文化に関心を抱いていたのである。

シーボルトは、日本語の特色を知るためには日本の近隣諸国の言語も知る必要があると考えた。彼は朝鮮語についても調べている。長崎には船が遭難して日本の沿岸に漂着した朝鮮人たちがいた。取り調べは長崎で行われることになっていたので、遭難者達は長崎で一時期を過ごし、それから機会を得て故国へ帰還した。無教養な水夫が多かったが、かなり知的な人々もいた。シーボルトは彼らを訪問して、朝鮮語の単語、発音などを調べ、ハングル文字についても研究した。ヨーロッパ人としては最初の朝鮮語の研究である。^{(6)(MF脚註6追記)}

一方、彼はアイヌ民族に関心が深かった。⁽⁷⁾日本の北部に住んでおり、生活状態も言語も日本人と異なる民族ということで、大いに研究意欲をそそられたのである。彼は、出島に着任して早々に江戸の将軍の侍医の一人の桂川甫賢（かつらがわほけん）（1797年生～1845年没）と文通を開始し、アイヌ語辞書も入手したことが窺える。⁽⁸⁾

その他、桂川甫賢とは江戸参府時に接見し、215.『花彙』をオランダ語に翻訳してシーボルトに渡したことが知られる。⁽⁹⁾また、「iv 自然史関連」でふれるが、『日本書籍目録』の254.『蝦夷本草之図』は、桂川甫賢の手稿である。

シーボルトは、文政9年（1826）の江戸参府の折、北方地方の探検家として知られる最上徳

内（1754年生～1836年没）と江戸で面会し、4月16日（太陰暦3月10日）、彼から蝦夷の海と樺太の略図を借りたこと、4月21日（太陰暦3月15日）の項で、「数日間、朝の時間を老友最上徳内とエゾ語の編纂のことで過ごす」と記録している[10]。彼は、後述するように語彙集329.『蝦夷ヶ嶋言語』の作成に関わったが、資料は現在、ライデン大学図書館に保存されている。

[写真6参照：アイヌ語関連の語彙集（ライデン大学図書館蔵）]

ⅲ．地図類

シーボルトが1829年2月13日（太陰暦1月10日）、ジャワのオランダ領東インド政庁に宛てて作成した報告で示しているように、日本での収集書籍類は、地図類（「E 地図、絵図、展望図など約110」）・自然史（「D 自然学 約70」）関連のものが多い[11]。シーボルトは日本という国の地誌を知るために、多くの地図類を購入した[12]。

今日、「伊能図」（大日本沿海輿地全図）は有名であるが、それは幕府の管轄下にあり、当時、一般の人が利用できるものではなかった。「伊能図」に正確さで劣るとはいえ、実用的な地図類は各種出版されており、入手は比較的容易であった。シーボルトは、77.「越後国絵図」、78.「佐渡国絵図」、79.「丹波国絵図」、69.「尾張国絵図」といった「b 地方地図」（各地方の地図）の他、56.「改正日本興地路程全図」、57.「新版日本国大絵図」、58.「日本辺界略図」といった日本全体の地図（「a．一般地図」）を入手している。

その一方で、江戸に関しては105.「分間江戸大絵図」、107.「分間懐宝御江戸絵図」、111.「文政改正御江戸大絵図」、115.「駿河台小川町之図」といった大絵図・懐中図・町絵図など各種を手に入れていた（「b．江戸地誌」）。さらに124.「江戸御城内御住屋之図」のように江戸城の本丸御殿の図面まで入手していた。シーボルトは自分が将来刊行する日本に関した研究論文において、地図がどれほど重要か、十分に知っていた。それらが無ければ、日本という国の地誌的、地理的な記述はできないからである。

文政11年（1828）、いわゆる「シーボルト事件」の摘発により、出島に奉行所の役人達が数回立ち入って、入念な探索を行い、シーボルトが高橋景保（1785年生～1829年没）から貰っていた日本地図、蝦夷地の地図などを押収した。しかし、それだけではなかった。禁制品とされる各種の物品を押収している。探索と押収は1828年12月17日・同18日（太陰暦11月11日・12日）、1829年2月8日・同14日・同17日・同21日・3月4日（太陰暦1月5日・11日・14日・18日・29日）と繰り返し行われた[13]。

呉秀三によるシーボルトの伝記『シーボルト先生その功業と生涯』には、どのような物が押収されたかリストがある。数カ所に分散して示されているので、以下にまとめてみた。【地図・地誌】、【書物】、【画図】以上3つに関したものは次の通りである[14]。

【地図・地誌類】
大日本輿地図3枚、日本国切図9枚、蝦夷地図1枚、カラフト島図1枚、三国通覧（日本・朝鮮・唐土・平蝦夷・カラフト・カムサッカ・山丹ノ辺ヲ認候図ヲ写候様相見候図）1枚、琉球国図1枚、朝鮮国図1枚、大日本細見指掌全図1枚、版本細見指掌の凡例、新増細見京絵図1枚、長州下関小倉辺より測量切図、長州下関小倉三所絵図之写、分間江戸大絵図1枚、大坂の地図1枚、和蘭字を書いたる地図1枚、大日本道中行程見記（折本）1冊、江戸名所絵1枚、日本の旅行の書物1冊、絵図一袋9枚、地図4枚、東韃紀行1冊、北夷紀行之内抜書1冊、和蘭字に書いたる蝦夷・樺太の気候を記せる書物1冊、晴雨昇降之表1袋1冊、和州芳野山勝景図（折本）1冊、浪花筱応道撰但日本図之序1枚、同凡例但大日本図之事1枚、道中独案内図（折本）1冊、日本廻国の詳記の書物1冊、花路一覧之図（折本）1冊、大和名所の書物7冊

【書物】
装束図式2冊、満州字書、中国人・蝦夷人の絵70包、書物（町尽）1冊、書物（百人一首）1箱、絵の書物1冊、公家の図1枚、日本国物産の図絵5冊、夜啼石敵討記1冊、無間ノ鐘由来記1冊、書物1冊、或書物の序文1通、中山刀雉子1冊、大坂戦争の絵本1冊、武者絵の書物3冊、有名な人物の書の書物1冊、草と花の書物1冊、

【画図】
東海道の絵6枚、江戸の景色の絵1枚、名所の絵2枚、桶狭間合戦略記1枚、桶狭間古跡記1枚、大黒天の下絵1枚、恵比寿天の下絵1枚、武器の下絵2枚、僧侶の絵1枚、僧の衣類及び武具の絵1枚、小形官服之武者絵1包、鞍を置きたる馬の下図1枚、絵図（名前が不明）9枚、錦絵3枚

　最初の「大日本輿地図3枚、日本国切図9枚、蝦夷地図1枚、カラフト島図1枚」は幕府天文方の要職にあった高橋景保から入手したものである。これらの海外持ち出しは、国禁として幕府から押収されても仕方がなかった。(MF脚註17) しかし、それだけではなかった。各種の地図・地誌類が押収されたことがわかる。「琉球国図1枚」、「朝鮮国図1枚」といった地図だけはなく、「江戸名所絵」のような当時の観光案内にあたるものも没収された。また、日本人の「装束図式」、「武者絵の書物」や「武器の下絵」なども押収されたのである。つまり、シーボルトにとっては、高橋景保から贈られた地図類の他に、多種のものが押収されたことになる。

　しかし、『日本書籍目録』をみると、彼は多くの地図類・名所図会・紀行類をはじめ多数の資料を持ち帰っている。押収された書籍類中、【地図・地誌類】に「東韃紀行1冊」「北夷紀行之内抜書1冊」、【書物】に「満州字書」など、北方地方の研究に役に立つものが含まれている。しかし、彼のコレクションからすると、ごく一部で、それらが無くてもひどく困ることはなかった。

どのようにして押収を免れて、膨大な書籍類、写生図類を無事にオランダにもたらすことができたのか、筆者にはよく判らない。但し、シーボルトが乗船する予定であった蘭船コルネリス・ハウトマン号は1888年9月18日（太陰暦8月10日）長崎で座礁したものの、翌1889年2月24日、シーボルトの積荷89箱（内67箱が博物学的収集品・図画類、残り22箱は植物）が積み込まれて出帆し、バタヴィアに到着した。また、シーボルトが1830年1月3日（太陰暦1829年12月9日）、日本追放という状態で長崎を離れたが、その際に書籍類を伴っていたことが知られる。

　つまり、「シーボルト事件」摘発よりも前に書籍類を含めた荷物を発送していたのではなかった。それゆえ、探索時にはそれらはすべて出島にあったのである。

　シーボルトはしたたかな人で、安易に妥協はしなかった。先に述べたように、持ち帰った地図類の中には江戸城に関するもの（124.「江戸御城内御住屋之図」）、「vi. 最上徳内からの贈り物」で後述するように、最上徳内による詳細なカラフトの地図などもあった。そうしたものが見つかって江戸に送られたならば、厄介なことになったであろう。[写真7参照：56.『改正日本輿地路程全図』、58.『日本辺界略図』（ライデン大学図書館蔵）]

iv. 自然史関連

　『日本書籍目録』によると、シーボルトが収集した自然史に関した書籍類と写生画類はおよそ100タイトルで、冊子数は約350もある。先に触れたように1829年2月13日（太陰暦1月10日）インド政庁への報告では70点とあるのに増加したのは、自然史関連の写生画集を別扱いにしていたからである。フィッセル、ブロムホフが収集したものの中には自然史関連のものは無かった。すべてがシーボルトの収集品である。『日本書籍目録』通し番号の第194番から293番にかけて「第三部　自然科学書」がリストされている。

　内容は様々である。江戸時代の日本における自然史研究は中国の影響下にあった。明の李時珍（1518年生〜1593年没）の『本草綱目』は没後の1596年に刊行された。中国では実用植物学の「本草学」が伝統的に研究されていた。李時珍はそれまでの本草書を調べて取捨選択を行い、自分でも観察を行って正確をきして、『本草綱目』を執筆した。実用性の無い動物や植物も一部には収録されており、本草学の伝統をやや離れた革新性がある。『本草綱目』は日本に輸入され、徳川幕府に仕えた林羅山（1583年〜1667年没）は家康に献上している。家康は単なる武将ではなく、学問に理解と関心が深い教養人・蔵書家であった。

　林羅山は、『本草綱目』で記述されている動物や植物が日本のどういう動植物に該当するかを調べて『多識編』と題された本を刊行している（2巻2冊寛永7年〈1630〉刊、『新刊多識編』5巻3冊寛永8年〈1631〉刊）。『本草綱目』を活用するためには、必要なことであった。

　こうした背景もあって『本草綱目』は日本の自然史研究においてバイブルとも言うべき重要

な存在になった。江戸時代の日本の自然史研究者は『本草綱目』の分類システムにそって動植物を分類していた。なお、『本草綱目』以外の各種の中国の自然史に関係する文献類も日本に輸入されて、重宝された。それらは極めて高価であったから、日本で和刻本が作成刊行された。原文には無い返り点などが加えられ、読みやすくされている。そうした加筆は当時のもっと優れた自然史研究者、例えば小野蘭山（1729年生〜1810年没）のような人によって行われた。[(17)]

　シーボルトが入手した書籍類の中には195.『校正本草綱目』を初めとして、次のような和刻本が含まれている。194.『大観証類本草』、196.『本草淮』、197.『毛詩草木鳥獣虫魚疏』、203.『通志昆虫草木略』、205.『本草彙言』、206.『南方草木状』などが挙げられる。これらの書物はシーボルトには利用できないものであった。中国語・漢文に明るくないと読むことはできない。それでも彼が入手していたのは、自分には活用できなくても、将来役に立つと考えたからである。日本の自然史研究は中国の強い影響下にある。日本における自然史研究の状態を研究するためには、そうした文献に目を通す必要があり、誰かが研究することがあろうと思ってのことであった。［写真8参照：和刻本の例：203.『通志昆虫草木略』（ライデン大学図書館蔵）］

　それら和刻本とは別に日本人が執筆した書物もある。貝原益軒による211.『大和本草新校正』、平賀源内による214.『物類品隲』、小野蘭山による207.『本草綱目啓蒙』、あるいは210.『本草和解』、220.『本草薬名備考和訓鈔』といった対象がかなり広いものと、特定の植物だけを扱ったものとがある。後者に関しての例を挙げると、菊に関した224.『百菊譜』・225.『花壇養菊集』、朝顔の図鑑の226.『牽牛品』・228.『朝顔譜』・229.『花壇朝顔通』、モクタチバナの類の図鑑である234.『橘品類考』・235.『橘品』がある。

　平和な江戸時代には各種の園芸植物、庭園植物が広く栽培され、色々な園芸品種が作り出されていた。そうした植物に関した書籍が各種刊行されていたのである。シーボルトは日本に多様で優れた園芸・庭園植物があることを知り、ヨーロッパにそれらを導入したいと思うようになった。出島から生きた園芸植物をオランダに向けて発送すると共に、園芸植物を扱った書籍類も集めたのである。伊藤伊兵衛の236.『広益増補地錦抄』は小型の冊子本であるが、さまざまな園芸植物が図示されている。平仮名のつづけ字で記されている植物名は、彼には読めなかった。幸い、彼の門人がカタカナのルビを付けてくれたので、シーボルトにとって役に立つものになった。［写真9：236.『広益増補　地錦抄』（ライデン大学図書館蔵）］

　一方、シーボルトが日本人の自然史研究者から貰った各種の図譜類がある。シーボルトが偉いのは、当時の一流の自然史研究者たちとうまく接触していたことである。

　例えば、尾張藩の武士で薬園担当の水谷助六（1779年生〜1833年没）とは文通をしていた。そして、各種の植物の標本類（400種近くに及ぶもの）や種子類を貰うだけではなく、写生画集も貰っていたのである（例：258.『本草写真』・259.『本草抜粋』）。助六は当時の日本ではもっと

も優れた自然史研究者であった。嘗百社という自然史愛好家のグループの盟主であり、物産会を開催して、啓蒙的な活動も行っていた。彼がシーボルトに与えた標本の中には木曾や白山に産し、長崎では入手できないものがいろいろと含まれていた。そのお陰で、シーボルトの植物標本コレクションは随分と内容豊なものになった。助六は写生画の妙手であった。対象とする植物の形態的特色をうまく把握した絵を描くことができた。一見したところ、粗雑に見えても、特色を押えているので、どういう種を描いたのかが判るのである。シーボルトは1826年の江戸参府時に往路、帰路の2回助六と彼の門人の大河内存真、伊藤圭介らと会っている。[18]

また、シーボルトは江戸で栗本瑞見（1756年生〜1834年没）に会っている。彼は将軍の侍医の一人であったが、医師としてよりも、優れた自然史研究者として幕府内で高く評価され、尊敬を集めていた。彼もまた写生画の妙手であった。大名や旗本の中に自然史に興味を抱く人々がいた。そうした人々は自ら写生を行ったり、画家に描かせたりして、図譜を作成し、将軍に献上することがあった。幕府の中枢にいる栗本瑞見はそうしたものを閲覧することができた。彼は見るだけではなく、それらを模写して、自分のコレクションに加えたのである。栗本瑞見は動物にも植物にも興味があり、生涯におびただしい写生画を描いている。彼がとりわけ興味を抱いていたのは魚類であった。シーボルトは栗本瑞見から魚や甲殻類の絵を見せて貰っている。そして、267.『蟹蝦類写真』・272.『魚類写真』といった瑞見が原図を描いた甲殻類と魚類の図譜を入手している。[19]

シーボルトが自然史研究者から貰った写生画集は日本の自然史研究の歴史を知る上で貴重である。江戸時代に数多くの写生図集が作成されていた。夏が高温多湿になる日本では標本の保存が困難であった。腐敗したり、害虫に冒されて価値を失ったりすることが多かった。そのために、写生画にして残すのが一般的であった。しかし、明治以降にそれらの多くが失われてしまい、ごく一部しか残っていない。文明開化の時代になると、江戸時代の作品は何もかも時代遅れのつまらないものとされて、切り捨てられた。加えて、関東大震災や第二次世界大戦による東京の空襲で、多くの資料が焼失した。

『日本書籍目録』に記載されたシーボルト収集の写生画集の作者と点数を示すと次の通りである。作者名（タイトル数・冊子数）の順で示している。これらはシーボルトに贈られたために現存できたのである。日本にあったなら、失われてしまったことであろう。

　　栗本瑞見（2点5冊）、水谷助六（4点9冊）、大窪昌章（4点5冊）、宇田川榕菴（6点7冊）、
　　桂川甫賢（6点9冊）、大河内存真（3点3冊）、黒田斉清（3点3冊）、作者未詳（8点）

写生図集はシーボルトが刊行した『Fauna Japonica』（日本動物誌）と『Flora Japonica』（日本植物誌）の参考資料として役立っている。しかし、それらの写生画が図版の原画として用いられたことは無かった。標本あるいは川原慶賀に特別に描かせた正確な写生図に基づいて図版は作成された。[20]

シーボルトは、川原慶賀に描かせただけでなく、先に述べたように日本人の自然史研究者たちから写生画集を貰っている。自然史研究者の多くは絵に巧みで、学術的な質が高いものを多く描いている。着色された自然史関係の図譜は印刷費がかかり、採算に乗らないので、ごく一部以外は出版されなかった。写生画の図譜類は模写・転写されることが多く、模写や転写を通じて広まることで、自然史研究の発展に大きな寄与をしたのである。[写真10参照：自然史研究者、桂川甫賢・水谷助六・大窪昌章・栗本瑞見から贈られた図譜類（6種）]

v. 門人たちの草稿類の種本として用いられたもの

シーボルトは美馬順三、高野長英、高良齋らに自分の日本の研究に役に立つようなテーマで、オランダ語による草稿類の執筆を依頼していた。草稿類について、昭和13年当時のシーボルト研究をまとめた『シーボルト研究』（岩波書店　1938年刊）に所収された緒方富雄・大島蘭三郎ほかによる「門人がシーボルトに提供したる蘭語論文の研究」（61～274頁）に言及がある。それらはシーボルトにとって『Nippon』を執筆する上でかなり役に立ったのである。(21) 門人達は依頼を受けると書籍などを調べて執筆した。門人が書いたものは『シーボルト研究』でも「蘭語論文」と表現されるが、論文よりもレポート、あるいは翻訳文と表現するのが適切と思われる。

数は少ないが、門人たちの草稿類執筆に用いられた書籍あるいは草稿類が『日本書籍目録』に含まれており、ライデン大学図書館に保存されている。(MF脚註28) 以下、筆者が確認できた資料に関して、目録番号『日本書籍目録資料名』（著者名〈ライデン大学図書館所蔵番号〉）→「蘭語論文名」（門人名）の順で列記する。なお、門人の蘭語論文名は『シーボルト研究』における表題略記に従った。

・446.『飲膳摘要』（小野蘭山〈Ser. 891〉）→　「飲膳摘要」（高野長英）
・465.『染物之法　早稲作法　茶製法』（筆者未詳〈Ser. 892〉）
　　→「日本に於ける茶樹の栽培と茶の製法」（高野長英）
・270.『虫類写集』（大河内存真〈Ser. 1024〉）→「日本産昆虫図説　日本産蜘蛛図説」（石井宗謙）
・283.『天狗爪石雑考』（木内重暁〈Ser. 1032〉）→「天狗爪石略記」(22)（高良齋）

その他、488.『鍼灸説約』(MF脚註30)（石井宗謙〈Ser. 1100〉）は、蘭語論文「灸法略説」（美馬順三・戸塚亮齋・石井宗謙(MF脚註30)）と関係すると考えられるが、筆者は未見なので、レポート類との関係がはっきりしないため明記を控えた。しかし、シーボルトは日本の鍼灸に関心があり、江戸でその方面の大家として知られる石坂宗哲に会っている。(23)

上記の内、465.『染物之法　早稲作法　茶製法』は誰が執筆したのか未詳だが、短い草稿類のよせ集めであるが、それぞれが高野長英によって翻訳されている。高野長英による製茶の草

稿は、緒方富雄が『シーボルト研究』(岩波書店)の中で詳しく記述している。緒方は、シーボルトによる『日本書籍目録』における465.『染物之法・早稲作法・茶製法』とあるものが、種本ではないかと推定している。筆者が確認したところ、まさにその通りで、高野長英が書いたものは『染物之法　早稲作法　茶製法』の忠実な訳に他ならないことが分かった。但し、種本に著者は記されていなかった。［写真11参照：465.『染物之法　早稲作法　茶製法』(ライデン大学図書館蔵)］

vi．最上徳内からの贈り物

　最上徳内は、シーボルトに特別な好意を抱いた。そして、彼が大切にしていた地図類や北方地方の紀行記のようなものをそっくり贈っている。並外れた好意を示したのは、シーボルトなら、それらを学術研究に活用してくれると確信したからであった。シーボルトにとって特に有り難かったのは、北方地方の精密な地図が含まれていたことである。前記のように彼はアイヌ人に興味があったが、それだけではなかった。蝦夷地や樺太の地理学的なことにも大いに関心があった。樺太が島であり、半島ではないことは日本人達には知られていたが、ヨーロッパではまだ決着が着いていなかった。

　シーボルトは、文政9年(1826)江戸参府の折、最上徳内から島であることを示す地図類を見せられて、大喜びした。

　また、シーボルトは高橋景保から日本全体の伊能図、北方地方の地図を入手した。しかし、先に述べたように「シーボルト事件」によって、それらは押収されてしまった。蝦夷地や南千島に関した部分だけは押収される前に徹夜してコピーした。但し、他の地域を模写する時間的余裕は無かった。シーボルトが樺太の地形について『Nippon』で報告できたのは、最上徳内から貰った詳細な地図があったおかげである。

　最上徳内から贈られた資料で『日本書籍目録』に掲載されているのは、次の10タイトルである。

　　176.『蝦夷拾遺』、177.『蝦夷図』、180.『唐太島』、181.『薩哈連島之図』、183.『黒龍江中之州并天度』、192.『東察加之図』、193.『北海』、328.『蝦夷方言』(白虹齊)、340.『論語彝訓巻之首』、433.『度量衡説統』。

　その他、シーボルトが徳内と一緒になって作成したアイヌ語の単語集、329.『蝦夷ケ嶋言語』がある。

　また、書籍ではないが、ライデンにある国立植物標本館には、樹木材標本がある。薄い板にその植物の絵が描かれ、植物名が記入されている。蝦夷産の樹木の場合は、アイヌ語名もある。美麗に作られたもので、シーボルトが蝦夷など北方地方の植物について記述した際の重要な資料であった。

これらの内で特に重要なのは、183.『黒龍江中之州并天度』と 177.『蝦夷図』である。前者は間宮林蔵（1780 年生〜1844 年没）が作った樺太の地図を徳内がコピーしたものである。周知の通り、間宮林蔵は、偉大な探検家であった。徳内は生涯で 2 回、樺太に渡航したとされているが、その第 2 回目にあたる文化 5 年（1808）、徳内・林蔵を含めた計 6 名は、幕府から命じられて樺太見分を行った。徳内は同年中に松前に帰着して越冬したが、松田伝十郎と間宮林蔵は、翌文化 6 年（1809）樺太の北部まで探索した。林蔵は、強靱な身体、冷静な判断力と観察力、熱意の持ち主であり、画才もあった。樺太の海峡を発見し、ひとりで対岸の黒龍江の沿岸部も調査して『東韃地方紀行』を記したことが知られる。(33)

　徳内は、地図を作成することを意図して、可能な限りデータを得て帰国して、蝦夷の地図を作成した。より詳細なものは、幕府天文方の高橋景保に提出された。そのコピーをシーボルトは景保から贈られていたが、押収されてしまった。182.『黒龍江中之州并天度』と徳内の蝦夷図の中に含まれる別の樺太の地図 2 葉を活用して、シーボルトは『Nippon』で樺太の詳しい地図を紹介することができたのである。(34)

［写真 12 参照：193.『北海』・177.『蝦夷図』（ライデン大学図書館蔵）］

［写真 13 参照：182.『黒龍江中之州并天度』（ライデン大学図書館蔵）］

［写真 14 参照：シーボルトから押収された間宮林蔵による樺太の地図（国立公文書館蔵）］

3. シーボルト収集和古書とライデンにおける整理と現状

　シーボルトが入手した書籍類の一部はシーボルトによってウィーンとパリの図書館に贈られた。しかし、シーボルトの日本に関した研究のために集められたものであるから、大部分は彼の手元にあった。その後にシーボルトによって寄贈されて、オランダ国の所有物になった。現在はライデン大学図書館貴重書室とライデンにあるオランダ国立民族学博物館に分散保存されている。ごく少数であるが、目録出版後に失われたものがある。『日本書籍目録』には、271.『蛛類説図』があるが、これはライデンに保存されていない。279.『唐婦人所謂リキンカムヒツナカイ二獣之図』も行方不明である。(MF脚註45)［写真 15 参照：ライデン大学図書館］

　シーボルト収集の書籍類を含む日本から到来したものを整理して、整理番号を与えたのはホフマンの弟子であり、日本語学者のセルリエ（Lindor Serrurier、1846 年生〜1901 年没）であった。セルリエは、1877 年〜1880 年はキューレーターとして、1880 年〜1896 年は館長としてライデンの国立民族学博物館に勤務した。彼は 1896 年に E. J. Brill 社から目録『Bibliothèque japonaise: catalogue raisonné des livres et des manuscrits japonais enrégistrés à la bibliothèque de l'université de Leyde』を出版した。それには 1,263 タイトルの日本の書籍や写生図、手稿類が収録されている。漢字あるいは仮名の書名が示され、読みがローマ字で記されて

いる。続けて、内容が簡単にフランス語で紹介されている。文献は内容順にグループ化されてリストされている。最初が事典・辞書類、続いて語学関連、地理学と行った具合である。自分が調べたい分野のものがまとめてリストされているので、書名を知らない場合でも、どういうものがあるかを探すのに便利である。[**写真 16 参照**：L. Serrurier『Bibliothèque japonaise』(ライデン大学図書館蔵)]

オランダ国立民族学博物館へ移管された書籍、写生図類には新しく整理番号が与えられた。[MF脚註46] シーボルト収集品は1に続いて番号がある。例えば、水谷助六の植物写生画集『本草写真』(『日本書籍目録』の248番目に掲載)には1-4312という番号が与えられている。ブロムホフ、フィッセルの場合は360に続けて番号が示されている。[MF脚註47] 例えば、ブロムホフが描かせた昆虫の図譜の番号は360-959である。ライデン大学図書館貴重書室にあるものは現在でもセルリエが与えた整理番号に従って保存されている。閲覧したいと思ったら、その整理番号で請求すればよい。

セルリエの目録が刊行されて丁度100年目の1996年にH. Kerlenが『オランダ国内所蔵明治以前日本関係コレクション目録、Catalogues of pre-Meiji Japanese books and maps in public collections in the Netherlands』を刊行した。これはオランダ国内に保存されている文献類を対象とし、本文だけでも918ページもあり、合計1,962タイトルが収録されている。書名のアルファベット順に紹介されているが、著者名・所蔵している機関名・刊行者・刊行年・(本の)大きさ・ページ数などが示されている。この目録では書名によってリストされているので、書名が判っている場合には便利であるが、書名がはっきりしないものを探し出すのは面倒である。Kerlenはライデン大学図書館に960タイトル、国立民族学博物館に970タイトル、ライデンの国立植物標本館に45タイトルあると述べている。

4. おわりに―総合的調査研究の必要性について―

筆者はライデン大学図書館貴重書室にのべ百数十日通って、主として自然史に関した資料を調べた。これまでも『日本書籍目録』やSerrurierによる目録でどういうものがあるか、書名や名称は知ることはできた。しかし、それだけでは内容は判らない。借り出して閲覧し、具体的な内容を知って、驚いたことが再三あった。

例えば、Serrurierによる目録の整理番号 No.932 の文書である。これにはタイトルが無い。Serrurierは気象に関したものと目録に書いている。調べてみると1826年(文政9年)における江戸の気象観測のデータで、気圧・気温・天候が1月1日から記録されている。[MF脚註*48] 江戸時代の日本の気候を知るのに役に立つ資料と判明した。1日も休むことなく1年間の観測結果が記録されている。ライデン大学図書館にあるのは1826年の一ヶ年の記録だけであるが、より

長期間にわたって、江戸では気象観測が行われていたに違いない。⁽³⁵⁾

　最上徳内がシーボルトに贈呈した地図や記録などのうち、地図類は研究者諸氏によって調査されている。しかし、他のものは筆者の知る限りでは調査研究されていない。島谷良吉『最上徳内』には徳内がシーボルトに渡したものの中に「北海」があることが示されている。⁽³⁶⁾島谷は『日本書籍目録』の第193番目に『北海』がリストされているのを知って紹介したのである。しかし、現物を知らないので、『北海』を地図として示したのであった。実際に筆者が閲覧すると『北海』というタイトルで地図と冊子3冊がファイルされている。^{（MF脚註＊51）}冊子には徳内がロシア人と親しく接して、色々と聞き出したことがかなり詳細に記録されており、ロシア正教に関したものも含まれている。原資料を閲覧していない島谷はそうしたことを知るはずもなかった。最上徳内がどういう人物であったかを知るために『北海』は実に興味深いものであることを指摘しておく。しかし、筆者の知る限りでは、この資料を調査研究した人はいないし、内容が紹介されたこともなかった。

　今後、『日本書籍目録』を土台として、ライデン大学図書館と国立民族学博物館にあるシーボルトらが収集した書籍・写生画について、L. Serrurier、H. Kerlen の目録よりもより具体的に内容を紹介した新目録が作成されるならば、シーボルトついてだけではなく、様々な学問分野で役に立つものになるであろう。^{（MF脚註＊52）}現在は映像の時代である。最終的には、目録だけではなく、画像によってそれらが紹介されることが望ましい。日本の国立国会図書館でも所蔵する古典籍の文献や資料類の画像を順次にネットで公開している。筆者は、そうした状態になるのが理想的であると考えている。⁽³⁷⁾いずれにせよ、これまでに刊行されたものよりも、内容を詳しく紹介した目録あるいは総合的な解説書が作成されるならば、シーボルトが収集した書籍や写生画がより広く活用できることになる。

　調査範囲はライデン大学図書館と国立民族学博物館だけに限定されてはならないし、学際的に行う必要があろう。近年、国文学研究資料館が主催となって国際連携研究が行われていると聞いたが、⁽³⁸⁾ライデンの国立自然史博物館には川原慶賀による自然史関連の写生画が所蔵されている。⁽³⁹⁾シーボルト収集和古書類が現存する大英図書館やフランス国立図書館だけでなく、ドイツでも調査を行う必要がある。例えば、ミュンヘンにある国立民族学博物館にはシーボルト『Nippon』の原画となった『人物画帖』が保存されており、ボフムのルール大学東アジア研究学部にはシーボルト・アーカイブが存在し、ブランデンシュタイン城には様々な手稿や写生画が保存されている。⁽⁴⁰⁾各国にある資料を網羅的に調査して、新目録に加えられねばならない。

　シーボルトは日本にとって恩人の一人であり、その活動は自然史から外交に至るまで、実に多彩であったにも関わらず、総合的な調査の実行が未だに行われていないのが現状である。今後、彼が日本から持ち帰った書籍・写生画についての学際的・国際的な総合調査が行われることを筆者は強く要望するものである。

【 注 】

(1) 杉本つとむ『杉本つとむ著作選集10　西洋人の日本語研究』八坂書房　1999年　387～389頁

(2) 『Nippon』の原注には、『和漢三才図会』をはじめとした書物が記されていることが、緒方富雄『シーボルト「日本」の研究と解説』(講談社　1977年　41～42頁) などに指摘されている。

(3) 呉秀三『シーボルト先生　その生涯及び功業』1　東洋文庫103　平凡社　1967年　88～94頁。

(4) 杉本つとむ「商館長、H・ドゥーフと蘭日対訳辞典の訳編」『杉本つとむ著作選集10　西洋人の日本語研究』八坂書房　1999年　289～296頁

(5) 岸本恵美「シーボルトの日本語研究」『新・シーボルト研究Ⅱ　社会・文化・芸術篇』八坂書房　2003年。

(6) シーボルト著『Nippon』Ⅶには、「高麗の情報」が記されており「日本の海岸に漂着した高麗商人たちへの訪問」(6～9頁) が含まれる。なお、朝鮮人が一時収容されていたのは、「出島近くの対馬藩の屋敷」である(宮崎克則「【復元】シーボルト『NIPPON』の配本」『九州大学総合研究博物館研究報告』3号　2005年3月)。

(7) シーボルトのアイヌ語研究として代表的な論述は次の通りである。黒田源次「シーボルト先生のアイヌ語研究」『シーボルト研究』岩波書店　1938年　315～352頁、金田一京助「シーボルト先生とアイヌ語学」『シーボルト研究』岩波書店　1938年　353～426頁、杉本つとむ「シーボルトと日本語・アイヌ語研究」『杉本つとむ著作選集10　西洋人の日本語研究』八坂書房　1999年　303～324頁。

(8) シーボルトは、1823年8月12日 (太陰暦7月7日) 出島に上陸したが、翌1824年11月26日付バタヴィア政庁への報告書で「私はボタニクス (桂川甫賢) 博士が私の希望を叶えて最近贈ってくれた貴重なアイヌ語辞書を所有しております。この辞書は蝦夷にいる日本人役人が使用するため、皇帝の命令により、江戸で印行されたので、非常に権威あるものです。」と記している (栗原福也訳「出島からバタヴィアへ―シーボルトの日本調査報告一八二三、二四年―」『新・シーボルト研究Ⅱ』八坂書房　2003年　370頁)。

(9) 大島蘭三郎「五　桂川甫賢訳　花彙」『シーボルト研究』岩波書店　1938年　117～125頁。

(10) シーボルト著　斎藤信訳『江戸参府紀行』東洋文庫87　平凡社　1967年　197頁。

(11) 栗原福也訳『シーボルトの日本報告』東洋文庫784　平凡社　2009年　293～299頁。

(12) 沓沢宣賢「ライデンに於けるシーボルト蒐集地図について」『東海大学紀要　文学部』33号　1980年　東海大学　74～90頁。

(13) 呉秀三『シーボルト先生　その生涯及び功業』1　東洋文庫103　平凡社　1967年　279～282頁、石山禎一「シーボルト生涯・業績および関係年表」『新・シーボルト研究Ⅰ』八坂書房　2003年、石山禎一・宮崎克則「シーボルトの生涯とその業績関係年表1 (1796～1832年)」『西南学院大学国際文化論集』26巻1号　西南学院大学学術研究所　2011年9月。

(14) 呉秀三『シーボルト先生　その生涯及び功業』1　東洋文庫103　平凡社　1967年　261～262頁・267～270頁・323～324頁。

(15) 梶輝行「シーボルト事件―商館長メイランの日記を中心に―」『新・シーボルト研究Ⅱ』2003年　86頁。

(16) 文学的・民族学的コレクション5,000点以上のほか、多数の動物標本類を持ち帰った。標本発送については、オランダ国立自然史博物館の標本受け入れ台帳から、その状況がわかる（山口隆男「シーボルトと日本の自然史研究」『新・シーボルト研究Ⅰ』八坂書房　2003年　49～50頁）。

(17) 小野蘭山については、小野蘭山没後二百年記念誌編集委員会編『小野蘭山』八坂書房　2010年、に詳しい。

(18) 山口隆男「尾張学派との接触」（「シーボルトと日本の自然史研究」）『新・シーボルト研究Ⅰ』八坂書房　2003年　43～44頁。

(19) 山口隆男「「ファウナ・ヤポニカ」甲殻類編で参照された図譜「蟹蝦類写真」について」『CALANUS』特別号Ⅲ　熊本大学　2001年。

(20) 山口隆男「川原慶賀と日本の自然史研究Ⅰ　シーボルト，ビュルゲルと「ファウナ・ヤポニカ魚類編」」『CALNUS』12号　1994年、山口隆男「シーボルトと日本の植物学」『CALANUS』特別号Ⅰ・Ⅱ　熊本大学　1997・1998年、山口隆男・加藤僖重ほか『シーボルト収集植物標本リスト』『CALANUS』特別号Ⅴ　熊本大学　2003年。

(21) 例えば、高野長英による「蘭語論文」である「日本に於ける茶樹の栽培と茶の製法」は、『Nippon』第4巻9編の基となった（シーボルト著・中井晶夫訳「第9編：茶の栽培と製法」『日本第4巻』雄松堂　1978年　127～142頁）。

(22) 高良齋による蘭語論文「天狗爪石略記」について、大島蘭三郎は「三　高良齋稿　日本疾病志」（『シーボルト研究』岩波書店　1938年）の解説中で「高家に蔵せられている」（90頁）と記す。

(23) シーボルトは1826年4月21日（太陰暦3月15日）、「幕府の針医者石坂宗哲とその他の医師・知人ら来訪」と記している（斎藤信訳『江戸参府紀行』東洋文庫87　平凡社　1967年　197頁）。

(24) 緒方富雄「七　高野長英稿　日本に於ける茶樹の栽培と茶の製法」『シーボルト研究』岩波書店　1938年　135～179頁。

(25) 緒方富雄「七　高野長英稿　日本に於ける茶樹の栽培と茶の製法」『シーボルト研究』岩波書店　1938年　144頁。

(26) 当時のヨーロッパにおける日本地図やシーボルトとの関係の概説は、中村拓「欧米人に知られたる江戸時代の実測日本図」『地学雑誌』78号　1969年、宮崎克則・福岡アーカイブ研究会編「第四章　地図をめぐって」『ケンペルやシーボルトたちが見た九州、そしてニッポン』海鳥社　2009年　164～186頁、などがある。当時の欧州における蝦夷地・樺太の認識とシーボルトの意図については、島谷良吉『最上徳内』人物叢書174　吉川弘文館　1977年　251～258頁、に記

述がある。

(27) 1826 年 4 月 16 日（太陰暦 3 月 10 日）江戸滞在中、シーボルトは「最上徳内から蝦夷の海と樺太島の略図が描いてある二枚の画布をわれわれに貸してくれた」「実に貴重な宝ではあるまいか」と記している（シーボルト著　斎藤信訳『江戸参府紀行』東洋文庫 87　平凡社　1967 年　194 頁）。

(28) 呉秀三「二十二　シーボルト事件一．高橋作左衛との贈答往来」『シーボルト先生　その生涯及び功業』1　東洋文庫 103　平凡社　1967 年　213～236 頁。

(29) 呉秀三『シーボルト先生　その生涯及び功業』1　東洋文庫 103　平凡社　1967 年　285 頁。

(30) 船越昭生「シーボルト資料カラフト図に関する若干の検討」『奈良女子大学地理学研究報告』1 号　奈良女子大学文学部地理学教室　1979 年　81～98 頁。

(31) 329.『蝦夷ヶ嶋言語』は、最上徳内だけでなく、桂川甫賢の校閲も経て成立したという（黒田源次「シーボルト先生のアイヌ語研究」『シーボルト研究』岩波書店　1938 年　343 頁）。

(32) 山口隆男・加藤僖重「最上徳内がシーボルトに贈呈した樹木材の標本」『CALANUS』特別号 II　熊本大学　1998 年。

(33) 島谷良吉『最上徳内』人物叢書 174　吉川弘文館　1977 年、洞富雄・谷沢尚一編注『東韃地方紀行：他』東洋文庫 484　平凡社　1988 年。

(34) 『Nippon』第 2 冊には、「樺太島とマンコー河口：最上徳内と間宮林蔵の原図による」の掲載がある。また、その作成に関する論考には、蘆田伊人・箭内健次「シーボルト作成の地圖」『シーボルト研究』岩波書店　1938 年　427～480 頁、がある。

(35) 1826 年の記録の他にも「1828 年 1 月～9 月の気象観測」がボフム大学図書館に所蔵されていることが図版で報告されている（石山禎一・宮崎克則「シーボルトの生涯とその業績関連年表 1（1796-1832 年）」『西南学院大学国際文化論集』26 巻 1 号　西南学院大学学術研究所　2011 年 9 月　203 頁）。

(36) 島谷良吉『最上徳内』人物叢書 174　吉川弘文館　1977 年　239 頁。

(37) ライデン大学図書館における資料電子化の現状と展望については、奥田倫子「ライデン大学図書館特別コレクション室における研究促進とデジタル化」『カレントアウェアネス』311 号　日本図書館協会　2012 年 3 月、に詳しい。

(38) 鈴木淳「国際連携研究「オランダ国ライデン伝来のブロンホフ、フィッセル、シーボルト蒐集日本書籍の調査研究」」『国文研ニューズ』22 号　国文学研究資料館　2011 年 2 月。

(39) 山口隆男「ライデンにある川原慶賀の自然史画（1996 年度〔洋学史学会〕大会記録（長崎））」『洋学』5 号　洋学史学会　1996 年、山口隆男「川原慶賀と日本の自然史研究：I．シーボルト，ビュルゲルと「ファウナ・ヤポニカ魚類編」」『CALANUS』12 号　熊本大学　1997 年 1 月。

(40) 宮崎克則「シーボルト『NIPPON』の原画・下絵・図版」『九州大学総合研究博物館研究報告』9 号　九州大学　2011 年 3 月。

「シーボルトの日本収集書籍コレクションの概略について」写真および解説

資料名は『　』内に記し、直前に『Catalogus librorum et manusciptorum Japonicum a Ph. Fr. de Siebold collectorrum, annexa enumeratione illorum, qui in Museo Regio Hagano ervantur』の掲載番号を付した。また、「L. Serrurier 目録」は『Bibliotheque japonaise』（E. J. Brill 社　1896 年）をさす。資料名の後（　）内に「L. Serrurier 目録」に掲載された整理番号を付した。

写真 5：『和漢三才図会』表紙、その他（ライデン大学図書館蔵）
Fig. 5—The cover of *Wakan sansai zue*. Courtesy University Library Leiden.

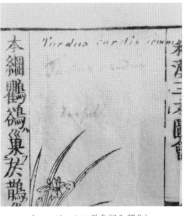

（シーボルトの学名記入部分）

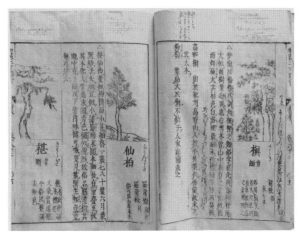

「1. Wakan san sai dsu e」(UL, Ser. 1)

【1.『和漢三才図会』（L. Serrurier 目録№ 1、ライデン大学図書館蔵）】

　大坂の医師の寺島良安が編集作成した百科事典である。105 巻、81 冊で構成されている大著で、1712 年頃に刊行された。シーボルトもホフマンも重宝して活用している。漢文で記されているが、平易な文なので、漢文の素養があまり無くても内容をある程度理解することができる。

　また、簡単ではあるが、絵がある。動物、植物を扱った巻にはシーボルト、ホフマンが学名や説明を書き入れている場合が多い。ここに示すのは第 1 巻の表紙、鳥類を扱った第 43 巻のクロツグミを扱った箇所、植物を扱った第 82 巻のマキ類に関した箇所である。クロツグミはシーボルトがオランダに送った標本によってライデンの国立自然史博物館の館長のテンミンクが 1831 年に新種として発表した鳥である。つまり、シーボルトと関係が深い動物である。シーボルトは、それが和漢三才図会に記述されていることを知った。彼は、クロツグミの絵のところに学名を記入している。第 82 巻のマキ類の解説の欄外に書き入れがあるが、これもシーボルトによるものである。彼は植物を扱った『Flora Japonica』（日本植物誌）の解説を書くための資料として『和漢三才図会』を調べたことが分かる。

写真6：アイヌ語関連の語彙集（ライデン大学図書館蔵）
Fig 6—Vocabulary of the Ainu language. Courtesy University Library Leiden.

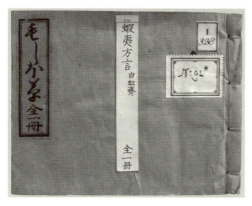
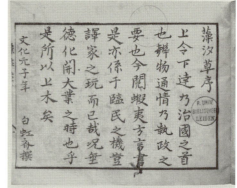
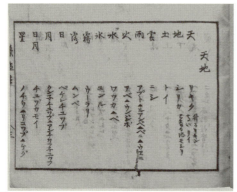

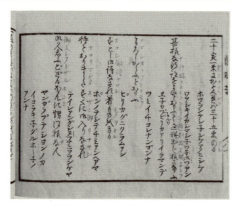

「328. Jezo fôgen」(UL, Ser. 92)

【6-A：328.『蝦夷方言』（原題「もしほ草」、L. Serrurier 目録№ 92、ライデン大学蔵）】
　1792年に刊行された和語 - アイヌ語語彙集である。横166 mm、縦126 mm ある。103丁。著者はアイヌ語通詞の上原熊治郎である。この人の生没年は不明であるが、アイヌ語によく通じていた。『もしほ草』は蝦夷地に来た和人に役立つように編集されている。アイヌ語と和語は単語がまるで異なっており、互いに全く異なる言語である。蝦夷地に来た和人には全く理解できないものであった。熊治郎は単語だけでなく、文例も示しており、アイヌ語の習得を助ける工夫をしている。蝦夷地の松前にいた熊治郎が刊行するのは困難だったため、最上徳内が出版を助けたのであった。彼は序文を書いて、そこに白虹斉という自分の号を書き入れている。『藻汐草』と徳内については、黒田源次「シーボルト先生のアイヌ語研究」（『シーボルト研究』岩波書店　1938年）に詳しい。

シーボルトの日本収集書籍コレクションの概略について

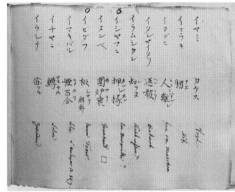

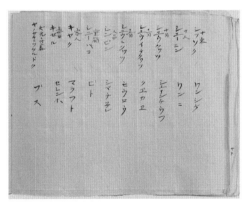

「329. Jezogasima kotoba」(UL, Ser. 93)

【6-B：329.『蝦夷ヶ嶋言語』(L. Serrurier 目録№ 93)】

　『もしほ草』を底本にして編集された語彙集である。2 部分からなっている。350 頁あるが、空白で全く記入が無い頁もある。第 1 部は 246 頁あり、アイヌ語－和語－ドイツ語の語彙集である。イロハ順にアイヌ語の単語が上段に示され、それに対応する和語が中段に記されている。下段にはドイツ語がシーボルトによって記入されている。合計 2,488 語がある。第 2 部はアイヌ語が上段に示され、その下和語が記されている。ドイツ語は記されていない。第 2 部は 78 頁に 663 語があるが、最後の単語が「ヤ」で始まる語であり、いろは順の末尾にあたる「セ」や「ス」ではなく、完結には至っていない。『蝦夷ヶ嶋言語』はアイヌ語の権威の金田一京助が研究し、その成果は「シーボルト先生とアイヌ語学」『シーボルト研究』（岩波書店　1938 年）に収録されている。

写真7：56.『改正日本輿地路程全図』、58.『日本辺界略図』（ライデン大学図書館蔵）
Fig. 7—*Kaisei Nihon yochi rotei zenzu* (Hoffmann No. 56) and *Nihon henkai ryakuzu* (Hoffmann No. 58)

シーボルトが入手していた地図類のうち、興味深いもの2点を紹介する。

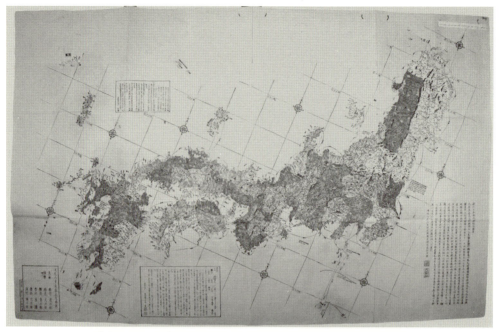

(UL. Ser. 220)

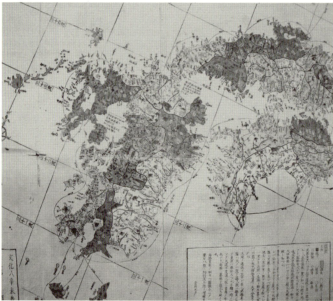

「56. Kai-sei Nippon jo-dsi-ro-tei zen-dsu」（中国・四国・九州部分拡大）

【7-A：56.『改正日本輿地路程全図』（L. Serrurier 目録№220、ライデン大学図書館蔵）】
　水戸藩の長久保赤水（1717-1801）が編集した日本地図で、1779年に出版された。ライデン大学図書館には、この地図の異なる版が何種類もある。宮緯度経度も記入され、伊能図が作成されるまでは、もっとも優れた日本地図であった。シーボルトにとっても役に立ったのである。伊能図は幕府の所蔵物で一般に公開されたことはなく、それによって印刷物が作成されてこともなかった。江戸時代の人々にとって、この『改正日本輿地路程全図』は極めて重要な存在であった（宮崎克則撮影）。

シーボルトの日本収集書籍コレクションの概略について

(UL, Ser. 228)

「58. Nippon fen-kai rjak-dsu」(東日本部分拡大)

【7-B：58.『日本辺界略図』(L. Serrurier 目録№ 228、ライデン大学図書館蔵)】
　当時の幕府天文方高橋景保が主体になって作成した日本および周辺の地図である。島の形がはっきりと判っていなかったカラフトの地形が間宮林蔵の調査によって明らかになった。その成果が盛り込まれた地図で、銅版画である。作成されたのは1809年である。朝鮮の地形は正確さが劣るが、その程度の地図しか日本には伝来していなかった。
　これら2図は共に『Nippon』に複製されたことをふまえ、詳しい言及がある(宮崎克則「シーボルト『NIPPON』の色つき図版」『九州大学総合研究博物館研究報告』5号　2007年)。

写真8：和刻本の例：203.『通志昆虫草木略』（ライデン大学図書館蔵）
Fig. 8—Hoffmann 203 as an example of a *wakokubon*. Courtesy University Library Leiden.

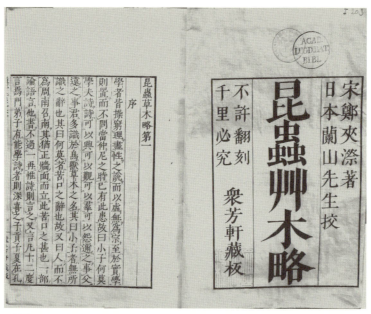

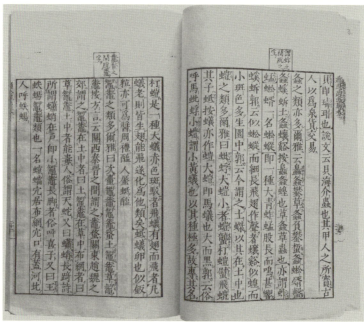

「203. T'ûngtshi kuêntsch'ông ts'aomǔ liǒ」（UL, Ser. 967）

【203.『通志昆虫草木略』（L. Serrurier 目録№. 967、ライデン大学図書館蔵）】
　扉には「昆虫草木略」とあって、通志の2字が欠けている。しかし、表紙には「通志昆虫草木略」とある。中国渡来のものに小野蘭山が返り点などを附記し、内容をチェックした。小野蘭山は江戸時代におけるもっとも優れた自然史研究者である。シーボルトが日本に来たときにはすでに亡くなっていた。中国渡来のものは高価でかつ白文では日本人には読みにくかった。そのままではうまく読めないから、小野蘭山その他の著名な学者、研究者が協力して、返り点を加筆したより安価な和刻本が作成され、日本の学術の発展に大きな寄与したのである。

写真9：236.『広益増補　地錦抄』（ライデン大学図書館蔵）
Fig. 9—Hoffmann 236 – *Kōeki jikinshō*. Courtesy University Library Leiden.

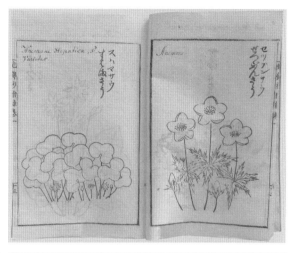

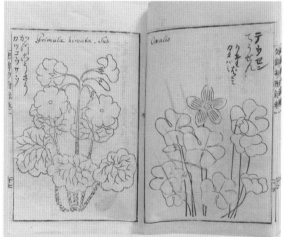

「236. Kwôjeki zôhô, Tsikin seô」（UL, Ser. 1052）

【236.『広益増補 地錦抄』全28冊（L. Serrurier 目録№1052『地錦抄附録』、ライデン大学図書館蔵）】
　『地錦抄』は、江戸時代の代表的な園芸書である。江戸の有名な植木商、伊藤伊兵衛の著作。小形本で、各種の園芸植物の園芸品種が多くの図版によって紹介された。図版は白黒で彩色は無い。和名と簡単な解説がある。日本の園芸・庭園植物に関心があり、オランダに戻ってから、それらを同地に導入するのに努力したシーボルトにとって、役に立つものであった。彼は平仮名で附記されている名前を読むことができなかったので、門人か知人に依頼してカタカナ名を記入して貰っている。
　『地錦抄』には伊藤伊兵衛三之丞著『花壇地錦抄』（1695）、伊藤伊兵衛政武著『増補地錦抄』（1710）、『広益地錦抄』（1719）、『地錦抄附録』（1733）の計4シリーズがある。最初に刊行されたのは『花壇地錦抄』であったが、シーボルトは入手していない。伊藤伊兵衛政武の3シリーズは入手している。『広益地錦抄』は8冊、『増補地錦抄』は8冊、『地錦抄附録』は4冊で構成されている。奇麗な花が咲く植物だけとは限らず、薬草類、実用植物なども含まれている。ここに示すのは最後に刊行された『地錦抄附録』である。表紙の色は、地錦抄シリーズは同じ青い色が使われていたようである。また、内容を示す紙片が表紙に貼付けてあり、どういう植物が収録されているのか、本を開かなくても判るように利用者の利便が図られているのも同じである。
　『地錦抄附録』第1冊に含まれる4図版を紹介しているが、シーボルトが左上に学名を記入している。学名の記入があるのは一部の図だけで、どれにも書き入れているのではない。

写真 10：自然史研究者、桂川甫賢・水谷助六・大窪昌章・栗本瑞見から贈られた図譜類（6種）
Fig. 10—Some albums in the Siebold collection donated by Japanese natural history researchers, Katsuragawa Hoken, Mizutani Sukeroku, Ōkubo Masaaki, and Kurimoto Zuiken.

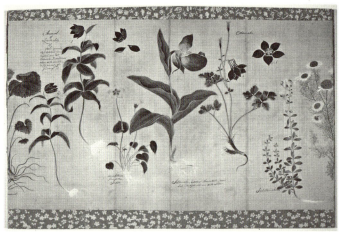

「254. Jezo honzōno dsu」(UL, Ser. 1003)

【10-A-a：254. 桂川甫賢『蝦夷本草之図』(L. Serrurier 目録№1003『蝦夷草木之図』、ライデン大学図書館蔵)】
　桂川甫賢はシーボルトの計6点の図譜を贈っている。その他にシーボルトの求めに応じて、数十枚の植物写生画を描いて、シーボルトに送り届けている。ここに示すのは「蝦夷草木之図」と題されたもので、絹に描き、折帖装に製本された台紙に貼り込まれており、実に美麗である。シーボルトに贈ることを念頭において作成された。台紙は縦 410 mm に横 320 mm で、貼ってある絹の幅は紙と同じであるが、縦は 260 mm で2冊ある。
　上掲図は小林豊章（源之助）が作画した「蝦夷草木図」の模写図のうちの2丁である。小林源之助は1792年に蝦夷に派遣され、最上徳内と一緒にカラフトにも渡っている。絵に巧みであったので、蝦夷地のいろいろなもの、動植物の絵を作成するようにと指示されていた。江戸に戻ってから植物図譜を幕府に提出したが、好評で、模写図がいくつも作成された。桂川甫賢の祖父の桂川甫周も模写している。幕府に提出された献上本は現在、失われている。甫賢が献上本、甫周本のどちらを模写したかはよくわからないが、甫周本とは植物の順序などがかなり異なっている。シーボルトが理解できるように、植物名、地名その他がオランダ語で記入されている。第1冊に描かれている植物は47種。
　シーボルトは『Nippon』第VII部の第5章、蝦夷・樺太および日本領千島の天産物に植物リストを示している。そこには、顕花植物が342種、隠花植物が12種リストされている。出典の一つがこの『蝦夷本草之図』（L. Serrurier 目録№1003）であった。この『蝦夷本草之図』には、別の蝦夷の植物図も含まれている。冊子に作画されているが、描かれている植物は13点である。

シーボルトの日本収集書籍コレクションの概略について

No Title（RMvV 1-4496）

【10-A-b：（仮称）『鳥とモグラの図譜』（ライデン国立民族学博物館蔵、所蔵館資料番号1-4496）】
　桂川甫賢から贈られた資料。表紙にはタイトルは記されていないため、『日本書籍目録』との関係は未詳。『鳥とモグラの図譜』は筆者山口による仮称である。冊子の大きさは横390、縦286 mm。21図ある。うち1図は白化したモグラであるが、残り20図は鳥で、20種が描かれている。甫賢の自筆は5図だけで、残りは転写図。
　ここに示す図の一つはライチョウの絵である。ライチョウは日本中部の日本アルプスの高山にだけ生息している。氷河時代の遺留種として貴重な存在である。図の右に文化10年（1813）に江戸城の西の丸に献上されたことが記されている。模写図である。出典は不明。美麗に描かれているが、鳥学の見地からすると問題がある。ライチョウは夏と冬で羽の色が大きく変化する。冬羽はほとんど白色である。ここに示す図では夏羽が描かれている。手前がオスで後ろがメス。雄では中央部に黒い羽根がある。ここには黒い羽根は生じない。従って、誤りである。『鳥とモグラの図譜』はシーボルト『Fauna Japonica』（日本動物誌）の「鳥類編」を執筆したシュレーゲルが調査した。そして標本は無かったが、日本にライチョウがいるとリストしている。
　もうひとつの絵は甫賢の自筆図で、左がヒガラ、コガラである。どちらも正確で学術的である。

「258. Honzō sjasin」(RMvV 1-4312)

【10-B-a：258.『本草写真』(L. Serrurier 目録№ 979、ライデン国立民族学博物館蔵、所蔵館資料番号 1-4312)】
　水谷助六（1779-1833）は尾張藩の 200 石の武士。薬草園を担当していた。当時における最も優れた自然史研究者であった。興味の幅が広く、日本だけではなく、海外のものにも関心をよせていた。シーボルトは水谷助六と積極的に接触して、図譜類だけはなく、多数の植物標本を貰っている。
　シーボルトは植物図譜を 8 冊、鳥のシギ類の図譜 1 冊、計 9 冊も貰ったのであった。それらの中で、この『本草写真』はもっとも完成度が高く美麗なので 4 図を紹介している。計 22 丁半に、合計 60 の植物が描かれている。

シーボルトの日本収集書籍コレクションの概略について

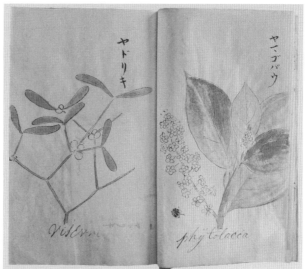

「259. Honzo batsusui」(UL, Ser. 979)

【10-B-b：259.『本草抜翠』(L. Serrurier 目録№ 979、ライデン大学図書館蔵)】
　水谷助六からシーボルトがもらった植物写生図集であり、『本草抜翠』のタイトルで5冊がファイルされている。この冊子は、表紙の貼紙に「水谷助六　No. 13」と記される。102の植物が描かれているが、すべてに属名が助六によって記入されている。ここに示すのは第9丁裏〜10丁表（pp.18-19）、13丁裏〜14丁表（pp.26-27）である。ヤマゴボウ（Phytolocca）、ヤドリギ（Viscum）、クサツゲ（Buxus）、ウマノスズクサ（Aristolochia）と4植物に記入されている属名は適切である。
　シーボルトは『江戸参府紀行記』で次のように述べている（斎藤信訳、1967）。「私はとくに2冊の肉筆の画帳に注目した。それは日本植物のコレクションであるが、すべて正確にリンネによる名称で分類し、すべての植物に属名をあげていた。102の同定のうちで私はたった四つの誤りを指摘することができただけであった。」シーボルトは2冊と述べているが、属名の記入があるのは1冊だけで、勘違いをしている。シーボルトは参府旅行の途中で、助六に3月29日に会っている。助六はシーボルトに会うために名古屋から郊外の熱田のそばの宿場町の宮まで来てくれたのであった。

シーボルトの日本収集書籍コレクションの概略について

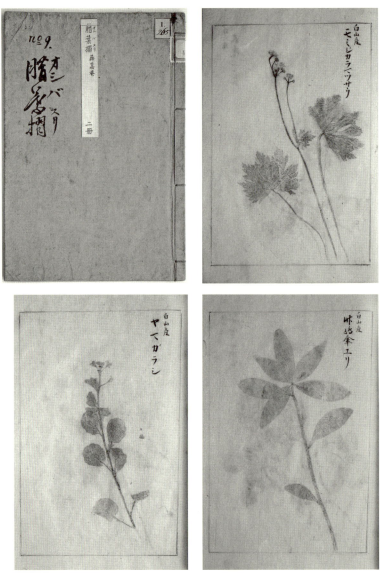

「265. Osiba suri」(RMvV 1-4317)

【10-C-a：265.『腊葉摺』(L. Serrurier 目録№ 991、ライデン国立民族学博物館蔵、所蔵館資料番号 1-4317)】
　作者の大窪昌章（1802-1841）は尾張藩の下級武士である。彼はシーボルトに会っていないと思われるが、交流はあり、昆虫の図譜、植物の図譜、印葉図を贈っている。ここに示すのは印葉図である。冊子の装丁にしてあるものと、製本されていない大きな紙10枚からなるものの2点がある。
　印葉図は植物の拓本で、形を整えて乾燥した植物に墨を塗って、写し取ったのである。左右が反転した鏡像になる。印葉図は標本よりも取り扱いに便利なので、当時の日本ではかなり盛んに作られていた。また同じものを何枚も作ることができた。大窪昌章は、いわば「自然史おたく人間」で、動植物の研究に熱中して比較的短い生涯を終えている。彼は、各種の植物が豊富なことで知られる石川県の白山（2,702 m）で採集を行なった。製本された『腊葉摺』にはその際に収集した各種の植物が含まれている。紙の大きさは縦241 mm、横170 mmである。

シーボルトの日本収集書籍コレクションの概略について

「260. Honzo bătsusui」(UL, Ser. 975)

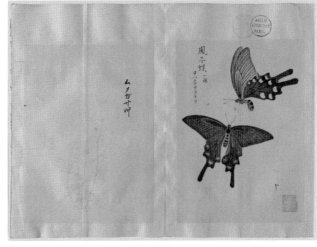

（第2図）　　　　　　（第1図）

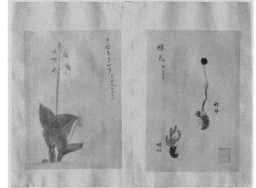

（第23図）

【10-C-b：260.『本草抜翠』(L. Serrurier 目録№. 975、ライデン大学図書館蔵)】
　計18丁の冊子で、半丁の大きさは縦268mm、横181mm。蝶の絵が2点、植物が27種描かれている。この写生画集の前半は大窪舒三郎昌章の養父の大窪太兵衛忠陳が描いている。後半は舒三郎である。
　第1・2図は太兵衛の絵。他は舒三郎の絵。一部の絵にはシーボルトが学名を書き入れている。第23図は「蝉花セミタケ」である。これは冬虫夏草として知られるもので、昆虫に菌類が寄生して生じる。セミから上方に伸びているのが菌体である。漢方薬として重宝されている。日本にも各地に産するが、発見するのが難しい。

「267. Kaika rui Sjasin」(UL, Ser. 1018)

(第2巻第32図)

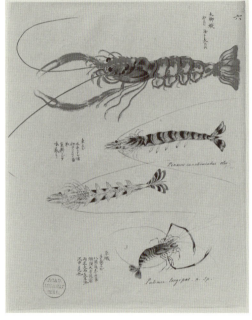

(第2巻第16図)

【10-D：267.『蟹蝦類写真』（L. Serrurier 目録№ 1018、ライデン大学図書館蔵）】

　2巻からなる写生図集で、主に甲殻類が描かれている。シーボルトは『江戸参府紀行記』で、1826年4月25日に栗本瑞見（1756-1834）がシーボルトらの宿舎の長崎屋に来たことを「幕府の本草家栗本瑞見はたくさんの植物の絵巻とたいへん多くの日本や支那の魚類・すばらしい甲殻類の画集を私に見せてくれる」と述べている（斎藤信訳、1967）。栗本瑞見は将軍の侍医であったが、医師としてより、自然史研究者として知られていた。画技に巧みで、おびただしい数の絵を描いている。

　『蟹蝦類写真』は瑞見の自筆ではない。模写図である。シーボルトは4月25日に見せて貰い、欲しくなったと思われる。『蟹蝦類写真』にはオランダ製の紙が使用されている。おそらく、シーボルトはオランダ製の紙を瑞見に渡して、模写を依頼したと思われる。自然史関連の絵を描くためには、絵の具が滲む和紙よりも、滲まないオランダ製の紙の方がより適していた。瑞見の原画を職業的絵師が模写したと思われる。シーボルトは『蟹蝦類写真』を大切にしていた。製本は、されていない。カバーに包まれている。第1巻には32枚、第2巻には12枚が含まれている。絵の数は第1巻が149、第2巻が59である。紹介している第29図の原画は瑞見の自筆。他の2図は模写図である。『蟹蝦類写真』の第1巻の1-30図の大きさは縦33.5 cm、横25.8 cmである。第31・32図はその4倍の大きさでカブトガニとタラバガニが実物大に描かれている。第2巻の紙はやや不揃いで、縦31 cm、横は25-29 cmである。

写真 11：465.『染物之法　早稲作法　茶製法』（ライデン大学図書館蔵）
Fig. 11—Hoffmann 465 Somemono no hō. Courtesy University Library Leiden.

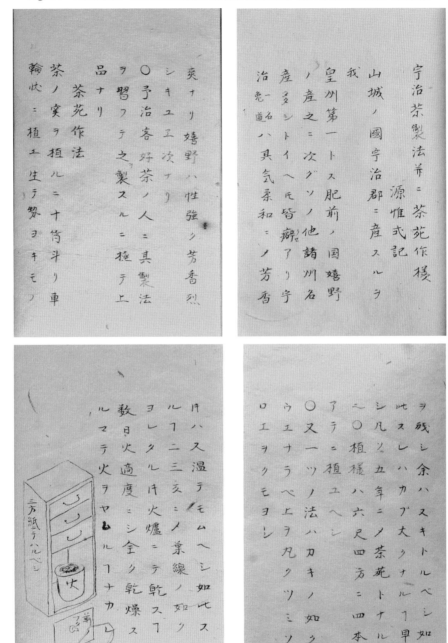

「465. c. Tsja tsukûri nori」(UL, Ser. 892)

【465.『染物之法　早稲作法　茶製法』（L. Serrurier 目録№ 892、ライデン大学図書館蔵）】
　「早稲作法、茶製法、染物之法」と内容を書いた紙が表紙に貼付けてある。作者は不明。高野長英がシーボルトに依頼されて翻訳した文書の原本である。長英は忠実に翻訳している。
　ここに示すのは「茶製法」に関した箇所である。シーボルトは日本の茶に大きな関心を寄せていた。長英の翻訳文は執筆時に資料の一つとして役に立った。

写真 12：193.『北海』・177.『蝦夷図』（ライデン大学図書館蔵）
Fig. 12—Hoffmann 193 *Hokkai* and 177. *Ezo zu* Courtesy University Library Leiden.

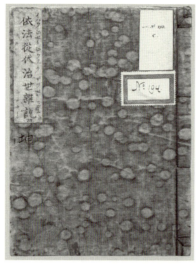

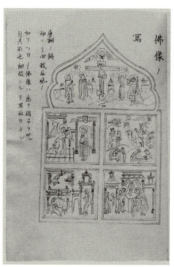
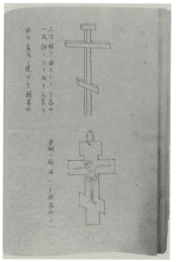

「193. Fŏ kai」(UL, Ser. 194)

【12-A：193.『北海』（L. Serrurier 目録№194、ライデン大学図書館蔵）】
　このタイトルで地図と 3 点の小冊子がファイルされている。冊子の内「依法従代治世雑記、坤」という題名の資料を紹介している。この冊子は 19 丁半（39 頁）で、縦 205 mm、横 155 mm の大きさである。最初の 4 丁は徳内が天明 6 年（1786）丙午孟春に松前から厚岸を経由して 3 月 23 日に国後島に到着したことが記され、次に択捉島に行きロシア人に接したことが記されている。3 名のロシア人が礼儀正しく徳内らを迎えたこと、徳内も礼をもって接したこと。言葉は通じなかったことが記されている。
　そのロシア人のスケッチが 2 丁に亘ってあるが、なかなか良い出来の絵である。衣類・靴の様子が示され、姓名も記されている。その次がイコンの図である。仏像の写とされ、十字架に架けられているキリスト・聖母マリアに懐妊を告げる天使・キリストの出産などの図が細かく写し取られている。その次に身に付け、礼拝の対象にしている十字架のスケッチがある。絵は、彩色されていない。また、キリスト教についての簡単な解説がある。但し「基督教」「天主教」とった直接的な表現は避けられている。「此ヲ以テ参合スルニ蓋シ妖法邪宗ニハ有ラス乎」といって好意的である。しかし、当時としては、かなり大胆な表現であるため、私的な手稿であったことが窺える。

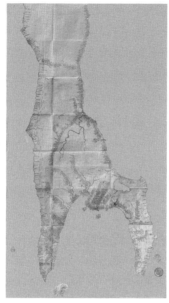

『Nippon』

(UL, Ser. 205)
(上：第5図／右：第4図)

「177. Jezono dsu」

(UL, Ser. 205)

【12-B：177.『蝦夷図』（L. Serrurier 目録№. 205、ライデン大学図書館蔵）】

　5点の地図が含まれている。どれもかなり大きい。5点の内訳は次の通りである。

　第1図：蝦夷西南之地（南蝦夷）縦1,039 mm 、横1,117 mm である。「エゾニシミナミノチ」のルビがある。青森県北部から札幌の北までが示されている。極めて細い線、文字（カタカナあるいは漢字）で記される。大きな地図であるから、1枚ではなく何枚もの紙を巧妙に貼りあわせてそれに描き込まれた。水系は入念に記入されているが、山は示されていない。

　第2図：蝦夷東北之地（東蝦夷）「エゾヒガシキタノチ」のルビがある。縦619 mm 、横929 mm。国後・歯舞・色丹・根室半島・知床などが示されているが、それらの地名は記されていない。

　第3図：蝦夷西北之地（北蝦夷）「エゾニシキタノチ」のルビがある。縦626 mm 、横619 mm。北の地方、宗谷・網走・知床・礼文島が示されている。地名は細かく記され、水系も大きな河は蛇行した状態で丁寧に示されている。

　第4図：夷北島之南浜（南唐太）「エゾキタシマノミナミハマ」のルビがある。縦804 mm、横584 mm。地名は実に詳しく、驚く程に詳細である。しかし、地域差があり、東海岸に比較して西はおおまかに記される。水系も詳しいのは南部だけで、北部はおおまかになっている。

　第5図：蝦夷北島之北浜（北唐太）「エゾキタシマノキタハマ」のルビがある。縦1,067 mm、横901 mm。間宮海峡が示されている。主な山や河は、赤字・漢字で記されている。間宮海峡は実際よりもかなり広く示されている。因みに間宮海峡という地名は樺太がロシア領になった現在では使用されていない。なお、間宮海峡・黒龍江、それ自体を示す名前は記されていない。間宮海峡と反対側、つまり北樺太の東海岸は、地名がほとんど記入されていない。

　上掲図版では、5点の地図の内、第4・5図を示している。原図では水のあるところは薄い水色、陸地は薄い赤褐色に着色されている。しかしコントラストが十分ではなく、細かく折り畳まれているために、地図自体に凹凸があり、陰影が生じて全体をうまく撮影することができなかった。そのため筆者は画像加工を施し、地形の輪郭を明確にしてみた。この処置によって、樺太の地形がかなり判りやすくなった。なお、シーボルトは『Nippon』に含まれる地図類の中で、樺太、間宮海峡に関した箇所の画像を加えている（右の図版）。

写真13：182.『黒龍江中之州并天度』（ライデン大学図書館蔵）
Fig. 13—Hoffmann 182. *Kokriukō nakanosu narabini Tendo* Courtesy University Library Leiden.

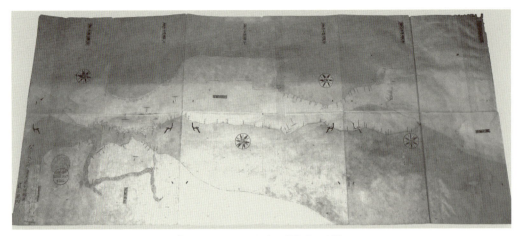

「182. Kok-riu-kô tsiu-siu」（UL, Ser. 215）

（最上徳内落款・印章部分拡大）

【182.『黒龍江中之州并天度』（L. Serrurier 目録№. 215）】
　「黒龍江中之州并天度」の名前がある樺太の地図。左下に最上徳内の書き入れがあり、徳内が間宮林蔵と接触して手に入れたものであることが判る。この地図はライデン大学図書館の所蔵品であるが、現在はライデン市内に開館したシーボルト・ハウスにあって、展示されている。

写真 14：シーボルトから押収された間宮林蔵による樺太の地図（国立公文書館蔵）
Fig. 14—Mamiya Rinzō's map of Karafuto that was confiscated. Courtesy National Archives Tokyo.

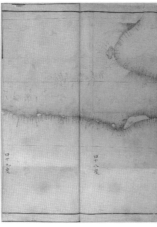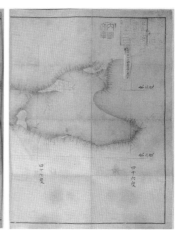

【間宮林蔵「カラフト島図」（国立公文書館蔵）、178-0316】
　これは東京の国立公文書館にある間宮林蔵による樺太の地図である。幕府天文方の高橋景保がシーボルトに贈った資料に含まれていた。出島に長崎奉行所の役人が、シーボルトから押収して江戸に送ったのである。その地図が現在は国立公文書館に所蔵されている。作成者が同じであるから、写真13『黒龍江中之州并天度』と似た地図である。
　間宮林蔵は、樺太の東海岸（画像では東方向が上）の調査はしていないので、この地図では空白になっている。写真12-Bで紹介している最上徳内の地図では東海岸もきちんと示されている。

写真 15：ライデン大学図書館（2011年4月18日筆者撮影）
Fig. 15—The University Library at Leiden.

　ライデン大学図書館の建物は地下1階、地上3階である。写真ではわかりにくいが、中央に出入り口がある。右側にドーム屋根が見えるが、貴重書室はドーム下の3階にある。

写真 16：L.Serrurier『Bibliotheque japonaise』（ライデン大学図書館蔵）
Fig. 16—L. Serrurier title page *Bibliotheque Japonaise* - UBL

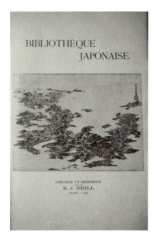

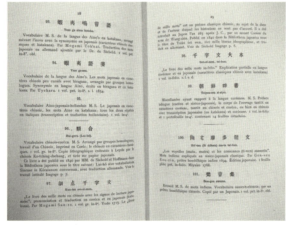
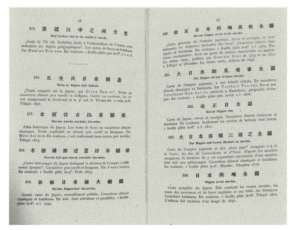

　L. Serrurier による日本書籍類の目録。1896 年に刊行された。タイトルと扉、第 28-29 頁、56-57 頁を紹介している。目録は 298 頁あり、収録されている書目は 1,263 タイトルある。シーボルトらが江戸期に収集したものだけではなく、明治時代になってから入手された資料が、かなりの数含まれている。

Overview of the books collected by Siebold

Dr. Takao Yamaguchi

I. Introductory

In 1845, Philipp Franz von Siebold (1796-1866) published the *Catalogus librorum et manuscriptorum japonicorum a Ph. Fr. de Siebold collectorum, annexa enumeratione illorum, qui in Museo Regio Hagano servantur*, a catalogue compiled with the assistance of J. J. Hoffmann (1805-78), comprised of 594 titles. As can be inferred from the title, it covers, in addition to his own collection, also the books collected earlier by Blomhoff and Fisscher. The first, Jan Cock Blomhoff (1779-1853), had been Opperhoofd at Deshima from 1817 to 1823, making the Court Journey to Edo twice, in 1818 and in 1822. On the latter occasion, he was accompanied by Johan van Overmeer Fisscher (1800-48), who served in various functions on Deshima from 1820 to 1829. King Willem I of the Netherlands had already bought the ethnographical collections of these two collectors earlier. Upon closer investigation of this catalogue, we find that it contains 70 titles that were collected by Fisscher, identified by a cross, and 31 titles collected by Blomhoff, marked with an asterisk, with three titles apparently figuring in both collections. However, in the preface to the catalogue, Siebold states that these figures would be 60 and 29 respectively. We can thus conclude that there is a slight difference in understanding between Hoffmann and Siebold, although we will have to await further research to find out the reasons for this difference. Anyway, when we accept the latter's view, this would result in the figure of 503 [MF: 505] titles for what could be called 'the Siebold collection of books.' And although the last number in the catalogue is 594, nine numbers appear twice, making the total number of books in this catalogue equal to 603.[1]

Among the books that Siebold acquired is *Wakan sansai zue* (No. 1 in the *Catalogus librorum*), comprised of 105 parts in 81 volumes. Somewhat smaller are the *Kinmo zui taisei* (No. 3), 21 parts in 9 vols., and the *Keisei zusetsu* (No. 439), in 30 vols. This is only a small selection of the multi-volume works. Counting the number of volumes, Siebold collected a total of more than 1500 volumes.[2]

---

1 MF: Indeed, the catalogue is numbered from 1 to 594. However, taking into account a few multiple entries under one number as well as a number of overlapping numbers, the total would amount to 615. In the preface Siebold states that he collected 525 books. Adding the 29 books collected by Blomhoff and the 60 books collected by Fisscher, as Siebold indicates, gives a total of 614 titles. That is probably as close as we can get, 614 or 615. Working, for example, with my count of the marks in the catalogue, yielding figures like 32 for Blomhoff and 69 for Fisscher, or with my count of the marks in the list of titles at the end, yielding 25 and 63 respectively, would only further complicate this exercise.

As for its contents, the *Catalogus librorum* is subdivided into eleven sections and each entry is provided with brief explanatory notes. The first Section deals with Encyclopaedic works, Section II with Historical and geographical works, III Natural history, IV Grammar and dictionaries, V Theology and works on moral aspects, VI Poetry, VII Communal customs and systems, VIII Economy, IX Numismatics, X Medicine and pharmaceutics, and XI Woodblock prints.

In this contribution I would like to discuss some aspects of the Siebold collection of books that cannot be so easily understood from this subdivision, in Part II. Then, under the heading of the 'accessibility and condition of Siebold's collection of books in Leyden,' I will make some observations on traces of the Siebold collection of books after his death, Part III. In the 'Conclusion,' I will discuss the necessity of comprehensive research, Part IV, also expanding on the perspectives of Siebold research.

II. Aspects of the Siebold collection of books

The *Catalogus librorum* is subdivided into eleven sections. Here I would like to discuss some aspects of the collection of books that may not be directly obvious from this categorization, focusing on: 1—Encyclopaedias; 2—Japanese and Ainu languages; 3—Maps; 4—Books related to natural history; 5—Sources used for the essays written by Siebold's pupils; and 6—The presents of Mogami Tokunai, in short, six themes.

II. 1 Encyclopaedic works

The first section of the *Catalogus librorum* covers encyclopaedic works and is comprised of, among others, the following four works: *Wakan sansai zue* (No. 1), *Zōho kashiragaki-Kinmō zui* (No. 2), *Zōho kashiragaki-Kinmō zui taisei* (No. 3), and *Morokoshi Kinmō zui* (No. 4). As I will demonstrate below, it is quite clear that Siebold had a great interest in the *Wakan sanzai zue*. Sugimoto Tsutomu already indicated that *Zōho kashiragaki-Kinmō zui taisei* had been very useful for Hoffmann.[3]

As for *Wakan sansai zue*, this was an innovative *magnum opus* edited by Terajima Ryōan (born 1654-?), a medical doctor in Osaka. The '*sansai*' in the title indicates 'heaven, earth, and man,' *ten chi jin*, and it is an encyclopaedia with lemmas. As for the '*zue*' in the title, this indicates that it is also comprised of (many) illustrations, as an important characteristic of this work. Although written in classical Chinese, *kanbun*, it is a relatively simple writing and, consequently, it was not very difficult to understand even for those who didn't master *kanbun* or Chinese. It contains descriptions that are still useful for the people of today. We may assume that *Wakan sansai zue* was both a useful and an important source for Siebold. This is only confirmed by the regular references to the work in his *Nippon*.[4] Although Siebold could not read *kanbun*

---

2 MF: In my count this would total some 1800 volumes.
3 Sugimoto 1999, pp. 387-389.
4 From the notes in *Nippon* it is evident that Siebold used books such as *Wakan sanzai zue*. This was already pointed out by, among others, Iwao et al (ed.) 1977, pp. 41f.

texts, he benefited from the assistance of both Hoffmann and Ko-tsching Dschang (dates unknown). [Fig. 5]

II. 2 Books treating the Japanese and the Ainu languages

Although Siebold was certainly interested in the Japanese language, it is a real pity that he was not gifted with some better talent for languages. He obviously had much larger capacities than most other people, but apparently not the talent to make a reputation in linguistics. Yet, in Nagasaki, interpreters such as Yoshio Gonnosuke absolutely had a great talent in languages. It was he who would teach Siebold the basics and the characteristics of the Japanese language.[5] Before Siebold even arrived in Deshima, Opperhoofd Doeff (1777-1835, on Deshima 1801-17) was quite advanced in Japanese, obviously thanks to his long residence in Deshima. With the assistance of among others Yoshio Gonnosuke, he even edited a Dutch-Japanese dictionary. This, the so-called 'Doeff Halma' dictionary, would ever since play a major role in Dutch-Japanese cultural exchanges.

In shipwrecking on his return journey to the Netherlands, Doeff not only lost his wife, but also all of his possessions. We may well assume that this concerned a sizeable collection, not only comprised of what he assembled himself, but also of the many various gifts that he had received from his large circle of Japanese friends. Undoubtedly, there must have been a large number of remarkable objects, as well as the drafts of his Dutch-Japanese dictionary. And still, all was lost to the sea.[6]

Whereas Doeff may consider himself a pioneer for editing a Dutch-Japanese dictionary, it must be said that Siebold's objectives were even more pretentious. In his 'Nihongo yōryaku,' in *Verhandelingen van het Bataviaasch Genootschap*, 11, 1826, for example, he introduces Chinese characters, their pronunciation and part of speech, as well as the grammar of the Japanese language. Moreover, in a table at the end of this contribution, he presents a list of words in Chinese, in Korean, Manchurian, Ainu, Japanese, and in the Ryūkyūan languages.[7] From this, we may well conclude that there was a very distinct difference between Doeff and Siebold as regards their approach to the Japanese language. Siebold was not so much interested in making a dictionary, his interest was wider, rather concerned with the characteristics and structure of the Japanese language, as well as with the Japanese culture.

Siebold realized that he also had to study the languages of the tributary countries so as to be able to grasp the characteristics of Japanese.

He therefore also investigated Korean. In Nagasaki there were always quite a few Ko-

---

5 Kure 1967-68 I (1967), pp. 88-94.
6 Sugimoto 1999, pp. 289-296 (「商館長 H. ドゥーフと蘭日対訳辞典の訳編」['Opperhoofd H. Doeff and his Editing of the Dutch-Japanese Dictionary']). [MF: Incidentally, Siebold is not the first researcher of the Korean language in Europe. Even prior to Siebold, Europe was aware of the Korean language and its "Hangul" script. In particular, linguist scholars in Paris had a considerable knowledge of the Korean language. Naturally, Blomhoff and Fisscher introduced and made reference to the Korean language.]
7 Kishimoto 2003.

reans that had shipwrecked on the Japanese coasts. They were normally interrogated in Nagasaki and so they were obliged to stay there until they were allowed to return again to their home country. Most often, they were seamen with hardly any education. But occasionally there would be some educated persons among them. By visiting these shipwrecked Koreans, Siebold had an opportunity to research Korean words, their pronunciation, and the characteristics of the Korean language. In this respect, he was the first European to investigate the Korean language.[8]

Otherwise, he also had a very large interest in the language of the Ainu who lived in the northern parts of Japan.[9] The circumstance that both their way of living and their language were different from the Japanese stimulated Siebold to research them. Shortly after arriving in Deshima in 1823, he started corresponding with the court physician Katsuragawa Hoken (1797-1844). The fact that he managed to obtain an Ainu dictionary from Hoken is a clear indication of his interest in the Ainu.[10] Moreover, we also know that Siebold met with Hoken during the court journey of 1826 (Bunsei 9). It was on this occasion that Hoken gave him his translation into Dutch of *Kai* (No. 215).[11] We also know that *Ezo honzō no zu* (No. 254) was a draft MS by Katsuragawa Hoken, about whom more in II-4.

On the occasion of the court journey, Siebold also met with Mogami Tokunai (1754-1836) who was known for having explored the northern parts of Japan. According to his notes, on April 21st (3/15), Siebold received the loan of a sketch of the waters around Ezo and Karafuto from Tokunai: 'For several days now, I spend the mornings in the company of my old friend Mogami Tokunai in order to discuss the edition of the Ezo language.'[12] It thus becomes clear that Siebold was involved in making a vocabulary, the *Ezogashima gengo* (No. 329), to which I will come back below. This manuscript is preserved in the University Library of Leyden. [Fig 6]

II. 3 Maps

According to Siebold's report to the Government at Java, dated February 13th, 1829 (1/10), most of the books that he collected

---

8 *Nippon* VII includes 'some information from Korai,' such as 'the visit to Korean merchants, driven to the coast of Japan' (pp. 6-9). The relief centre where those Koreans were housed provisionally was located in the house of the Lord of Tsushima, near Deshima (Miyazaki 2005. [MF: As for the suggestion that Siebold were the first to investigate the Korean language, again, I am afraid, this is a fairytale. Before Siebold's encounters with Koreans, both a provisional understanding of the Korean language, as well as knowledge of the *hangŭl* script had been introduced into Europe, most recently by both Blomhoff and Fisscher, more generally even long before. Certainly, the Parisian linguists were quite well informed about Korean.]

9 Major publications on Siebold's Ainu Language Studies are Kuroda 1938, pp. 315-52); Kindaichi 1938, pp. 353-426); Sugimoto 1999, pp. 303-24 (「シーボルトと日本語・アイヌ語研究」['Siebold and His Research on Japanese and Ainu Languages']).

10 In his report to the Government in Batavia of November 11th 1824 (9/21), Siebold states: 'I have come to own a precious Ainu dictionary that Dr. Botanicus (Katsuragawa Hoken) gave to me on my request. This Dictionary was printed in Jedo and is the best one could get. It was made on the order of the Emperor [= Shogun] for the use of his Japanese servants stationed in Ezo.' Citation from Kurihara (tr.) 2003, p. 370.

11 Ōshima 1938, pp. 117-25.

12 Siebold/Saito 1967, p. 197.

were related to maps, plans and views (c.110) and natural history (c.70).[13] He bought this large number of maps in order to get to know the geography of Japan.[14] Nowadays, the so-called Inō-map, or *Dai Nippon enkai yochi zenzu*, is widely known, but at the time, it was residing with the *bakufu* and not available for general use. Although less accurate than the Inō-map, various other practical maps were actually easily available. In addition to quite a few maps of the provinces that Siebold acquired, such as of the province of Echigo, *Echigo no kuni no ezu* (No. 77), of Sado, *Sado no kuni ezu* (No. 78), Tanba, *Tanba no kuni ōezu* (No. 79), or Owari, *Owari no kuni ezu* (No. 69) [See *Catalogus librorum* Section II C-b, Special geographical maps], he also obtained maps of all of Japan, such as *Kaisei Nihon yochi rotei zenzu* (No. 56), *Shinpan-Nihonkoku ōezu* (No. 57) and *Nihon henkai ryakuzu* (No. 58) [See *Catalogus librorum* Section II C-a, General geographical maps]. As for the capital city of Edo, Siebold acquired several maps, even up to a plan of the Inner quarters of Edo castle, titled *Edo gojō osumai no zu* (No. 124), as well as of districts, such as *Bunken Edo ōezu* (No. 105), *Bunken-Kaihō OEdo ezu* (No. 107), *Bunsei kaisei-OEdo ōezu* (No. 111, ex Fisscher), or *Surugadai Ogawamachi no zu* (No. 115) [See *Catalogus librorum* Section II D-b, Topographical works on Edo]. Naturally, Siebold was aware of the importance of maps for his future publications on Japan. Without these, his geographical and historical description of Japan would not have been possible.

Following the so-called Siebold Incident of 1828 (Bunsei 11), the maps of Japan and of Ezo that Siebold had received from the court astronomer Takahashi Kageyasu Sakusaemon (1785-1829) were confiscated and carefully investigated by the officials of the Nagasaki magistrate. However, that was not the end of it. Many more diverse items that could not be exported from Japan were also confiscated. Investigations and confiscations took place repeatedly, e.g. on December 17th and 18th, 1828 (11/11 and 12), February 8th, 14th, 17th, and 21st, and on March 4th of 1829 (Bunsei 12, 1/5, 11, 14, 18, 29).[15] In his *Dr. von Siebold: His Life and Contributions*, Kure Shūzō published a list of all the confiscated items. As these are only mentioned passim, I here intend to list all these items in the following:[16]

Maps and Topography:
Dai Nihon (Japan) *yochi no zu*, 3 sheets; *Nihonkoku kirizu*, 9 sheets; *Ezo* (Hokkaidō) *chizu*, 1 sheet; *Karafutotō* (Sakhalin) *no zu*, 1 sheet; *Sankoku tsūran*, 1 sheet; *Ryūkyūkoku* (Okinawa) *no zu*, 1 sheet; *Chōsenkoku* (Korea) *no zu*, 1 sheet; *Dai Nihon saiken shishō zenzu*, 1 sheet; *Shinzō saiken Kyō* (Kyoto) *ezu*, 1 sheet; *Chōshū Shimonoseki Kokura atari yori sokuryō* (a survey) *kirizu*; *Chōshū*

13　Kurihara (tr.) 2009, pp. 293-99.
14　Kutsuzawa 1980, pp. 74-90.
15　Kure 1967-68, pp. 279-82; Ishiyama 2003; Ishiyama/Miyazaki 2011.
16　Kure 1967-68, pp. 261f., 267-270, 323f. [MF: I must admit that I could not come up with an adequate translation of all these titles, so it may still be good to check with Kure, and probably also with *Naikaku bunko bunsei zakki* (内閣文庫文政雑記)].

Shimonoseki Kokura sankasho ezu no sha (copies); *Bunken Edo ōezu*, 1 sheet; *Osaka no chizu*, 1 sheet; A map with annotations in Dutch, 1 sheet; *Dai Nihon dōchū kōtei* (distances along the main roads) *kenki*, 1 vol., folding album; Famous places of Edo, 1 sheet; A Japanese travelogue, 1 volume; An envelope with maps, 9 sheets; Maps, 4 sheets;

Todatsu (East Tartary) *kikō*, 1 vol.; Excerpts from a Travel Account to the Northern Parts of Ezo, 1 vol.; Records of the climate in Hokkaido and Karafuto, in Dutch, 1 vol.; A graph of the fluctuation in the weather conditions, 1 envelope, 1 vol.; *Washū Yoshinoyama shōkei no zu*, 1 vol., folding album; Idem, introductory notes to the *Dai Nihonzu*, 1 sheet; *Dōchū hitori annaizu* (Travel by yourself), 1 vol., folding album; A full account of tours or pilgrimages in Japan, 1 vol.; *Yamato meisho*, 7 vols.

Books:

Shōzoku zushiki, 2 vols.; *Manshū jisho*; Pictures of Chinese and people from Hokkaido, 70 packages; A Street index, 1 vol.; *Hyakunin isshu*, 1 vol., in a box; A Picture book, 1 vol.; A Picture of a court noble, 1 sheet; *Nihonkoku bussan no zue*, 5 vols.; *Yonaki ishi katakiuchi no ki*, 1 vol.; *Buma no kagami yurai no ki*, 1 vol.; A book, 1 vol.; The Preface to a book, 1 copy; *Nakayama tō no kiji*, 1 vol.; *Osaka kassen no ehon*, 1 vol.; Pictures of warriors, 3 vols.; A Book on the writings of famous men, 1 vol.; A Book on plants and flowers, 1 vol.

Pictures:

Pictures along the Tōkaidō, 6 sheets; Edo sceneries, 1 sheet; Famous places, 2; A Simple view of the battle of Okehazama, 1; the Vestiges of the battle of Okehazama, 1; A Sketch of the god Daikokuten, 1; A Sketch of the god Ebisu, 1; Sketches of weapons, 2; A Picture of a Buddhist priest, 1; The Various types of clothing of priests and armour, 1; Small size pictures of warriors in official uniforms, 1 bundle; A Sketch of a saddled horse, 1; Paintings (name unclear), 9; Woodblock prints, 3.

Indeed, Siebold received the first maps in the above list, the *Dainihon yochizu* (in 3 sheets), *Nihonkoku kirizu* (9 sheets), *Ezo chizu* (1 sheet), and the map of the Island of Karafuto (1 sheet) from the court astronomer Takahashi Kageyasu. And indeed, it was strictly forbidden by the Tokugawa shogunate to export these maps out of Japan.[17] But this wasn't all. Eventually many more maps and topographical works were confiscated. These were not only maps of Ryūkyū (1 sheet) or Korea (1 sheet). Even works such as *Edo meishoe*, obviously contemporary guides to the city of Edo, were confiscated. Moreover, this was also the case with works containing illustrations of traditional clothing of the Japanese, or of portraits of warriors, or sketches of weapons and the like. In other words, many more items were confiscated from Siebold than just the maps that Takahashi had given him. Nevertheless, as can be inferred from the *Catalogus librorum*, Siebold still managed to bring back quite a number of documents, such as maps, guides, and travelogues.

---

17 MF: Yet, so far nobody has been able to show me the relevant passage in any official decree.

Among the confiscated topographical works, there was, among others, a Travel Account of the Eastern Parts of Tartary, *Tōdatsu kikō* (1 vol.), or Excerpts from a Travel Account to the Northern Parts of Ezo (1 vol.), and the *Manshū jisho*, that would have been very useful for his research on the northern parts of Japan. However, these only represented a small part of the Siebold collection and their being confiscated would hardly affect his research.

I wouldn't know how Siebold, in spite of all that was confiscated, still managed to bring back such a large collection of books and drawings to the Netherlands. What I do know is that the Dutch ship *Cornelis Houtman* stranded at Nagasaki on September 18th, 1828 (Bunsei 11, 8/10) and only arrived at Batavia from Nagasaki on February 24th, 1829 (Bunsei 12, 1/21), bringing 89 crates belonging to Siebold (67 of them containing ethnographical items, paintings and drawings, the remaining 22 crates containing plants).[18] Moreover, we also know that Siebold brought his collection of books with him when he departed from Nagasaki on January 3rd 1830 (Bunsei 12, 1829/12/9), being banned from Japan.[19] We can thus conclude that he did not ship his collection of books before they were subjected to inspection in the course of the Siebold Incident. At the time of the investigations, the books were just all available at Deshima.

Yet, Siebold was also a shrewd man who would not easily compromise. As already said above, among the maps that he managed to bring back to the Netherlands, there was even one of Edo castle (No. 124), as well as detailed maps of Karafuto by Mogami Tokunai that will be discussed into more detail in paragraph II-6 below. When these would also have been discovered and forwarded to Edo, the problems would have been even bigger. [Fig. 7]

II. 4 Books related to natural history

The *Catalogus librorum* gives some one hundred titles, or circa 350 vols. as the number of books and drawings on natural history collected by Siebold. Earlier, quoting the report to the government of February 13th, 1829 (1/10), I mentioned that this number was only 70. However, the difference with the earlier cited report is due to the circumstance that no drawings were included there. As for the books that Blomhoff and Fisscher collected, none of these deal with natural history. Consequently, all of the books on natural history are part of the Siebold collection.[20] The *Catalogus librorum* registers this collection as Section 3—Natural history books, numbered from 194–293.

The nature of these books is highly varied. In the Edo period, natural history research in Japan was strongly influenced by China. The *Honzō kōmoku*, compiled in the Ming Dynasty by Ri Jichin (1518-93), was only published posthumously, in 1596. The practi-

---

18 Kaji 2003, p. 86.

19 Besides the literary and ethnographical collections, Siebold brought many specimens of Flora and Fauna of Japan to the Netherlands. As for these, one can get an insight from the inventory of new acquisitions preserved in the Naturalis Biodiversity Centre (Yamaguchi 2003, pp. 49f.).

20 MF: This is not altogether correct, Fisscher did bring back a copy of the *Honzō kōmoku* from Japan, figuring as No. 103 in his MS Catalogue.

cal application of plants, *honzōgaku*, or also *materia medica*, was traditionally well researched in China. Ri studied all earlier publications on *honzōgaku*, made a selection of these, and then authored the *Honzō kōmoku* based on his own observations. This work also records a selection of animals and plants that were not of direct practical use. Yet, this deviation from traditional *honzōgaku* made his work revolutionary. When it found its way to Japan, it was Hayashi Razan (1583-1657) who introduced it to Tokugawa Ieyasu (1543-1616), the latter probably best known as a warlord, but also an intellectual and a collector of books. Razan then investigated which animals and plants of Japan would be represented in *Honzō kōmoku*. Consequently, he then published the *Tashikihen* (2 parts in 2 vols.) in 1630 (Kanei 7) and later, in 1631 (Kanei 8), the *Shinkan tashikihen* (5 parts in 3 vols.). These were necessary to be able to profit from the *Honzō kōmoku*.

Because of its background, the *Honzō kōmoku* took a position of the highest importance in the natural history research in Japan, almost like the Bible. All natural history research in Edo-period Japan would categorize plants and animals after the system of *Honzō kōmoku*. Also some various other Chinese publications on natural history were introduced into Japan and came to be appreciated as well. As these books were extremely expensive, people in Japan would make copies from locally cut blocks, *wakokubon*. Since these also included marks to assist in the reading of the classical Chinese text, *kanbun*, these *wakokubon* were considerably easier to read. These indications were provided by some of the most excellent researchers of natural history at the time, such as Ono Ranzan (1729-1810).[21]

In addition to the *Kōsei honzō kōmoku* (No. 195), the Siebold collection of books also contains *wakokubon* such as *Taikan shorui honzō* (No. 194), *Honzōkai* (No. 196), *Mōshi sōmoku chōjū chūgyoso* (No. 197), *Tsūshi konchū sōmokuryaku* (No. 203), *Honzō igen* (No. 205), and *Nanpō sōmokujō* (No. 206). These books couldn't be read unless one were familiar with Chinese and *kanbun*. Consequently, it is obvious that Siebold couldn't use these books himself. Nevertheless, he brought these works to the Netherlands as he estimated that they might be of use in the future. Since Japanese natural history research was strongly influenced by China, these books are also necessary for an understanding of the development of this research in Japan. Siebold hoped that there would sometime be someone to get to see these books. [Fig. 8]

Apart from such *wakokubon*, the Siebold collection of books is also comprised of books written by Japanese authors. Works such as the *Yamato honzō shinkōsei* by Kaibara Ekken (1630-1714, No. 211), *Butsurui hinshitsu* by Hiraga Gennai (1728-79, No. 214), *Honzō kōmoku keimō* by Ono Ranzan (No. 207), *Honzō wage* (No. 210), and *Honzō yakumei bikō wakunshō* (No. 220), discuss a wide array of subjects. But there are also works dealing exclusively with plants. Examples are the *Hyakkikufu* (No. 224) and

---

21 About Ono Ranzan, see: *Ono Ranzan* 2010.

Kadan yōgikushū (No. 225), both dealing with chrysanthemums, or illustrated works on morning glories, such as *Asagaohin* (No. 226), *Asagaofu* (No. 228), and *Kadan asagaotsū* (No. 229), or even on tangerines, such as *Kitsuhin ruikō* (No. 234) and *Kitsuhin* (No. 235).

In the peaceful Edo-period, various horticultural and garden plants were cultivated. In turn, books were also published on the various newly cultivated varieties of horticultural plants. As Siebold came to realize that Japan had excellent and very diverse horticultural and garden plants, he got the idea to also introduce these into Europe. He therefore exported living horticultural plants to the Netherlands and also collected books on these plants. The small booklet *Kōeki jikinshō* (No. 236) by Itō Ihei has illustrations of various horticultural plants. With the names of the plants written in cursive running script, Siebold could not read these. However, as the book also gives the reading in *katakana*, it was still very useful for Siebold. [Fig. 9]

Quite some albums of drawings were presented to Siebold by various researchers. These only confirm that he was in contact with the foremost natural history researchers in Japan of the time. He corresponded for example with Mizutani Sukeroku (1779-1833), a samurai in charge of the herbarium of the Owari clan. Sukeroku not only provided Siebold with almost 400 specimens of plants, but also with albums such as the *Honzō shashin* (No. 258) and *Honzō bassui* (No. 259).[22] As the most excellent natural history researcher in Japan of his day, he was the chairman of a group of amateurs of natural history, the Shōhyakusha, organizing exhibitions of products that were offered for sale, as well as being engaged in instruction activities. Providing Siebold with specimens of plants that were indigenous to Kiso and Hakuzan (Toyama Prefecture) that Siebold could not obtain from Nagasaki, he considerably contributed to Siebold's collection. His understanding of the distinguishing features of plants made Sukeroku a master in drawing. And although his drawings might seem somewhat coarse at first sight, it is still directly clear which kind of plant Sukeroku actually drew. In 1826 Siebold met twice with Sukeroku, both on his way to Edo and on the way back to Nagasaki. Sukeroku was then accompanied by his pupils Ōkōchi Sonshin (1796-1883) and Itō Keisuke (1803-1901).[23]

In Edo, Siebold met with Kurimoto Zuiken (1756-1834), one of the shogun's court physicians, a well respected and appreciated natural history researcher in the *bakufu* and a master in drawing. Quite some daimyo and *hatamoto* had an interest in natural history. They either made drawings themselves or had someone make drawings for them, in this way making albums that they would then dedicate to the shogun. Through his important position in the *bakufu*, Zuiken had access to these albums which he would not

---

22 MF: Various works titled *Honzō shashin* are preserved both at the National Museum of Ethnology, as 1-4312, and at the Leiden University Library, as Ser 970; the *Honzō bassui* is to be found at the Leiden University Library, as Ser 979.
23 Yamaguchi 2003, pp. 43f.

only investigate, but also would copy, adding these copies to his own collection. Although he was interested in flora and fauna and drew very much in his life, his primary interest was concerned with fish. Siebold had an opportunity to see his drawings of fish and crustaceans and managed to obtain *Kaikarui shashin* (No. 267) and *Gyorui shashin* (No. 272), albums of drawings by Zuiken.[24]

The albums of drawings that Siebold obtained from various natural history researchers represent most important source material for the history of natural history research in Japan. Many such albums were made during the Edo-period. Especially since Japanese summers are hot and humid, it was not easy to preserve actual specimens. These would often rot or loose their value due to insects. Therefore it became common practice to make drawings of plants and animals. By the Meiji period, however, objects from the Edo period were often considered as of no value and so they were lost. Then came the great Kantō earthquake and the bombing of Tokyo during the war, so that even more got lost. Now only a small portion has been preserved.

In the following, I will list the albums in the *Catalogus librorum*, by author/maker, with the number of titles, and the number of volumes. These were only preserved since Siebold obtained them, otherwise they would all have been lost in Japan.

Kurimoto Zuiken: 2 titles, 5 vols.

Mizutani Sukeroku: 4 titles, 9 vols.
Ōkubo Masaaki (1802-41): 4 titles, 5 vols.
Udagawa Yōan (1798-1846): 6 titles, 7 vols.
Katsuragawa Hoken: (6 titles, 9 vols.
Ōkōchi Sonshin: 3 titles, 3 vols.
Kuroda Narikiyo (1795-1851): 3 titles, 3 vols.
Anonymous: 8 titles.

These drawings must have been of great use in the preparation of the *Flora* and *Fauna japonica*. However, they were not used as the direct examples for these publications. The illustrations in these publications are directly based on both the specimens and on the drawings that Siebold had commissioned specifically from Kawahara Keiga.[25] As for the drawings in the albums, these were very skilled, both artistically and scientifically. Yet, only few were eventually published, as it would be too costly to publish natural history albums in colour. Nevertheless, these albums were often copied and even as copies, they contribute to the development of natural history research. [Fig. 10]

II. 5 The books used by pupils of Siebold as source material

Siebold asked Mima Junzō (1794-1825), Takano Chōei (1804-50), Kō Ryōsai (1799-1846), *et al.* to write in Dutch on themes that would be of use for his own Japan research. Already in 1938, Ogata Tomio, Ōshima Ransaburō, *et al.* paid attention to these MSS.[26] These must have been of great

---

24 Yamaguchi 2001. [MF: The *Kaikarui shashin* and *Gyorui shashin* are now preserved in the University Library Leiden, as Ser 1018, and Ser 1013].
25 Yamaguchi 1997; Yamaguchi 1997-98; Yamaguchi/Kato et al 2003.
26 Ogata/Ōshima et al 1938, pp. 61-274.

value for Siebold when writing his *Nippon*.[27] When asked, his pupils would search for relevant literature and come up with a Dutch translation. Although Ogata and Ōshima refer to these MSS as theses, it seems more correct to use terms such as 'report,' or 'translation.'

Although not so many in number, at least some of the MSS of his students or the books that they used are listed in the *Catalogus librorum* and have been preserved in the University Library of Leyden.[28] I will here list those that I could identify, in the order of the Hoffmann *Catalogus*, citing their title, shelf number, the title in Dutch, and the name of the pupil. The Dutch titles are here quoted after Ogata and Ōshima.

446 *Inzen tekiyō*, by Ono Ranzan (UB Ser 891) > *Inzen tekiyō*, by Takano Chōei, 1804–50

465 *Somemono no hō, wasetsukuri no hō, chaseihō*, by Anon. (UB Ser 892) > Cultivation of tea plants and the process of making tea in Japan, by Takano Chōei

270 *Chūrui shashū*, by Ōkōchi Sonshin (UB Ser 1024) > Illustrated description of indigenous insects of Japan, Idem for spiders from Japan, by Ishii Sōken, 1796–1861

283 *Tengu tsumeishi no zakkō*, by Kiuchi Jūgyō (UB Ser 1032) > Miscellaneous thoughts on fossilized *tengu* nails, by Kō Ryōsai.[29]

Moreover, it seems likely that also the following belong to this group:

488 *Shinkyū setsuyaku*, by Ishii Sōken[30] (UB Ser 1100) seems to be related to a Dutch language translation of *Kyūhō ryakusetsu* by Mima Junzō, Totsuka Ryōsai, and Ishii Sōken, but as I did not see this report myself, I rather abstain from adding it to the above list. Yet we know that Siebold was interested in Japanese acupuncture and would meet in Edo with Ishizaka Sōtetsu who was then a respected expert in this profession.[31]

As for *Somemono no hō, wasetsukuri no hō, chaseihō* (No. 465), its author is not known. It is a collection of various MSS, each translated by Takano Chōei. Ogata Tomio discussed the MS of Takano Chōei on the process of making tea in Japan in *Siebold kenkyū*.[32] Ogata assumes that No. 465 *Somemono no hō, wasetsukuri no hō, chaseihō* would be the source of Takano Chōei's work.[33] I can confirm that the MS of Takano Chōei is, indeed, a faithful translation of this work and that no name of an author is given. [Fig. 11]

II. 6 Presents of Mogami Tokunai

Mogami Tokunai had a special liking for

---

27 A thesis written in Dutch, for example,「日本に於ける茶樹の栽培と茶の製法」[Cultivation and Production of Tea in Japan] by TAKANO Chōei, became the basis of Siebold's *Nippon* Vol. IV-9 (Ph. Fr. von Siebold, *Nippon* (tr. Nakai Akio, Yūshōdō, 1978, pp. 127–42).

28 MF: There seem to have been at least 45 such "theses," as can be inferred from an inventory preserved at the Burg Brandenstein Archives (V-e 93).

29 As for a Dutch thesis by Kō Ryōsai「天狗爪石略記」[Short discourse on a fossilized tooth] Ōshima Ranzaburō writes that the manuscript has been preserved in the Kō family (Ōshima 1938, p. 90).

30 MF: This Ishii Sōken must be Ishizaka Sōtetsu, *c*.1789–1844.

31 Siebold noted that he visited Ishizaka Sōtetsu, acupuncturist to the Shogun, and the others on April 21st, 1826 (3/15). Siebold/Saitō 1967, p. 197.

32 Ogata 1938, pp. 135–179.

33 Ogata 1938, p. 144.

Siebold and presented him with the maps and his travelogues of the northern parts of Japan that he had cherished. Such a demonstration of a special friendship stemmed from his conviction that Siebold would use these for his general research. For Siebold this was especially favourable as he thus obtained accurate maps. As already said above, he was interested in the Ainu and in the geographical aspects of Ezo and Karafuto. At the time when this was still a mater of discussion in Europe, the Japanese knew that Karafuto was an island, not a peninsula.[34] Siebold was therefore very excited when Mogami Tokunai – on the occasion of the court journey of 1826 (Bunsei 9) – showed him the maps that proved that Karafuto was an island.[35]

Siebold had obtained the so-called Inō-zu map of Japan and maps of the northern parts of Japan from Takahashi Kageyasu.[36] However, these were confiscated in the course of the Siebold Incident, as already remarked above. Yet, without any sleep, he managed to copy the maps of Ezo and the southern Kuriles (or at least the relevant parts) before these were confiscated.[37] But he had no time to also copy the remaining parts of Japan. Nevertheless, thanks to the detailed maps that he had obtained from Tokunai, he could still provide us with an accurate account of the geographical situation of Karafuto in his *Nippon*.[38]

The *Catalogus librorum* has ten titles of items that were given to Siebold by Tokunai:

Ezo shūi (No. 176);[39] *Ezo no zu* (No. 177); *Karafutotō* (No. 180); *Sagarintō no zu* (No. 181); *Kokuryūkō naka no shū narabi ni tendo* (No. 183); *Kamusasuka no zu* (No. 192); *Fokai* (No. 193); *Ezo hōgen* (No. 328);[40] *Rongo ikun* (No. 340); and *Doryōkō settō* (No. 433). Moreover, the *Catalogus librorum* also has the *Ezogashima gengo* (No. 329), a vocabulary of Ainu words that Siebold made together with Tokunai.[41]

Apart from these books, Tokunai also gave Siebold specimens of trees, drawn on thin wooden planks with their names, still preserved in the Naturalis collection. In the case of trees originating from Ezo, their names were indicated in the Ainu language. These specimens were very well made and were an important source for Siebold when describing the plants of Ezo and the north of Japan.[42]

The most important gifts of Tokunai are the maps in Nos. 183 and 177. The first,

---

34 As for the maps of Japan available in Siebold's days, see among others: Nakamura 1969; Miyazaki, et al (eds.) 2009, pp. 164-86. For the understanding of Europeans of Jezo and Karafuto, and for Siebold's intention with the maps of these islands, see: Shimatani 1977, pp. 251-8.
35 During his stay in Edo, Siebold noted on April 16th (3/10) 1826, that Mogami Tokunai lent him two sketches of the waters around Jezo and of the Island of Karafuto. What a treasure indeed. (Siebold/Saitō 1967, p. 194).
36 Kure 1967-68. I (1967), pp. 213-36.
37 Kure 1967, p. 285.
38 Funakoshi 1979, pp. 81-98.
39 MF: actually, this book is from the Fisscher collection and obviously not a present of Tokunai to Siebold.
40 MF: again, both copies are from the Fisscher collection.
41 Hoffmann 329『蝦夷ヶ嶋言語』[Language of the Island Jezo] came into being not only through the efforts of Tokunai, but also thanks to the editorial work of Katsuragawa Hoken. (Kuroda 1938, p. 343).
42 Yamaguchi/Kato 1998.

Kokuryūkō naka no shū narabi ni tendo, is a copy by Tokunai after the map of Karafuto by Mamiya Rinzō (1780-1844). As is well known, Mamiya Rinzō was a great explorer of whom it is said that he made the journey to Karafuto twice. In the second expedition, in 1808 (Bunka 5), six persons were involved, among whom Tokunai and Rinzō, to execute a survey of the land of Karafuto by order of the *bakufu*. Whereas Tokunai himself returned to Matsumae to hibernate, Matsuda Denjūrō and Mamiya Rinzō stayed in Karafuto to explore the area until the far northern parts until 1809 (Bunka 6). Physically, Rinzō was very strong and he also possessed the means of a sharp judgment and a keen observation. Moreover, he had both a passion and a talent for making drawings. He not only discovered the Strait of Karafuto, he also crossed it all by himself and explored the mouth of the Amur River. He published his findings in his Travel Account of the Eastern Parts of Tartary, *Tōdatsu chihō kikō*.[43]

Tokunai had the intention to make a map of Ezo and so he returned to Edo with as many data as he could gather to make this. He then gave his most detailed map to the court astrologer Takahashi Kageyasu. In turn, Kageyasu gave a copy of this map to Siebold, which would later be confiscated. It was then thanks to the map in No. 183 above, and the maps of Ezo that he had obtained from Tokunai, that Siebold could present an accurate map of Karafuto in *Nippon*.[44] [Fig. 12] [Fig. 13] [Fig. 14]

III. The Siebold Collection of books: its accessibility and condition in Leyden

Although Siebold donated part of his collection of books to the libraries of Vienna and Paris, he retained the larger part for his own researches. Later these were donated to become the property of the Kingdom of the Netherlands. Nowadays, this collection is split up: one part is preserved in Leiden University Library, the other in the National Museum of Ethnology. However, some books were apparently lost after the catalogue was published, such as for example Spiders, *Churui no zu* (No. 271) and Depiction of the Quadrupeds Known as Likinkamui and Tsunakai in the Language of Karafuto (No. 279).[45] [Fig 15].

It would be the Japanologist Lindor Serrurier (1846-1901), a pupil of Hoffmann's, who would arrange the books and documents that Siebold had assembled and provide them with a continuing numbering. Serrurier was also the curator (1877-80) and later director (1880-96) of the Leiden National Museum of Ethnography. In 1896 he published the *Bibliothèque japonaise. Catalogue raisonné des livres et des manuscrits japonais enrégistrés à la Bibliothèque de l'Université de Leyde*, with E.J. Brill. In that

---

43 Shimatani 1977; Mamiya/Hora et al 1998.
44 One finds a lithograph in Siebold's *Nippon* (Vol. VII), titled, 'Die Insel Kraft (Sedhalien) und die Mündung des Mankô (Amur) von Mocami Tokunai und Mamia Rinzo.' On the process of the making of this map, see among others: Ashida/Yanai 1988, pp. 427-80.
45 MF: it may sound somewhat illogical–but that is the problem when splitting up the collection: one loses the overview. Yet, this album of spiders is still preserved in the Museum of Ethnology. As for the Depiction of the Quadrupeds, I don't know.

catalogue he lists 1263 titles of Japanese books, drawings and MSS. These are listed with their titles in *kanji* and *kana* syllabary and their reading provided in Western script. Then follow notes on the contents for each title in French. The catalogue is arranged by subject, starting with encyclopaedic works, dictionaries, language, geographical works, etc. It is in so far practical as one can quite easily and simply gain an overview of the titles in each category, without any necessary notion of some exact title. [Fig. 16]

As for the books and drawings that were placed in the Museum of Ethnology, these were given new inventory numbers.[46] The Siebold collection then starts with the numeral 1. For example, *Honzō shashin* (*Catalogus* No. 248), Album of Drawings of Plants by Mizutani Sukeroku, has the inventory number 1-4312. As concerns the collections of Blomhoff and Fisscher, these have an inventory number starting with 360.[47] E.g., an album of insects that Blomhoff commissioned has the inv. no. 360-959. The shelf marks of the University Library still correspond with the Serrurier numbering. So when one would like to consult one of the books, one can simply ask for the number given in the Serrurier catalogue.

In 1996, exactly 100 years after the publication of the Serrurier catalogue, H. Kerlen published his *Catalogue of pre-Meiji Japanese books and maps in public collections in The Netherlands*. This catalogue lists all Japanese books, maps, and manuscripts preserved in the Netherlands, 918 pp. of text and in total 1962 titles. This catalogue is arranged in strictly alphabetical order of titles, giving the name of the author, the publisher, the format, the number of pages, etc., as well as identifying the institution where the book is preserved. As this catalogue is arranged according to the titles of the books, it is especially useful for those who already know the title they are looking for. However, if one doesn't know an exact title, this is some disadvantage. In his Introduction, Kerlen informs us that some 960 titles have been preserved in the University Library, some 970 titles in the National Museum of Ethnology, and some 45 titles in the Rijksherbarium of dried plants.

IV. By way of conclusion: about the need of a comprehensive investigation of the Siebold collections

This writer visited the special collections of the University Library more than a hundred times to investigate the literature on natural history. Consulting the catalogues of Hoffmann and Serrurier, I knew beforehand what they had. However, judging from the catalogues, one cannot always have any inkling as to the contents, and time and again I was in for a surprise. As an example I

---

46 MF: As is explained by Serrurier himself in the preface to the catalogue, it is rather that he in 1881, as the new director of the museum, took the initiative to place part of the Museum's Siebold collection in the University Library–not the other way around–keeping only those works that he considered useful for the study of the ethnography of Japan. Cf. his preface, p. vi.

47 MF: It must be said though, that, apart from only a few volumes of popular novels from the collection of Fisscher, no books whatsoever can be found under the inventory number of 360; all of the books in these two collections have now been integrated into the Siebold collection.

may cite Serrurier 932, an untitled work. According to Serrurier this would be a document concerned with meteorology. On closer inspection I came to understand that it was the meteorological data for Edo of 1826 (Bunsei 9), complemented with notes on such aspects as pressure, temperature, and the weather, from January 1st of that year.[48] This represents the meteorological observations for a full year, without any interval and is important material for an insight in the weather conditions of the Edo period. Although only the records of 1826 have been preserved in the University Library, I suspect hat this kind of observation would have been done over a longer period in the Edo period.[49]

As concerns the maps and documents that Mogami Tokunai gave to Siebold, these have already been subject to investigation by various experts. However, as for the material of a different nature, as far as I have come to understand, this has never been researched. In his biography on Mogami Tokunai, Shimatani Yoshikichi states that *Hokkai* figured among the presents he made to Siebold.[50] Shimatani came to suggest this since he noticed that a work titled *Hokkai* was registered as No. 193 in the Hoffmann *Catalogus librorum*. But as he never had the original in his hands, he cited *Hokkai* as being a map. When I requested this work myself, I found that it is actually comprised of both a map and three pamphlets.[51] These pamphlets contain written information that Tokunai managed to obtain from Russians, such as, among others, on Russian Christianity. I would like to add that *Hokkai* is a very interesting source for an understanding of Mogami Tokunai as a person. However, as far as I know, nobody has ever bothered to research this material or publish its contents.

It would be extremely useful for research of the Siebold collection, as well as for research in various fields, if a catalogue were available with a more concrete listing of the contents of the books and plates preserved in the University Library and the Museum of Ethnology than is to be found in the Hoffmann, Serrurier, and Kerlen catalogues.[52]

Now is the time for digitized images. In the end it would be good if these books and documents would not only be available through a catalogue, but also through digitized images. Nowadays, the National Diet Library of Japan steadily makes its books and documents accessible through the internet. I believe that this would also be the ideal accessibility for books and documents in the Siebold collection.[53] Anyway, if there would be a better catalogue, the books and drawings that Siebold collected would be more widely used.

---

48 MF: This already would have been less of a surprise if only one would have read the explanatory notes in French.
49 Besides the records of 1826, it is reported that Ruhr University Bochum preserves the records of the weather from January through September of 1828 (Ishiyama/Miyazaki 2011, p. 203).
50 Shimatani 1977, p. 239.
51 MF: Again, this is exactly the information that Hoffmann provides in his catalogue, admittedly in Latin. Serrurier 194 has even more detailed notes on the three pamphlets, in French.
52 MF: As may be inferred from my annotations above, the information is certainly given and available, it is just a matter of some basic understanding of the Latin and/or French languages.
53 About the perspectives of digitization of the books in the University Library of Leiden, see: Okuda 2012.

This research shouldn't be restricted to the material preserved in the University Library of Leiden and in the National Museum of Ethnology. It should be done in a scientific way. I recently heard that the National Institute of Japanese Literature, Kokubunken, has taken some initiative.[54] But drawings by Keiga related to natural history are also preserved in the Naturalis Museum in Leiden.[55] Moreover, it is also necessary to conduct such research in Germany. For example, there is an Album of People in the National Museum of Ethnology in Munich that even served as a basis for illustrations in Nippon. And then there is also a Siebold Sammlung in the Ruhr University at Bochum as well as numerous MSS and drawings in the Burg Brandenstein Archives.[56] All these materials in various countries should be investigated integrally.

We Japanese must be grateful to Siebold. However, his activities were so diverse, ranging from natural history to diplomatic matters, so that some really comprehensive research hasn't been done yet. This writer really hopes that some interdisciplinary and international research may be conducted on the books and drawings that Siebold brought with him to Europe from Japan.

captions for the figures (pp. 176～195)

Fig. 5—The cover of *Wakan sansai zue*. Courtesy University Library Leiden.

Fig. 6—Vocabulary of the Ainu language.

Fig. 7—*Kaisei Nihon yochi rotei zenzu* (Hoffmann No. 56) and *Nihon henkai ryakuzu* (Hoffmann No. 58)

Fig. 8—Hoffmann 203 as an example of a *wakokubon*. Courtesy University Library Leiden.

Fig. 9—Hoffmann 236 - *Kōeki jikinshō*. Courtesy University Library Leiden.

Fig. 10—Some albums in the Siebold collection donated by Japanese natural history researchers, Katsuragawa Hoken, Mizutani Sukeroku, Ōkubo Masaaki, and Kurimoto Zuiken.

Fig. 11—Hoffmann 465 *Somemono no hō*. Courtesy University Library Leiden.

Fig. 12—Hoffmann 193 *Hokkai* and 177. *Ezo zu* Courtesy University Library Leiden.

Fig. 13—Hoffmann 182. *Kokriukō nakanosu narabini Tendo* Courtesy University Library Leiden.

Fig. 14—Mamiya Rinzō's map of Karafuto that was confiscated. Courtesy National Archives Tokyo.

Fig. 15—The University Library at Leiden.

Fig. 16—L. Serrurier title page *Bibliothèque japonaise*. Courtesy University Library Leiden.

(English Trans. by Matthi Forrer)

---

54 Suzuki 2011.
55 Yamaguchi 1996b; Yamaguchi 1997.
56 Miyazaki 2011.

「シーボルトの日本収集書籍コレクションの概略について」に対する脚註・追記

マティ・フォラー
（Matthi Forrer）

※ 本稿の註番号はマティ・フォラーによる英訳脚註番号（197～211頁）に対応しており、「＊」は、原文に注がないため、追記として新たに付したことを示す。

脚註＊1
MF：『日本書籍目録』は、通し番号で、収録書物は1から594番までということになっている。しかし、一番号下に複数の書物がリストアップされていたり、また、番号の重複があったりするため、これを精査すると、収録総数は614，または、615タイトルということになる。シーボルト自身は、同目録序文で、525タイトルを集めたとしている。これにシーボルトがブロムホフ、及び、フィッセルの収集品とするもの、それぞれ29と60を足すと、総計は614となる。こうして見ると、私の計算した総計とほぼ一致するが、私の調査では、目録に収録されているシーボルトの収集品は505、ブロムホフ、及び、フィッセルの収集品はそれぞれ32と63タイトルとなるため、総数がほとんど一致するからと喜べない。さらに詳細な調査が必要である。

脚註＊2
MF：私の計算では1800巻になる。

脚註7 追記
MF：ちなみにシーボルトは、ヨーロッパで最初の朝鮮語研究者ではない。シーボルト以前のヨーロッパは、朝鮮語やハングル文字の存在について知っており、とりわけパリの言語学者らは、朝鮮語についてかなりの知識を持っていた。もちろんブロムホフやフィッセルも朝鮮語に言及し、紹介している。

脚註＊17
MF：しかしながら、そのような御触書があったのかは、いまだ誰に聞いても定かではない。

脚註＊20
MF：これは誤りである。フィッセルは『本草綱目』を日本で購入している。フィッセルの手稿目録の103番として記録されている。

脚注＊22
MF：『本草写真』と題された複数の書物があり、ライデン国立民族学博物館（RMvV1-432）と、ライデン大学図書館（Ser. 970）にある。『本草抜粋』は、ライデン大学図書館にある（Ser. 979）。

脚注＊24
MF：『蟹蝦類写真』と『魚類写真』は、現在ライデン大学図書館に保存されている（Ser. 1018、Ser. 1013）。

脚註＊28
MF：これら門人による蘭語論文は少なくとも45本あることがブランデンシュタイン家文書に保存されている目録から推察できる（所蔵館資料番号 V-e 93）。

脚註＊30
MF：「石井宗謙」ではなく、「石坂宗哲」の誤りであろう。

「シーボルトの日本収集書籍コレクションの概略について」に対する脚註・追記

脚註＊39
MF：しかし、この本は、フィッセルが持ち帰ったものである。したがって、徳内がシーボルトに贈呈した本ではない。

脚註＊40
MF：上記同様、両方ともフィッセルのコレクションである。

脚註＊45
MF：コレクションを分割して保存する場合に生じる問題である。そのために全体像が失われてしまうのだ。ただ、蜘蛛の画帖については、たしかにライデン国立民族学博物館にあることを追記しておく（所蔵館資料番号未詳）。一方、四足動物の記述に関しては、私も所在を把握していない。

脚註＊46
MF：セルリエ自身が、目録序文で説明しているように（vi 頁）、民族学博物館のシーボルト書籍コレクションを民族学に寄与するものを除いて大学図書館に移行するというのは、むしろ彼が提案したことであり、その逆ではない。

脚註＊47
MF：柳亭種彦の合巻物を除き、ブロムホフとフィッセルの「書籍」コレクションはライデン国立民族学博物館の360番系（旧王立骨董陳列室所蔵品）所蔵番号に登録されていないことを明記しておく。2人の書籍コレクションは、シーボルトコレクションに合流し、現在は「1」ではじまる数字で、シーボルトコレクションとして登録されている。

脚註＊48
MF：セルリエのフランス語の解説にある情報で、驚くには値しない。

脚註＊51
MF：同様に、これもホフマンが目録に記載している情報である。また、セルリエに至っては、目録の194番でこの3冊の小誌について詳細な記述をしている。

脚註＊52
MF：先の追記にも記したとおり、ホフマンにしても、セルリエにしても各々の目録において、収集品に関して、必要な情報は提供している。研究する側は、彼らの解説（ラテン語、及び、フランス語）を正確に解読しようとする姿勢が必要であろう。

Bibliography —Two posthumous articles by Dr. Yamaguchi Takao—

Dr. Matthi Forrer

Ashida/Yanai 1938
ASHIDA Koreto & YANAI Kenji「シーボルト作成の地図」『シーボルト研究』['Maps Made by Siebold', in: *Siebold Research*]（Iwanami shoten, 1938）

Barbinger/Furuta 1986
BARBINGER, Franz, 'Johann Joseph Hoffmann (1805-1878): ein Würzburger Orientalist', tr. by FURUTA Kei as「日本語学者列伝　ホフマン伝（1）〜（3）」『日本語学』['Biography of Japanologists: Hoffmann (1)-(3)', in: *Japanology*] 44-46（June-Sep. 1986）

Exhibtiion Catalogue 1980
『川原慶賀展：鎖国の窓を開く出島の絵師』[*Kawahara Keiga: the Deshima Painter Who Opens the Window of the Country of Seclusion*]（Seibu Art Museum, 1980）

Exhibition Catalogue 1987
『川原慶賀展：幕末の"日本"を伝えるシーボルトの絵師』[*Kawahara Keiga: Siebold's Painter Who Transmitted Late Edo 'Japan'*]（Seibu Art Museum, 1987）

Forrer 2007
FORRER, Matthi「葛飾北斎とシーボルトの出会い」『北斎』['Siebold's Encounter with Hokusai', in: *Hokusai*]（Tokyo Shimbun, 2007. Exhibition Catalogue）

Forrer/Kouwenhoven 2000
FORRER, Matthi & KOUWENHOVEN, Arlette, *Siebold and Japan*（Leyden, 2000）

Funakoshi 1979
FUNAKOSHI Akio「シーボルト資料カラフト図に関する若干の検討」『奈良女子大学地理学研究報告』['Some notes on the map of Karaft collected by Siebold', in: *Bulletin on Geographical Studies Nara Women's University*] 1（1979）

Furuta 2004
FURUTA Kei「ヨハン・ヨゼフ・ホフマン―生涯と業績」『お茶の水女子大学人文科学紀要』['Johann Josef Hoffmann: his Life and Contributions', in: *Bulletin for the Humanities, Ochanomizu Women's University*] 57（Mar. 2004）

Hashimoto 2013
HASHIMOTO Kenichiro「『北斎漫画』考その成立と影響―シーボルト著『NIPPON』図版篇を中心として―」『北斎研究所研究紀要』['Thoughts on Hokusai Manga: how it came to being and its influences, based on the illustrations in Siebold's Nippon', in: *Bulletin from the Hokusai Research Centre*] 5（Jan. 2013）

Hata 1990
HATA Shinji「150年前の"現代人"」『ヨーロッパに眠る日本の宝』['A "modern" man from 150 years ago', in: *Japanese Treasures Dormant in Europe*]（Nagasaki Prefectural Art Museum, 1990. Exhibition Catalogue）

Holthuis/Sakai 1970
HOLTHUIS, L.B. & SAKAI Toshikazu『シーボルトと日本動物誌：日本動物史の黎明』[*Siebold and His "Fauna Japonica": the Dawn of the Natural History of Japanese Animals*].（Gakujutsusho shuppankai, 1970）

Inuki 1996
INUKI Jun「シーボルト生誕二百周年の歩み―シーボルトと長崎―」『鳴滝紀要』['Towards the 200th Commemoration Day of the Birth of Siebold: Siebold and Nagasaki', in: *Narutaki Bulletin*] 6（1996）

Ishiyama 2003

Bibliography —Two posthumous articles—

ISHIYAMA Yoshikazu「シーボルトの生涯・業績および関係年表」『新・シーボルト研究』['Siebold's Life and Contributions, with a chronology', in: *New Siebold Research*]（Yasaka shobō, 2003. II）

Ishiyama/Miyazaki 2011
ISHIYAMA Yoshikazu & Miyazaka Katsunori「シーボルトの生涯とその業績関係年表（1796-1832）」『西南学院大学国際文化論集』['A Chronology related to Siebold's life and contributions I (1796-1832)', in: *Bulletin of the Dept. International Culture, Seinan Gakuin University*] 26-1 (Sept. 2011)

Itazawa 1938
ITAZAWA Takeo「シーボルトの第一回渡来の使命と彼の日本研究特に日蘭貿易の検討について」『シーボルト研究』['Siebold's Mission during His First Stay in Japan, and His Research, Especially His Considerations on the Dutch-Japanese Trade', in: *Siebold Research*]（Iwanami shoten, 1938）

Itazawa 1960
── 『シーボルト』[*Siebold*]（Yoshikawa Kōbunkan, 1960. Series Jinbutsu sōsho 45）

Iwao et al (ed.) 1977
IWAO Seiichi et al (ed.)『シーボルト「日本」の研究と解説』[*Research and Comments on Siebold's Nippon*]（Kōdansha, 1977）

Iwao (ed.) 1977-1996
IWAO Seiichi (ed.)『シーボルト「日本」』[*Siebold 'Nippon'*]（Yūshōdō shoten, 1977-1996. 9 vols.）

Kagesato 1993
KAGESATO Tetsuro「川原慶賀と長崎派」『日本の美術』['Kawahara Keiga and the Nagasaki School', in: *Japanese Art*] 329 (Gyōsei, Oct. 1993)

Kaji 2003
KAJI Teruyuki「シーボルト事件—商館長メイランの日記を中心に」『新・シーボルト研究』['The Siebold Incident Considered from the Diary of Meylan, Opperhoofd of Deshima', in: *New Siebold Research*]（Yasaka shobō, 2003. II）

Kaneko 1982
KANEKO Atsuo『シーボルトの絵師―埋れていた三人の画業』[*Painters of Siebold: The forgotten Business of Three Painters*]（Seichōsha, 1982）

Kaneshige 2003
KANESHIGE Mamoru『シーボルトの町絵師慶賀』[*Keiga, the Nagasaki Painter of Siebold*]（Nagasaki Shimbunsha, 2003）

Kimura 1976
KIMURA Yojiro「シーボルトと川原慶賀―植物図の関連」『蘭学資料研究会研究報告』['Siebold and Kawahara Keiga: Drawings of Plants', in: *Bulletin of the Research Society on Materials Related to Dutch Studies*] 309 (1976)

Kimura 1981
── 『シーボルトと日本の植物　東西文化交流の源泉』[*Siebold and Japanese Plants: the Fountain of the Cultural Exchange between the East and West*]（Kōwa shuppan, 1981）

Kimura/Ohba 2000
KIMURA Yojiro and OHBA Hideaki『シーボルト「フローラ・ヤポニカ」日本植物誌』[*Siebold's "Flora Japonica"*]（Yasaka shobō, 2000）

Kindaichi 1938
KINDAICHI Kyosuke「シーボルト先生とアイヌ語学」『シーボルト研究』['Dr. von Siebold and His Ainu Language Studies', in: *Siebold Research*]（Iwanami shoten, 1938）

Kishimoto 2003
KISHIMOTO Emi「シーボルトの日本語研究」『新・シーボルト研究』['Siebold's Research on Japanese Language', in: *New Siebold Research*]（Yasaka shobō, 2003. II）

Kōda 1940
KŌDA Naritomo「ヨハン・ヨゼフ・ホフマン」『科学ペン』['Johann Josef Hoffmann', in: *Science Pen*] 15-12 (Dec. 1940)

Koga 1933

KOGA Jujiro『長崎絵画全史』[*History of Nagasaki Painting*]（Kitamitsu shobō, 1933）

Körner/Takeuchi 1974
KÖRNER, Hans [*Die Würzburger Siebold. Eine Gelehrtenfamilie des 18. und 19. Jahrhunderts*]（Neustadt a.d. Aisch, 1967）, tr. by TAKEUCHI Seiichi as『シーボルト父子伝』[*A biography of father and sons Siebold*]（Sōzōsha, 1974）

Kure 1967-68
KURE Shuzō『シーボルト先生其生涯及功業』[*Dr. von Siebold, His Life and Contributions*]（Heibonsha, 1967-1968. 3 vols.）

Kurihara (tr.) 2003
KURIHARA Fukuya (tr.)「出島からバタヴィアへ―シーボルトの日本調査報告 1823, 24 年―」『新・シーボルト研究』['From Deshima to Batavia: Siebold's reports on His Research in Japan for 1823 and 1824', in: *New Siebold Research*]（Yasaka shobō, 2003. II）

Kurihara (tr.) 2009
── (tr.)『シーボルトの日本報告』[*Siebold's Reports from Japan*]（Heibonsha, 2009. Series Tōyō bunko 784）

Kuroda 1938
KURODA Genji「シーボルト先生のアイヌ語研究」『シーボルト研究』['Research on Ainu Language by Dr. von Siebold', in: *Siebold Research*]（Iwanami shoten, 1938）

Kutsuzawa 1980
KUTSUZAWA Nobutaka「ライデンに於けるシーボルト蒐集地図について」『東海大学紀要文学部』['On the Maps Collected by Siebold Preserved in Leyden', in: *Bulletin from Tokai University Dept. Humanities*] 33（1980）

Kutsuzawa 1996
──「シーボルト渡来百年記念祭に関する一考察―外務省外交史料館所蔵史料を中心に」『鳴滝紀要』['A thought on the 100th commemoration of Siebold's arrival in Japan, based on the materials preserved in Diplomatic Archives of the Ministry of Foreign Affairs of Japan', in: *Narutaki Bulletin*] 6（Mar. 1996）

Mamiya/Hora et al 1998
MAMIYA Rinzo『東韃地方紀行他』[*A Journey to East Tartary &c.*] ed. by HORA Tomio & YAZAWA Shoichi（Heibonsha, 1998. Series Tōyō bunko 484）.

Miyanaga 1984
MIYANAGA Takashi「ヨハン・ヨゼフ・ホフマン―ライデンの日本学者―」『法政大学教養部紀要人文科学偏』['Johann Josef Hoffmann: A Leyden Japanologist', in: *Bulletin for Humanities, Dep. Liberal Arts, Hōsei University*] 50（Jan. 1984）

Miyasaka 1991
MIYASAKA Masahide「研究ノート：シーボルトの日誌「漁村小瀬戸への調査の旅」（草稿）について」『鳴滝紀要』['Research Notes: On Siebold's Research *Journey to the Fisherman Village of Kozeto* (Draft) in Diary of Siebold', in: *Narutaki Bulletin*] 1（1991）.

Miyazaki 2005
MIYAZAKI Katsunori「復元シーボルト『NIPPON』の配本」『九州大学総合研究博物館研究報告』['A Reconstruction of the Distribution of Siebold's "Nippon"', in: *Bulletin of the University Museum Kyushu*] 3（Mar. 2005）

Miyazaki 2006
MIYAZAKI Katsunori「シーボルト『NIPPON』の山々と谷文晁『名山図譜』」『九州大学総合研究博物館研究報告』['The mountains depicted in Siebold's *Nippon* and *Meizan zufu* of Tani Bunchō', in: *Bulletin of the University Museum Kyushu*] 4（2006）

Miyazaki et al (eds.) 2009
MIYAZAKI Katsunori & Fukuoka Archive Research Group (eds.)「第四章　地図をめぐって」『ケンペルやシーボルトたちが見た九州、そしてニッポン』['Chapter 4 Around Maps', in: *Kyushu, and Japan seen by Kaempher and Siebold*]（Kaichōsha, 2009）

Miyazaki 2011
MIYAZAKI Katsunori「シーボルト『NIPPON』の

原画・下絵・図版」『九州大学総合研究博物館研究報告』['Original Paintings, Sketches and Lithographs of Siebold's "*Nippon*"', in: *Bulletin of the University Museum Kyushu*] 9（Mar. 2011）

Nakamura 1969
NAKAMURA Taku「欧米人に知られたる江戸時代の実測日本地図」『地学雑誌』['Japanese Maps based on Land Surveying in the Edo Periode known to the Europeans', in: *Earth Science*] 78（1969）

Nakanishi 1999
NAKANISHI Akira「シーボルト事件判決時の法的根拠『鳴滝紀要』」['Juridical Evidence Employed in the Siebold Incident', in: *Narutaki Bulletin*] 9（1999）

New Seabold Research 2003
Ishiyama et al（ed.）『新・シーボルト研究』[*New Siebold Research*]（Yasaka shobō, 2003. 2 vols.）

Ogata 1938
OGATA Tomio「七　高野長英稿　日本に於ける茶樹の栽培と茶の製法」『シーボルト研究』[7 Written by TAKANO Choei, Cultivation and Production of thee in Japan, in: *Siebold Research*]（Iwanami shoten, 1938）

Ogata/Ōshima 1938
Ogata Tomio, Ōshima Ransaburō, *et al.*,「門人がシーボルトに提供したる蘭語論文の研究」『シーボルト研究』['Research of Dutch-language theses written by pupils of Siebold and given to Siebold', in: *Siebold Research*]（Iwanami shoten, 1938, pp. 61-274.）

Ohba 2003
OHBA Hideaki「シーボルトと彼の日本植物研究」『新・シーボルト研究』['Siebold and his research on Japanese plants', in: *New Siebold Research*]（Yasaka shobō, 2003. I）

Okuda 2012
OKUDA Tomoko「ライデン大学図書館特別コレクション室における研究促進とデジタル化」『カレントアウェアネス』['Digitlization and stimulation for Research in the Department of Special Collection in Leyden University', in: *Current Awareness*] 311（Mar. 2012）.

Ono Ranzan 2010
Editorial Committee of the Book in Commemoration of the 200th Anniversary of the Death of Ono Ranzan（eds.）『小野蘭山』[*Ono Ranzan*]（Yasaka shobō, 2010）

Ōshima 1938a
OSHIMA Ranzaburo「三　高良齋稿　日本疾病志」『シーボルト研究』[3 'Kō Ryosai, Korte naamlyst en beschryving van alle op Japan voorkomende merkwaerdige ziekten. In het hollantsch opgesteld. Door Koo Riosai', in: *Siebold Research*]（Iwanami shoten, 1938）

Ōshima 1938b
──「五　桂川甫賢訳　花彙」『シーボルト研究』['5 Vocabularies Flowers, translated by Katsurakawa Hoken', in: *Siebold Research*]（Iwanami shoten, 1938）

Saito 1979
SAITO Shin「シーボルト『日本』の最終刊年とその全体構想について」『シーボルト「日本」』[On the Last Year of the "Nippon" Publication and Siebold's Perspective of "Nippon", in: *Siebold 'Nippon'*] 6（Yūshōdō shoten, 1979）

Shimatani 1977
SHIMATANI Yoshikichi『最上徳内』[*MOGAMI Tokunai*]（Yoshikawa Kōbunkan, 1977. Series Jinbutsu sōsho 174）.

Siebold Research 1938
Japanisch-Deutsche Gesellschaft『シーボルト研究』[*Siebold Research*]（Iwanami shoten, 1938）

Siebold/Saito 1967
SIEBOLD, Ph. Fr. von『江戸参府紀行』[*A Court Journey to Jedo*] tr. by SAITO Shin.（Heibonsha, 1967. Series Tōyō bunko 87）

Sueki 1979
SUEKI Fumihiko「『仏像図彙』解説」『シーボルト

「日本」』['Explanations on *Butsuzō zui*', in: *Siebold 'Nippon'*] 4（Yūshōdō shoten, 1977-1996.）

Sueki 1999

――「シーボルト・ホフマンと日本宗教」『季刊日本思想史』['Siebold/Hoffmann and Japanese Religions', in: *History of Japanese Thoughts*] 55（Nov. 1999）

Sugimoto 1999

SUGIMOTO Tsutomo『杉本つとむ著作選集10巻西洋人の日本語研究』[*Selected works of SUGIMOTO Tsutomu. Vol. 10: Japanese Studies by Europeans*]（Yasaka shobō, 1999）

Suzuki 2011

SUZUKI Jun「国際連携研究"オランダ国ライデン伝来のブロンホフ、フィッセル、シーボルト蒐集日本書籍の調査研究"」『国文研ニュース』[International Research 'Research on the books collected by Blomhoff, Fisscher and Siebold Preserved in the Netherlands', in: *News from the National Institute of Japanese Literature*] 22（Feb. 2011）

Yamaguchi (ed.) 1993

YAMAGUCHI Takao（ed.）『シーボルトと日本の博物学甲殻類』[*Siebold and Japanese Natural History: Crustacea*]（The Carcinological Society of Japan, 1993）

Yamaguchi 1996a

YAMAGUCHI Takao「シーボルトと日本の動物学」『鳴滝紀要』['Siebold and Japanese Fauna', in: *Narutaki Bulletin*] 6（1996）

Yamaguchi 1996b

――「ライデンにある河原慶賀の自然史画」『洋学』['Natural History Paintings of Kawahara Keiga Preserved in Leyden', in: *Annals of the Society of the History of Western Learning in Japan*] 5（1996）

Yamaguchi 1997

――「川原慶賀と日本の自然史研究：シーボルトとビュルゲルと「ファウナ・ヤポニカ魚類編」」『合津マリンステーション報カラヌス』['Siebold, Bürger, and "*Fauna Japonica*" (pisces)', in: *Calanus: Bulletin of the Aitsu Marine Station, Kumamoto University*] 12（Jan. 1997）

Yamaguchi 1997-98

――「シーボルトと日本の植物学」『合津マリンステーション報カラヌス』['Siebold and Japanese Botany', in: *Calanus: Bulletin of the Aitsu Marine Station, Kumamoto University*] Special Number I & II（1997 & 1998）

Yamaguchi/Kato 1998

YAMAGUCHI Takao & KATO Nobushige「最上徳内がシーボルトに贈呈した樹木材の標本」『合津マリンステーション報カラヌス』['Specimina of the trees given by MOGAMI Tokunai to Siebold', in: *Calanus: Bulletin of the Aitsu Marine Station, Kumamoto University*] Special Number II（1998）

Yamaguchi 2001

YAMAGUCHI Takao「「ファウナ・ヤポニカ」甲殻類編で参照された図譜「蠏蝦類編写真」について」『合津マリンステーション報カラヌス』['The study of Suiken's *Kai-ka Rui Siya-sin* Repeatedly reffered to in the Crustacea volume of *Fauna Japonica*', in: *Calanus: Bulletin of the Aitsu Marine Station, Kumamoto University*] Special Number III（2001）

Yamaguchi 2003

――「シーボルトと日本の自然史研究」『新・シーボルト研究』['Siebold and His Research on the Natural History in Japan', in: *New Siebold Research*]（Yasaka shobō, 2003. I）

Yamaguchi/Kato et al 2003

Yamaguchi/Kato et al「シーボルト収集植物標本リスト」『合津マリンステーション報カラヌス』['List of Botanical specimens collected by Siebold', in: *Calanus: Bulletin of the Aitsu Marine Station, Kumamoto University*] Special Number V（2003）

Yamaguchi 2007

――「シーボルト、ビュルガー、川原慶賀と日本の魚類学」『鳴滝紀要』['Siebold, Bürger, Kawahara Keiga and Japanese Ichthyology', in: *Narutaki Bulletin*], 17（2007）

シーボルトがフィッセルから借用した書籍一覧
A Provisional List of the Books Collected by Overmeer Fisscher, now to be found in the Siebold Collection

マティ・フォラー（Matthi Forrer）作成 (註1)

日本書籍目録 (Cat. Hoff.) 本文掲載番号	書籍名 (『 』内は郭成章の石版目録を通行字体で表記、〔 〕内はセルリエ目録あるいは原本表記による)	刊年西暦 (「MS.」は手稿、「n. d」は作成年代未詳)	フィッセル手稿目録 (MS. Cat. Overmeer Fisscher)	セルリエ目録〔Ser〕ライデン国立民族学博物館資料番号、（備考）
Cat. Hoff. 001 (註2)	『和漢三才図会』	1713	F 101	〔Ser 1**〕
Cat. Hoff. 003	『頭書増補訓蒙図彙大成』	1789	F 007	1-4290
Cat. Hoff. 006	『文化補刻万海節用字福蔵』	1816	F 001	〔Ser 7〕
Cat. Hoff. 007	『新撰増益都会節用百家通』	1819	F 002	〔Ser 12〕
Cat. Hoff. 009	『増字倭漢節用無双嚢』	1799	F 003	〔Ser 5〕
Cat. Hoff. 011	『彙刻書目』	1818	F 006	〔Ser 19〕
Cat. Hoff. 016	『日本王代一覧』	1803	F 024	〔Ser 424〕
Cat. Hoff. 017	『日本書紀』	1798	F 079	〔Ser 421〕
Cat. Hoff. 019	『掌中和漢年契』	1801	F 067	〔Ser 466〕
Cat. Hoff. 020	『和年代皇紀絵章』	n. d.	F 035	〔Ser 426〕
Cat. Hoff. 021	『太平記』	1631	F 105	〔Ser 439〕
Cat. Hoff. 022	『甲陽軍鑑』	1659	F 104	〔Ser 440〕
Cat. Hoff. 023	『平家物語』	c. 1800	F 074	〔Ser 434 I/II〕
Cat. Hoff. 024	『島原記』	n. d.	F 038	〔Ser 441〕
Cat. Hoff. 030	『紀年指掌』	1826	F 071	〔Ser 472〕
—	『〔改正倭玉真艸字引大成〕』	1820	F 068 (註3)	〔Ser 32〕
Cat. Hoff. 033	『万歴〔暦〕両面鑑』	1825	F 068	〔Ser 482〕
Cat. Hoff. 056	『改正日本輿地路程全図』	1811	F 000 イ (註4)	〔Ser 220〕
Cat. Hoff. 063	『河内国細見小図』	1802	F 063	〔Ser 261〕
Cat. Hoff. 064	『河内国絵図』	n. d.（文政）	F 064	〔Ser 260〕
Cat. Hoff. 066	『和泉国絵図』	1824	F 066	〔Ser 262〕
Cat. Hoff. 069	『尾張国絵図』	n. d.（文政）	F 069	〔Ser 266-I/Ser 266-II〕（2枚）
Cat. Hoff. 072	『武江略図』	1824	F 072	〔Ser 268〕
Cat. Hoff. 077	『越後国絵図』	n. d.（文政）	F 077	〔Ser 274〕
Cat. Hoff. 096	『都寺社全図』	1730	F 096	〔Ser 389〕
Cat. Hoff. 102	『新改内裏図』	1817	F 102	〔Ser 312〕
Cat. Hoff. 105	『分間江戸大絵図』	1772	F 000 ホ	〔Ser 315A〕
Cat. Hoff. 111	『文政改正御江戸大絵図』	1824	F 000 ヘ	〔Ser 321〕（フィッセル蒐集図書は転売か？）
Cat. Hoff. 122	『いろは分独案内江戸町づくし』	1821	F 000 チ	〔Ser 335〕
Cat. Hoff. 126	『増修大坂指掌図』	1797	F 000 ヌ	〔Ser 345〕（ブロムホフ蒐集図書）
Cat. Hoff. 127	『新板増補大坂之図』	1787	F 000 ロ	〔Ser 344〕
Cat. Hoff. 138	『日光御山総絵図』	n. d.（文政）	F 000 リ	〔Ser 381〕
Cat. Hoff. 161	『東海道分間絵図』	1772	F 000 ハ	〔Ser 410A〕
Cat. Hoff. 162	『東海木曾両道中懐宝図鑑』	1807	F 000 ト	〔Ser 412〕 or 1-4304
Cat. Hoff. 164	『大日本道中行程指南車』	1820	F 000 ニ	〔Ser 403A〕 or 1-4305

Cat. Hoff. 166	『道中独案内』	1822	F 000 ル	〔Ser 404〕
Cat. Hoff. 176	『蝦夷拾遺』	MS.	F 061 & F 062	〔Ser 196〕(2 部のうち 1 部紛失か、1 copy lost?)
Cat. Hoff. 183	『唐太島之図』	MS.	F 000	〔Ser 214〕
Cat. Hoff. 190	『古今沿革地図』ほか13点	1788 ほか	F 000 カ	〔Ser 182〕
Cat. Hoff. 195	『校正本草綱目』	1603	F 103	1-4307
Cat. Hoff. 222	『〔湖上石話〕雲根志』	1773, 1779 & 1801	F 034	1-4308
Cat. Hoff. 297	『新増字林玉篇〔大全〕』	1820	F 005	〔Ser 27〕
Cat. Hoff. 300	『急用間合真字〔引〕玉篇大成』	1819	F 023	〔Ser 30〕
Cat. Hoff. 301	『和漢音釈書言字考節用集』〔増補合類大節用集〕	1766	F 033 & F065	〔Ser 38〕& 1-4323A/B
Cat. Hoff. 304	『〔増字百倍〕早引節用集』	1823	F 004	〔Ser 39C〕
Cat. Hoff. 306	『訳文筌〔蹄〕』	1715	F 031	〔Ser 37〕
Cat. Hoff. 312	『雑字類編』	1764	F 095	1-4326
Cat. Hoff. 321 (註5)	『画引十体千字文綱目』	1756	F 059	〔Ser 113〕&〔Ser 113A〕
Cat. Hoff. 324a (註6)	Nieuw verzameld Japans en Hollandsch woordenboek (新輯和蘭辞書)	1810	F 072	1-4329
Cat. Hoff. 324b	『訳鍵』	1810	F 021 & F 022	〔Ser 61 dubbel〕& 1-4331
Cat. Hoff. 328 (註7)	『蝦夷方言〔もしほ草〕』	1804	F 056	〔Ser 92〕,〔Ser 92*〕& 1-4333
Cat. Hoff. 337b	『四書』	1812	F 055	〔Ser 607〕
Cat. Hoff. 340b	『論語彝訓巻之首』	1822	F 000	1-4337
Cat. Hoff. 341b	『菜根譚』	1825	F 044	〔Ser 651〕
Cat. Hoff. 342b	『絵本孝婦伝』	1806	F 082	〔Ser 635〕
Cat. Hoff. 343 (註8)	『増補諸宗仏像図彙』	1796	F 036 & F 078	1-4339
Cat. Hoff. 344	『類葉百人一首教文庫』	1817	F 076	〔Ser 10〕
Cat. Hoff. 347	『雑話教訓鑑』	1776	F 092	〔Ser 626〕
Cat. Hoff. 348	『近世貞婦伝』	1800	F 090	〔Ser 626*〕
Cat. Hoff. 349	『世談雑説』	1754	F 091	〔Ser 623〕
Cat. Hoff. 350	『つれづれ草』	1737	F 027	〔Ser 622〕
Cat. Hoff. 351	『絵本金花談』	1806	F 028	〔Ser 637〕
Cat. Hoff. 352	『絵本鏡山〔烈〕女功』	1803	F 075	〔Ser 631〕
Cat. Hoff. 353	『巨勢金岡名技伝』	1808	F 084	〔Ser 1147〕
Cat. Hoff. 354	『文化新板伊勢物語』	n. d.（文化）	F 043	〔Ser 632〕& 1-4344（2部）
Cat. Hoff. 355	『本朝蠢物語』	1774	F 089	〔Ser 425〕
Cat. Hoff. 356	『遠乃白浪』	1822	F 073	〔Ser 668〕
Cat. Hoff. 358	『和漢古今角偉談』	1784	F 085	〔Ser 1027〕
Cat. Hoff. 359	『艶廓通覧』	1800	F 083	〔Ser 809〕
Cat. Hoff. 360	『松陰快談』	1821	F 052	〔Ser 646〕
Cat. Hoff. 361	『東牖子』	1803	F 087	〔Ser 629〕
Cat. Hoff. 362	『間情偶寄』	1801	F 054	〔Ser 683〕
Cat. Hoff. 363	『笑府』	1768	F 100	〔Ser 625〕
Cat. Hoff. 375	『一谷嫩軍記』	1767	F 046	〔Ser 775〕
Cat. Hoff. 376	『姉若草妹初音本町糸屋娘』	1813	F 049	〔Ser 777〕

Cat. Hoff. 377	『近江源氏先陣館』	1769	F 047	〔Ser 776〕
Cat. Hoff. 378	『仮名手本忠臣蔵』	1748	F 048	1-4354
Cat. Hoff. 379	『双蝶々曲輪〔日〕記』	1749-	F 051	〔Ser 774〕
Cat. Hoff. 380	『菅原伝授手習鑑』	1746	F 050	〔Ser 773〕
Cat. Hoff. 381	『京都歌舞〔伎〕新狂言外題年鑑』	n.d.（文政）	F 000	〔Ser 787〕
Cat. Hoff. 385	『歌道名目〔抄〕』	1713	F 086	〔Ser 752〕
Cat. Hoff. 386	『正徹物語』	1790	F 000	〔Ser 701〕
Cat. Hoff. 389	『歌林雑木抄』	1696	F 080	〔Ser 699〕
Cat. Hoff. 404	『狂歌画自満』	1824	F 058	1-4363
Cat. Hoff. 405	『狂歌関東百題集』	1813	F 040	〔Ser 747〕
Cat. Hoff. 406	『狂歌扶桑集』	n.d.（文政）	F 045	〔Ser 749〕
Cat. Hoff. 407	『宋詩清絶』	1813	F 053	1-4366
Cat. Hoff. 408	『〔増訂〕宋詩礎』	1803	F 017	〔Ser 695〕
Cat. Hoff. 409	『詩礎諺解』	1805	F 094	〔Ser 760〕
Cat. Hoff. 410	『袖珍略韻大成』	n.d.	F 026	〔Ser 759〕
Cat. Hoff. 411	『制度通』	1792	F 032	〔Ser 800〕
Cat. Hoff. 412	『骨董集』	1815	F 020	1-4368
Cat. Hoff. 416	『小笠原諸礼大全』	1810	F 088	1-4371
Cat. Hoff. 417	『京大坂茶屋諸分調方記』	n.d.（元禄）	F 000	〔Ser 815〕
Cat. Hoff. 428	『万世江戸町鑑』	1826	F 060	〔Ser 509〕
Cat. Hoff. 451	『妙術博物筌』	n.d.（寛政）	F 025	〔Ser 876〕
Cat. Hoff. 463	『立華正道集』	1784	F 019	1-4642
Cat. Hoff. 473	『珍貨孔方鑑』	1729	F 010	1-4643
Cat. Hoff. 474	『寛政孔方鑑』	1805	F 011	〔Ser 564E〕
Cat. Hoff. 476	『珍銭奇品図録』	1817	F 012	〔Ser 572〕
Cat. Hoff. 477	『孔方図鑑』	1728	F 014	〔Ser 564〕
Cat. Hoff. 478	『〔和漢〕古今泉貨鑑』	1804	F 008	〔Ser 569〕
Cat. Hoff. 480	『金銀図録』	1823	F 015	〔Ser 571〕
Cat. Hoff. 482	『〔古今図鑑〕古銭価附』	1805	F 013	〔Ser 568〕
Cat. Hoff. 483（註9）	『銭範』	1793	F 070	〔Ser 567〕
Cat. Hoff. 485	『西洋銭譜』	1790	F 009	1-4644
Cat. Hoff. 488	『鍼灸説約』	1812	F 016	1-4645
Cat. Hoff. 503	『画筌』	1721	F 081	1-4400
Cat. Hoff. 531	『画本虫撰』	1823	F 041	1-4428（註10）
Cat. Hoff. 534	『〔再板絵本〕初心柱立』	1794	F 042	〔Ser 1257〕
Cat. Hoff. 543	『花鳥写真図会』	1805	F 097	1-4438
Cat. Hoff. 544	『花鳥画譜』	n.d.（化政期？）	F 000	1-4439
Cat. Hoff. 547	『〔伝神開手〕北斎漫画』	1814-1818	F 039	1-4442 （初編から十編まで）
Cat. Hoff. 554	『〔伝神開手〕北斎画式』	1819	F 039	1-4452
Cat. Hoff. 559	『絵本写宝袋』	1720	F 029 & 030	1-4457 & 1-4457B
Cat. Hoff. 567	『〔新板〕絵本武勇桜』	1756	F 037	〔Ser 1172〕
Cat. Hoff. 568	『絵本多武峯』	1793	F 057	〔Ser 1178〕
Cat. Hoff. 570	『絵本鶯宿梅』	1740	F 029	1-4652A/B
Cat. Hoff. 571	『絵本フチハカマ』	1823	F 098	〔Ser 1218〕
Cat. Hoff. 573	『絵本婚礼道シルベ』	1813	F 018	1-4461
Cat. Hoff. 580	『花容女職人鑑』	n.d.（文政）	F 099	1-4463

【 註 】

註1－このリストはもともとフィッセルの蒐集書籍の再構築を目的とした作成したもので、フィッセルの手稿目録（ライデン国立民族学博物館蔵、パリ国立図書館に草稿あり）とシーボルト関係文書（ブランデンシュタイン家文書、ボッフムルール大学シーボルト文書）に基づく。今回、故山口博士の調査を一歩進めるため『日本書籍目録』の番号順に並べ替えて、ここに掲載した。調査がまだ進行中であることは、先に述べたとおりである（「山口博士の遺稿英訳にあたって」2頁参照）。フィッセルの蒐集書籍は、一部の例外を除き、すべてシーボルトコレクションとして、ライデン国立民族学博物館、または、ライデン大学図書館に保存されている（ちなみにこれはブロムホフの蒐集書籍についても同じである）。このシーボルトコレクションとされる書籍群に、ブロムホフとフィッセルの蒐集書籍が混在することは、すでにそれぞれの蔵書印の存在から明らかである。そして、この書籍の「混在」からわかることは、シーボルトは日本研究のために必要な図書をすべて一堂に集め、手元に置いていたということである。つまり、自分が持ち帰った書籍だけでなく、すでにブロムホフとフィッセルがハーグの王立骨董陳列室に寄贈、あるいは、売却していた書籍もライデンの自宅に持っていたということだ。そしてそれら日本研究のための参考文献をホフマンにまとめさせたものがこの『日本書籍目録』であった。シーボルトは、オランダに戻ってからも書籍を補充し、重複が出れば、それを売却した。これがウィーン国立図書館をはじめ、オランダ国外にもシーボルト、あるいはフィッセルの蒐集書籍が存在する理由であるが、この点についてはさらに精査が必要である。

註2－シーボルトはオランダに戻ったあと、この書籍を一部購入した（UBL Ser 1）。これは1838年10月、ハインリッヒ・ビュルガーから購入した書籍114点のうちの1点である（ブランデンシュタイン家文書K3-37）。

註3－フィッセル本と見られるが、手稿目録に題名が明記されていないため、さらに詳細な調査が必要である。

【Notes】

1 - This list is primarily based upon the MS Catalogue made up by Johan van Overmeer Fisscher (copies preserved in the National Museum of Ethnology, Leiden, and in the Bibliothèque Nationale, Paris [an early draft version]), as well as documents in the Burg Brandenstein Siebold Archives and the Siebold Archives in Ruhr University Bochum. In tune with the research of the late Dr. Yamaguchi, this list is here presented according to the numbering of the *Catalogus librorum*. I must, however, add immediately that what I can present here is nothing more than the present state of ongoing research that is still in need to be finalized. The collection of books made by Fisscher is primarily preserved in two locations, as part of the 'Siebold collection of books,' in the National Museum of Ethnology, Leiden, as well as in the Library of Leiden University. The same by the way also applies to the collection of books made by Jan Cock Blomhoff. It is only from the stamped seals inside these books that we can distinguish which books in the Siebold collection originally formed part of the collections made by Blomhoff or by Fisscher. Yet, from this "mixture," we can understand which books Siebold considered of value for the study of Japan. These were not only the books that he himself brought from Japan. He would soon also borrow books from the collections of Blomhoff and Fisscher that were kept as part of their collections in the Royal Cabinet of Curiosities in The Hague and bring these to his home. All these books were then listed in his *Catalogus librorum* with the help of Dr. Hoffmann. Occasionally, he would also sell those books that he came to consider as duplicates to foreign institutions, such as, for example, the National Library in Vienna. Consequently, it is essential to also search for books originally collected by Fisscher in various foreign collections.

2 - Siebold only managed to purchase a copy after returning to the Netherlands, actually buying it from Dr. Heinrich Bürger (1804-1858), his assistant in Japan, in October 1838, together with 113 other books (Burg Brandenstein Archives, K3-37).

3 - As quite some books in the Fisscher catalogue are not identified by their title, serious further investigation is often necessary.

註4－フィッセルの項の「000」は、フィッセルが蒐集したことが蒐集ラベルやその他の資料から明らかだが、本人の手稿目録では特定できない書籍を示す。また、そのうち「イロハ」の追記記載がある書籍は、シーボルト自身が王立骨董陳列室から借用した書籍リスト（1836年4月21日付け）で、フィッセルから借用したと明言している書籍を示す（ブランデンシュタイン家文書 SAM 21-9.）。

註5－2部現存する。Ser 113 には、フィッセルの蔵書印が確認できるだけでなく、フィッセルが手書きで「1826年10月購入」と記している。ただし、フィッセルの手稿目録によって特定することは今のところ不可能。Ser 113Aの方には、フィッセルの蔵書印もなければ、シーボルトの蔵書印もない。来歴は不明である。

註6－324a の書籍名は郭の石版刷目録には掲載されていないため、「Cat. Hoff. 本文の書籍名表記」（邦訳）の順に記した。

註7－フィッセルは手稿目録で『蝦夷方言』を2部購入したとしている。しかし、オランダには、ライデン国立民族学博物館に1部（フィッセルの蔵書ラベル付き）、ライデン大学図書館に2部（いずれにもフィッセルの蔵書印あり）、すなわちフィッセルの持ち帰った『蝦夷方言』が合計3部現存する。ちなみに、ケルレン 1080a の所蔵番号（UB [Ser] 7954）は誤りである。

註8－註2に同じ（UBL Ser 592）。ただし、シーボルトがいつ、誰からこの書籍を購入したかはわからない。

註9－『日本書籍目録』は、この本をブロムホフからの借用図書としているが、ライデン大学図書館に現存するものはフィッセルの蒐集図書である。

註10－ライデン国立民族学博物館に現存するのはシーボルト蒐集書籍1部のみであるため、フィッセルの蒐集書籍は転売した可能性がある。

4 - The Fisscher books identified as '000' are books that cannot be identified positively from his catalogue. The numbering like 'i-ro-ha' was given by Siebold himself in a list of books from the Blomhoff and Fisscher collections figuring in the Catalogus, provided to the Director of the Royal Cabinet, R.P. van de Kasteele, and dated April 21st, 1836 (Burg Brandenstein Archives, SAM 21-9.1, 2).

5 - This book is represented in two copies, and though not identified by any Ex libris, there is a MS note stating that Fisscher obtained the copy in Ser 113 in the 10th month of 1826. Yet, this cannot be confirmed in the MS Catalogue of the Fisscher catalogue. As for the copy in Ser 113A, this has neither a stamp identifying it as a book from the Fisscher collection nor any stamp or seal to identify it as part of the Siebold collection.

6 - As the title of the book No. 324a is not given in the list written by Ko, it is here translated after the reading in the *Catalogus librorum*.

7 - The Fisscher MS Catalogue lists two copies of the *Ezo hōgen*. However, there are three copies, all in the Leiden University Library. One copy features the Ex libris label identifying it as No.56 in the Fisscher collection. Another copy has the stamped seal indicating that it comes from the collection of Fisscher. Yet another one (Kerlen 1080a [is Ser 92*, not Ser 7954]) without any seal or stamp, has the notes in red ink referred to by Fisscher in his other copy.

8 - See Note 2 (UBL Ser 592). It is unknown that Siebold bought this book from whom and when.

9 - In the *Catalogus librorum* this book is indicated as from the Blomhoff collection. In fact, the copy in the Leiden University Library has the stamp identifying it as from the Fisscher collection.

10 - Because only a part of Siebold's collection of books remain at the Leiden Museum of Ethnology, there is a possibility that Fisscher's collection was resold.

掲載図版一覧（List of the Illustrative Plates）

【巻末掲載図版】
*1 掲載頁：pp. *3〜82* はカラー図版（Color）、pp. *83〜146* はモノクロ図版（Monochrome）
*2 目録番号：ラテン語本文番号（Cat. Hoff. No.）
*3 所蔵館資料番号：所蔵館略記は次の通り。UL＝ライデン大学図書館（Universiteitsbibliotheek Leiden）、
　　RMvV＝ライデン国立民族学博物館（Rijksmuseum voor Volkenkunde）
*4 撮影者：略記（Photographed by）は次の通り。F＝マティ・フォラー（Matthi Forrer）、
　　M＝宮崎克則（Miyazaki Katsunori）、T＝高杉志緒（Takasugi Shio）、Y＝山口隆男（Yamaguchi Takao）

*1 掲載頁(p)	*2 目録番号	『日本書籍目録』表題 (Title)(掲載部分・原資料表題等)	掲載資料形状 (Type)	掲載箇所 (Figure)	寸法（Size）縦(Length)×横(Breadth) cm	*3 所蔵館資料番号 (Identification No. of Ownership Institution)		*4 撮影者
						UL	RMvV	
3	47	諸国奇談西遊記（袋）	木版（1枚）	全5冊の袋	（袋）22.2×36.3	Ser. 233 C		T
3	48	諸国奇談東遊記（袋）	木版（1枚）	全5冊の袋	（袋）22.4×37.2	Ser. 233 B		T
4	58	日本辺界略図	銅板・手彩色（1舗）	1舗（全図）	23.8×35.7	Ser. 228		T
3	95	天明再板京都めぐり（袋）	木版多色摺（1枚）	全2冊の袋	（袋）18.5×14.7	Ser. 296		T
5	125	自上古到今世難波大坂十二図	手稿、墨書手彩色（2舗）	13舗の内 2舗	「浪華上古図」（紙寸）26.3×40.8、「浪華図」（紙寸）27.3×17.3	Ser. 341		T
6	140	日本名所の絵（袋・全図）	袋（木版1枚）、木版多色摺（1枚）	1枚	（袋）21.7×29.0、（図）42.7×56.3	Ser. 364		T
7	143	和州吉野山名勝図	折本、木版手彩色	1冊の内 表紙・1図	（表紙）30.7×16.8	Ser. 369		T
8	147	江戸隅田川両岸一覧図	折本、木版手彩色	2冊の内 上巻2図	（表紙）25.0×19.7	Ser. 378		T
9	149	名山図譜	袋綴、木版手彩色	3冊の内 第3冊2図	（表紙）29.7×19.6	Ser. 365		M
10〜16	152	富士之景	折本・手稿、絹本著色	1冊（全図）	（表紙）29.2×37.7		1-4302	M
83〜87	153	采草閑筆	折本・手稿、紙本墨書	1冊（全図）	（表紙）31.0×22.2		1-4303	T
17	181	薩哈連島之図	手稿（1舗）	1舗（表紙、全図）	（表紙）13.7×9.0、（紙寸）36.4×54.0	Ser. 213		T
18	192	東察加之図	手稿（1舗）	1舗（表紙、全図）	（表紙）19.0×13.0、（紙寸）75.6×51.5	Ser. 186		T
19	246	夏草冬蟲図	折本、木版多色摺	1冊の内 2図	（表紙）19.1×16.1	Ser. 1023		T
20	253	梅桜類花写真	折本・手稿、絹本著色	1冊の内 2図（第1図、第13図）	（表紙）31.4×40.8		1-4311	M

225

掲載図版一覧

21〜25	254	蝦夷本草之図	折本・手稿、絹本著色	2冊の内第1冊（全丁）	（台紙）41.0×32.0	Ser. 1003		Y
26	258	本草写真	袋綴・手稿、紙本著色	1冊（3図、表紙〜2丁表）	（表紙）22.7×16.0		1-4312	T
27〜35	260	本草抜粋	折本・手稿、紙本著色	1冊（全図）	（表紙）27.0×18.2	Ser. 975b		T
36〜37	261	本草抜粋（原資料表題は「本草推写」）	袋綴・手稿、紙本著色	1冊（全図）	（表紙）24.9×20.1	Ser. 975a		T
38〜39	265	腊葉揚	袋綴・手稿、紙本墨書・墨摺	2冊の内1冊（5図）	（表紙）24.2×17.0		1-4317	M
40	282	石ニ化魚之図	木版多色摺（1枚）	1枚	（表紙）23.4×16.2、（紙寸）31.8×45.7		1-4319	M
41〜47	293	鶉十八品真写	袋綴・手稿、紙本著色	1冊（全図）	（表紙）22.7×16.0		1-4320	M
48	325	江戸ハルマ	袋綴、木版墨書	全23冊の内第1冊（1オ〜2オ）	（表紙）26.1×17.8	Ser. 62 A I		T
49〜56	371	キフ子本地	巻子・手稿、紙本著色・金泥	3巻の内上巻（本文全紙）	（上巻題箋）17.7×3.5、（上巻縦）33.2、（上巻紙幅）表紙26.2、1紙49.0、2紙49.5、3紙50.2、4紙49.0、5紙50.0、6紙47.2、7紙49.7、8紙49.7、9紙49.5、10紙47.5、11紙49.4、12紙49.7、13紙49.3、14紙48.2、15紙49.2、16紙46.8、17紙49.3、18紙49.3、19紙49.8、20紙49.5、21紙24.5、22紙50.0、23紙46.0、24紙55.3		1-4352	T
88〜94	371	キフ子本地	巻子・手稿、紙本著色・金泥	3巻の内中巻（本文全紙）	（中巻題箋）17.7×3.4、（中巻縦）33.3、（中巻紙幅）表紙26.8、1紙48.2、2紙42.8、3紙50.0、4紙46.7、5紙49.2、6紙48.6、7紙49.4、8紙43.75、9紙50.0、10紙47.5、11紙22.0、12紙49.5、13紙46.5、14紙49.3、15紙48.2、16紙49.8、17紙46.0、18紙19.8、19紙49.8、20紙47.5、21紙49.0、22紙34.7		1-4352	T

掲載図版一覧

95〜102	371	キフ子本地	巻子・手稿、紙本著色・金泥	3巻の内下巻（本文全紙）	（下巻題箋）17.7×3.5、（下巻縦）33.3、（下巻紙幅）表紙27.0、1紙48.7、2紙48.8、3紙49.5、4紙49.3、5紙46.5、6紙49.5、7紙47.4、8紙49.4、9紙49.4、10紙50.3、11紙47.2、12紙49.0、13紙49.1、14紙47.3、15紙49.7、16紙50.0、17紙49.7、18紙19.2、19紙49.0、20紙47.0、21紙50.2、22紙48.0、23紙49.2、24紙34.8	1-4352	T
57〜62	397	絵本和歌合（吉原女郎歌準）	折本、木版多色摺（九ツ切版摺物）貼込	1冊（全図）	（表紙）21.2×15.2	1-4361	M
63〜64、103〜105	417	京大坂茶屋諸分調方記	袋綴、木版墨摺	全一冊（横本）	（表紙）7.0×15.7	Ser. 815	T
65	438	佩文耕織図	袋、折本、木版多色摺	袋、2冊表紙、第1冊第1図	（表紙）34.6×25.5	1-4390	M
106〜108	448	日州養蜂図	折本、銅版摺4枚貼込	2冊の内1冊（全1丁）	（表紙）30.8×38.2、（銅版刷紙寸）17.8×27.3	1-4393a	T
109〜110	448	日州養蜂図	袋綴・手稿、墨書	2冊の内1冊（全丁）	（袋綴）29.1×20.0		T
66	453	鼓銅図録	袋綴、木版多色摺	1冊（1オ〜2オ）	（表紙）27.3×18.3	1-4635	M
67	459	瓶花図彙	袋綴、木版手彩色	2冊の内乾巻（1オ〜2オ）	（表紙）33.2×24.2	1-4638	M
111〜127	465	染物之法 早稲作法 茶製法	袋綴・手稿、紙本墨書	1冊（本文全丁）	（表紙）16.2×11.5	Ser. 892	T
128〜135	466	酒作之事	袋綴・手稿、紙本墨書	1冊（本文全丁）	（表紙）23.7×18.5	Ser. 897	T
136〜139	467	紙作之法	袋綴・手稿、紙本墨書	1冊（本文全丁）	（表紙）23.1×19.0	Ser. 896	T
140〜141	468	塗之法	袋綴・手稿、紙本墨書	1冊	（表紙）25.3×19.5	Ser. 895	T
68	471	張公捕魚	折本、紙本著色	1冊（第1図、9図）	（表紙）42.0×53.2	1-4394	T
69〜70	493	和蘭全軀内外分図	折本、木版手彩色	2冊の内「別録験号」（1オ、2オ、4ウ〜5オ）	（表紙）25.7×15.1、（最大）37.0×30.0	Ser. 1128	T

掲載図版一覧

142〜146	493	和蘭全軀内外分図	袋綴、木版墨摺	2冊の内「驗号」(1オ〜10オ、43ウ〜奥付)	(表紙) 15.0×25.5	Ser. 1128		T
71	533	絵本筆二色	袋:木版多色摺、本:袋綴・木版墨摺	袋、2冊の内上巻1図	(袋) 21.0×16.7、(表紙) 21.4×15.3	Ser. 1180		T
72〜73	535	桜花画帖	折本、木版多色摺	1冊 (3図)	(表紙) 25.3×16.5		1-4430	T
74	555	秀画一覧	袋綴、木版多色摺	1冊 (2ウ〜3オ、25ウ〜奥付)	(表紙) 26.0×17.2		1-4453	T
75	558	鳥山石燕画譜	袋綴、木版多色摺	1冊 (30ウ〜32オ)	(表紙) 31.0×31.1		1-4456	T
76〜78	582	猿楽之図	折本・手稿、絹本著色	1冊 (全図)	(表紙) 34.7×22.7		1-4465	T
79〜82	583	江戸風美人姿	折本、木版多色摺 (九ツ切版浮世絵) 貼込	1冊 (全図)	(表紙) 21.3×15.2		1-4466	T

掲載図版一覧

【論文掲載写真】 （Figures of the articles）
＊撮影者略記（Photographed by） F＝マティ・フォラー（Matthi Forrer）、Y＝山口隆男（Yamaguchi Takao）

山口隆男「シーボルトの初回来日と収集書籍類について」（pp. 17〜19）

写真(Fig.) No.	キャプション（Caption）	資料所蔵先(Ownership Institution)	所蔵館資料番号(Identification number)	＊撮影者
1	ヨセフ・ホフマン（Johann Joseph Hoffmann）	ライデン大学(Leiden Universiy)	—	—
2	「郭成章　Ko Tsching Dschang」（『Nippon』Ⅰ）	福岡県立図書館(Fukuoka Prefectual Library)	—	—
3	『仏像図彙』（*Buts zo dsu i*）	ライデン大学図書館(Leiden Universiy Library)	Ser. 592	Y
3	Buddha-Pantheon von Nippon Buts zo dsu i（『Nippon』Ⅴ）	福岡県立図書館(Fukuoka Prefectual Library)	—	—
4	「筥根嶺」、「御嶽」（『名山図譜』 *Mei zan zufu*）	ライデン大学図書館(Leiden Universiy Library)	Ser. 365	Y
4	「HAKONE-TOGE」、「MI-TAKE」（『Nippon』Ⅵ）	福岡県立図書館(Fukuoka Prefectual Library)	—	—

マティ・フォラー「「シーボルトの初回来日と収集書籍類について」に対する脚註・追記」（p. 34）

写真(Fig.) No.	キャプション（Caption）	原資料名：（Title）Hoff. 目録№『資料名』	資料所蔵先(Ownership Institution)	所蔵館資料番号(Identification number)	＊撮影者
1a	ブロムホフコレクションの蔵書印(The stamp identifying books from the Blomhoff Collection)	＊574『隅田川両岸一覧』下巻1丁表	ライデン国立民族学博物館(National Museum of Ethnology)	1-4654	F
1b	フィッセルコレクションの蔵書印(The stamp identifying books from the Fisscher Collection)	＋559『絵本写宝袋』4巻1丁表	ライデン国立民族学博物館(National Museum of Ethnology)	1-4457	F
1c	シーボルト蒐集図書（1929年バタヴィア政庁報告分）の付箋（A sample note of the books in the original Siebold Collection)	502『漢画独稽古』1丁表見返〜1丁表	ライデン国立民族学博物館(National Museum of Ethnology)	1-4399	F
2a	フィッセルによる手稿目録の書籍部分(The Fisscher Catalogue of his books collected in Japan)	—	ライデン国立民族学博物館(National Museum of Ethnology)	—	F
2b	フィッセルコレクションの石版刷蔵書ラベル(A sample Ex libris, designed by Fisscher)	＋559『絵本写宝袋』4巻に貼付	ライデン国立民族学博物館(National Museum of Ethnology)	1-4457	F

掲載図版一覧

山口隆男「シーボルトの日本収集書籍コレクションの概略について」(pp. 175〜194)

写真 (Fig.) No.	キャプション (Caption) Cat. Hoff. 目録№.『書籍名』又は資料名等	資料所蔵先 (Ownership Institution)	所蔵館資料番号 (Identification number)	＊撮影者
5	1.『和漢三才図会』	ライデン大学図書館 (Leiden Universiy Library)	Ser. 1	Y
6A	328.『蝦夷方言』(原題「もしほ草」)	ライデン大学図書館 (Leiden Universiy Library)	Ser. 92	Y
6B	329.『蝦夷ヶ嶋言語』	ライデン大学図書館 (Leiden Universiy Library)	Ser. 93	Y
7A	56.「改正日本輿地路程全図」	ライデン大学図書館 (Leiden Universiy Library)	Ser. 220	Y
7B	58.『日本辺海略図』	ライデン大学図書館 (Leiden Universiy Library)	Ser. 228	Y
8	203.『通志昆虫草木略』	ライデン大学図書館 (Leiden Universiy Library)	Ser. 967	Y
9	236.『公益増補 地錦抄』	ライデン大学図書館 (Leiden Universiy Library)	Ser. 1052	Y
10-A-a	254. 桂川甫賢『蝦夷本草之図』	ライデン大学図書館 (Leiden Universiy Library)	Ser. 1003	Y
10-A-b	(仮称)『鳥とモグラの図譜』	ライデン国立民族学博物館 (National Museum of Ethnology)	1-4496	Y
10-B-a	258.『本草写真』	ライデン国立民族学博物館 (National Museum of Ethnology)	1-4312	Y
10-B-b	259.『本草抜粋』	ライデン大学図書館 (Leiden Universiy Library)	Ser. 979	Y
10-C-a	265.『腊葉摺』	ライデン国立民族学博物館 (National Museum of Ethnology)	1-4317	Y
10-C-b	260.『本草抜翠』	ライデン大学図書館 (Leiden Universiy Library)	Ser. 975	Y
10-D	267.『蟹蝦類写真』	ライデン大学図書館 (Leiden Universiy Library)	Ser. 1018	Y
11	465.『染物之法 早稲作法 茶製法』	ライデン大学図書館 (Leiden Universiy Library)	Ser. 892	Y
12A	193.『北海』	ライデン大学図書館 (Leiden Universiy Library)	Ser. 194	Y
12B	177.『蝦夷図』	ライデン大学図書館 (Leiden Universiy Library)	Ser. 205	Y
13	182.『黒龍江中之州并天度』	ライデン大学図書館 (Leiden Universiy Library)	Ser. 215	Y
14	間宮林蔵「カラフト島図」	国立公文書館 (National Archives of Japan)	178-0316	
15	ライデン大学図書館、2011年4月18日撮影 (The University Library at Leiden)	―	―	Y
16	L. Serrurier『Bibliothèque japonaise』	ライデン大学図書館 (Leiden Universiy Library)	OOSHSS A 56	Y

索　引
Index

1. 本索引は、「書名索引」「人名索引」から成る。
2. 項目の配列はアルファベット順とした。
3. 漢字は全て通行の字体で記した。
4. 原則としてラテン語本文・論文中の表記・記載に基づいて収録することに重きを置き、和文書名がラテン語本文と日本語読み（ローマ字大文字表記）で著しく異なる場合は、日本語読みの項目を立て（　）内にラテン語本文表記・記載を記した。
5. ラテン語本文に日本語以外の読み（主として中国語読み）が記されている場合は、〔　〕内に記した。
6. 論文中の参考文献における現代の書籍・論文、研究者は「Bibliography」に記し、立項していない。
7. 「書名索引」について
   - ラテン語本文と石版刷目録の記載が異なる場合は、〔　〕内に漢字で石版刷目録の記載を記し、石版刷目録の脱字は【　】に記した。
   - 原文の書名が欧文（ラテン語・仏語等）の場合、欧文の表記に基づき立項した。
   - 書名の原文表記が明らかに誤記と分かる場合、〈　〉内に正しい書名を記した。
8. 「人名索引」について
   - 本文中に同一人物の別称がみられる場合は、一項目にまとめた。
   - ラテン語本文が誤記・脱字・号による記載等で分かりにくい場合、〔　〕内に正しい表記・名字・通称等を漢字で記入して補った。

書名索引
Title Index

【A】

Adsuma nisigi je →AZUMA NISHIKI E

Adsuma nisigi je atsume →AZUMA NISHIKIE ATSUME

Adsuma nisigi je, bizin sugata →AZUMA NISHIKIE BIJIN SUGATA

Akino kuni Itsukusima kei 安芸国厳島景 53, 84, 119

Annalium Itinerum →RYOKO NENDAI KI

Asagavono fu 朝顔譜 59, 86, 127, 167, 205

AWAJI NO KUNI EZU (Awadsino kuni jedsu) 淡路国絵図 50, 83, 114

Awano kuni je dsu 阿波国絵図 50, 82, 114

AZUMA NISHIKI E (Adsuma nisigi je) 東錦絵 78, 96, 158

AZUMA NISHIKIE ATSUME (Adsuma nisigi je atsume) 東錦絵集 79, 96, 159

AZUMA NISHIKIE BIJIN SUGATA (Adsuma nisigi je, bizin sugata) 東錦絵美人容貌 78, 96, 158

【B】

Baibin 梅品 59, 86, 127

BANCHO NO EZU (Ban tsjôno jedsu) 〔東都〕番町之絵図 52, 84, 117

Bango sen 蛮語箋 64, 89, 136

BANKAKU SHOMEN KAGAMI 万鄙笑面鑑 97

BANKOKU DAIZENZU〔Wàn-kuē tà tsïuén tú〕万国大全図 56, 85, 123

BANSEI EDO CHOKAN (Jorodsujo Jedo matsino kagami) 万世江戸町鑑 70, 92, 146, 222

BANSHU AKASHI-MAIKO HAMA NO ZU (Fansiu Akasi Maikono famano dsu) 播州明石 舞子浜之図 54, 85, 120

BEI NAN KYU TORITSU BOKUCHO〔Mì Nân kūng tùliŭ mēïë〕米南宮杜律墨帖 63, 89, 135

Benkak Kivan →HENGAKU KIHAN

Bibliothèque Japonaise 171, 172, 177, 196, 209, 230

BIJIN E GOJUSAN TSUGI (Bizin je gozjusan tsugi) 美人絵五十三駅 79, 96, 159

BITTCHU NO KUNI EZU (Bitsiuno kuni jedsu) 備中国絵図 50, 83, 114

Bizenno kuni jedsu 備前国絵図 50, 83, 114

Bizin je gozjusan tsugi →BIJIN E GOJUSAN TSUGI

BOCHO NISHU NO KI (Wô Tsjô ni siu no ki) 防長二州之記 49, 82, 112

Boksen sôgwa〔写真学筆〕墨僊叢画 76, 95, 155

BONGO JU (Fangonatsume) 梵言集 64, 89, 136

Buke finagata 武家雛形 70, 92, 146

BUKO RYAKUZU (Musasino rjak-dsu) 武江略図 50, 82, 114, 220

Bukô san buts si〔Wùkiâng ts'àn wū tschi〕武江産物志 72, 92, 147

Bunbô bsansui kwa bu 文鳳山水画譜 76, 95, 154

Bun-ken Jedo oho jedsu 分間江戸大絵図 51, 83, 116, 164, 201, 220

Bun-ken kwai-bô, won Jedo no jedsu 分間 懐宝御江戸絵図 51, 83, 116, 164, 201

Bun-ken, won Jedo no je 分間御江戸絵 51, 83, 116

Bun-kwa kai sei, won Jedo no jedsu →OEDO EZU

BUNRIN SETSUYO HIKKAI TAIZEN 新刻 文林節用筆海大全 81

Bunsei Bu kan 文政武鑑 70, 92, 145

Bun-sei kai sei, won Jedo oho jedsu →OEDO OEZU

Bun-sei sin kai, Setsiu Ohosakano zen dsu →SESSHU OSAKA ZENZU

Bunsei zjuitsi nen rjakrekiko 文政十一年略暦候 70, 92, 145

Bunsei zjuitsi (tsutsinoje ne no) tosi rjakreki zjusitsini kô 文政十一(戊子)年略暦十七二候 70, 92, 145

BUPPIN SHIKIMEI (Butsbin sikimei) 物品識名 58, 86, 126

BUPPO SOBUN 仏法双六〔仏法双文〕 97

BUTSURUIHINSHITU (Butsruibinsits) 物類品隲 58, 86, 126, 167, 204

【C】

Catal. librorum Bibl. regiae sinicorum (ORITSU TOSHOKAN NO CHUGOKUSHO MOKUROKU「王立図書館の中国書目録」) 62, 132

Catalogues of pre-Meiji Japanese books and maps in public collections in the Netherlands『オランダ国内所蔵明治以前日本関係コレクション目録』 172, 210

Catalogus librorum et manuscriptorum Japonicorum a Ph. Fr. de Shiebold collectorum (Catalogus librorum) シーボルト収集日本書籍目録、日本書籍目録 1, 4, 5, 7, 10, 12, 21, 23, 25, 27-30, 32, 161-163, 165, 166, 168-173, 177, 185, 197, 198, 202, 203, 206-208, 211, 213, 223, 224, 225

CHA SEIHO (Tsja tsukûri nori) 茶製法 73, 93, 149, 169, 170, 191, 207, 227, 230

CHANO YUNO ZU (Tsjanojuno dsu) 茶湯之図

書名索引（Title Index）

78, 96, 158
CHASEKI SOKA SHU（Sasiki sasibanano atsumé）茶席挿花集　59, 87, 128
CHIKUHU SHOROKU（Tsikubu sjôrok）竹譜詳録　75, 95, 154
CHINKA KOHO KAN（Tsinkwa kôfô kan）珍貨孔方鑑　73, 93, 150, 222
CHINSEN KIHIN ZUROKU（Tsin sen kibin dsu rok［Tschĭn ts'iên kĭp'ĭn t'ú lŭ］）珍銭奇品図録　73, 93, 150, 222
CHIYO ICHIGEN（Tsijô itsigen）知要一言　74, 94, 152
CHOGON KA（Tsjôkon uta［Tsch'ánghén kô］）長恨歌　67, 90, 141
CHO HINRUI SHOKI（Teo binrui seoki）鳥品類小記　61, 88, 132
CHO NIJU SHASHIN（Teô nizju sjasin）蝶二十写真　60, 87, 130
CHOJU RYAKUGA SHIKI（Teôsiu rjak gwasiki）鳥獣略画式　76, 95, 155
CHOKO HOGYO（Tsjôko sunadori）張公捕魚　73, 93, 150, 227
CHOSEI KARIN SHO（Tsjôsei kwarin seô）長生花林抄　59, 86, 127
CHOSEN JISHO（Tsjozen zisjo）朝鮮辞書　64, 89, 136
CHOSEN MONOGATARI（Tsjôsen monogatari）朝鮮物語　55, 85, 122
CHU KAINO ZU（Tsui kaino dsu）虫蟹之図　60, 87, 130
CHURUI SETSUZU（Tsiurui setsdsu）蛛類説図　61, 87, 130, 171, 209
CHURUI SHASHU（Tsiurui sjasju）虫類写集　60, 87, 130, 169, 207
Chuya yosoou-IROMACHI NIMEN KAGAMI 昼夜化粧　青樓両面鏡　97

【D】

Dai-fei ki　→TAIHEI KI
DAI HANNYA HARAMITA［Tápanshōpolomitoking］大般若波羅蜜多　65, 137
DAI HANNYA RISHU［Mahâpradschnâritsch］大般若理趣　65, 137
DAI HANNYA RISHU BUN［(Tíschī) Tápanshū lits'úfên］(大唐) 大般若理趣分　65, 90, 137
Daiku finagata 大工雛形　70, 146
Dai Nippon Dai-fei-ki mei-sjô bu-jû kurabe 大日本太平記名将武勇競　47, 81, 110
Dai Nippon dô-tsiu kô-tei sai-ken ki 大日本道中行程細見記　54, 85, 121

Dai Nippon dô-tsiu kô-tei si-nan-kuruma 大日本道中行程指南車　54, 85, 121, 220
Dai Nippon kai riku tsû ran 大日本海陸通覧　54, 85, 121
Dai Nippon sai-ken si-sjô zen-dsu 大日本細見指掌全図　49, 82, 113
Dai Nippon tsi-zin mei sjô jû si kagami 大日本知仁名将勇士鑑　47, 81, 110
Dairino dsu 新改　内裏図　51, 83, 116, 220
Daisaifu Ten man gu won kei naino jedsu　→DAZAIFU TENMANGU GOKEIDAI NO EZU
Daisai honzô meisu　→TAISEI HONZO MEISO
Daisen fajabiki setsjô sju　→TAIZEN HAYABIKI SETSUYO SHU
DAISHIN BANNEN ITTO CHIRI ZENZU［Tà-Ts'ing wan-nién ĭt'ông tĭ-li ts'iuén t'ú］大清万年一統地理全図　56, 85, 123
Dannoura kabuto-kun 壇浦兜軍　67, 91, 141
DAZAIFU TENMANGU GOKEIDAI NO EZU（Daisaifu Ten man gu won kei naino jedsu）太宰府天満宮御境内之絵図　54, 85, 121
DOCHU HITORI ANNAI ZU（Dô-tsiu fitori an-nai）道中独案内　55, 85, 121, 221
DOCHUKI（Tô-tsiu ki）道中記〔東海道〕　53, 84, 119
DORYOKO SEKKO（Doreôkô sets tô［Tŏliànghêng schuĕ t'ŏng］）度量衡説統　71, 92, 146, 170, 208
Dsjojô sibo Mijako Meisjo tsukusi　→MIYAKO MEISHO TSUKUSHI
Dsukai, Bujô benrjak　→ZUKAI BUYO BENRYAKU

【E】

ECHIGO NO KUNI EZU（Jetsigono kuni jedsu）越後国絵図　50, 83, 114, 164, 201, 220
EDO DOCHU MEISHO ZU E 新板　江戸道中名所図会　97
EDO FU BIJIN SUGATA（Jedo fû bizin sugata）江戸風美人姿　78, 96, 158, 228
EDO FUKEI（Jedo fukei）江戸風景　79, 96, 159
EDO GOJONAI GOSUMAI NO ZU（Jedo go sjô nai go sumaino dsu）江戸御城内御住屋之図　52, 84, 117, 164, 166, 201
EDO HAKKEI（Jedo fatsukei）江戸八景　79, 96, 159
EDO HARUMA（Jedo-Halma）江戸ハルマ　64, 89, 135, 226
EDO OMITSUKE RYAKUZU（Jedo won metsuke rjak dsu）江戸御見附略図　52, 84, 117
EDO SANPU KIKO 江戸参府紀行　187, 190
EDO SHOKUNIN UTA AWASE（Jedo sjoknin, uta-

233

書名索引（Title Index）

avase）江戸職人歌合　　72, 93, 148
EDO SUMIDAGAWA RYOGAN ICHIRAN ZU（Jedo Sumidagawa rjô-gan itsi ran dsu）江戸隅田川両岸一覧図　　54, 84, 120, 225, 229
EHON AZUMA ASOBI（Jehon, Adsuma asobi）画本東都遊　　78, 96, 158
EHON BEION ROKU（Jehon beiwon rok [Hoeí pèn mìngēn lū]）〔童蒙教訓〕絵本米恩録　　72, 93, 148
EHON BUYU ZAKURA（Jehon, Mukô sakura）絵本武勇桜　　77, 96, 157, 222
EHON EDO SAKURA（Jehon, Jedo sakura）絵本江戸〔都〕桜　　78, 96, 158
EHON EIBUTU SEN（Jehon jeibuts sen）絵本詠物選　　76, 95, 154
EHON FUDENO NISHIKI（Jehon fudeno nisiki）絵本筆二色　　76, 95, 155, 228
EHON FUJIBAKAMA（Jehon, Futsibakama）絵本フチハカマ　　78, 96, 157, 222
EHON GENPAI MUSHA SOROE（Jehon, Gen Fei musja sorove）絵本源平武者揃　　77, 96, 157
EHON GENSHO MEIYO SO（Jehon, Gensjô meijo zô）絵本源将名誉草　　77, 96, 157
EHON HITSUYO（Jehon fitsjô）画本必用　　75, 94, 153
EHON HYAKUNIN ISSHU（Jehon Fjaknin itsu sju）絵本百人一首　　68, 91, 143
EHON JIKI SHOHO（Jehon dsik si bô）絵本直指宝　　75, 94, 152
EHON JORURI ZEKKU（Jehon Zjôruri zetsuku）絵本浄瑠璃絶句　　77, 95, 156
EHON KAGAMIYAMA RETSUJO KO（Jehon Kagamijama retzjokô）絵本鏡山烈〔列〕女功　　66, 90, 139, 221
EHON KEIKO CHO（Jehon keiko tsjô）絵本稽古帳　　76, 95, 154
EHON KINKA DAN（Jehon Kinkwa dan）絵本金花談　　66, 90, 139, 221
EHON KOFUNO DEN（Jehon kôfuno ten）絵本孝婦伝　　66, 90, 138, 221
EHON KOKORONO TANE（Jehon sinnôno tane）絵本心農種　　76, 95, 155
EHON KONREI MICHI SHIRUBE（Jehon, Konrei mitsisirube）絵本婚礼道シルベ　　78, 96, 157, 222
EHON MUMEI（Jehon mumei）画本無名　　76, 95, 155
EHON MUSHA WARAJI（Johon, Musja waratsi）絵本武者鞋　　78, 96, 157
EHON MUSHI ERAMI（Jehon musino erabi [Hoá pèn tsch'ùng tschuén]）画本虫撰　　76, 95, 154, 222
EHON NO YAMAGUSA（Jehon no jamagusa）絵本野山草　　76, 95, 154
EHON OSHUKU BAI（Jehon, Usuguijadoru mume）絵本鶯宿梅　　78, 96, 157, 222
EHON RYOHITSU（Jehon rjô bits）絵本両筆　　77, 95, 156
EHON SHAHO FUKURO（Jehon sjabô fukuro）画本写宝袋　　77, 96, 156, 222, 229
EHON SHUCHU HINA GENJI（Jehon, siu tsiu, Fina Gen si rok zju dsjô）〔絵本袖中　雛源氏〕六十帖　　77, 96, 157
EHON SUMIDAGAWA RYOGAN ICHIRAN（Jehon, Sumidagawa rjôgan itsiran）絵本隅田川 両岸一覧　　78, 96, 158
EHON TE KAGAMI（Jehon te kagami）絵本手鑑　　76, 95, 155
EHON TEBIKI GUSA（Jehon tebikinogusa）絵本手引草　　76, 95, 155
EHON TONO MINE（Jehon, Tabuno mine）絵本多武峯　　77, 96, 157, 222
EHON WAKA AWASE（Jehon Waka awase）絵本和歌合　　68, 91, 143, 227
EHON YORITOMO ISSHO KI（Jehon, Joritomo itsu seô ki）絵本頼朝一生記　　77, 96, 157
EIEI CHUKEINO ZU（Jeijei tsiukeino dsu [Ingwei tschûng kìng t'ú]）栄衛中経図　　74, 94, 151
EIYU ZU E（Jeijû dsu e）英雄図会　　77, 95, 156
EMA HINAGATA（Jemūma finagata）絵馬雛形　　65, 89, 137
Encyclopaediam エンサイクロペディア〔百科事典〕　　41, 103
ENKAKU TSURAN（Jenkwak dsuran）艶廓通覧　　66, 90, 140, 221
EZO DAN HIKKI（Jezo tan fitsu ki）蝦夷談筆記　　55, 85, 122
EZO GASHIMA KOTOBA（Jezo gasima kotoba）蝦夷ヶ嶋言語　　64, 89, 136, 164, 170, 176, 179, 200, 208, 230
EZO HOGEN（Jezo fôgen/Mo sivo kusa）蝦夷方言〔もしほ草・藻汐草・モシボクサ〕　　64, 89, 136, 170, 178, 179, 208, 221, 224, 230
EZO HONZO NO ZU（Jezo honzô no dsu）蝦夷本草之図　　60, 87, 129, 163, 184, 200, 226, 230
EZO KAIHIN NO KEI（Jezo kai bin no kei）蝦夷海浜之景　　55, 85, 122
EZO NO ZU（Jezo no dsu）蝦夷図　　55, 85, 122, 170, 171, 192, 193, 208, 230
EZO SHUI（Jezo sju wi）蝦夷拾遺　　55, 85, 122,

書名索引（Title Index）

170, 208, 221

【F】

Fai bun kô sjokno dsu　→HAIBUN KOSHOKU ZU
Fajabiki setsjô sju　→HAYABIKI SETSUYO SHU
Fak buts zen　→HAKUBUTSU SEN
Fama-tsjo, Kanda, Nippon-basi kita no dsu　→HAMACHO KANDA NIHONBASHI KITA NO ZU
Fangonatsume　→BONGO JU
Fansiu Akasi Maikono famano dsu　→BANSHU AKASHI-MAIKO HAMA NO ZU
Fauna Japonica　日本動物誌　12, 16, 29, 168, 185, 206, 219
Fei-ke monogatari　→HEIKE MONOGATARI
Fisiu Nagasakino dsu　→HISHU NAGASAKI ZU
Fitomono rjakgwa siki　→JINBUTSU RYAKUGA SHIKI
Fjak kikno fu　→HYAKU KIKU HU
Fjaknin itsu sju　→HYAKUNIN ISSHU
Fjaknin itsu sju Kokura monko　→HYAKUNIN ISSHU OGURA BUNKO
Fjakninitsu sju mineno kakebasi　→HYAKUNIN ISSHU MINENO KAKEHASHI
Flora Japonica　日本植物誌　12, 16, 29, 168, 177, 206, 216
Fôgjok Fjaknin itsu sju　→HOGYOKU NHYAKUNIN ISSHU
Fô kai　→HOKKAI
Fokino kuni jedsu　→HOUKI NO KUNI EZU
Fô-sjo no Udsijasu zidai Bu-siu Jedo no jedsu　→HOJO NO UJIYASU JIDAI BUSHU EDO NO EZU
FUJIN KANBYO SHO（Funin kwanbjô sio [Fùschín huánpíng schu]）婦人患病書　74, 94, 152
FUJI NO KEI（Fusino kei）富士之景　54, 84, 120, 225
FUJIYAMA NO ZU（Fusijama no dsu）富士山図　54, 84, 120
Funin kwanbjô sio　→FUJIN KANBYO SHO
Furukotono basi　→KOGEN TEI
FURYU EAWASE TEBIKINO SONO（Fûriu jeavase, Tebikino sono）風流絵合 手引の園　77, 96, 156
Fusijama no dsu　→FUJIYAMA NO ZU
Fusino kei　→FUJI NO KEI
Futats teôteô kuruwa ki 双蝶曲輪日記〔双蝶蝶曲輪記〕　67, 91, 141, 222

【G】

Gagen kazikak　雅言仮字格　63, 89, 134
Gajù man rok　→GAYU MANROKU

Gakgoron [Hiōjùlun]　学語編〔学語論〕　63, 89, 134
GAKYOKU HANA MUSUME, TAMANO ASOBI（Kagjok Fana musubi, Tamano asobi）雅曲花結〔娘〕玉のあそび　72, 93, 148
GASEN（Kwazen）画筌　74, 94, 152, 222
GASHI KAIYO（Gwasikwaijô）画史会要　75, 94, 153
GATO HYAKKA CHO（Kwado fjak kwa teô）画図百花鳥　76, 95, 154
GAYU MANROKU（Gajù man rok [Jà jeu moénlũ]）雅遊漫録　70, 92, 145
GAZU HYAKKI TSUREZURE BUKURO（Jedsu fjakki Tsuredsure fukuro）画図百器 徒然袋　77, 96, 156
GEISHI（Keisi [K'ïngtschi]）鯨志　59, 87, 129
Gen Mei kwateo [Juên Ming hoá tiaò] 元明華鳥　75, 94, 153
GETSUREI HAKUBUTU SEN（Gwatsrei fakbutszen [Juēlíng pōwùtsïuên]）月令博物筌　70, 92, 145
Gjorui sjasin　→GYORUI SHASHIN
Gunden senzimon　→KUNTEN SENJIMON
GUNSEI NO ZU　軍政之図　84
GUNSHO RUIJU（Gunsjo ruiseô [Kiuntschu luits'ông]）群書類従　70, 92, 145
Gwasikwaijô　→GASHI KAIYO
Gwatsrei fakbutszen　→GETSUREI HAKUBUTU SEN
GYOKKAI SETUYOU JIRINGURA（Kjok-kai sets-jô zi-rin zô）玉海節用字林蔵　45, 81, 107
GYORUI SHASHIN（Gjorui sjasin）魚類写真　61, 88, 130, 168, 206, 213

【H】

HAIBUN KOSHOKU ZU（Fai bun kô sjokno dsu [Peiwên Kêngtschī t'û]）佩文耕織図　71, 92, 147, 227
Haikai sitsibu atsume　俳諧七部集　69, 91, 143
HAKUBUTSU SEN（Fak buts zen）博物筌〔荃〕　46, 81, 108
Halima Fimedsino dsu　→HARIMA HIMEJI NO ZU
Halima mei-sjo sjun-ran-dsu e　→HARIMA MEISHO JUNRAN ZUE
Halimano kuni jedsu　→HARIMA NO KUNI EZU
Halimano kuni oho jedsu　→HARIMA NO KUNI OEZU
HAMACHO KANDA NIHONBASHI KITA NO ZU（Fama-tsjo, Kanda, Nippon-basi kita no dsu）浜町神田日本橋北之図　52, 84, 117
HANAGATACHI ONNA SHOKUNIN KAGAMI

書名索引（Title Index）

(Kwajônjo sjoknin kagami) 花容女職人鑑 78, 96, 158, 222

HARIMA HIMEJI NO ZU (Halima Fimedsino dsu) 播磨姫路之図 53, 84, 119

HARIMA MEISHO JUNRAN ZUE (Halima mei-sjo sjun-ran-dsu e) 播磨名所巡覧図会 48, 82, 112

HARIMA NO KUNI EZU (Halimano kuni jedsu) 播磨国絵図 50, 83, 114

HARIMA NO KUNI OEZU (Halimano kuni oho jedsu) 播磨国大絵図 50, 83, 114

HAYABIKI SETSUYO SHU (Fajabiki setsjô sju) 早引節用集 62, 88, 133, 221

HEIKA ZUI (Ikebana dsui) 瓶花図彙 72, 93, 149, 227

HEIKA ZUZEN (Ikebana dsuzen) 瓶花図全 72, 93, 149

HEIKE MONOGATARI (Fei-ke monogatari) 平家物語 47, 81, 110, 220

HENGAKU KIHAN (Benkak Kivan) 扁額軌範 65, 89, 137

HIEI ZAN ENRYAKUJI ZU (Sin fan, Fijei-san Jen-raksi) 新板 比叡山延暦寺 51, 83, 116

Hiêntsïng ngeù ki →KANJO GUKI

HISHU NAGASAKI ZU (Fisiu Nagasakino dsu) 肥州長崎図 53, 84, 119

Historia naturalis →HONZO KOMOKU

HITOMESENGEN (Kai-sei, Fito-me sen-gen) 改正 一目千軒 53, 84, 118

HOGYOKU NHYAKUNIN ISSHU (Fôgjok Fjaknin itsu sju) 宝玉百人一首 68, 91, 142

HOJO NO UJIYASU JIDAI BUSHU EDO NO EZU (Fô-sjô no Udsijasu zidai Bu-siu Jedo no jedsu) 北条氏康時代武州江戸絵図 52, 83, 117

HOKKAI (Fô kai) 北海 56, 85, 123, 170–172, 192, 208, 210, 230

Hoksai gwasiki 北斎画式 77, 95, 156, 222

Hoksai mangwa 北斎漫画 12, 30, 33, 76, 95, 155, 215, 222

Hoksai sjasin gwabu 北斎写真画譜 77, 95, 156

HOKUUN MANGA (Hokun mangwa) 北雲漫画〔編〕 77, 95, 156

HONCHO HIKI MONOGATARI (Honteôfiki monogatari) 本朝蕚物語 66, 90, 139, 221

HONCHO KOKUGUN KENCHI ENKAKU ZUSETSU (Hon-tsjô kok-gun ken-tsi jen-kak dsu-sets) 本朝国郡建置沿革図説 47, 81, 110

Honmatsi Itoja musume〔姉若草妹初音〕本町糸屋娘 67, 91, 141, 221

Honteôfiki monogatari →HONCHO HIKI MONOGATARI

Hon-tsjô kok-gun ken-tsi jen-kak dsu-sets →HONCHO KOKUGUN KENCHI ENKAKU ZUSETSU

Honzô batsusui・Honzô batsusui［Pèn ts'aô pā ts'ui］本草抜萃 60, 87, 130, 167, 187, 189, 205, 213, 226, 230

Honzô gensi［Pènts'aô juênschí］本草原始 58, 86, 126

HONZO IGEN［Pèn ts'aô weijên］本草彙言 57, 86, 125, 167, 204

Honzô itsika gen 本草一家言 61, 88, 131

Honzô Jakumei bikô Wagun seô 本草薬名備考和訓鈔 58, 86, 127, 167, 204

HONZO KAI［Pèn ts'aô hoèi］本草滙 57, 86, 124, 167, 204

Honzô keimô meisu 本草啓蒙名疏 58, 86, 126

HONZO KOMOKU (Historia naturalis) 校正 本草綱目 56, 86, 124, 167, 204, 221

HONZO KOMOKU［Pen ts'aô kang mū］本草綱目 56, 124, 166, 167, 203, 204, 213

Honzô kômok keimô 本草綱目啓蒙 57, 86, 126, 167, 204

Honzôkwai mokrok【本】草会目録 61, 88, 132

Honzô sjasin 本草写真 60, 87, 129, 130, 167, 172, 186, 205, 210, 213, 226, 230

Honzô Wakai 本草和解 58, 86, 126, 167, 204

Honzô Wameô 本草和名 58, 86, 126

Honzô Wameô sju 本草和名集 61, 88, 131

Hoŭ kíng →KAKYO

HOUKI NO KUNI EZU (Fokino kuni jedsu) 伯耆国絵図 50, 83, 114

HYAKU KIKU HU (Fjak kikno fu) 百菊譜 58, 86, 127, 167, 204

HYAKUNIN ISSHU (Fjaknin itsu sju) 百人一首 68, 91, 142

HYAKUNIN ISSHU MINENO KAKEHASHI (Fjak-ninitsu sju mineno kakebasi) 百人一首峯のかけはし 68, 91, 142

HYAKUNIN ISSHU OGURA BUNKO (Fjaknin itsu sju Kokura monko) 百人一首小倉文庫 68, 91, 142

【I】

ICHINOTANI FUTABA GUN KI (Itsinotani futaba kun ki) 一谷嫩軍記 67, 91, 141, 221

Idsumi mei-sjo dsu-e →IZUMI MEISHO ZUE

Idsumino kuni je dsu →IZUMI NO KUNI EZU

Idsumino kuni oho je-dsu →IZUMI NO KUNI OEZU

IGANSAI KAIHIN (Ikansai kai bin) 怡顔斎介【品】 59, 87, 129

書名索引（Title Index）

IGANSAI OHIN（Ikansai ôbin）怡顔斎桜品　59, 86, 128
IGANSAI RANPIN（Ikansai ranbin）怡顔斎蘭品　59, 86, 127
Ikebana dsui　→HEIKA ZUI
Ikebana dsuzen　→HEIKA ZUZEN
Ikebana fiden no jama no nisigi 生花秘伝 野山錦　72, 93, 149
Ikebana koromonoka　→SOKA KOROMONO KA
Ikebana tsisuzino fumoto　→SOKA CHISUJINO FUMOTO
IKKAKU SANKO［Ïkiō tsuàn k'aò］一角篆考　59, 87, 128
IKOKU SHOMOKU［Wei k'ě schû mū］彙刻書目　46, 81, 108, 220
IMAYO BIJINNO KAGAMI（Imajo bizinno kagami）今様美人鑑〔鏡〕　78, 96, 158
Imose jama 妹背山　67, 91, 141
Inabano kuni jedsu 因幡国絵図　50, 83, 114
Inisive jori imajomade Naniva Ohsaka zjū ni dsu　→JOKO YORI KONSEI NI ITARU NANIWA OSAKA JUNI ZU
Inzen takujô［In schén ts'ëjao］飲膳摘要　72, 92, 148, 169, 207
IPPITSU GAFU（Itsubits gwabu）一筆画譜　77, 95, 156
Irofa wake fitori annai, Jedo matsi tsukusi いろは分 独案内 江戸町づくし　52, 84, 117, 220
IROHA GUMI MATOI TSUKUSHI（Irofa kumi matove tsukusi）〔江戸本所深川〕いろは組纏つくし〔両面摺〕　70, 92, 146
IROHA JIKOROKU（Irofazi kôrok）以呂波字考録　63, 89, 134
IROHANO GORUI（Irofano gorui）以呂波之五類　63, 89, 134
IROHA TENRI SHO（Irofa tenri seo）イロハ天理鈔　63, 89, 134
Isagoge in Bibl. Jap.　→NIHONGO ZOSHO HENO JOSETSU
Isagoge in Biblioth. Jap.　→NIHONGO ZOSHO HENO JOSETSU
Isemonogatari〔文化新板〕伊勢物語　66, 90, 139, 221
Isininaru uwono dsu 石ニ化魚之図　61, 88, 131, 226
Itsinotani futaba kun ki　→ICHINOTANI FUTABA GUN KI
Itsubits gwabu　→IPPITSU GAFU
Iwamino kuni jedsu 石見国絵図　50, 83, 114
IZUMI MEISHO ZUE（Idsumi mei-sjo dsu-e）和泉名所図会　48, 81, 111

IZUMI NO KUNI EZU（Idsumino kuni je dsu）和泉国絵図　49, 82, 114, 220
IZUMI NO KUNI OEZU（Idsumino kuni oho je-dsu）和泉国大絵図　49, 82, 113

【J】

Jabinwô siu rok　→YAKUHIN OUSHU ROKU
Jakken　→YAKUKEN
Jak mei sjô ko　→YAKUMEI SHOKO
JAKOTSU SHASHIN（Sjakotsno sjasin）蛇骨之写真〔蛇骨写真〕　61, 88, 131
Jamakasju, rui tai　→SANKASHU RUIDAI
Jamasakurano sets　→YAMAZAKURANO SETSU
Jamasirono kuni je dsu　→YAMASHIRO NO KUNI EZU
Jamato fumi sive Nippon sjo ki　→NIHON SHOKI
Jamato honzô sinkiôsei　→YAMATO HONZO SHINKOSEI
Jamatokotoba　→YAMATO KOTOBA
Jamato mei-sjô dsu-e　→YAMATO MEISHO ZUE
Jamato nen-dai kwô-ki kwai-sjô　→YAMATO NENDAI KOKI ESHO
Jamátono kuni je dsu　→YAMATO NO KUNI EZU
Jamátono kuni sai-ken je dsu　→YAMATO NO KUNI SAIKEN EZU
Jamato uta Rinja sju　→YAMATO UTA REIYA SHU
Janaka Motomimarujama Woisigawa katanodsu　→YANAKA HONGO MARUYAMA KOISHIKAWA HEN NO ZU
Javeno jamabiko　→YAENO YAMABIKO
Jedo fatsukei　→EDO HAKKEI
Jedo fû bizin sugata　→EDO FU BIJIN SUGATA
Jedo fukei　→EDO FUKEI
Jedo go sjô nai go sumaino dsu　→EDO GOJONAI GOSUMAI NO ZU
Jedo-Halma　→EDO HARUMA
Jedo katsikei itsiran　→TOTO SHOKEI ICHIRAN
Jedo sjoknin, utaavase　→EDO SHOKUNIN UTA AWASE
Jedo Sumidagawa rjô-gan itsi ran dsu　→EDO SUMIDAGAWA RYOGAN ICHIRAN ZU
Jedo won metsuke rjak dsu　→EDO OMITSUKE RYAKUZU
Jedsu fjakki Tsuredsure fukuro　→GAZU HYAKKI TSUREZURE BUKURO
Jehon, Adsuma asobi　→EHON AZUMA ASOBI
Jehon beiwon rok　→EHON BEION ROKU
Jehon dsik si bô　→EHON JIKI SHOHO
Jehon fitsjô　→EHON HITSUYO

237

書名索引（Title Index）

Jehon Fjaknin itsu sju →EHON HYAKUNIN ISSHU
Jehon fudeno nisiki →EHON FUDENO NISHIKI
Jehon, Futsibakama →EHON FUJIBAKAMA
Jehon, Gen Fei musja sorove →EHON GENPAI MUSHA SOROE
Jehon, Gensjô meijo zô →EHON GENSHO MEIYO SO
Jehon, Jedo sakura →EHON EDO SAKURA
Jehon jeibuts sen →EHON EIBUTU SEN
Jehon, Joritomo itsu seô ki →EHON YORITOMO ISSHO KI
Jehon Kagamijama retzjokô →EHON KAGAMIYAMA RETSUJO KO
Jehon keiko tsjô →EHON KEIKO CHO
Jehon Kinkwa dan →EHON KINKA DAN
Jehon kôfuno ten →EHON KOFUNO DEN
Jehon, Konrei mitsisirube →EHON KONREI MICHI SHIRUBE
Jehon, Mukô sakura →EHON BUYU ZAKURA
Jehon mumei →EHON MUMEI
Jehon musino erabi →EHON MUSHI ERAMI
Jehon no jamagusa →EHON NO YAMAGUSA
Jehon rjô bits →EHON RYOHITSU
Jehon sinnôno tane →EHON KOKORONO TANE
Jehon sjabô fukuro →EHON SHAHO FUKURO
Jehon te kagami →EHON TE KAGAMI
Jehon tebikinogusa →EHON TEBIKI GUSA
Jehon Waka awase →EHON WAKA AWASE
Jehon Zjôruri zetsuku →EHON JORURI ZEKKU
Jehon, siu tsiu, Fina Gen si rok zju dsjô →EHON SHUCHU HINA GENJI
Jehon, Sumidagawa rjôgan itsiran →EHON SUMIDAGAWA RYOGAN ICHIRAN
Jehon, Tabuno mine →EHON TONO MINE
Jeijei tsiukeino dsu →EIEI CHUKEINO ZU
Jehon, Usuguijadoru mume →EHON OSHUKU BAI
Jeijû dsu e →EIYU ZU E
Jeki mon zen →YAKU MON ZEN
Jemûma finagata →EMA HINAGATA
Jenkwak dsuran →ENKAKU TSURAN
Jetsigono kuni jedsu →ECHIGO NO KUNI EZU
Jezo fôgen →EZO HOGEN
Jezo gasima kotoba →EZO GASHIMA KOTOBA
Jezo honzô no dsu →EZO HONZO NO ZU
Jezo kai bin no kei →EZO KAIHIN NO KEI
Jezo no dsu →EZO NO ZU
Jezo sju wi →EZO SHUI
Jezo tan fitsu ki →EZO DAN HIKKI
JII〔Tsèlui・Tsèwei〕字彙 62, 88, 132

JINBUTSU RYAKUGA SHIKI（Fitomono rjakgwa siki）人物略画式 75, 95, 154
JINDAI KI ASHI KABI（Kami-jo-bumi asikabi）神代紀葦牙 46, 81, 108
Jodogawa ryô-gan sjô-kei dsu-e →YODOGAWA RYOGAN SHOKEI ZUE
Johon, Musja waratsi →EHON MUSHA WARAJI
JOKO YORI KONSEI NI ITARU NANIWA OSAKA JUNI ZU（Inisive jori imajomade Naniva Ohsaka zjū ni dsu）自上古到今世難波大坂十二図 52, 84, 118, 225
Jomeiri dankô basira →YOMEIRI DANGO BASHIRA
Jorodsujo Jedo matsino kagami →BANSEI EDO CHOKAN
Josivara bizin midate gozjusan tsugi →YOSHIHARA BIJIN MITATE GOJUSAN TSUGI
Josivara keisei Jedo bizin je →YOSHIHARA KEISEI EDO BIJIN E
Judok honzô dsusets →YUDOKU HONZO ZUSETSU
JUGYO SHUKUSHA（Siugjo sjuksja）獣魚縮写 61, 88, 131
JU KIN CHU SHASHIN（Zju kin tsiu sjasin）獣禽虫写真 60, 87, 130
JUSO CHOHO KI（Sjuso teôfôki）〔増補〕呪詛調法記 65, 90, 138

【K】

KACCHU CHAKUYO BEN（Kattsiu tsjakjô ben〔Kiātscheú tschôjúng pién〕）甲冑着〔著〕用弁 71, 92, 146
KACHO GACHO（Kwateô kwateô）花鳥画帖 76, 95, 155
KACHO GAFU（Kwateô kwabu）花鳥画譜 76, 95, 155, 222
KACHO GASHIKI（Kwa teo gwa siki）花鳥画式 75, 94, 152
KACHO SHASHIN ZUE（Kwateô sjasin dsue）花鳥写真図会 76, 95, 155, 222
KADAN ASAGAO TSU（Kwadan Asagavono dsu）花壇朝顔通 59, 86, 127, 167, 205
KADAN SOBOKU EZU（Kwadan sômok jebu）花壇草木絵図 59, 128
KADAN TAIZEN（Kwadan daizen）花壇大全 59, 87, 128
KADAN YOUKIKU SHU（Kwadan jôkik siu）花壇養菊集 58, 86, 127, 167, 205
Kadômei mok seô 歌道名目抄〔鈔〕 68, 91, 142, 222

書名索引（Title Index）

KA GA 花画　97

Kagjok Fana musubi, Tamano asobi　→GAKYOKU HANA MUSUME, TAMANO ASOBI

KA I（Kwa wi）花彙　58, 86, 126, 163, 200

KAIGYO KO ZUE（Kaigjo kô dsu-e）海魚考図絵　61, 88, 131

KAIGYO SHASHIN（Kaigjo sjasin）海魚写真　61, 88, 131

KAIHO CHINSEN KAGAMI（Kwaibo tsinsen kagami）懐宝珍銭鑑　73, 94, 151

KAIHO KYO EZU（Kwai bô Kjô no jedsu）懐宝京絵図　51, 116

Kaika rui sjasin 蟹蝦類写真　60, 87, 130, 168, 190, 206, 213, 219, 230

Kai-sei, Fito-me sen-gen　→HITOMESENGEN

Kaisei kôfô dsu kan 改正孔方図鑑　73, 93, 150

Kai-sei Nippon dsu 改正日本図　49, 82, 113

Kai-sei Nippon jo-dsi-ro-tei zen dsu 改正日本輿地路程全図　49, 82, 113, 164, 166, 180, 201, 212, 220, 230

KAISHU（Kaisiu [Haì tsïeû]）海鰌　61, 88, 132

Kaitsukusi urano nisigi 貝ツクシ 浦のにしき　68, 91, 143

Kaizô dsu fu [Kiaì tsáng t'û fú] 解臓図賦〔譜〕　74, 94, 151

KAJI ON SHUTSUYAKU（Kuwazi on sjutsjak）火事御出役〔定火消御役御大名火消　御場所附　イロハ番組〕　70, 92, 146

KAKUBIKI JITTAI SENJIMON KOMOKU（Kwain zjutai senzimon kômōk）画引十体千字文綱目　63, 89, 135, 221

KAKYO [Hoũ king] 花鏡　57, 86, 125

Kamakura seô kaino dsu 鎌倉勝概図　53, 84, 119

Kami-jo-bumi asikabi　→JINDAI KI ASHI KABI

Kamijono masa koto 神代正語　46, 81, 109

Kami tsukûru fô 紙作之法　73, 93, 149, 227

KAMUSAKKA NO ZU（Kan-tsa-ka no dsu）東察加之図　56, 85, 123, 170, 208, 225

Kanafiki setsjô sju 仮名引節用集　62, 88, 133

Kanatehon Tsiusingura 仮名手本忠臣蔵　67, 91, 141, 222

KANGA HITORI GEIKO（Kangwa fitori keiko）漢画独稽古　74, 94, 152, 229

KANGA SHINAN（Kangwa sinan [Hánhoá tschì nan]）漢画指南　74, 94, 152

KANGA SHINAN NIHEN（Kangwa sinan niben）漢画指南二編　74, 94, 152

K'anghi tsètièn　→KOKI JITEN

KANJO GUKI [Hièntsïng ngeù kí] 間情偶寄　66, 90, 140, 221

KANSEI KOHO KAN（Kwansei kôfô kan）寛政孔方鑑　73, 93, 150, 222

KANSHOKU SHOSHIN SUGOROKU 官職昇進双六　97

Karafutono ivajuru Likinkamūi, Tsūnakai ni-siuno dsu 唐夫人所謂リキンカムヒ　ツナカヒ二獣之図　61, 88, 131, 171, 209

Karafuto sima 唐太島　55, 85, 122, 170, 208

Karafuto sima no dsu 唐太島之図　55, 85, 122, 221

KARAKU ICHIRAN ZU（Kwa-rak itsi-ran dsu）花洛一覧図　51, 83, 116

Karin zatsmok seô 歌林雑木抄　68, 91, 142, 222

Kasaneno irome かさねのいろめ　70, 92, 145

Kasira gaki, zû-bo, Kin mô dsu i　→KINMO ZUI

Kasira gaki, zû bo, Kin mô dsu i dai sei　→KINMO ZUI TAISEI

Kasô tôtsiu no dsu 夏草冬虫図　60, 87, 129, 225

KASSHI JUNKAN ZU（Katsu-si zjun kwan dsu）甲子循環図　47, 81, 110

Kattsiu tsjakjô ben　→KACCHU CHAKUYO BEN

KAWACHI MEISHO ZUE（Kwatsi mei-sjo dsu-e）河内名所図会　48, 81, 111

Kawátsino kuni je-dsu 河内国絵図　49, 82, 113, 220

Kawátsino kuni sai ken sjo dsu 河内国細見小図　49, 82, 113, 220

KEIJO GAEN（Keisjô kwajen）京城画苑　76, 95, 155

Keisai sokwa 蕙斎麁画　75, 94, 153

Keisi　→GEISHI

KENGYU HIN（Kengo bin）牽牛品　59, 86, 127, 167, 205

Kensi kwajen 建氏画苑　75, 95, 154

Kensi kwajen kai sak dsu 建氏画苑海錯図　75, 95, 154

Kieù-hoàng pen-ts'aò　→KYUKO HONZO

KIFUNENO HONJI（Kibuneno Hondsi）キフ子本地　67, 90, 140, 226, 227

Kiino kuni mei-sjo dsu-e 紀伊国名所図会　48, 82, 112

Kiino san-sui kei kwan 紀伊山水景〔奇〕観　54, 84, 120

Ki nen si sjô 紀年指掌　47, 81, 110, 220

Kin fu 菌譜　61, 88, 131

Kingin dsu rok 金銀図録　73, 93, 150, 222

KIN JU GYO SHASHIN（Kin siu gjo sjasin）禽獣魚写真　61, 88, 131

KINMO ZUI（Kasira gaki, zû-bo, Kin mô dsu i）頭書増補　訓蒙図彙　11, 45, 81, 107, 162, 198

KINMO ZUI TAISEI（Kasira gaki, zû bo, Kin mô dsu i dai sei）頭書増補　訓蒙図彙大成　11,

書名索引（Title Index）

45, 81, 107, 161, 162, 197, 198, 220
Kin siu gjo sjasin →KIN JU GYO SHASHIN
KISHU KOYA SAN KONGO BUJI SAIKEN ZU (Kisiu Kôjasan Kongô busi saiken dsu) 紀州 高野山金剛峯寺細見図 54, 85, 120
KISOJI MEISHO ZUE (Kisodsi mei-sjo dsu-e) 木曾路名所図会 48, 82, 111
KITSUHIN (Kitsbin) 橘品 59, 87, 128, 167, 205
KITSUHIN RUIKO (Tatsibana binrui kô) 橘品類考 59, 87, 128, 167, 205
Kiusiuno dsu →KYUSHU NO ZU
Kjô kate gotono bana →KYOKA TEGOTONO HANA
Kjôka Fusan sju →KYOKA FUSO SHU
Kjôka je ziman →KYOKA E JIMAN
Kjôka Kwantô fjaktai sju →KYOKA KANTO HYAKUDAI SHU
Kjok-kai sets-jô zi-rin zô →GYOKKAI SETUYOU JIRINGURA
Kjô midsu →KYO NO MIZU
Kjôto kabuki sin kjôgen ge-tai nen kan →KYOTO KABUKI SHIN KYOGEN GEDAI NENKAN
Kjôto meguri →KYOTO MEGURI
Kjôto si-sjô no dsu →KYOTO SHISHO ZU
KODO ZUROKU (Kotô dsurok) 鼓銅図録 72, 93, 148, 227
KOEKIZOHO JIKIN SHO (Kwôjeki zôbô, Tsikin seô) 広益増補 地錦抄 59, 87, 128, 167, 183, 205, 212, 230
Kôfô dsu kan →KOHO ZUKAN
KOGEN TEI (Furukotono basi) 古言梯 63, 88, 134
Ko Gunkino dsu kai [Kù kiûn k'itschi t'û kiai] 古軍器之図解 71, 92, 147
KOHO ZUKAN (Kôfô dsu kan [K'ùngfâng t'û kién]) 孔方図鑑 73, 93, 150, 222
Kôjasan sai ken jedsu →KOYA SAN SAIKEN EZU
Kô-jô gun kan →KOYO GUNKAN
Kôkaino Irofa →KUKAINO IROHA
KOKI JITEN [K'anghi tsètièn] 康熙字典 62, 88, 132
Kokin sju 古今集 68, 142
Kokin sju tovokagami 古今集遠鏡 68, 91, 142
Kôkjô →KOKYO
KOKKEI MANGA (Kotsukei mankwa) 滑稽漫画 72, 93, 148
KOKON ENKAKU CHIZU [Kù-kin jên-kë tí-tû] 古今沿革地図 56, 85, 123, 221
KOKON EZU, ZOKU HYAKKI (Kokon jedsu, Tsukudsugu fjaktsu ki) 古今〔今昔〕画図続百鬼 77, 96, 156
Kokon senkwa kan [Kùkin t'siuênhó kién] 古今泉貨鑑 73, 93, 150, 222
Kokon takano koto 古今鷹之事 59, 87, 128
KOKURYUKO NAKANOSU (Kok-riu-kô tsiu-siu) 黒竜江中之洲〔并天度〕 55, 85, 122, 170, 171, 194, 195, 208, 209, 230
KOKYO (Kôkjô [Hiao king]) 孝経 65, 90, 138
Konze tei fu zen 近世貞婦伝 66, 90, 139, 221
KORIN HYAKU ZU (Kwôrin fjak dsu) 光琳百図 76, 95, 155
Ko san-rjôno dsu-e 古山陵之図 49, 82, 112
Ko sen, atavi tsuku 古銭価附 73, 93, 150, 222
Koseno Kanaoka Meiki tsutave 巨勢金岡 名技伝 66, 90, 139, 221
KOSHIN SETSU (Kwôsin sets) 広参説 74, 94, 151
ko si-kei dsu 古史系図 46, 81, 109
Kotô dsurok →KODO ZUROKU
Koto semeno tan〔阿古屋〕琴責めの段 67, 141
KOTSUBO KANE (Seôfei nori) 小坪規矩 71, 92, 146
Kotsukei mankwa →KOKKEI MANGA
Kot tô sju [Kōtòng tsī] 骨董集 69, 92, 144, 222
KO YAMATO HONZO (Kwô Jamato honzô) 広倭〔穉〕本草 58, 86, 126
KOYA SAN SAIKEN EZU (Kôjasan sai ken jedsu) 高野山細見絵図 54, 85, 120
KOYO GUNKAN (Kô-jô gun kan) 甲陽軍鑑 47, 81, 110, 220
KUKAINO IROHA (Kôkaino Irofa) 空海之いろは 63, 89, 134
Kù-kin jên-kū tí-tû →KOKON ENKAKU CHIZU
Kuniguni sibawi vanjei sumô 諸〔都〕国芝居繁栄数望 68, 91, 141
KUNTEN SENJIMON (Gunden senzimon) 訓点千字文 28, 33, 63, 89, 135
KUSA BANA RYAKUGA SHIKI (Sôkwa rjakgwa siki) 草花略画式 75, 94, 154
Kutsin no sets →KYUSHIN NO SETSU
Kuwazi on sjutsjak →KAJI ON SHUTSUYAKU
Kwadan Asagavono dsu →KADAN ASAGAO TSU
Kwadan daizen →KADAN TAIZEN
Kwadan jôkik siu →KADAN YOUKIKU SHU
Kwadan sômok jebu →KADAN SOBOKU EZU
Kwado fjak kwa teô →GATO HYAKKA CHO
Kwai bô Kjô no jedsu →KAIHO KYO EZU
Kwaibo tsinsen kagami →KAIHO CHINSEN KAGAMI
Kwain zjutai senzimon kômôk →KAKUBIKI JIT-

書名索引（Title Index）

TAI SENJIMON KOMOKU
Kwajônjo sjoknin kagami　→HANAGATACHI ONNA SHOKUNIN KAGAMI
Kwa-rak itsi-ran dsu　→KARAKU ICHIRAN ZU
Kwan-sei kai-sei Miwodsukusi　→MIO TSU KUSHI
Kwansei kôfô kan　→KANSEI KOHO KAN
Kwa teo gwa siki　→KACHO GASHIKI
Kwateô kwabu　→KACHO GAFU
Kwateô kwateô　→KACHO GACHO
Kwateô sjasin dsue　→KACHO SHASHIN ZUE
Kwatsi mei-sjo dsu-e　→KAWACHI MEISHO ZUE
Kwa wi　→KA I
Kwazen　→GASEN
Kwô Jamato honzô　→KO YAMATO HONZO
Kwôjeki zôbô, Tsikin seô　→KOEKIZOHO JIKIN SHO
Kwôrin fjak dsu　→KORIN HYAKU ZU
Kwôsin sets　→KOSHIN SETSU
KYOKA E JIMAN（Kjôka je ziman）狂歌画自満　69, 91, 143, 222
KYOKA FUSO SHU（Kjôka Fusan sju）狂歌扶桑集　69, 91, 143, 222
KYOKA KANTO HYAKUDAI SHU（Kjôka Kwantô fjaktai sju）狂歌関東百題集　69, 91, 143, 222
KYOKA TEGOTONO HANA（Kjô kate gotono bana）狂歌手毎之花　69, 91, 143
KYO NO MIZU（Kjô midsu）京之水　51, 83, 115
KYO NO ZU（Sin bô, Kjôno dsu）新補 京之図　51, 83, 116
KYO OEZU（Mijako oho je-dsu）〔新撰増補〕京大絵図　51, 83, 115
KYOTO KABUKI SHIN KYOGEN GEDAI NENKAN（Kjôto kabuki sin kjôgen ge-tai nen kan）京都歌舞伎〔妓〕新狂言外題年鑑　68, 91, 141, 222
KYOTO MEGURI（Kjôto meguri）〔天明再板〕京都めぐり　51, 83, 115, 225
KYOTO SHISHO ZU（Kjôto si-sjô no dsu）〔文化改正〕京都指掌図　51, 83, 115
KYUKO HONZO［Kieù-hoàng pen-ts'aò］救荒本草　57, 86, 125
KYUSHIN NO SETSU（Kutsin no sets［Kieú tschîn tschi schuĕ］）九鍼之説　74, 94, 152
KYUSHU NO ZU（Kiusiuno dsu）九州之図　49, 82, 113

【L】

Lĭ taí ssé-tsĭ t'ŭ　→REKIDAI JISEKI ZU
Liukiu dan　→RYUKYU DAN
Liukiu honzô no dsu　→RYUKYU HONZO NO ZU
Liukiu sômok sjasin so kô　→RYUKYU SOMOKU SHASHIN SOKO
Luihō　→RUIGO

【M】

MACHI HIKESHI BAN GUMI（Matsi fikesi ban gumi）町火消番組　70, 92, 146
Mahâpradschnâritsch　→DAI HANNYA RISHU
MAKO INKYO［Mâkuâng júnking］麻光韻鏡　63, 89, 134
Man-bô ni-men kagami 万宝二面鑑　48, 81, 111
Man-bô sets-jû fu-ki zô〔増字百倍〕万宝節用富貴蔵　45, 81, 108
Manjo sju　→MANYO SHU
Man-kai sets-jô zi fuk-zô〔文化補刻〕万海節用字福蔵　45, 81, 108, 220
MANKAI SETSUYO HYAKKA SEN 新増広益 万会節用百家選　81
Man-reki rjô-men kagami 万暦〔歴〕両面鑑　48, 81, 111, 220
Mantai fôkan［Wántaí paò kièn］万代宝鑑　70, 92, 145
MANYO SHU（Manjo sju）万葉集　68, 91, 142
Maôschī　→MOSHI
Maôschī ming-wū t'ù jūe　→MOSHI MEIBUTSU ZUSETSU
Matsi fikesi ban gumi　→MACHI HIKESHI BAN GUMI
Matsukage kwaidan［Sûngĭn Kuait'ân］松陰快談　66, 90, 140, 221
Matsumaë Jezo no dsu 松前蝦夷之図　55, 85, 122
Meika kwabu 名家画譜　75, 94, 153
Mei san dsu bu 名山図譜　12, 20, 30, 31, 54, 84, 120, 217, 225, 229
Meôzjuts fakbuts zen　→MYOJUTSU HAKUBUTSU SEN
Mija finagata　→MIYA HINAGATA
Mijako mei sjo dsu e　→MIYAKO MEISHO ZUE
Mijako oho je-dsu　→KYO OEZU
Mijako Ohosaka tsjaja sjo bunteôfô ki　→MIYAKO OSAKA CHAYA SHOBUN CHOHOKI
Mijako rin sen mei sjo dsu e　→MIYAKO RINSEN MEISHO ZUE
Mijako si-sja zen dsu　→MIYAKO JISHA ZENZU
Mikawano kuni je dsu 参河国絵図　50, 82, 114
Mimasakano kuni jedsu 美作国絵図　50, 114
Mimasakano kuni jedsu 美濃〔美作国〕絵図　82
Mĭ Nân kūng tùliù mētïë　→BEI NAN KYU TORITSU BOKUCHO
MIO TSU KUSHI（Kwan-sei kai-sei Miwodsukusi）

241

書名索引（Title Index）

寛政改正 みをつくし　53, 84, 118
Mitsinoku kuni Sivokama Matsusimano dsu　→MUTSU NO KUNI SHIOGAMA MATSUSHIMA ZU
MIYA HINAGATA（Mija finagata）宮雛形　70, 92, 146
MIYAKO JISHA ZENZU（Mijako si-sja zen dsu）都寺社全図　51, 83, 115, 220
MIYAKO MEISHO GURUMA（Zô-bô je-ire Mijako mei-sjo kuruma）増補絵入 都名所車　51, 83, 115
MIYAKO MEISHO TSUKUSHI（Dsjojô sibo Mijako Meisjo tsukusi）〔女用至宝〕都名所尽　66, 90, 138
MIYAKO MEISHO ZUE（Mijako mei sjo dsu e）都名所図会　50, 83, 115
MIYAKO OSAKA CHAYA SHOBUN CHOHOKI（Mijako Ohosaka tsjaja sjo bunteôfô ki）京大坂茶屋諸分調方記〈茶屋諸分調方記〉　70, 92, 145, 222, 227
MIYAKO RINSEN MEISHO ZUE（Mijako rin sen mei sjo dsu e）都林泉名勝図会　50, 83, 115
Morokosi kin-mô dsu i 唐土訓蒙図彙　45, 81, 107, 162, 198
MOSHI（Maôschî）毛詩　57, 124, 125
MOSHI HINBUTSU ZUKO（Môsi bin-buts dsu kô,〔Maôschî p'in-wǔ t'ǔ k'aò〕）毛詩品物図攷　57, 86, 125
MOSHIHO GUSA　→EZO HOGEN
MOSHI MEIBUTSU ZUSETSU〔Maôschî ming-wǔ t'ù jūe〕毛詩名物図説　57, 86, 125
MOSHIO GUSA　→EZO HOGEN
MOSHI RIKUSHI SOMOKU SO ZUKAI（Môsi, Liksi sô mok so dsu kai,〔Maôschî Lǔ-schī ts'aô-mū sū t'ǔ kiai〕）毛詩陸氏草木図解　57, 86, 125
MOSHI SOMOKU CHOJU CHUGYO SO（Môsi sô mok teo ziu gjô so,〔Maôschî ts'aô mū niaò scheù tsch'ǔng jū sǔ〕）毛詩草木鳥獣虫魚疏　57, 86, 124, 167, 204
Môsi, Liksi sô mok so dsu kai　→MOSHI RIKUSHI SOMOKU SO ZUKAI
Môsi bin-buts dsu kô　→MOSHI HINBUTSU ZUKO
Môsi sô mok teo ziu gjô so　→MOSHI SOMOKU CHOJU CHUGYO SO
Mo sivo kusa　→EZO HOGEN
Mume sakurano rui kwa sjasin　→UME SAKURA-NO RUIKA SHASHIN
Musasino banasi 武蔵野話　48, 82, 111
Musasino rjak-dsu　→BUKO RYAKUZU
MUSHA KAGAMI（Musja kagami）武者鑑　78, 96, 157
Musino kagami 虫鑑〔鏡〕　59, 87, 129
Musja kagami　→MUSHA KAGAMI
MUTSU NO KUNI SHIOGAMA MATSUSHIMA ZU（Mitsinoku kuni Sivokama Matsusimano dsu）陸奥国塩釜〔竈〕松島図　54, 84, 120
MYOJUTSU HAKUBUTSU SEN（Meôzjuts fakbuts zen）妙術博物筌　72, 93, 148, 222

【N】

Nachrichten über Kôrai, Japan's Bezüge mit Kôraischen Halbinsel und mit Schina 高麗についての報告：日本の朝鮮半島及び中国との関係　123
Nagasaki gjô-jak nitsi-ki 長崎行役日記　48, 82, 112
NAGATACHO NO EZU（(Tôdo) Nagada matsino jedsu）〔東都〕永【田】町之絵図　52, 84, 117
Nànfang ts'aòmu tschoùng　→NANPO SOMOKU JO
NANHEI, BUNBO KAIDO SOGA（Nanfei, Bunbô kaido sôkwa）南兵文鳳 街道双画〈南岳文鳳街道双画〉　76, 95, 155
NANPO SOMOKU JO〔Nànfang ts'aòmu tschoùng〕南方草木状　57, 86, 125, 167, 204
NANYU KI（Nan-ju ki）〔諸国奇談〕南遊記　49, 82, 112
Nari katatsino dsu sets　→SEIKEI ZUSETSU
Nen-dai Ki 年代記　47, 81, 110
Nieuw verzameld Japans en Hollandsch Woordenboek door den Vorst van het Landschap Nakats（SHINSHU WARAN JISHO 新輯和蘭辞書〔蘭語訳撰〕）　64, 135, 221
NIHON GO JISHO（vocabularia Japonica）日本語辞書　41, 103
NIHONGO ZOSHO HENO JOSETSU（Isagoge in Biblioth. Jap.）日本語蔵書への序説　64, 135, 136
NIHON NENDAI KI（Annales japonici）日本年代記　46, 109
NIHON SHOKI（Jamato fumi sive Nippon sjo ki）日本書紀　46, 81, 109, 220
NIHON ZOSHO（Bibliothecae Japonicae）日本蔵書　46, 109
NIJUSHIHAI JUNPAI ZUE（Nizjusibai sjunbaidsue）二十四輩順拝図会　65, 89, 137
NIKKO EKIRO RISU NO HYO（Ni-kwô jeki-ro ri-sû-no beô）日光駅路里数之表　55, 85, 121
NIKKO OYAMA SOUEZU（Nikwô won-san sôno jedsu）日光御山総絵図　53, 84, 119, 220
NIKKOSAN SOMOKU SHASHIN（Nikwôsan sômok sjasin）日光山草木写真　60, 87, 129

書名索引（Title Index）

Ni-kwô jeki-ro ri-sûno beô →NIKKO EKIRO RISU NO HYO
Nin men zô dsu sets 人面瘡図説　74, 94, 151
Ninzin sjasin 人参写真　60, 87, 129
Nippon 日本　2, 4, 10, 12, 16-20, 29-31, 33, 162, 169-171, 173, 174, 176, 181, 184, 193, 198, 207-209, 212, 215-218, 229
Nippon fen-kai rjak-dsu 日本辺界略図　49, 82, 113, 164, 166, 180, 181, 201, 212, 225, 230
Nippon mei-sjo no je 日本名所之絵　53, 84, 119, 225
Nippon motsimaru teôzja sju 日本持丸長者集　73, 93, 149
Nippon no kusaki 日本草木　60, 87, 129
Nippon sankai meibuts dsu e 日本山海名物図会　71, 92, 147
Nippon sivodsino ki 増補 日本汐路之記　55, 85, 122
Nippon sjokin sinsja 日本諸禽真写　61, 88, 132
Nippon someirono fô 日本染色法　72, 93, 149
Nippon wô-dai itsi-ran・Nippon wôdai itsi ran 日本王代一覧　46, 47, 81, 109, 220
NISSHU YOHONO ZU (Nitsu sin jôfôno dsu) 日州養蜂図　72, 93, 148, 227
Nizjusihai sjunbaidsue →NIJUSHIHAI JUNPAI ZUE
NOGYO ZENSHO (Nôgeo zensjo [Nûngniĕ tsïuên schǔ]) 農業全書　71, 92, 147
Nôka geozi [Nûng kiá niĕ ssé] 農稼〔嫁〕業事　71, 92, 147
Nôka jeki [Nûng kiá ī] 農家益　71, 92, 147
Notono kuni jedsu 能登国絵図　50, 82, 114
NURINO HO (Nuru fô) 塗之法　73, 93, 149, 227

【O】

OCHINO SHIRANAMI (Wotsino siranami) 遠乃白波〔浪〕　66, 90, 139, 221
OEDO EZU (Bun-kwa kai sei, won Jedo no jedsu) 文化改正 御江戸絵図　51, 83, 116
OEDO EZU (Sai fan, Sin kai won Jedo no jedsu・Sai-fan sin-kai, won Jedo no jedsu) 再版 新改御江戸絵図　51, 52, 83, 116
OEDO MEISHO HITORI ANNAI KI (Sin fan, won Jedo mei-sjo fitori annai ki) 新板 御江戸名所独案内記　52, 84, 117
OEDO OEZU (Bun-sei kai sei, won Jedo oho jedsu) 文政改正 御江戸大絵図　52, 83, 116, 164, 201, 220
OGASAWARA SHOREI TAIZEN (Wokasa vara sjo-rei daizen) 小笠原諸礼大全　69, 92, 144, 222
Ohosaka Abeno katsusen no dsu →OSAKA ABENO GASSEN NO ZU
Ohosaka matsi kagami →OSAKA MACHI KAGAMI
Ohosaka matsi-tsiu Ohoso tsumori-mune san-jô →OSAKA MACHIJU OZUMORI MUNA SANYO
Ohosaka Mijako mei-buts awase sumô →OSAKA MIYAKO MEIBUTU AWASE SUMO
Ohosakano gawa-kutsi jori Nagasaki madeno sen-ro →OSAKA KAWAGUCHI YORI NAGASAKI MADE FUNAJI
Ohosaka rjô-gave te-kata fen-ran →OSAKA RYOGAE TEGATA BINRAN
Ohosaka siro no dsu →OSAKAJO NO ZU
Okino kuni jedsu 隠岐国絵図　50, 83, 114
O-lan sin-jeki tsi-kiu zen dsu →OURAN SHINYAKU CHIKYU ZENZU
Omi Gensi sendsin Jakáta 近江源氏先陣館　67, 91, 141, 222
Omi mei-sjo dsu-e 近江名所図会　48, 82, 111
Omino fatsikei dsu 淡海八景図　54, 85, 120
Ômino kuni jedsu 近江国絵図　50, 82, 114
Ômino kuni oho-jodsu 近江国大絵図　50, 82, 114
On gen, buk Gjo kiûni mairu Gjo jôke gjo jaknin tsuku 御元服御宮参御用掛御役人附　70, 92, 145
OSAKA ABENO GASSEN NO ZU (Ohosaka Abeno katsusen no dsu) 大坂〔城之図〕安部之合戦之図　53, 84, 118
OSAKAJO NO ZU (Ohosaka siro no dsu) 大坂城之図　53, 84, 118
OSAKA KAWAGUCHI YORI NAGASAKI MADE FUNAJI (Ohosakano gawa-kutsi jori Nagasaki madeno sen-ro) 大坂川口ヨリ長崎迄舟路　55, 85, 122
OSAKA MACHIJU OZUMORI MUNA SANYO (Ohosaka matsi-tsiu Ohoso tsumori-mune san-jô) 繁花市中 大凡積胸算用　53, 84, 118
OSAKA MACHI KAGAMI (Ohosaka matsi kagami) 大坂町鑑　53, 84, 118
OSAKA MIYAKO MEIBUTU AWASE SUMO (Ohosaka Mijako mei-buts awase sumô) 大坂都名物合角力　53, 119
OSAKA NO ZU (Sin-ban zô-bô, Ohosakano dsu) 新板増補 大坂之図　52, 84, 118, 220
OSAKA RYOGAE TEGATA BINRAN (Ohosaka rjô-gave te-kata fen-ran) 大坂両替手形便覧　53, 118
OSAKA SISHO ZU (Zô-sin, Ohosaka si sjô dsu) 増修大坂指掌図　52, 84, 118, 220
OSHIE HAYA GEIKO (Osije fajageiko) 押絵早稽古

書名索引（Title Index）

72, 93, 148
OSHIE TEKAGAMI（Osijeno tekagami）押画手鑑　75, 94, 153
Osiba suri 腊葉揚　60, 87, 130, 188, 226, 230
Osome Fisamatsu Fanakurabe ukinano jomiuri おそめ久松　花競浮名の読販　67, 90, 140
OSON GAFU（Wôton kwabu）鶯䳕画譜　76, 95, 155
Otoba Tansitsi. Womina besi Tatoveno avasima 音羽丹七　女郎花喩粟島　67, 90, 140
OURAN SHINYAKU CHIKYU ZENZU（O-lan sin-jeki tsi-kiu zen dsu）喎蘭新訳地球全図　56, 85, 123
Owarino kuni je dsu 尾張国絵図　50, 82, 114, 164, 201, 220
OYUTON KAISHO SENJIMON［Wângjeû tûntschìschû Tsiän dsū wên］汪由敦楷書千字文　63, 89, 135

【P】

Pèn ts'aô hoèi　→HONZO KAI
Pen ts'aô kang mū　→HONZO KOMOKU
Pèn ts'aô weìjên　→HONZO IGEN

【R】

RANEN TEKIHO（Ranjen tekifô）蘭畹摘方　59, 87, 128
REIGYOKU HYAKUNIN ISSHU AZUMA NISHIKI（Reikjok Fjaknin itsusju adsumanisigi）〔文化新版〕麗玉百人一首吾妻錦　66, 90, 138
REKIDAI JISEKI ZU（Lĭ taí ssé-tsī t'ú）歴代事跡図　56, 85, 123
RIKKA SEIDO SHU（Ritsukwa seidô sju）立華正道集　72, 93, 149, 222
RIKUBUTSU SHINSHI（Rikbuts sinsi）六物新志　59, 87, 128
Rjôbu Sindô kukets Sjô　→RYOBU SHINTO KUKETSU SHO
Rongo［Lûnjú］論語　65, 90, 138
Rongo ikun makino fazime［Lûnjú îhiún kiuén tschi scheù］論語彝訓巻之首　65, 90, 138, 170, 208, 221
RUIGO［Luihô］類合　64, 89, 136
RUIYO HYAKUNIN ISSHU KYOBUNKO（Ruijevu Fjaknin itsusju keomonko）類葉百人一首教文庫　66, 90, 138, 221
RYOBU SHINTO KUKETSU SHO（Rjôbu Sindô kukets Sjô［Liàngpú schîntao K'eùkiuē tschaô］）〔改正〕両部神道口決鈔　65, 89, 137
RYOKO NENDAI KI（Annalium Itinerum）旅行年代記　40, 103
RYUKYU DAN（Liukiu dan）琉球談　55, 85, 122
RYUKYU HONZO NO ZU（Liukiu honzô no dsu）琉球本草之図　60, 87, 129
RYUKYU SOMOKU SHASHIN SOKO（Liukiu sômok sjasin so kô）琉球草木写真素稿　60, 87, 129
RYUTEI SEIGAN RYO SENSEI MYOHIN 笠亭晴岩両先生妙品　97

【S】

Sadono kuni jedsu 佐渡国絵図　50, 83, 114, 164, 201
SAHARIN TO NO ZU（Sāgalen sima no dsu）薩哈連島之図　55, 85, 122, 170, 208, 225
Sai fan, Sin kai won Jedo no jedsu　→OEDO EZU
Sai ken 細見　52, 117
Sai kou dan［Ts'aí kên t'ún］菜根譚　65, 90, 138, 221
Sai-fan sin-kai, won Jedo no jedsu　→OEDO EZU
Sai-ju ki　→SAIYU KI
Saiken Wotokojama Fôzjôje dsurok 細見　男山放生会図録　65, 89, 137
Sai-kok zjun-rei sai-ken dai sen 西国順礼細見大全　55, 85, 121
SAISO KANHITSU（Sai zô kan bits）采草閑筆　54, 84, 120, 225
SAIYU KI（Sai-ju ki）〔諸国奇談〕西遊記　48, 82, 112, 225
Sake tsukúru koto 酒作之事　73, 93, 149, 227
Sakurabana kwateô 桜花画帖　76, 95, 155, 228
Samekava seikan rok 鮫皮精鑑録　72, 93, 148
SANGOKU TSURAN ZUSETSU（San-kok tsu-ran dsu ki）三国通覧図記　55, 85, 122
SANJUROKKA SHU（Sanzjurok utano atsume）三十六歌集　68, 91, 143
Sankai meisan dsu e［Schān haì mĭngts'àn t'û hoeí］山海名産図会　71, 92, 147
SANKASHU RUIDAI（Jamakasju, rui tai）山家集類題　68, 91, 143
San-kok tsu-ran dsu ki　→SANGOKU TSURAN ZUSETSU
Sanrei Kukets［Sân lì k'eùkiuē］三礼口訣　69, 92, 144
San rjô si　→SANRYO SHI
SANRYO SHI（San rjô si）山陵志　49, 82, 112
SANSAI IKKAN ZU［Sân-ts'aí ī-kuân tû］三才一貫図　55, 85, 123
San-sui ki-kwan 山水奇観　54, 84, 120
San tai kwa bu 三体画譜　77, 95, 155
Santei zôbô seo zii［Sânting tsêngpù siaô tsèweì］冊

書名索引（Title Index）

定増補小字彙　62, 88, 133
Sân-ts'aí ï-kuán tû　→SANSAI IKKAN ZU
Sanzjurok utano atsume　→SANJUROKKA SHU
Sarugakno dsu 猿楽之図　78, 96, 158, 228
Sasairono tsjoku kojomide 笹色〔酒〕猪口暦手　67, 90, 140
Sasiki sasibanano atsumé　→CHASEKI SOKA SHU
Schân haí kîng　→SENGAIKYO
Schî-king　→SHIKYO
Schïwǔ pen-ts'aò　→SHOKUMOTSU HONZO
Sechsblätteriger Windschirm mit neuen Figuren aus der flotten Welt　→UKIYO SHINGATA ROKUMAI BYOBU (Ukijo sinkata rok mai bjôfu) 浮世新形六枚屏風
Sedan zavusets 世談雑説　66, 90, 139, 221
Sei do dsû〔Tschí tú t'ûng〕制度通　69, 92, 144, 222
Seijô sen bu　→SEIYO SEIPU
SEIKEI ZUSETSU (Nari katatsino dsu sets〔Tsch'îng hîng t'û schuĕ〕) 成形図説　71, 92, 147, 161, 197
Seiseidô Honzôkwai mokrok 生々堂　本草会目録　61, 88, 132
SEISHOKU ZENSHO (Seisjok zensjo) 生植〔檀〕全書　60, 87, 130
SEIYO SEIPU (Seijô sen bu〔Sijang ts'ïen p'ù〕) 西洋銭譜　73, 94, 151, 222
Sendai Kinko no ki 仙台　きんこの記　60, 87, 129
Sengaikjô〔Schân haì kîng〕山海経　67, 79, 90, 140, 159
SENJIMON OHON〔Tsïän dsŭ wên, tápèn〕千字文大本　64, 89, 136
Senkô bansi 千紅万紫　68, 91, 142
SEN PAN (Sen van〔Ts'ïên fán〕) 銭範　73, 93, 151, 222
Sen zi mon〔Tsïän dsŭ wên〕千字文　63, 89, 135
Seôfei nori　→KOTSUBO KIKU
Seôhon sitate fatsiben　→SHOHON JITATE HACHIHEN
Seôhon sitate sitsiben　→SHOHON JITATE SHICHIHEN
Seô zok dsu siki　→SHO ZOKU ZU SHIKI
SESSHU OSAKA CHIZU (Zo-siu kai-sei, Setsiu Ohosaka dsino dsu) 増修改正　摂州大坂地図　52, 84, 118
SESSHU OSAKA ZENZU (Bun-sei sin kai, Setsiu Ohosakano zen dsu) 文政新改　摂州大坂全図　52, 84, 118
Setsno kuni mei-sjo oho je dsu　→SETTSU NO KUNI MEISHO OEZU

Setsu-jô gun-tan 摂陽群談　48, 81, 111
Setsu mei-sjo dsu-e　→SETTSU MEISHO ZUE
SETTSU MEISHO ZUE (Setsu mei-sjo dsu-e) 摂津名所図会　48, 82, 111
SETTSU NO KUNI MEISHO OEZU (Setsno kuni mei-sjo oho je dsu) 摂津国名所大絵図　50, 82, 114
SHABEN YOROKU (Sjaben jorok) 楮鞭余録　58, 86, 126
SHASEI KEDAMONO ZUGA (Sjasei kedamono no dsu e〔Sièseng scheú t'ú hoá〕) 写生獣図画　76, 95, 154
SHASHIN NAGAKUJIRA ZU (Sjasin nagakuzirano dsu) 写真長鯨之図〔写真長鯨図〕　61, 88, 131
SHASHIN ZUISHU (Sjasin suisju) 写真随集　61, 88, 131
SHICHIFUKU SHICHINAN ZU E (Sitsi-fuk sitsi-nan dsu-e) 七福七難図会　66, 90, 139
SHIGI JUHACHIHIN SHINSHA (Sigi zjufatsibin sinsja) 鷸十八品真写　61, 88, 132, 226
SHIKYO (Schï-king) 詩経　57, 124, 125
SHIMOTSUKE NO KUNI NIKKOSAN NO ZU (Simôsa kunino Nikwôsanno dsu) 下総〔野〕国日光山之図　53, 84, 119
SHINGO SHU〔Ts'ïngjutsi〕清語集　64, 89, 137
SHIN HONZO KOMOKU (Sin Pèn ts'aô kang-mü) 新本草綱目　56, 124
SHINKOKU SHINSHO ZENSHU〔Sînk'ĕ Ts'îng schû ts'iuên tsï〕新刻清書全集　64, 89, 136
SHINKYU BASSUI TAISEI (Sinkiu fatsusui daisei〔Tsch'înkieù päts'uí tátsching〕) 鍼灸抜粋大成　74, 94, 151
SHINKYU KOKYO SHINGU SHU (Sinkiu kwôkeô singu sju〔Tsch'în kieù Kuang hiä schînkiù tsï〕) 鍼灸広狭神倶集　74, 94, 151
SHINKYU SETSUYAKU (Sinkiu setsjak〔Tsch'în kieù schuĕjô〕) 鍼灸説約　74, 94, 151, 169, 207, 222
SHINKYU ZUKAI (Sinkiu dsu kai〔Tsch'în kieù t'û kiai〕) 鍼灸図解　74, 94, 152
SHINSEN YAMATO KOTOBA (Sinsen Jamatokotoba) 新撰　大和詞　63, 89, 134
SHINSHU WARAN JISHO 新輯和蘭辞書〔蘭語訳撰〕　→Nieuw verzameld Japans en Hollandsch Woordenboek door den Vorst van het Landschap Nakats
SHINSOU JIBIKI TAISEI 改正倭玉　真艸字引大成　220
SHISHO (Sisjo〔Ssè schû〕) 四書　65, 90, 138, 221
SHISO GENKAI (Ziso genkai〔Sch'îts'ù jén kiai〕) 詩

書名索引 (Title Index)

礎諺解　69, 91, 144, 222
SHITAYA ASAKUSA HEN NO ZU (Sita-ja Asagusa katano dsu) 下谷浅草辺之図　52, 83, 117
SHITSUTAN MATA TAIMON (Sitvan mata tiwen) 悉曇摩多体文　64, 89, 136
SHOCHIN GAJO (Siutsin gwateo) 聚珍画帖　75, 94, 153
SHOCHU WAKAN NENKEI (Sjô-tsiu Wa-Kan nenkei) 掌中和漢年契　47, 81, 109, 220
SHO FU (Siáofu) 笑府　67, 90, 140, 221
SHOGUN NIJUGO MIEI (Sjôgun nizjugo mijei) 将軍二十五容貌　78, 96, 158
SHOHON JITATE HACHIHEN (Seôhon sitate fatsiben) 正本製八編　67, 90, 140
SHOHON JITATE SHICHIHEN (Seôhon sitate sitsiben) 正本製七編　67, 90, 140
SHOKUMOTSU HONZO〔Schīwŭ pen-ts'aò〕食物本草　57, 86, 125
SHOKUNIN TSUKUSHI HOKKU AWASE (Sjoknin tsukusi, fotsuku avase) 職人尽発句合　72, 93, 148
SHOKU SENGIN WAKASHU RUIDAI (Sjoksengin Wakasju rui tai) 続撰吟和歌集類題〔韻〕　68, 91, 142
SHOSHOKU GAKAN (Sjosjok kwakan) 諸職画鑑　75, 94, 153
SHOTETSUNO MONOGATARI (Sjôtetsno monogatari) 正徹物語　68, 91, 142, 222
SHO ZOKU ZU SHIKI (Seô zok dsu siki〔Tschoāng schŏ tû schī〕) 装束図式　70, 92, 145
SHUCHIN RYAKUIN TAISEI (Siutsinrjak in daisei〔Sieú tschîn liŏjún tá tsch'ìng〕) 袖珍略韻大成　69, 91, 144, 222
SHUGA ICHIRAN (Siugwa itsiran) 秀画一覧　77, 95, 156, 228
SHUGYOKU CHIE KAI (Sjugjok tsije kai〔Schījütschī hoeí hai〕) 拾玉智恵海　73, 93, 149
SHUN JU 春秋　56, 123
SHUYODO MONZOKAI MOKUROKU (Siujôdô Honzôkwai mokrok) 修養堂 本草会目録　61, 88, 132
Siáofu　→SHO FU
Siba, Atago sita katano dsu 芝愛宕〔岩〕下辺之図　52, 84, 117
Sifo tsukúru fô dsu　→ZOEN HOZU
Sigi zjufatsibin sinsja　→SHIGI JUHACHIHIN SHINSHA
Si-kok ben-reino dsu 四国徧礼之図　55, 85, 121
Simabaraki 島原記　47, 81, 110, 220

Simano kuni je dsu 志摩国絵図　50, 82, 114
Simôsa kunino Nikwôsanno dsu　→SHIMOTSUKE NO KUNI NIKKOSAN NO ZU
Sin ban, Nippon-kok oho je-dsu 新板日本国大絵図　49, 82, 113, 164, 201
Sin-ban zô-bô, Ohosakano dsu　→OSAKA NO ZU
Sin bô, Kjôno dsu　→KYO NO ZU
Sin fan, Fijei-san Jenraksi　→HIEI ZAN ENRYAKU-JI ZU
Sin fan, won Jedo mei-sjo fitori annai ki　→OEDO MEISHO HITORI ANNAI KI
Sink'ĕ Ts'ĭng schú ts'iuên tsī　→SHINKOKU SHINSHO ZENSHU
Sinkiu dsu kai　→SHINKYU ZUKAI
Sinkiu fatsusui daisei　→SHINKYU BASSUI TAISEI
Sinkiu kwôkeô singu sju　→SHINKYU KOKYO SHINGU SHU
Sinkiu setsjak　→SHINKYU SETSUYAKU
Sinkok Kinsi kwabu 新刻 金氏画譜　75, 94, 153
Sin Pèn ts'aô kang-mū　→SHIN HONZO KOMOKU
Sinsen Jamatokotoba　→SHINSEN YAMATO KOTOBA
Sinzi gjokben daisei〔Tschíntsè jūp'iên tátsch'ìng〕〔急用間合〕真字玉篇大成〈真字引玉篇大成〉　62, 88, 133, 221
Sin-zô sai-ken Kjô no je-dsu〔文化改正〕新増細見京絵図　51, 83, 116
Sinzô Zilin gjokben〔Sintsêng Tsèlin jūpiên〕新増字林玉篇　28, 33, 62, 88, 133, 221
Sisei zilin sjuin〔Sseschîng Tsèlin tsíjún〕四声字林集韻　62, 88, 133
Sisjo　→SHISHO
Sita-ja Asagusa katano dsu　→SHITAYA ASAKUSA HEN NO ZU
Si ten wô si Karanno dsu 四天王寺伽藍図　54, 85, 120
Sitsi-fuk sitsi-nan dsu-e　→SHICHIFUKU SHICHINAN ZU E
Sitvan mata tiwen　→SHITSUTAN MATA TAIMON
Siugjo sjuksja　→JUGYO SHUKUSHA
Siugwa itsiran　→SHUGA ICHIRAN
Siujôdô Honzôkwai mokrok　→SHUYODO MONZOKAI MOKUROKU
Siutsin gwateo　→SHOCHIN GAJO
Siutsinrjak in daisei　→SHUCHIN RYAKUIN TAISEI
Sjaben jorok　→SHABEN YOROKU
Sjakotsno sjasin　→JAKOTSU SHASHIN
Sjasei kedamono no dsu e　→SHASEI KEDAMONO

書名索引（Title Index）

ZUGA
Sjasei kwateô Sjo sin fasira date →SYASEI GACHO SHOSHIN HASHIRA DATE
Sjasin nagakuzirano dsu →SHASHIN NAGAKUJIRA ZU
Sjasin suisju →SHASHIN ZUISHU
Sjôgun nizjugo mijei →SHOGUN NIJUGO MIEI
Sjoknin tsukusi, fotsuku avase →SHOKUNIN TSUKUSHI HOKKU AWASE
Sjo kok tate-jokoki koto;gohori sirono kazu tsuku →SYOSHU KEII GUNJOSU TSUKI
Sjoksengin Wakasju rui tai →SHOKU SENGIN WAKASHU RUIDAI
Sjosjok kwakan →SHOSHOKU GAKAN
Sjôtetsno monogatari →SHOTETSUNO MONOGATARI
Sjô-tsiu Wa-Kan nen kei →SHOCHU WAKAN NENKEI
Sjugjok tsije kai →SHUGYOKU CHIE KAI
Sjuso teôfôki →JUSO CHOHO KI
SOKA CHISUJINO FUMOTO（Ikebana tsisuzino fumoto）挿花 千筋之麓　72, 93, 149
SOKA KOROMONO KA（Ikebana koromonoka）挿花衣之香　72, 93, 149
SOKA NO ZU 草華之図　97
SOKA SHIKI（Sôkwa siki）草花式　58, 86, 127
SOKANO ZU（Sô kwano dsu）草花之図　60, 87, 97, 130
SOKEN GAFU（So tsjun kwa bu）素絢画譜　76, 95, 154
Sôken kisjô［Tschoâng kién kî schàng］装剣奇賞　72, 93, 148
Sôkwa rjakgwa siki →KUSA BANA RYAKUGA SHIKI
Sô kwano dsu →SOKANO ZU
Sôkwa siki →SOKA SHIKI
Somemonono fô 染物の法　73, 93, 149, 169, 170, 191, 207, 227, 230
Sômok kibin kagami 草木奇品家雅見　59, 87, 128
Sômok seifu 草木性譜　58, 86, 126
SOSHI SEIZETSU［Súng schî tsïng tsiuē］宋詩清絶　69, 91, 143, 222
SOSHI SO（Sôzino fasira［Súng schî tsù］）宋詩礎　69, 91, 144, 222
Sô Siseki kwabu 宋紫石画譜　75, 94, 153
So tsjun kwa bu →SOKEN GAFU
Sôzino fasira →SOSHI SO
Sôzi ruiben →ZOJI RUIHEN
Sugavara tenzju tenaravi kagami 菅原伝授手習鑑　67, 91, 141, 222

SUKIYA HINAGATA（Sukija finagata）数寄屋雛形　71, 92, 146
Sumô seôsets, Kwats kongô den 角觝詳説活金剛伝　71, 92, 147
Súng schî tsïng tsiuē →SOSHI SEIZETSU
Suruga tai Wogawa matsino dsu 駿河台小川町之図　52, 83, 117, 164, 201
SYASEI GACHO SHOSHIN HASHIRA DATE（Sjasei kwateô Sjo sin fasira date）写生画帖 初心柱立〔絵本初心柱立〕　76, 95, 155, 222
SYOSHU KEII GUNJOSU TSUKI（Sjo kok tate-jokoki koto; gohori sirono kazu tsuku）諸国経緯郡城数附　49, 82, 112

【T】

TAIHEI KI（Dai-fei ki）太平記　47, 81, 109, 110, 220
TAIKAN SHORUI HONZO［Tà-kuon Tsching-lui pèn-ts'aò］大観証類本草　56, 86, 124, 167, 204
TAISEI HONZO MEISO（Daisai honzô meisu）泰西本草名疏　58, 86, 127
Taisen fu［Tuí tsiuên p'ù］対泉譜　73, 93, 150
TAIZEN HAYABIKI SETSUYO SHU（Daisen fajabiki setsjô sju）大全早引節用集　62, 88, 133
TAJIMA NO KUNI EZU（Tatsimano kuni jedsu）但馬国絵図　50, 83, 114
Tàjuĕ keûtschung tschù i scheù kiō t'û →UCHIKOSHI KOCHUSHUTSU IJU TSUNOHONE ZU
TAKADA KEIHO GAFU（Takeda Keibo kwabu）高田敬輔〔甫〕画譜〈敬輔画譜〉　75, 94, 153
Tà-kuon Tsching-lui pèn-ts'aò →TAIKAN SHORUI HONZO
Tana finagata 棚雛【形】　71, 92, 146
Tanbano kuni jedsu 丹波国絵図　50, 83, 114, 164, 201
Tangono kuni Amanobasi tateno dsu 丹後国天橋立之図　53, 84, 119
Tangono kuni jedsu 丹後国絵図　50, 83, 114
Tápanshō lits'úfên →DAI HANNYA RISHU BUN
Tápanshōpolomitoking →DAI HANNYA HARAMITA
Tatsibana binrui kô →KITSUHIN RUIKO
Tatsimano kuni jedsu →TAJIMA NO KUNI EZU
Tà-Ts'ing wan-nién it'ông ti-li tsïuên t'û →DAISHIN BANNEN ITTO CHIRI ZENZU
Teika sen kinjevu seô 定家撰錦葉鈔　66, 90, 139
Teito gakei itsiran 帝都雅景一覧　76, 95, 154
Tenguno tsumeisi satsukô 天狗爪石雑考　61, 88, 131, 169, 207
Teo binrui seoki →CHO HINRUI SHOKI

書名索引 (Title Index)

Teô nizju sjasin →CHO NIJU SHASHIN
Teôsiu rjak gwasiki →CHOJU RYAKUGA SHIKI
Titsinghianae ティツイング集　40, 103
(Tôdo) Nagada matsino jedsu →NAGATACHO NO EZU
Tôfû Wakok fjaknjo［Táng fûng Hôkuē pēniü］当風和国百女　69, 92, 144
Tô-ju ki →TOYU KI
Tôjûsi →TOYUSHI
Tôkaidô bun-ken jedsu 東海道分間絵図　54, 85, 121, 220
Tôkaidô gozjusan jeki 東海道五十三駅　79, 96, 159
Tô-kai dô mei-sjo itsi ran 東海道名所一覧　53, 84, 119
Tô-kai-dô mei-sjo dsu-e 東海道名所図会　48, 82, 111
Tô-kai-dô jeki ro-ri-sûno beô 東海道駅路里数之表　55, 85, 121
Tôkai, Kiso rjô-dô-tsiu kwai bô dsu kan 東海木曾両道中懐宝図鑑　54, 85, 121, 220
TOKAI SETSUYOU HYAKKA TSU (To-kwai setsjô fjak-ka tsû)〔新撰増益〕都会節用百家通　45, 81, 108, 220
Tô-tsiu ki →DOCHUKI
TORI TO MOGURA NO ZUFU 鳥とモグラの図譜　185, 230
TORIYAMA SEKIEN GA (Torijama Sekijen gwa) 鳥山石燕画〈鳥山石燕画譜〉　77, 96, 156, 228
Tôsei bizin gwateo 当世美人画帖　78, 96, 158
TOSEI GAKO CHOSHU 当世画工帖集　97
TOTO SHOKEI ICHIRAN (Jedo katsikei itsiran) 東都勝景一覧　78, 96, 158
TOYU KI (Tô-ju ki)〔諸国奇談〕東遊記　49, 82, 112, 225
TOYUSHI (Tôjûsi) 東牖〔牏〕子　66, 90, 140, 221
Tsch'ü tsieu →SHUN JU
Tsèlui / Tsèwei →JII
Tsiän dsü wên, tápèn →SENJIMON OHON
Tsijô itsigen →CHIYO ICHIGEN
Tsikubu sjôrok →CHIKUHU SHOROKU
Tsikusi ki-kô →TSUKUSHI KIKO
Tsĭngjutsī →SHINGO SHU
Tsinkwa kôfô kan →CHINKA KOHO KAN
Tsin sen kibin dsu rok →CHINSEN KIHIN ZUROKU
Tsiurui setsdsu →CHURUI SETSUZU
Tsiurui sjasju →CHURUI SHASHU
Tsjanojuno dsu →CHANO YUNO ZU
Tsja tsukûri nori →CHA SEIHO
Tsjôkon uta →CHOGON KA
Tsjôko sunadori →CHOKO HOGYO

Tsjôsei kwarin seô →CHOSEI KARIN SHO
Tsjôsen monogatari →CHOSEN MONOGATARI
Tsjozen zisjo →CHOSEN JISHO
Tsui kaino dsu →CHU KAINO ZU
TSUKIJI HATCHOBORI NIHONBASHI MINAMI NO ZU (Tsuku dsi, Batsjô fori, Nipponbasi minami no dsu) 築地八丁〔町〕堀日本橋南之図　52, 84, 117
TSUKUSHI KIKO (Tsikusi ki-kô) 筑紫紀行　48, 82, 112
Tsumesirusi 爪印　53, 119
Tsuredsure gusa つれづれ草　66, 90, 139, 221
TSUSHI KONCHU SOMOKU RYAKU［T'ûngtschi kuèntsch'ông ts'aòmū lió］通志昆虫草木略　57, 86, 125, 167, 182, 204, 230
Tsûsin kwabu 通神画譜　65, 89, 137

【U】

UCHIKOSHI KOCHUSHUTSU IJU TSUNOHONE ZU［Tàjuĕ keütschung tschū i scheù kiŏ t'ú］打越溝中出異獣角骨図　61, 88, 131
UKIYO SHINGATA ROKUMAI BYOBU (Ukijo sinkata rok mai bjôfu) 浮世新形六枚屏風 (Sechsblätteriger Windschirm mit neuen Figuren aus der flotten Wel)　67, 90, 140
UME SAKURANO RUIKA SHASHIN (Mume sakurano rui kwa sjasin) 梅桜類花写真　60, 87, 129, 225
Unkonsi 雲根志　58, 86, 127, 221

【V】

Verzeichniss der Chinesischen und Mandschuischen Bücher und Handschriften der Königl. Bibliothek zu Berlin (BERURIN ORITSU TOSHOKAN ZOU CHUGOKUGO・MANSHUGO NO SYOSEKI・SHUKOU MOKUROKU「ベルリン王立図書館蔵中国語・満州語の書籍・手稿目録」)　56, 62, 124, 132
vocabularia Japonica →NIHON GO JISHO

【W】

Wakan kokon kakwi dan 和漢古今角偉談　66, 90, 139, 221
Wa-Kan nen-kei［Hô-Hán nién-k'ï］和漢年契　46, 81, 109
Wa-Kan nen reki zen 和漢年歴箋　47, 81, 111
Wa Kan san sai dsu e［Hô Hún sûn ts'ai tú hoei］和漢三才図会　2, 4, 11, 12, 28, 33, 45, 81, 107, 161, 162, 174, 177, 197, 198, 212, 220, 230
Wa Kan sen wi 和漢泉彙　73, 93, 150

書名索引（Title Index）

Wa-Kan sets-jô mu-sô bukuro〔増字〕倭漢節用無双嚢 46, 81, 108, 220
Wa-Kan sjo kwa itsi ran〔増補〕和〔倭〕漢書画一覧 46, 81, 108
Wa Kan wonseki siogen zikô 和漢音釈書言字考節用集 11, 12, 28, 29, 33, 62, 88, 133, 221
WAKOKU HYAKUJO (Wakok fjaknjo) 和〔倭〕国百女 78, 96, 158
Wa Lan kotoba sjo →WARAN JISHO
Walan zenku naigwaibun no dsu →WARAN ZENKU NAIGAIBUN NO ZU
Wa nen kei 和年契 46, 109
Wângjeû tûntschischû Tsiän dsü wên →OYUTON KAISHO SENJIMON
Wàn-kuē tà tsʻiuén tû →BANKOKU DAIZENZU
Wa siu Josino jama mei-sjo dsu →WASHU YOSHINOYAMA MEISHO ZU
WARAN JISHO (Wa Lan kotoba sjo) 和蘭辞書 64, 89, 135
WARAN ZENKU NAIGAIBUN NO ZU (Walan zenku naigwaibun no dsu) 和蘭全軀内外分合図 74, 94, 151, 227, 228
Wase tsukuri nori 早稲作法 73, 93, 149, 169, 170, 191, 207, 227, 230
WASHU YOSHINOYAMA MEISHO ZU (Wa siu Josino jama mei-sjo dsu) 和州〔洲〕吉野山名勝図 53, 84, 119, 225
Wei kʻē schû mū →IKOKU SHOMOKU
Wokasa vara sjorei daizen →OGASAWARA SHOREI TAIZEN
Wôton kwabu →OSON GAFU
Wotsino siranami →OCHINO SHIRANAMI
Wô Tsjô ni siu no ki →BOCHO NISHU NO KI

【Y】

YAENO YAMABIKO (Javeno jamabiko) 八重山彦〔婦〕〈八重山吹〉 69, 91, 143
YAKUHIN OUSHU ROKU (Jabinwô siu rok) 薬品応手録 74, 94, 152
YAKUKEN (Jakken [ikiʻèn]) 訳鍵 64, 89, 135, 221
YAKUMEI SHOKO (Jak mei sjô ko [Jō ming tschʻing hu]) 薬名称呼 74, 94, 151
YAKU MON ZEN (Jeki mon zen) 訳文筌〈訳文筌蹄〉 62, 88, 134, 221
YAMASHIRO NO KUNI EZU (Jamasirono kuni je dsu) 山城国絵図 49, 82, 113
YAMATO HONZO SHINKOSEI (Jamato honzô sinkiôsei) 大和本草新校正 58, 86, 126, 167, 204

YAMATO KOTOBA (Jamatokotoba) やまと詞 63, 89, 134
YAMATO KOTOBA (Jamatokotoba) 大和詞 63, 89, 134
YAMATO MEISHO ZUE (Jamato mei-sjô dsu-e) 大和名所図会 48, 81, 111
YAMATO NENDAI KOKI ESHO (Jamato nen-dai kwô-ki kwai-sjô) 和年代皇紀絵章 47, 81, 109, 220
YAMATO NO KUNI EZU (Jamátono kuni je dsu) 大和国絵図 49, 82, 113
YAMATO NO KUNI SAIKEN EZU (Jamátono kuni sai-ken je dsu) 大和国細見絵図 49, 82, 113
YAMATO UTA REIYA SHU (Jamato uta Rinja sju) 和歌 怜野集 68, 91, 142
YAMAZAKURANO SETSU (Jamasakurano sets) 山桜説 60, 87, 130
YANAKA HONGO MARUYAMA KOISHIKAWA HEN NO ZU (Janaka Motomimarujama Woisigawa katanodsu) 谷中本郷丸山小石川辺之図 52, 83, 117
YODOGAWA RYOGAN SHOKEI ZUE (Jodogawa ryô-gan sjô-kei dsu-e) 澱川両岸 勝景図会 54, 84, 120
YOMEIRI DANGO BASHIRA (Jomeiri dankô basira [Kiáschī tʻan hŏ tschù])〔新板後篇〕嫁入談合柱〔桂〕 69, 92, 144
YOSHIHARA BIJIN MITATE GOJUSAN TSUGI (Josivara bizin midate gozjusan tsugi) 吉原美人見立五十三駅 78, 96, 158
YOSHIHARA KEISEI EDO BIJIN E (Josivara keisei Jedo bizin je) 吉原傾城江戸美人画 78, 96, 159
YUDOKU HONZO ZUSETSU (Judok honzô dsu-sets) 有毒本草図説 58, 86, 126

【Z】

ZATSUWA KYOKUN KAN (Zatwa, Keokun Kagami) 雑話 教訓鑑 66, 90, 139, 221
Ziso genkai →SHISO GENKAI
Zju kin tsiu sjasin →JU KIN CHU SHASHIN
Zô-bô je-ire Mijako mei-sjo kuruma →MIYAKO MEISHO GURUMA
ZOEN HOZU (Sifo tsukûru fô dsu) 造塩法図 73, 93, 150
ZOHO GORUI DAISETSUYOSHU〈増補合類大節用集〉→Wa Kan wonseki siogen zikô 和漢音釈書言字考節用集
ZOHO SHIBUN CHOHO KI (Zôbô Simon tsiubô ki) 増補詩文重宝記 62, 88, 133
ZOHO SHOSHU BUTSUZO ZUI (Zôbô sjosiu, Butszô

書名索引 (Title Index)

dsui) 増補諸宗　仏像図彙　12, 18, 19, 29, 31, 33, 65, 89, 137, 218, 221, 229

ZOJI RUIHEN (Sôzi ruiben) 雑字類編　63, 89, 134, 221

Zô-sin, Ohosaka si sjô dsu　→OSAKA SISHO ZU

Zo-siu kai-sei, Setsiu Ohosaka dsino dsu　→SESSHU OSAKA CHIZU

ZOZOKU DAI KOEKI GYOKUHEN (Zôsjok daikwôjeki Gjokben [Tsêng sū tá kuangī Jūpiên]) 増続大広益玉篇　62, 88, 132

ZUKAI BUYO BENRYAKU (Dsukai, Bujô benrjak [Tûkiaí, Wùjúng pién liŏ]) 図解武用弁略　71, 92, 146

人名索引（Personal name Index）

人名索引
Personal name Index

【A】

AIKAWA MINWA（Avigawa Minkwa）合川珉和 65, 89, 90, 137

Akamidsu →NAGAKUBO SEKISUI

AKATSUKI NO KANENARI（Keô sjô sei）暁鐘成 54, 84, 120, 148

Akimidsu Tsjareo 秋水茶寮 59, 86, 127

Akizato Ritô 秋里籬島 48, 50, 81, 82, 83, 111, 112, 115

Akizato Sjunfuk 秋里舜福 51, 115

ANTOKUTENNO（Mikadonis Antok interitus）安徳天皇 67, 141

Asaina Jûkavo 朝比奈夕顔 75, 94, 152

Asano Javei 浅野弥兵衛 50, 114

ASAO ENSHI 浅尾遠視 93

Asija Jamabito →TAKAYASU ROOKU

Avigawa Minkwa →AIKAWA MINWA

【B】

BABA SADAYOSHI（B. Sadajasi）馬〔場〕貞由 64, 135

BLOMHOFF, JOHANNEN COCK ヤン・コック・ブロムホフ 1, 2, 4, 21, 31, 32, 34, 41, 50, 51, 103, 115, 161, 166, 172, 197, 199, 200, 203, 210, 213, 214, 219, 220, 223, 224, 229

Bok kan sai Sjuzin 墨憨斎主人 67, 90, 140

Boksen 墨僊 76, 155

Buddha 仏陀 64, 136

Bunbô →KAWAMURA BUNPO

BUNCHODO 文徴堂〔吉田新兵衛〕 95

Buniu Sokei →MONNO SOKEI

Bunjano Sigetada →BUNYANO SHIGETAKA

Buntsjô →TANI BUNTYOU

BUNYANO SHIGETAKA（Bunjano Sigetada）文屋茂喬 69, 91, 143

Burger ビュルゲル 219, 223

Burôden Motonari 文楼田元成〔文桜、田元成、加保茶元成〕 73, 93, 150

【C】

CLEYER, ANDREAS アンドレアス・クライエル 39, 41, 101, 103

Coenraad Jacob Temminck C. J. テンミンク 6, 14, 177

Confucius 孔子 56, 63, 123, 135

【D】

Danaka Nobu →TAMIYA CHUSEN

DAZAI SHUNDAI 太宰純〔春台〕 90

DONDONTEI WATARU（Tontontei）鈍々亭〔和樽〕 69, 91, 143

DORA SANJIN（Tôra Sanzin）洞羅山人 66, 90, 140

Dosan →MANASE DOSAN

【E】

ENDLICHER, STEPHANO ステファン・エントリッヘル 41, 104

Étienne Fourmont E. フールモン 62, 132

【F】

Fajamidsu Sjungeôsai →HAYAMI SHUNGYOSAI

Fajasi Moriatsu →HAYASHI MORIATSU

Fajasi Sivei →HAYASHI SHIHEI

Fan ai dô no Sjuzin →HANAIDO SHUJIN

Fan Kwa an →HANKA AN

Farubok Itsuwo →OOKA SHUNBOKU

Fasegawa Mitsinobu →HASEGAWA MITSUNOBU

Fata Kasimaru →HATAKASHIMARU

Fatotani Firaki Sensei →HIRAGA GENNAI

Fatsne →HATSUNE

Firase Tetsusai →HIRASE TESSAI

Firazumi Senan →HIRAZUMI SENAN

Fisamatsu →HISAMATSU

Fisija Feisitsi →HISHIYA HEISHICHI

FISSCHER, VAN OVERMEER ファン・オーフェルメール・フィッセル 1, 2, 4, 21, 28-31, 33, 34, 41, 46, 56, 104, 109, 124, 161, 166, 197, 199, 200, 203, 208, 210, 213, 214, 219, 220, 223, 224, 229

Fizi gawa Moro nobu →HISHIKAWA MORONOBU

Fôgawa Zinujemon →YOSHIKAWA KOREKATA

Foken Tatsibana Jasukuni →TACHIBANA YASUKUNI

Fokiô Farugawa →OOKA SHUNSEN

Fokio Sjunbok →OOKA SHUNBOKU

Fôkiô Tsiuwa →NISHIMURA CHUWA

Fokjô Wôsan →HOKKYO OZAN

Forida Rensan →HOTTA RENZAN

Fori Seiken →HORII KEN

Fôsan →HOZAN

Fô-sjô no Udsi jasu →HOUJOU UJIYASU

Fôtei Jazin →HOTEI YAJIN

Fotsutari Seki →HOTTA RENZAN

人名索引（Personal name Index）

Fudsibajasi Daisuke →HUJIBAYASHI TAISUKE
Fudsivara Kunifasira →SHIRAO KUNIHASHIRA
FUJITANI MITSUE（Fudsi tani Mitsuje）富士谷御杖 68, 143
FUJIWARANO TEIKA（Teika）〔藤原〕定家 66, 139
FUJIWARANO UMAKI（Fudsivara no Umaki）藤原宇万伎 63, 134
FUJIWARA YASUCHIKA 藤原泰周 93
FUKAE SUKEHITO（Fukaje Fozin）深江輔仁 58, 86, 126
Fukuzawa Yukichi 福沢諭吉 10, 26, 32
Futsi Zai kwan →HUCHI ZAIKAN

【G】

GAMO HIDEZANE 蒲生秀實 82
Gen →MINAMOTO
GENJO SANZO〔Hiuên tsàng fùng〕玄奘三蔵〔三蔵法師、玄奘老人〕64, 65, 90, 136, 138
Genrjusai Taito →KATSUSHIKA TAITO
Genseô Rôzin →GENJO SANZO
GENSHO 源昭 89
GENSHOUTENNOU（imperatori Gensio）元正天皇 46, 109
Gensiu siwô →NAGAKUBO SEKISUI
Gensju →NAGAKUBO SEKISUI
GEN SO〔Jang Kueifei〕玄宗 67, 141
Gjokkô →HUCHIGAMI KYOKKOU
GODAIGOTENNO（Mikado Godaiko）後醍醐天皇 69, 144
GO SOSEN（Zisôzen）児素仙 58, 86, 127

【H】

HANAIDO SHUJIN（Fan ai dô no Sjuzin）汎愛堂主人 63, 89, 134
HANAWA HOKIICHI（Kenkjô Fomiitsi）検校〔塙〕保己一 70, 92, 145
HANKA AN（Fan Kwa an）伴花菴 68, 91, 143
HASEGAWA MITSUNOBU（Fasegawa Mitsinobu）長谷川光信 77, 96, 157
HATAKASHIMARU（Fata Kasimaru）秦檜丸 53, 84, 119
HATSUNE（Fatsne）初音 67, 141
HAYAMI SHUNGYOSAI（Fajamidsu Sjungeôsai）速水春暁斎 65, 89, 93, 137
HAYASHI MORIATSU（Fajasi Moriatsu）林守篤 74, 94, 152
HAYASHI RAZAN 林羅山〔道春〕65, 90, 138, 166, 204
HAYASHI SHIHEI（Fajasi Sivei）林子平 55, 85, 122
HAYASHI SHUNSAI（Sjunzai Rinsjo）春斎林恕〔林春斎〕46, 81, 109
HEIREIAN（Kadsura Reian）薛荔菴 60, 87, 130
Hendrick Doeff H. ドゥフ 163, 199
Hîhân 毘舍 57, 125
HIRAGA GENNAI（Fatotani Firaki Sensei）鳩溪平賀先生〔平賀源内〕58, 86, 126, 167, 204
HIRASE TESSAI（Firase Tetsusai）平瀬徹斎 71, 147
HIRATA ATSUTANE（Tairano Atsutane）平〔田〕篤胤 46, 81, 109
HIRAZUMI SENAN（Firazumi Senan）平住専庵 45, 57, 81, 107, 125
HISAMATSU（Fisamatsu）久松 67, 140
HISHIKAWA MORONOBU（Fizi gawa Moro nobu）菱川師宣 69, 92, 96, 144
HISHIYA HEISHICHI（Fisija Feisitsi）菱屋平七 48, 82, 112
Hiuên tsàng fùng →GENJO SANZO
Hiuên tsûng →YOKIHI
H.Kerlen H. ケルレン 172, 173, 210, 211, 224
HOFFMANN, J. ヨハン・ホフマン 2, 4, 5, 8-11, 15, 17, 18, 21, 25-28, 32, 37, 42, 101, 104, 161, 162, 171, 177, 180, 182, 183, 191, 192, 194, 197-199, 207, 209-212, 214-218, 220, 223, 229
Hokkei Sensei →TOTOYA HOKKEI
HOKKYO OZAN（Fokjô Wôsan）法橋王山〔岡田玉山〕69, 92, 144
Hoksai →KATSUSHIKA HOKUSAI
Hokun →KATSUSHIKA HOKUUN
HORII KEN（Fori Seiken）堀井軒 72, 148
HOTEI YAJIN（Fôtei Jazin）芳亭野人 59, 87, 128
HOTTA RENZAN（Forida Rensan）堀田連山〔堀田里席〕77, 78, 96, 157
HOUJOU UJIYASU（Fô-sjô no Udsi jasu）北条氏康 52, 117
HOZAN（Fôsan）絳〔縫〕山〔小枝繁〕78, 96, 157
HUCHI ZAIKAN（Futsi Zai kwan）淵在寛〔淵在寬〕57, 86, 125
HUCHIGAMI KYOKKOU（Gjokkô）〔淵上〕旭江 54, 84, 120
HUJIBAYASHI TAISUKE（Fudsibajasi Daisuke）藤林泰助 64, 135
Hūng tsé Tsch'ing 洪自誠 65, 90, 138
Hû Schángli 湖上李〔李漁〕66, 90, 140

【I】

ICHIOKA TAKEHIKO（Itsioka Takefiko）市岡孟彦

人名索引 (Personal name Index)

63, 89, 134
Ikeda Josijuki Tôzô 池田義之冬蔵　74, 94, 151
Ikeda Tourisai 池田東籬斎〔池田東籬亭〕66, 138
imperatori Gensio →GENSHOUTENNOU
imperatoris Mongolici Kublaikhan →KUBIRAI
imperatoris Tenmu →TENMUTENNO
imperatrice Zingu →JINGUKOUGOU
IMURA KATSUYOSHI (Wimura Katsukits) 井村勝吉　76, 95, 154
Inaba Mitsidatsu Sinjemon 稲葉通龍新右衛門　72, 93, 148
INOUE CHOKU (Winouve Okina) 井上翁〔井上直、井上老先生〕71, 92, 146
IRIE GYOKUSEN (Irije Kjoksen) 入江玉蟾　72, 93, 149
Ishii Souken 石井宗謙　169, 207
Isisaka Sôtets (Kan sei Sen sei) 石坂宗哲〔竿斎先生〕74, 94, 151, 152, 169, 175, 207, 213
Itô Ifei 伊藤伊兵衛　59, 86, 87, 127, 128, 167
Itô Keiske 伊藤圭介〔舜民〕58, 60, 61, 86, 87, 88, 127, 129, 132, 168, 205
Itô Tsjôin 伊藤長胤　69, 91, 144
Itsioka Takefiko →ICHIOKA TAKEHIKO
Itsi sai Satô →SAITOU ISSAI
Itsufon Dajemon →NIHON ZAEMON
IWAKI HYOGONO KAMI HIDEKATSU (Iwagi Fiogono Kami Fidekatsu) 岩城兵庫守秀勝　66, 139
Iwasaki Tsunemasa (Iwasaki Tokiva) 岩崎常正　50, 59, 72, 82, 87, 92, 114, 128, 147
IWASE SEISAI〔岩瀬〕醒斎〔山東京伝〕92

【J】

Jamagutsi So tsiun →YAMAGUCHI SOKEN
Jamanaka Tsiu Sajemon →YAMAGUCHI CHU ZAEMON
Jamasaki Ujemon →YAMASAKI UEMON
Jamasita Sekitsiu →YAMASHITA SEKICHU
Jamasita Sigemasa →YAMASHITA SHIGEMASA
Jang Kueifei →GEN SO
Jano Sadatosi →YANO SADATOSHI
Jaô K'ò tsching 姚可成　57, 86, 125
Jasida Kitsifei →YASUDA KICHIHEI
J.H. Donker Curtius D. クルチウス　10, 26, 27, 32
JIKUJO (Tsikuzjô) 竺常〔大典顕常〕63, 134
JINGUKOUGOU (imperatrice Zingu) 神功皇后　47, 109
Jônan Densiu →SHIMADA MITSUFUSA
Jorigiri Sanzin →KYOGO SANJIN
Joritomo →MINAMOTONO YORITOMO

JORURI HIME (Zjôruri fime) 淨瑠璃姫　77, 156
Ju 禹　79, 159
Jukinaga →SHINANO NO ZENJI YUKINAGA
JULIEN, STANISLASIO スタニスラス・ジュリアン　41, 104

【K】

Kadsura Reian →HEIREIAN
Kadsuragawa →KATSURAGAWA
Kadsuragawa Fosan →KATSURAGAWA HOSAN
Kadsuragawa Hoken →KATSURAGAWA HOKEN
KAEMPFER, ANGELBERTUS エンゲルベルト・ケンペル　39, 41, 101, 103, 217
KAGAMI SHIKO (Tôkwa Sekkei) 東華切稽〔東華坊、各務支考〕63, 89, 134
KAHO SANJIN (Kwafô Sonzin) 華鳳山人　69, 92, 144
KAIBARA ATSUNOBU (Kaibara Toksin) 貝原篤信　51, 53, 58, 69, 70, 72, 83, 86, 92, 93, 115, 119, 126, 144, 145, 148, 167, 204
Kajaaki Njotei →KASHIWAGI JOTEI
KAMATA KANSAI (Kamada Teisan) 鎌田禎斎〔環斎〕62, 88, 133
KAMIYA HIROYOSHI (Kaija Filojosi) 神谷弘孝　64, 135
KANDENSHI KOKEI (Kanten Si kôkei) 閑田子蒿蹊〔伴蒿蹊〕72, 93, 148
K'ang hi 康熙　71, 147
Kan jo sai →KENRYOTAI
KANO TANYU (Taniu)〔狩野〕探幽　75, 153
Kan sei Sen sei →ISIZAKA SOTETSU
Kanten Si kôkei →KANDENSHI KOKEI
KASHIWAGI JOTEI (Kajaaki Njotei) 柏木如亭〔柏昶如亭〕69, 91, 143
KATORI NABIKO〔楫〕取魚彦　88
KATSURAGAWA (Kadsuragawa) 桂川　60, 61, 87, 88, 130
KATSURAGAWA HOKEN (Kadsuragawa Hoken) 桂川甫賢　60, 74, 87, 94, 129, 151, 163, 168, 169, 174, 176, 184, 185, 200, 206, 208, 212, 218, 230
KATSURAGAWA HOSAN (Kadsuragawa Fosan) 桂川甫三　64, 136
KATSUSHIKA HOKUSAI (Hoksai) 葛飾北斎　12, 15, 16, 23, 29, 30, 32, 53, 76-78, 84, 95, 96, 119, 155, 156, 158, 215
KATSUSHIKA HOKUUN (Hokun)〔葛飾〕北雲　77, 156
KATSUSHIKA TAITO (Genrjusai Taito)〔葛飾〕玄龍斎戴斗　77, 95, 156
Kavamura Bunbô →KAWAMURA BUNPO

253

人名索引 (Personal name Index)

Kavaseki Wizju →KAWAZEKI KOREMITSU
Kawahara Keiga 川原慶賀 7, 12, 14, 16, 23, 29, 33, 168, 169, 175, 206, 212, 215, 216, 219
KAWAMURA BUNPO (Kavamura Bunbô) 河村文鳳〔河邑文鳳〕 76, 95, 154, 155
Kawatsi ja Gisuke 河内屋儀助 50, 114
KAWAZEKI KOREMITSU (Kavaseki Wizju) 川関惟充 66, 90, 139
Kazawori Masaka 風折政香 51, 83, 116
Kei an Kimura Sjuntok 桂菴木村俊篤 59, 87, 128
Keisai Kitawo Masajosi (Kunsai Seôsin) 蕙斎北尾政美〔蕙斎紹真〕 53, 75, 76, 84, 94, 95, 119, 153-155
Kenkjô Fomiitsi →HANAWA HOKIICHI
KENRYOTAI (Kenrjô tai/Kan jo sai) 建凌岱〔孟喬、寒葉斎、建部綾足〕 74, 75, 94, 95, 152, 154
Kensi 建氏 75, 154
Keô sjô sei →AKATSUKI NO KANENARI
Kijobarano Ogaze →KIYOHARANO OKAZE
Kijovara Tsiukjo →KIYOHARA SHIGEO
KIKKYU GASANJIN (Kikkiu Kwasanzin/Kikuoka Kwasanziu) 菊丘臥山人 65, 66, 90, 138, 139
KIKURAKU TEI 菊楽亭 91
Kimura Kôkjô 木村孔恭 71, 147
KIMURA MUNEZANE (Kivara Sôtei) 木原宗真 74, 94, 151
Kimura Rijemon 木村理右衛門 55, 122
Kimura Siutok 木村周篤 72, 149
KINEYA UHEI (Kinuja Uvei) 杵屋右兵衛 77, 156
Kinda →UEKIYA KINTA
Kino Fidenobu 紀秀信 65, 89, 137
Kino Josinobu 紀信吉 77, 157
Kinosita Jositomo 木下義俊 71, 92, 146
KINOUCHI SHIGEAKI (Kiutsi Tsiukjô/Kinoudsi Seôban) 木内重暁〔小繁〕 58, 61, 86, 88, 127, 131, 169
Kinsi 金氏 75, 153
KINUGAWA TAIJIN (Koromogava Dainin) 衣川大人 68, 91, 142
Kinuja Uvei →KINEYA UHEI
Kitagawa Sjunsei 北川春成 65, 89, 137
Kitagawa Utamaro 喜多川歌麿 76, 95, 154
KITAO SHIGEMASA (Kitawo Sigemasa/Kôsuigen Sigemasa) 北尾重政〔紅翠軒〕 76, 77, 95, 96, 155, 157
Kiutsi Tsiukjô →KINOUCHI SHIGEAKI
Kivara Sôtei →KIMURA MUNEZANE
KIYOHARANO OKAZE (Kijobarano Ogaze) 清原雄風 68, 91, 142
KIYOHARA SHIGEO (Kijovara Tsiukjo) 清原重巨 58, 86, 126
Kjoktei Makin →KYOKUTEI BAKIN
Kjufou Keiden →YORITA KYUHO
Klaproth, J. クラプロート 41, 56, 62, 103, 124, 132
KO ANKOKU 孔安国 90
Kobajasi Tsjôsiu 小林長周 54, 84, 120
Kobô daisi →KUKAI
Kógen Keian →MINAMOTO YOSHIYASU
Kô Genriu 高玄竜 59, 87, 129
KOJIMA JOSUI (Kosima Zjo sui) 児島如水 71, 92, 147
KOJURO SEIAN (Kozju Rôseian) 壺十楼成安 78, 96, 158
Kôkai →KUKAI
Komatani Sanzin →MAKISHIMA AKITAKE
KONDO JUZO (Kontô Ziudsiû) 近藤重蔵〔守重〕 73, 93, 150
Kô Rjô sai →KO RYOSAI
Koromogava Dainin →KINUGAWA TAIJIN
KO RYOSAI (Kô Rjô sai) 高良斎 74, 94, 152, 169, 206, 207, 218
Koseno Kanaoka 巨勢金岡 66, 139
Kosima Zjo sui →KOJIMA JOSUI
Kôsuigen Sigemasa →KITAO SHIGEMASA
Kotendono sjunin 壺天堂主人 59, 86, 127
KO TSCHING DSCHANG 郭成章〔乾草堂主人〕 5, 9-12, 17, 21, 25, 27-29, 31, 33, 42, 104, 162, 199, 220, 224, 229
Kozju Rôseian →KOJURO SEIAN
KUBIRAI (imperatoris Mongolici Kublaikhan) 忽必烈汗 47, 109
KUKAI (Kôkai/Kobô daisi) 空海〔弘法大師〕 63, 134
Kunsai Seôsin →KEISAI TSUGUZANE
Kunseô sai 薫松斎〔薫杉軒、石川大浪〕 75, 94, 153
Kunzan Kiukei →MIYAMOTO KUNZAN
Kuōpō・Kuōp'o 郭璞 67, 79, 90, 140, 159
Kurida Toman →KURITA HIJIMARO
Kurimoto Suiken 栗本瑞見 60, 61, 87, 88, 130, 168, 169, 184, 190, 205, 206, 212
KURITA HIJIMARO (Kurida Toman) 栗田土満 46, 81, 108
Kuroda Narikiyo 黒田斉清 168, 206
Kú sieû lo 顧修郎〔顧修〕 46, 108
KUTSUKI MASATSUNA 朽木昌綱 151
Kwafô Sonzin →KAHO SANJIN
Kwakiuken Sjuzin →NAKANISHI TAKAFUSA
Kwakki Sensei →SAITOU KAKKI

人名索引（Personal name Index）

Kwangjok siunin 観嶽主人　47, 81, 110
Kwansai Kamada　→KAMATA KANSAI
Kwok Pui-lan 郭佩蘭　48, 57, 81, 86, 111, 124
Kwôrin　→OGATA KORIN
KYOGO SANJIN（Jorigiri Sanzin）據梧散人　62, 88, 133
KYOKUTEI BAKIN（Kjoktei Makin）曲亭馬琴　77, 96, 157

【L】

LANGLESII ラングレス　40, 102
Lindor Serrurier L. セルリエ　18, 20, 171-173, 177-194, 196, 209-212, 214, 220, 230
Li Schi tsching 李時珍　56, 86, 124, 166, 203
Lù-fù Ngân schí 呂撫安世　55, 85, 123
Lui kung pao 雷公炮　58, 86, 126
Lŭ ki 陸璣　57, 86, 124, 125
Lŭ schî 陸氏　57, 125

【M】

MAKISHIMA TERUTAKE（Makinosima Terutake/Komatani Sanzin）槙島昭武〔駒谷散人〕　11, 62, 88, 133
Malte-Brunii マルテ・ブルン　40, 103
Mamiya Rinzou（Mamija Rinzô）間宮林蔵　55, 85, 122, 171, 181, 194, 195, 209, 212, 230
MANASE DOSAN（Dosan）〔曲直瀬〕道三　58, 126
MANO TOKEI（Tokei Sensei）〔真野〕桃渓先生　75, 94, 153
MARUYAMA OUJU（Wôsiu）〔円山〕応受　54, 85, 120
MASUDA KO（Masida kô）増田綱　72, 93, 148
MATSUMIYA KANZAN（Sugano Jôfo）松宮観山〔菅縄、藤仍縄〕　55, 85, 122
Matsuoka Dsiôun（Matsuoka Tsiuan/Matsuoka Gendats [Dsiôan]）〔怡顔斎〕松岡恕庵〔玄達、成章〕　57, 59, 61, 86-88, 125, 127-129, 131
Matsusita Kenrin 松下見林　57, 124
Meiïngtsû 梅膺祚　62, 88, 132
Midsutani Fôfun　→MIZUTANI SUKEROKU
Midsutani Sukerok　→MIZUTANI SUKEROKU
Mijasaki Antei　→MIYAZAKI YASUSADA
Mikado Godaiko　→GODAIGOTENNO
Mikadonis Antok interitus　→ANTOKUTENNO
Mima Junzou 美馬順三　169, 206, 207
Minamato Jositsune 源義経　77, 156
MINAMOTO（Gen）源（[Minamoto]）　77, 157
MINAMOTO YOSHIYASU（Kógen Keian）江源慶安〔源慶安〕　65, 89, 137

Minamoto Joritomo 源頼朝　66, 77, 139, 157
Minamoto Masataka　→OKUDAIRA MASATAKA
Mi Nan kung 米南宮〔米芾〕　63, 135
MINEGISHI RYUFU（Minokisi Rjôfo）峰岸龍父　59, 86, 127
MIYAMOTO KUNZAN（Kunzan Kiukei）〔宮本〕君山宮瓊　74, 94, 152
MIYAZAKI YASUSADA（Mijasaki Antei）宮崎安貞　71, 92, 147
MIZUTANI SUKEROKU（Midsutani Sukerok/Fôfun）水谷助六〔豊文〕　58, 60, 61, 86-88, 126, 129, 130, 132, 167-169, 172, 184, 186, 187, 205, 206, 210, 212
Mogami Sansi 最上山子〔片山兼山〕　63, 89, 135
Mogami Toknai（Siranizi sai）最上徳内〔白虹斎〕　55, 56, 60, 64, 65, 71, 72, 85, 89, 90, 92, 122, 123, 130, 136, 138, 146, 148, 162-164, 166, 170, 171, 173, 176, 178, 184, 192, 194, 195, 198, 200, 203, 207-209, 211, 214, 218, 219
MONNO SOKEI（Buniu Sokei）文雄僧谿　63, 89, 135
Morisima Tsiurô 森島中良　55, 85, 122
Mori Sjunkei 森春渓　59, 86, 87, 127
Mori Teisai 毛利貞斎　62, 88, 133
Motoki si i 本木子意〔本木了意〕　74, 94, 151
MOTOORI NORINAGA（Motowi Noritake/Motoworino Norinaga）本居宣長　46, 68, 81, 91, 109, 142
MUCHI KONSAI（Mutsi Konsai）鞭近斎　61, 88, 131
Murase Kaibo 村瀬海輔　69, 91, 144

【N】

NAGAKUBO SEKISUI（Gensiu siwô/Akamidsu/Sekisui Sensei）長久保赤水〔玄珠子王、赤水先生、赤水長、長赤水、長玄珠子王〕　48, 49, 56, 82, 85, 112, 113, 123, 180
NAGANO HOZAN（Tojojama Nagano Sensei）長野豊山〔豊山長野先生〕　66, 90, 140
Nakadsi Undsiku 中路雲軸〔岫〕　75, 94, 153
NAKAE TOJU（Ohoje Fensen）大江頤軒〔中江藤樹〕　58, 86, 126
Nakagawa Aritsūne 中川有恒　72, 93, 148
Nakamura Kan zi sai 中村敢耳斎　49, 82, 113
NAKANISHI TAKAFUSA（Kwakiuken Sjuzin）華文軒風子主人〔中西敬房〕　59, 81, 128
Nakatani Kôsan 中谷顧山　73, 93, 150
Nanfei 南兵〔渡辺南岳〕　76, 155
Nanki Njosui 南紀如水〔梶取屋次右衛門〕　59, 87, 129

255

人名索引（Personal name Index）

NANRITEI KIRAKU 南里亭其楽　96
NAOMI GENSHU (Tsiok Kairiu) 直海龍〔直海元周〕　58, 86, 126
NEPVEU ネーブブー　40, 102
NIHON ZAEMON (Itsufon Dajemon) 日本左衛門　66, 139
Ninomija Komaki 二宮熊木　54, 84, 120
NISHIMURA CHUWA (Fôkiô Tsiuwa)〔西村〕法橋中和　48, 111
Nisikame son　→SON HIKEN
Nisikowori Matsubuts　→SAIRIKYO MIBUTSU
Nitschü mu 倪朱謨　57, 86, 125
Niva Tokei (Tanba-no Tôkei) 丹羽桃渓　48, 49, 81, 82, 111, 113
NOTANSAI (Tsjô Tansai) 濃淡斎　59, 86, 127

【O】

OEDA RYUHO (Ohojeda Riûfô) 大枝流芳　70, 92, 145
OGASAWARA (Wokasawara) 小笠原
OGASAWARA SADATAKA (Sadamune Kiutaka) 貞宗弓高〔小笠原貞宗〕　69, 144
OGATA KORIN (Kwôrin)〔尾形〕光琳　76, 155
OGAWA KYUHO (Okava Kiufo) 雄川丘甫　72, 148
OGYU SORAI (Sorai Sensei)〔荻生〕徂徠先生　62, 134
Ohodsuki Gendak　→OTSUKI GENTAKU
Ohojeda Riûfô　→OEDA RYUHO
Ohoje Fensen　→NAKAE TOJU
Ohokôtsi Sonsin　→OKOCHI ZONSHIN
Ohokubo Dafeije　→OKUBO TAHEI
Ohokubo gjô　→OKUBO SHIBUTSU
Ohokubo Sjôsanrô　→OKUBO JOSABURO
Ohokura Nagatsune　→OKURA NAGATSUNE
OMURA SHIGETOMI　→OMURA SHIGETOMI
Ohooka Mitsinobu　→OOKA MICHINOBU
Ohu Ason Amaro　→ONO YASUMARO
Okada Roksuke 岡田陸助　48, 81, 111
Okada Tôseki 岡田東虎　66, 90, 139
Oka Genfô　→OKA TANSAI
Okamoto Itsufôsi 岡本一抱子　74, 94, 151
OKA TANSAI (Oka Genfô) 岡元鳳〔岡澹斎〕　57, 86, 125
Okava Kiufo　→OGAWA KYUHO
OKOCHI ZONSHIN (Ohokôtsi Sonsin) 大河内存真　60, 61, 88, 130, 132, 168, 169, 205-207
OKUBO JOSABURO (Ohokubo Sjôsanrô) 大窪舒三郎〔昌章〕　61, 87, 130, 168, 169, 184, 188, 189, 206, 212

OKUBO SHIBUTSU (Ohokubo gjô) 大窪行〔詩仏〕　69, 91, 144
OKUBO TAHEI (Ohokubo Dafeije) 大窪太兵衛　60, 87, 130, 189
OKUDAIRA MASATAKA (Minamoto Masataka) 源〔奥平〕昌高　64, 135
OKURA NAGATSUNE (Ohokura Nagatsune) 大蔵永常　71, 92, 147
OMURA SHIGETOMI (Ohomura Naritomi) 大村成富　73, 93, 150
ONO RANZAN (Wono Lanzan) 小野蘭山〔蘭山小野、職博〕　57, 58, 72, 86, 125, 126, 148, 151, 167, 169, 175, 182, 204, 207, 218
ONO TSUNENORI (Tsunenori/Sjok kô) 小野職孝〔蕙畝〕　57, 58, 74, 86, 92, 94, 126, 151
ONO YASUMARO (Ohu Ason Amaro) 太朝臣安万侶　46, 109
ONOUE OHATSU (Wonoë Ofats) 尾上おはつ　66, 139
OOKA MICHINOBU (Ohooka Mitsinobu) 大岡道信　75, 94, 153
OOKA SHUNBOKU (Fokio Sjunbok/Farubok Itsuwo) 法橋春ト〔大岡春ト、春ト一翁〕　75, 76, 94, 95, 153, 155
OOKA SHUNSEN (Fokiô Farugawa) 法橋〔大岡〕春川　58, 86, 127
Osome おそめ　67, 140
OSON (Wôton) 鶯邨〔酒井抱一〕　76, 155
Otoba 音羽　67, 140
OTOMONO YAKAMOCHI (Udaiven Jakamotsi) 右大弁〔大伴〕家持　68, 142
OTSUKI GENTAKU (Ohodsuki Gendak) 大槻玄沢〔茂質〕　59, 60, 87, 128, 129
OZAWA TOICHI (Wozawa Tôitsi) 小沢東市〔小沢辰元〕　73, 93, 94, 150, 151

【R】

Remusat, Abel アベル・レミューザ　45, 107
RHEEDE, JOHANNEN FREDERICUM VAN ヨハン・フレデリック・ファン・レーデ　40, 103
RIKO (Tungjen Likaò) 東垣李杲〔李杲、李東垣〕　57, 86, 125
Riu Kosai　→RYUKOSAI
Riuseki Anu　→RYUSEKI AN
Riutei Tanefiko　→RYUTEI TANEHIKO
ROKUJU EN 六樹園〔石川雅望〕　91
Rôkwa teino Sjuzin　→UDAGAWA YOAN
RYUKOSAI (Riu Kosai) 立好斎〔如圭〕　77, 95, 156
RYUSEKI AN (Riuseki Anu) 流石庵〔河村羽積〕

人名索引（Personal name Index）

73, 93, 150
RYUTEI TANEHIKO（Riutei Tanefiko）柳亭種彦 67, 90, 140, 214

【S】

Sadamune Kiutaka →OGASAWARA SADATAKA
SAIGYO SHONIN（Saigjô sjônin）西行上人 68, 91, 143
SAIRIKYO MIBUTSU（Nisikowori Matsubuts）西來居未仏 78, 96, 158
Saito Sin sajemon 斎藤甚左衛門 50, 114
SAITOU ISSAI（Itsi sai Satô）一斎佐藤〔佐藤一斎〕 47, 81, 110
SAITOU KAKKI（Kwakki Sensei）〔斉藤〕鶴磯先生 48, 82, 111
Sakawi Liusei 酒井立生 61, 88, 131
SAKURAI SESSEN 櫻井雪鮮 92
Satomatsu sai Itsiba →TEISHO SAI ICHIBA
Schi Hoang ti →SHI KOTEI
Schi tsung →SEISO
Seisei Suima 生々瑞馬 66, 90, 139
SEISO（Schi tsung）世宗 71, 147
Seki sui Sensei →NAGAKUBO SEKISUI
SEKKEI（Setskei）雪渓〔宋紫石〕 75, 153
Seô buts 生仏 47, 110
Seôzjurô Sjuzin →SHOJURO SHUJIN
Setskei →SEKKEI
SHAKU RYOTEI（Sjak Reôtei）釈了貞 65, 89, 137
SHI KOTEI〔Schi Hoang ti〕始皇帝 79, 159
SHIMADA MITSUFUSA（Jônan Densiu）雍南田充〔島田光房〕 58, 86, 126
SHINANO NO ZENJI YUKINAGA（Jukinaga）〔信濃前司〕行長 47, 110
SHIN NYO HO SHINNO（Sin mjô kô sinwô）真如法親王 63, 134
SHIRAO KUNIHASHIRA（Fudsivara Kunifasira）藤原〔白尾〕国柱 71, 92, 147
SHOJURO SHUJIN（Seôzjurô Sjuzin）松寿楼主人 71, 92, 147
SHOKUSANJIN（Sjoksan Sensei）蜀山先生〔蜀山人〕 68, 91, 142
SHOTETSU（Sjôtets）正徹 68, 142
SHOTOKU TAISHI（Sjôtok Daisi）聖徳太子 78, 158
SIEBOLD, PH. FR. DE フィリップ・フランツ・フォン・シーボルト 1-16, 18, 20-34, 37, 42, 74, 101, 104, 152, 161-177, 179, 180, 182-191, 193, 195-220, 223, 224, 229, 230
Simajosi Ankô →TERASHIMA RYOUAN

Simidsu Kanzi 志水閑事 58, 86, 127
Sin Kôsei 信更生 62, 88, 133
Sin mjô kô sinwô →SHIN NYO HO SHINNO
Siranizi sai →MOGAMI TOKUNAI
Sivoja Kisuke 塩屋義助 48, 111
Sjak Reôtei →SHAKU RYOTEI
Sjok kô →ONO RANZAN
Sjoksan Sensei →SHOKUSANJIN
Sjôtets →SHOTETSU
Sjôtok Daisi →SHOTOKU TAISHI
SHUNSAI RINJO →HAYASHI SHUNSAI
SLOANE, JOHANNIS ハンス・スローン 39, 101
Soksai Tôzin 息斎道人〔息斎李〕 75, 95, 154
SON HIKEN（Nisikame son）西甌孫〔孫丕顕〕 63, 89, 135
Sorai Sensei →OGYU SORAI
Sugano Jôfo →MATSUMIYA KANZAN
SUGAWARANO MICHIZANE（Sugavara）菅原〔道真〕 67, 141
SUGITA GENPAKU（Sugida）杉田〔玄白〕 59, 128
SUHARAYA MOHEI（Suwara ja movei）須原屋茂兵衛 47, 70, 111, 145
Suzuki Sôun 鈴木宗云 74, 94

【T】

TACHIBANA KUNIO（Tatsibana Kuniwô）橘国雄 54, 85, 120
TACHIBANA MORIKUNI（Tatsibana Morikuni/Tatsibana Jusei）橘守国〔有税〕 75, 77, 78, 94, 96, 152, 156, 157
TACHIBANA MOROE（Tatsibana Moroje）橘諸兄 68, 91, 142
TACHIBANA NANKEISHI（Tatsibana Nan kei si）橘南谿子 48, 49, 82, 112, 113
TACHIBANA YASUHARU（Tatsibana Tô siun）橘保春 54, 85, 120
TACHIBANA YASUKUNI（Foken Tatsibana Jasukuni）法眼橘保国 76, 95, 154
Tairano Atsutane →HIRATA ATSUTANE
T'aiseè 大宛 79, 159
TAKADA KEIHO（Takeda Keibo）高田敬輔 75, 153
Takada Masanori 高田政度 55, 85, 122
Takahashi Kageyasu 高橋景保 164, 165, 170, 171, 181, 195, 202, 208, 209
Takano Chiouei 高野長英 169, 170, 175, 191, 206, 207, 218
TAKAYASU ROOKU（Asija Jamabito）芦屋山人〔蘆屋山人、高安蘆屋〕 46, 81, 109

人名索引 (Personal name Index)

Takebara Sinfan →TAKEHARA NOBUSHIGE
Takebara Sjunsensai 竹原春泉斎　65, 89, 137
Takebara Sjun tsjô zai 竹原春朝斎　48-50, 81, 83, 111, 113, 115
TAKEDA INABANO JO 竹田因幡禄〔掾〕　91
Takeda Keibo →TAKADA KEIHO
TAKEDA SHINMATSU 竹田新松　91
Takeda Singen 武田信玄　47, 110
TAKEHARA NOBUSHIGE (Takebara Sinfan) 竹原信繁〔春朝斎〕　54, 85, 120
TAKEMOTO CHIKUGONO JO 竹本筑後〔掾〕　91
TAKEMOTO GIDAYU 竹本義太夫　91
TAMAMIZU GENJIRO 玉水源次郎　91
TAMIYA CHUSEN (Danaka Nobu) 田仲宣〔田宮仲宣〕　62, 88, 133
Tanba Jorisudsi 丹波頼理　58, 86, 127
Tanba-no Tôkei →Niva Tokei
T'ang Schin wi 唐慎微　56, 86, 124
TANI BUNTYOU (Buntsjô) 谷文晁　12, 20, 30, 31, 54, 84, 120, 217
Taniu →KANO TANYU
Tansitsi 丹七　67, 140
Tatsibana Jusei →TACHIBANA MORIKUNI
Tatsibana Kuniwô →TACHIBANA KUNIO
Tatsibana Morikuni →TACHIBANA MORIKUNI
Tatsibana Moroje →TACHIBANA MOROE
Tatsibana Nan kei si →TACHIBANA NANKEISHI
Tatsibana Tô siun →TACHIBANA YASUHARU
Teika →FUJIWARANO TEIKA
TEISHO SAI ICHIBA (Satomatsu sai Itsiba) 貞松斎一馬　72, 93, 149
TENMUTENNO (imperatoris Tenmu) 天武天皇　46, 109
TERASHIMA RYOUAN (Simajosi Ankô) 寺島良安　11, 45, 81, 107, 162, 177, 198
Tessan 鉄山　60, 87, 130
THUNBERG, CAROLUS PETRUS カール・ペーテル・トゥーンベリ　40, 41, 58, 102, 103, 127
TITSINGH, ISACUS ティツイング　40, 102, 103
Tojoda Jokei →TOYOTA YOKEI
Tojojama Nagano Sensei →NAGANO HOZAN
Tojokuni →UTAGAWA TOYOKUNI
Tojotake Jetsizen Seorok →TOYOTAKE CHIKUZEN SHOJO
Tojotomi Fidejosi 豊臣秀吉　47, 110
Tokei Sensei →MANO TOKEI
Tôkwa Sekkei →KAGAMI SHIKO
Tontontei →DONDONTEI WATARU
Tôra Sanzin →DORA SANJIN

Torijama Sekijen →TORIYAMA SEKIEN
Torijama Sekijen Tojofusa →TORIYAMA SEKIEN
Torijama Tojofusa →TORIYAMA SEKIEN
Torikavi Tôzai 鳥飼洞斎　49, 113
TORIYAMA SEKIEN (Torijama Sekijen Tojofusa) 鳥山石燕豊房　77, 96, 156
Tosa Hidenobu 土佐秀信　12, 18, 29
To sjun →HAYASHI RAZAN
TOTOYA HOKKEI (Hokkei Sensei) 〔魚屋〕北渓先生　69, 143
TOYOTAKE CHIKUZEN SHOJO (Tojotake Jetsizen Seorok) 豊竹越前少禄〔掾〕　67, 91, 141
TOYOTA YOKEI (Tojoda Jokei) 豊田養慶　58, 86, 126
Tscheû-fân Hièn wamg 王西楼　57, 86, 125
Tsch'ing fû jaô 陳扶揺　57, 86, 125
Tsching kiä tsi 鄭夾漈　57, 86, 125
Tschîn Nânpîn 沈南蘋　75, 153
Tschung kù 帝台　79, 159
Tschûng siù tìng 徐鼎　57, 86, 125
Ts'iën jùn tschí 錢允治　57, 86, 125
Tsikuzjô →JIKUJO
Tsiok Kairiu →NAOMI GENSHU
Tsjô Tansai →NOTANSAI
Tsunenori →ONO TSUNENORI
Tsuruoka Rosui 鶴岡蘆水　54, 84, 120
Tungjen Lìkaò →RIKO

【U】

UCHUBEN SUKETO (Utsiufen Sukemotsi) 右中辨資任　68, 91, 142
Udagawa Jôan (Wutagawa Joan/Rôkwa teino Sjuzin) 宇田川榕菴〔弄花亭主人〕　59-61, 87, 88, 128-131, 168, 206
Udaiven Jakamotsi →OTOMO YAKAMOCHI
UEKIYA KINTA (Kinda) 〔種樹家〕金太　59, 87, 128
Unrôsi 雲桜子〔雲棲子〕　74, 94, 151
UTAGAWA TOYOKUNI (Tojokuni) 〔歌川〕豊国　67, 90, 140
Utsiufen Sukemotsi →UCHUBEN SUKETO

【W】

Wakagusa 若草　67, 141
Wâng Hūsūn 汪鶴孫　64, 89, 137
Wângjeūtūn 汪由敦　63, 135
Wang Schi tschin 王世貞　56, 124
Watanave no Kuruvu 渡部狂　63, 134
WILHELMO, FREDERICO フリードリヒ・ウィルヘルム　39, 101

人名索引 (Personal name Index)

Williem I, King 国王ウィレム I 世　159, 161, 197
Wimura Katsukits　→IMURA KATSUYOSHI
Winouve Okina　→INOUE CHOKU
Wokasawara　→OGASAWARA
Wô kwa san 黄華山　51, 83, 116
Wonoë Ofats　→ONOUE OHATSU
Wono Lanzan　→ONO RANZAN
Wôsiu　→MARUYAMA OUJU
Wôton　→OSON
Wozawa Tôitsi　→OZAWA TOICHI
Wutagawa Joan　→UDAGAWA YOAN

【Y】

YAMAGUCHI SOKEN (Jamagutsi So tsiun) 山口素絢　76, 95, 154
YAMANAKA CHU ZAEMON (Jamanaka Tsiu Sajemon) 山中忠左衛門　72, 149
YAMASAKI UEMON (Lanzai Jamasaki Ujemon) 蘭斎山崎右衛門　46, 81, 108
YAMASHITA SEKICHU (Jamasita Sekitsiu) 山下石仲〔石仲子守範〕　76, 95, 154
YAMASHITA SHIGEMASA (Jamasita Sigemasa) 山下重政　50, 82, 114
YANAGAWA JUZAN 柳川重山　96
YANO SADATOSHI (Jano Sadatosi) 矢野貞利　50, 114
YASUDA KICHIHEI (Jasida Kitsifei) 安田吉兵衛　51, 115
YOKIHI (Hiuên tsûng) 楊貴妃　67, 141
YORITA KYUHO (Kjufou Keiden) 九峰寄田〔寄田九峯〕　75, 94, 153
YOSHIKAWA KOREKATA (Fôgawa Zinujemon) 芳川〔維堅〕甚右衛門　73, 93, 150
Yoshio Gonnosuke 吉雄権之助　163, 199
YUZUKI TOKIWA 柚木常盤　87

【Z】

Zisôzen　→GO SOSEN
Zjôruri fime　→JORURI HIME

図版　493 和蘭全軀内外分図（UL, Ser. 1128　験号　43ウ～44ウ・裏表紙見返し・裏表紙）

（験号　10ウ～43オ　省略）

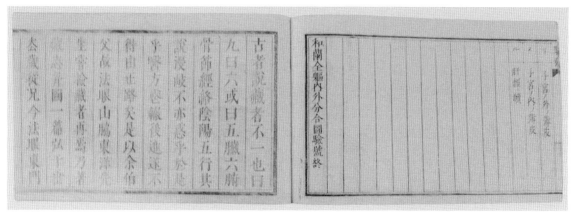

（験号　44オ［跋文1オ］）　　　　　　　　　　（験号　43ウ）

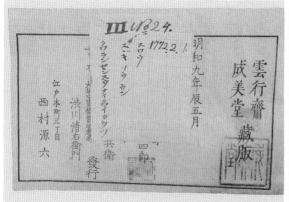

（験号　裏表紙見返し［貼紙］）

（験号　44ウ［跋文1ウ］）

（験号　裏表紙）

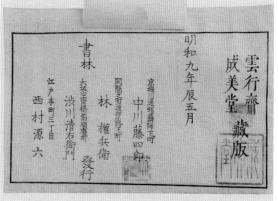

（験号　裏表紙見返し［奥付］）

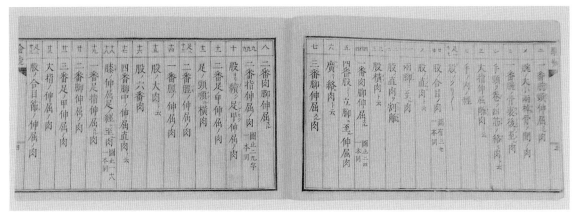

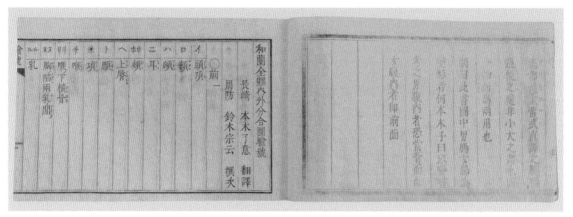

図版 493 和蘭全軀内外分合図（UL, Ser. 1128 験号 4ウ～7オ）

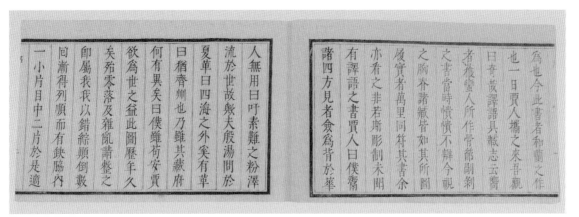

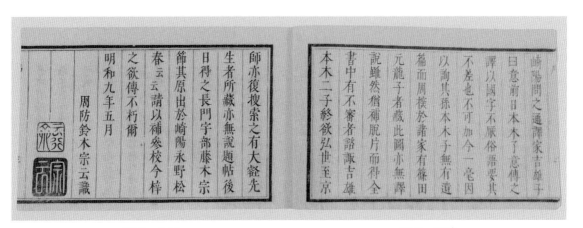

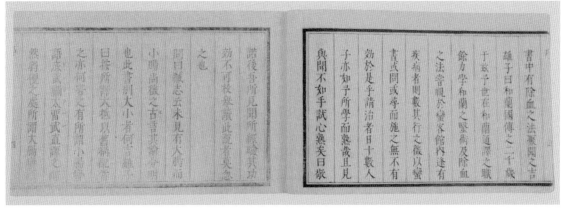

図版 493 和蘭全軀内外分図 (UL, Ser. 1128 験号 表紙・1オ)

493 和蘭全軀内外分図　UL, Ser. 1128（外題「驗號」・内題「和蘭全軀内外分合圖驗號」）

（験号　表紙）

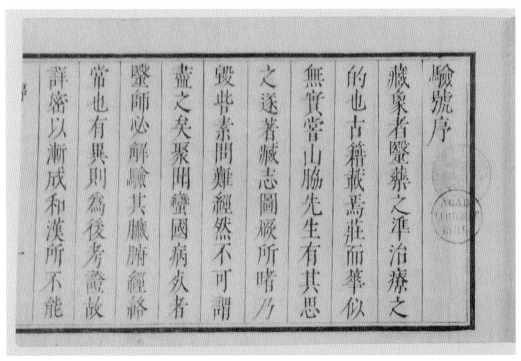

（験号　1オ）

図版 468 塗之法（UL. Ser. 895 2ウ〜4オ）

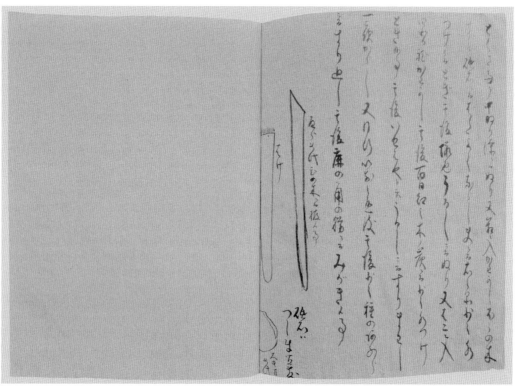

（2ウ）　　（3オ）

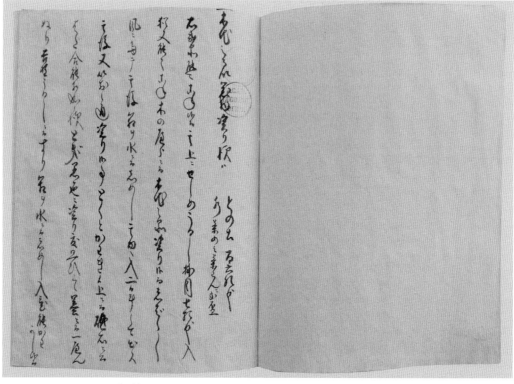

（3ウ）　　（4オ）

図版 468 塗之法（UL, Ser. 895 表紙・1オ〜2オ）

468 塗之法　UL, Ser. 895　＊左開き

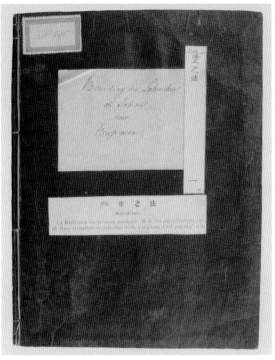

（表紙）

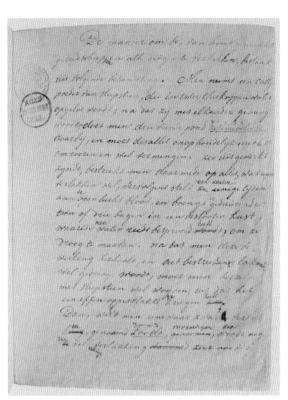

（1オ）

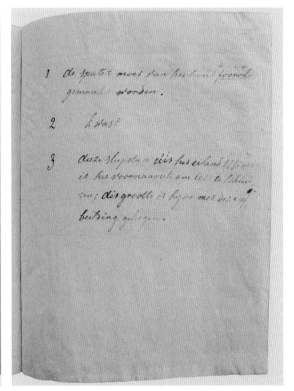

（2オ）

図版 467 紙作之法（UL, Ser. 896 6ウ～7ウ・裏表紙）

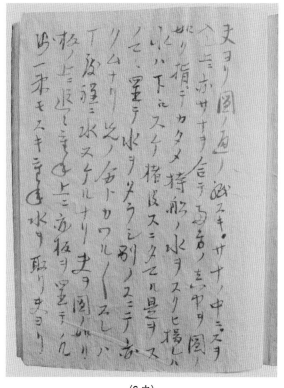
(6ウ)

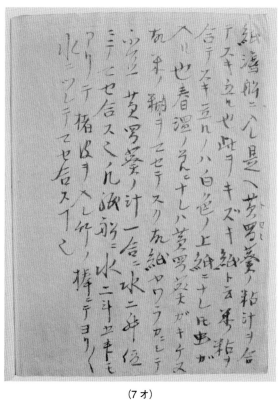
(7オ)

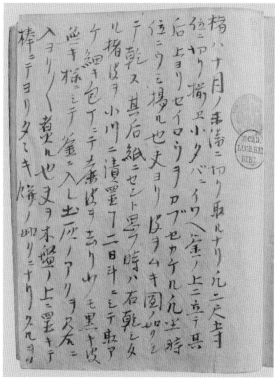
(7ウ)

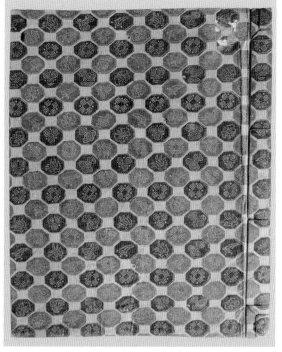
(裏表紙)

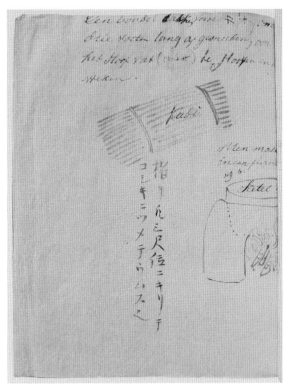

(4ウ)

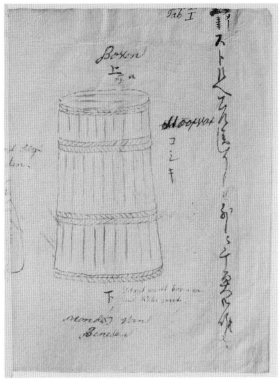

(5オ)

※5ウは白

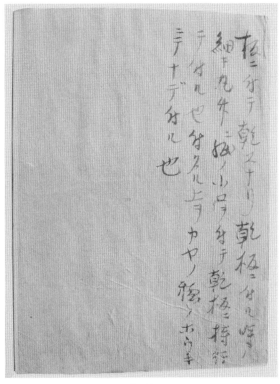

(6オ)

図版　467 紙作之法（UL, Ser. 896　2ウ～4オ）

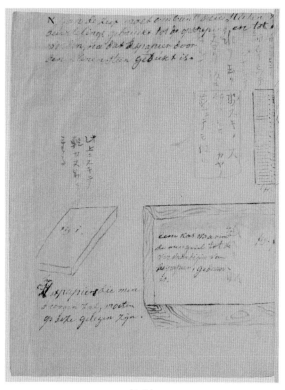

(2ウ)

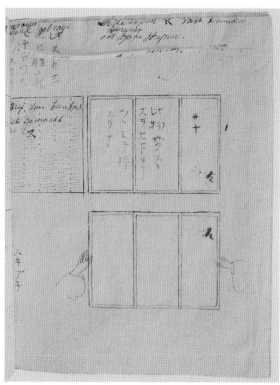

(3オ)

※3ウは白

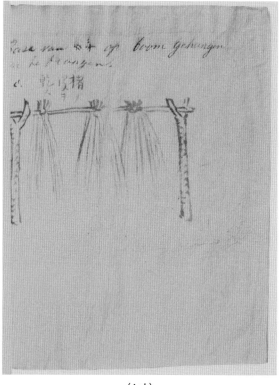

(4オ)

図版　467 紙作之法（UL. Ser. 896　表紙・1オ・1ウ・2オ）

467 紙作之法　UL. Ser. 896　＊左開き

（表紙）

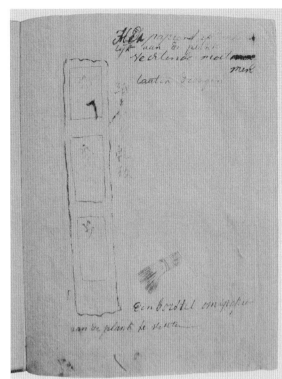

（1オ）

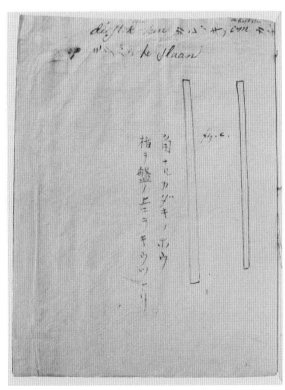

（1ウ）

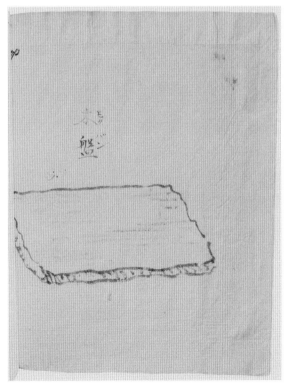

（2オ）

図版 466 酒作之事（UL, Ser. 897 8ウ〜9ウ・裏表紙）

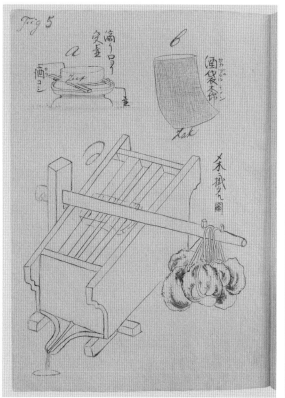

（9オ）

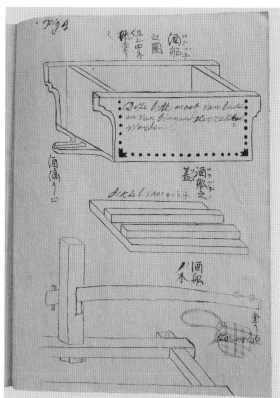

（8ウ）

（裏表紙）

（9ウ）

図版　466 酒作之事（UL. Ser. 897　6ウ：貼込5ウ・7ウ・8オ）

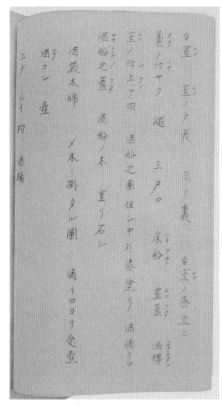

(6ウ：貼込5ウ)

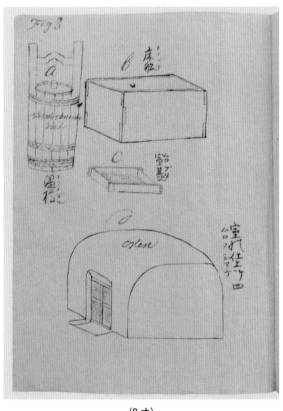

(8オ)

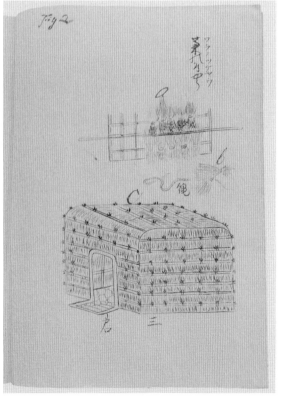

(7ウ)

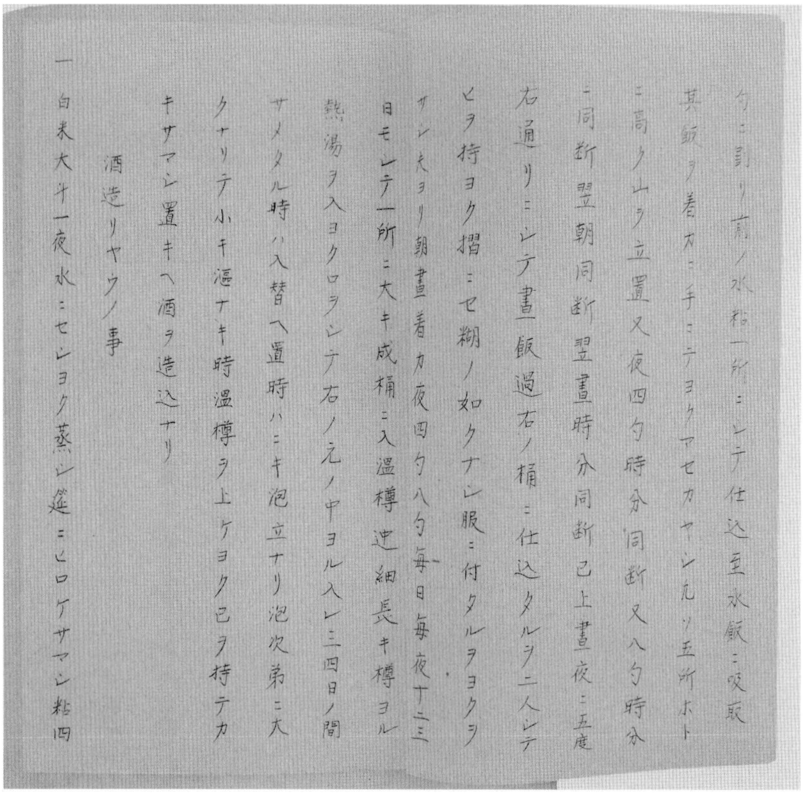

（6ウ：貼込3ウ）

ラニ割リ煎リ水和シ一所ニシテ仕込至水飯ニ交反
其飯ノ香方ニ手ニテヨクアセカヤシ丸メ五所ホト
ニ高ク山ク立置又夜四ツ時分同断又へ々ツ時分
一同断翌朝同新翌朝昼時分同断己上昼夜ニ五度
右通リニシテ昼飯過右ノ桶ニ仕込タルヲ入レテ
ヒヲ持ヨクニテ糊ノ如クナシ服ニ付タルヲヨクラ
サシ々ヨリ朝昼晩方夜四ツ八ツ毎日毎夜十三
日モシテ一所ニ大キ成桶ニ入温樽迚細長キ樽ヨリ
熱湯ヲ入ヨクロラシテ右ノ元ノ中ヨル入レ三四日ノ間
サメタル時ハ入替へ置時ハニキ泡立ナリ泡次弟ニ大
クヽリテ小キ泡ナキ時温樽ヲ上ケヨクテカ
キサマシ置キへ酒ヲ造込ナリ
　　酒造リヤウノ事
一白米大キ十一夜水ニセシヨク蒸シ莚ニヒロケサマシ粘四

（6ウ：貼込4オ）

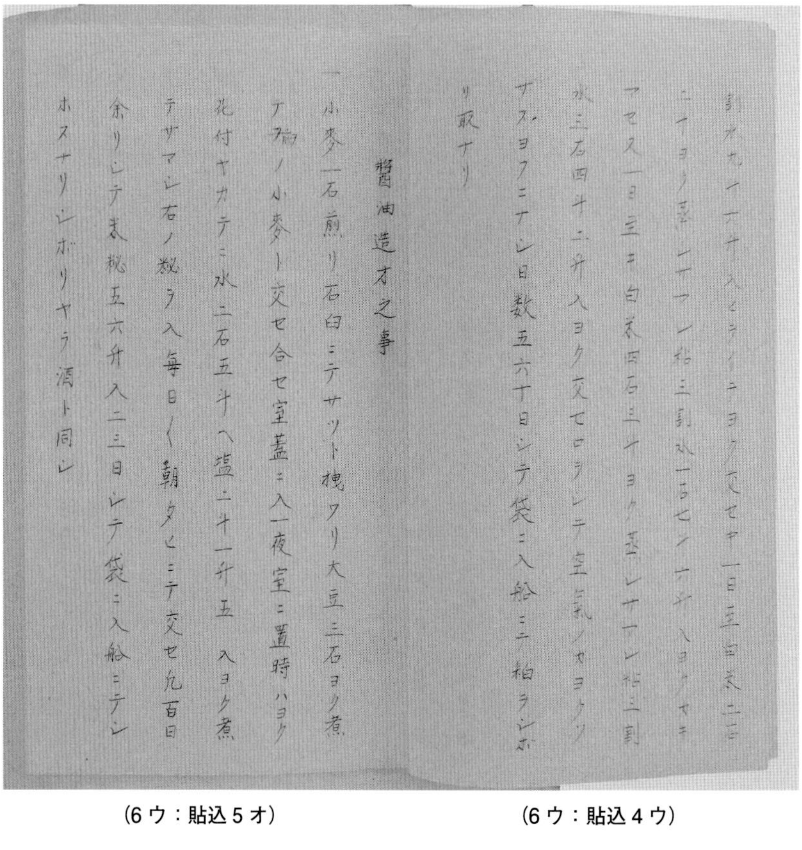

割方九十一斗入ヨウニヨクシテセリ一日ヨ米三斗
ニテラ昆シニテマシ粘三斗パヒセニヒヨクヤキ
水五石四十二升入ヨクヨセロランテ宣気ヨヨク
ヤスヨクニナシ日数五六十日シテ笶ニ入船ニ粕ヲシホ
リ取ナリ

（6ウ：貼込4ウ）

　　醤油造才之事
一小麦一石煎リ石臼ニテサット挽ワリ大豆三石ヨク煮
テ桶ノ小麦ト交セ合室盖ニ入一夜室ニ置時ハヨク
花付ヤカテニ水一石五十へ塩二十一升五へヨク煮
テサマシ右ノ殻ヲ入毎日く朝夕ニテ交セ九百日
余リシテ麦桃五六升入ニ三日レテ笶ニ入船ニテシ
ホスナリシホリヤウ酒ト同レ

（6ウ：貼込5オ）

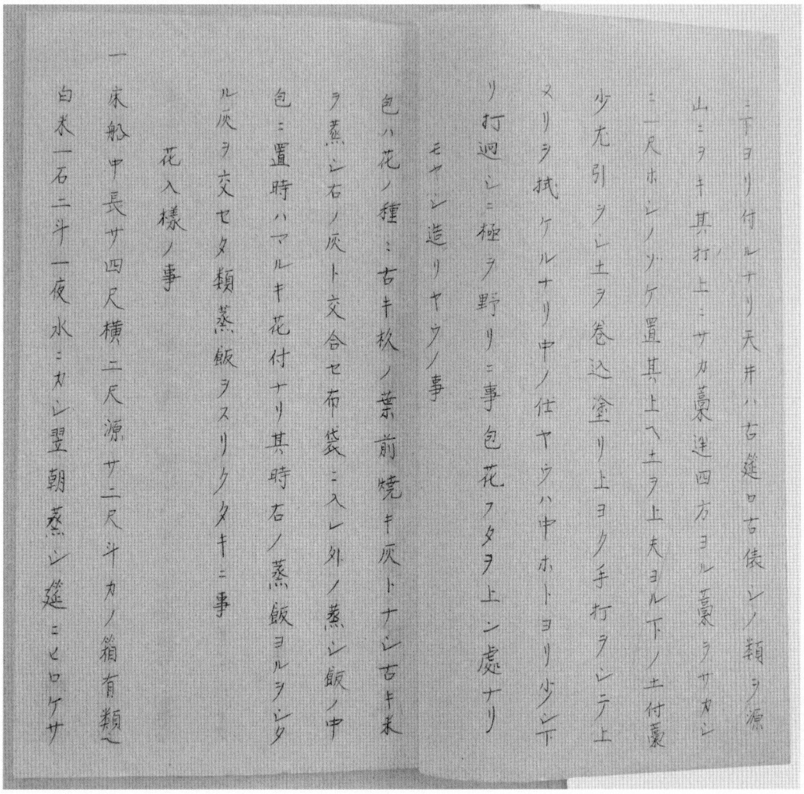

図版　466　酒作之事（UL, Ser. 897　6ウ：貼込1ウ～3オ）

(6ウ：貼込1ウ)

ヨリ付ケテ十リ天井ハ古延口古俵ニシノ頬ヲ源
山ニヲキ其打上ニサカ薬ヲ四方ヨリ豪ヲサカン
三一尺ホシノケ置其上ヘ土ヲ上夫ヨリ下ノ土付豪
少ヽ引タレ土ヲ巻込塗リ上ヨク手打タレテ上
メリヲ拭ケルナリ中ノ仕ヤウハ中ホドヨリ少シテ
リ打廻シニ種ヲ野リニ事包花ヲタヲ上ン處ナリ
モヤレ造リヤウノ事

色ハ花ノ種ニ古キ枚ノ葉前焼キ灰トナシ古キ米
ヲ蒸ニ石ノ灰ト交合セ布袋ニ入レ外ノ蒸シ飯ノ中
色ニ置時ハマルキ花付ナリ其時石ノ蒸飯ヨルヲシタ
ル灰ヲ交セタ麺蒸飯ヲスリクタキニ事

花入様ノ事

一床船中長サ四尺横二尺深サ二尺斗カノ箱有類ニ
白米一石二斗一夜水ニカシ翌朝蒸シ筵ニヒロケサ

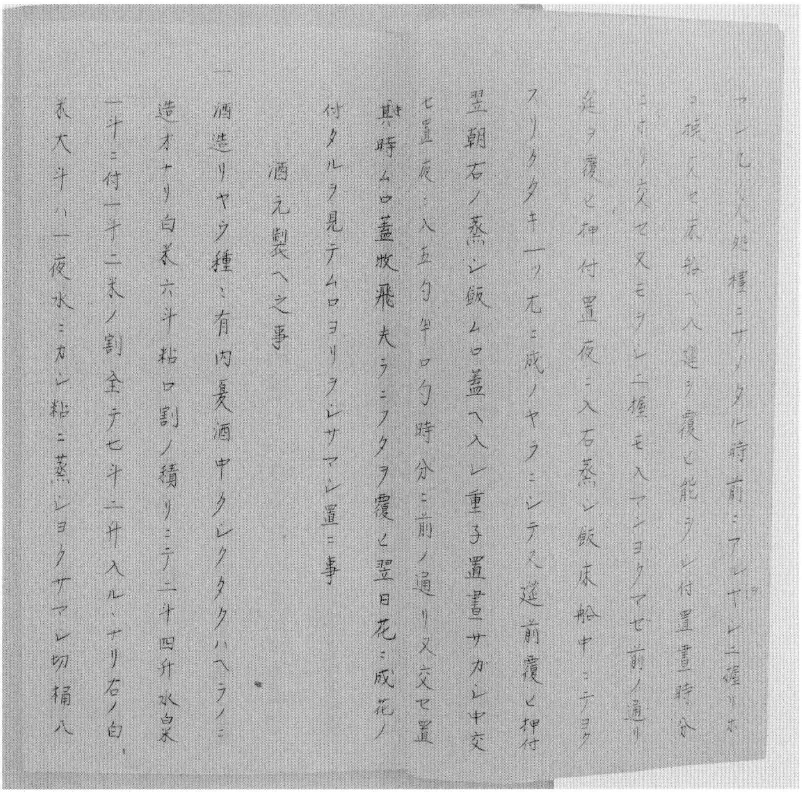

(6ウ：貼込2オ)

(6ウ：貼込2ウ)

マシ又處ニ種ニサマシタル時前ニアンサレニ寝シ
二種タシ末ヲ扨ハ入違ヲ寝シ能ク付置昼時分
ニモヲ交セテ又モヲシ二種モ入アンヨクマセ前ノ通リ
延ヲ覆と押付置置夜ニ入石蒸シ飯床中ニテヨク
スリタクキ一ツ元ニ成ヤウニシテス延前霞ヲ押付
翌朝右ノ蒸シ飯ムロ蓋ヘ入レ重子置畫サカシ中交
セ置夜ニ入五ツ斗ニノ時分ニ前ノ通リ又交セ
其時蓋放飛夫ニニ又ヲ覆と翌日花ニ成花ノ
付タルヲ見テムロヨリヲレサマシ置ニ事

酒元製ヘノ事

(6ウ：貼込3オ)

一酒造リヤウ種ニ有内長夏酒中クレクタクハヘラニ
造オナリ白米六斗粘ロ割ノ積リニテ二十四升水泉
ニ付テ一十二米ノ割全テ七十二升入ル・ナリ右ノ白
米大斗ハ一夜水ニカシ粘ニ蒸シヨクサマシ切稲ハ

図版 466 酒作之事（UL, Ser. 897 6ウ・7オ・6ウ：貼込1オ）

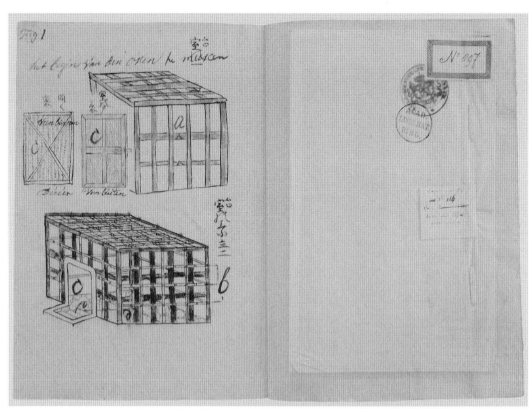

(7オ)　　　　　　　　　　　　(6ウ)

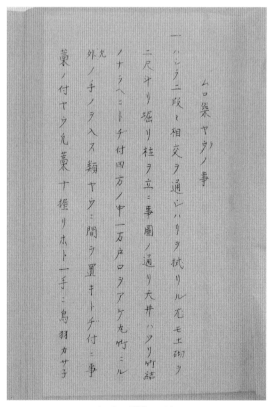

(6ウ：貼込1オ)

ムロ築ヤウノ事
一 ハシラ二段ニ相交ラ通シハリヲ拭リル尤モ土砌ヲ
二尺斗リ堀リ柱ヲ立ニ事図ノ通リ天井ハツリ竹結
ノナラヘニトヂ付四方ノ中一万戸ロヲアケ九竹ミル
外ノチノ子ヲ入ス類ヤウニ間ヲ置キトヂ付ニ事
九
藁ノ付ヤウ九藁十握リホト一手ニ烏羽カサ子

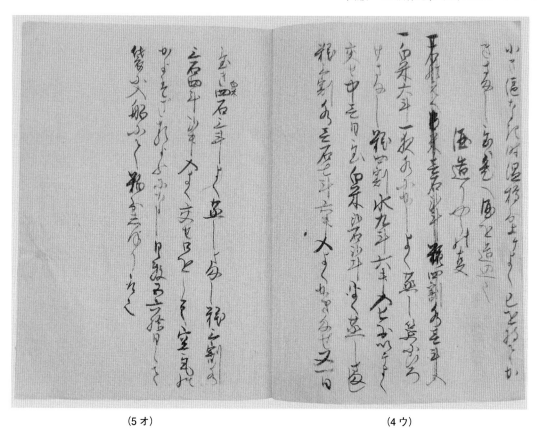
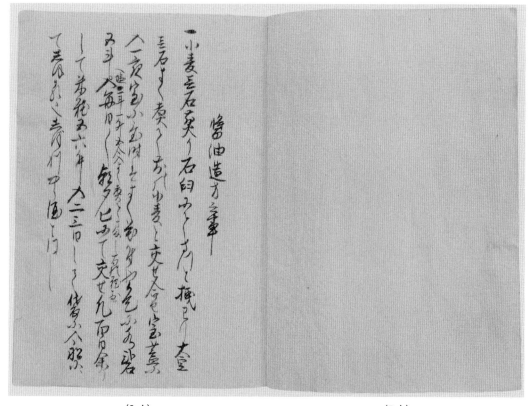

図版 466 酒作之事 (UL, Ser. 897 2ウ〜4オ)

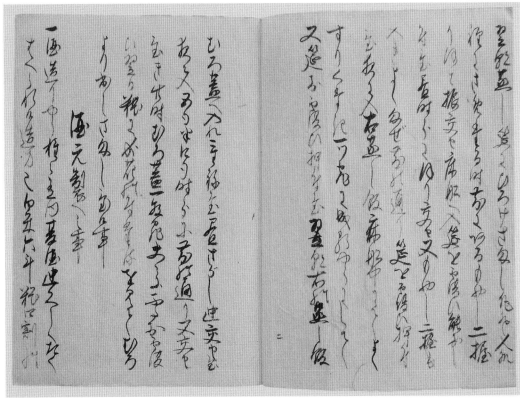

(3オ)　　　　　　　　　(2ウ)

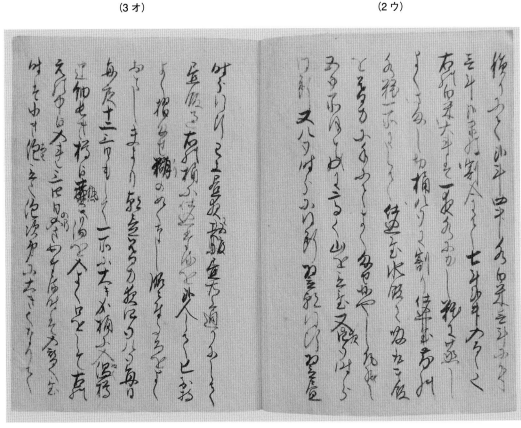

(4オ)　　　　　　　　　(3ウ)

図版　466 酒作之事（UL, Ser. 897　表紙・1オ〜2オ）

466 酒作之事　UL, Ser. 897

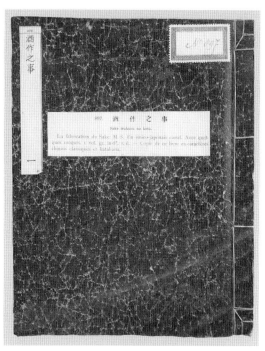

（表紙）

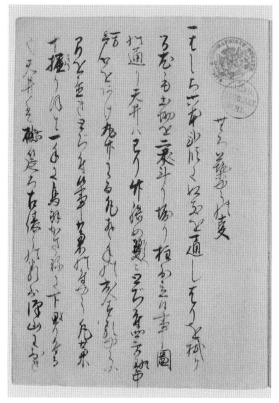

（1オ）

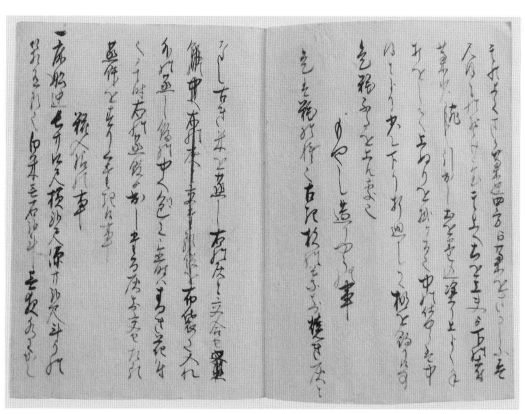

（2オ）　　　　　　　　　　　（1ウ）

(36ウ)

イレガミ

髪短クメ足ラサル者ハ結ヒ難キ故ニ
之ヲ用テ補フ

ビンカヅラ

髪薄フメ結ヒ難キモ之ヲ用テ鬢毛
ヲ助ケ地ヲ覆フ

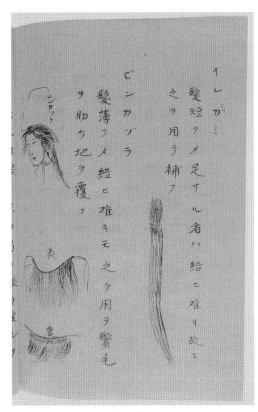

(37オ)

其法三味線ノ糸ヲ弓ニ張リ髪毛ヲ
アミ付ケルニ毛四五本アテ取リテ
如此ノアミテシノ固メ両ノ端ヲ能
ク止メ線ノ両端ヲ鋸状ニ造リ緒ヲ
通ス様ニスヘシ

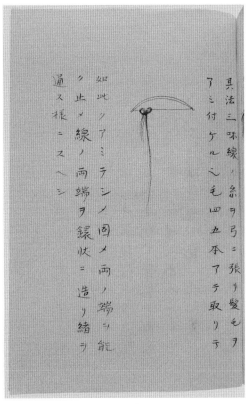

(37ウ)

洗髪ヲ結フ論

惣メ女ノ物ハ飽易ク又移リ易キ故
ニ其ノ風俗日々ニ異ニシ此ヲ以テ委曲
ニ尽シ難シ尤モ今用ルヽ物ハ古ヨ
リ通メ用ル處ニ近世流行ノ洗ヒ髪
ハ甚タ乱レ易シテ旦ツ髪乱レ色山
キハ不好故ハ乱レハ非禮之色山シキハ
魂ニ殺合ハ隠隠遁気食ノ爪ニ薫シ
此爪多ハ遊女ヨリ始ルモノヽ
ナラス洗髪ハ古実アリ大ニ忌

(38オ・ウ白)

ヘキナリ男女共ニ尤リ是禮式家秘
事ナル故ニ此扇ニ記セス

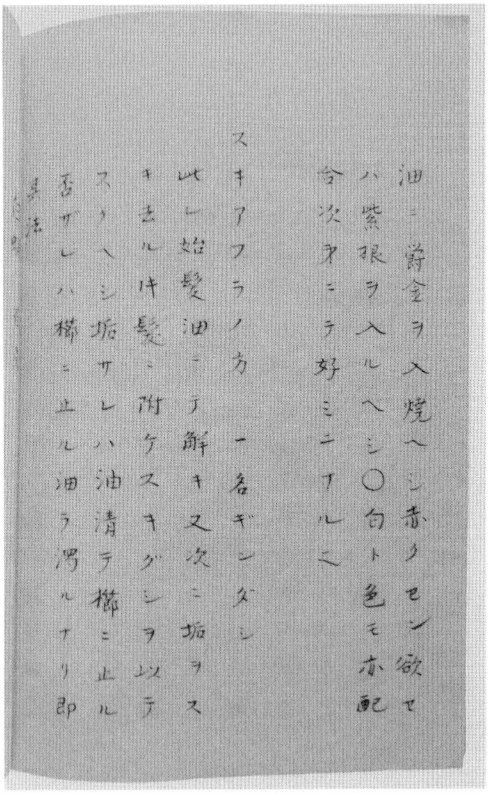
油ニ紛金ヲ入焼ヘシ赤クセン欲セ
ハ紫根ヲ入ルヘシ○白ト色モ亦配
合次第ニテ好ミニナル之
スキアフラノ方　一名ギンダシ
此レ始髪油ニテ解キ又次ニ垢ヲス
キ去ル件髪ニ附ケスキグシヲ以テ
スクヘシ垢サレハ油清テ櫛ニ止ル
否サレハ櫛ニ止ル油ヲ濁ルナリ即
異法
(34 ウ)

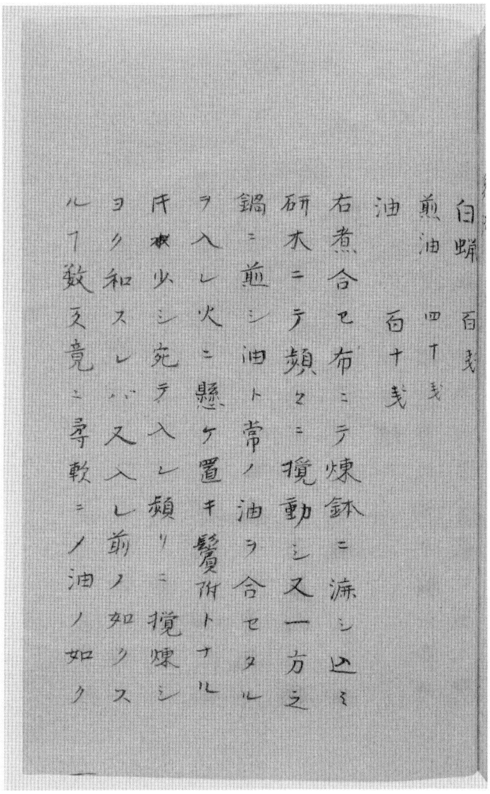
白蝋　百戔
煎油　四十戔
油　百十戔
右煮合セ布ニテ煉鉢ニ漉シ込ミ
研木ニテ頻々ニ攪動シ又一方之
鍋ニ煎シ油ト常ノ油ヲ合セタル
ヲ入レ火ニ懸ケ置キ髪附トナル
件少シ宛テ入レ頻リニ攪煉シ
ヨク和スレハ又入レ前ノ如クス
ルコト数叉竟ニ等軟ニノ油ノ如ク
(35 オ)

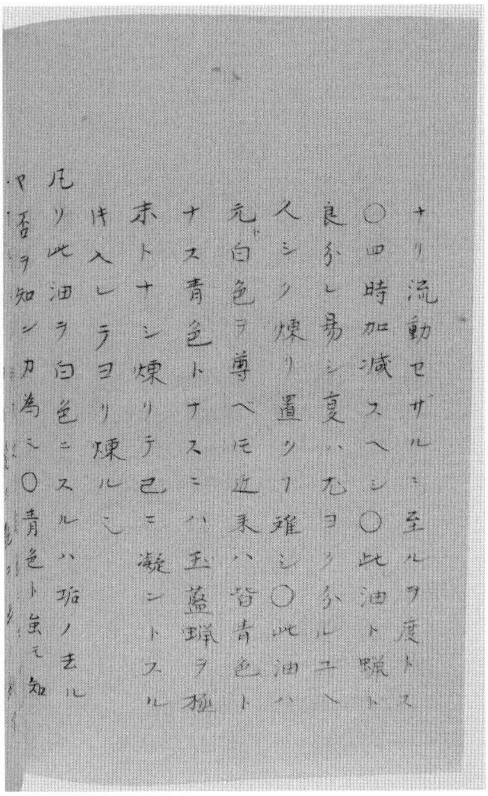
ナリ流動セザルニ至ルヲ度トス
○四時加減スヘシ○此油ト蝋ト
良分レ易シ夏ハ尤ヨク分ルユヘ
久シク煉リ置クコト難シ○此油ハ
元白色ヲ尊ヘトモ近来ハ皆青色ト
ナス青色トナスニハ玉藍蝋ヲ極
末トナシ煉リテ已ニ凝ントスル
件入レテヨリ煉ル之
凡ソ此油ヲ白色ニスルハ垢ノ去ル
ヤ否ヲ知ンカ為ニ○青色ト虫モ知
(35 ウ)

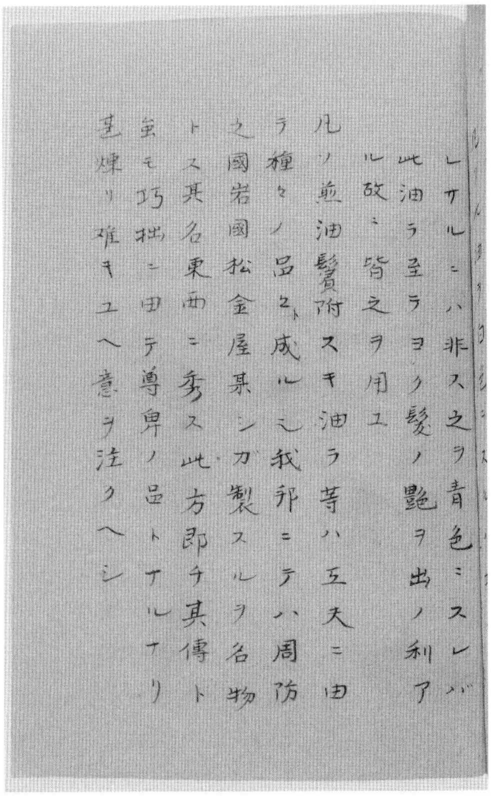
レナルニハ非ス之ヲ青色ニスレハ
此油ヲ至ラヨク髪ノ艶ヲ出ノ利ア
ル故ニ皆之ヲ用ユ
凡ソ煎油髪附スキ油ヲ等ハ五夫ニ田
ヲ種々ノ品之ト成ル之我邦ニテハ周防
之國岩國松金屋某シガ製スルヲ名物
トス其名東西ニ秀ス此方即チ其傳ト
虫モ巧拙ニ由テ尊卑ノ品トナルナリ
其煉リ難キユヘ意ヲ注クヘシ
(36 オ)

(32ウ)

ナリ其法
油 三斤 白止 淀近油ニ一夜
右煎ノ句ニ移レハ可ニ白芷ヲ入
レサレハ蝋ノ臭気消ヘズ滓ヲ出
リテ
白蝋 二斤 ハゼヌハミソ蝋良
油ニ入レ煉鉢ニ入レ未々温ナルトキ
焼ノ煉鉢ニ入レ能煮解シ布ニテ漉シエ
ニテ頻ニ攪動シテ煉ルヘシソノ
熱ノ醒加減ヲ知リテオノ／＼頗リ
…

(33ウ)

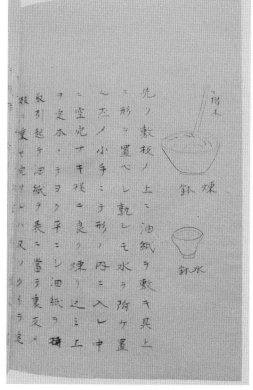
煉鉢
水鉢

先ノ敷板ノ上ニ油紙ヲ敷キ其上
ニ形ヲ置ベシ軟キモ水ヲ附ケ置
キタノ小手ニテ形ノ内ニ入レ中
ニ空气ナキ様ニ良ク煉リ込シ上
ニ定水ニテヨク平ニシ油紙ヲ
取引起テ油紙ノ表ニ當テ裏文ヘ
…

(33オ)

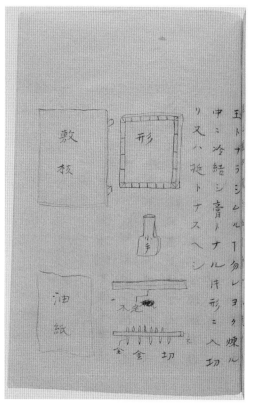
敷板　形
油紙
不定　金金切

玉トナルヲシルノ…ヨク煉ル
中ニ冷結シ青ノナルトキニ入切
リ又ハ挺トナスヘシ
…

(34オ)

木ニ方子ニシ切金ヲ形ノ理文ニ當
テ縦横ニ切リ形ヲ出メ紙ニ包ム
モ度ニ器水ヲヌルヘシ…ナリ
粘着ノ形チトナスヘシ
膏剤ノ句ト能チ付ヘキハ油ヲ入
○之句ニテ中ノ油ヲ煎シ油ヲ減ス
ヘシ○蝋ハ寒暑ニヨリテ加減ア
リ此量ハ春秋ノ中和ノ時ノ量ニ意ヲ
用ユベシ○色ハ貢ニセント欲レハ
…

(30ウ)

此中ニ浸シ置ベシ赤色ヲ為セハ可
レ之ヲ小器ニ入レ火ニ燻メ又一ノ器
ニ五倍子ノ粉ヲ盛リ革ヲカケ
歯ニ付ベシ深黒色トナルヲ度トス
尤モ歯ヲヨク磨キ汚物ヲ落シ置
テ付クヘシ

歯磨　ハミガキ
此レ男女夫ニ用テ歯ヲ白クスルノ具
ニ歯ハ匂モ尊ク故ニ男子モ常ニ用
江○女モ未タ歯ヲ染ル中ハ之ヲ用

(31オ)

此中ニ漬シ置ベシ赤色ヲ為セハ可
ユ其法
鹿角灰ヲヨク水飛ノ匂ヲ入レ又ハ
乾紅ヲ入用ユ

梅花油　バイクワアブラ
此レ髪ヲ解ク件ニ此油ヲ手ニ附ケ
髪ニ塗リ附テ櫛ニテ解ノ心具方
椿実油　一升　又胡麻油モ用ユ
耳松　三奈　各十一匁
大茴香　各二十二匁　丁子　五匁

(31ウ)

甕ニ入凡二畫一夜ニ〆後布ニテ
濾之餅ハ任ノ與フベシ○福ハ絹
甑ニ入ル味細刀ニ剉ミ焼酎ヲ手ニ入
レ茶ニモミ附ケヲヨク湿メラシメ
油ニ交へ之ヲトクリノ中ニ入レ
口ヲ封シ釜ノ中ニ居ヘ間ニ湯ヲ
入レ武火ニテ蒸シ出スナリ

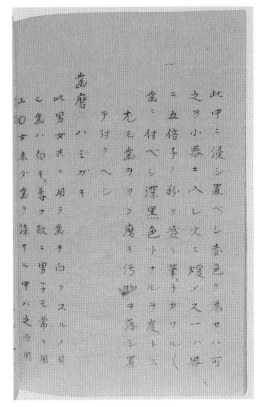

(32オ)

鬢附
此レ髪ヲ結フ時擦スハヘラニ子ギ
付ケテ髪ニスリ櫛ニテ刀千付テ結

凡焼手油ハ国々家々ニテ異ナリ香
具ノ配合製煉ニ田テ種々ノ品トナ
リ在モ亦異ニ工夫ヲ造ルベシ
龍脳末　五匁　麝香末　五分
入置片ハ最上ノ品トナルナリ

香之具ニ供ス
○油絞リテ温ナル件ニ

(28ウ)

ル器ノ中ニ入レ白色ヲ移スヘシ
下品ハ白亜土千是ホノ末ヲ以精製
ノ交ユルヽ
和漢三才圖會ニ出ル法ハ鉛ヲ戦状ニ
作リ串ニ貫キ壺ノ内ニ酢ヲ入レ其空
上ニ串ヲ斜ニ掛ケロヲ密封シ置ケハ
鉛錆テ白粉ヲ發ス之ヲ掃ヒ取ルトス
此ヘ其製ハ迂遠ナリ只シ極テ上品
トハナルヘシ乎未々試ミス

(29オ)

紅ヘニ
製法別ニ詳ニ○用ヒ樣筆ニテ唇ニ
付クルニヘ唇ノ全面ニ付シハ口廣ク
ナリテ塊ニ下唇ノ中央ニ半月状ニ
付レハ甚良ナリ○又頬紅ハ紅ヲ少
シトキ眼ノ上瞼見シ頬ノ辺ニシ水
ニトキ交ヘ薄桃色トナシ少
シヅヽ眼ノ上瞼ニ付眉掃ニテ良クテラスヘシ

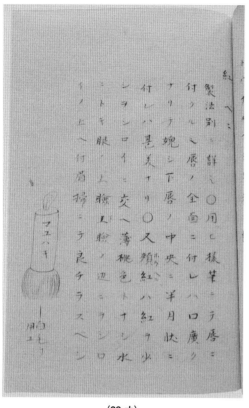

マユハキ
眉ニ用ヒ

(29ウ)

黛 マユスミ
一 眉ハ遠山ノ眉トテ薄キニ長ク
又蛾眉トライカイコノ眉ノ如ク中
高ク千月ヲ伏セルカ如キヲ貴シ
又々蛭ノ眉トテ細長ク貴シ七三
ツノ形ヲ具ヘ作ルヘシ足ラサル處
ニ黛ヲ用ユ其方
蒲ノ葉出テ後テ根ト葉ノ附際ニ
花ノ含ムキ取り置キ祐レルヲ
中ヲ用ケハ黒キ彩アリ之ヲ

(30オ)

又ハ墨ニモスリ付ケモ
テ付クルヽ
又胡桃仁ニ火ヲ付ケ其煙ヲ茶碗
ニ受ケテ用ルモノアリ
又肥松ヲ焼テ用ユ
○又鬢除ノ富士形ヲモ作ル毎剪ノ生下
ノ辰ニ付クルヽ
鉄漿ハグロ
鉄ヲ焼キ水ヲ壷ニ入酒ヲ少シ入レ
リ頬ノ生下リ等ニモ赤々用ユ

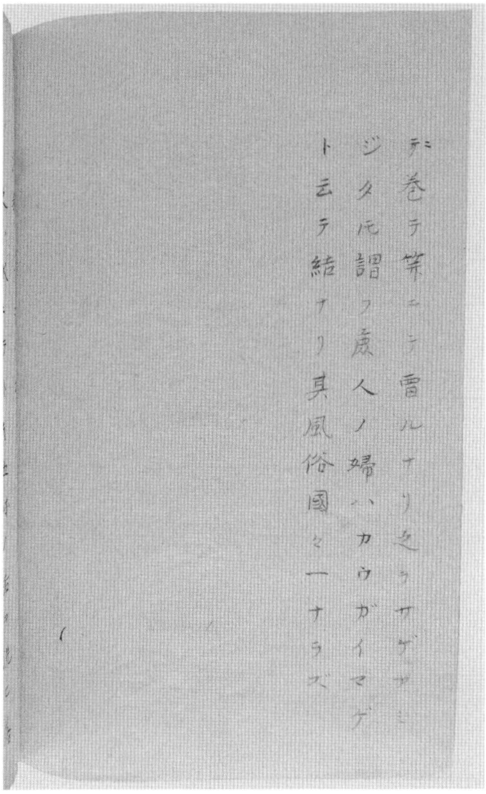

(26ウ)

テ巻ラ笄ニテ雪ル ナリ云ウサゲサミ
ジタ此謂フ處人ノ婦ハカウガイマゲ
ト云テ結ナリ其風俗國々一ナラズ

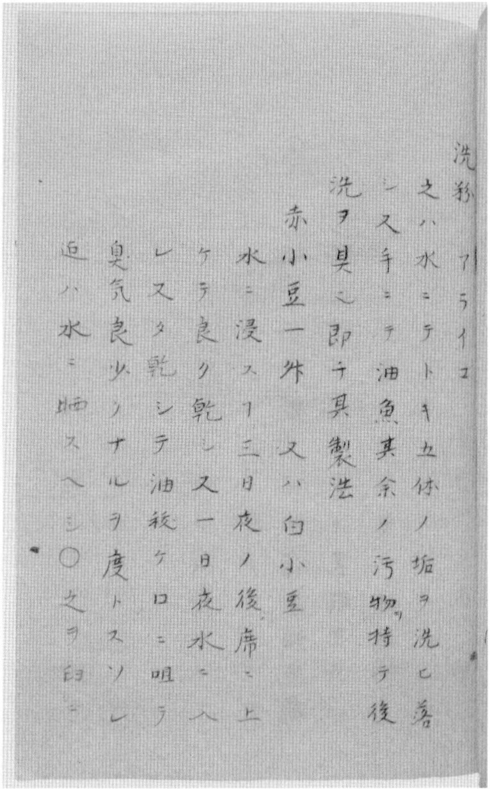

(27オ)

洗粉ノフライニ
之ハ水ニテトキ五体ノ垢ヲ洗ヒ落
シ又手ニテ油魚其余ノ汚物ヲ持テ後
洗ヲ具シ即チ其製造
赤小豆一作又ハ白小豆
水ニ浸シ三日夜ノ後席ニ上
ケテ良ク乾シ又一日夜水ニ入
レタ乾シテ油袋ケロニ咽レ
臭気良少ナルヲ度トスソレ
近ハ水ニ晒スヘシ○之ヲ曰ニ

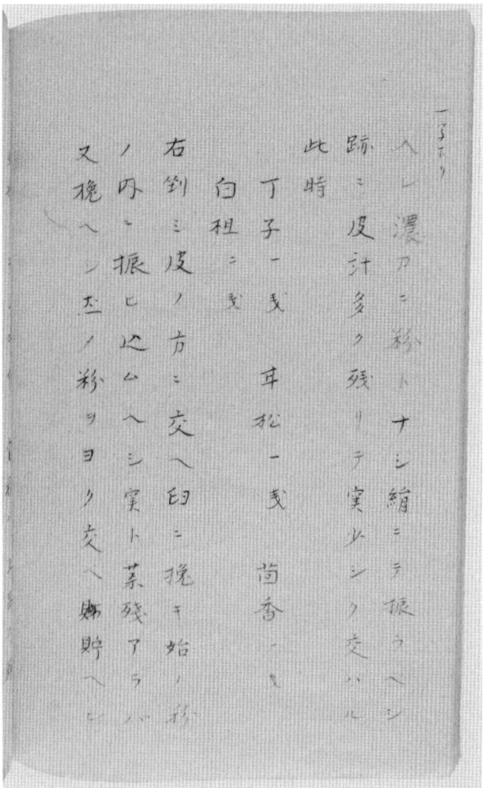

(27ウ)

入レ濃ノニ粉トナシ絹ニテ振ウヘン
跡ニ反汁多ク残リテ実少シノ定ハル
此時
丁子一戈　年松一戈　茴香ニ戈
白柏ニ戈
右釣ニ度ノ方ニ交ヘ臼ニ挽キ始ノ粉
ノ内ニ振ヒ込ムヘシ実ト茶残アラハ
又挽ヘリ盃ノ粉ヲヨク交ヘ梅貯ヘレ

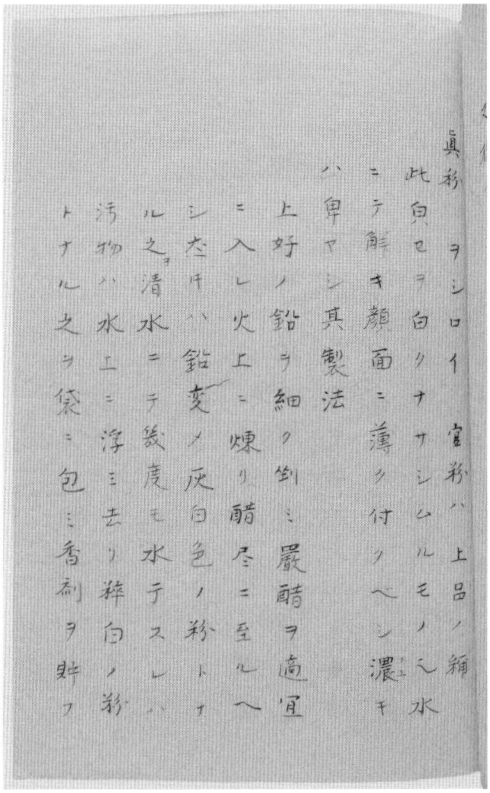

(28オ)

眞粉ヲシロイ
此白セヲ白クナシハルモノヘ水
ニテ解キ顔面ニ薄ク付ヘシ濃キ
ハ卑ヤシ其製法
上好ノ鉛ヲ細ク剉ミ嚴酢ヲ適宜
ニ入レ火上ニ煉り酢盡シニヘ
シたハ鉛変メ灰白色ノ粉トナ
ルレハ之清水ニテ笈度モ水テスレ
ハ汚物ハ水上ニ浮ミ去ノ粋白ノ粉
トナル之ヲ袋ニ包ミ香剤ヲ貯フ

図版 465 染物之法 (UL. Ser. 892 25オ〜26オ)

(25オ)

婦人粧身之篇

逹者真甫集

凡ソ女ノ身ヲツクルハ髪ヲ梳ケヅリ面
ニ真粉ヲ傅シ唇ニ紅サシ髪ニ油シ眉ヲ黛
ス命婦ハ髪ニ笄サシ歯ニ鉄漿シテ子
アリハ眉ヲ掃フ貴人ニ仕エルモノモ
ノハスヘ面ニ紅粉ヲ傅ヘス亡婦ハ髪ヲ
極ク散ニシ又ハチヤセンノ
形ニ結ヒテ芹サシ又面ハ染シ尼唇

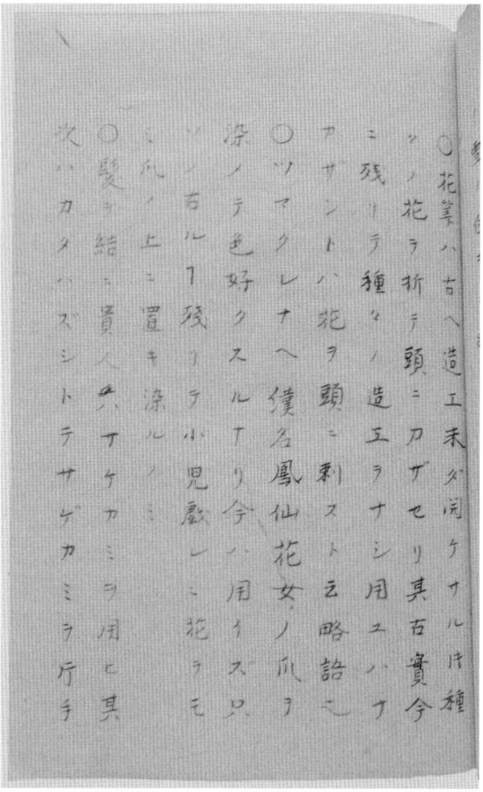

※ 24オ・ウは白

(25ウ)

ニ紅サセハ面ニ彩ヒス面ニカレハ
唇ニ紅サヘス是ヲ庁粧ト謂フ之ヲ
ノ人ニ見エレハ甚非禮ナリ
○木朝ノ夕額ヲ富士山ノ形ニ作リ
富士擶規ト散テ奉ツル此花咲也姫
物語ニノ貞節ニ習ワシメトス夫ト
ヨリテ按スルニ此説非ナリ大夫モ
女ハ色ノ白キヲ貴シトス心故ニ
ノ雪ノ白キニ愛テカクハスルナル

(26オ)

○花葉ハ古ヘ造工未タ開ケサル作種
ニノ花ヲ折戸頭ニ刀ザセリ其百實今
ニ残リテ種々ノ造エラナシ用ユハ
アサント花ヲ頭ニ剩スト云略語ニ
○ツマクレナヘ倭名鳳仙花女ノ爪ヲ
深メテ色好クスルハ今ハ用スル
ノ古ルノ上ニ置キ染ルニ花ヲモ
ノ爪ニ上リテ小兒戲レニ花ヲモ
○髪ヲ結ニ貴人ハナケカミヲ用ヒ其
次ハカタハズシトラサゲヒ手

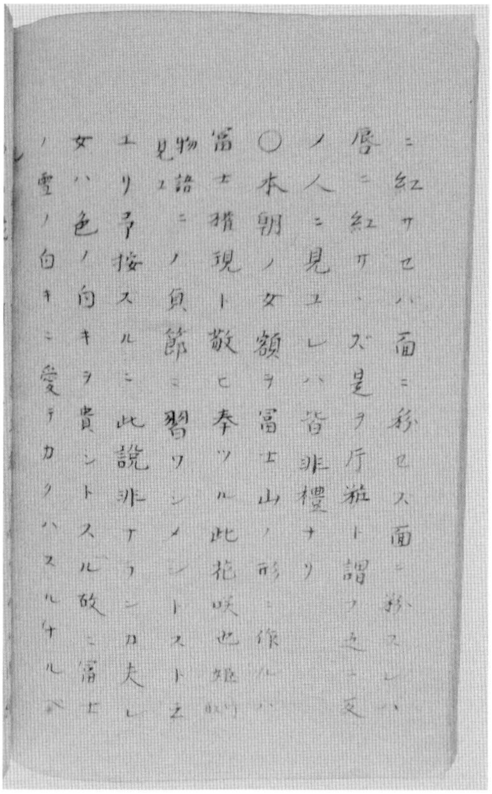

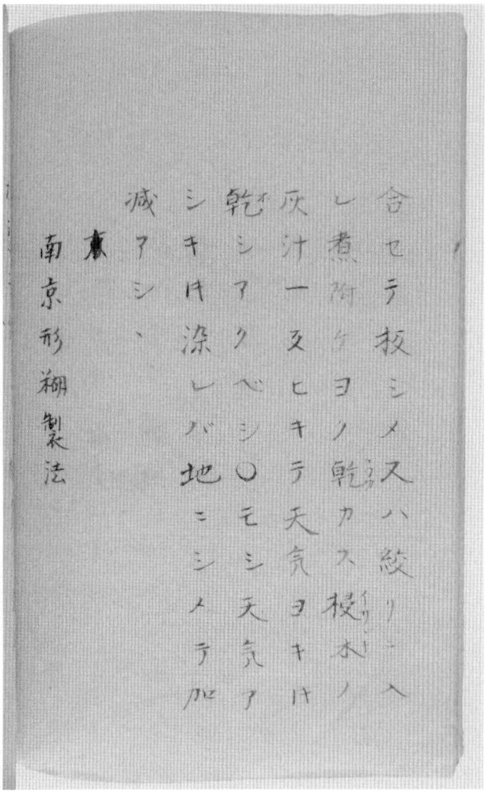

(21ウ)

合セテ扨シメスハ絞リニ入
シ煮附ケヨリノ桜ホリノ
灰汁一ヲヒキテ天気ヨキ
乾シマクベシ○モシ天気ア
シキ付染レバ地ニシメテ脱
減アシ、

南京形糊製法

(22オ)

南京形糊製法

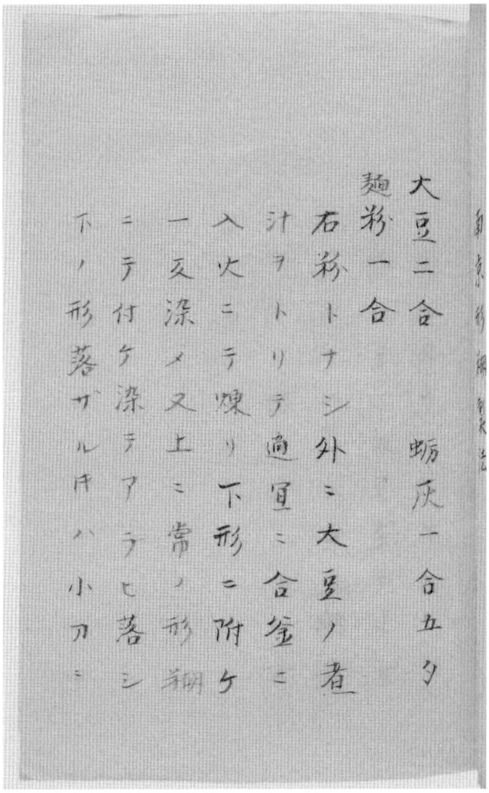

大豆二合　　蛎灰一合五夕
麺粉一合
右粉トナシ外ニ大豆ノ者
汁ヲトリテ適宜ニ合シ
入火ニテ煉リ下形ニ附ケ
一反染メ又上ニ常ノ形糊
ニテ付ケ染テアラヒ落シ
下ノ形落ザルギハ小刀ニ

(22ウ)

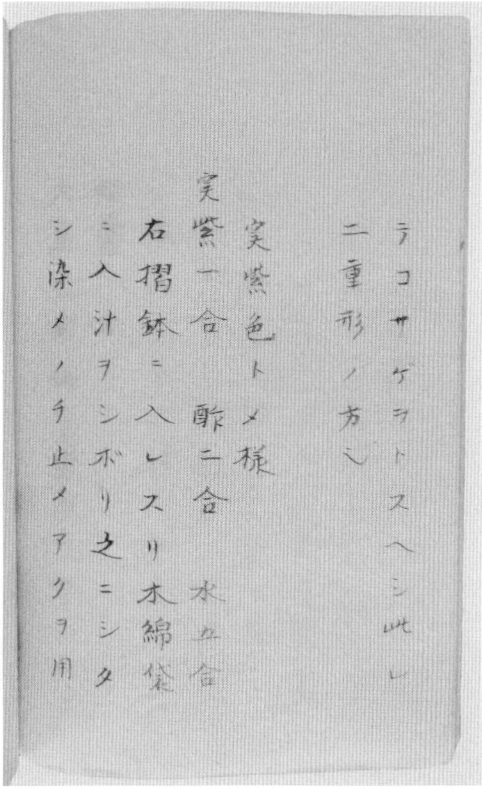

テコサゲヨトスヘシ此レ
二重形ノ方ヘ

実紫色トメ様
実紫一合　　酢二合
右摺鉢ニ入レスリ木綿袋　水五合
ニ入汁ヲシボリ之ニシタ
シ染メノチ止メアクヲ用

(23オ) ※23ウは白

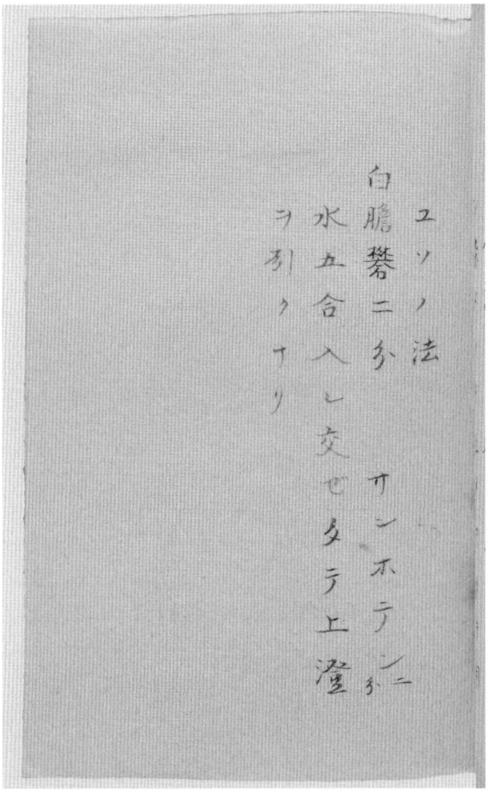

ユソノ法
白膽礬二分　サンホテンニ分
水五合入レ交ゼテ上澄
ヲ別ノナリ

図版　465 染物之法（UL, Ser. 892　19ウ〜21オ）

（19ウ）
本灰三外ヒカエ右ノ灰汁
ヲ一外入レ酒ヲ五タマシ
ヨクニカキマセ余リ五
合ヲ一合アテ五日ニ入ル
ナリ
○コレ早出シノ法ナリ
○比分量ヲ出シ藍ノ色薄ク
ナル件入ル件ハ委ク深ク藍

（20オ）
ツイヘナシ
　蒸絣ノ法
木綿一端ニ附キ水二外山灰
五タヽバコ灰二タ蛎灰一タ
酒少シ青笹ノ葉少シ
石水二外ヲ釜ノ内ニ入レ
沸騰スル件右ノ五味ヲ入レ
釜ノ上ニコシキヲカケ中ニ

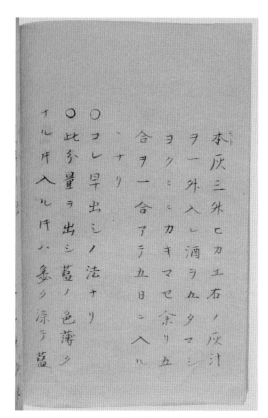

（20ウ）
品物ヲ入レ暫ク蒸スニツヤ
ヨク藍コユクナルヿ妙ニ
村雲染様
此ノ枚ジメ絞リノ法ナリ
一端分ニ付キ
蘇枋三十弐
一番水一外入レ四合ノ
二番水七合入レ三合ノ

（21オ）
三番水五合レ二合ニ煎
シトリ各交ゼアワセス
四合ニ前結メ
紫根二十弐湯ニテ一夜刀
シ翌日湯ヲハヘアトヘ榊
ノ灰汁ヲ一合入レ紫根ニ
カケル件ハ紅ラリシ右
ノ蘇枋ノ釜ノ中ヘ入レ煮

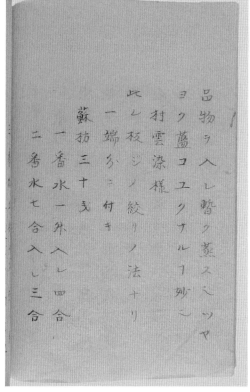

(16ウ)

竹木花ノマヽニ焼クコフ花
炭ト名ク瓦瓶ナリ
〇之ヲ焼ントスハ先其物
切リトル鮮体ニ雲母石ノ粉
ヲヨクヌリ付ケ毛䒳ニ入レ
間タラヌヤウ又ハ細キ切リ
ワラニテツメ蓋ヲ泥ニテ
ヨクヌリ中ニ火ノ入ラヌ様

(17オ) ※17ウは白

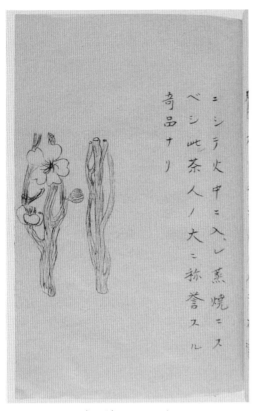

ニシテ火中ニ入レ蒸焼ニス
ベシ此茶人ノ大ニ称誉スル
奇品ナリ

(18オ) ※18ウは白

染物之法

(19オ)

藍落シ込ノ法
是ハ藍早出シノ法ヘ〇又出
シ藍余分染テ後青色ノ分子
スクナクナルトキ一処ニ集メ
染メトル法ヘ
タバコ三十匁黒焼ニシ湯
二升入灰汁一升五合ニタ
ラシ藍ツチノ通リニ出シ

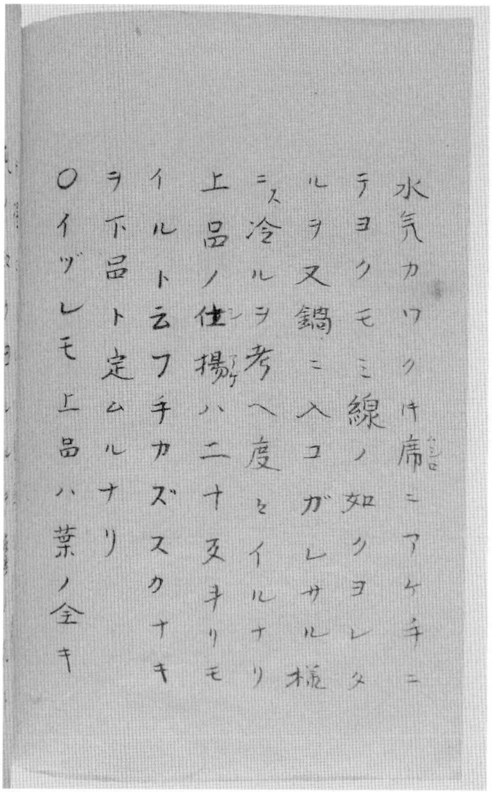
水気カワク时扁ニアケ干ニ
テヨクモミ線ノ如クヨレタ
ルヲ又鍋ニ入コガレサル様
ニ冷ルヲ考ヘ度ヽイルナリ
上品ノ仕揚ハ二十夂ヨリモ
イルト云フ手カズスクナキ
ヲ下品ト定ムルナリ
○イヅレモ上品ハ葉ノ全キ

(14ウ)

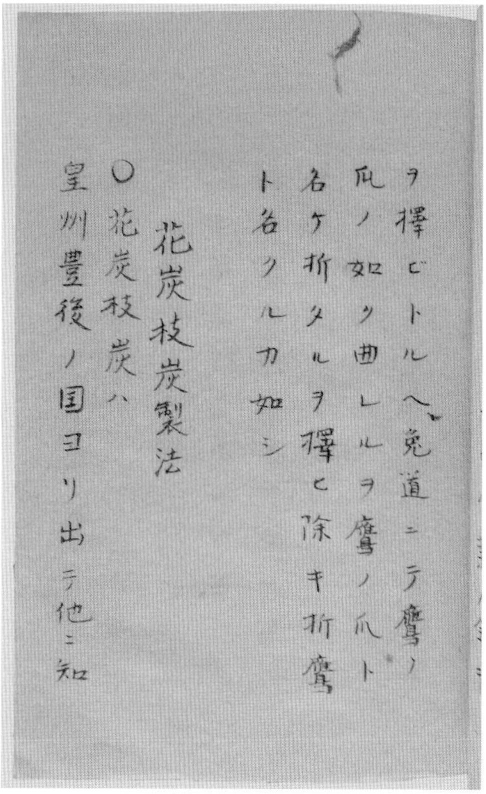
ヲ擇ビトルヘ、免道ニテ鷹ノ
爪ノ如ク曲レルヲ鷹ノ爪ト
名ケ折タルヲ擇ヒ除キ折鷹
ト名クルカ如シ
花炭枝炭製法
○花炭枝炭ハ
皇州豊後ノ国ヨリ出テ他ニ知

(15オ)

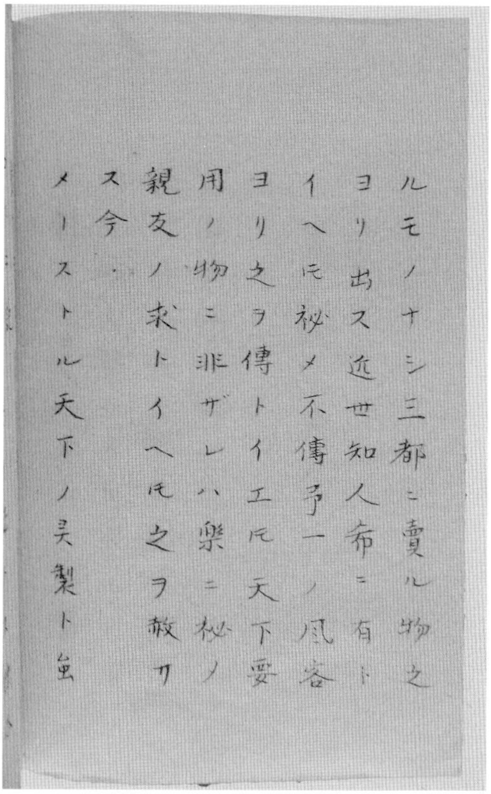
ルモノナシ三都ニ賣ル物之
ヨリ出ス近世知人希ニ有ト
イヘ氏秘メ不傳予一ノ風客
ヨリ之ヲ傳トイエ氏天下要
用ノ物ニ非ザレハ樂ニ秘ノ
親友ノ求トイヘ氏之ヲ赦サ
ス今・
メースト ル天下ノ美製ト虫

(15ウ)

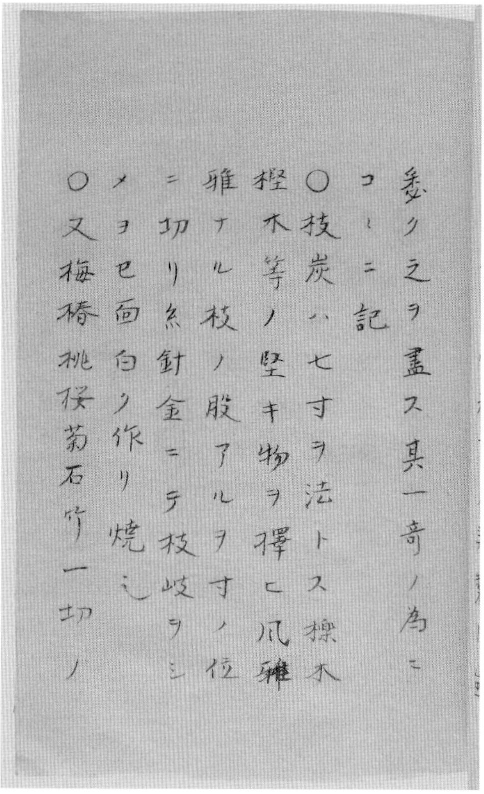
悉ク之ヲ盡ス其一奇ノ為ニ
コヽニ記
○枝炭ハ七寸ヲ法トス櫟木
樫木等ノ堅キ物ヲ擇ヒ凡雜
雅ナル枝ノ股アルヲ寸ノ位
ニ切リ糸針金ニテ枝岐ヲシ
メヨセ面白ク作リ焼ヽ
○又梅椿桃桜菊石竹一切ノ

(16オ)

【12ウ】

片ハ又温テモムヘシ如ニス
ルフ二三爻ニノ棄線ノ如
ヨシタル片火爐ニテ乾スレ
數日火適度ニシ全ク乾燥ス
ルマテ火ラヤムルコトナカレ

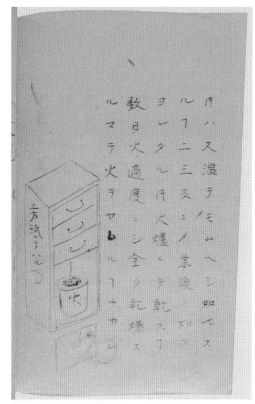

【13オ】

○ヨク乾モノ器ニ入外気通
紙ニテ厚クハルヘシ又長雨ノ
廻リ木ニテ作リ底
シアマリ厚キハアシ、此舟ニ茶ヲ入
レ乾スナリ

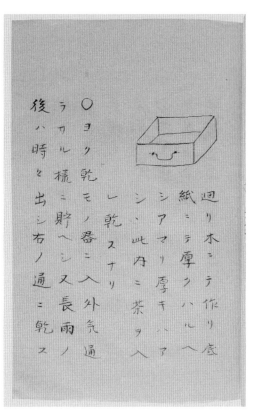

後ハ時々出シ右ノ通ニ乾ス
ラカル樣ニ貯ヘシ

【13ウ】

ヘシ、ヒタラサレハヒ子クサク
テルナリ
○挽茶ヒキヽハアシ、用ル
前晩ヒキ用ユレハ至テ香合ヨ
シ
○茶ヲ植ルノ地ハ深山ノ流
ヲ帯タル谷野ノ雲霧深キ處
ヲ最上トス尤モ日陰ハムシ

【14オ】

人家ニ近キホトアシ、
嬉野茶製法
予嬉野通行ノ時茶屋ニ止宿
シ製法ヲ問ヒ精シク習フト
イヘニ未タ試ミズ
○其製法葉ヲトリ鉄鍋ニ入レ
燒火ニカケシキリニイリテ

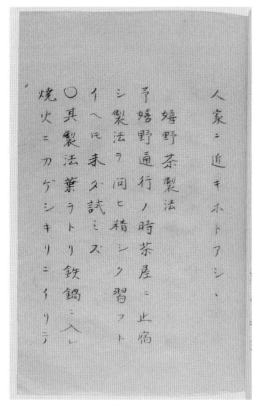
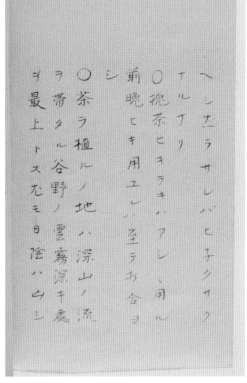

(10ウ)

○コヘノ仕様ハイワン油カ
ス茶ニ交エ根ノ辺リヲ掘リ
車コヘニスヘシ其余通例ノ
コヘモ可シ
茶ノ芽ノツミ様
春芽ヲ生ズル〻ヨク生スル
ハ五六寸次ハ三四寸斗リノ
寸根ヨリツミトルヘシ本ノ

(11オ)

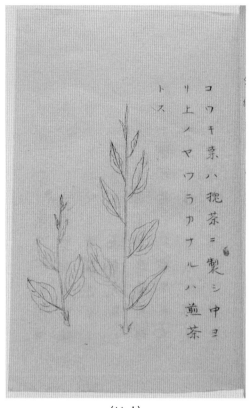

コワキ葉ハ挽茶ニ製シ中ヨ
リ上ノヤワラカナルハ煎茶
トス

(11ウ)

先ノ少キ葉ト茎ノヤワラカ
ナル処ハ一処ノアツメ製シ
センチャトナスニ下品トイ
モヨク製スレハ随引用ユル
ニ足リ○マツ葉ヲ煎茶ノ部
挽茶ノ部ト定メトルキニ下
ヨリ葉ノコワリヲ以テ挽茶
三品ニモワケ煎茶

(12オ)

モ石ノ通リニシ別〻ニ製エ
ルナリ又葉ノコワリ〻時ト
ヲ考ヘ製スレハ數種ナルヘ
○マツ葉ノロエメル葉ヲ
鉄鍋ニ入ヒ火ニ上ヒ水氣ハ
ナル・マコゲヌ様ニイリ
テ後ムシロニアゲチニ細
ニヨレルマテモミベシ冷ル

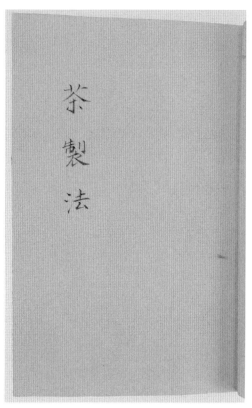

茶製法

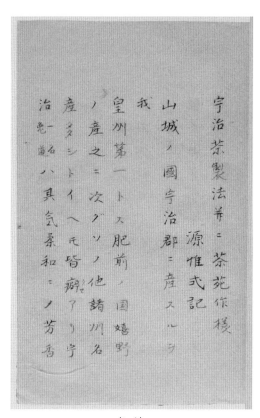

宇治茶製法并ニ茶苑作様
　　　　　　源惟式記
山城ノ国宇治郡ニ産スルヲ
我
皇州第一トス肥前ノ国嬉野
ノ産之ニ次グソノ他諸州名
産多シトイヘ氏皆後レリ宇
治亮道名ハ其気柔和ニノ芳香

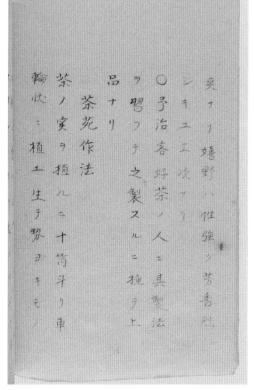

炙ナリ嬉野ハ性強ク芳香炙
シキユヘニ次ナリ
○宇治客好茶ノ人ニ其製法
ヲ習フテ之製スルニ極テ上
品ナリ
　茶苑作法
茶ノ実ヲ植ルニ十筋斗リ車
輪状ニ植エ生テ勢ヲキモノ

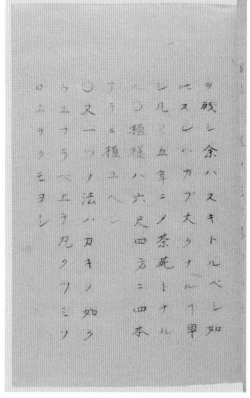

ヲ残シ余ハスキトルベシ如
セスレハカブ大クナル丁早
シ凡ソ五年ニノ茶苑トナル
ナリ○植様ハ六尺四方ニ四本
ヅヽ植ユヘシ
了又一ツノ法ハ刀キノ如ク
ウエテナラベ上ヲ凡クツミシ
ロヲエテクモヨシ

図版 465 染物之法 (UL. Ser. 892 5ウ〜7オ)

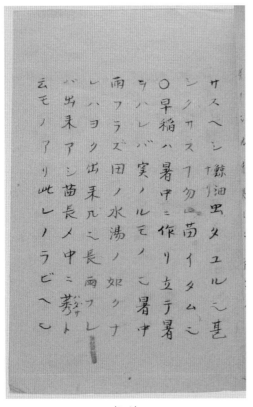

(6オ)

モ足アルナハ干鰯油糟ナド
少シ入ルヽナリ入レ過ルトキ
田ニフリコムニ具ナリ一日水
ヲ落シオクヘシ又弱クナルニ
切リ処ヽニサスモヨシ
〇植テノチ長雨フレハ中サ
シト云テ苗ノ中ヲ食コム虫
付クコノ片処ヽニ油コヘヲ

(5ウ)

サスヘシ懈怠油虫タユルニ悪
シクサスヲ勿論苗イタミニ
〇早稲ハ暑中ニ作リ立テ暑
中ニ実ノルモノニ暑中
ハレバ実ノルモノニ暑中
雨フラズ田ノ水湯ノ如クナ
レハヨク出来シ長雨フレ
バ出来アシ苗メ中ニ葵[?]
云モノアリ此レノラビヘシ

(7オ) ※7ウは白

片ニ附トルヘシ

(6ウ)

早ク抜キ去ヘシ早ヲ害スル
ナリシ
〇穂出ルニ雨フレハアシ
ホミツ入ルトキホクサル
穂出テ花咲キ実熟スルニ
水ヲ皆落シ田ヲ乾ベシ大ラ
サレハ実リアシヽ
〇ヨク熟シ蘂黄色ニカレ

図版 465 染物之法（UL, Ser. 892 3ウ〜5オ）

(3ウ)

十日ニ苗ヲトリ田ニ植カエ
ル之時ハ五月梅雨ニ入テ五
六日ヲヨシトス

(4オ)

苗代ハ泥ヲヨクヤキマゼ底
ニ州ヲヨク踏ミコムヘシヲ
正月不二月ノ初カタニ作リ
ラクヘシ太ノ種ヲマク什泥
ヨク齊リ合申テ間ニアハス
ヘシ
植田ハ梅雨マヘ迄ニ耕シコ
ヘカヒ水ヲ仕カケヲクヘシ

(4ウ)

苗トリ様苗ヲ両ノ大指食指
ニ因ム位ニタバネヲクヘシ
植様ハ土地ノ厚薄ニ從フ
ヘキ土ノ厚サ一尺ナレハ苗
ノ間一尺隔テ植ユヘシ五寸

(5オ)

ナレハ苗五すヘダテウユヘ
シ余ハ皆此例ニ
苗ハ一カブニ五本ヲ植ヱ
苗地ニアリツカハ根ノ州ヲ
トリ去ヘシ州アレハ苗栄ユ
ヘシナシコヘハ初ノ耕スヰ
ニ州ノ馬ノ敷州糞等ヲ交廬
セヨクモノヲ入ラ耕シ植テ

図版　465 染物之法（UL. Ser. 892　表紙・1オ〜3オ）

465 染物之法　UL. Ser. 892

（表紙）

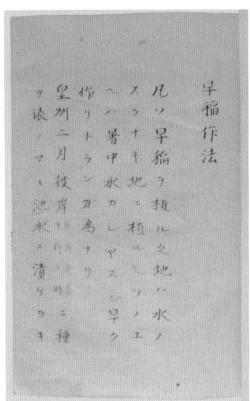
（2オ）

早稲作法

凡ソ早稲ヲ植ルノ地ハ水ノ
スクナキ地ニ植ルヘシソノユ
ヘハ暑中水カレヤスシ早ク
作リトランガ為ナリ
皇州二月彼岸前行ノ時籾ニ種
ヲ俵ノマヽ池水ニ漬ケラキ

（1オ）※1ウは白

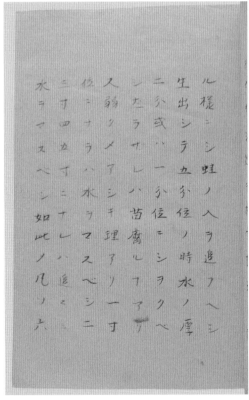
（3オ）

ル様ニシ蛙ノ入ヲ追フヘシ
生出シテ五分位ノ時水ノ厚
二分或ハ一分位ニシテヘ
シタラサレハ苗腐ルフアリ
人弱メアシテ理了リ一寸
位ニナレハ水ヲマスヘシニ
三寸四五寸ニマスヘシ如此ノ凡ノ六
水ヲマスヘシ

（2ウ）

芽少シ出ルトキヲ考ヘヨリ上
ケ筵ニ入レホノ蒸ニ入レ水ノ
タラヌヲ乾シテ苗代ニマキ
ヌリ
○苗代ハ泥土ヨクカキナ
ラシ中ヲ一面ニ四角ニ作
リ四方ニ溝ヲ作リ平面ノ種
ヲマキシ処ニ水一寸斗リア

図版　448 日州養蜂図（RMvV 1-4393　袋綴　4ウ・裏表紙見返し・裏表紙）

（裏表紙見返し）　　　　　　　　（4ウ）

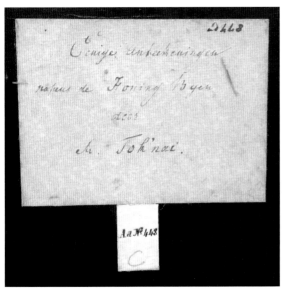

（裏表紙のラベル部分）

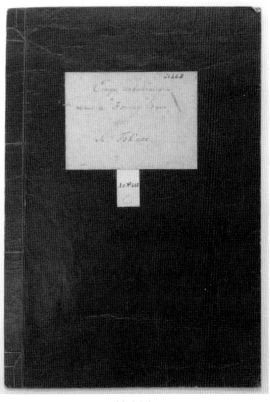

（裏表紙）

図版 448 日州養蜂図（RMvV 1-4393 袋綴 2ウ～4オ）

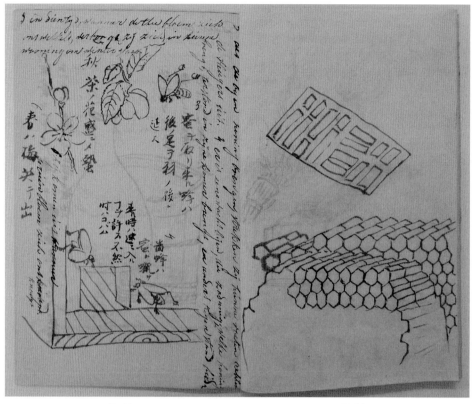

(3オ)　　　　　　　　　　　　　(2ウ)

(4オ)　　　　　　　　　　　　　(3ウ)

図版　448 日州養蜂図（RMvV 1-4393　袋綴　表紙・1オ〜2オ）

448 日州養蜂図　RMvV 1-4393（袋綴）

（1オ）

（表紙）

（2オ）　　　　　　（1ウ）

図版　448 日州養蜂図（RMvV 1-4393　折帖　第 1 図拡大～第 4 図拡大）

（第 2 図拡大）　　　　　　　　　　　　　　　　（第 1 図拡大）

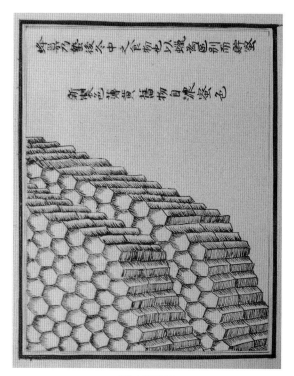

（第 4 図拡大）　　　　　　　　　　　　　　　　（第 3 図拡大）

図版　448 日州養蜂図（RMvV 1-4393　折帖　表紙・第1図〜第4図）

（表紙）

448

日州養蜂図　RMvV 1-4393（折帖）

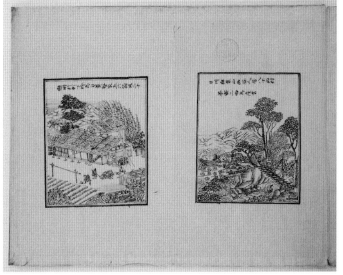

（第1図・第2図）

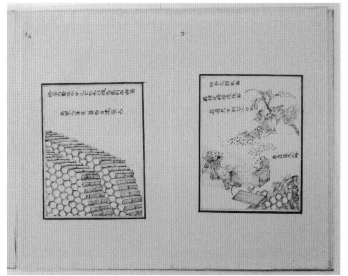

（第3図・第4図）

図版　417 京大坂茶屋諸分調方記（UL. Ser. 815　11ウ〜14オ）

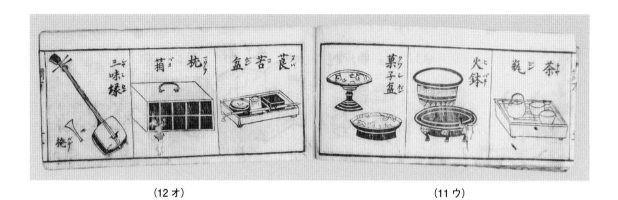

（12オ）　　　　　　　　　　　　　　　　（11ウ）

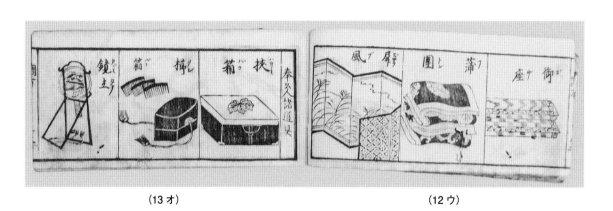

（13オ）　　　　　　　　　　　　　　　　（12ウ）

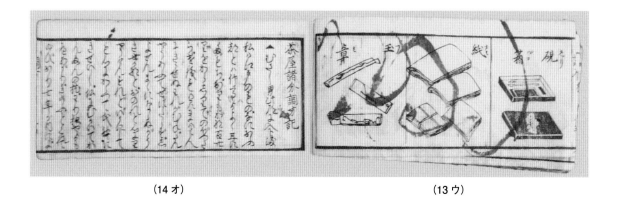

（14オ）　　　　　　　　　　　　　　　　（13ウ）

図版　417 京大坂茶屋諸分調方記（UL, Ser. 815　8ウ〜11オ）

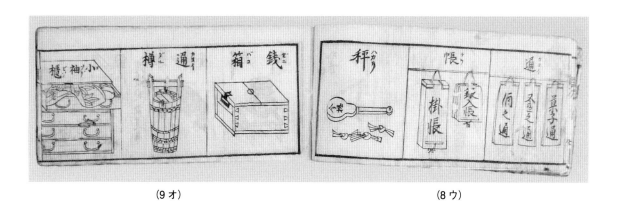
（9オ）　　　　　　　　　　　　（8ウ）

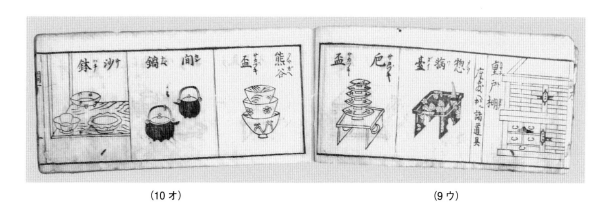
（10オ）　　　　　　　　　　　　（9ウ）

（11オ）　　　　　　　　　　　　（10ウ）

417 京大坂茶屋諸分調方記　UL. Ser. 815

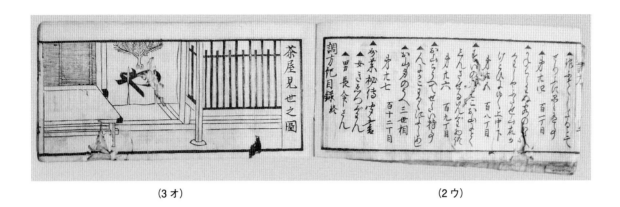

（3オ）　　　　　　　　　　　　　　（2ウ）

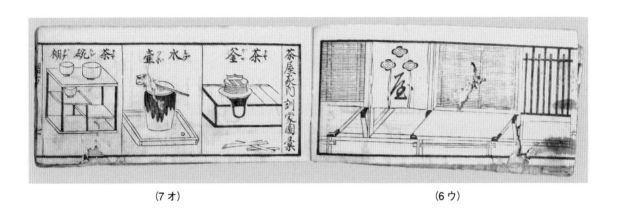

（7オ）　　　　　　　　　　　　　　（6ウ）

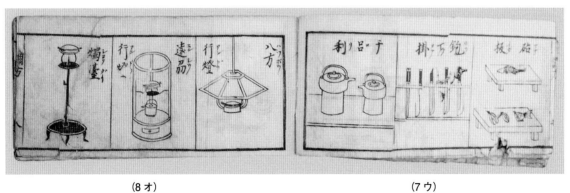

（8オ）　　　　　　　　　　　　　　（7ウ）

図版　371 キフ子本地（RMvV 1-4352　下巻　第22紙〜第24紙）

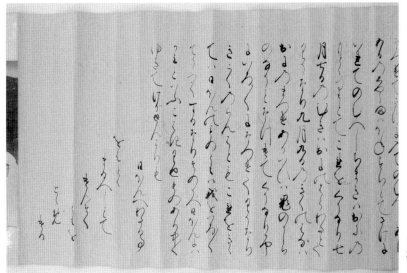
（第22紙）

（第23紙）

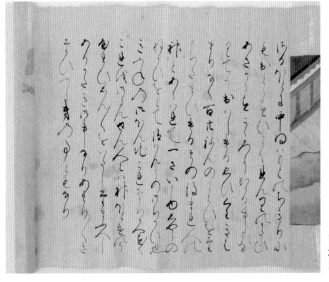
（第24紙）

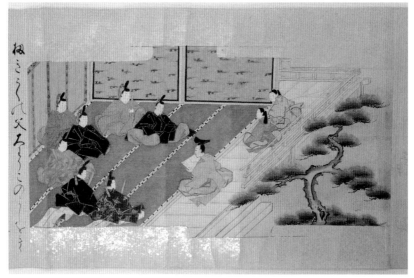

(第19紙)

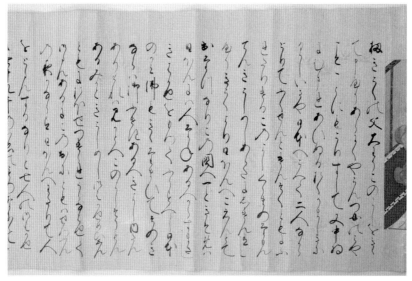

(第20紙)

(第21紙)

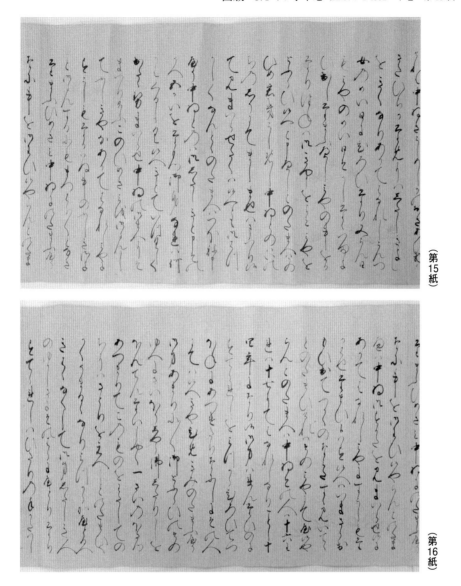

図版　371 キフ子本地（RMvV 1-4352　下巻　第15紙～第18紙）

図版 371 キフ子本地（RMvV 1-4352　下巻　第12紙〜第14紙）

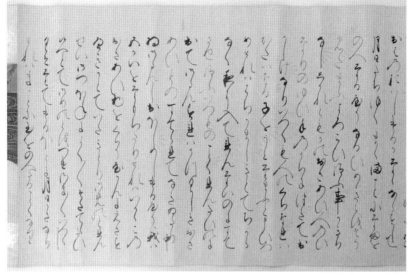

（第12紙）

（第13紙）

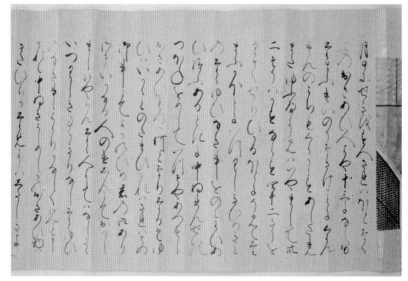

（第14紙）

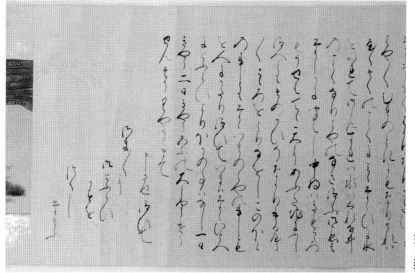

(第9紙)

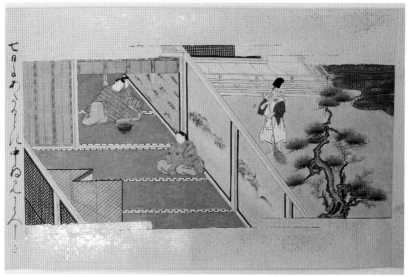

(第10紙)

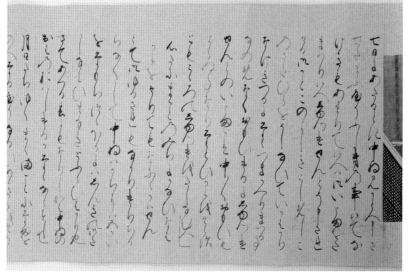

(第11紙)

図版　371 キフ子本地（RMvV 1-4352　下巻　第6紙〜第8紙）

（第6紙）

（第7紙）

（第8紙）

図版　371 キフ子本地（RMvV 1-4352　下巻　第3紙〜第4紙）

（第3紙）

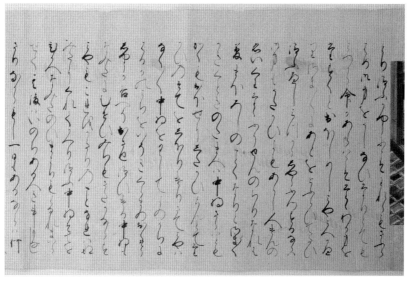

（第4紙）

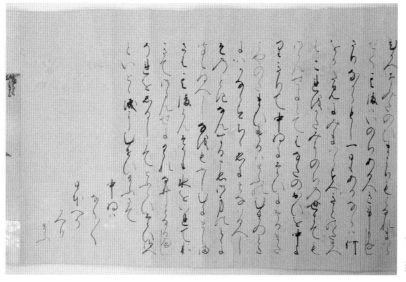

（第5紙）

図版 371 キフ子本地（RMvV 1-4352　下巻　巻姿・外題・第1紙・第2紙）

371 キフ子本地　RMvV 1-4352　下巻

（外題）

（巻姿）

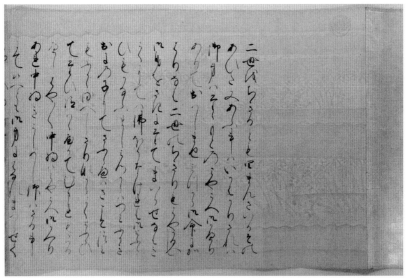
（第1紙）

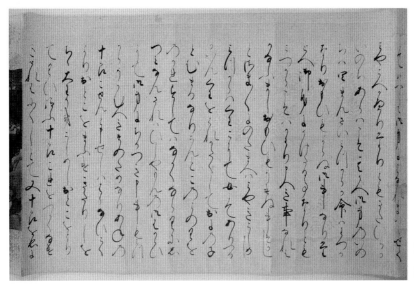
（第2紙）

図版　371 キフ子本地（RMvV 1-4352　中巻　第20紙〜第22紙）

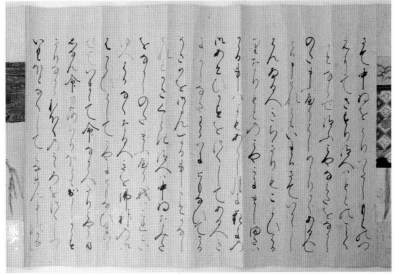

（第20紙）

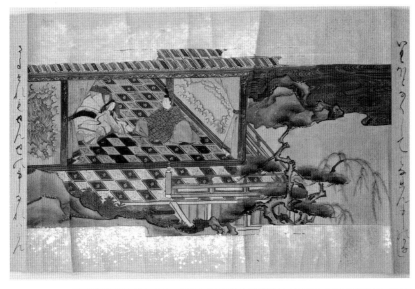

（第21紙）

（第22紙）

図版 371 キフ子本地（RMvV 1-4352 中巻 第16紙〜第19紙）

（第16紙）

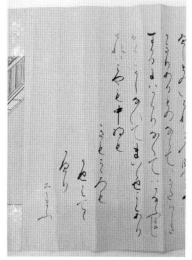

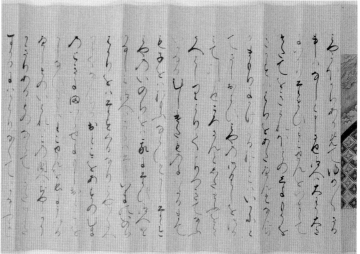

（第17紙・第18紙）

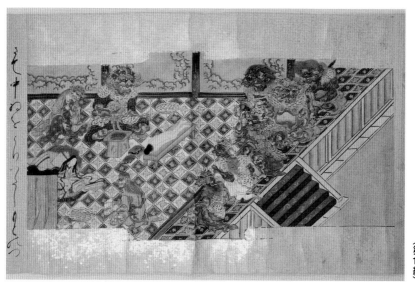

（第19紙）

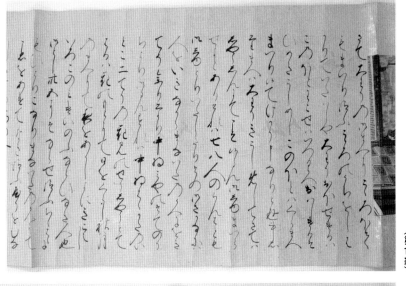

（第13紙）

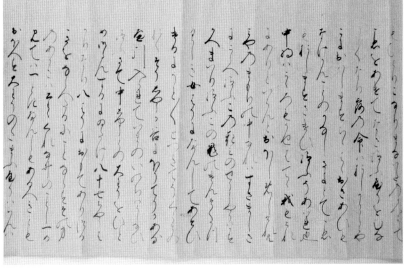

（第14紙）

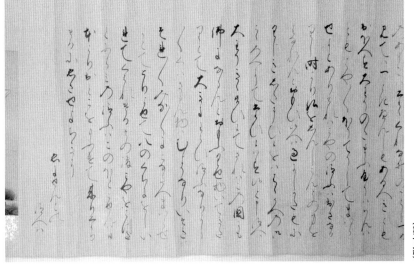

（第15紙）

図版　371 キフ子本地（RMvV 1-4352　中巻　第9紙〜第12紙）

（第9紙）

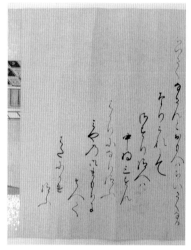

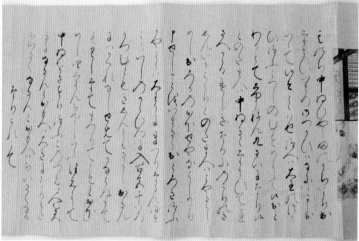

（第10紙・第11紙）

（第12紙）

図版　371 キフ子本地（RMvV 1-4352　中巻　第6紙〜第8紙）

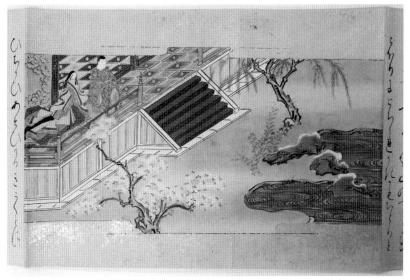

（第6紙）

（第7紙）

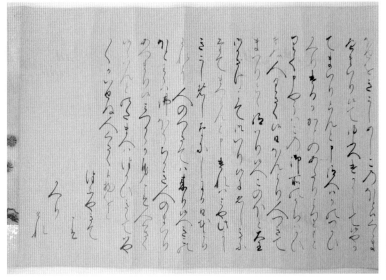

（第8紙）

図版　371 キフ子本地（RMvV 1-4352　中巻　第3紙～第5紙）

（第3紙）

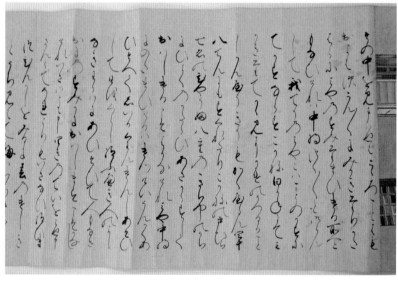

（第4紙）

（第5紙）

図版　371 キフ子本地（RMvV 1-4352　中巻　巻姿・外題・第1紙・第2紙）

371 キフ子本地　RMvV 1-4352　中巻

（外題）

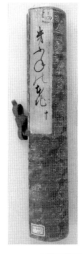
（巻姿）

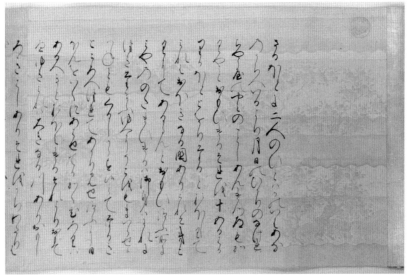
（第1紙）

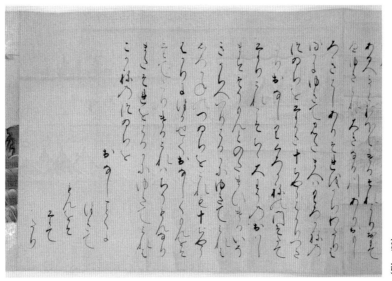
（第2紙）

図版 153 采草閑筆（RMvV 1-4303 図8・図9）

（図8）

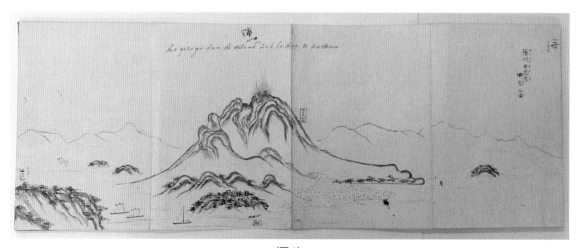

（図9）

図版　153 采草閑筆（RMvV 1-4303　図6・図7）

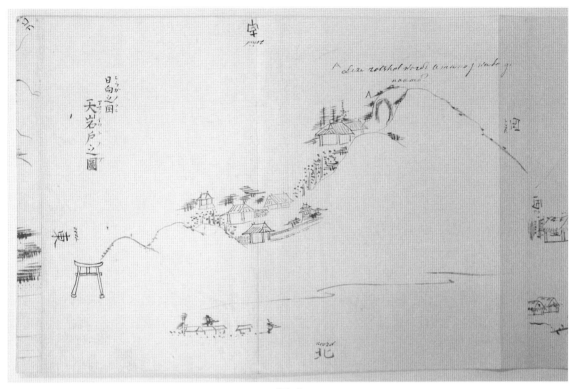

（図6）

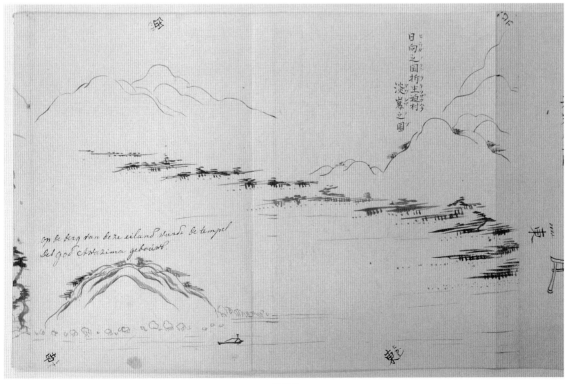

（図7）

図版 153 采草閑筆（RMvV 1-4303 図4・図5）

（図4）

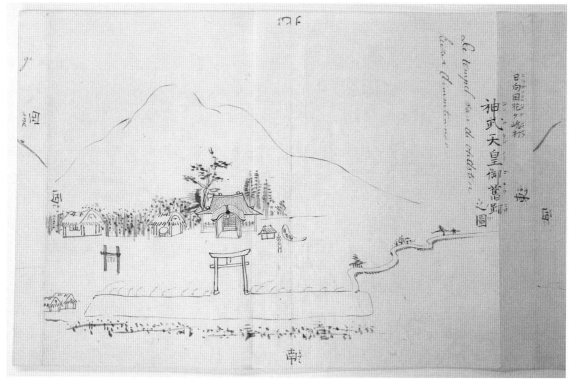

（図5）

図版 153 采草閑筆（RMvV 1-4303 図2・図3）

（図2）

（図3）

図版 153 采草閑筆（RMvV 1-4303 表紙・裏表紙・図1）

153 采草閑筆　RMvV 1-4303

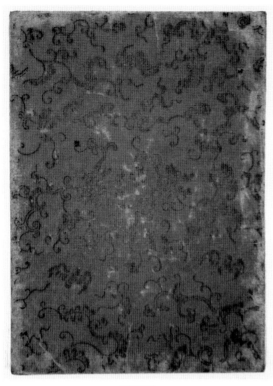

（裏表紙）

（表紙）

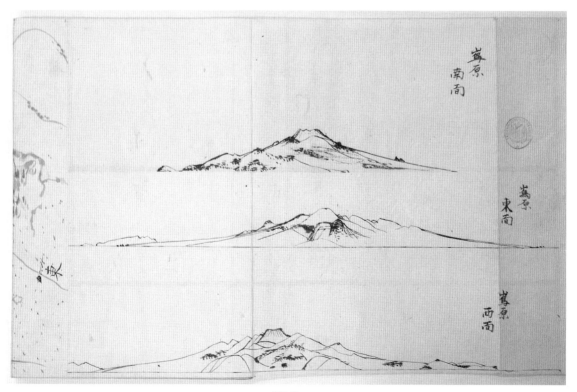

（図1）

図版 583 江戸風美人姿（RMvV 1-4466 8ウ～9ウ・裏表紙）

（9オ）　　　　　　　　　　　　（8ウ）

（裏表紙）

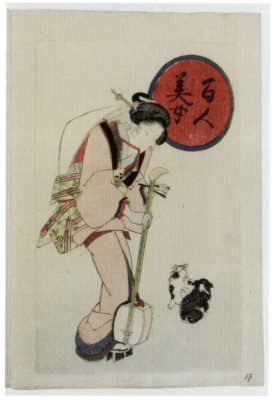

（9ウ）

図版　583 江戸風美人姿（RMvV 1-4466　5ウ〜8オ）

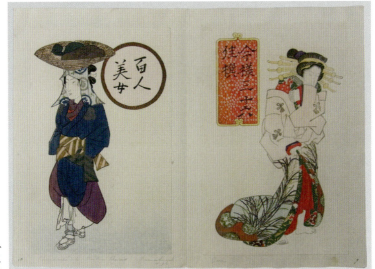

（6オ）　（5ウ）

（7オ）　（6ウ）

（8オ）　（7ウ）

図版 583 江戸風美人姿（RMvV 1-4466 2ウ〜5オ）

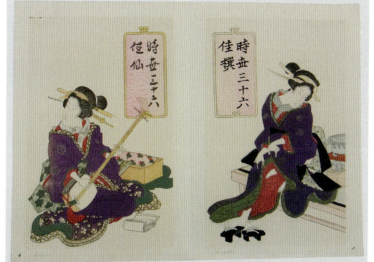

図版　583 江戸風美人姿（RMvV 1-4466　表紙・1オ～2オ）

583 江戸風美人姿　RMvV 1-4466

（1オ）

（表紙）

（2オ）　　　　　　　　　　　　　　　（1ウ）

図版　582 猿楽之図（RMvV 1-4465　4ウ〜6オ）

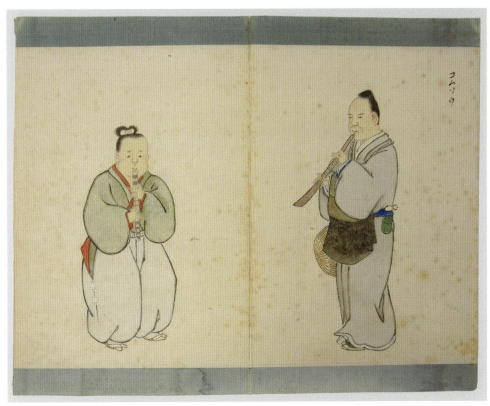

（5オ）　　　　　　　　　　　　　　（4ウ）

（6オ）　　　　　　　　　　　　　　（5ウ）

図版 582 猿楽之図（RMvV 1-4465 2ウ〜4オ）

（3オ）　　　　　　　　　　　　（2ウ）

（4オ）　　　　　　　　　　　　（3ウ）

図版　582 猿楽之図（RMvV 1-4465　表紙・裏表紙・1ウ・2オ）

582 猿楽之図　RMvV 1-4465

（裏表紙）

（表紙）

（2オ）　　　　　　　　　　　　　　　　（1ウ）

図版　558 鳥山石燕画譜 (RMvV 1-4456)

558 鳥山石燕画譜　RMvV 1-4456　(29ウ・30オ)

(30ウ・31オ)

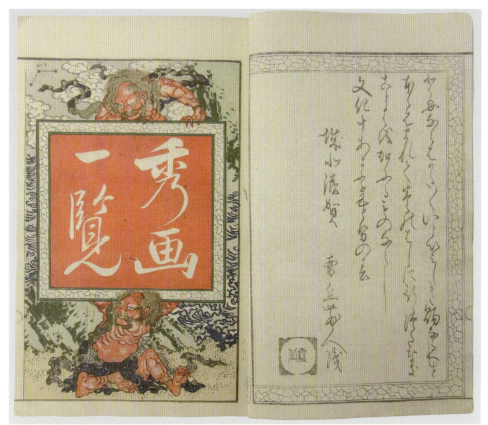

図版　535 櫻花画帖（RMvV 1-4430　図2・図3）

(図2)

(図3)

図版　535 櫻花画帖（RMvV 1-4430　表紙・見返し・図1）

535 櫻花画帖　RMvV 1-4430

（見返し）

（表紙）

（図1）

533 絵本筆二色　UL. Ser. 1180

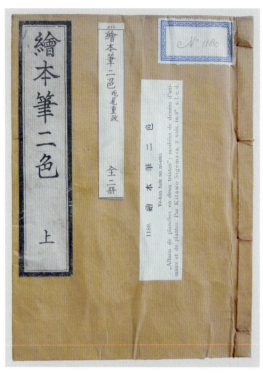

（上　表紙）

（袋）

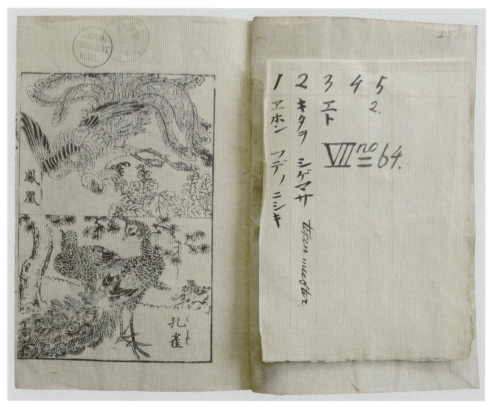

（上　1オ）　　　　　　　　　　　（上　見返し）

図版　493 和蘭全躯内外分図（UL. Ser. 1128　別録験号　2オ・4ウ・5オ）

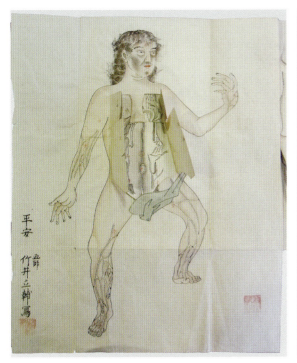

（同　展開撮影）

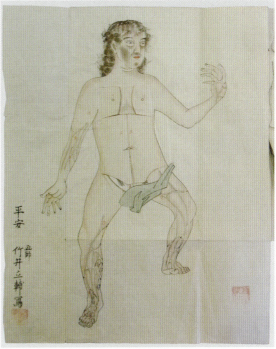

（別録験号　2オ）

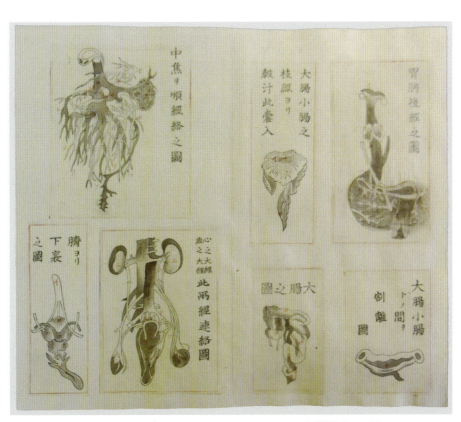

（別録験号　5オ）　　　　　　　　　　（別録験号　4ウ）

図版　493 和蘭全軀内外分図（UL, Ser. 1128　別録験号　表紙・裏表紙見返し・1 オ）

493 和蘭全軀内外分図　UL, Ser. 1128

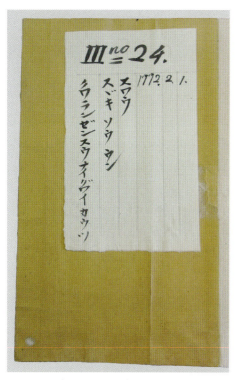

（別録験号　裏表紙見返し）

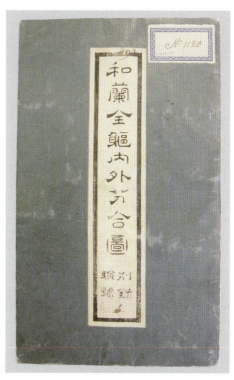

（別録験号　表紙）

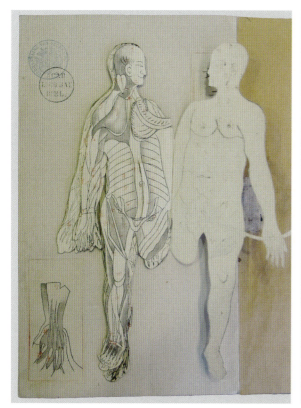

（同　展開撮影）

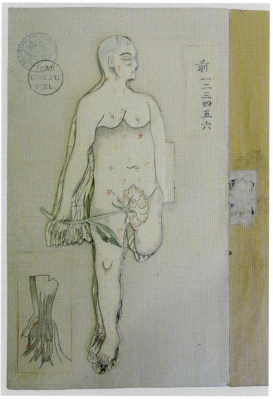

（別録験号　1 オ）

図版 471 張公捕魚（RMvV 1-4394）

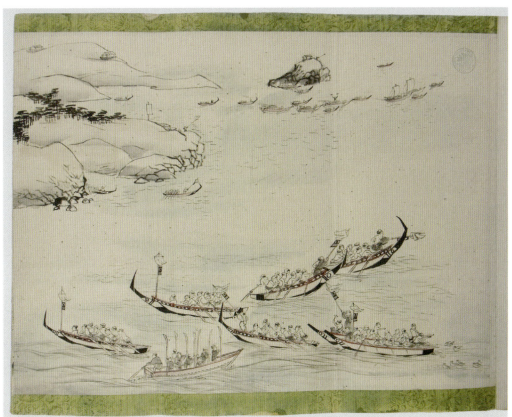

（第1図）

（第9図）

図版　459 瓶花図彙（RMvV 1-4638）

459 瓶花図彙　RMvV 1-4638

（乾　1オ）

（乾　表紙）

（乾　2オ）　　　　　　　　　（乾　1ウ）

453 鼓銅圖錄　RMvV 1-4635

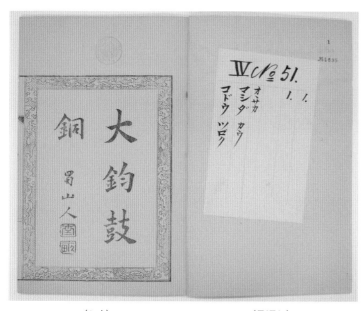

（1オ）　　　　　　　　　（見返し）

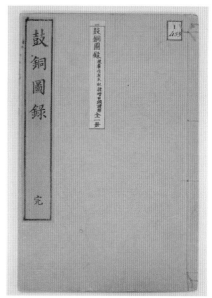

（表紙）

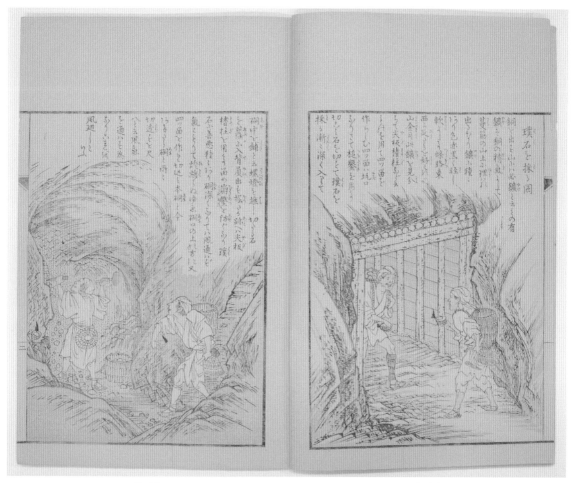

（2オ）　　　　　　　　　（1ウ）

図版　438 佩文耕織図（RMvV 1-4390）

438 佩文耕織図　RMvV 1-4390

（表紙）

（袋）

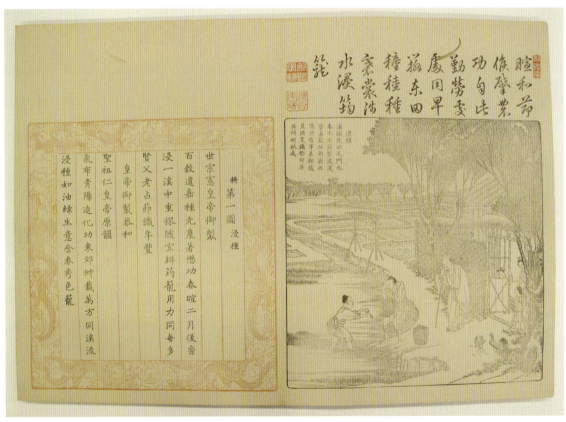

（第1図）

図版　417 京大坂茶屋諸分調方記（UL. Ser. 815　末丁オ・末丁ウ・裏表紙見返し・裏表紙）

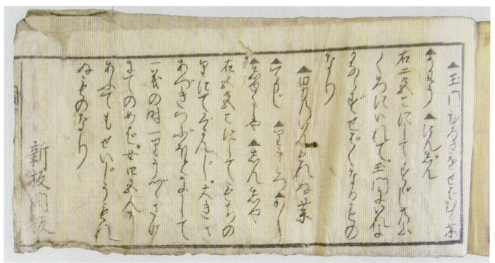
（末丁オ）

（末丁ウ）

（裏表紙見返し）

（裏表紙）

417 京大坂茶屋諸分調方記　UL, Ser. 815

（表紙）

（見返し）

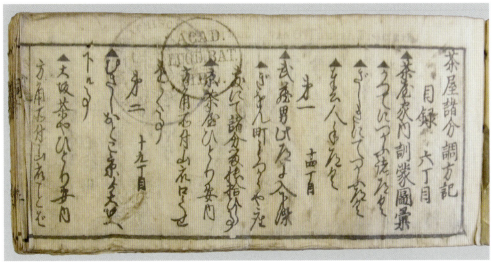

（１オ）

図版 397 絵本和歌合（吉原女郎歌準）（RMvV 1-4361 9ウ・裏表紙見返し・裏表紙）

（裏表紙見返し） （9ウ）

（裏表紙）

図版　397 絵本和歌合（吉原女郎歌準）（RMvV 1-4361　7ウ〜9オ）

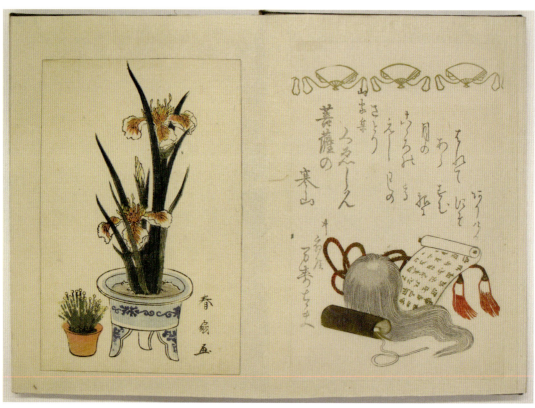

（8オ）　　　　　　　　　　　　　　　　（7ウ）

（9オ）　　　　　　　　　　　　　　　　（8ウ）

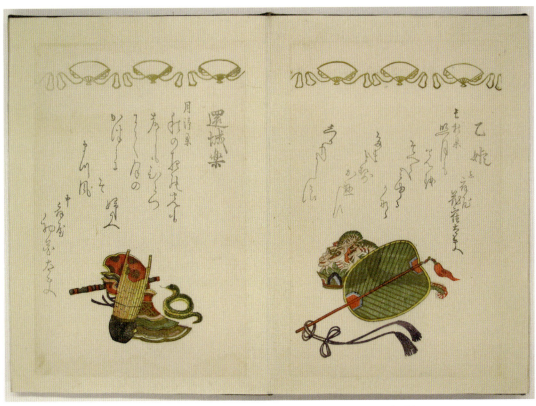

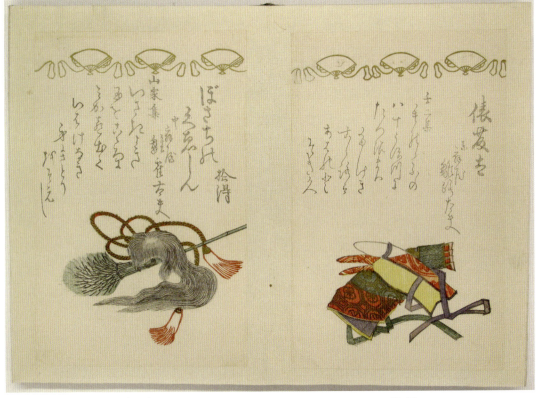

図版　397 絵本和歌合（吉原女郎歌準）（RMvV 1-4361　3ウ〜5オ）

（4オ）　　　　　　　　　　　　　　　　　　　（3ウ）

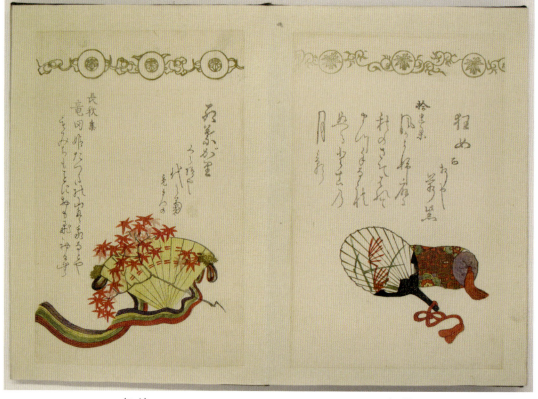

（5オ）　　　　　　　　　　　　　　　　　　　（4ウ）

図版　397 絵本和歌合（吉原女郎歌準）（RMvV 1-4361　1ウ～3オ）

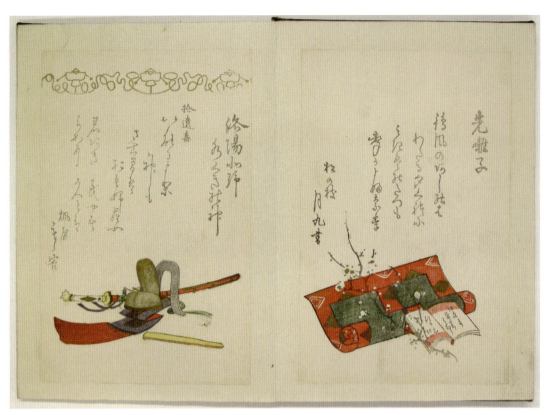

（2オ）　　　　　　　　　　　　（1ウ）

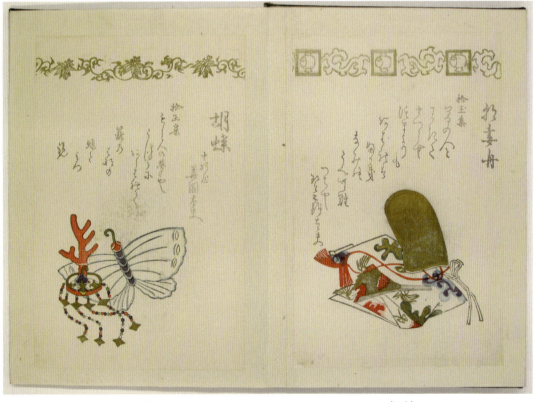

（3オ）　　　　　　　　　　　　（2ウ）

図版　397 絵本和歌合（吉原女郎歌準）（RMvV 1-4361　表紙・見返し・1オ）

397
絵本和歌合（吉原女郎歌準）

RMvV 1-4361

（表紙）

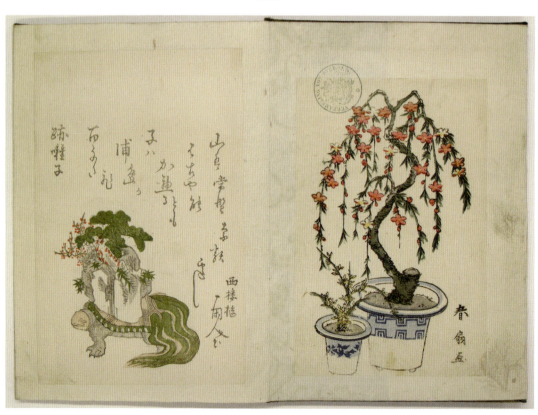

（1オ）　　　　　　　　　　　　（見返し）

図版　371 キフ子本地（RMvV 1-4352　上巻　第22紙〜第24紙）

（第22紙）

（第23紙）

（第24紙）

図版 371 キフ子本地（RMvV 1-4352　上巻　第18紙〜第21紙）

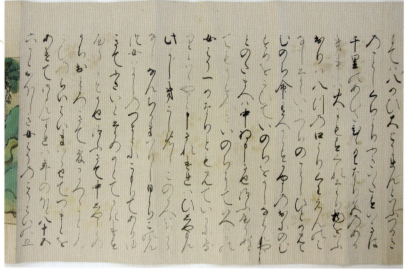
（第18紙）

（第19紙）

（第20紙・第21紙）

図版　371 キフ子本地（RMvV 1-4352　上巻　第15紙～第17紙）

（第15紙）

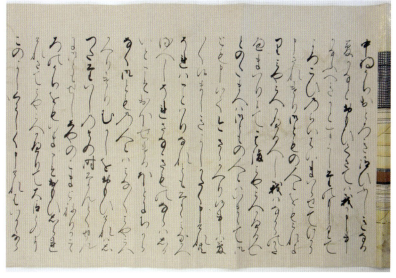

（第16紙）

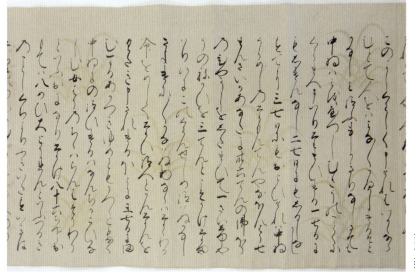

（第17紙）

図版　371 キフ子本地（RMvV 1-4352　上巻　第12紙〜第14紙）

（第12紙）

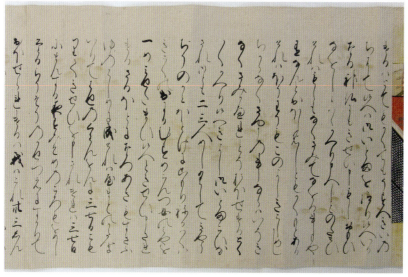

（第13紙）

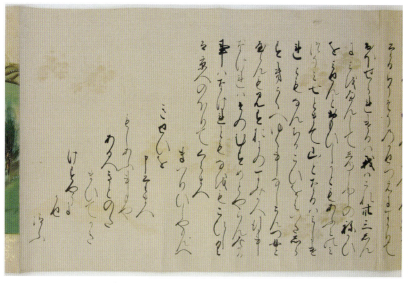

（第14紙）

図版 371 キフ子本地（RMvV 1-4352 上巻 第9紙～第11紙）

（第9紙）

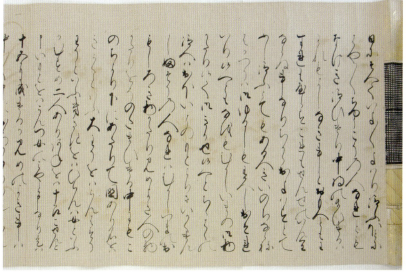

（第10紙）

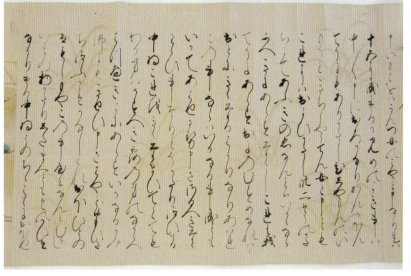

（第11紙）

図版 371 キフ子本地（RMvV 1-4352　上巻　第6紙〜第8紙）

（第6紙）

（第7紙）

（第8紙）

(第3紙)

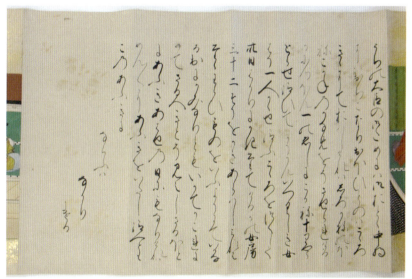

(第4紙)

(第5紙)

図版　371 キフ子本地（RMvV 1-4352　上巻　巻姿・外題・第1紙・第2紙）

371 キフ子本地　RMvV 1-4352　上巻

（外題）

（巻姿）

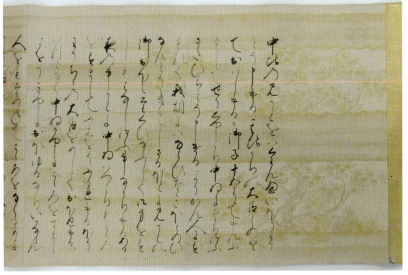
（第1紙）

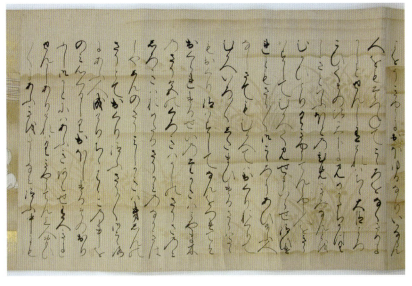
（第2紙）

325 江戸ハルマ　UL. Ser. 62 A I

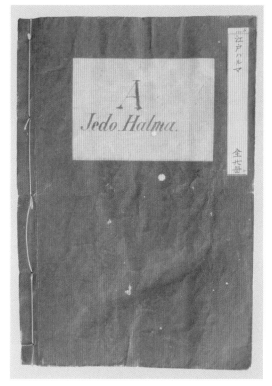

（表紙）

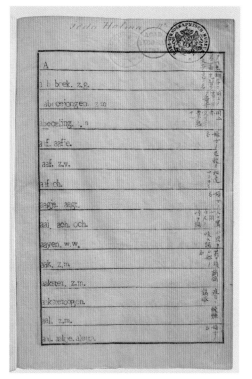

（1オ）

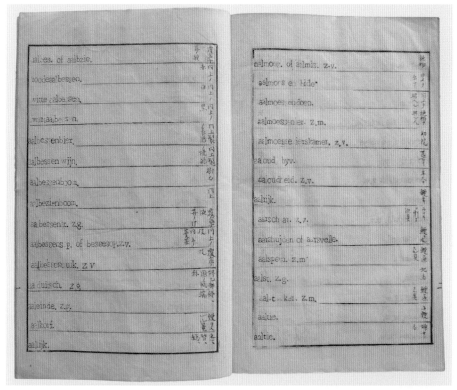

（1ウ）　　　　　　　　　　　　（2オ）

図版 293 鷸十八品真写（RMvV 1-4320 16ウ〜18ウ・奥書）

図版　293 鷸十八品真写（RMvV 1-4320　12 ウ〜16 オ）

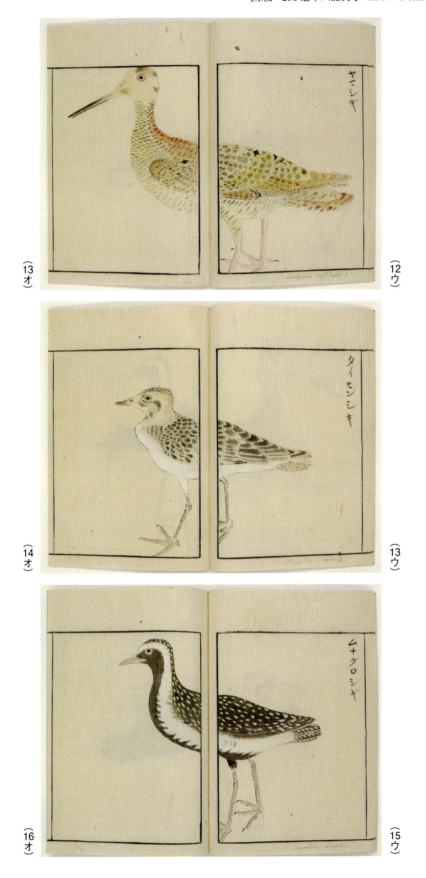

図版 293 鷸十八品真写（RMvV 1-4320 9ウ〜12オ）

45

図版　293 鷸十八品真写（RMvV 1-4320　6ウ～9オ）

図版　293 鷸十八品真写（RMvV 1-4320　3ウ〜6オ）

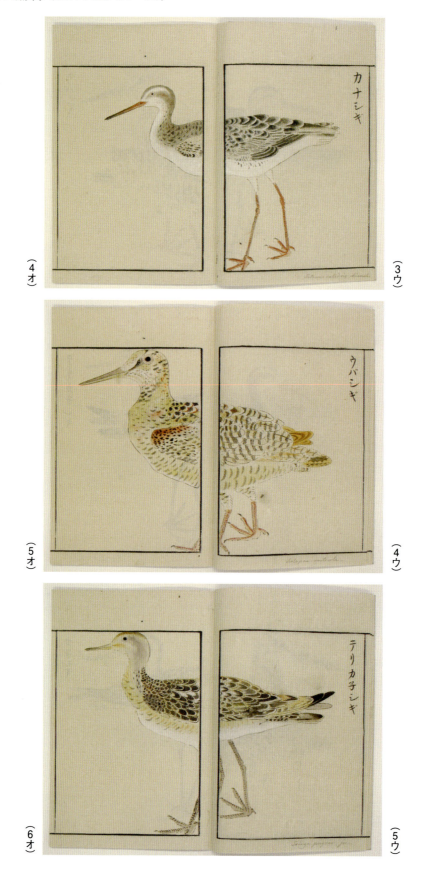

図版 293 鷸十八品真写 (RMvV 1-4320 1ウ〜3オ)

(2オ)　　　　　　　　　　　　　　　　(1ウ)

(3オ)　　　　　　　　　　　　　　　　(2ウ)

図版 293 鷸十八品真写（RMvV 1-4320　表紙・裏表紙・見返し・1オ）

293 鷸十八品真写　RMvV 1-4320

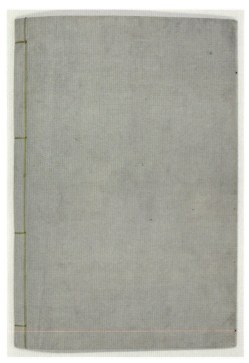

（裏表紙）　　　　　　　　　　　　　（表紙）

（1オ）　　　　　　　　　　　　　（見返し）

282 石ニ化魚之図　RMvV 1-4319

（裏表紙）

（表紙）

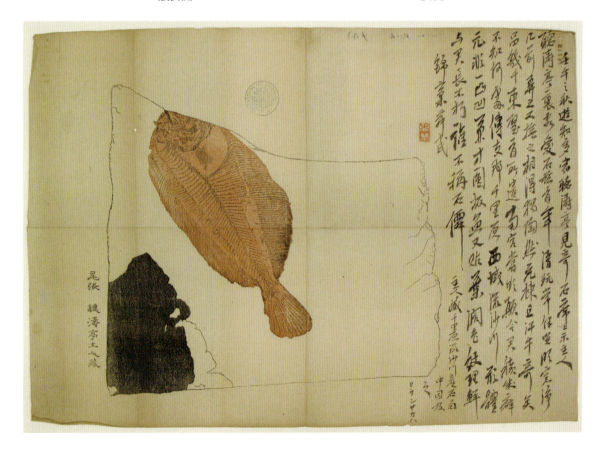

図版 265 腊葉揚（RMvV 1-4317 2ウ〜4オ）

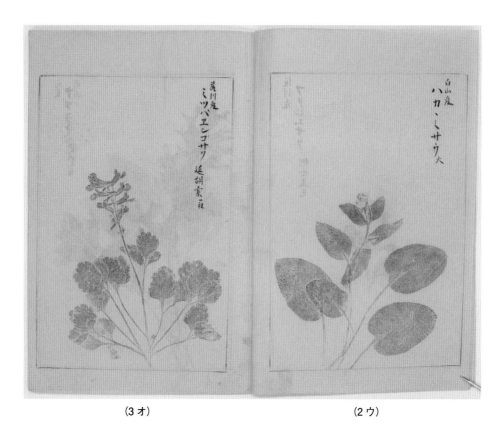

（3オ）　　　　　　　　　（2ウ）

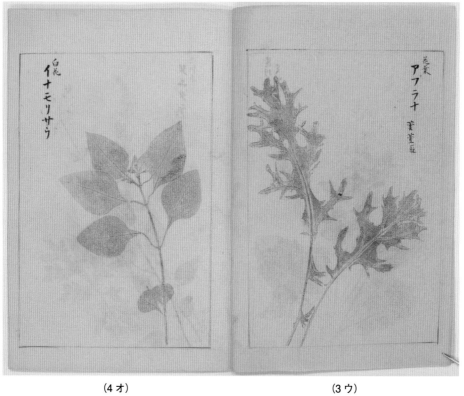

（4オ）　　　　　　　　　（3ウ）

図版　265 腊葉搨（RMvV 1-4317　表紙・1オ〜1ウ）

265 腊葉搨　RMvV 1-4317

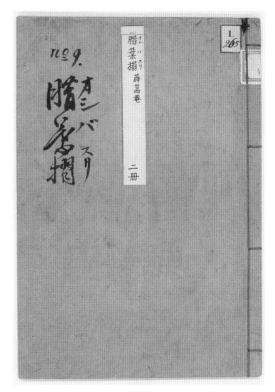
（表紙）

（1オ）

（2オ）　　　　　　　　　　　（1ウ）

図版 261 本草推写（UL, Ser. 975a 図4〜図7）

（図5） （図4）

（図7） （図6）

図版　261 本草推写（UL, Ser. 975a　表紙・図1～図3）

261 本草推写　UL, Ser. 975a

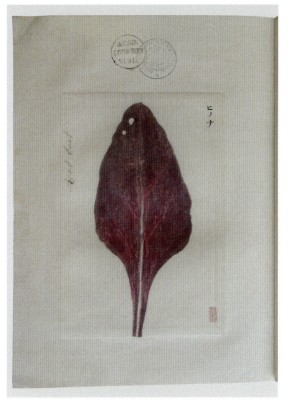

（図1）

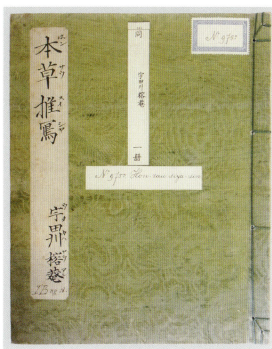

（表紙）

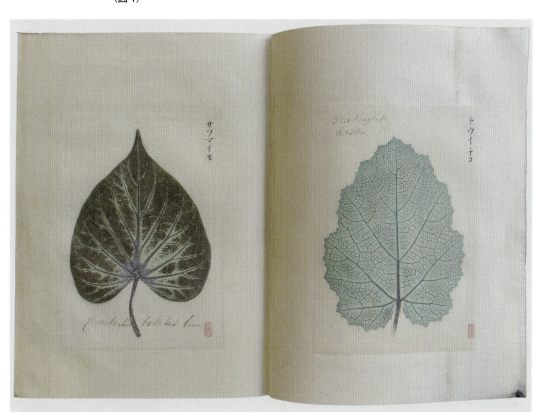

（図3）　　　　　　　　　　　　　　　（図2）

図版 260 本草抜粋（UL, Ser. 975b 図 31～図 33・奥書）

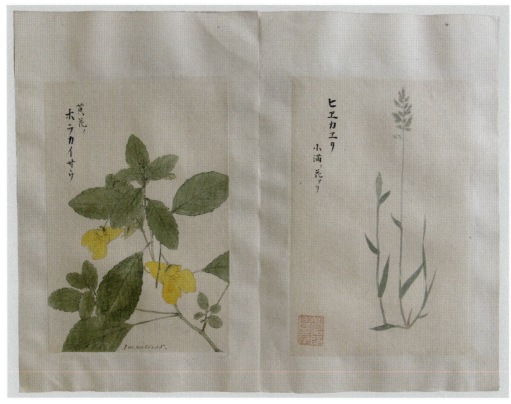

（図 32）　　　　　　　　　　　　　　　（図 31）

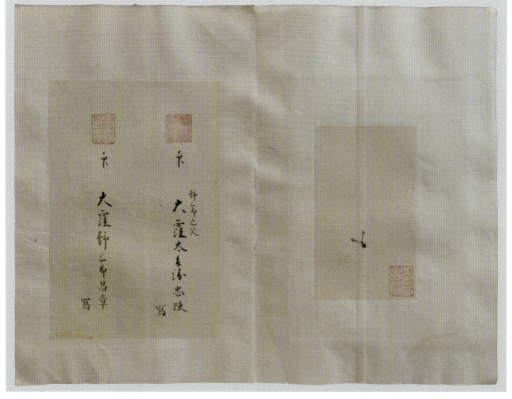

（奥書）　　　　　　　　　　　　　　　（図 33）

図版　260 本草抜粋（UL. Ser. 975b　図 27 〜図 30）

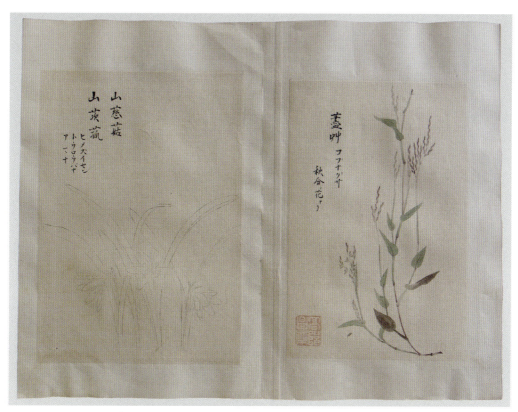

（図 28）　　　　　　　　　　　　　　　　（図 27）

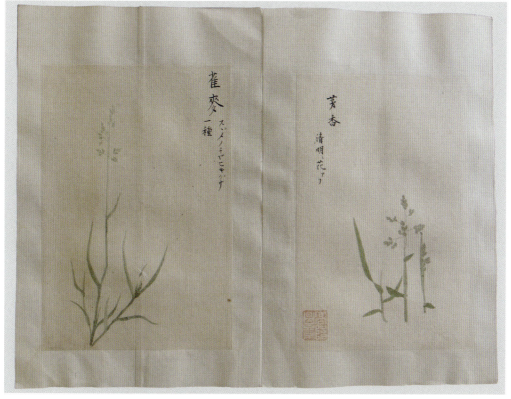

（図 30）　　　　　　　　　　　　　　　　（図 29）

図版　260 本草抜粋（UL, Ser. 975b　図 23 〜図 26）

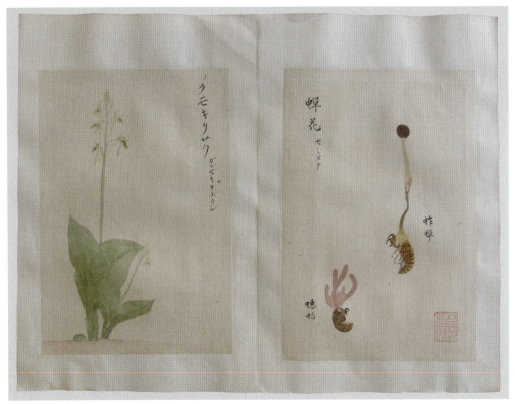

（図 24）　　　　　　　　　　　　（図 23）

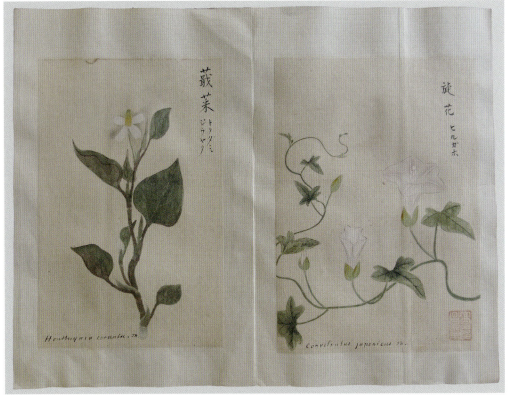

（図 26）　　　　　　　　　　　　（図 25）

図版　260 本草抜粋（UL, Ser. 975b　図 19 〜図 22）

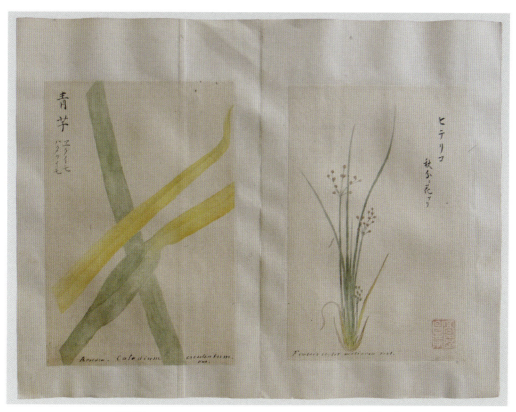

（図 20）　　　　　　　　　　　　　　　　（図 19）

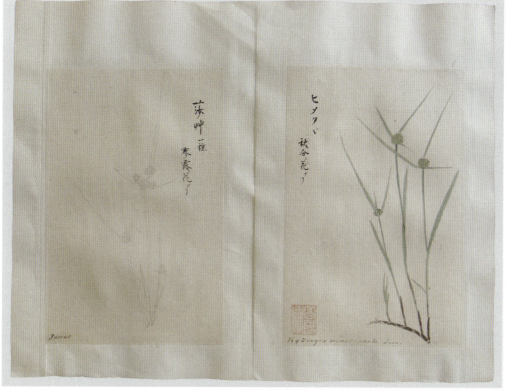

（図 22）　　　　　　　　　　　　　　　　（図 21）

図版　260 本草抜粋（UL. Ser. 975b　図15〜図18）

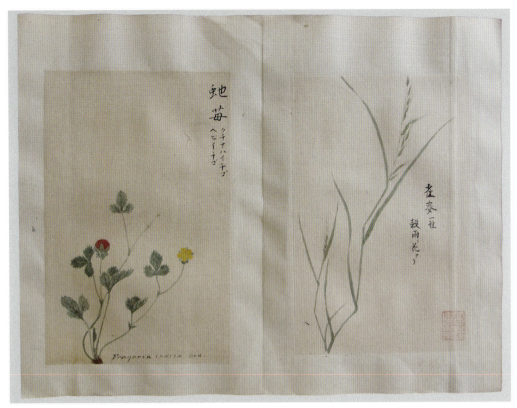

（図16）　　　　　　　　　　　　　　　（図15）

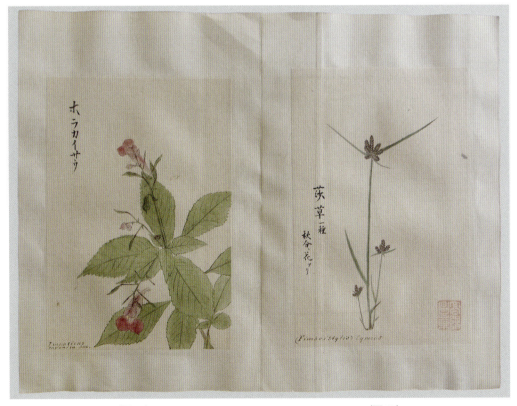

（図18）　　　　　　　　　　　　　　　（図17）

図版　260 本草抜粋（UL, Ser. 975b　図11〜図14）

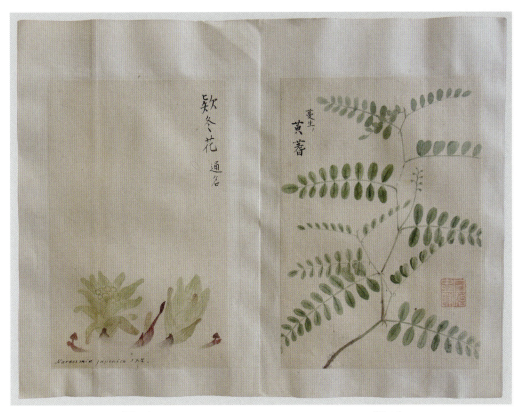

（図12）　　　　　　　　　　　（図11）

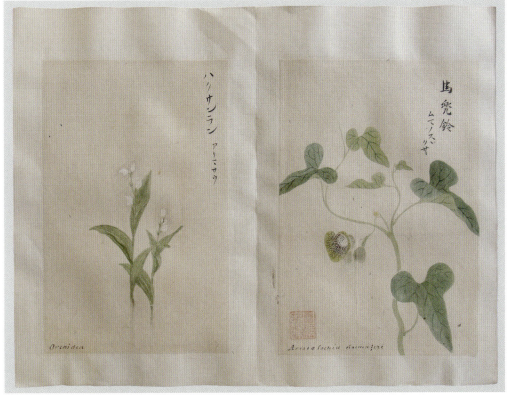

（図14）　　　　　　　　　　　（図13）

図版　260 本草抜粋（UL, Ser. 975b　図 7〜図 10）

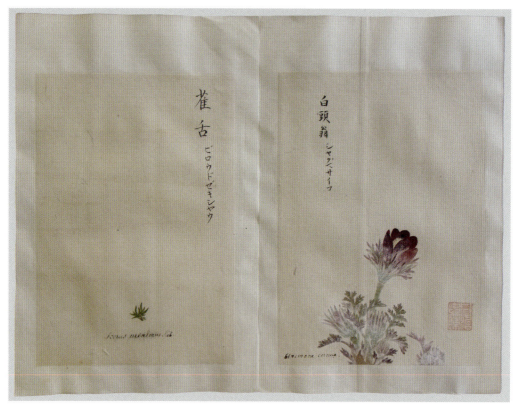

（図 8）　　　　　　　　　　　　　　（図 7）

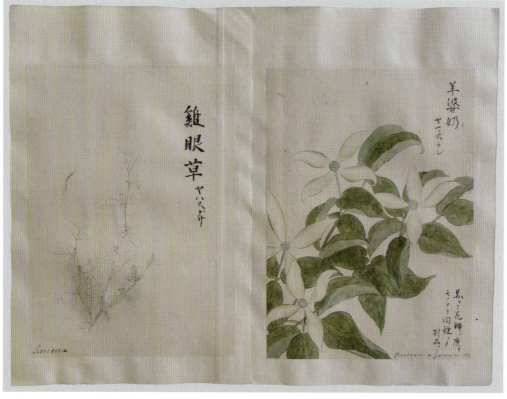

（図 10）　　　　　　　　　　　　　（図 9）

図版　260 本草抜粋（UL, Ser. 975b　図3〜図6）

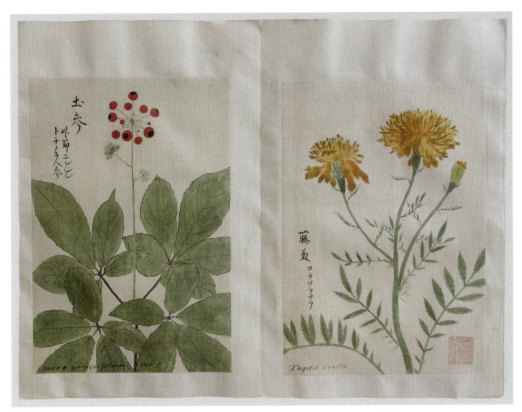

（図4）　　　　　　　　　　　　　　（図3）

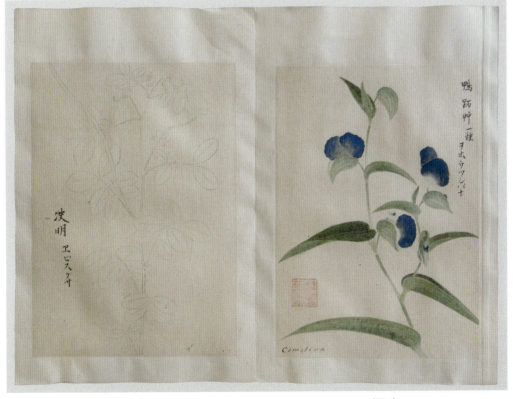

（図6）　　　　　　　　　　　　　　（図5）

図版　260 本草抜粋（UL, Ser. 975b　表紙・裏表紙・図1・図2）

260 本草抜粋　UL, Ser. 975b

（裏表紙）

（表紙）

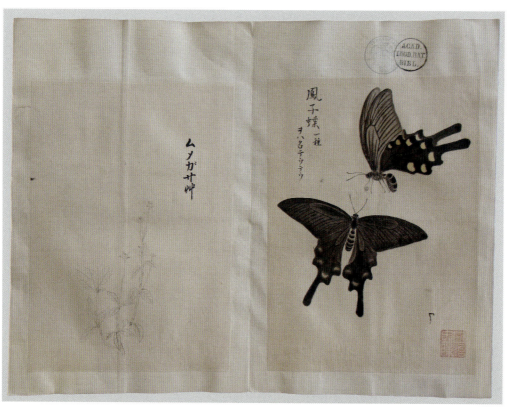

（図2）　　　　　　　　　　　　　　　　（図1）

258 本草写真　RMvV 1-4312

（1オ）

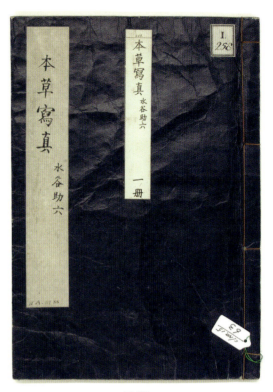

（表紙）

（2オ）　　　　　　　　　　（1ウ）

図版 254 蝦夷本草之図(UL, Ser. 1003 第1冊 図9・図10)

(第1冊 図9)

(第1冊 図10)

図版 254 蝦夷本草之図（UL.Ser.1003 第1冊 図7・図8）

（第1冊 図7）

（第1冊 図8）

図版　254 蝦夷本草之図（UL, Ser. 1003　第1冊　図5・図6）

（第1冊　図5）

（第1冊　図6）

(第1冊 図3)

(第1冊 図4)

図版　254 蝦夷本草之図（UL, Ser. 1003　第 1 冊　図 1・図 2）

254 蝦夷本草之図　UL, Ser. 1003

（第 1 冊　図 1）

（第 1 冊　図 2）

図版 253 梅櫻類花写真（RMvV1-431）

253 梅櫻類花写真 RMvV1-431

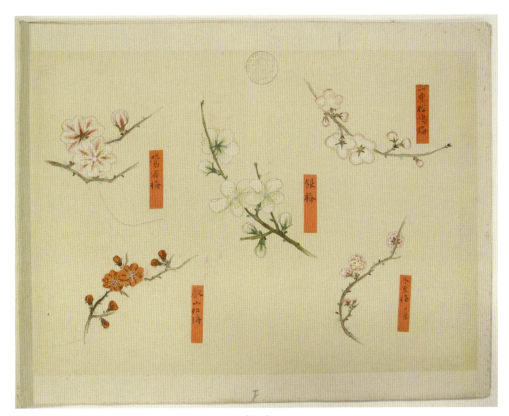

（図1）

（図13）

246 夏草冬蟲図　UL, Ser. 1023

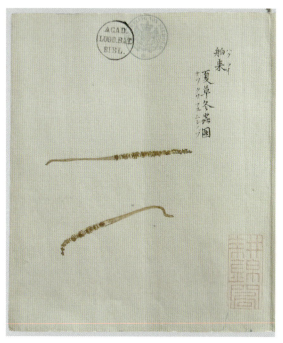

（2オ）

（表紙）

（3オ）　　　　　　　　　　　　　（2ウ）

192 東察加之図　UL, Ser. 186

（裏表紙）

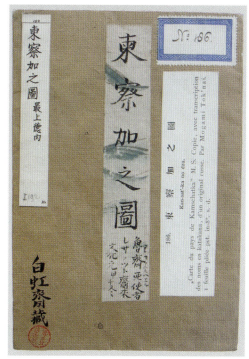

（表紙）

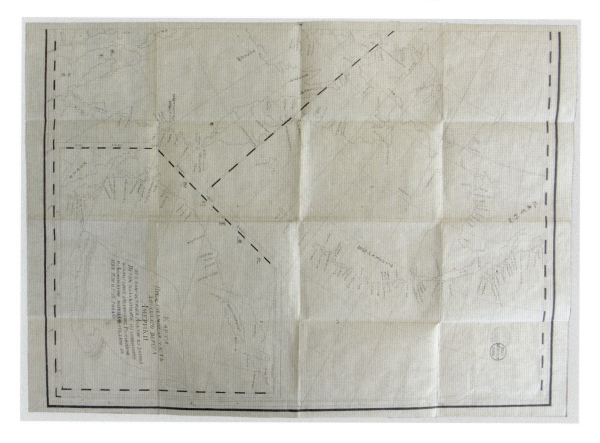

図版　181 薩哈連島之図（UL, Ser. 213）

181 薩哈連島之圖　UL, Ser. 213

（裏表紙）

（表紙）

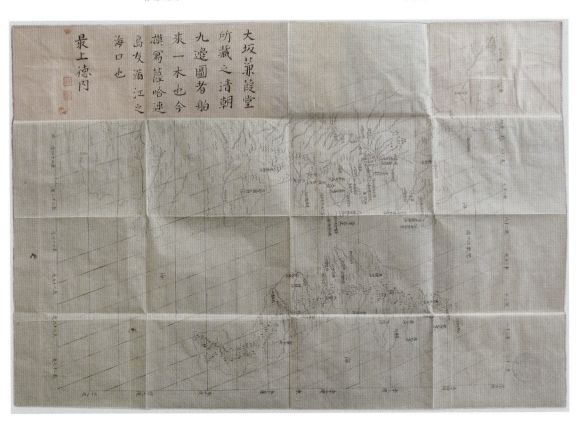

図版 152 富士之景（RMvV 1-430 秋景・冬景）

（秋景）

（冬景）

16

図版 152 富士之景（RMvV 1-430 春景・夏景）

（春景）

（夏景）

図版　152 富士之景（RMvV 1-430　第九）

（第九）

（第九：部分拡大）

図版 152 富士之景（RMvV 1-430 第七・第八）

（第七）

（第八）

図版 152 富士之景（RMvV 1-430 第四・第六）

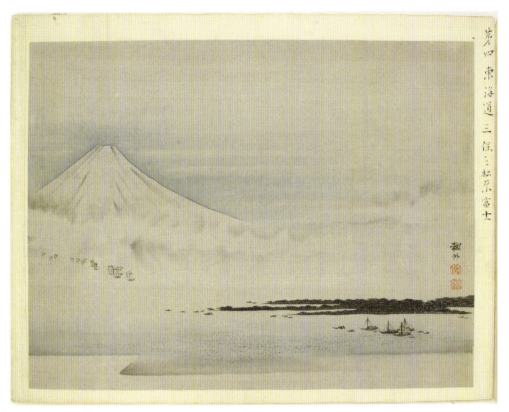

（第四）

（第六）

図版　152 富士之景（RMvV 1-430　第一・第三）

（第一）

（第三）

図版　152 富士之景（RMvV 1-430　表紙・第五）

（表紙）

（第五）

図版　149 名山図譜（UL, Ser. 365）

（1巻、2図「冨士山」）

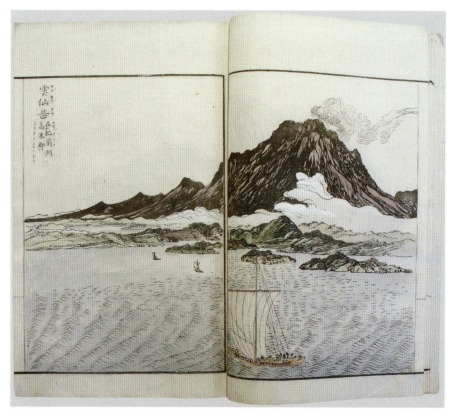

（3巻、8図「雲仙岳」）

図版　147 江戸隅田川両岸一覧図（UL, Ser. 378）

147 江戸隅田川両岸一覧図　UL, Ser. 378　上巻（9 ウ～11 オ）

（10 オ）　　　　　　　　　　　　　　　　　（9 ウ）

（11 オ）　　　　　　　　　　　　　　　　　（10 ウ）

図版　143 和州吉野山名勝図（UL, Ser. 369）

143 和州吉野山名勝図　UL, Ser. 369

（見返し）　（表紙）

（11 オ）　（10 ウ）

140 日本名所の絵　UL, Ser. 364

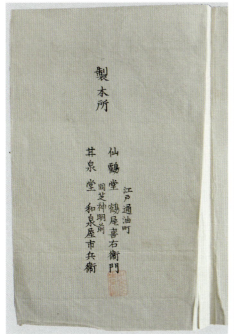

（袋：刊記）

（袋：表題）

図版　125 自上古到今世難波大坂十二図（UL, Ser. 341）

125 自上古到今世難波大坂十二図　UL, Ser. 341

（「浪華上古図」）

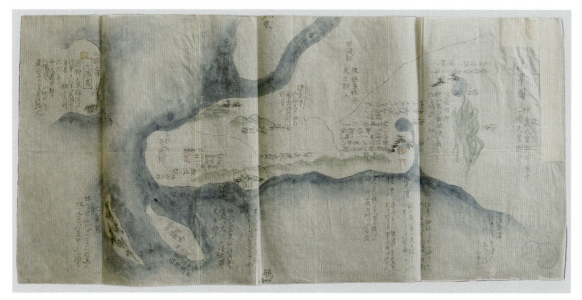

（「浪華図」）

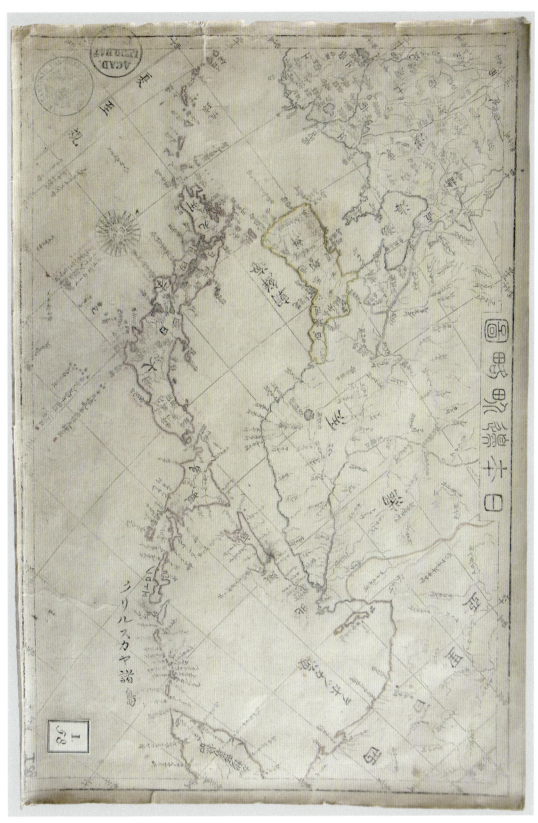

図版 58 日本辺界略図（UL, Ser. 228）

図版　47 諸国奇談西遊記（UL, Ser. 233C）・48 諸国奇談東遊記（UL, Ser. 233B）・95 天明再板京都めぐり（UL, Ser. 296）

48 諸国奇談東遊記（袋） UL, Ser. 233B

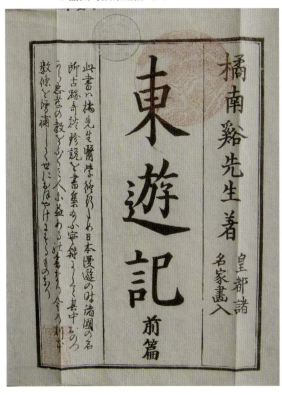

47 諸国奇談西遊記（袋） UL, Ser. 233C

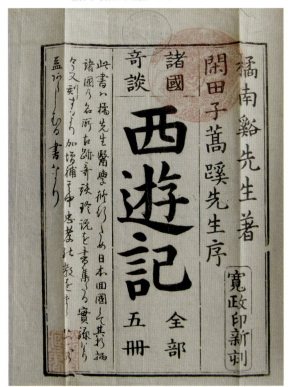

95 天明再板京都めぐり（袋） UL, Ser. 296

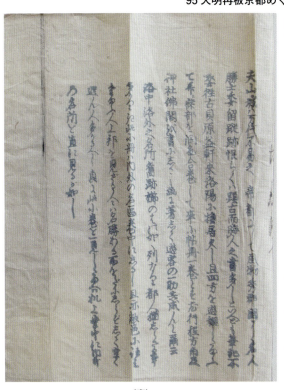

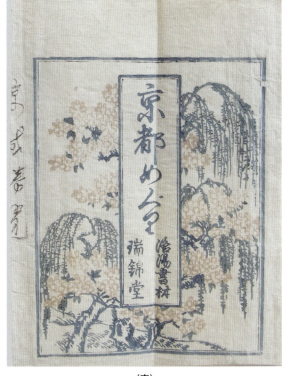

（裏）　　　　　　　　　　　　　　　　（表）

《凡例》

1. 掲載方針
   (1) 図版掲載の順番は原文（ラテン語本文・石版刷目録）に従い、右開きに掲載した。
   (2) 掲載資料の選定・掲載箇所については、中野三敏が行った。

2. 目録番号・資料名
   (1) 掲載資料の冒頭図版（ゴチック体）と各頁の柱（明朝体）に、原文（石版刷目録）で表記された番号（アラビア数字）と資料名（漢字と仮名、双方通行の字体）を記した。
   (2) 掲載資料の該当部分が分かりにくい場合はゴチック体で（　）の中に当該部分を記した。また、刊本や袋綴じの写本等は丁数、丁付が無い折帖は掲載図の順番あるいは資料に記載された表記番号、巻子本は紙数を記した。
   　（例）**47 諸国奇談西遊記（袋）　　152 富士の景（第五）**
   　　　　371 キフネ本地（第１紙）

3. 所蔵館・所蔵館請求番号
   (1) 掲載資料の冒頭図版と各頁の柱に明朝体で、所蔵館略称と資料館請求番号を記した。
   (2) 図版は、ライデン国立民族学博物館あるいはライデン大学図書館が所蔵する資料を撮影して掲載した。所蔵館の略称は、以下のとおりである。

   　　RmvV：Rijksmuseum Volkenkunde, Leiden（Rijksmuseum voor Volkenkunde）
   　　　　（National Museum of Ethnology［Netherlands］　ライデン国立民族学博物館）
   　　UL 　：Universiteitsbibliotheek Leiden
   　　　　（Leiden University Library　ライデン大学図書館）

   (3) 資料に対する所蔵館請求番号は、各所蔵館で使用している記載（番号・記号）に従って記した。
   　（例）RmvV 1-430　（RmvV：ライデン国立民族博物館　1-430：所蔵館整理番号）
   　　　　UL, Ser. 233C　（UL：ライデン大学図書館　Ser. 233C：所蔵館整理番号）

4. 縮尺・法量
   (1) 一定の縮尺率で掲載せず、資料毎に縮尺を変えた。
   (2) 本文を大きく同率掲出することを優先した。従って、表紙は綴部分等、左右が本文版面より大きい場合もあり、同率掲出が困難な場合は適宜収まる縮率に調整した。
   (3) 表紙の大きさ等、法量については、「掲載図版一覧」（225頁）を参照されたい。

図　版

Illustrative Plates

【著編者一覧】

監修：中野三敏
編集：高杉志緒／宮崎克則
ラテン語和訳：家入敏光
執筆：山口隆男／マティ・フォラー
英訳：マティ・フォラー／デビット・キャリシャー

本書の出版にあたり、下記の諸機関・各氏に御協力いただきました。
記して謝意を表します。

【協力者一覧】

掲載資料所蔵機関（五十音順）
　公益財団法人東洋文庫
　国立公文書館
　福岡県立図書館
　ライデン国立民族学博物館
　ライデン大学
　ライデン大学図書館

協力者（五十音順・敬称略）
　浅野秀剛／大場秀章／奥田倫子／金子和正／久留島浩
　日高薫／邦子フォラー／山口晶子／山村義照

※本書は、第39回（平成22年度）公益財団法人三菱財団人文科学研究助成「ライデンに現存するシーボルト収集和古書の書誌学的研究」の研究報告書であり、資料調査・出版にあたり、公益財団法人三菱財団の助成を受けた。

シーボルト蒐集和書目録

2015年3月10日　初版発行　　　　定価（本体20,000円＋税）

監修　中　野　三　敏
編集　高杉志緒・宮崎克則

発行所　株式会社　八木書店 古書出版部
代表　八　木　乾　二
〒101-0052 東京都千代田区神田小川町3-8
電話 03-3291-2969（編集）-6300（FAX）

発売元　株式会社　八　木　書　店
〒101-0052 東京都千代田区神田小川町3-8
電話 03-3291-2961（営業）-6300（FAX）
http://www.books-yagi.co.jp/pub/
E-mail pub@books-yagi.co.jp

印刷　精興社
製本　博勝堂

ISBN978-4-8406-0049-1

A Listing of Siebold's Collection of Japanese Books
—Papers on Siebold and Japanese Translation of Latin Used—

Supervised by :
  Mitsutoshi Nakano
Edited by :
  Shio Takasugi
  Katsunori Miyazaki
Translated from Latin to Japanese by :
  Toshimitsu Ieiri
Written by :
  Takao Yamaguchi
  Matthi Forrer
Translated from Japanese to English by:
  Matthi Forrer
  Dabid Kalischer

Special thanks to :

  Fukuoka Prefectual Library
  Leiden Universiy (Universiteit Leiden)
  Leiden Universiy Library (Universiteitsbibliotheek Leiden)
  National Archives of Japan
  National Museum of Ethnology (Netherlands)
    (Rijksmuseum Volkenkunde)
  Toyo Bunko (The Oriental Library)

  Shugo Asano
  Kuniko Forrer
  Kaori Hidaka
  Kazumasa Kaneko
  Hiroshi Kurushima
  Hideaki Ohba
  Tomoko Okuda
  Akiko Yamaguchi
  Yoshiteru Yamamura

Published by :
  Yagi Bookstore Ltd.
  3-8 Kanda-Ogawamachi, Chiyoda-ku, Tokyo, Japan.
  Printed in Japan

  (This Publication is subsidized by the Mitsubishi Foundation.)